LEARN
Office 2000

John Preston
Sally Preston
Robert Ferrett

PRENTICE
HALL

Learn Office 2000

© 2000 Prentice Hall

A division of Pearson Education

Upper Saddle River, NJ 07458

Library of Congress Catalog No: 98-89125

ISBN: 1-58076-263-8

03 02 01   4

Screens reproduced in this book were created using Collage Plus from Inner Media, Inc., Hollis, NH.

Credits

Publisher:
Robert Linsky

Executive Editor:
Alex von Rosenberg

Operations Manager:
Christine Moos

Series Editors:
John Preston, Sally Preston, Robert L. Ferrett

Senior Product Manager:
Cecil Yarbrough

Senior Editor:
Karen A. Walsh

Project Editors:
Karen A. Walsh
Laura N. Williams

Copy Editor:
Lunaea Hougland

Indexer:
Larry Sweazy

Marketing Team:
Nancy Evans, Susan L. Kindel, Kris King

Software Specialist:
Angela Denny

Team Coordinator:
Melody Layne

Designer:
Louisa Klucznik

Layout:
Wil Cruz
Jeannette McKay

About the Authors

John Preston is an Associate Professor at Eastern Michigan University in the College of Technology, where he teaches microcomputer application courses at the undergraduate and graduate levels. He has been teaching, writing, and designing computer training courses since the advent of PCs, and has authored and co-authored more than two dozen books on Microsoft Word, Excel, Access, and PowerPoint. He is a series editor for the *Learn 97* and *Learn 2000* books. He has received grants from the Detroit Edison Institute and the Department of Energy to develop Web sites for energy education and alternative fuels. He has also developed one of the first Internet-based microcomputer applications courses at an accredited university. He has a BS from the University of Michigan in Physics, Mathematics, and Education, and an MS from Eastern Michigan University in Physics Education. He is ABD in the Ph.D. degree program in Instructional Technology at Wayne State University.

Sally Preston is President of Preston & Associates, a computer software-training firm. She utilizes her extensive business experience as a bank vice president in charge of branch operations along with her skills in training people on new computer systems. She provides corporate training through Preston & Associates and through the Institute for Workforce Development at Washtenaw Community College where she also teaches computer courses part-time. She has co-authored more than 20 books on Access, Excel, PowerPoint, and Word including the *Learn 97* books, *Learn 2000* books, *Office 2000 Essentials*, and *Access 2000 Essentials*. She has an MBA from Eastern Michigan University.

Robert L. Ferrett is the Director of the Center for Instructional Computing at Eastern Michigan University. His center provides computer training and support to faculty at the university. He has authored or co-authored nearly 30 books on Access, PowerPoint, Excel, and Word, and was the editor of the *1994 ACM SIGUCCS Conference Proceedings*. He has been designing, developing, and delivering computer workshops for more than a decade. He has a BA in Psychology, an MS in Geography, and an MS in Interdisciplinary Technology from Eastern Michigan University. He is ABD in the Ph.D. program in Instructional Technology at Wayne State University.

Trademark Acknowledgments

All terms mentioned in this book that are known to be trademarks or service marks have been appropriately capitalized. Prentice Hall cannot attest to the accuracy of this information. Use of a term in this book should not be regarded as affecting the validity of any trademark or service mark.

Acknowledgements

In addition to the editing and production team listed on the credits page, the authors want to acknowledge the contributions of the students in the technical writing program at Eastern Michigan University. These students, under the instruction and guidance of their professor, Ann Blakeslee, provided a valuable review of an early draft of the manuscript for this book. The following students participated in this project:

Stephanie Somerville	Lisa M. Smith
Hanna Gilberg	Rocky Peterson
Charles Vescoso	Amy L. Johnson
Mary Lacey	Mary Wolfe
Don Hughes	Steve Morgan
Keun-Hae Lee	

Philosophy of the Learn Series

The *Learn* series has been designed for the student who wants to master the basics of a particular software package quickly. The books are very visual in nature because each step is accompanied by a figure that shows the results of the step. Visual cues are given to the student in the form of highlights and callouts to help direct the student to the location in the window that is being used in a particular step. Explanatory text is minimized in the actual steps, but is included where appropriate in additional pedagogical elements. Every lesson includes a variety of exercises to immediately give the student a chance to practice the skills that have just been learned.

Structure of a Learn Series Book

Each of the books in the *Learn* series is structured the same way. The following elements comprise the series:

Introduction

Each book has an introduction. This consists of an introduction to the series (how to use this book), a brief introduction to the Windows operating system, and an introduction to the software.

Lesson Introduction

The introduction to each lesson includes a lesson number, a title, a list of tasks covered in the lesson, and a brief introduction to the main concept or purpose of the lesson.

Task Introduction

The tasks included in a lesson are shown on the opening page of the lesson. As you proceed through the lesson, the purpose of each task is explained in the "Why would I do this?" section at the beginning of the task.

Visual Summary

A screen capture or printout of the results of the lesson is included at the beginning of the lesson to provide an example of what is accomplished in the lesson.

"Why would I do this?"

At the beginning of each task is a "Why would I do this?" section, which is a short explanation of the relevance of the task. The purpose is to show why this particular element of the software is important and how it can be used effectively.

Figures

Each step has an accompanying figure that is placed below the step. Each figure provides a visual reinforcement of the step that has just been completed. Buttons, menu choices, and other screen elements used in the task are highlighted or identified.

Pedagogical Elements

Three recurring elements are found in the Preston Ferrett *Learn* series:

 In Depth: Provides a detailed look at a topic or procedure, or another way of doing something.

 Quick Tip: Provides a faster or more efficient way of doing something.

 Caution: Presents areas where trouble may be encountered, along with instructions on how to recover from or avoid these mistakes.

Glossary

New words or concepts are printed in italic the first time they are encountered. Definitions of these words or phrases are included in the Glossary at the back of the book.

End-of-Lesson Material

The end-of-lesson material consists of four elements: Comprehension, Reinforcement, Challenge, and Discovery exercises.

Comprehension exercises are designed to check the student's memory and understanding of the basic concepts in the lesson. Next to each exercise is a notation that references the task number in the lesson where the topic is covered. The student is encouraged to review the task referenced if he is uncertain of the correct answer. The Comprehension section contains the following three elements:

True/False Questions   There are ten true/false questions that test the understanding of the new material in the lesson.

Visual Identification   A captured screen or screens gauge the familiarity with various screen elements introduced in the lesson.

Matching   Ten matching questions are included to check familiarity with concepts and procedures introduced in the lesson.

Reinforcement exercises provide practice in the skills introduced in the tasks. These exercises generally follow the sequence of the tasks in the lesson. Because each exercise is usually built on the previous exercise, it is a good idea to do them in the order in which they are presented.

Challenge exercises test the student's ability to apply skills to new situations with less detailed instruction. These exercises challenge students to expand their skill set by using commands similar to those they've already learned.

Discovery exercises are designed to help students learn how to teach themselves new skills. In each exercise, the student discovers something new that is related to the topic taught in the lesson.

Welcome to the Learn On-Demand Series

Congratulations on choosing the Learn On-Demand series from Prentice Hall. The On-Demand software in the back of your book gives you the opportunity to learn while you work. This unique software provides computer-based training using the content from this book. To learn more, read the product information booklet included with the CD.

CD-ROM Disc

The CD-ROM disc in the back of the book contains the supporting data files. It also contains files that are used by the learner to complete the lessons. The files used by the learner are located in the **Student** folder. In the **Student** folder, you will find **Lesson** folders that are numbered to match the lessons in the book. The files needed for each lesson can be found in the lesson folder that corresponds to the lesson number in the book.

Annotated Instructor's Manual

If you have adopted this text for use in a college classroom, you will receive, upon request, an *Annotated Instructor's Manual* (*AIM*) at no additional charge. The *Annotated Instructor's Manual* is a comprehensive teaching tool that contains the student text with margin notes and tips for instructors and students. The *AIM* also contains suggested curriculum guides for courses of varying lengths, answers to the end-of-chapter material, test questions and answers, and PowerPoint slides. Data files and solutions for each tutorial and exercise, along with a Windows NT presentation, are included on disk with the *AIM*. Please contact your local representative or write to us on school or business letterhead at Prentice Hall, One Lake Street, Upper Saddle River, NJ 07458.

Introduction to Office 2000

There are several versions of Microsoft Office 2000 available: the Small Business edition, the Standard edition, the Professional edition, and the Premium edition. These come with a variety of programs, although all versions include Word and Excel. The version that is installed on your computer will determine to which of the following Office components you will have access:

Program	What the program does
Word	Word is a program known as a **word processor**. Word processors are the most commonly used productivity programs. They are used to create documents that are mainly text-based, although graphics can also be added to documents. Word processors can be used to create letters, memos, research papers, simple newsletters, and even Web pages.
Excel	Excel is a **spreadsheet** program that is usually used to process, analyze, and chart numbers, although it can also be used to sort through lists of data. Spreadsheets can be used to track sales, create financial models, or create a home or business budget.
PowerPoint	PowerPoint is a **presentation manager**. Presentation managers enable you to create professional-quality computer slide presentations, overhead transparencies, and even Web slide shows.
Access	Access is a **database**. Databases are used to store and present large amounts of information. This information can be sorted, searched, and categorized. Databases are often used for such things as inventories, address lists, and research data.
Outlook	Outlook is an **information manager**, a program that can take charge of your day-to-day scheduling. It can be used to track business contacts, supervise your email, keep track of appointments, and store a task list. Outlook helps a busy person organize his activities.

Publisher	Publisher is a **desktop publisher**, which is a program used to organize and present different kinds of information. Desktop publishing programs combine text and graphics to create such things as newsletters, posters, greeting cards, and even Web pages.
FrontPage	FrontPage is a sophisticated, powerful **Web creation and management tool**. It gives you maximum flexibility in the design and layout of Web pages, and provides the oversite tools to manage the site after it goes online.
PhotoDraw	PhotoDraw is a **graphics software** package. It can be used to create original drawings. It can also be used to enhance and modify images from a scanner, a digital camera, or even a downloaded (copyright-free) image.

The combination of programs will be determined by the version of Office that you have installed. One of the great strengths of Office 2000 is the interchangeability of information among the various programs. For example, you might create a document using Word, and then place a logo that you created in PhotoDraw at the top of the first page. You could also insert a small data set created in Access, and a table or chart created in Excel. Finally, you might put the new document on the Web as a Web page.

With Office 2000, you can save your documents in a format that enables them to be viewed and used on the Web. Anyone with a Web browser can view your documents. You can also edit the documents as necessary because of Office's capability to "round trip" the documents to the Web and then back into the original Office program without losing any of the functionality of the file formats.

The Concept of This Book

This book is designed for students who are new to Office 2000 and would like to know how to use it in real-life applications. The authors have combined their many years of business experience and classroom teaching to provide a basic step-by-step approach that leads to the development of skills advanced enough to be useful in the workplace. They have designed the book so that you will be successful immediately and will create something useful in the beginning lesson in each section of the book. The first two lessons provide an introduction to using the Windows operating system and managing files. The third lesson is an overview of Office and explains common features and tools used in the Office environment. The main content of the book introduces the student to using Word, Excel, Access, and PowerPoint. In each section you learn the basic components of that particular program and how to create documents, spreadsheets, databases, and presentations. The authors recognize that few people can remember everything that they learn in class, so they introduce the extensive Help system early in the book and use it in exercises throughout the book. This enables you to learn how to use the Help system to find answers to questions about using Office 2000.

Table of Contents at a Glance

Table of Contents

Lesson: 1

Working with Windows

Introduction

Windows is the operating system that coordinates the activities of your computer. It controls how your screen is displayed, how you open and close programs, the startup and shutdown procedures for your computer, and general navigation techniques for moving around.

Before you can use Microsoft Office 2000 effectively, you will need to have at least a basic familiarity with the Microsoft Windows operating system. You need to know how to work with the Start button and taskbar, and how to open, close, move, and resize windows. You also need to know how to use both the left and right buttons on your mouse.

In this lesson, you learn how to use the mouse. You also learn how to use the Start button and the taskbar, and how to manipulate windows. You also learn how to use some of the Help features available in Windows. Finally, you learn how to shut down your computer.

TASK *1*

Starting Windows and Using the Mouse
Why would I do this?

In most cases, starting Windows is an automatic procedure. You turn on the machine and Windows (whichever version you are using) eventually appears. The mouse and keyboard are two of the common input devices used to interact with Windows.

Your screen will look different from the Windows screens displayed throughout this lesson because your computer has different software installed and different shortcuts on the desktop.

In this task, you learn how to start Windows and use the mouse.

> **Caution:** If you are using a computer in a lab or on a network, a box—called a *dialog box*—may open and ask for a username and password. In many cases, you can press Esc or click the Cancel button, which will bypass the security. If this doesn't work, ask your instructor or network administrator how to proceed.

1 Turn on your computer. After showing several screens of text and the Windows opening screen, the Windows desktop is displayed. The desktop consists of shortcut *icons* (small graphic symbols that represent programs) that run programs, a *taskbar* at the bottom of the screen, and a *Start button* on the left edge of the taskbar. There are also shortcut icons on the right side of the taskbar. Finally, somewhere on the desktop you will see an arrow. This is the *mouse pointer*, often just called the pointer, which you will use to select or activate things on the screen. The look of the screen will vary depending on which version of Windows you are using. The figures in this lesson show Microsoft Windows 98.

> **In Depth:** The taskbar may not appear at the bottom of the desktop. If you cannot see the taskbar, it may have been hidden. To see it, move the mouse pointer to the bottom of the screen. The taskbar should pop up.
>
> The taskbar also may not appear at the location shown in the figures. It may have been moved to the top or one of the sides of the desktop.

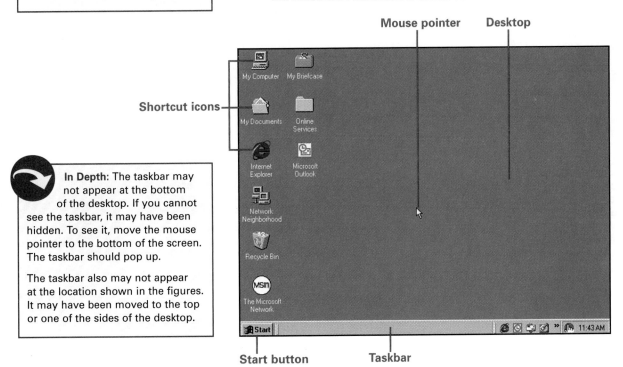

2 Move the mouse across a flat surface such as a mouse pad to control the pointer on your screen. Position the pointer in the center of the **My Computer** icon on the desktop, and click once using the left mouse button. The icon turns dark, indicating that it has been selected, and a *ScreenTip* may be displayed, depending on the version of Windows installed on your computer. A ScreenTip is a message that pops up on the screen to identify an icon, button, or some other part of a window. *My Computer* is one of two ways to get to the programs and documents stored on your computer. The My Computer icon looks like a miniature computer.

ScreenTip

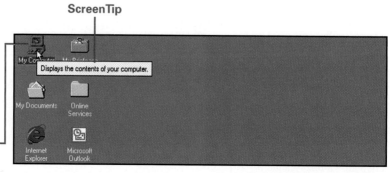

My Computer icon is selected

3 With the mouse pointer still pointing to **My Computer**, click twice in rapid succession using the left mouse button. The My Computer *window* is displayed. A window is a box that displays information or a program. A window consists of a *title bar* containing the window name, a *menu bar*, and usually one or more *toolbars*. A *status bar* at the bottom of the window gives additional information. When a window is open, the name of the window is displayed on the taskbar at the bottom of the desktop.

Menu bar   Title bar   Close button

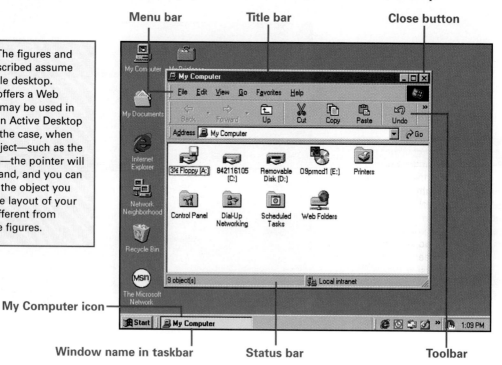

My Computer icon

Window name in taskbar   Status bar   Toolbar

4 Click the **Close** button in the upper-right corner of the My Computer window title bar. The My Computer window closes.

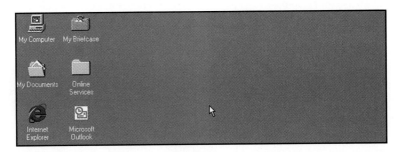

5 Click the right mouse button on the **My Computer** icon. A *shortcut menu* is displayed. Shortcut menus are used to perform operations quickly without having to use the menu bar or the toolbar. On this shortcut menu, the Open command is displayed in bold because it is the default action that occurs when you double-click on this icon.

The command in bold is the default action

Shortcut menu

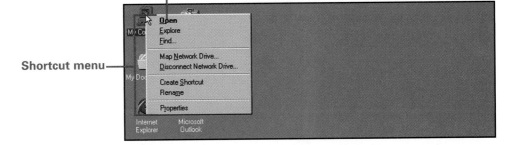

6 Move the mouse pointer over the word **Open** in the shortcut menu. The Open command is highlighted, which means it is selected.

The Open command is selected

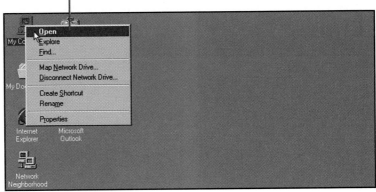

7 Click the left mouse button once. The My Computer window is displayed. This performs exactly the same task as double-clicking on the icon. In both Microsoft Windows and Microsoft Office, nearly every procedure and task can be performed two, three, or even four different ways!

Close button

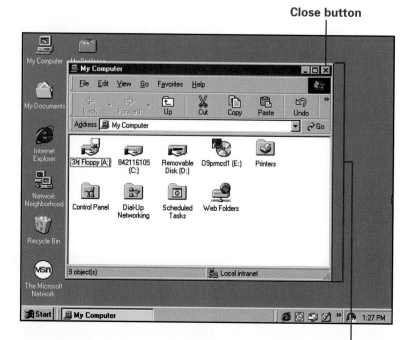

My Computer window opens

8 Click the **Close** button in the My Computer window title bar. The window closes. Leave your computer on for the next task.

Using the Start Button

Why would I do this?

The Start button is a very important part of the Windows desktop. You can use it to launch programs, set up your printer, get help, and shut down your computer.

In this task, you use the Start button to open a built-in application that acts as an online calculator.

1 Move the pointer to the **Start** button and click it once using the left mouse button. The Start menu is displayed. Notice that some of the options have arrows on the right. These arrows indicate that there is a *submenu* containing programs or more folders within that folder. A submenu is a second-level menu activated by selecting a menu item.

The items at the top of the Start menu will be different from those on your screen. The user can customize this area with shortcuts to programs and files. Once the Start menu is displayed, you can let go of the mouse button.

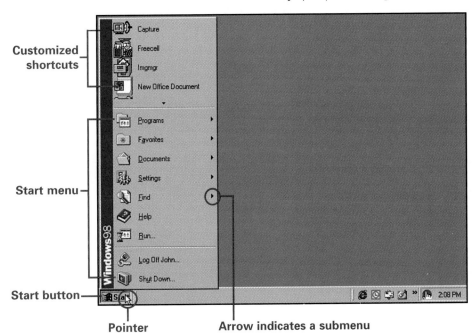

Customized shortcuts

Start menu

Start button

Pointer

Arrow indicates a submenu

2 Move the pointer up to the **Programs** menu option, but do not click the mouse button. The Programs menu is displayed. Your Programs menu will look somewhat different because your computer will have different programs installed. The folders at the top contain more programs, more folders, or some of each.

Folders   Programs submenu

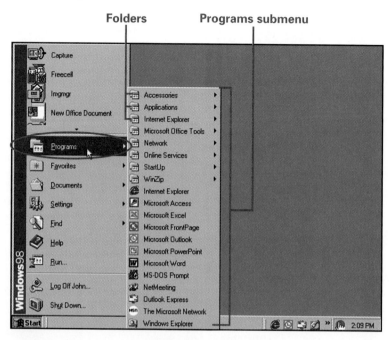

3 Move the pointer up to the **Accessories** menu option, but do not click the mouse button. The Accessories submenu is displayed.

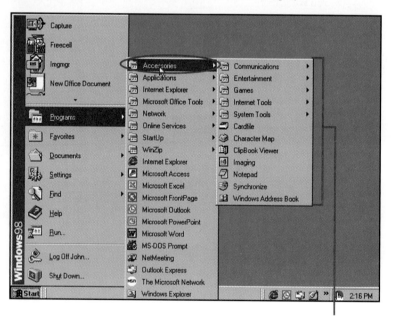

Accessories submenu

4 Move the pointer into the **Accessories** submenu and move down to the **Calculator** option. The Calculator option is highlighted.

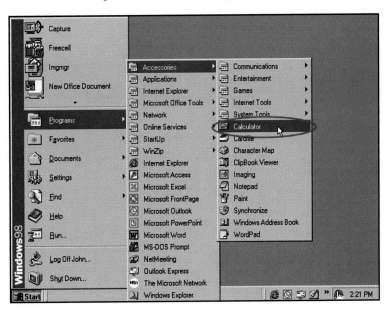

5 Click the **Calculator** option with the left mouse button. The Calculator window is displayed. Try using the calculator. Point and click on numbers and keys just as you would press keys on a calculator.

Close button

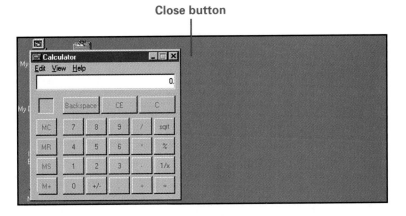

In Depth: You can use the Accessories programs from the Start menu while you are using other Office programs. For example, you might want to make a quick calculation while you are typing a document into Microsoft Word. You can go to the Start button and open the calculator (as you did above), make the calculation, and then place the answer in your Word document without ever closing Word!

6 Click the **Close** button to close the calculator. The open desktop is displayed. Leave the computer on for the next task.

Resizing and Moving a Window
Why would I do this?

Another skill you need to have is the ability to resize and move windows. When a window opens on your screen, it generally opens to the same size and shape as it was when last used. If you are using more than one window at a time, you may want to increase or decrease the size of the window so that you can see the information you need. Moving a window on your desktop is another way to help you see what you need.

In this task, you open, resize, and move the My Computer window.

① Double-click the **My Computer** icon on the desktop. The My Computer window opens.

Caution: The My Computer window may open in a view that fills the screen. If this is the case, click the Restore button, which is the middle button on the right end of the title bar, to return the window to its normal size.

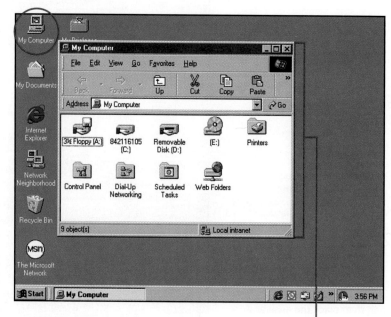

My Computer window

2 Move the pointer to the lower-right corner of the window. The pointer changes to a diagonal two-headed arrow. When the mouse pointer is in this shape, you can click and drag the item to which you are pointing to change its size and shape.

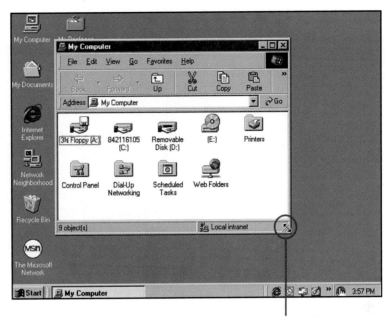

Two-headed pointer

3 Hold down the left mouse button and drag diagonally up and to the left. When you release the left mouse button, the window will be resized to the size of the thick gray outline. Resize your window to approximately the same size as the one in the figure.

Outline of resized window

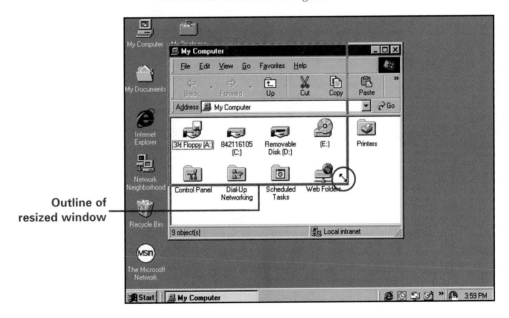

4 Release the left mouse button. The My Computer window is resized. Notice that scrollbars are displayed on the right side and bottom of the window. These appear whenever there is more in the window than can be displayed in its current size. Next, you will move the window.

In Depth: You can also resize a window by clicking and dragging on one side of the window at a time. To increase or decrease the width of the window, click and drag on the left or right side. To change the height of a window, click and drag on the top or bottom edge of the window.

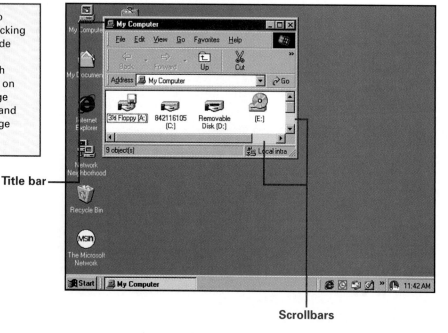

Title bar

Scrollbars

5 Move the pointer to an open space on the **My Computer** title bar. Click and drag down and to the right. When you release the left mouse button, the window will be moved to the location indicated by the thick rectangle in the figure. Depending on the settings on your computer, the full window may be displayed as you move it across the desktop.

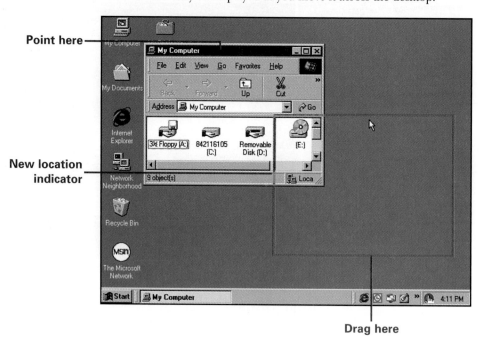

Point here

New location indicator

Drag here

6 Release the left mouse button. The My Computer window is moved. Leave My Computer open for the next lesson.

The My Computer window is moved

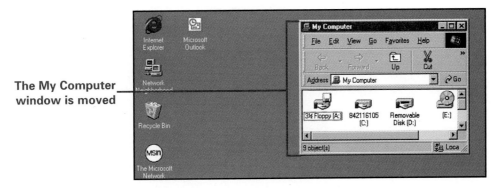

TASK 4

Scrolling a Window
Why would I do this?

In many cases, your computer will not be able to display all the information contained in a window, whether that window contains a word processing document, a Web page, or My Computer. Scrollbars are included if the information in a window stretches beyond the right or bottom edges of the window. The *horizontal scrollbar* enables you to move left and right to view information too wide for the screen. The *vertical scrollbar* enables you to view information too long for the screen.

In this lesson, you use the scrollbars in the My Computer window to look at information that won't fit on the screen.

1 With the **My Computer** window open, point to the down arrow at the bottom of the vertical scrollbar, and click. The items at the bottom of the window scroll up so that you can see the folders and icons that were not visible before. You can click and hold down the left mouse button to scroll rapidly in a window that has many items that are not visible.

Scroll box   Vertical scrollbar

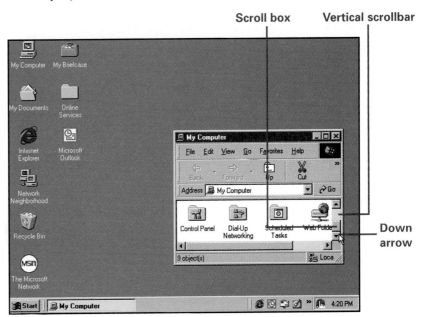

Down arrow

2 Click and hold down the left mouse button on the up arrow on the same scrollbar. You move up in the list until the first item is displayed.

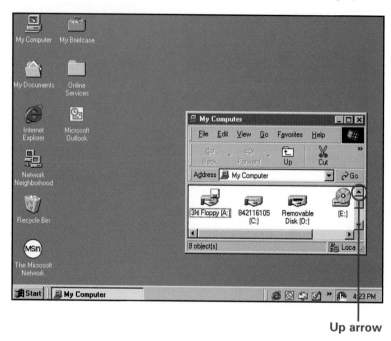

Up arrow

3 Click and hold down the right arrow on the horizontal scrollbar at the lower-right corner of the window. The window scrolls to display the information on the right.

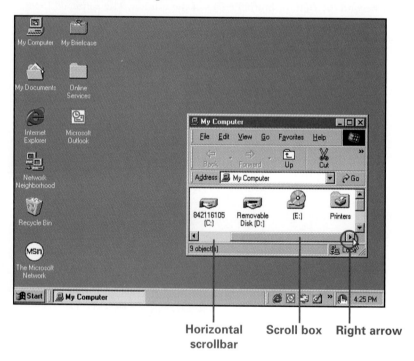

**Horizontal   Scroll box   Right arrow
scrollbar**

4 Click and hold down the left arrow on the same horizontal scrollbar. The window scrolls back to the left edge of the information.

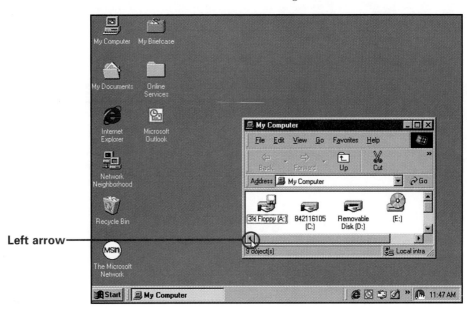

Left arrow

5 On the vertical scrollbar, click the *scroll box* with the left mouse button and drag down. The scroll box enables you to move quickly up or down a window. The relative location of the scroll box indicates your relative location in the window. It also gives you more control as you scroll because you can see the information as it moves up or down the window. Leave the My Computer window open for the next task.

Quick Tip: You can move up or down a screen at a time by clicking in the gray area above or below the scroll box.

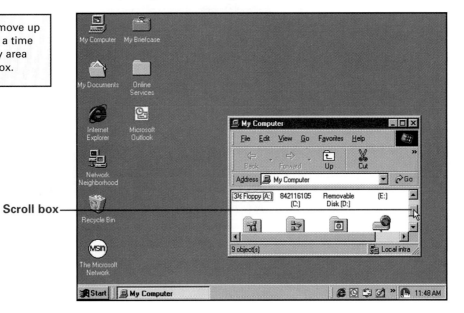

Scroll box

TASK 5

Maximizing, Restoring, Minimizing, and Closing a Window
Why would I do this?

In Task 4, you resized the My Computer window. You can also *maximize* the window, which enables the window to take up the whole screen; and *restore* the window, which takes it back to the size it was before being maximized. You can also *minimize* a window, removing it entirely from the screen and storing it on the taskbar until it is needed again.

In this lesson, you maximize, restore, minimize, and finally close the My Computer window.

① Place the pointer on the **Maximize** button in the upper-right corner of the My Computer window. The Maximize button is the middle button in the group of three. When you point to it, a ScreenTip is displayed.

Minimize button   **Maximize button**

② Click the **Maximize** button. The My Computer window now occupies the entire screen. The Maximize button is now the Restore button, and has a different look.

Restore button——

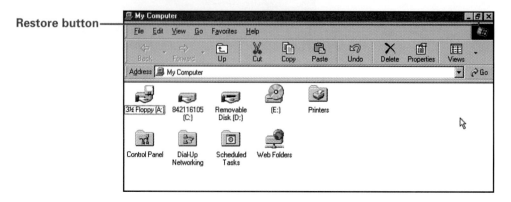

3 Click the **Restore** button. The window returns to the size it was before you clicked the Maximize button.

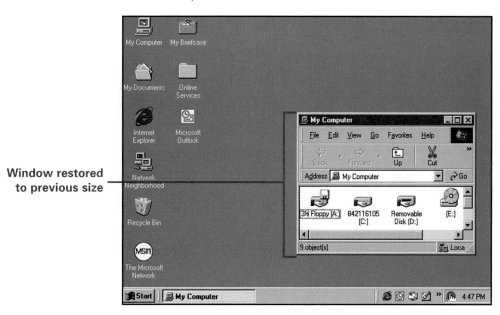

Window restored to previous size

4 Click the **Minimize** button. The My Computer window is still open, but, it is stored on the taskbar at the bottom of the screen. The window has not been closed, just temporarily hidden.

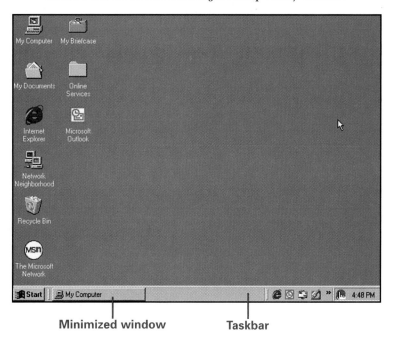

Minimized window   Taskbar

5 Click the **My Computer** button on the taskbar. The window reappears in the same location it was in when you clicked the Minimize button.

In Depth: Dialog boxes and windows serve distinct purposes. Dialog boxes ask you for some type of decision—if you want to accept changes, what size something should be, how you want an item formatted. These responses always deal with a single item or task. A window, on the other hand, contains information that can be used over and over again—a document, a list of available programs, a calculator. Because windows can be used multiple times, they all have Minimize buttons so they can be stored on the taskbar but not closed. Dialog boxes do not have Minimize buttons, because they focus on a particular task.

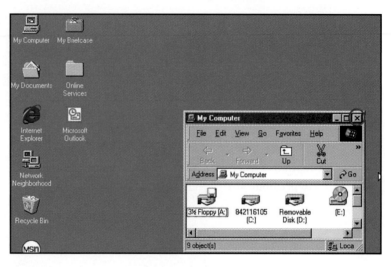

6 Click the **Close** button in the upper-right corner of the My Computer window. The window is closed.

TASK 6

Using the Taskbar to Work in Multiple Windows
Why would I do this?

One of the really nice features of the Windows operating system is the capability for the user to have more than one window open at a time. This is particularly important when using Microsoft Office, because you can have more than one application open at a time and easily move information between applications.

In this task, you open two of the Office applications and quickly move from one to the other.

1 Click the **Start** button and move the pointer to the **Programs** menu choice. The **Programs** submenu is displayed.

Microsoft Word shortcut ——

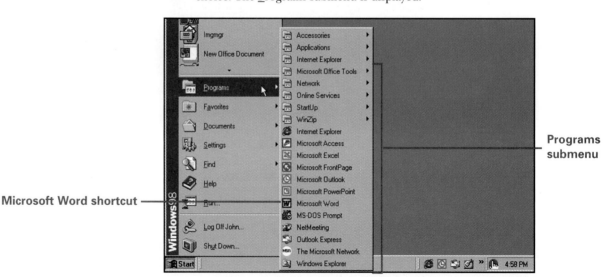

Programs submenu

Quick Tip: The way you open the Microsoft Office applications depends on how your computer has been set up. You may have a shortcut so that you can start the programs from the top of the Start menu. You may also have shortcuts on the desktop. If there is a shortcut for Microsoft Word on the desktop, you can double-click it with the left mouse button instead of using the Start menu.

2 Move the pointer to **Microsoft Word** and click it. Microsoft Word is opened. There is also a Microsoft Word button on the taskbar. The Word window may or may not be maximized. If it is not, click the **Maximize** button. The button on the taskbar displays Document1 as the default name for the Word document when it is first opened.

Microsoft Word
in title bar

Microsoft Word button

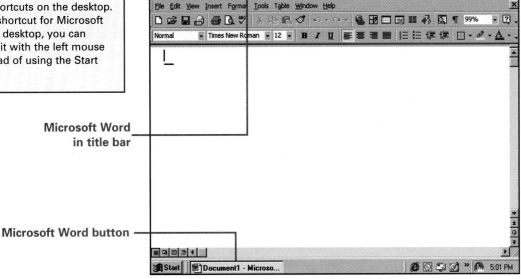

3 Click the **Start** button, go to the **Programs** menu option, and then click **Microsoft Excel**. After a moment, Microsoft Excel is opened. You now have buttons for both Word and Excel on the taskbar. The Excel window may or may not be maximized. If it is not, click the **Maximize** button.

The buttons on the taskbar are displayed from left to right in the order the programs were opened.

Microsoft Excel
in title bar

Microsoft Excel button

Microsoft Word
button

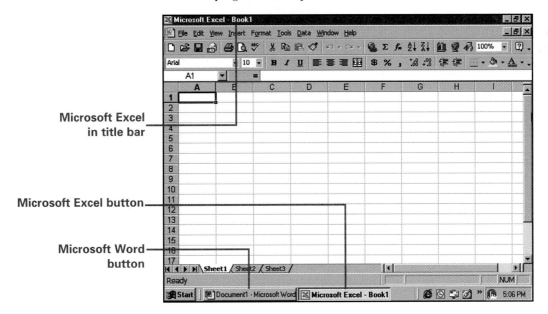

4 Click the **Microsoft Word** button on the taskbar. You are immediately taken to the Microsoft Word window. The program was open but hidden, so it did not have to be reloaded. The button for the program looks indented and is displayed in a lighter color.

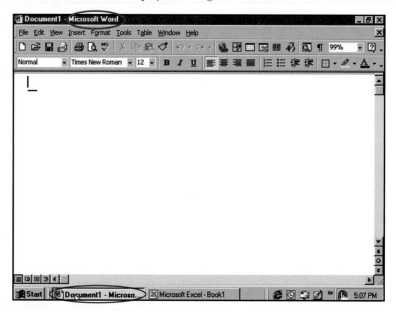

5 Click the **Microsoft Excel** button on the taskbar. The Excel window is displayed. You can have more than two programs open at the same time.

Close button

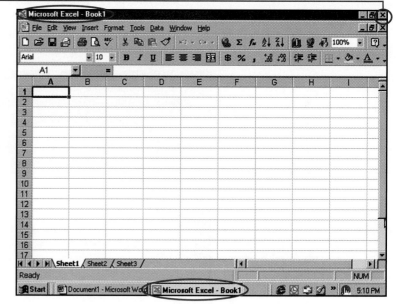

> **Quick Tip:** In addition to using the taskbar to move between open applications, you can also hold down ⟨Alt⟩ on the keyboard and quickly press and release ⟨Tab⟩ to scroll between open programs. When you see the program you want, release the ⟨Alt⟩ key and that program will be displayed on your screen. Each time you press ⟨Tab⟩, it scrolls to a different open program.

6 Click the **Close** button to close Excel. The Microsoft Word window is displayed again.

Close button

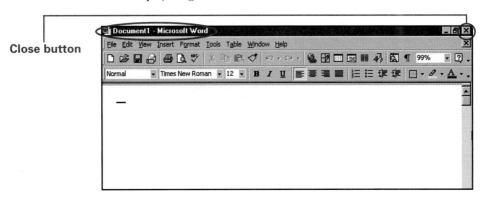

7 Click the **Close** button to close Word. You know there are no more programs open because the taskbar is empty.

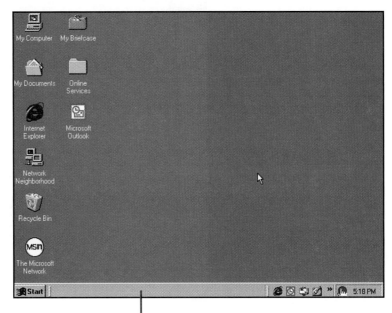

No buttons show on the taskbar

TASK 7

Using the Windows Help System
Why would I do this?

There are many more things you can do with Windows. If you want to do something in Windows but don't know how, Windows has a Help feature that can guide you. There are three separate Help functions included in the Windows Help file. The first is a Contents section that is similar to the Table of Contents in a book. The second is an Index of key terms that might help you find a topic if you know the proper terminology. The third is a Find (Search) feature that enables you to look for individual words in the Help text. This last feature is particularly important if you don't know the correct words and phrases to use with the Index feature.

In this task, you look up a topic in the Contents section, and then move to the Index section to look for Help on a specific topic.

1 Click the **Start** button and click the **Help** option. Windows Help is displayed. There are three tabs: Contents, Index, and Search (called Find in the older versions of Windows). Click the **Contents** tab, if necessary. The Contents page contains Help in a format similar to a Table of Contents in a book.

Contents tab   Index tab   Search tab

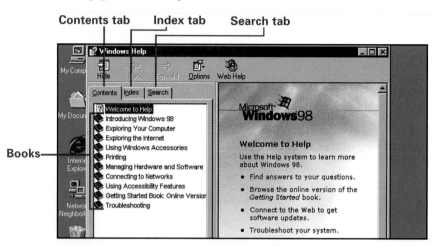

Books

In Depth: The look of the Help window varies depending on which version of Windows you are using. For example, the Contents tab contains five books in Windows 95 and ten books plus an introduction in Windows 98. The way these books are activated is also different. In Windows 95, you need to double-click on the book or select the book and click the Open button. If you are using Windows 98, you simply need to click once on the book. This demonstrates the progression of the Windows operating system toward a Web metaphor.

2 Click the **Introducing Windows** book if you are using Windows 98; double-click if you are using an older version. The Introducing Windows book is opened to display additional topics that are also in the form of books.

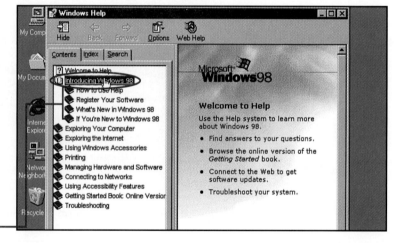

Topics in the
Introducing Windows book

3 Click the book in the first topic until you see a chapter displayed. The chapter will consist of a page with a question mark. The chapter topics will be different for different versions of Windows.

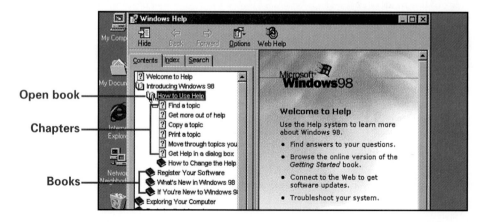

Open book

Chapters

Books

4 Click a chapter to open it. Read the information for the Help topic you have chosen. If necessary, use the scrollbar to view the rest of the topic.

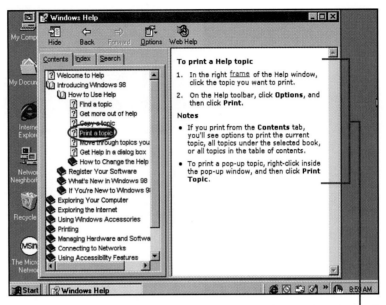

Selected topic displayed

5 Click the **Index** tab. The alphabetical index list is displayed. The Index tab enables you to type the word or phrase to locate the topic you need. As you type, related topics are displayed in the bottom part of the window. The index limits you to searches for words and phrases that Microsoft has predetermined.

Type the word or phrase here———

Related topics are shown here———

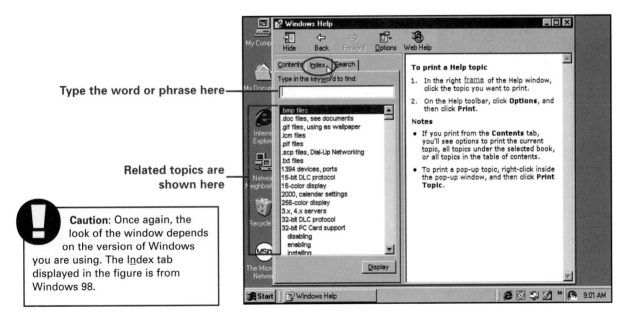

! **Caution:** Once again, the look of the window depends on the version of Windows you are using. The Index tab displayed in the figure is from Windows 98.

6 Type **Start** in the box at the top of the dialog box. Related topics are shown in the box below.

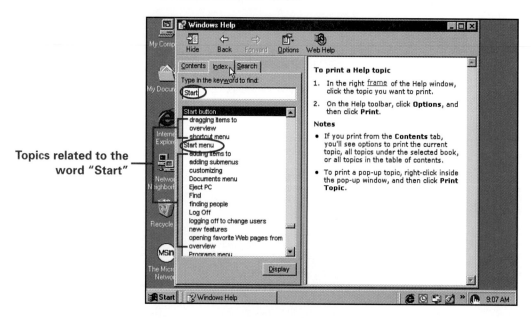

Topics related to the word "Start"

7 Double-click **customizing** from the Start menu topics. Read the instructions about customizing the taskbar and Start menu.

Caution: In Windows 95 Help, when you double-click customizing, a Topics Found dialog box opens. Double-click the topic **Customizing the taskbar or Start menu,** or single-click it and then click the **Display** button.

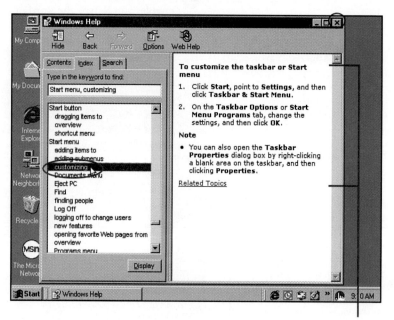

Topic displayed

In Depth: The third (Find/Search) tab in the Windows Help enables you to look through the Help text for individual words. This is particularly useful when you don't know the proper terminology for what you want to do.

8 When you are finished, click the **Close** button on the **Help** window. Help closes, and the open desktop is displayed.

TASK 8

Shutting Down Your Computer
Why would I do this?

It is important that you shut down your computer properly. To do this, you need to use the Shut Down option from the Start menu. The Shut Down option gives the computer a chance to close down many of the programs that are going on in the background—programs that you probably don't even know are running. Simply turning off the computer can cause problems.

In this task, you shut down your computer using the proper procedure.

1 Click the **Start** button. The Start menu is displayed.

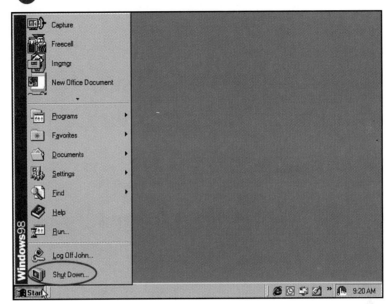

! **Caution:** Once again, the contents of the dialog box will depend on the version of Windows you are using. The dialog box shown in the figure is from Windows 98. The Windows 95 dialog box has a **Shut down the computer?** option.

2 Click **Shut Down** from the Start menu. The Shut Down Windows dialog box is displayed.

➜ **In Depth:** Sometimes you will need to restart your computer, in which case you should select the **Restart** option from the Shut Down Windows dialog box. If you are working in a lab or network environment, you may also have an option to shut down the computer and log on as a different user. If you have your own personal user login and password, you want to make sure you use this so that you have access to your files and any profiles or templates that you may have established in your network files.

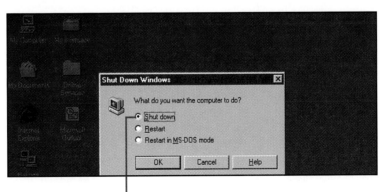

Shut Down option

3 Make sure the **Shut Down** (or **Shut down the computer?**) option is selected, and then click **OK** (**Yes** in Windows 95). The computer may shut down, or you may get a message telling you it is now safe to turn off your computer.

Lesson: 2

Windows Disk and File Management

Introduction

After you create something on your computer, you need to save it before you turn off the computer. When the power to the computer is turned off, the work you have done is lost unless it has been saved to a storage device. When you save your work, it is saved as a *file* and is usually stored on a disk drive. Most of the time, you store files on the *hard disk drive*, a *floppy disk drive*, or other type of storage device. If you are going to become a frequent computer user, you need to know how to use disks to store files effectively.

Your computer's hard disk drive, generally referred to as the hard drive, is the main storage device on your computer. It stores the programs that run on your computer, as well as the files that you save. It is usually identified on your computer with the notation C:\, but your computer may have more than one hard drive.

A floppy disk drive provides storage on a floppy disk, which is a small round, magnetized disk encased in hard plastic. You insert a floppy disk into the floppy disk drive and then save your files to that location. The floppy drive is generally identified on your computer with the notation A:\. If the computer you are using has two floppy drives, the second one will be identified as B:\. The advantage of using a floppy disk is the capability to take the disk with you and use it in other computers. Before you can use a floppy disk, it needs to be *formatted* so that it is ready to receive files. Most new disks are already formatted using a method that the IBM company made popular and that is also used by Windows. Some disks are already formatted for use in Apple computers and may be reformatted for use with Windows. Reformatting a disk permanently erases any files that are on the disk.

This book assumes that you are using a floppy disk to store the files you create for this book, although you may be using a hard drive, a network drive, or some other type of storage device. This enables you to work in the classroom, at home, at work, or in an open lab because you take your files with you. It is especially important that you know how to copy, paste, rename, and even delete files.

This book comes with another type of storage device, a *CD-ROM* disc. CD-ROM stands for Compact Disc-Read Only Memory. This is a storage device from which you can read and open files, but you cannot save files to these discs. In some lessons in this book, you will open a file from the CD-ROM disc and then save it to your floppy disk. In other lessons, you will copy the file from the CD-ROM disc to the floppy disk and then open it. You will need to know how to copy files from your CD-ROM disc onto a floppy disk.

In this lesson, you format a floppy disk and create two folders. You copy files from the CD-ROM disc onto the floppy disk, where you rename, move, change properties, and delete the files and folders.

Formatting a Disk

Why would I do this?

When you purchase a floppy disk, it will most likely be formatted for use on a Windows-based machine. (These disks are often labeled "IBM formatted.") There are instances, however, when you need to format the disks yourself. Formatting a disk sets it up to receive data. It also identifies and isolates any bad spots on the disk, and creates an area for a disk *directory*. The directory identifies the location of each of the files on the disk, so when you want to open a file, the computer knows where to find it. If there is any information on the disk, formatting will erase it.

In this task, you use Windows Explorer to format a floppy disk.

1 Place a floppy disk in drive **A:**. Drive A:\ is the floppy drive on your computer. It doesn't matter if the disk is new or used. If it has been previously used, or is formatted for use on an Apple computer, make sure any files on the disk are no longer needed.

> ! **Caution:** The edge with the sliding cover is inserted first. If you attempt to insert the disk upside down, it will not go in. Turn it over and try again.

Accessories

2 Click the **Start** button, move to the **Programs** option, and select **Windows Explorer**. The Windows Explorer program opens. Maximize the window if necessary. Windows Explorer provides a way to view your files. It provides a hierarchical view that enables you to see the relationship between files and folders. (You'll learn about folders in Task 2.)

Address box indicates currently selected drive or folder   **Title bar**   **Toolbar**

Menu bar

Address bar

– indicates that drive or folder is expanded

Drive icon

+ indicates that drive or folder is collapsed

List of drives and folders

Contents of the selected disk drive

Name	Size	Type	Modified
Books		File Folder	8/2/98 11:35 AM
Cdrom		File Folder	2/6/98 8:26 PM
Collwin		File Folder	8/17/98 3:58 PM
Dos		File Folder	3/30/95 12:00 PM
ExcelP1		File Folder	11/11/98 11:40 AM
IntroProjs		File Folder	1/15/99 7:52 AM
My Documents		My Docume...	2/7/98 7:43 PM
Program Files		File Folder	2/7/98 7:03 PM
Sally		File Folder	9/28/98 9:30 AM
Sound144		File Folder	3/30/95 12:00 PM
Temp		File Folder	6/8/95 10:11 AM
Tools_95		File Folder	6/8/96 5:38 PM
Ver2to95		File Folder	2/11/98 6:59 PM
Windows		File Folder	3/30/95 12:00 PM
Windrvs		File Folder	3/30/95 12:00 PM
Wlwin		File Folder	6/8/95 12:38 AM

3 If you can't see the icon that says 3 1/2 Floppy (A:), use the up arrow at the top of the vertical scrollbar in the Folders side of the window to move to the top of the list. The drive A icon should be visible near the top of the Folders area on the left side of the Windows Explorer window.

3 1/2 Floppy
(A:) drive   **Vertical scrollbar**

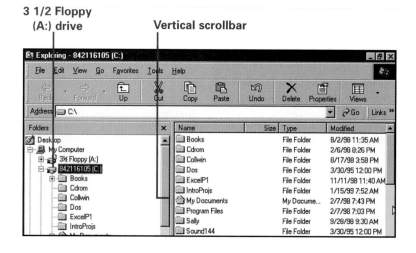

4 Right-click on the floppy disk icon or name. A shortcut menu is displayed. One of the options is Format. The options available in the shortcut menu will vary depending on what version of Windows you are using and what other programs you have installed on your computer.

Drive A icon ——

Format command ——

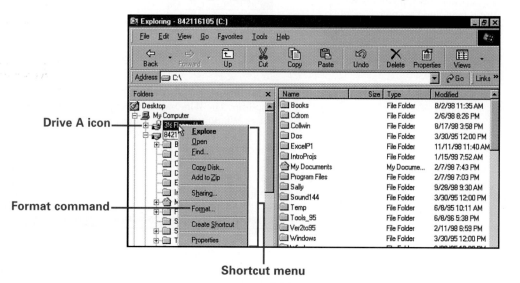

Shortcut menu

5 Click **Format**. The Format dialog box is displayed. Several options are available. You can do a Quick (erase) format, which erases the existing files on a previously formatted disk. You can also copy system files to the disk so that it can be used to boot your computer. Use the **Full format** option the first time a disk is formatted or if you are reformatting an Apple disk.

The capacity of the disk is detected automatically. If you are formatting a very old disk, the capacity might be 720Kb instead of 1.44Mb.

Disk capacity   **Start button**

Title indicates what
will be formatted

Full format option

Requests summary
information

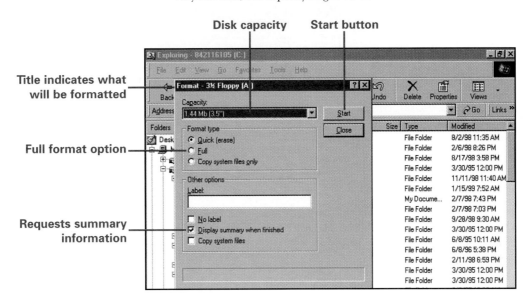

6 Select the **Full** format type and the **Display summary when finished** option, if necessary, and then click **Start**. Windows begins to format the disk. A bar at the bottom of the Format dialog box shows you the progress of the format, which will take a couple of minutes. When the formatting is complete, a Format Results dialog box is displayed.

Available space on the disk

Caution: The title bar of the Format dialog box includes the name of the disk that will be formatted, in this case 3 1/2 Floppy (A:). If it has anything else, do not proceed. Close the dialog box, go back to step 3, and make sure you first click on the 3 1/2 floppy disk icon before continuing.

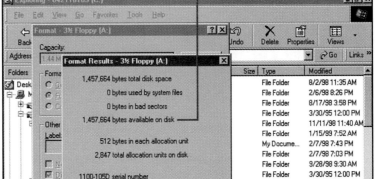

In Depth: Currently, the most common disk capacity for floppies is 1.44Mb, which can hold approximately 1,440,000 bytes of information. Older disks, called double density disks, have a capacity of 720Kb or 720,000 bytes.

7 Click the **Close** button in the Format Results dialog box. The program returns to the Format dialog box. If you wanted to format another disk, you would insert the new disk and repeat the process.

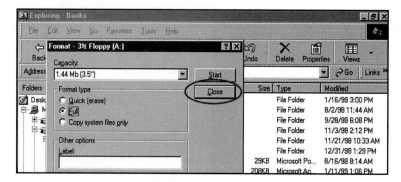

In Depth: When you are working in a program and try to save a file, if the disk you use is unreadable, Windows will automatically ask you if you want to format the disk the first time you try to open it.

If you use an Apple formatted disk, the computer will be unable to read it and will ask you if you want to format it. Before you reformat it, make sure it does not have files that you want to preserve. Formatting it will remove all the information on the disk and set it up to be readable by a Windows computer.

8 Click the **Close** button in the Format dialog box. You now have a clean disk ready to use.

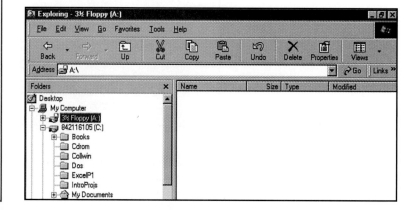

Creating a New Folder
Why would I do this?

Folders are used to organize files or other folders. As you use the computer more, you will build up a collection of files that you want to save. If you put all of the files in one place, searching for the right one might be difficult. Folders enable you to store your important files by type or by subject, and make handling your files more manageable. In most cases, you will use folders on hard drives or other drives with large capacities. You can, however, create folders on floppy disks. The procedure is the same regardless of where you create them.

In this task, you create two folders on the floppy disk you formatted in Task 1.

1 With the Windows Explorer window open, click on the icon for drive **A:**. You may have to scroll up to find the drive A:\ icon. A:\ shows in the address box, and the contents area on the right is empty because you just formatted the disk. Notice that the taskbar button for Explorer now shows 3 1/2 Floppy.

Address box shows drive A:

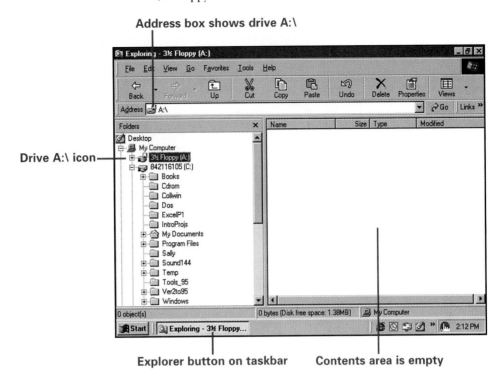

Drive A:\ icon

Explorer button on taskbar   **Contents area is empty**

2 Move the pointer to the contents area and click the right mouse button. A shortcut menu is displayed. The contents of the shortcut menu will depend on the version of Windows that you are using.

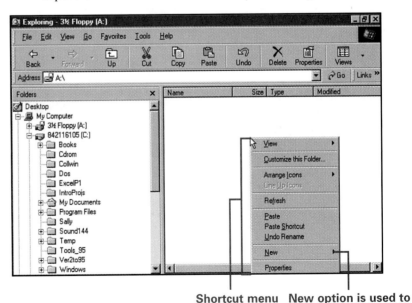

Shortcut menu   **New option is used to create folders**

3 Move the pointer to the **New** option. A submenu is displayed, showing the things you can create from this shortcut menu. The top of the submenu will give you the option of creating a new folder or shortcut. The contents of the bottom part of the submenu will be determined by the programs you have installed on your computer.

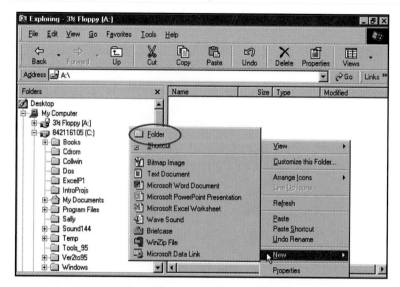

4 Move the pointer to the **Folder** option and click it with the left mouse button. A new folder is created with the name in the Edit mode.

Box around folder name indicates it is ready to be edited

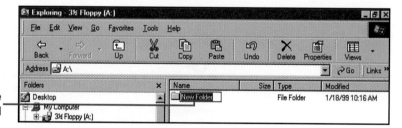

5 Type **Word Documents** over the default New Folder name and press ↵Enter). The folder now has a meaningful name.

Caution: If you accidentally press ↵Enter before you have a chance to name the folder, you can rename it. Click the folder once with the left mouse button to select it, choose **File**, **Rename** from the menu, and type a new filename.

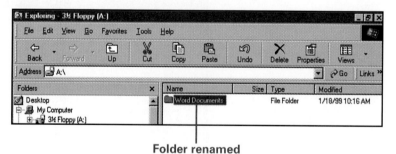

Folder renamed

6 Choose **File**, **New** from the menu. The same submenu you used in the shortcut menu is displayed.

New option   Folder option on submenu

Drop-down menu list——

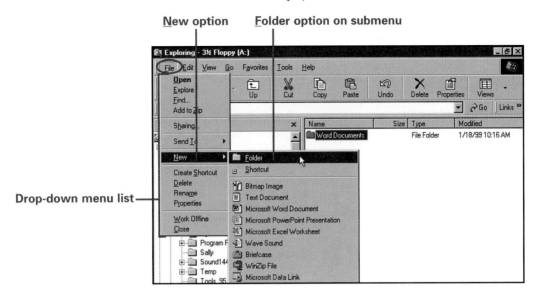

7 Select **Folder** from the submenu. Call the new folder **Excel Documents** and press ↵Enter. You now have two folders and no files on your disk.

Folder icon ——

New folder is renamed ——

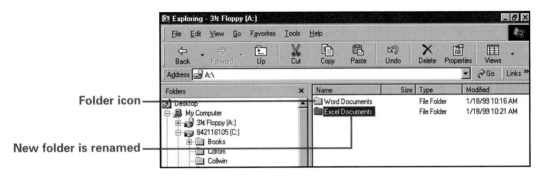

8 Click the **Name** column selector in the contents area of the Windows Explorer window. The folders are sorted in alphabetical order. If you were to click the Name column selector again, it would sort the folders in descending (z-to-a) order.

Leave the Windows Explorer window open for the next task.

Other column selectors can be used for sorting

In Depth: You can click any of the column selectors in the contents area to sort the files and folders. Clicking once on the Size column selector, for example, sorts the files by size, smallest to largest. Clicking it again sorts the files from largest to smallest. Because folders have no size, they are either all shown first or all shown last.

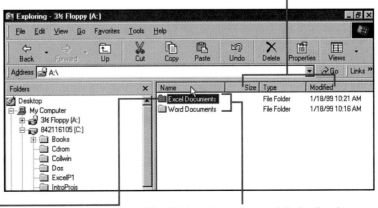

Name column selector ——

The folders have been alphabetized

TASK 3

Copying a File
Why would I do this?

You will often need to copy files from one location to another. As you work on your computer you will need to make backup copies of important files. You can do this by copying a file from a hard disk to a floppy disk, a network drive, or even a recordable CD. As you work through this book, you will want to make copies of your files to have them as backup files. You may also want to copy files to the hard drive on your own computer. In either case, knowing how to copy files is an important skill in using a computer. There are several different methods that can be used.

In this task, you copy a file from your student CD-ROM disc to the floppy disk you formatted in Task 1.

1 Place the CD-ROM disc that came with your book in the CD drive of your computer. Click the arrow on the right of the **Address** box in the Windows Explorer window and click the CD-ROM drive. The Windows Explorer window displays the folders that are on that disc. You will have several folders displayed in the contents area on the right side of the window.

Quick Tip: You can also select the CD-ROM disc from the list of folders in the **Folders** section of the Windows Explorer window. The drive letter of your CD-ROM may be different from the one showing in the figure.

CD-ROM selected

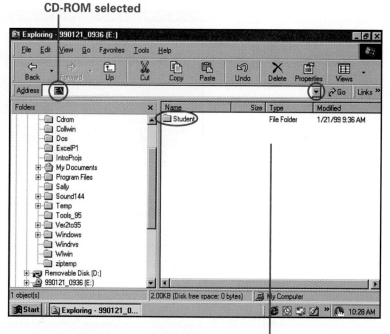

Folders on the CD-ROM disc shown here

2 Double-click the **Student** folder. A list of folders for each lesson used in this book is displayed.

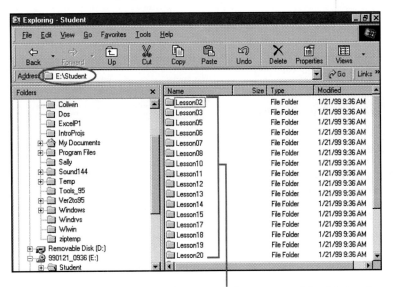

Folders numbered to match lessons used in this book

3 Double-click the folder for **Lesson02**. The files used in this lesson are displayed. Your screen may show additional files with the ones listed on the screen. Notice that the Address box shows the path to this list of files.

Address box shows the location of this group of files

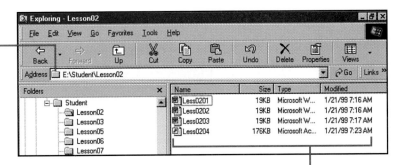

Files for Lesson02 folder displayed on the contents side of the window

In Depth: The files you see may show three letters following the filename, such as .doc. These letters are known as the *file extension*, and nearly all files have these extensions. Files created by Microsoft Office programs have a standard set of extensions that identify the type of program used to create the file. For example, Microsoft Word documents end in .doc, whereas PowerPoint presentations end with .ppt.

If you want to turn the extensions off, choose **View, Folder Options** from the menu, and then click the **View** tab, if necessary. Click the check box to the left of the phrase **Hide file extensions for known file types**. In this book, it is assumed that the file extensions are turned off.

④ Right-click **Less0201** and select **Send To** from the shortcut menu. A submenu is displayed showing the locations you can send the file. You are going to send this file to your floppy drive.

In Depth: If you are using disk space on a hard drive or network drive to store your files, you will need to use a different procedure. Several methods can be used, but the easiest is to select the file, use the **Edit**, **Copy** command from the menu (or click the **Copy** button), go to the destination drive and folder, and then use the **Edit**, **Paste** command from the menu (or click the **Paste** button).

Drive A:\ option

Selected file

Send To submenu

⑤ Select and click the **3 1/2 Floppy (A)** option. The file is copied to your floppy drive. Now you will repeat the procedure to copy two more files.

Dialog box showing the file is being copied

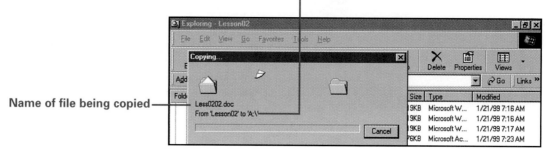

⑥ Right-click on the **Less0202** file, choose **Send To** from the shortcut menu, and then select and click the **3 1/2 Floppy (A)** option. The Less0202 file is copied to your floppy disk.

Shows where the file is being copied from and to

Name of file being copied

7 Right-click on the **Less0203** file, choose **Send To** from the shortcut menu, and then select and click the **3 1/2 Floppy (A)** option. The Less0203 file is copied to your floppy disk.

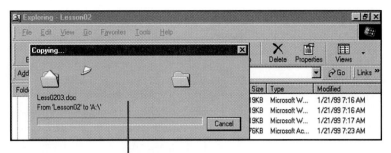

Less0203.doc is copied to the A:\ drive

8 Click the icon for drive **A** in the **Folders** section of the Windows Explorer window. Notice the three files that have been copied are now on the floppy disk. The files also remain on the CD-ROM disc. Copying does not remove the file from its original location, no matter where you are copying from and to. Leave your Windows Explorer open to drive A for the next task.

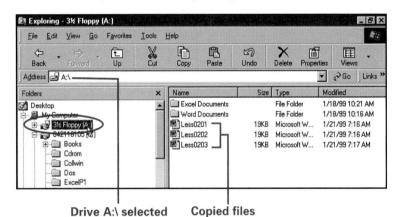

Drive A:\ selected   **Copied files**

TASK 4

Renaming a File or Folder

Why would I do this?

In Task 3, you copied a file from one location to another. You may copy files to make backups. You may also copy files that you want to change while preserving the original file. In that case, you will want to rename the file after it has been copied.

In this task, you rename a file you copied to your floppy drive in Task 3.

1 With the Windows Explorer window open, click the drive **A** icon, if necessary. The files and folders on your floppy drive are listed on the right side of the Windows Explorer window.

Folders

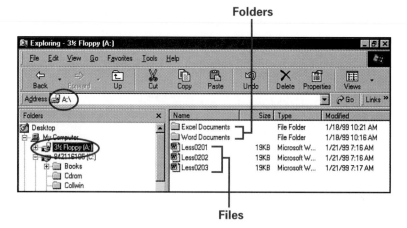

Files

2 Right-click on the **Less0201** file. The file is selected and a shortcut menu is displayed.

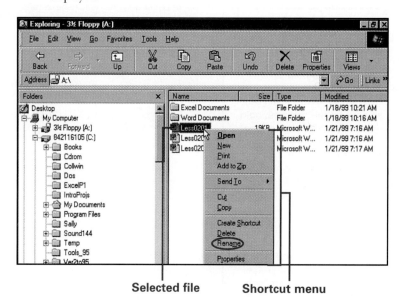

Selected file   Shortcut menu

3 Select **Rename** from the shortcut menu. The shortcut menu disappears and the filename is in the Edit mode.

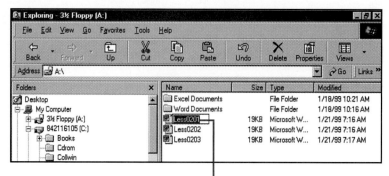

Filename in Edit mode

4 Type **Sample Word Document** over the existing name and press ⏎Enter. The first letter you type removes the entire original name. After you press ⏎Enter, a Confirm File Rename warning box is displayed asking if you are sure you want to rename a read-only file. You will learn how to change this file attribute in Task 5.

Warning box regarding renaming read-only file

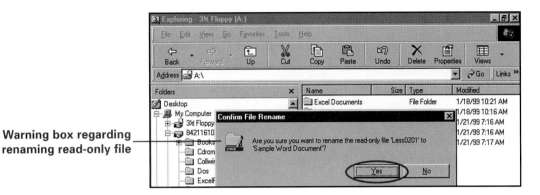

5 Click **Yes**. The warning box closes and the file is renamed.

In Depth: If your filename is longer than the Name column in the contents area of the Windows Explorer window, the right side of the filename will appear to be cut off. Don't worry, it's still there. If you want to see the entire filename, click on the line to the right of the Name column selector and drag to the right. You can resize any of the columns in the contents area.

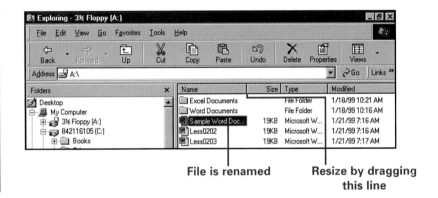

File is renamed   **Resize by dragging this line**

6 Click once on the **Excel Documents** folder. The folder is selected.

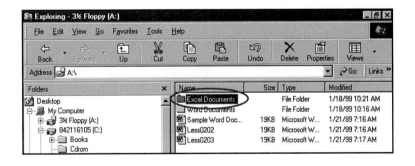

7 Choose **File**, **Rename** from the menu. The folder name is now in the Edit mode.

Quick Tip: There is a third way to rename a file or folder. You can click the file or folder once with the left mouse button, wait a second, and then click on it again and type in a new name. If you click too quickly, however, you will open the folder.

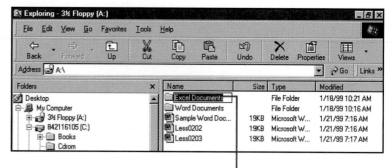

Folder name in Edit mode

8 Click to the left of the word **Documents** and drag to the right until you have selected the entire word.

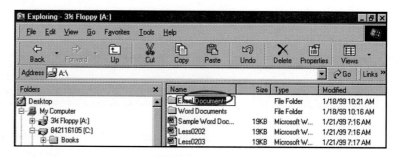

9 Type **Spreadsheets** over the word **Documents** and press ↵Enter. If you accidentally selected the space before the word **Documents**, you will have to put a space back in. The name of the folder has been changed. It doesn't matter which of the two methods of renaming files and folders you use, so use whichever is more comfortable for you. Leave Windows Explorer open for the next task.

In Depth: There are several restrictions for naming files or folders. A filename can contain up to 255 characters, including spaces, although the filename cannot begin with a space. It also cannot contain the following characters:
\ / : * ? " < > |

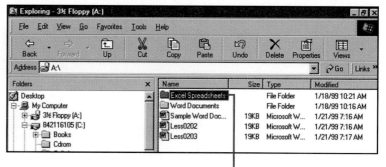

Folder is renamed

TASK 5

Changing File Properties
Why would I do this?

Each file has certain properties that are established when the file is created. These include the date and time the file was created, the last time it was modified, the last time it was accessed, the type of file, and the file location. There are also attributes that are set which may need to be changed. Files from a CD-ROM disc have the attribute of read-only.

In this task, you learn how to change the attribute property of a Word file.

1 Right-click the **Sample Word Document** file and click the **Properties** option on the shortcut menu. The Properties dialog box opens to the Summary page that displays the title of the document, its author, and other information. There are several tabs across the top of the dialog box.

Caution: If your properties dialog box opens to a different tab, click the summary tab to view this figure.

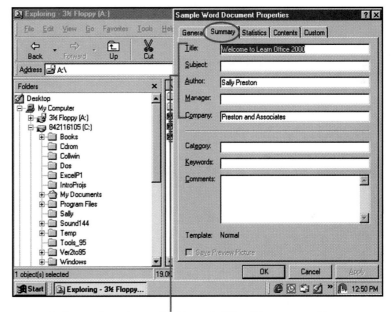

Information about the Sample Word Document file

2 Click the **General** tab. Notice that the attributes for this file show Read-only. The Read-only attribute prevents someone from opening and changing a file. To be able to use this file, you need to first remove the Read-only attribute.

Read-only check box————

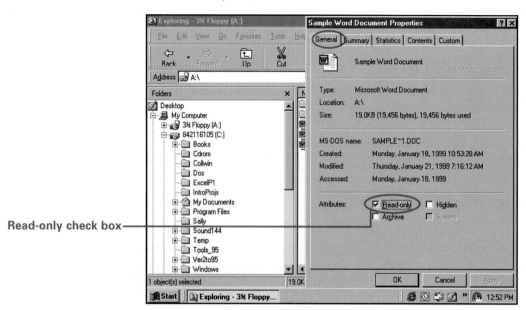

3 Click the **Read-only** check box to deselect it.

Read-only attribute
has been removed————

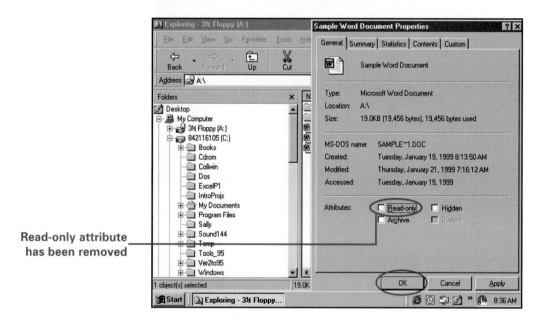

4 Click **OK**. The attribute for this file is changed and the Properties dialog box closes. Now change the attribute of the other two Word files on your floppy disk.

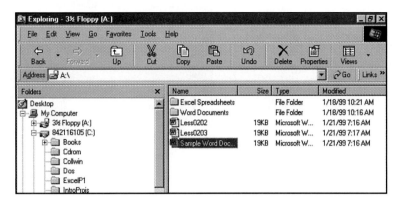

5 Right-click on file **Less0202** and choose **Properties** from the shortcut menu. The Properties dialog box opens.

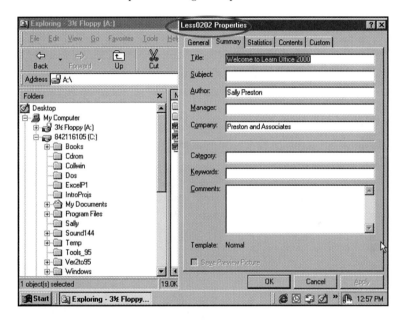

6 Click the **General** tab and deselect **Read-only** in the Attributes area. Then click **OK**.

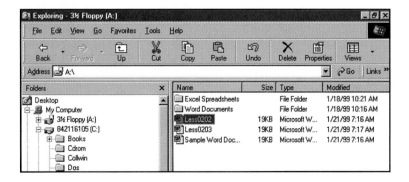

7 Repeat this process and remove the **Read-only** attribute for **Less0203**.

In Depth: As you saw in Task 4, if you attempt to rename a file that is read-only, a dialog box opens asking you to confirm that you want to rename a read only file. This also happens when you attempt to move a file that has a read-only attribute.

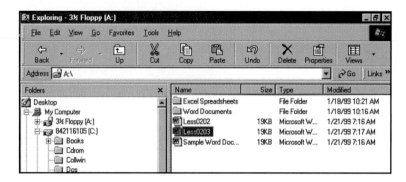

TASK 6

Moving a File

Why would I do this?

You have copied three files to your floppy disk. They are all Microsoft Word documents that should be in the Word Documents folder. You can move files, or even folders, from one folder to another, or up or down one folder level on the same disk drive.

In this task, you move the three documents into the Word Documents folder.

1 Click on the **Sample Word Document** file and drag it over the top of the **Word Documents** folder. The Word Documents folder is selected, and the name and icon of the file being dragged are visible over the folder name.

Highlighted folder   Document being dragged

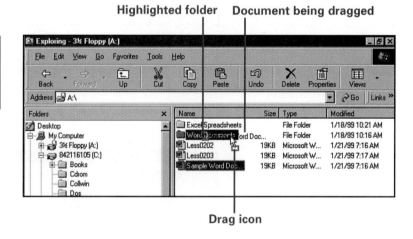

Drag icon

Caution: The look of the filename and icon being dragged vary in different versions of Windows.

2 Release the mouse button. The file disappears.

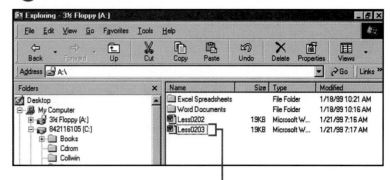

The Sample Word Document file no longer shows

3 Double-click the **Word Documents** folder to open it. Its contents, the file you just moved to the folder, are displayed in the contents pane. Look at the drive icon on the folders side of the window. Its plus sign has now changed to a minus sign, its folders are displayed, and the selected folder, Word Documents, now has an open folder icon. The Address box, which always displays the address and name of the open object, now shows the Word Documents folder on drive A:\.

– indicates this
drive is expanded
Open folder icon

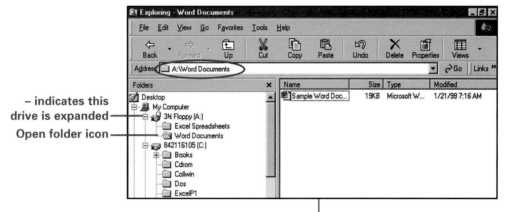

Word file has been moved

> ❗ **Caution:** A plus sign next to a drive icon in the Folders side of an Explorer window indicates that the drive contains folders. (The same thing applies to any folder that has a plus sign next to it.) Clicking the plus sign expands the view of the drive or folder on the Folders side of the window, displaying the folders or subfolders it contains. At the same time, the plus sign changes to a minus sign, indicating that the view is expanded. To see files that the drive or folder contains, you must open it by clicking it on the Folders side or double-clicking it on the contents side of the window.

4 Click once on the **3 1/2 Floppy (A:)** icon. The two remaining files are displayed with the two folders.

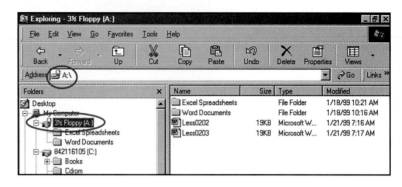

5 Click the **Less0202** file, hold the ⬆Shift key down, and click the **Less0203** file. Both remaining files are selected.

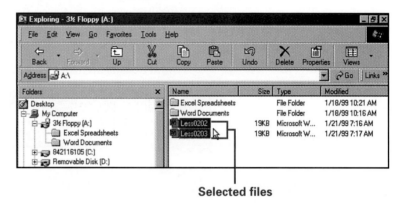

Selected files

6 Click and hold down the left mouse button on one of the two files, and drag them up to the **Word Documents** folder until it is selected, then release the mouse button. Both files disappear.

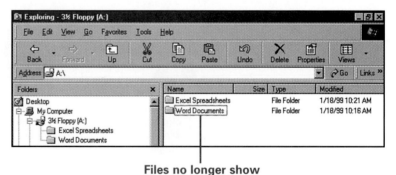

Files no longer show

7 Click on the **Word Documents** folder in the **Folders** area on the left side of the Windows Explorer window. All three files are now in the Word Documents folder. Leave Windows Explorer open for the next task.

In Depth: You can also move a file using the cut-and-paste method. To do this, select the file, and then choose **Edit**, **Cut** from the menu (or click the **Cut** button). Move to the new drive or folder, and then choose **Edit**, **Paste** from the menu (or click the **Paste** button).

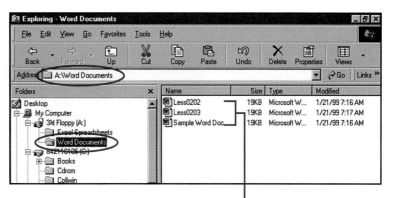

Word files moved to Word Documents folder

TASK 7

Deleting a File or Folder
Why would I do this?

When you are certain you no longer need a file, it is a good idea to remove it from the disk, whether it is a floppy disk or a hard drive. If you leave it on a disk too long, you tend to forget what was in the file. If you don't remove files, your disks can fill up. You can delete files in several ways.

In this task, you use two different methods to delete a file and a folder from your floppy disk.

1 With the **Word Documents** folder open, right-click the **Sample Word Document** file. A shortcut menu is displayed.

Selected file

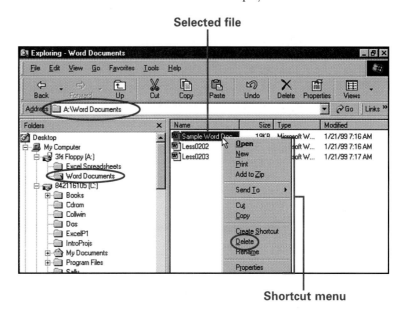

Shortcut menu

2 Select **Delete** from the shortcut menu. A dialog box is displayed asking if you are sure that you want to delete the file.

Confirms request to delete the file ——————

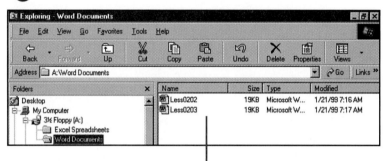

3 Click the **Yes** button. The file is deleted from the disk.

Quick Tip: You can also click the **Delete** button on the Windows Explorer toolbar to delete files.

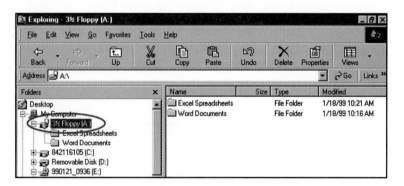

Sample Word document file is removed

4 Click once on the **3 1/2 Floppy (A:)** icon. The two file folders are displayed in the contents area.

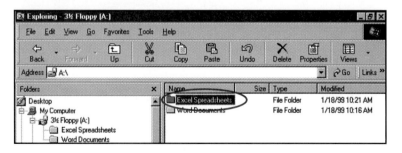

5 Click once on the **Excel Spreadsheets** folder using the left mouse button. The folder is selected.

6 Press ⌈Del⌋ on the keyboard. A dialog box is displayed asking if you are sure you want to delete the folder and all its contents. When you delete a folder, you also delete any files in that folder.

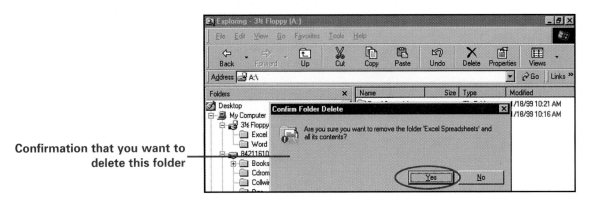

Confirmation that you want to delete this folder

7 Click the **Yes** button to confirm the deletion. The folder is deleted from the disk. Leave Windows Explorer open for the next task.

In Depth: Sometimes you will try to delete a file and Windows Explorer will display a dialog box that says that the file cannot be deleted. This usually means that the file is open. You must close a document before you can delete it.

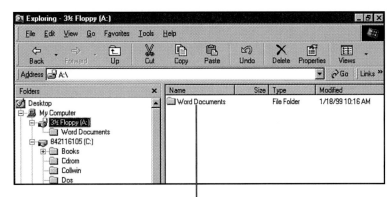

Excel Spreadsheets folder is removed

TASK 8

Copying a Floppy Disk
Why would I do this?

If you are saving your files on a floppy disk, you will want to make backup copies of your files. If you have access to a hard drive, you can copy files from a floppy disk to a temporary location on the hard drive, and then put a new floppy disk in the drive and copy the files from the hard drive to the new disk. There is, however, an easier way to duplicate an entire floppy disk. Before you begin this task, make sure you have an empty formatted disk available. When you use this procedure, everything on the destination disk is overwritten with the contents of the source disk.

In this task, you make a copy of an entire floppy disk.

1 Right-click on the **3 1/2 Floppy (A:)** icon. A shortcut menu is displayed.

Copy Disk command—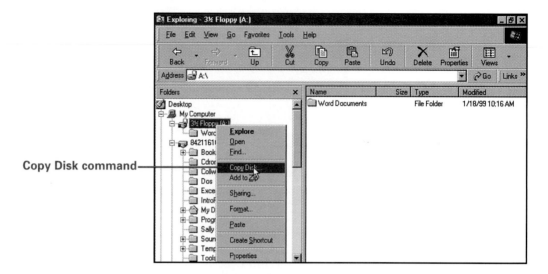

2 Select **Copy Disk** from the shortcut menu. A dialog box is displayed asking what you want to copy from and to.

Source   Destination

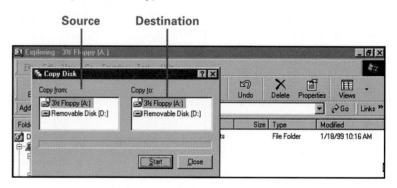

3 Click **3 1/2 Floppy (A:)** in the **Copy from** box and click the **Start** button. The program reads the disk you want to copy, known as the *source disk*, into memory. The program then asks you to insert the disk you want to copy to, called the *destination disk*.

Dialog box directing you to insert the destination disk

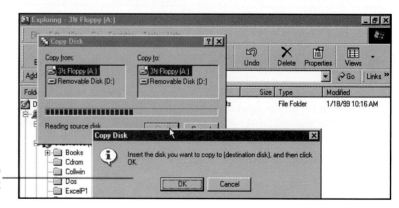

4 Remove the source disk and insert the destination disk; then click **OK**. The contents of the source disk are copied to the destination disk. When the Copy Disk procedure is finished, the Copy Disk dialog box displays a message that the copy was successful.

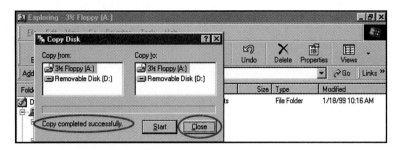

5 Click the **Close** button to close the Copy Disk dialog box. You now have an identical copy of your original disk.

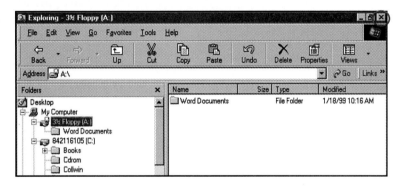

6 Click the **Close** button to close Windows Explorer. If you are finished using the computer, click the **Start** button and select **Shut Down**.

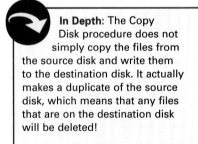

In Depth: The Copy Disk procedure does not simply copy the files from the source disk and write them to the destination disk. It actually makes a duplicate of the source disk, which means that any files that are on the destination disk will be deleted!

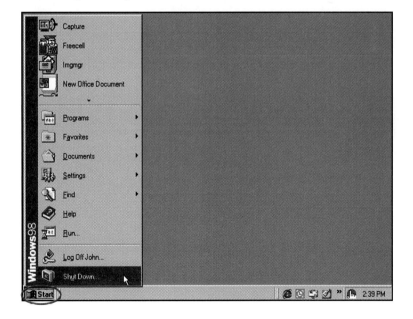

Lesson: 3

Office 2000 Basics

Task 1 Launching and Exiting an Office Application

Task 2 Opening and Saving an Existing Document with a New Name

Task 3 Using Menus and Toolbars

Task 4 Printing a Document Using the Toolbar Button and the Menu

Task 5 Using the Office Assistant Help Feature

Introduction

Many of the techniques and procedures you use in one Office 2000 application will work in most or all of the other applications. (Note: The term *application* refers to one of the parts of the Office suite, such as Word or Excel. In this book, it is used synonymously with the word *program*). For example, you will use the same procedures to activate a menu in Word as you do in Excel and PowerPoint. The toolbars are used in the same way, and some of the more common buttons (Print, Copy, Paste, Undo, and several others) that you will learn about in the following lessons are exactly the same in every application.

There are also differences between the applications. No two have exactly the same menu options, although all have many similarities. Some buttons are common to many of the programs, but are missing from one or two others. For example, PowerPoint does not use the Print Preview feature, which is used in many other applications.

One of the main strengths of the Microsoft Office 2000 suite is consistency of the programs and the way they work together. A chart created in Excel can easily be inserted into a Word document or a PowerPoint presentation. An outline in Word can be used as the backbone of a PowerPoint presentation. A table of information in Access can be sent to Excel for numerical analysis.

Another strength of the Office suite is the capability to save files created in most applications in a format that can be read on the World Wide Web. You can create a Web page using Word, Publisher, or Front Page. You can create a Web slideshow using PowerPoint, and you can publish Access data pages that can be read, searched, and sorted by people all over the world.

In this lesson, you will look at some of the features common to all (or nearly all) of the Microsoft Office 2000 applications.

Launching and Exiting an Office Application
Why would I do this?

To work in one of the Microsoft Office 2000 applications, it first needs to be opened. Starting an application is referred to as *launching* the program. This is usually done using the Start button on the taskbar. All Office applications can be launched in exactly the same way. The exit procedure is also consistent for all Office applications.

In this task, you launch Microsoft Word and exit it.

1 Click the **Start** button and move to the **Programs** option. A submenu is displayed. It doesn't matter if Windows Explorer or any program is open. You can launch any Office application with one or more programs open.

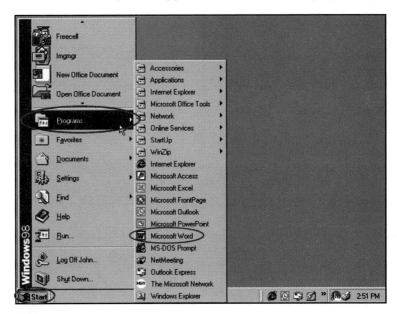

In Depth: You may have two toolbars displayed, instead of the one that is shown in the following figures. This issue will be addressed in Task 3. Your work area may also look different, with a ruler down the left side of the screen. There are several different views you can choose when working in Word, and the one that is displayed is the last one that was used on that machine. This will be addressed in the Word section of this book. Finally, you may have a paper clip icon somewhere on your screen. This is the Office Assistant; ignore it for now.

In some of the applications, such as Access and PowerPoint, you will have to answer questions before you get to the window in which you will enter information. In Word and Excel, however, a blank document (or worksheet) is displayed as soon as the program is launched.

2 Select **Programs** and click **Microsoft Word** from the submenu. The Microsoft Word window is opened to a new document. The document is given a default name, such as Document1. This name is displayed in both the title bar and the taskbar.

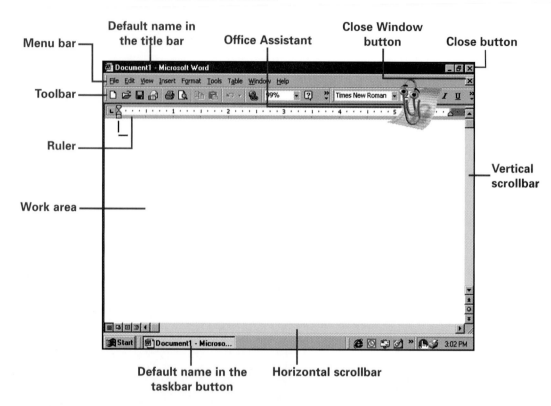

Menu bar —
Default name in the title bar
Office Assistant
Close Window button
Close button

Toolbar —

Ruler —

Vertical scrollbar

Work area —

Default name in the taskbar button
Horizontal scrollbar

3 If the window does not fill the screen, click the **Maximize** button on the title bar. (It will be the middle button on the right end of the bar; see Task 5 in Lesson 1 if you need review.) this gives you the largest area to work in.

When the window is maximized, the Maximize button changes to a Restore button

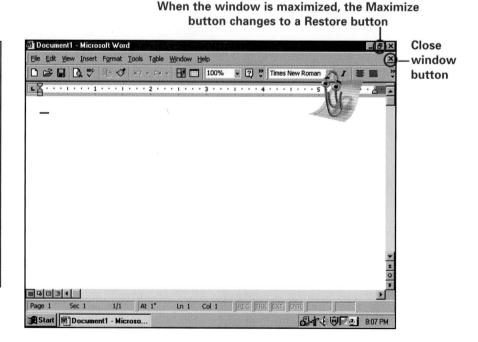

Close window button

Caution: You may not see the default name in the taskbar if the taskbar is hidden. If the taskbar is hidden, move your pointer to the bottom of the screen. The taskbar will pop up. If you want to display or hide it, right-click in an open area of the taskbar and select **Properties** from the shortcut menu. Click the **Auto hide** check box to turn the Auto hide feature on or off. The taskbar will be displayed in the figures through the end of this lesson, then turned off for the rest of the book. This is to give you the maximum viewing area for the figures.

4 Click the **Close Window** button on the right edge of the menu bar. The Close Window button is just below the Close button in the title bar. The document closes, leaving the Microsoft Word window open.

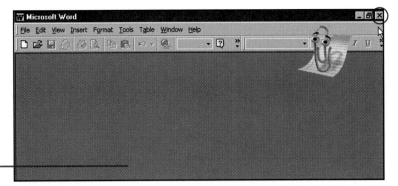

No document is active

5 Click the **Close** button in the upper-right corner of the screen. This closes Microsoft Word. The open desktop is displayed.

TASK 2

Opening and Saving an Existing Document with a New Name
Why would I do this?

In Task 1, you launched Microsoft Word, which automatically opened a blank document that could be used to create a new document. Once a document is created and saved to a disk, you may want to open it again so you can edit it, print it, or read it. In this book, you open files from the CD-ROM disc that came with your book and save the files with a new name on your floppy disk. As you progress through a lesson, you can save the changes with the click of a button.

In this task, you use the Open dialog box to copy a file from your CD-ROM disc to your floppy disk. You then open the document, make a change, and save the change. This is the document you will be using for the rest of this lesson.

1 Click the **Start** button, choose **P**rograms, then select **Microsoft Word**. Word opens to a blank document.

Open button

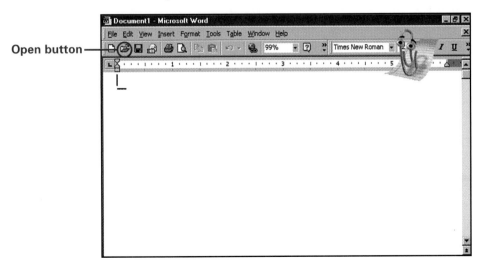

2 Make sure the CD-ROM disc that came with your book is inserted in the CD-ROM drive. Then click the **Open** button on the toolbar. The Open dialog box is displayed.

Look in box——

List arrow——

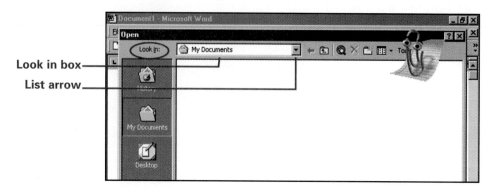

3 Click the list arrow at the end of the **Look in** box and select the CD-ROM drive from the list. The folders on the CD-ROM disc are displayed.

CD-ROM drive selected——

Folders listed here——

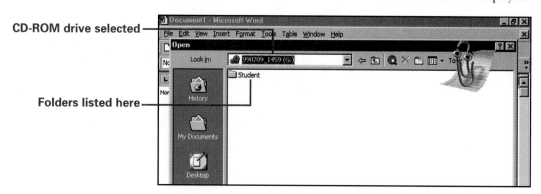

4 Double-click on the **Student** folder to display the contents of the folder. Each lesson in this book has a separate subfolder that contains all of the files that are related to that particular lesson. These are the same folders you saw in Lesson 2 when you used Windows Explorer.

Student folder selected

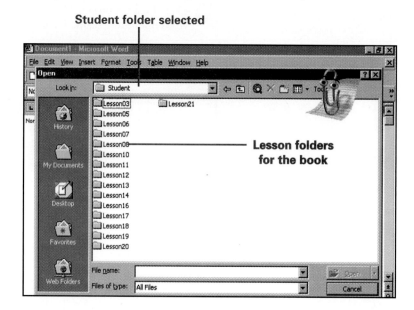

Lesson folders for the book

5 Double-click **Lesson03** to open the folder for this lesson. A list of Word files is displayed. The **03** in the filename designates this as a file for Lesson 3. The last number in the filename identifies the sequence in which the file is used in the lesson. The same numbering pattern is used throughout the book.

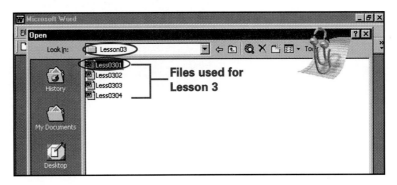

6 Select **Less0301** and click the **Open** button. The file opens as a read-only file. If you try to save it, a message will tell you the disc is write-protected. Before you can begin to use this file, you need to save it with a new name on your floppy disk.

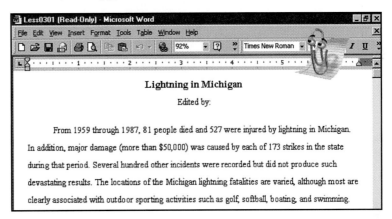

7 Choose **File**, **Save As** from the menu. The Save As dialog box opens, showing the same list of files as in the Open dialog box. These two dialog boxes are very similar, except one is used to open files and the other is used to save files. To save this file, you need to choose locations you can optionally change its name at the same time.

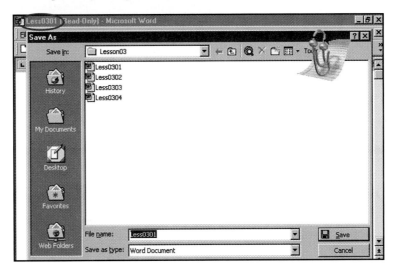

8 Make sure there is a formatted floppy disk in drive A. Then click the list arrow at the end of the **Save in** box and select **3 ½ Floppy (A:)**. The contents of the disk in the A drive are displayed.

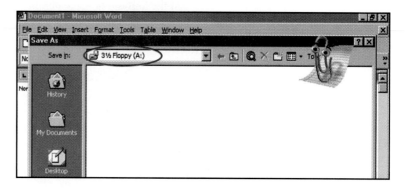

9 Click and drag across the name in the **File name** box to select the filename.

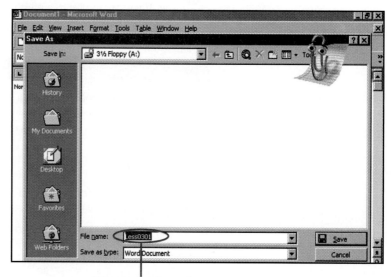

Filename selected

10 Type **Lightning Data** in the **File name** box.

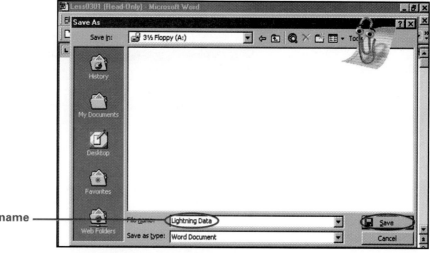

New filename

11 Click the **Save** button. The file is saved with the new name on your floppy disk, and is no longer a read-only file.

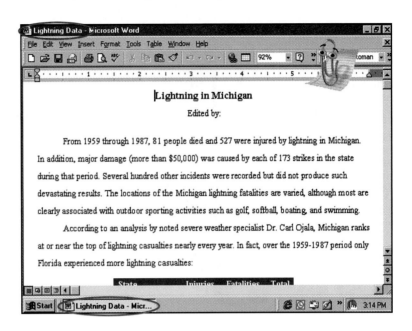

12 Click the pointer to the right of **Edited by:** and type your name. The pointer is now in the form of an I-beam. When you position the I-beam pointer and click with the left mouse button, a flashing vertical line is inserted. This is known as the *insertion point*. When you start typing, the text will appear at the insertion point, not at the pointer location. This is true in all Office programs.

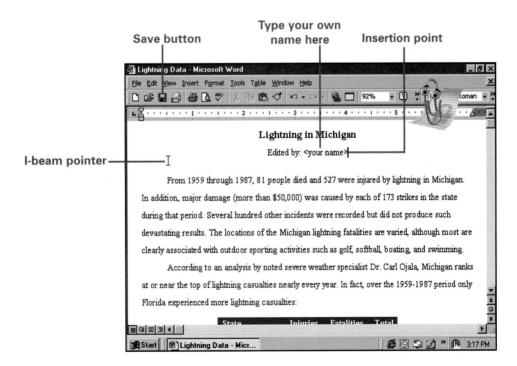

13 Click the **Save** button on the toolbar. (Look for the ScreenTip if you have trouble identifying the button.) The changes you just made to the document are saved. Leave the document open for the next task.

ScreenTip —

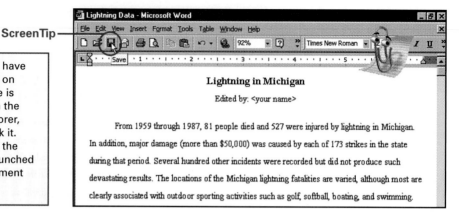

Quick Tip: Once you have the document saved on your floppy disk, there is a quick method to open it in the future. Open Windows Explorer, find the file, and double-click it. The application that created the file (in this case, Word) is launched automatically, and the document opens.

TASK 3

Using Menus and Toolbars

Why would I do this?

You have already used both menus and toolbars in the first two lessons of this book. In Lesson 2, for example, you used the File menu option to create a new document. Earlier in this lesson, you were asked to click buttons in a toolbar. The toolbars and menu bar have features that you will need to know to understand the way Office 2000 works.

In this task, you learn how to use the menu and how to use and modify a toolbar.

1 With the **Lightning Data** document open, click the **Tools** option in the menu bar. A fairly short drop-down menu is displayed. The options shown are the most commonly used <u>T</u>ools options and the ones most recently used on your computer. There are other <u>T</u>ools options that are not visible yet.

In Depth: The letter that is underlined in the menu option refers to a keyboard shortcut for that option. An alternative way to activate the menu is to press [Alt] and press the underlined letter, which activates the drop-down menu. You can then use the up and down arrows to move to menu choices and press [↵Enter] to select a command.

The Tools drop-down menu

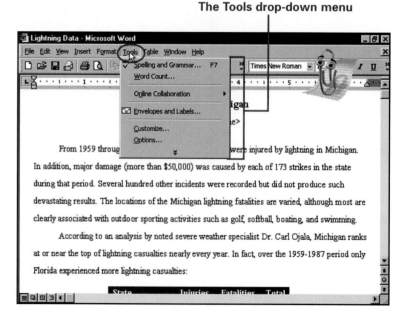

2 Leave the pointer on the **Tools** menu option for a couple of seconds. The Tools drop-down menu expands. The options with the dark gray background are the commands that were visible in the unexpanded drop-down menu. Those with a light gray background are less commonly used commands. This feature enables you to choose from the most commonly used commands in a short menu, but adds other options to be used when necessary. If you use one of these other options on a regular basis, it will show up in the short drop-down menu.

Notice that some of the commands in the Tools menu have arrows on the right side. This means that there is a submenu for that menu option.

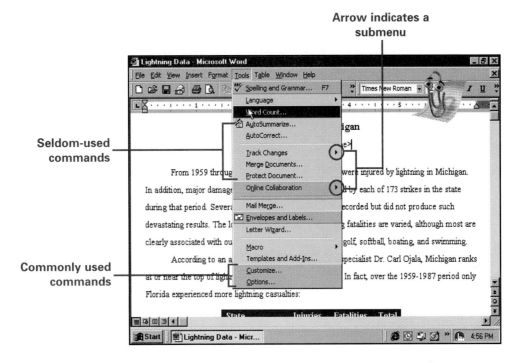

Arrow indicates a submenu

Seldom-used commands

Commonly used commands

3 Move the pointer anywhere in the document and click. When you have a menu open and want to close it, clicking outside the menu will turn it off. You can also press (Esc) to turn off a menu.

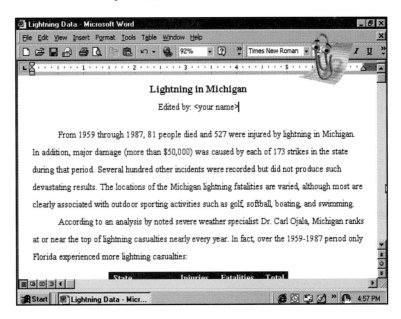

4 Click **View** and move the pointer down to the **Toolbars** option. A submenu is displayed showing the toolbars that are available. The ones that are open have check marks to the left. There is also a Customize option at the bottom of the submenu.

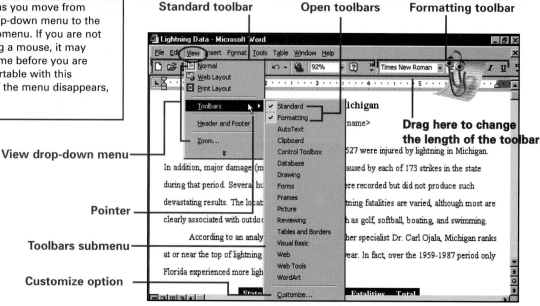

Standard toolbar   Open toolbars   Formatting toolbar

Drag here to change the length of the toolbar

View drop-down menu

Pointer

Toolbars submenu

Customize option

5 Move the pointer to the **Toolbars** submenu and select **Customize**. The Customize dialog box is displayed. This dialog box consists of three tabs— Tool**b**ars, **C**ommands, and **O**ptions.

Tabs used to access different pages of the dialog box

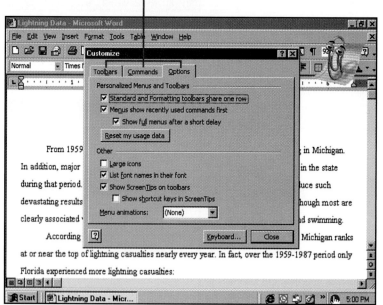

6 Click the **Options** tab, if necessary. The various toolbar options are displayed.

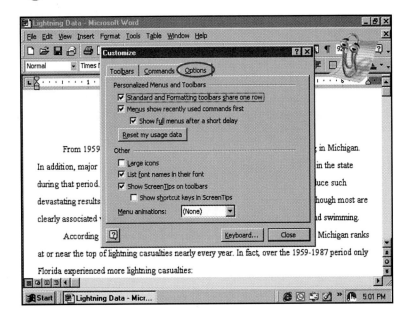

7 Click the check box to turn off the **Standard and Formatting toolbars share one row** option, if necessary. This will cause the Standard and Formatting toolbars to be displayed on separate rows. The second toolbar will decrease your work area slightly, but the convenience of seeing all of the buttons more than makes up for that. You should use this procedure to separate the main toolbars when you start the Excel and PowerPoint sections of this book. All of the figures from this point on will show the double toolbars when appropriate.

The row sharing option has been turned off

Close button

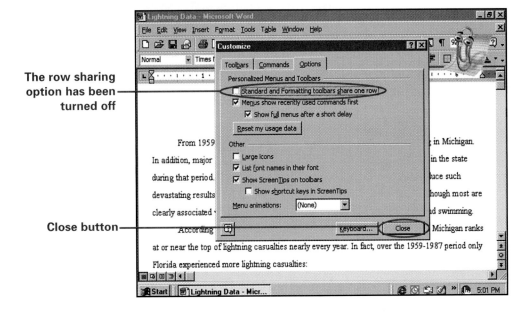

8 Click the **Close** button in the dialog box to turn it off. Notice that you now have two rows of toolbars. Also notice that some boxes on the toolbar have arrows on the right side, which are referred to as list arrows or down arrows.

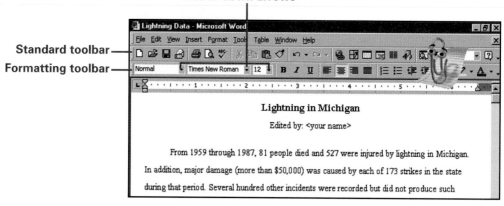

9 Click the down arrow on the **Font** box on the Formatting toolbar and release the mouse button. A drop-down list is displayed, showing some of the available fonts. There is also a vertical scrollbar at the right of the drop-down list. Try scrolling up and down to see the different fonts you will be able to use.

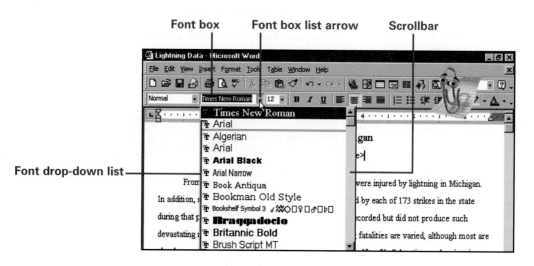

10 Click anywhere in the document to close the Font menu. Leave the document open for the next task.

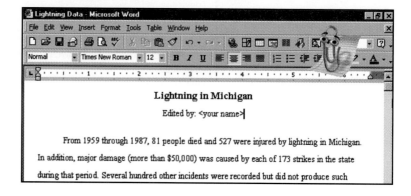

> ✓ **Quick Tip:** You can add or remove toolbars by right-clicking on any toolbar. This activates a shortcut menu that displays all of the available toolbars and the <u>C</u>ustomize option. Scroll down and select the toolbar you want to turn on or off and click it once. To test this, try turning on the **Drawing** toolbar, and then turn it back off.

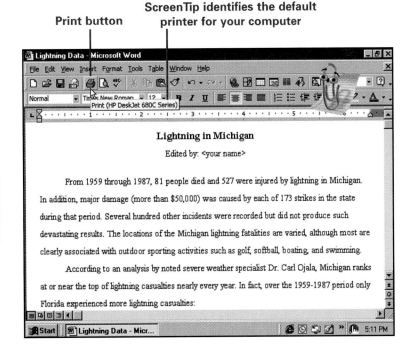

TASK 4

Printing a Document Using the Toolbar Button and the Menu
Why would I do this?

You will print documents for many different reasons—as draft copies for proofing, or as final documents, handouts, or even overhead transparencies. There are two different printing levels with most Office applications. The easiest way to print is to simply click the Print button. This sends a complete document to the printer. The problem with using the Print button is that it gives you little control over the process. You can also print using the Print command from the File menu. This gives you much more control and enables you to print specific pages or ranges of information. It also enables you to specify a printer and set the page layout.

In this task, you print the document you've been working on in this project using both the Print button and the menu command.

1 With the **Lightning Data** document still active, make sure your printer is turned on, then click the **Print** button on the Standard toolbar. The entire document is sent to the printer.

Caution: If the document does not print, it could mean that your printer is not turned on or is not connected properly. Check your connections and try again. If this does not work, you will need to make sure the correct printer is chosen in the Print dialog box, which you open in Step 2. If there are several printers available, ask your instructor or lab administrator which printer you should use.

Print button

ScreenTip identifies the default printer for your computer

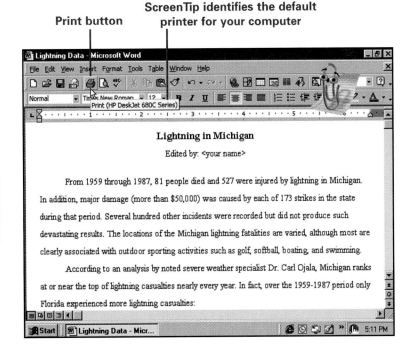

2 Choose **File**, **Print** from the menu. The Print dialog box is displayed. This dialog box enables you to choose a printer, specify the number of copies to be printed, select specific pages to print, and perform several other important tasks.

Current page option

Click here to select another printer

Select pages to print

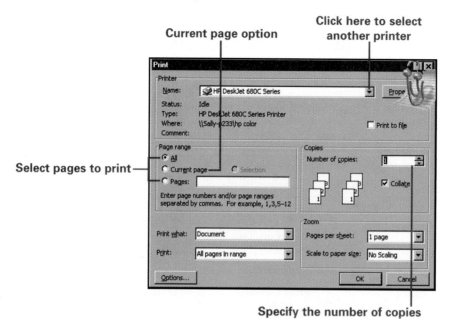

Specify the number of copies

3 Click the **Current page** option in the **Page Range** section. The page you print may not be the page showing on the screen. The program will print whichever page the insertion point is in.

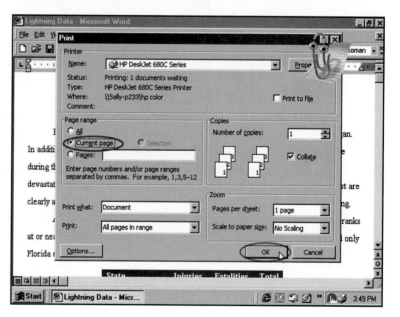

4 Click **OK** to print the current page. The dialog box closes and the page containing the insertion point is printed. Leave the document open for the next task.

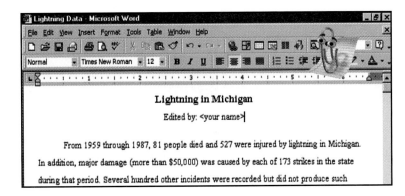

TASK 5

Using the Office Assistant Help Feature

Why would I do this?

In Lesson 1, you learned how to use Microsoft Help for Windows. There are several ways to get Help with your questions in any of the Office programs, including some of the procedures you used with Windows Help. The major Help source in Office applications is the Office Assistant, in addition to the Contents and Index options you saw in the Windows Help program. The Office Assistant is a program that enables you to ask questions in sentence form. When you ask a question of the Office Assistant, a series of possible related topics are displayed. You pick one of the topics and expand on it.

The Help that you see is specific to the application you are using. If you are using several applications at once, be sure to access Help from within the application where you need Help. Help enables you to learn as you use an application. You will find that using an Office application is an ongoing learning process, and Help can be an integral part of that learning. Sometimes when you use Help, it is useful to print the topic for future reference.

In this task, you use the Office Assistant to get Help.

In Depth: Occasionally, when you are typing a document or trying to perform a procedure, the Office Assistant will appear, even though you haven't called for it. Don't worry—the Office Assistant is just trying to be helpful. Read through the comment, and if it looks like it might be helpful, follow the onscreen instructions. If you do not want this Help, you can simply close the Help window. If you do not like these hints appearing on your screen, click the Office Assistant **Options** button and turn off the check boxes in the **Show tips about** section of the **Options** page.

1 If the Office Assistant is not displayed on your screen, select **Help**, **Show the Office Assistant** from the menu. The Office Assistant is displayed on the screen. You can move it by clicking and dragging it to a new location.

Office Assistant

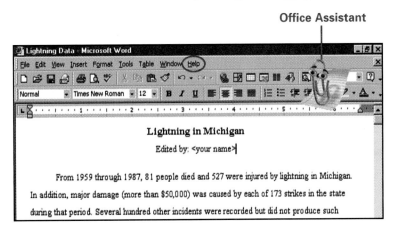

2 To get Help on a topic, click once on the Office Assistant with the left mouse button. A small dialog box is displayed, asking you what you would like to do. The list of topics you see may be different from the ones shown in the figure.

List of topics

Type question here

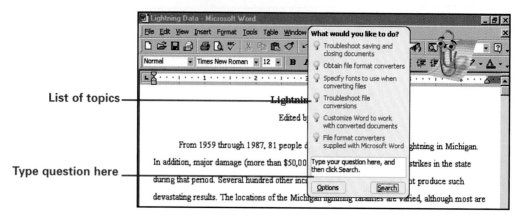

3 Type **How do I center text** in the box. The Office Assistant will look for keywords in your question and try to come up with answers. Notice that you do not have to add a question mark to your question.

Quick Tip: If you start to use the Office Assistant and change your mind, you can remove the dialog box from the screen by clicking anywhere in the document outside the dialog box.

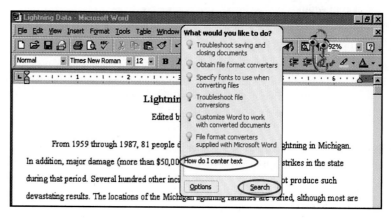

4 Click the **Search** button. The Office Assistant has looked at your question and anticipated possible answers. The most likely group of answers is shown on the screen. If the topic you are searching for does not appear in this list, click the **See more** button. The most likely answer to your question appears at the top of the list. Notice that by the end of the list the topics are getting less and less relevant to your question.

Topic buttons

A list of possible topics is displayed

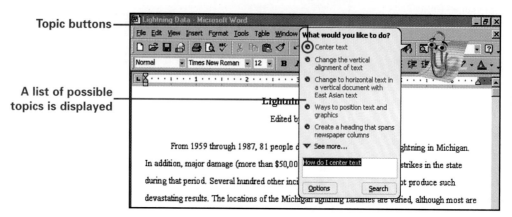

5 Click the button for the **Center text** topic. Several things happen. The document you are working on decreases in size and a Help window is displayed. Notice that some of the text is in blue. This means that the text is "hot" and more Help is available if you click the word or phrase. You can use the vertical scrollbar to move down the Help window.

Show button

A Help window explains the topic you select

Caution: Your Help window may be displayed on the right side of the screen, and may be a different width depending on how it was last used.

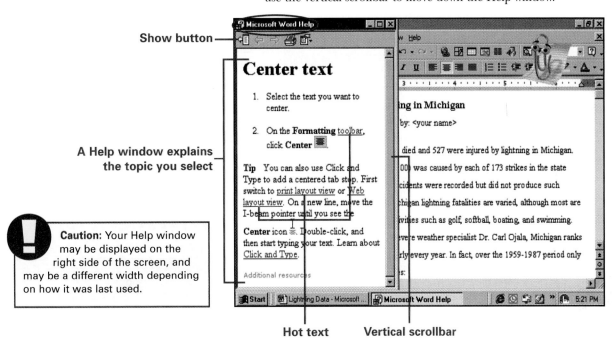

Hot text   Vertical scrollbar

6 Click the **Show** button. The Help window expands to include different types of Help. The Help window may also take up the entire screen. This Help is similar to the Windows Help you used in Lesson 1. The Index enables you to type in a word and see if it matches a predefined topic, while the Contents section reads like a book with chapters and topics. The Answer Wizard works just like the Office Assistant—you type in a question and the wizard displays a list of related topics. To move between these features, simply click the tabs at the top of the window. The Show button has changed to the Hide button. If you click the **Hide** button, the additional Help screen is removed from the screen.

Tabs for different Help options   Close button

Hide button

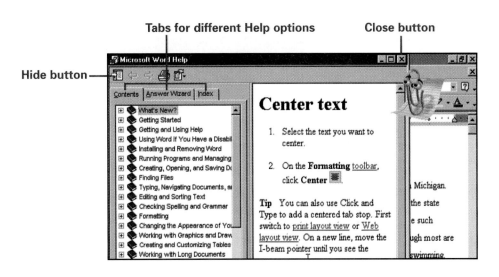

7 Click the **Contents** tab and click the ⊞ next to the topic **Getting and Using Help**. A page and four subtopics are displayed.

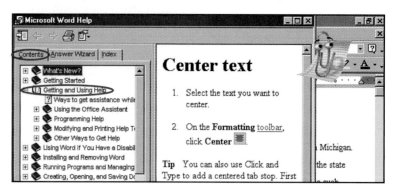

8 Click the ⊞ next to **Modifying and Printing Help Topics**, then click **Print a Help topic** from the pages that are displayed. The topic on the right changes to this selection. Scroll through this topic to learn how to print a Help topic. On occasion, you will be asked to print Help topics as you work through this book.

Print button

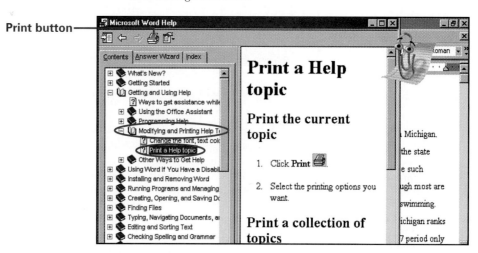

9 Click the **Print** button, make sure the **Print the selected topic** option is selected, and then click **OK**. The Print dialog box opens.

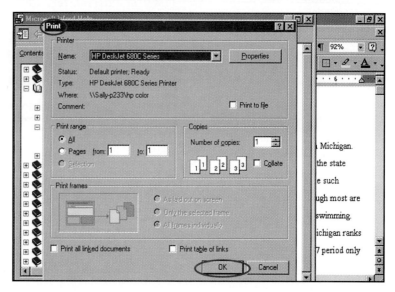

10 Make sure the printer is connected and turned on; then click **OK** to print this topic.

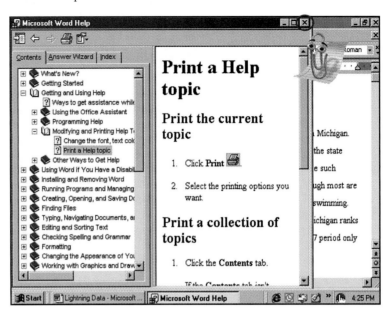

11 Click the **Close** button to close the Help window. The Help window closes, and the Office Assistant is still showing on your screen.

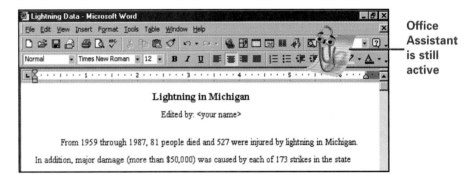

Office Assistant is still active

Quick Tip: You can open the Assistant by clicking the Office Assistant button on the toolbar. The Assistant is the gatekeeper for the rest of the Help options. To get to the Contents or Index options, you must first ask the Assistant a question and click **Search**. Once a topic is displayed, you can then click the **Show** button to expand the window to show the Contents and Index options. Chances are, though, that the Assistant will come up with a list of topics that is close to what you want.

In Depth: Some people do not like to have the Office Assistant on the screen at all. You can hide the Office Assistant by choosing **Help**, **Hide the Office Assistant**. To turn it off completely, click once on the Office Assistant and click the **Options** button. Click the check box for the **Use the Office Assistant** option at the top of the dialog box.

12 Right-click on the Office Assistant and choose **Hide** from the shortcut menu to remove the Assistant from the screen.

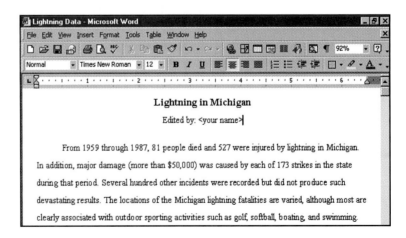

13 Close Word and shut down your computer if you are done working.

Introduction to Word

Microsoft Word is a word processing application program. A word processing program allows you to enter text and then change it by editing existing text, moving blocks of text, or changing the appearance of the letters. The document is stored electronically, so it can be duplicated, printed, copied, and shared with others more conveniently than paper documents.

How Word Processors Work

The computer screen is used to represent a page of paper. In Word, you can choose to work in a simulated page, called Print Layout view, that shows the page with its edges, margins, and any headers, footers, or automatic page numbers. This view uses an inch or so at each side to display the margins, so the available space for viewing each line is reduced. For this reason, most people work in the Normal view, which utilizes the full width of the screen for displaying text.

When you type on the keyboard, your text appears on the screen. A vertical, flashing line indicates the insertion point so that you can tell where your text will go when you start to type. A short, horizontal line marks the end of the existing text. When you are typing and reach the end of a line, just continue to type. The program decides whether the last word will fit. If it will not, it moves down to the next line. You press the ⏎Enter key when you get to the end of a paragraph or when you want to create empty lines to add extra space between paragraphs.

If you want to add words anywhere in an existing paragraph, move the insertion point to the desired location and start typing. The text that comes after your new text moves down the page automatically. The program determines where each new line of the paragraph will end and makes all the necessary adjustments to the paragraph. You can move the insertion point by using the four arrow keys on the keyboard or by moving the mouse pointer to the desired location and clicking the left mouse button one time.

To replace, move, delete, or enhance text, you need to select it first. After it is selected, you can press Del on the keyboard to delete it, or you can choose any of several buttons on the toolbar to change the size, color, alignment, font, or any number of other text characteristics.

Word has many additional features that you can use for special purposes. It is not necessary for you to learn them all. After you have mastered the basics, you can add the skills that are most useful in your pursuits.

Lesson: 4

Creating a Simple Document

Introduction

Microsoft Word can be used to do basic word processing tasks, such as writing a memo, an essay, or a letter. It is also a very robust program that can do the most complex word processing tasks, including creating sophisticated tables, embedding graphics, and linking to other documents and the Internet. After you have mastered the fundamental skills necessary to produce a basic document, you can build your word processing repertoire by adding advanced skills one at a time.

In this lesson, you learn how to create a new document and enter and edit text. You also learn how to save, print, and close a document.

Visual Summary

When you have completed this lesson, you will have created a short letter that looks like this:

July 5, 2000

The Lewis Family
1849 Hawken Blvd.
Ann Arbor, MI 48104

Dear Lewis Family:

Thank you for purchasing your swimming pool from Armstrong Pool, Spa, and Sauna. Your new pool is our top-of-the-line model, and should last thirty or forty years if properly maintained.

We hope you were completely satisfied with the installation. Dick and his crew have been installing swimming pools, spas, and saunas for us for a number of years, and no one does a better job!

Thanks again for choosing Armstrong Pool, Spa, and Sauna for your purchase. To show our appreciation, we will give you 10% off all pool chemicals and for one full year from the date of purchase of your pool!

Sincerely,

<your name>
Ann Arbor Manager
Armstrong Pool, Spa, and Sauna

TASK *1*

Opening a New Document and Entering Text
Why would I do this?

Word processing programs are used to create written documents—letters, memos, research papers, and so forth. When you launch Word, you automatically create a blank document where you can begin entering text. It is just like taking a blank piece of paper and writing with a pen or pencil, except that you write using a computer keyboard.

In this task, you learn to create a new document.

1 Launch **Microsoft Word**. A new document is displayed. The default name is **Document** followed by a number. The *insertion point* where you begin typing appears in the upper-left corner of the work area, and the end-of-document marker appears just below the insertion point. The *pointer,* showing the location of the mouse indicator, also appears on the screen. If you need assistance launching Word, refer to Lesson 3 of this book.

End-of-document marker   **Pointer**

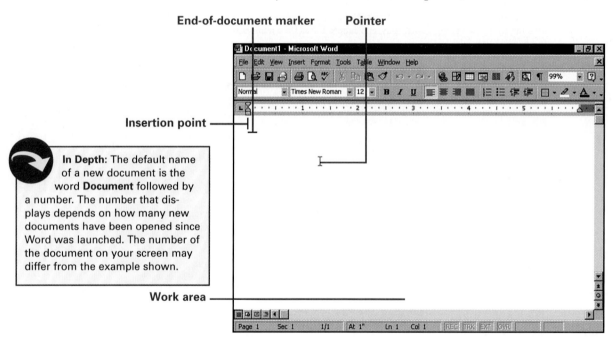

Insertion point

> **In Depth:** The default name of a new document is the word **Document** followed by a number. The number that displays depends on how many new documents have been opened since Word was launched. The number of the document on your screen may differ from the example shown.

Work area

2 Click the **Normal View** button if necessary, and make sure that the window size is maximized.

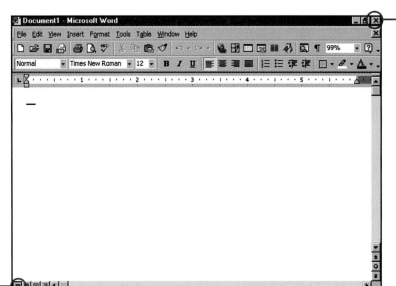

Restore button in maximized window

In Depth: The view buttons located on the status bar are used to change the way the document appears on your screen. The Normal view shows document formatting with a simplified page layout for quick and easy typing. The Print Layout view is used so that you can see how the text appears on the page and can edit margins, breaks between pages, and other print layout features.

Normal View button is selected

3 Type the following date: **July 5, 2000**. Notice that the text appears at the top of the new document.

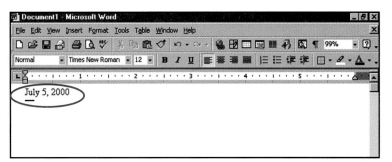

In Depth: Jagged underlines may appear below some of the text you have entered. A red jagged underline means that the word is not in the Office dictionary, and a green jagged underline means that the program thinks there may be a grammatical mistake. To verify that these options are turned on, click **Tools**, **Options** on the menu bar. Click the **Spelling & Grammar** tab and make sure there is a check mark in the box next to **Check spelling as you type** and in the box next to **Check grammar as you type**. Then click **OK** to close the Options dialog box.

4 Press ↵Enter. The insertion point and the end-of-document marker move down a line.

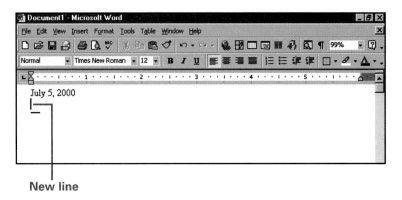

New line

⑤ Press ⏎Enter again to create a blank line, type **The Lewis Family**, and then press ⏎Enter. The new line of text is displayed.

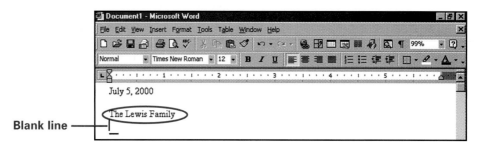

Blank line ——

⑥ Finish the address with the following text, pressing ⏎Enter twice after the postal code and the salutation.

1849 Hawken Blvd.
Ann Arbor, MI 48104

Caution: The Office Assistant may open on your screen at this point and ask if you need assistance writing a letter. Click the **Cancel** button to close the Office Assistant. The illustrations will be shown without the Office Assistant.

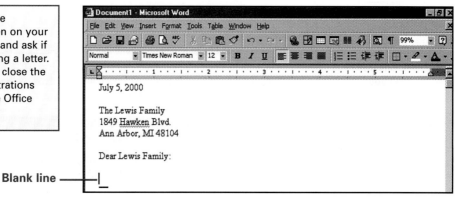

Blank line ——

In Depth: The insertion point for the text moves from one line to the next because of a feature called *word wrap*. With word wrap, the first word to extend beyond the right margin automatically moves to the next line. You do not press ⏎Enter until you get to the end of a paragraph. Pressing ⏎Enter marks the end of the paragraph with a special character that also includes information about the formatting of the entire paragraph.

The words on your screen may not wrap in the same way they do in the figure. This may be due to a difference in the document width or font size setting. It may also be due to the number of spaces used between sentences. Use one space between sentences in this text. Do not be concerned if the words wrap at a different place in the paragraph.

⑦ Type the following text. Press ⏎Enter after you have typed the entire paragraph. (Note: Misspell **purchaseing** in the first sentence, as shown in the following passage. You learn how to fix this type of error in a subsequent task.)

Thank you for purchaseing your swimming pool from Armstrong Pool, Spa, and Sauna. Your new pool is our top-of-the-line model, and should last thirty or forty years if properly maintained.

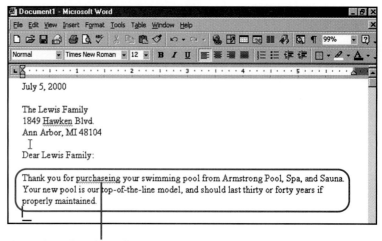

Intentionally misspelled word

8 Press ⏎Enter to create a blank line between the paragraphs. Then finish the letter by typing the following text, complete with grammar errors:

> **We hope you was completely satisfied with the installation. Dick and his crew have been installing swimming pools, spas, and saunas for us for a number of years, and no one does a better job!**
>
> **Thanks again for choosing Armstrong Pool, Spa, and Sauna for your purchase. To show our appreciation, we will give you 10% off all pool chemicals and pool toys for one full year from the date of purchase of your pool!**
>
> **Sincerely,**
>
> **<your name>**
> **Ann Arbor Manager**
> **Armstrong Pool, Spa, and Sauna**

Make sure you type your name in the third-to-last line.

> **Caution:** Depending on how your monitor is set up, the letter may be longer than can be displayed on the screen. If the top of the letter scrolls up out of sight when you type your name and title, don't be concerned. In the next task, you will learn how to move around in your document.

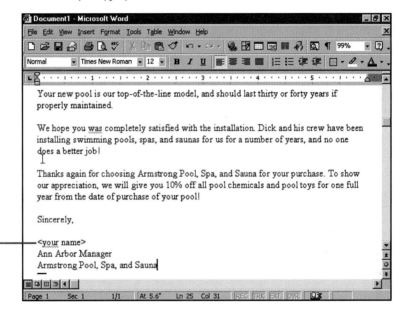

Type your own name here ⟶

TASK 2

Moving Around in a Document
Why would I do this?

When you typed the letter in the first task, the insertion point moved automatically as you typed or when you pressed the ⏎Enter key. When you reached the end of the letter, the screen automatically scrolled the text up and out of view so that you could see the new lines you were typing. You can move around in a document in many different ways so that you can select text, enter new text, edit existing text, or see different parts of your document. You can use the pointer to move the insertion point to a new location. You can use arrow keys to move up, down, left, or right in the text. You can also use the scrollbars or use combinations of keys that move you up or down a screen at a time. Knowing how to move around in your document enables you to enter and edit text much faster.

In this task, you learn how to use the scrollbar. You also learn how to move left and right one character at a time, up and down one line at a time, and up and down one screen at a time.

1 Click the arrow at the top of the vertical scrollbar several times to scroll to the top of your letter. Notice that the screen scrolls up one line at a time. If you click the arrow and hold down the left mouse button, your screen scrolls rapidly.

In Depth: The vertical scrollbar located at the right edge of the window and the horizontal scrollbar located at the bottom of the window can be used to move the portion of the document that shows on your screen. The vertical scrollbar moves the document up and down on your screen. The horizontal scrollbar moves the document left and right on your screen.

Vertical scrollbar

Horizontal scrollbar

2 Position the pointer on the blank line between the first and second full paragraphs and click once with the left mouse button. The insertion point is moved to the beginning of the blank line. If you begin typing, the words appear at the insertion point location, not at the pointer location.

Caution: When you first use Word, you may have a little trouble distinguishing between the pointer—which shows the movement or location of the mouse—and the blinking insertion point—which is the point at which you begin to type. Whatever you type always appears at the insertion point location, never at the pointer location. The mouse pointer appears as an I-beam on the document and as a white arrow when on the toolbars or at the edges of a document.

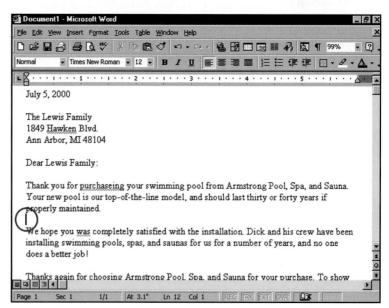

3 Press ⬆ on your keyboard four times. Notice that the insertion point is now just below the salutation. Using an arrow key changes the location of the insertion point in your document. If needed, the text showing on your screen will scroll up or down so that you can continue to see the insertion point.

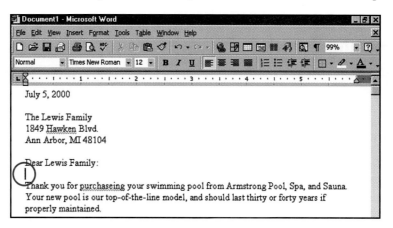

Caution: The PgDn and PgUp keys actually move the view one screen at a time, not one page of the document.

In Depth: Notice the box in the vertical scrollbar. This box lets you know your location in the document—it is at the top of the scrollbar when you are at the top of the document and at the bottom of the scrollbar when you are at the end of the document. In Print Layout view, the size of the box, relative to the length of the scrollbar, gives you an idea of how the currently visible portion of the document compares in size to the document as a whole (a small box means a large document).

You can point to the box, click and hold the left mouse button, and then drag the box up or down the scrollbar to move quickly to a new location in your document. A ScreenTip displays the current page number as you scroll through a multipage document. This action moves the text displayed on your screen, but it does not change the location of the insertion point. You need to click at the point where you want to begin to type to move the insertion point to that location.

4 Press PgDn to move down one screen. Notice that the insertion point moves and only the bottom of the document is now displayed.

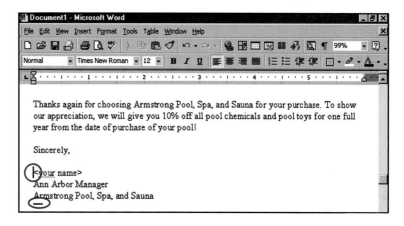

5 Press PgUp to move up one screen. Notice that the top of the letter is displayed and that the insertion point has moved back near the top of the letter. This feature is very helpful for longer documents.

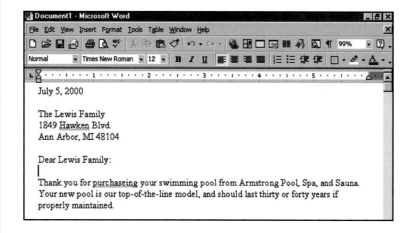

TASK 3

Correcting Errors Using the Backspace and Delete Keys
Why would I do this?

When you are creating a document, you will often make typographical errors that you want to correct immediately. You will also find changes that you want to make when you proofread what you've written. You can correct errors in several ways. The two most common methods are to use the ◀Backspace and Del keys. The ◀Backspace key deletes text to the left of the insertion point, and the Del key deletes text to the right of the insertion point.

In this task, you learn to edit text using the ◀Backspace and Del keys.

1 Use the skills you have just learned to place the insertion point immediately to the left of the word **toys** in the last full paragraph.

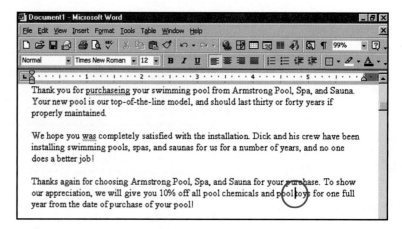

2 Press ◀Backspace once. Notice that the insertion point moves to the left and removes the space between the words **pool** and **toys**.

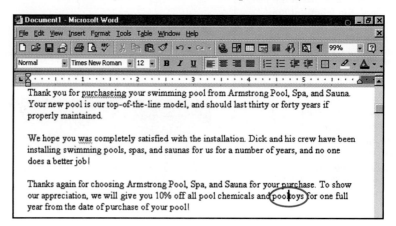

3 Press (◆Backspace) four more times. Notice that the word "pool" has now been deleted.

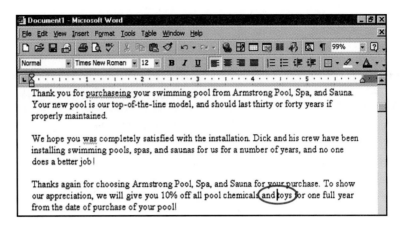

4 Press (Del) once. Notice that the first letter of the word **toys** to the right of the insertion point is removed, even though the insertion point didn't move.

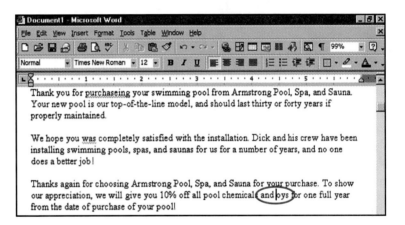

5 Press (Del) three more times. The word **toys** is now removed. Do not remove the space to the right of the word.

Two spaces with the insertion point between them

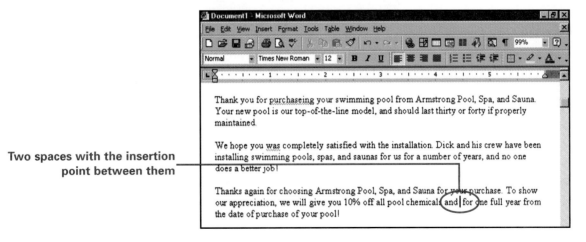

6 Type the word **accessories** at the insertion point. The new word is inserted at the insertion point, and the existing text is moved to the right.

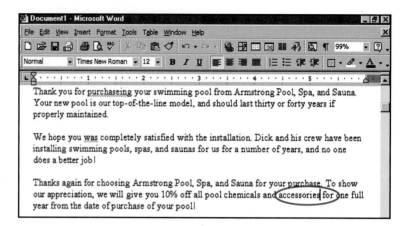

TASK 4

Correcting Spelling and Grammar Errors
Why would I do this?

Spelling and grammar errors in a document reduce the credibility and effectiveness of the message. Microsoft Word has two ways to check spelling and grammar. The first is a program that gives you a great deal of flexibility in checking and correcting the errors. The second is a shortcut that can save a considerable amount of time in a long document.

In this task, you learn how to use a shortcut menu to correct spelling and grammar errors.

1 Locate the misspelled word **purchaseing** in the first paragraph. Move the pointer onto the word and click with the right mouse button. A shortcut menu opens. The top section of the shortcut menu contains a suggestion for replacing the misspelled word.

In Depth: The spelling checker program uses a dictionary that has thousands of words in it. When you type a word that is not in its dictionary, the spelling checker program highlights the word with a red jagged underline. Just because the word is not in the program's dictionary does not mean that it is misspelled—it could be a proper noun, a technical term, or an unusual word.

Shortcut menu

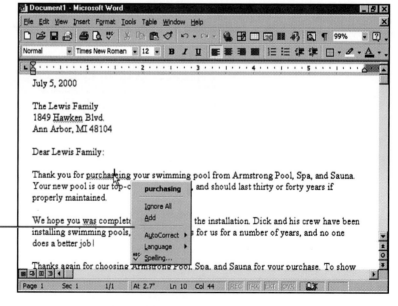

2 The suggestion is correct. Move the pointer to the word **purchasing** in the shortcut menu to select it.

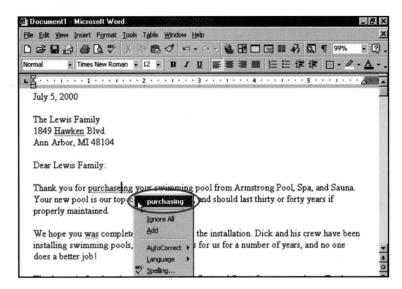

3 Click on the selected word with the left mouse button. The misspelled word is replaced with the correctly spelled word and the shortcut menu closes.

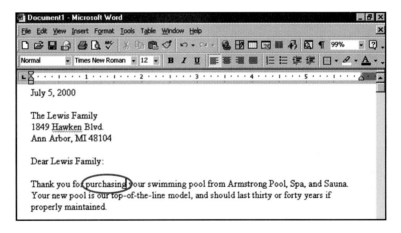

4 Right-click on the word **Hawken** in the address line. The shortcut menu opens with suggestions, but none of the suggestions are correct.

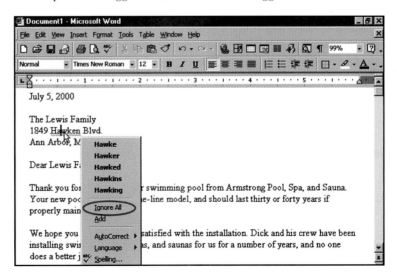

5 Click the **Ignore All** button to ignore all further occurrences of the word in this document. The red jagged underline disappears.

The red jagged underline is gone

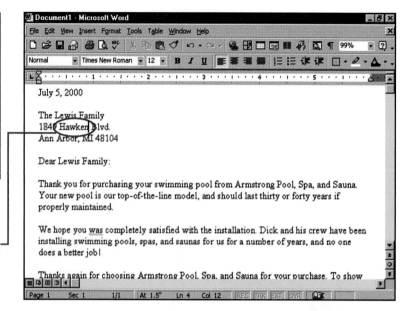

6 The green jagged underline indicates a grammar error. The same technique used to correct spelling errors can be used to correct grammar errors. Right-click on the word **was** in the second full paragraph. A shortcut menu is displayed.

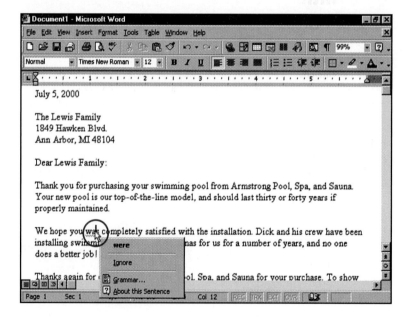

7 Click **were** in the shortcut menu to select it. This action replaces **was** in the sentence, and the green jagged underline disappears.

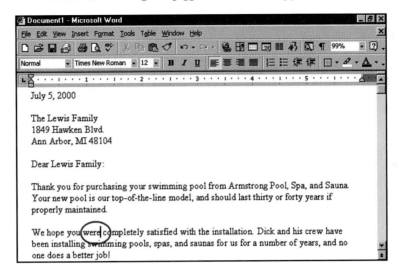

TASK 5

Saving, Printing, and Closing a Document

Why would I do this?

When you write a letter, memo, or other type of document, you generally want to save a permanent record of it for future reference. You can do this by saving a copy on a disk or printing it. As you are writing, the program works with RAM, which is temporary memory in your computer. If your computer suddenly stops working, or if you turn it off without saving your document, you may lose some of your work. To create a permanent record of your document, you need to save your work on a storage media that does not require continuous power, such as a hard disk or a floppy disk. The first time you save a document, you are asked to give the document a name.

You will also frequently need a printed copy of a document. A printed document is portable, easy to view, and does not require a computer. It can be mailed or faxed to other people. When you are finished with the document, you should close it before you turn off the computer. This allows the computer to close any other files automatically that it uses while you are editing the document.

In this task, you learn to save, print, and close a new document.

1 Click the **Save** button on the Standard toolbar. The Save As dialog box is displayed.

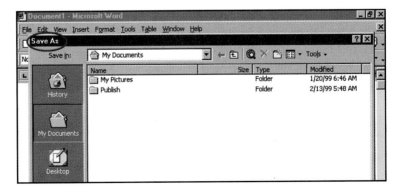

2 To specify where you want to save the file, click the down arrow to the right of the **Save in** box. A drop-down list opens.

List of possible storage sites

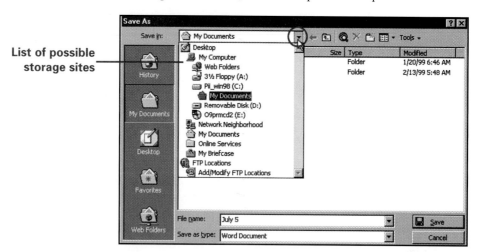

3 Choose the drive and folder where you want to store your document. In this case, **3 1/2 Floppy (A:)** has been selected.

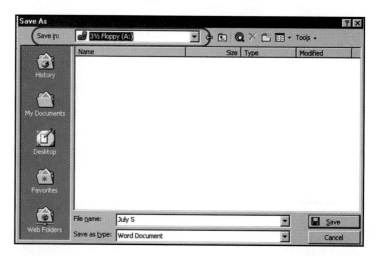

4 Place the insertion point in the **File name** box. Delete the suggested filename and type the following: **Lewis-Pool Purchase Letter**.

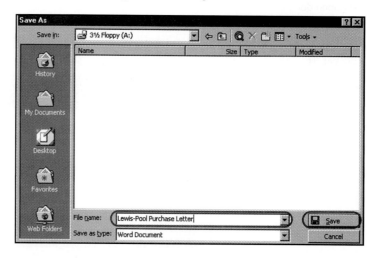

⑤ Click the **S**ave button in the dialog box. Notice that the name of the file in the Word title bar has changed.

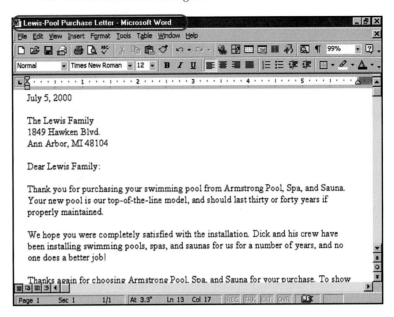

In Depth: Word has an AutoRecover feature that automatically saves a temporary backup version of your document every few minutes. This feature can be helpful in the event of a power failure. However, this setting may be changed or turned off, so you should save the document yourself to create a permanent record. Saving frequently is a good habit to acquire when working on a computer. After a file is first saved and given a name, you can quickly save the changes you make to your document by clicking the Save button on the Standard toolbar. It is important to remember that the temporary file that is created as you type will disappear if you close your file without saving it.

⑥ Make sure your printer is turned on. Then click the **Print** button on the Standard toolbar. The document is sent to the printer.

Close window button

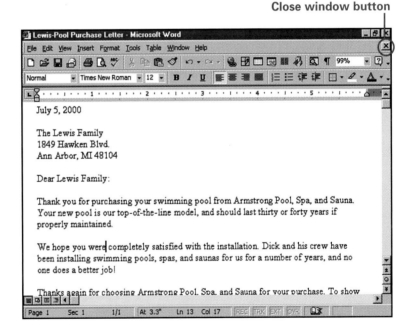

In Depth: If you have not saved your changes when you click the **Close** button, the program asks you whether you want to save them.

More than one document can be open at a time. Each document has a button on the Windows taskbar, and you can switch between open documents by clicking the taskbar button. When more than one document is open, the active document has a Close button in the title bar. Clicking it closes the document and displays the next open document. When only one document is open, Word 2000 displays a Close Window button in the menu bar and Close button in the title bar. The Close Window button closes the document, whereas the Close button in the title bar closes both the document and the application.

⑦ Click the document **Close Window** button at the right end of the menu bar. Make sure you don't click the application **Close** button in the title bar, which closes Word.

Comprehension Exercises

Comprehension exercises are designed to check your memory and understanding of the basic concepts in this lesson. You distinguish between true and false statements, identify new screen elements, and match terms with related statements. If you are uncertain of the correct answer, refer to the task number following each item (for example, T4 refers to Task 4) and review that task until you are confident that you can provide a correct response.

True-False

Circle either T or F.

T   F   **1.** When you launch Word, it automatically opens a blank document called **Document1**. **(T1)**

T   F   **2.** To create a blank line between lines of text, you press the **Insert Blank Line** button. **(T1)**

T   F   **3.** To move the insertion point in your document, you can use the arrow keys on your keyboard. **(T1)**

T   F   **4.** If you are typing a paragraph that will not fit on a single line, you press ⏎Enter at the end of each line of text. **(T1)**

T   F   **5.** The spelling checker program identifies any words not found in its dictionary, even if the words are proper names or technical terms. **(T4)**

T   F   **6.** When you type, the new characters go where the pointer happens to be when you start typing. **(T1)**

T   F   **7.** Del deletes the character to the right of the insertion point's current position. **(T3)**

T   F   **8.** ←Backspace causes all the text to the left of the insertion point to be moved to the left by one space each time ←Backspace is pressed. **(T3)**

T   F   **9.** Spelling errors are indicated by a red jagged underline, and grammar errors are indicated by a green jagged underline. **(T4)**

T   F   **10.** The first time you try to save a new document by pressing the **Save** button, the Save As dialog box opens to give you the opportunity to change the name and location of the file. **(T5)**

Identifying Parts of the Word Screen

Refer to the figure and identify the numbered parts of the screen. Write the letter of the correct label in the space next to the number.

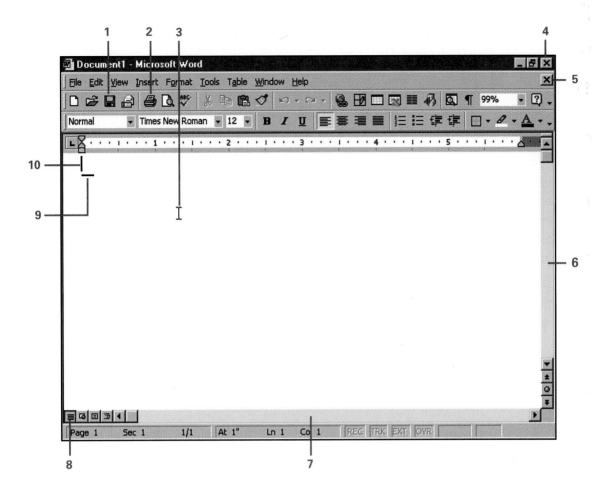

1. _____	**A.** Save button (**T5**)
2. _____	**B.** Vertical scrollbar (**T2**)
3. _____	**C.** Close Window button (**T5**)
4. _____	**D.** Horizontal scrollbar (**T2**)
5. _____	**E.** Pointer (**T1**)
6. _____	**F.** Print button (**T5**)
7. _____	**G.** End-of-document marker (**T1**)
8. _____	**H.** Insertion point (**T1**)
9. _____	**I.** Normal View button (**T1**)
10. _____	**J.** Close button (**T5**)

Matching

Match the following statements to the word or phrase that is the best match from the list. Write the letter of the matching word or phrase in the space provided next to the number.

1. __F__ Deletes the character to the left of the insertion point

2. __G__ Used to move the insertion around in the document one space or line at a time

3. __D__ Indicates that the sentence or phrase does not match the rules for structure that the program uses

4. __E__ Deletes the character to the right of the insertion point

5. __A__ Indicates the end of the document

6. __H__ Sends the document to the printer using the default settings

7. __B__ Stores the document on disk

8. __I__ Closes the document window but not the Word program

9. __C__ Indicates whether the word is in its dictionary

10. __J__ Moves the view of the document down one screen

A. End-of-document marker (T1)

B. Save (T5)

C. Spelling checker (T5)

D. Grammar check (T5)

E. [Del] (T3)

F. [◆Backspace] (T3)

G. Arrow keys (T2)

H. Print button (T5)

I. Close button at the right end of the menu bar (T5)

J. [PgDn] (T2)

K. [PgUp] (T2)

Reinforcement Exercises

Reinforcement exercises are designed to reinforce the skills you have learned by applying them to a new situation. Detailed instructions are provided along with a figure, where appropriate, to illustrate the result. The Reinforcement exercises that follow should be completed sequentially. Leave the document open at the end of each exercise for use in the next exercise until you are specifically directed to close it.

The following exercises produce and use a single document.

In these exercises, you launch Word and type a business letter from a bank executive to a customer. Refer to the figure to see how the text in the paragraphs wraps. Two intentional spelling mistakes and two intentional grammar errors are included in this text. These mistakes (as well as any additional typing errors you make) are corrected. The letter is then printed and saved.

R1—Launch Word and Enter a Date, Name, and Salutation

1. Launch Microsoft Word.

2. Type today's date—for example, **September 10, 2000**.

3. Press [◆Enter] to end the first line and move to the next line. Press [◆Enter] again to create a blank line between the date and the name and address lines.

4. Type the following name and address. Press [◆Enter] at the end of each line. If the Office Assistant appears, do not use it at this time.

   Bill Williams
   1835 Short Lake Road
   Ann Arbor, MI 48104

5. Press [◆Enter] twice after the postal code and type the salutation:

   Dear Mr. Williams:

6. Leave the document open for use in the next exercise.

R2—Enter the Body of the Letter

1. Place the insertion point to the right of the last (salutation) paragraph in your letter, press (⏎Enter) twice, and type the first full paragraph of the letter:

   Thank you for your letter concerning the rate on the Gold Card you hold with our bank.

2. Press (⏎Enter) twice, and then type the next paragraph:

   The account you have is a variable rate account. The rate are tied to the prime rate, as quated in the Wall Street Journal. It is going down to 11.8%, effective today, based on the recent decline in the prime rate. If you pay your credit card account in full each month, you can take advantage of the 25-day grace period before interest is assessed. The benefit is that accounts that are paid in full each month do not acumulate interest charges. This feature are not available on all variable rate accounts.

3. Press (⏎Enter). Unrecognized words are underlined in jagged red, and grammar errors are underlined in jagged green.

4. Press (⏎Enter) again, and then type the next paragraph:

   Thank you for taking the time to write to us to share your thoughts. If you have further questions, please call me at (734) 555-1234.

5. Press (⏎Enter) twice, then type the following:

   Sincerely,

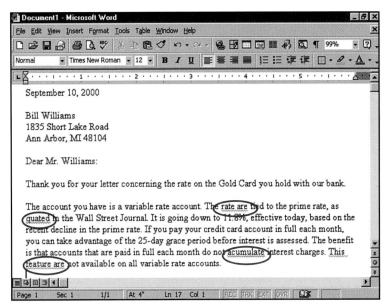

6. Press (⏎Enter) three times to make room for the signature, and then type the following. (Press (⏎Enter) at the end of each line.)

   Mary Nelson
   Vice President
   Branch Administration

7. Press (⏎Enter) twice, and then type the following:

   cc: Revolving Credit

8. Leave the document open for use in the next exercise.

R3—Move the View and the Insertion Point, and Correct Spelling and Grammar Errors

1. Use the vertical scrollbar, (↑), or (PgUp) to move the view to display the top half of the letter.

2. Right-click the words **rate are** and choose **rate is** from the shortcut menu.

3. Right-click the misspelled word **quated** and replace it with the first choice, **quoted**.

4. Right-click the misspelled word **acumulate** and select **accumulate**.

R4—Edit and Save the Document

1. Move the insertion point to Mary Nelson's name at the end of the document. Use (Del) or (⬅Backspace) to delete her name and type your name.

2. Click the **Save** button on the toolbar.

3. In the Save As dialog box, type **Letter to a Bank Customer** in the **File name** box.

5. Right-click the phrase **This feature are** and replace it with the first choice, **This feature is**.

6. Use the vertical scrollbar, (↓), or (PgDn) to move the view to display the bottom half of the letter.

7. Use this method to find and fix or ignore any other spelling or grammar errors that you may have made while typing the document. All red and green jagged underlines should be removed.

8. Leave the document open for use in the next exercise.

4. Select your floppy disk drive or the folder where you want to save the document.

5. Click the **Save** button.

6. Leave the document open for use in the next exercise.

R5—Print the Document and Close It

1. Make sure the printer that is hooked up to your computer is turned on.

2. Click the **Print** button on the toolbar.

3. Click the **Close Window** button at the upper-right corner of the document window to close the document.

4. Click the **Close** button at the upper-right corner of the Word title bar to exit Word.

Challenge

Challenge exercises are designed to test your ability to apply your skills to new situations with less detailed instruction. These exercises also challenge you to expand your repertoire of skills by using Word commands that are similar to those you have already learned. The desired outcome is clearly defined, but you have more freedom to choose the steps needed to achieve the required result.

C1—Working in the Print Layout View

Some people prefer to work entirely in Print Layout view rather than Normal view. In Print Layout view, the text is slightly smaller to display the page margins. The advantage to Print Layout view is that you can see how illustrations will be placed, how the text looks relative to the margins, and the placement of headers and footers.

Goal: To create a title page by using the Print Layout view.

1. Launch Word. If necessary, click the **Print Layout View** button on the horizontal scrollbar.

2. Press ⏎Enter to insert enough blank lines to move the insertion point down to the 4-inch mark on the vertical ruler. Click the **Center** button on the Formatting toolbar.

3. Type the name of the class you are taking. Press ⏎Enter and type your name.

4. Press ⏎Enter twice and type today's date.

5. Leave the file open for use in the next Challenge exercise.

C2—Using the Show/Hide ¶ Feature to Delete Blank Lines in a Document

Sometimes you will have blank lines in a document that you want to remove. In this Challenge exercise, you use the Show/Hide ¶ button to display the end-of-paragraph marks and delete some of the blank lines in your title page document.

Goal: To delete blank lines from the title page document.

1. Use the file created in the first Challenge exercise.

2. Click the **Show/Hide ¶** button on the Standard toolbar.

3. Position your mouse on the first empty line above the first line of text, and click the mouse.

4. Press ⬅Backspace five times. Notice that the text moves up on the page. You have removed five blank lines.

5. Move the insertion point to the top of the page and press Del three times. Three more lines are removed. You can use either the ⬅Backspace key or the Del key to remove blank lines.

6. Keep the file open for use in the next Challenge exercise.

C3—Saving a Document by Using a Different File Format

When you save a file in Word, it is saved with a **.doc** file extension. This tells the computer the type of file and the software that was used to create the file. Sometimes you will need to save a file in a different file format, so someone with a different word processing program can open and read the file. In this Challenge exercise, you will save the title page you created using the text format (.txt).

Goal: To save a file using the text format and open it in Notepad or WordPad.

1. Click **File**, **Save**.

2. Change the **Save in** box to the **3 1/2 Floppy (A:)** disk.

3. Type **Title Page** in the **File name** box.

4. Click the down arrow at the end of the **Save as type** box.

5. Select **Text Only**, then click **Save**. A warning will warn you that you may lose some formatting. Click **OK**. Close the document.

6. Launch **Notepad**, a simple word processing program that comes with Windows. Use WordPad if you do not have Notepad. (Use the **Start** button on the taskbar, choose **Programs**, **Accessories**.)

7. Click **File**, **Open**. In the Open dialog box, locate the **Title Page** file you just saved to your floppy. This dialog box works just like the Save As dialog box. Click on the filename and then click the **Open** button. Notice that you lost the centering format.

8. Print the document. Close the file and exit the program.

Discovery

Discovery exercises are designed to help you learn how to teach yourself a new skill. In each exercise, you discover something new that is related to the topic taught in this lesson. You may be directed to use built-in wizards or some of the extensive Help features provided in Word to discover new features and learn new skills with minimum assistance from books or instructors. The required outcome demonstrates your ability to apply the new skill. Choice of topic, design of presentation, and steps of execution are determined by the learner.

D1—Creating a Document in a Landscape Layout

Most documents are printed on a standard 8 1/2 by 11 sheet of paper using the portrait orientation. Sometimes you will need documents to print using the landscape orientation. In this case, it is best to create the document using the landscape orientation so you can see on the screen how the text will wrap.

In this Discovery exercise, you will use Help to find information on how to set the page so it uses a landscape orientation while you write.

Launch **Word** if necessary, open **Help**, and type **landscape orientation**. Choose the topic **Select the page orientation**. Click on the Office Assistant to close the yellow topic list. Print the topic, and then close the Help window. Follow the steps listed to change page orientation. You will see the orientation of the page in the Word window change. Repeat the procedure to change it back to portrait orientation.

D2—Using the Letter Wizard to Create a Letter Layout

If you are uncertain about the proper format for a letter, Word includes a wizard that can assist you. You can ask for Help and get instructions for creating a letter in the style you want. The wizard will guide you through the process, in which you answer a series of questions that enable the Word program to create the basic layout for your letter.

In this Discovery exercise, you use the assistance provided by the program to create a letter.

Click on the Office Assistant, or open it from the **Help** menu, and type, **How do I write a letter?**. Choose **Create a Letter**. Read the instructions on how to launch the Letter Wizard. If necessary, print the topic. Close Help, and then launch the **Letter Wizard** by choosing **File**, **New**, **Letters & Faxes**, **Letter Wizard**. When the Letter Wizard opens, do the following:

1. On the first page, select the **Letter Format** tab. Click the **Date line** box to include the current date.

2. Click the down arrow at the end of the box under **Choose a page design**. Select one of the options.

3. Click the down arrow at the end of the box under **Choose a letter style**. Select one of the options.

4. Click **Next** to move to the next page, where you type the recipient information. Type the name and address in the labeled boxes for your mom or dad, or for a friend.

5. In the Salutation area, select a greeting from the list or type one in the box. Try the option buttons to the right to see different greetings.

6. Click the **Next** button to move to the **Other Elements** page. (You can also click the **Other Elements** tab at the top of the dialog box.) Review the options available on

this page. Use one of the check boxes if you wish, and fill in the appropriate information. You can use more than one of the choices available on this page.

7. Click the **Next** button to move to the **Sender Info** page. Type your name and address in the appropriate boxes. In the Closing area, select a closing and any other options you want to include.

8. Click the **Finish** button. A letter layout is created based on the choices you made. If you made an error, you can choose **Rerun Letter Wizard** to change the selections you made for this letter. Notice that you can also make an envelope or a mailing label.

9. Put the insertion point before the body of the letter and type a new sentence.

10. Save the letter on your floppy disk with the name **Letter Wizard**. Close the letter.

D3—Increasing Your Speed with Shortcut Keys

If you are doing repetitive tasks, it is often much faster to use the keyboard shortcut keys than it is to take your hand off the keyboard to use the mouse. Use the Office Assistant to find and print out a list of common keyboard shortcut keys for formatting characters and paragraphs.

You can also learn keyboard shortcuts by looking at the right side of the menus. Three of the most useful keyboard shortcuts are Cut, Copy, and Paste. Look at the **Edit** menu and learn how to use the Cut, Copy, and Paste keyboard shortcuts.

Lesson: 5

Editing a Document

Introduction

You will probably need to alter nearly every document you create. These alterations will be necessary because you will make typographical errors or will want to delete, change, or add text. Word gives you many ways to edit a document. The most basic of these methods is the insertion, selection, deletion, and replacement of text. Word also provides ways to copy or move text.

In this lesson, you learn how to use several techniques to edit text in a document.

Visual Summary

When you have completed this lesson, you will have edited a document that looks like this:

New Technologies Affect Distance Education
The rapidly increasing capability of computers is affecting the way we communicate with each other. This year the Internet carried more personal mail than the US Postal Service and this article was dictated directly to a computer using voice dictation software. In this article we will look at how new technologies affect our ability to provide training when the instructor and the trainee are separated by distance or by incompatible time schedules.

Classroom Instruction
The most common format for training is an instructor standing in front of a class of trainees. This method is popular because it allows the instructor to adapt content and the pace of instruction to each individual group based on the verbal and nonverbal cues picked up from the audience. If a class is to be conducted at a distance, it needs to be done in such a way that the instructor can get feedback from the students in order to make necessary adjustments and students need to be able to interact with the instructor and their peers.

Some classes are now being taught using digital video conferencing. However, there are still significant limitations. The biggest limitation that must be addressed is that of

TASK 1

Opening an Existing Document and Saving It with a Different Name

Why would I do this?

Creating a document involves writing, proofreading, and editing. While writing is the first step, it is important to check your document carefully and then make any necessary changes. Often, you will create a draft of a document, save it and close it, and then edit it later. In some instances, you will want to open an existing document and use it as the basis for a new document. You can open an existing document, make changes to it, and then save it with a new name. This retains the original document without any changes, and creates a second document with a different name.

In this task, you learn to open a document that was created earlier and stored on a disk. You will save the document with a new name on a *floppy disk* in drive A:. Place a formatted disk in drive A: before you start this task.

In Depth: Computers store data on floppy disks in patterns of concentric circles called *tracks*. When the computer marks the locations of these tracks, it is called *formatting*. An older standard, called *double density*, spaces the tracks farther apart, and disks formatted with this standard hold 720 kilobytes of data. Currently, *high density* formatting is the most common, and these disks store 1.44 megabytes. This book assumes you are using high density disks formatted for Windows.

Other operating systems use different formatting schemes that may cause problems if used with Windows. For instance, Macintosh computers format their disks differently. At one time, IBM's name was more identifiable than Microsoft or Windows, and IBM used Microsoft's formatting method. You will still see disks labeled "IBM Formatted". This means they are formatted for use with the Windows operating system.

1 Launch **Word**. Word opens and an empty document called **Document1** is displayed. If your window differs in appearance from the one in the figure, click the **Normal View** button. If the Office Assistant appears, click **Help, Hide the Office Assistant**.

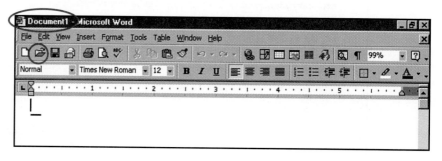

2 Place the CD-ROM disc that is included with this book in your computer and click the **Open** button. The Open dialog box is displayed.

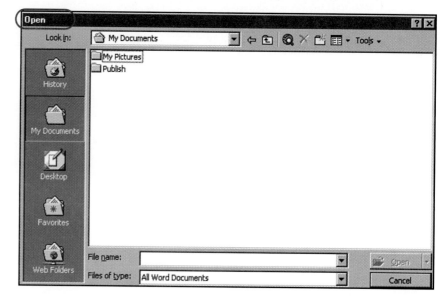

3 Click on the arrow to the right of the **Look in** list and click the drive where you have placed your CD-ROM disc. Locate the **Student** folder and double-click it. Double-click on the **Lesson05** folder to open it. The program displays all of the Word files that are provided for use in this lesson.

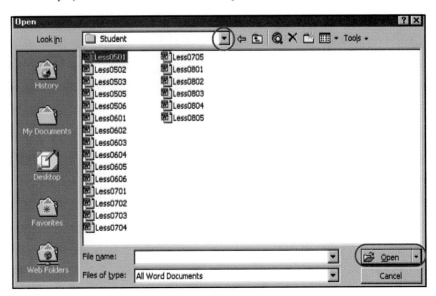

4 Locate the **Less0501** file and click to select it. Click the **Open** button in the Open dialog box. Word opens the file. The name of the file is shown in the title bar.

Caution: There are several different monitor settings that may affect the apparent size of the document. If the document appears to be too wide or too narrow for your screen, click the arrow on the right side of the **Zoom** box and select **Page Width** from the drop-down list.

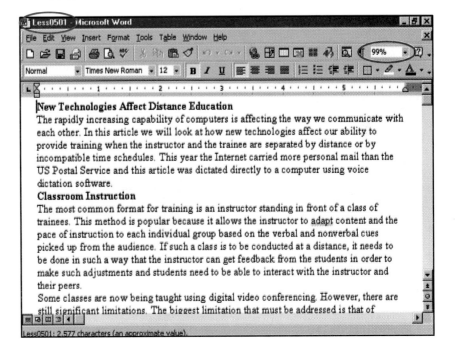

5 Choose **File**, **Save As** from the menu bar. The Save As dialog box is displayed.

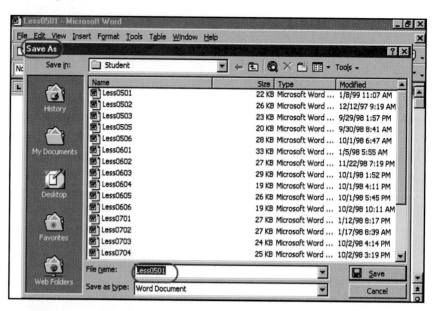

In Depth: Windows may be set to display or hide the file extensions. Word documents all have the extension .doc to identify them. If you see the file extensions on your files in the title bar, Open, and Save As dialog boxes, do not be concerned; your computer is not set to hide the extensions. This setting may be changed using My Computer's menu options: **View, Folder Options, View, Hide file extensions for known file types.** (This command may be slightly different, depending on the version of Windows you are using.)

In Depth: Files may be stored on a network server for several people to use. The network administrator can control who can read, change, or delete the files. If you are logged onto the network as a student who can read files but cannot change them, the filename of your document is followed by (Read-Only). This means that you can't make changes to the document until you have saved it to a different location, such as your own disk. Most compact discs are *CD-ROM*, which means Compact Disc–Read-Only Memory. Files that are opened from the CD-ROM disc supplied with the book must also be saved elsewhere before you can make changes.

6 Place the insertion point in the **File name** box, delete the default name, and type **New Technologies 1**. Select **3 1/2 Floppy (A:)** from the **Save in** drop-down list.

In Depth: You may see words or phrases on your screen displayed with green jagged underlines to indicate a grammar problem. These may be different from the figures shown in this book. Do not be concerned. The grammar checker in Word can be affected by editing changes as you work, and by the writing style level that has been selected on the Spelling and Grammar page in the Tools, Options dialog box. The default grammar setting for Microsoft Word is called Standard.

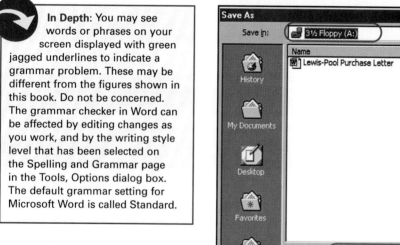
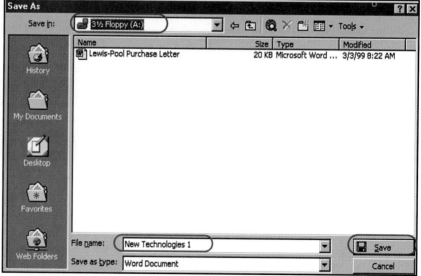

7 Click the **Save** button. The document is saved on the floppy disk, and the new name is displayed in the title bar.

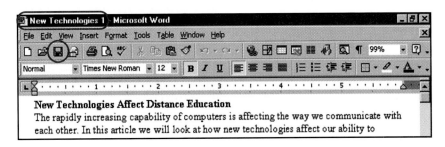

TASK 2

Inserting Text
Why would I do this?

In most cases, the first draft of a document is written quickly to record your initial thoughts. During the proofreading and editing process, you may want to expand on the existing text and add new ideas to your document. If you allowed the computer to wrap the text at the end of each line when you created the document, the program automatically adjusts the existing text to make room for whatever text you insert. This freedom to express your thoughts quickly and to then make extensive additions and changes is a major advantage of using a word processor over a typewriter.

In this task, you learn how to insert text into an existing document.

1 Click the down arrow on the vertical scrollbar to scroll down in the **New Technologies 1** file. Stop when the last paragraph and the end-of-document marker are displayed.

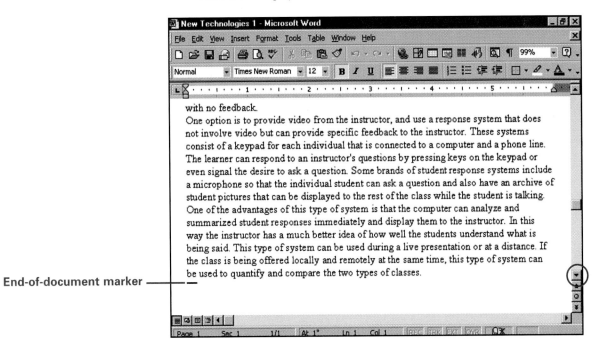

End-of-document marker

2 Place the insertion point just before the word **is** in the first line of the last paragraph.

Insertion point ——

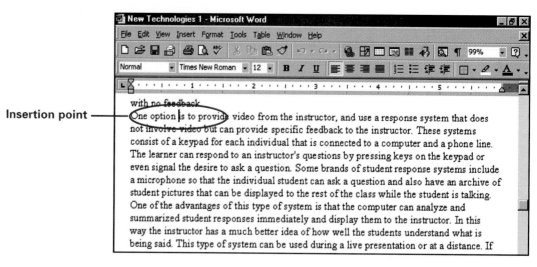

3 Type in the words **for distance courses** at the insertion point. Make sure you add a space at the end of the inserted text.

In Depth: When you are first learning to use the mouse, you may sometimes place the insertion point in the wrong location. You can use the right and left arrows on the keyboard to move the insertion point one character at a time to the right or left. You can also insert spaces by pressing Spacebar when needed.

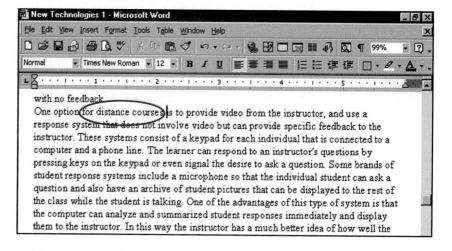

4 Use the up arrow on the vertical scrollbar to display the paragraph that begins, **Some classes are now being taught**.

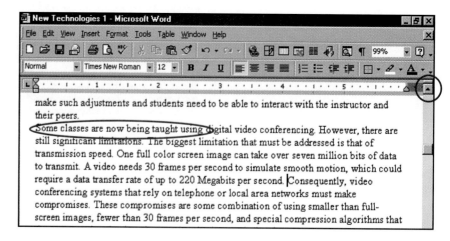

5 Place the insertion point just before the word **Consequently** in the fifth line of this paragraph.

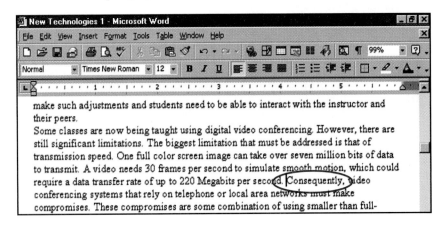

6 Type in the following sentence to help expand on the previous sentence: **This is four thousand times faster than the fastest modems that are used to connect home computers to the Internet, and it is approximately twice as fast as the entire capacity of most local area networks.**

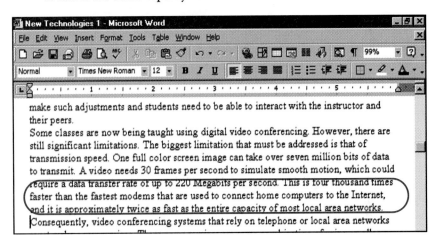

7 Click the **Save** button on the Standard toolbar to save your changes. The status bar indicates that the file is being saved.

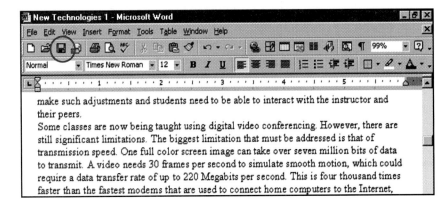

TASK 3

Selecting and Deleting Text

Why would I do this?

In Lesson 4, you learned how to use the Backspace and Delete keys to delete one character at a time. If you want to remove words, phrases, sentences, or even whole paragraphs, using these two procedures can be tedious. You can select and delete multiple characters in a way that will save you a great deal of time during the editing process.

In this task, you learn to select text and delete it.

1 Use the vertical scrollbar to move back to display the paragraph following the heading, **Classroom Instruction**.

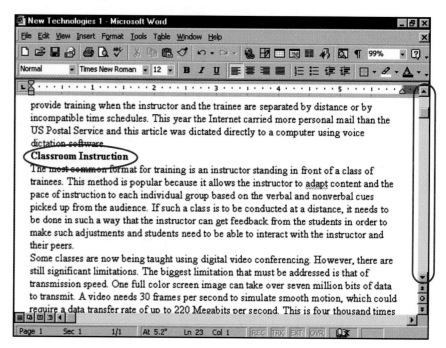

2 Double-click on the word **such** in the third sentence. The word, along with the following space, is selected.

Selected text —

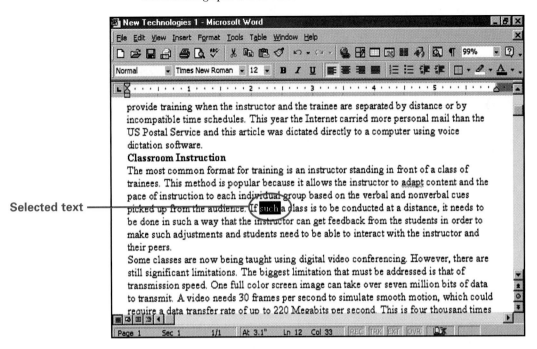

3 Press Del on your keyboard to delete the selected word. The selected word and space are removed from the document.

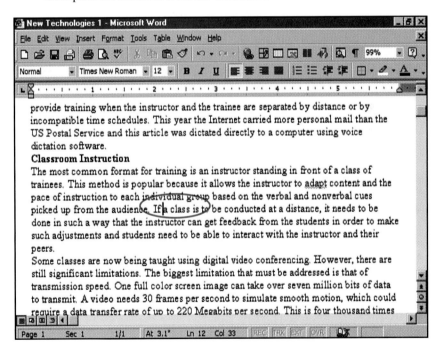

4 Use the down arrow on the vertical scrollbar to move to the bottom of the document. The end-of-document marker should be near the bottom of the screen.

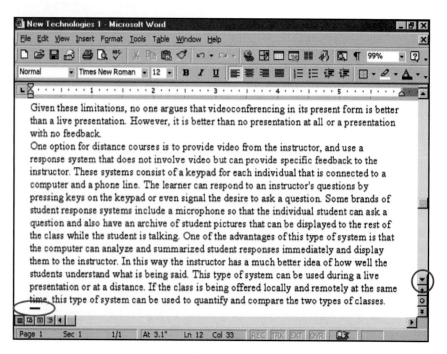

5 Move the pointer just to the left of the phrase **and summarized** in the last paragraph. Click and hold down the left mouse button. The pointer and the insertion point are now in the same location.

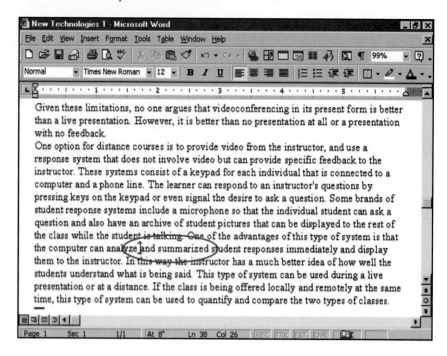

6 Drag to the right until you have selected the words **and summarized**, then release the left mouse button.

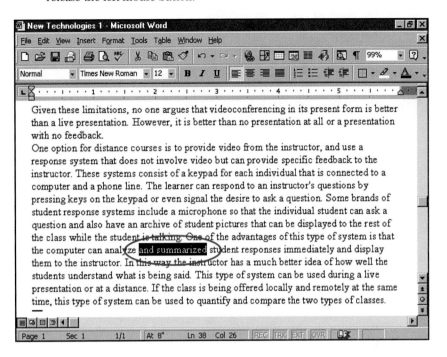

7 Press Del. The selected words are deleted. Only one space remains, because Word automatically adjusts spaces after a deletion.

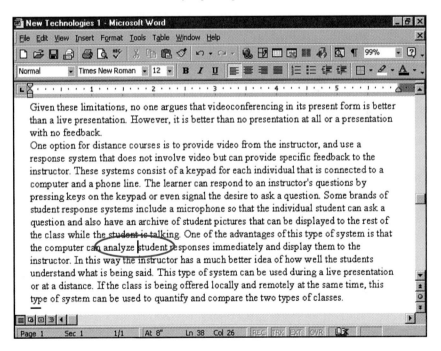

TASK **4**

Selecting and Replacing Text
Why would I do this?

Sometimes you think of a better word or phrase and want to make a replacement. You could select and delete the existing word or phrase and then insert its replacement, but it is faster to combine these two steps and simply select the old word or phrase and type in a new one.

In this task, you learn to select and replace existing text in a document.

1 Use the up arrow on the vertical scrollbar to move back to the top of the **New Technologies 1** document. Double-click on the second instance of the word **such** in the last full sentence of the second paragraph, as shown. The word, along with the following space, is selected.

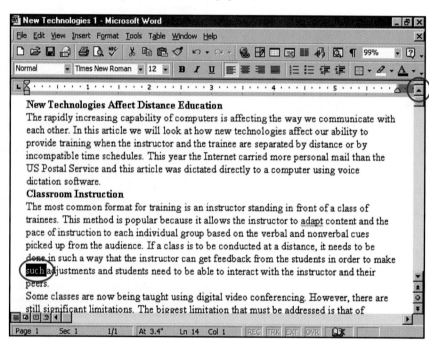

2 Type **necessary**. The new word replaces the selected word.

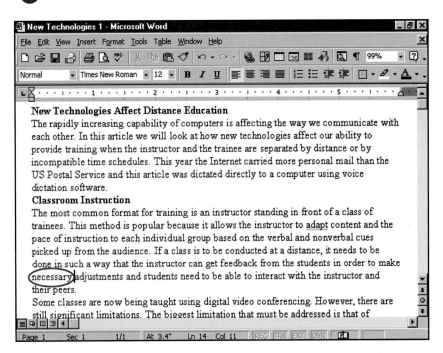

3 Scroll down to the bottom of the document. The end-of-document marker should be near the bottom of the screen. Locate the second-to-last sentence in the last paragraph. Click and drag across the words **This type of system** to select them.

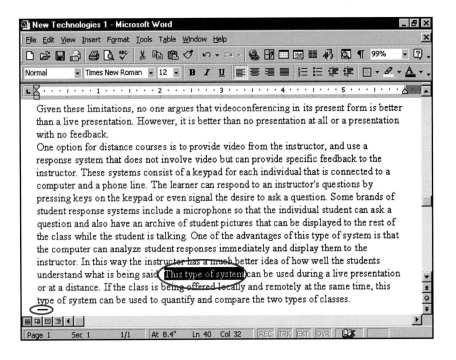

4 Type **Student response systems** to replace the words you selected. Click the **Save** button on the Standard toolbar to save your work.

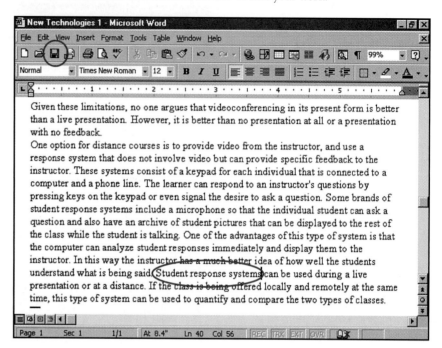

TASK 5

Moving Text Using Cut and Paste
Why would I do this?

If you want to relocate text in a document, you could use the skills you learned earlier in this lesson—that is, you could delete the text in its original location, move the insertion point to the new location, and retype the text. Moving the text using the *cut-and-paste* method is a quicker, easier way to relocate text without having to do any additional typing. This method removes the selected text from one location, stores it temporarily in a location known as the *Office Clipboard*, and then pastes the text to a new location when the Paste button is used.

In this task, you learn how to move text by cutting text from one location and pasting it in a new location.

1 Use the up arrow on the vertical scrollbar to move back to the top of the New Technologies 1 document.

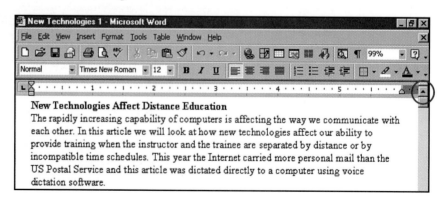

2 Click just to the left of the second sentence in the first full paragraph and drag down to the period at the end of the sentence, as shown in the figure. Make sure you include the period at the end of the sentence.

Include the period————

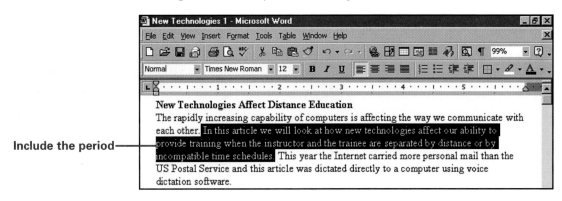

3 Click the **Cut** button on the Standard toolbar. The sentence disappears. It has been placed in an area known as the Office Clipboard for temporary storage.

In Depth: The Copy button, found just to the right of the Cut button on the Standard toolbar, also places selected text in the Office Clipboard, but it leaves the text in its original location as well. *Copy* is used to duplicate text. That text can then be pasted into another location in the same or a new document without any of the original text being moved. Notice that when no text is selected, the Copy and Cut buttons are dimmed and are not available for use. Text must first be selected for these buttons to be active.

Cut and copy buttons dimmed————

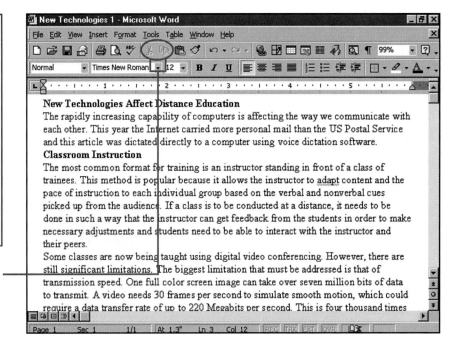

4 Place the insertion point to the right of the period at the end of the last sentence in the first paragraph, as shown in the figure.

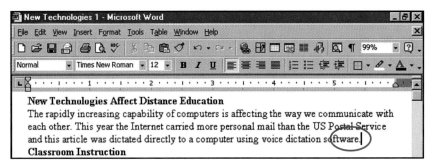

5 Click the **Paste** button in the Standard toolbar. Paste is a command that is used to insert text that is stored in the Office Clipboard. The sentence you cut is now pasted at the insertion point. Do not save your document at this time.

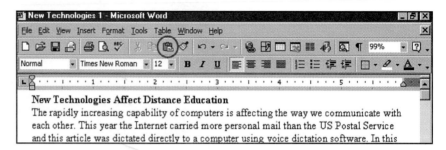

TASK 6

Using Undo and Redo
Why would I do this?

Sometimes you may accidentally delete text or paste something in the wrong location. On occasion, you may also make several changes in a document and then decide that you would rather not keep the changes you have made. Word gives you the option of undoing and redoing changes. This capability saves you from having to retype text.

In this task, you learn to undo and redo changes you have made.

1 With the top of the **New Technologies 1** document on the screen, move the pointer to the **Undo** button on the Standard toolbar. A ScreenTip that says **Undo Paste** is displayed. The Paste function was the last one you used.

Undo button ——
ScreenTip ——
Sentence that was moved ——

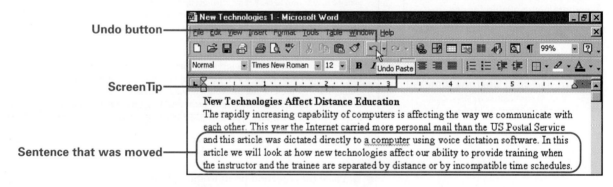

2 Click the **Undo** button on the Standard toolbar. The sentence that you pasted in Task 5 disappears.

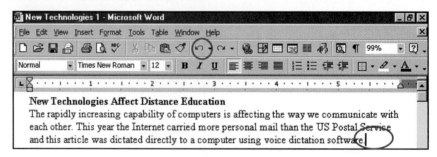

3 Click the **Undo** button again. The sentence you cut is now returned to its original location. You have undone the last two edits you made to the document. Notice that the Redo button is now active.

Redo button is active

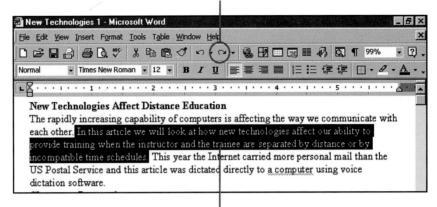

The sentence is returned to its original location

4 Click the **Redo** button twice to reverse the action of the last two undo commands. The cut and paste are redone. The Redo button has turned light gray, indicating that there are no more steps that can be redone.

Redo button is dimmed ————

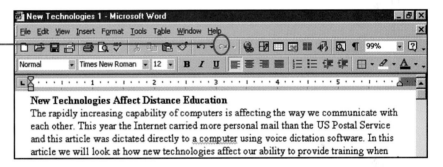

5 Click the **Close Window** button. A dialog box appears, asking if you want to save the changes you have made since the last time the document was saved.

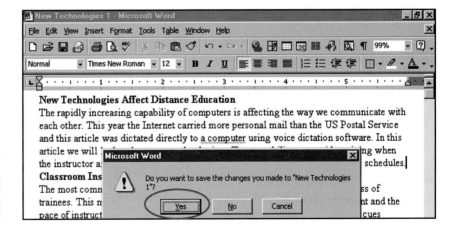

6 Click **Yes**. The document is saved and the window closed. The Word program remains open for use in the following exercises.

Comprehension Exercises

Comprehension exercises are designed to check your memory and understanding of the basic concepts in this lesson. You distinguish between true and false statements, identify new screen elements, and match terms with related statements. If you are uncertain of the correct answer, refer to the task number following each item (for example, T4 refers to Task 4) and review that task until you are confident that you can provide a correct response.

True-False

Circle either T or F.

T   F   **1.** To open a document that is stored on a floppy disk, you click the button on the Standard toolbar that looks like a small floppy disk. (**T1**)

T   F   **2.** The insertion point is indicated by the tip of the pointer arrow. New text goes wherever the pointer is when you start to type. (**T2**)

T   F   **3.** You may select an entire word by double-clicking on it. (**T3**)

T   F   **4.** When you make a mistake, you can reverse your error by clicking the **Undo** button. (**T6**)

T   F   **5.** If you want to undo a mistake, you must do so before you type anything else. The program can only undo one previous action. (**T6**)

T   F   **6.** The **Redo** button is the opposite of the **Undo** button. It allows you to change your mind and restore the actions that you chose to undo. (**T6**)

T   F   **7.** If you have made ten changes to the text and notice that the change you made six steps ago is wrong, you may click the list arrow next to the **Undo** button, pick that one action from the list, and undo it. The other actions are not affected. (**T6**)

T   F   **8.** If you are replacing selected text, you must always delete the selected text with the ⬚Del⬚ key before typing the new text. (**T4**)

T   F   **9.** The **Cut** button does the same thing as the ⬚Del⬚ key. (**T5**)

T   F   **10.** When you cut selected text, that text is stored in a memory area called the Office Clipboard. (**T5**)

Identifying Parts of the Word Screen

Refer to the figure and identify the numbered parts of the screen. Write the letter of the correct label in the space next to the number.

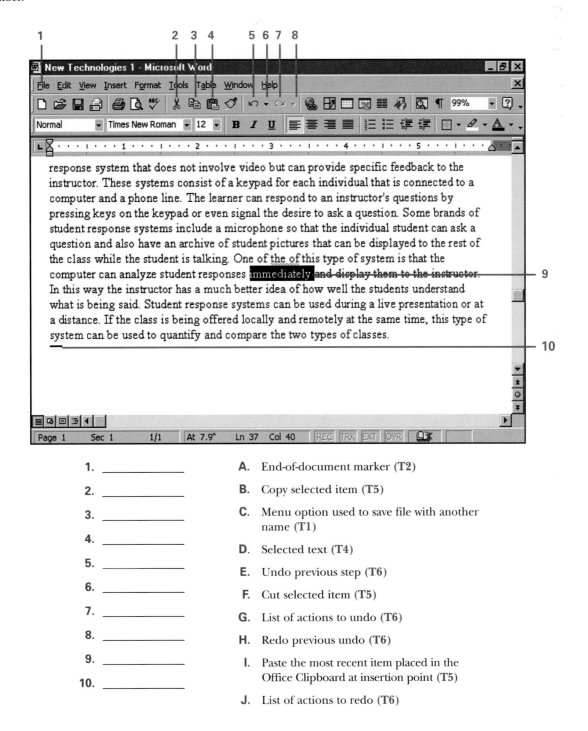

1. _____   **A.** End-of-document marker (**T2**)

2. _____   **B.** Copy selected item (**T5**)

3. _____   **C.** Menu option used to save file with another name (**T1**)

4. _____

5. _____   **D.** Selected text (**T4**)

6. _____   **E.** Undo previous step (**T6**)

7. _____   **F.** Cut selected item (**T5**)

8. _____   **G.** List of actions to undo (**T6**)

9. _____   **H.** Redo previous undo (**T6**)

10. _____   **I.** Paste the most recent item placed in the Office Clipboard at insertion point (**T5**)

J. List of actions to redo (**T6**)

Matching

Match the following statements to the word or phrase that is the best match from the list. Write the letter of the matching word or phrase in the space provided next to the number.

1. **G** Method that may be used to select a word

2. **D** An area that is used for temporary storage of information that has been cut or copied

3. **J** Reverses the undo action and returns the text to its condition prior to the undo

4. **A** Compact Disc–Read-Only Memory, a storage medium used to store programs, files, and other computer reference materials that cannot be changed

5. **E** Removes text from the document and stores it in the Office Clipboard

6. **B** Places the selected text in the Office Clipboard, while at the same time leaving it in the document

7. **E** Places the most recent item added to the Office Clipboard at the insertion point

8. **H** Reverses the previous action

9. **I** A file storage medium that can be easily removed from the computer, consisting of a flexible (floppy) plastic disk enclosed in hard plastic

10. **K** A vertical line that indicates where text goes if it is typed or dropped

A. CD-ROM (**T1**)

B. Copy (**T5**)

C. Double-click (**T8**)

D. Office Clipboard (**T5**)

E. Paste (**T5**)

F. Cut (**T5**)

G. Moving text (**T5**)

H. Undo (**T6**)

I. Floppy disk (**T1**)

J. Redo (**T6**)

K. Insertion point (**T1**)

Reinforcement Exercises

Reinforcement exercises are designed to reinforce the skills you have learned by applying them to a new situation. Detailed instructions are provided along with a figure, where appropriate, to illustrate the result. The Reinforcement exercises that follow should be completed sequentially. Leave the workbook open at the end of each exercise for use in the next exercise until you are specifically directed to close it.

R1—Open an Existing File and Save It Under a Different Name

1. Open the file **Less0502**, which is provided on the CD-ROM disc.

2. Use the **Zoom** button to change the document to **Page Width**, if necessary.

3. Use the **File**, **Save As** menu option to save the file on a floppy disk in drive A: with the name **New Technologies 2**.

R2—Insert Text into an Existing Document

1. Scroll to the beginning of the document.

2. Place the insertion point in front of the word **One** in the first paragraph.

3. Type **Edited by:**, followed by your name. The existing title will be forced to the right.

4. Press ⏎Enter.

5. Click the **Save** button to save your changes.

R3—Selecting and Deleting Text

1. Select the second full paragraph in the section on self-study. (This paragraph starts with the phrase "There are several".)

2. Press Del to delete the paragraph.

3. Click the **Save** button to save your work.

R4—Selecting and Replacing Text

1. Scroll down to the **Future Technologies** section.

2. Select the title **Future Technologies** and replace it by typing **Anticipated Increases in Transmission Speed**.

3. Click the **Save** button to save your work.

R5—Move Text Using Cut and Paste, Then Print the Page

1. Locate the sentence in the first paragraph that begins with "Many people try".

2. Move this sentence to the beginning of the paragraph using the cut-and-paste method.

3. Click **Undo** twice to return sentence to its original location.

4. Click **Redo** twice to move the sentence back.

5. Compare your document to the example in the figure.

6. Select **File**, **Print**, **OK** to print the page.

7. Click **Save** to save your changes.

8. Close the document and exit Word.

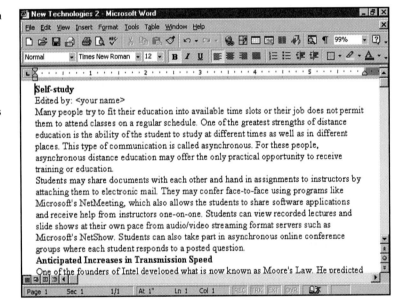

Challenge

Challenge exercises are designed to test your ability to apply your skills to new situations with less detailed instruction. These exercises also challenge you to expand your repertoire of skills by using Word commands that are similar to those you have already learned. The desired outcome is clearly defined, but you have more freedom to choose the steps needed to achieve the required result.

C1—Copy and Paste the Same Text to Two Locations

Sometimes you will want to cut or copy text from one part of a document and place it in several locations. You can use the skills that you learned in this lesson to copy the text and paste it in multiple locations.

Goal: To copy text from one part of a document and paste it in two other locations.

1. Launch **Word**. Locate and open the **Less0503** file that is in the **Student\Lesson05** folder on the CD-ROM disc that came with your book. Save the file as **Business Organizations** on your floppy disk.

2. Highlight the first use of the word **Advantages** and type **Benefits**.

3. Highlight the word **Benefits** you just typed. Click the **Copy** button.

4. Highlight the word **Advantages** under **Partnership** and click the **Paste** button. Highlight the word

Advantages under **Corporation** and click the **Paste** button again. **Benefits** replaces **Advantages** in both sections.

5. Repeat this process to replace the word **Disadvantages** with the word **Risks** under each topic.

6. Print the document and save your changes. Leave the document open for use in the next Challenge exercise.

C2—Undoing Multiple Changes

In this lesson, you learned how to use the Undo button to reverse a change you just made. You can also undo the last several changes by using the drop-down arrow next to the Undo button. In this Challenge exercise, you undo the changes you made to the **Business Organizations** document used in the previous exercise. If you did not do the previous exercise, do it now.

Goal: To use the Undo button to undo changes in a document.

1. With the **Business Organizations** document still open, click the down arrow next to the **Undo** button.

2. Select the last six actions to undo the changes made to the document.

3. Type your name at the bottom of the document.

4. Save the document on your floppy disk with the name **Business Org2** and leave it open for use in the next exercise.

C3—Printing Multiple Copies of a Document

Sometimes you need to print more than one copy of a document. You learned how to open the Print dialog box in this lesson. Here you use the Print dialog box to select two copies to print.

Goal: To print two copies of the **Business Org2** document.

1. With the **Business Org2** document still open, choose **File**, **Print**.

2. In the **Print** dialog box, change the **Number of copies** to **2**.

3. Press (←Enter) or click **OK**.

4. Close the document and close Word.

Discovery

Discovery exercises are designed to help you learn how to teach yourself a new skill. In each exercise, you discover something new that is related to the topic taught in this lesson. You may be directed to use built-in wizards or some of the extensive Help features provided in Word to discover new features and learn new skills with minimum assistance from books or instructors. The required outcome demonstrates your ability to apply the new skill. Choice of topic and steps of execution are determined by the learner.

D1—Opening a Document That Has a Different File Format

Files from other programs are saved with a different file format. If someone gives you a file created using a different word processing program, you need to know how to open it so you can work on it in Word. For example, files containing explanations about installing new software, called **Read Me** files, are usually saved as a text file with a .txt extension.

In this exercise, you learn how to open files that are in a different file format.

Launch **Word** and click the **Open** button. Locate the Word files for this lesson that are on the CD-ROM disc that came with your book. Click the drop-down arrow next to the **Files of type** box and scroll through the list to see the different file formats that can be selected.

First select **Text** files and see how the list of available files changes. Next, try **Encoded Text Files**, then try **Text with Layout**. Finally, change the **Files of type** box to **All Files**. Select the **Less0504** file, which shows the type as **Text Document**. If the Open dialog box does not show the Type column, use the **View** button on the dialog box toolbar to change the view to **Details**. Open this file. Add your name to the top of the document after the words **Alaska Journal**.
Now save the file on a floppy disk as a Word document and name it **My Alaska Journal**. Close the document.

D2—Deleting a Column of Text Using the ⟨Alt⟩ Key

When you are editing a document, you may need to remove a column of text. Rather than removing each item one by one, you can use ⟨Alt⟩ to select a column of text that can then be removed all at once. You can also use this same selection technique to apply a format or some other feature to a column of text. This process can be useful for files that are downloaded from the Internet or are in some other file format.

In this Discovery exercise, you will remove a column of days from the **Alaska Itinerary** document.

Locate and open the **Less0505** file that is in the **Student\Lesson05** folder on the CD-ROM disc that came with your book. Save the file on your floppy disk with the name **Alaska Itinerary**. Hold down the ⟨Alt⟩ key, and click and drag across the word **Monday**. Continue dragging downward to select the rest of the days of the week displayed on the left side of the page. You must press ⟨Alt⟩ continuously to select the column of text. Make sure all of the word **Wednesday** is selected; this is the widest point in the column. The last date is **Sunday, July 7**.

When all of the text is selected, release the mouse button and ⟨Alt⟩, then press ⟨Del⟩. The text is removed, and everything moves to the left. The July dates should be lined up on the left margin. If this is not the case, click **Undo** and try again. Change the title at the top of the page to **Alaska Itinerary for <your name>**. Save the document and print it. Then close the file.

D3—Printing Thumbnails

You may want to print several pages of a document on one or two sheets of paper to get an overview of how the document flows on the page or to use as a handout. This can be useful for outlines or other formats that contain a lot of whitespace. There is an option in the Print dialog box that enables you to select the number of pages per sheet. In this Discovery exercise, you will use this option to print "thumbnails" of an outline.

Locate and open the **Less0506** file that is in the **Student\Lesson05** folder on the CD-ROM disc that came with your book. Save it on your floppy disk with the name **Computer Upgrade**. Add your name at the bottom of the last page of the document. Open the **Print** dialog box and choose **4 pages** in the **Pages per sheet** box in the **Zoom** area. In the **Scale to paper size** box, select **Letter (8.5×11)**. Then click **OK** to print the document. Save the document, and close it. Exit from Word.

Lesson: 6

Formatting Text

Introduction

When you create documents, you want to have the ability to emphasize words, phrases, titles, subtitles, and so forth. In addition, you need to be able to give the text a professional look that conveys information quickly and is aesthetically pleasing.

Microsoft Word gives you many tools to help you format text effectively. You can emphasize text to make it stand out from the surrounding text. Formatting tools allow you to change line spacing, align text, and indent paragraphs in two distinct ways. You can align columns of text and format attractive, effective lists of information.

In this lesson, you learn how to use the most important Word formatting tools.

Visual Summary

When you have completed this lesson, you will have formatted a document that looks like this:

Introduction to the 1860 Alcona County Census

Census records contain large amounts of valuable information about our ancestors and their way of life. Fortunately, most of the actual census records (through 1920) are available on microfilm. Some of the original census books can be accessed, if a researcher knows where to look for them.

The problem with these records is:

- they are not readily available to the casual researcher
- the handwriting is difficult (sometimes impossible) to read
- the ink has faded or smudged
- indexes don't exist for some of the census years
- those indexes that do may be incomplete or difficult to use.

The following are the places, dates, and page numbers of the 1860 Alcona County

Federal census:

Black River	June
Harrisville Township	June
Yewell Place	June

1860 census publications

The Bureau of the Census published several volumes of abstracted data for each census year. The 1860 census resulted in a preliminary report and a four-volume compilation. Bibliographic information on each volume is listed below:

Preliminary Report on the Eighth Census. 1860., by Jos. C. G. Kennedy, Superintendent. (Washington: Government Printing Office, 1862).

Volume 1: Agriculture of the United States in 1860; Compiled from the Original Returns of the Eighth Census, under the Direction of the Secretary of the Interior, by Joseph C. G. Kennedy, Superintendent of the Census. (Washington: Government Printing Office, 1864).

Volume 2: Manufactures of the United States in 1860; Compiled from the Original Returns of the Eighth Census, under the Direction of the Secretary of the Interior. (Washington: Government Printing Office, 1865).

Volume 3: Population of the United States in 1860; Compiled from the Original Returns of the Eighth Census, under the Direction of the Secretary of the Interior, by Joseph C. G. Kennedy, Superintendent of the Census. (Washington: Government Printing Office, 1864).

Volume 4: Statistics of the United States (including Mortality, Property, &c.,) in 1860; Compiled from the Original Returns and being the Final Exhibit of the Eighth Census, under the Direction of the Secretary of the Interior. (Washington: Government Printing Office, 1866).

TASK *1*

Changing the Font, Font Size, and Font Style
Why would I do this?

Text formatting is used to emphasize important elements of a document. It helps you create effective, readable text. When you open the document used in this chapter, you will notice that it is difficult to read. At first glance, all of the text looks similar, even though it contains titles and subtitles. Changing the font and font size and adding emphasis by applying bold, italic, or underline characteristics to text help lead the reader through a document and aid in its overall organization.

In this task, you learn to format titles and subtitles by altering the look of the font.

1 Launch **Word** and click the **Open** button. Find **Less0601** on the CD-ROM disc in the **Student\Lesson06** folder and save it as **Book Introduction** on your floppy disk. Select **Page Width** from the **Zoom** button drop-down box, if necessary.

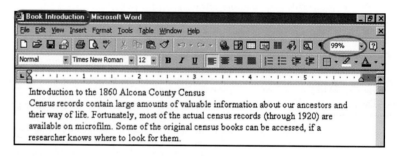

2 Select the first line of text, which is a title. Notice that the text is on a separate line at the beginning of the document, and that the line is not followed by a period.

Selected paragraph ────

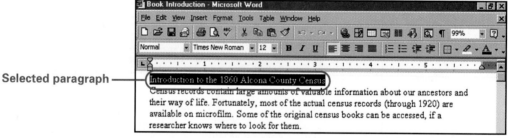

✓ Quick Tip: There are keyboard shortcuts for the major text formatting options. To boldface text, press Ctrl + B. You can use this shortcut to turn boldfacing on, then use the shortcut again to turn it off. This way, you do not have to take your hands off the keyboard. The shortcut for italics is Ctrl + I, and the shortcut for underline is Ctrl + U.

3 Click the **Bold** button on the Formatting toolbar. The selected text is now boldface, which makes it stand out from the rest of the text.

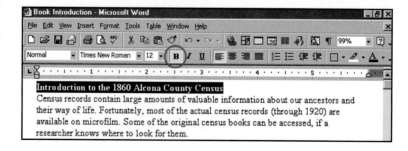

4 With the first line still selected, click on the arrow to the right of the **Font** box. A font drop-down list is displayed, showing the font name and appearance. The current font will be highlighted on your screen.

Font drop-down list

In Depth: If the font names are all displayed in the same font, choose **Tools**, **Customize** from the menu, click the **Options** tab, and select the checkbox next to **List font names in their font**.

Shows selected font ——

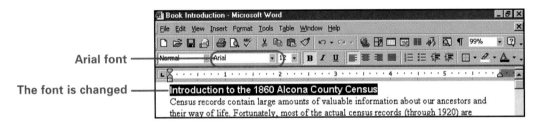

5 Scroll up to the top of the list and choose **Arial**. The font of the text is changed.

Arial font ——

The font is changed ——

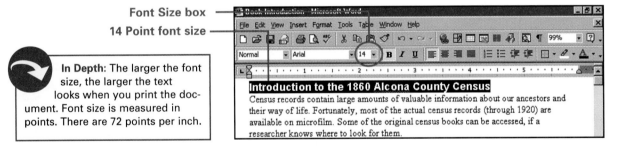

6 Click on the arrow to the right of the **Font Size** box. Choose **14** from the font size drop-down list. The size of the text is increased.

Font Size box ——
14 Point font size ——

In Depth: The larger the font size, the larger the text looks when you print the document. Font size is measured in points. There are 72 points per inch.

7 Highlight the first heading, **About this transcription**, and click the **Bold** button to boldface the text. Deselect the text by clicking anywhere else in the document. Notice that this one step enables you to recognize the subtitle quickly.

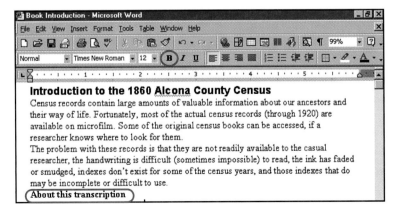

8 Highlight the second heading, **1860 census publications**, and click the **Bold** button to boldface the text. Deselect the text by clicking anywhere else in the document.

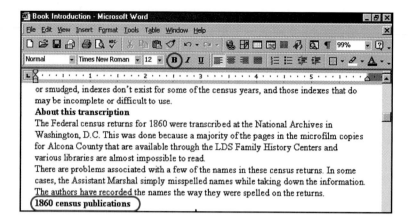

TASK 2

Aligning Text in a Paragraph
Why would I do this?

Most text is arranged on the page so that there is a uniform margin between the left edge of the paper and the beginning of each line. Because the words in each line are of different lengths, the right edge of the paragraph is usually uneven. Paragraphs like this are said to be aligned left, meaning the text lines up on the left side of the margin.

The computer calculates the length of a line and the available space between margins. If you want to center a line of text, the computer uses this information to position the line in the center of the available space. *Centering* is a type of alignment used to make titles distinct from other parts of the document and to attract the reader's attention.

If you are writing a newsletter or prefer to have the text line up on both sides, you can specify an alignment that is called *justified*. To accomplish this, the computer adjusts the size of the spaces between the words in each line. When you are trying to align text, it is important to remember that the computer does not consider a space to be a consistent size.

In this task, you learn how to center titles and to justify text.

1 With your **Book Introduction** file still active, select the first line, which is the title of the document.

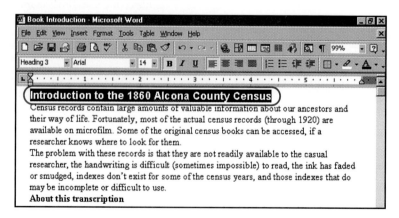

2 Click the **Center** button on the Formatting toolbar. The title is now centered in the document.

Centered text

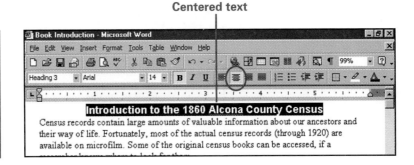

Quick Tip: There are keyboard shortcuts for text alignment options. To center text, press Ctrl+E. The shortcut for left-aligned is Ctrl+L, the shortcut for right-aligned is Ctrl+R, and the shortcut for justified is Ctrl+J.

Caution: Make sure you go to the end of the document, not just to the end of the screen. When you go below the bottom of the text, the screen scrolls down. Don't stop until you see the end-of-document marker and have the period at the end of the last line selected.

Quick Tip: On very long documents, scrolling to select a large portion of text can be cumbersome. A quicker method is to click at the beginning of the text that is to be selected. Position the pointer at the end of the text you want highlighted, and then hold down ◆Shift and click the left mouse button. All of the text from the insertion point to the location of the second click will be selected. Then you can apply the desired formatting to the selected text.

3 Click to the left of the second line of the document and hold the mouse button down. Drag down to the end of the document to select all but the first line.

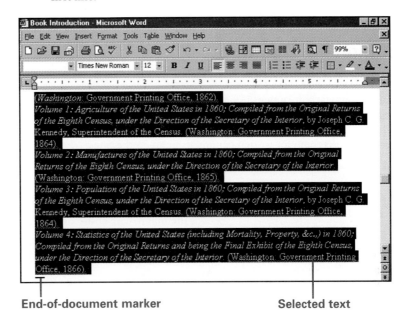

End-of-document marker   Selected text

4 Click the **Justify** button on the Formatting toolbar, scroll to the top of the document, and click anywhere on the text to deselect it. All of the selected text is now justified.

Justify button ——

Justified text ——

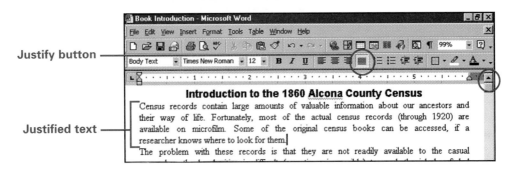

5 Click the **Save** button on the Standard toolbar to save your work up to this point.

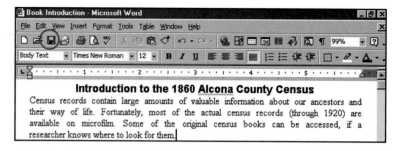

TASK 3

Changing Line Spacing
Why would I do this?

In many cases, you type a document using single-spacing, but change the spacing to double-spacing at a later time. Composing the document with single-spacing enables you to see twice as much text on the screen as you would with double-spacing. However, if you change to double-spacing before you print a copy of the document, the document is easier to edit. Double-spacing allows room for written comments between the lines.

In this task, you learn to change the line spacing in a document.

1 With your **Book Introduction** file still active, choose **Edit**, **Select All** from the menu. The entire document is now selected.

> ✔ **Quick Tip:** You can also use the Ctrl+A keyboard shortcut to select all the text in a document.

The whole document is selected ———

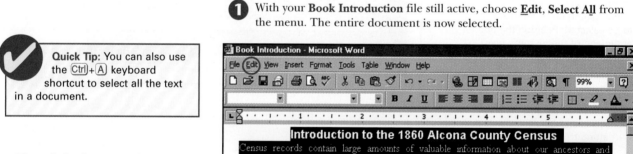

2 Choose **Format**, **Paragraph** from the menu. The Paragraph dialog box opens.

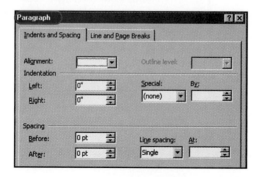

3 Select **Double** from the **Line spacing** drop-down list.

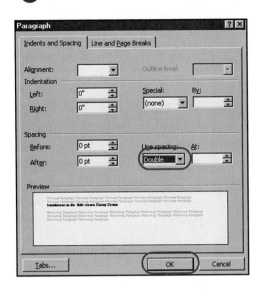

4 Click **OK**, then click anywhere in the document to deselect the text. Notice that the document is now double-spaced.

Double-spaced text ———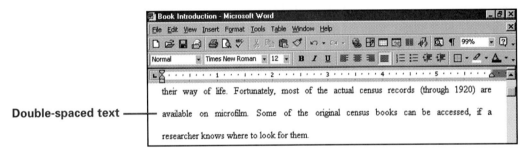

5 The bibliography at the end of the document should be single-spaced. Scroll down and select the text that extends from the first bibliography entry (the paragraph that begins **Preliminary Report**) to the end of the document.

Beginning of selected text is off the screen ———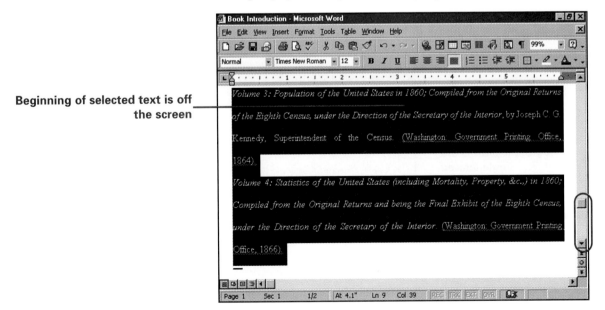

6 Choose **Format**, **Paragraph** from the menu. The Paragraph dialog box opens.

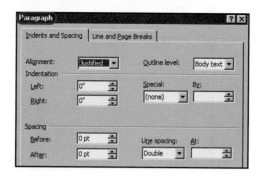

7 Select **Single** from the **Line spacing** drop-down list.

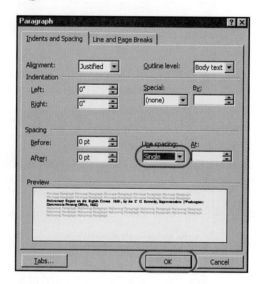

8 Click **OK**, and then click anywhere in the text to deselect the text. The bibliographic entries are again single-spaced. Click the **Save** button to save your work.

Bibliographic entries are single-spaced

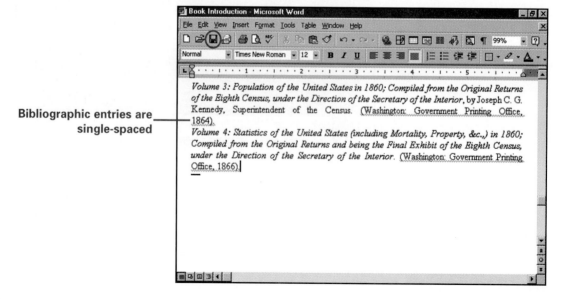

TASK 4

Creating a Bulleted List

Why would I do this?

A bulleted or numbered list helps draw the reader's attention to key points. Many people are busy and only glance at memos or letters they receive. The use of bulleted lists helps to ensure that the reader sees the most important points in a document. Word enables you to quickly create effective, professional-looking lists.

In this task, you learn how to create a bulleted list.

1 With your **Book Introduction** file still active, scroll to the top of the document and place the insertion point just to the right of the word **that** in the second full paragraph. Press Del to remove the space and enter a colon (:). The insertion point should be to the right of the colon.

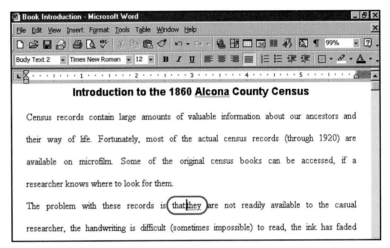

2 Press ↵Enter. A new paragraph is created, which begins with the phrase **they are not readily available**. This phrase will be the first item in a list of five items.

New paragraph ——

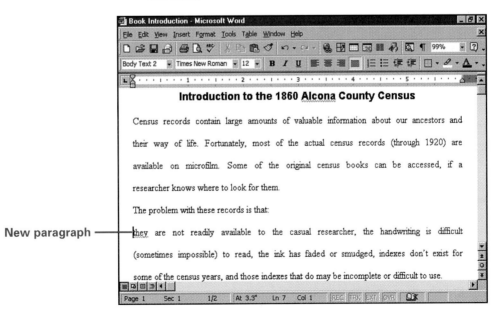

3 Select the comma and space after the word **researcher** in the same line and press ⏎Enter. The comma and space are deleted, and a new paragraph is created.

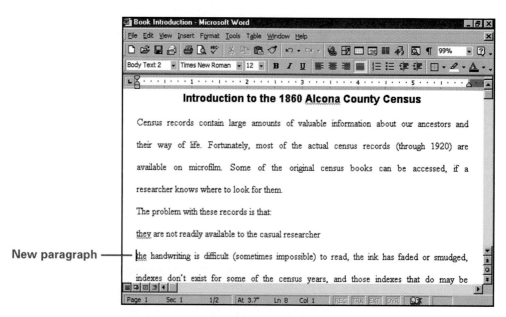

New paragraph

4 Select the comma and space after the words **to read** and press ⏎Enter. Another new paragraph is created.

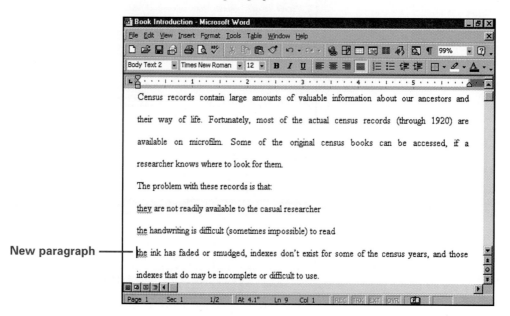

New paragraph

5 Select the comma and space after the word **smudged** and press ⏎Enter. Another new paragraph is created.

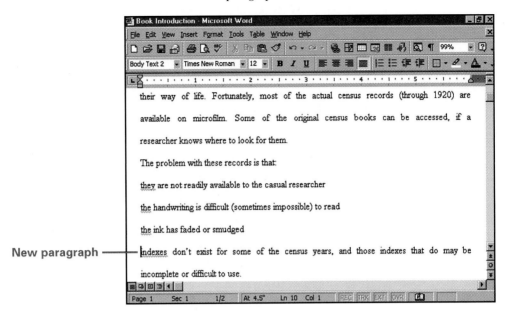

New paragraph ——

6 Select the comma and space after the words **census years** and press ⏎Enter. Another new paragraph is created. Press Del four times to delete the word **and** and the following space in the paragraph. Delete the period following the word **use**.

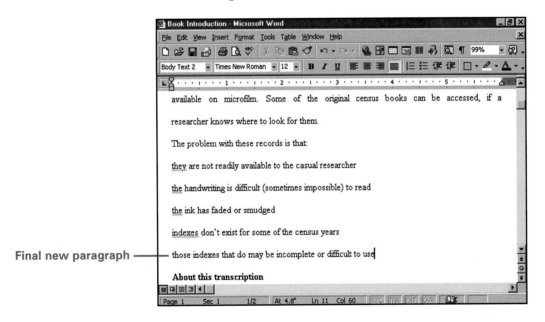

Final new paragraph ——

7 Select all five items that make up your new list.

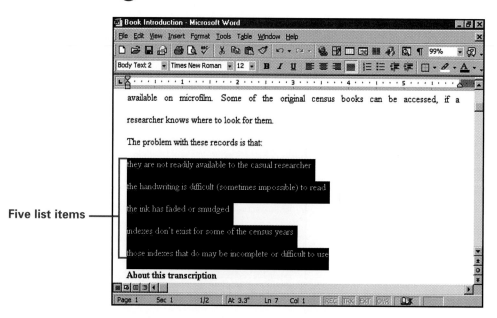

Five list items

8 Click the **Bullets** button on the formatting toolbar. Bullets are placed in front of the list items, and the list is indented 0.25 inches to the bullets and 0.5 inches to the text.

¼ inch indent to bullets   Bullets button   Decrease Indent button

½ inch indent to text

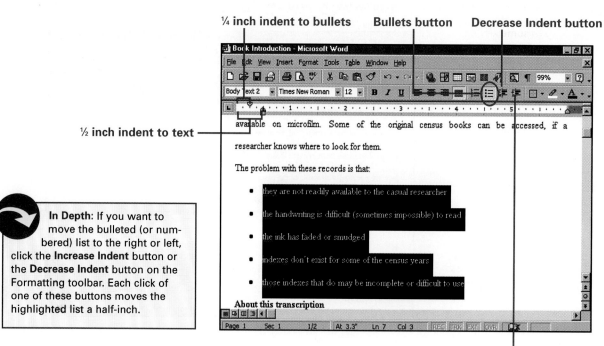

In Depth: If you want to move the bulleted (or numbered) list to the right or left, click the **Increase Indent** button or the **Decrease Indent** button on the Formatting toolbar. Each click of one of these buttons moves the highlighted list a half-inch.

Increase Indent button

9 With the list still selected, choose **Format**, **Paragraph** from the menu. The Paragraph dialog box opens. Select **Single** from the **Line spacing** drop-down menu.

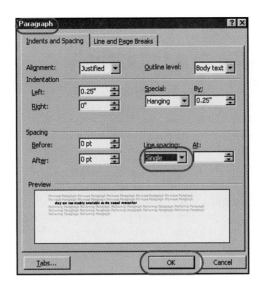

10 Click **OK** and click anywhere in the document to deselect the text. The bulleted list is now single-spaced. In Task 8, a space will be added after the fifth item to separate the bulleted list from the following subtitle.

In Depth: If the information in a list is in some kind of sequential order, you might consider using the **Numbering** button, which is to the left of the **Bullets** button. If the information is in no particular order, it is best to use a bulleted list.

The bulleted list is single-spaced

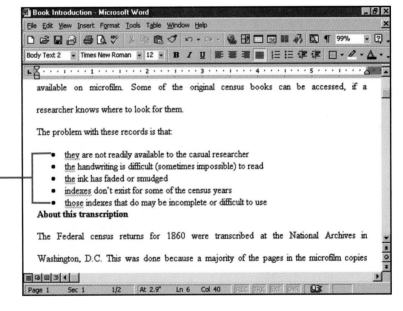

TASK 5

Indenting the First Line of a Paragraph
Why would I do this?

While some writing styles call for the first line of each paragraph to be aligned with the rest of the paragraph, others require that you indent the first line a certain distance. Many people indent the first line by typing five or six spaces. This method worked well on typewriters that always used the same size spaces, but it does not work well on computers that vary the size of spaces depending on the size of the paragraph's font.

Another method commonly used to indent the first line of a paragraph is to press Tab⇆. This method works well, but it has two drawbacks. If no tabs have been set, Word assumes that you want to move 0.5 inches to the right each time you press Tab⇆. If you try to edit this paragraph and set a tab for some other purpose, the indent lines up with the new tab. The real problem with using a tab to indent is evident when you try to use it to create hanging indents (paragraphs with all but the first line indented). Pressing Tab⇆ at the beginning of each subsequent line introduces tab characters that cause many problems if you try to change the length of the line by editing the text or changing the font size.

If you use the **Format**, **Paragraph** menu options, you can specify the size of the indent in inches, set a standard that can be applied to more than one paragraph, and avoid later editing problems.

In this task, you learn to indent the first line of a paragraph.

1 With your **Book Introduction** file still active, select the first two paragraphs (but not the title), as shown in the figure. This text includes the introduction to the bulleted list you created in Task 4, but not the list itself.

The first two paragraphs are selected —

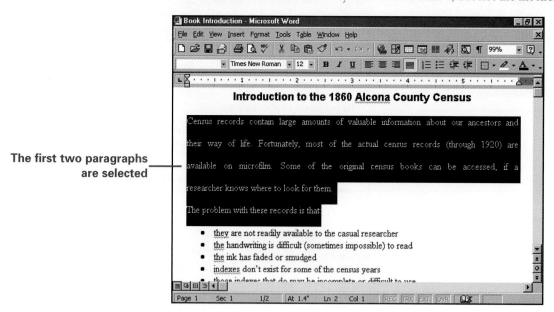

2 Select **Format**, **Paragraph** from the menu. The Paragraph dialog box opens. This is the dialog box you used to change the line spacing in Tasks 3 and 4.

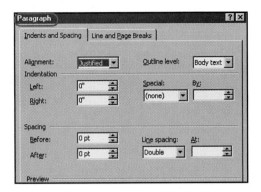

3 In the **Indentation** section, click the arrow on the right side of the **Special** drop-down list. Choose **First line**.

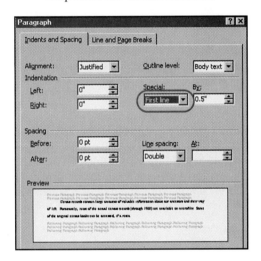

4 If necessary, click the up or down arrow on the right of the **By** box until you reach **0.5"**. This is the distance, in inches, that the first line of each selected paragraph will be indented.

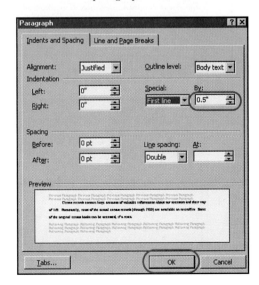

5 Click **OK** and click anywhere in the document to deselect the text. The selected paragraphs now have first lines indented half an inch.

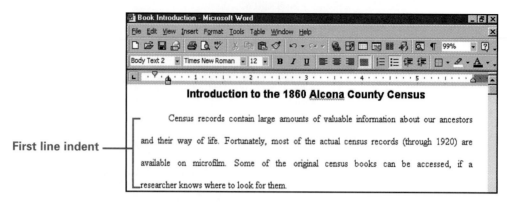

First line indent ———

TASK 6

Using the Format Painter
Why would I do this?

To apply a consistent look to your document, it is a good idea to have all of the paragraphs in the document formatted the same way. When you change the format of a paragraph, you will usually change the format of other paragraphs to match. If they are continuous, you can simply highlight all of the paragraphs and then do the formatting once. If the paragraphs are separated by lists, subtitles, tables, or other text that requires different formatting, a different technique can be used. The *Format Painter* is a tool that enables you to copy the formatting of one paragraph and paint it onto another paragraph. This tool can help you apply formatting characteristics quickly and easily.

In this task, you learn to use the Format Painter.

1 With your **Book Introduction** file still active, select the first full paragraph (but not the title). The first line in this paragraph is indented. You will apply the format of this paragraph to several other paragraphs in the document.

In Depth: When you press
↵Enter to mark the end of a paragraph, Word places a hidden character in the text. That character does more than just mark the end of the paragraph; it also stores the paragraph's formatting information. If the Format Painter is used to copy the format of a paragraph, the hidden paragraph mark must be included in the original selection. To see hidden characters, such as the paragraph mark, spaces, and tabs, press the **Show/Hide¶** button on the Standard toolbar.

Paragraph format to be copied ———

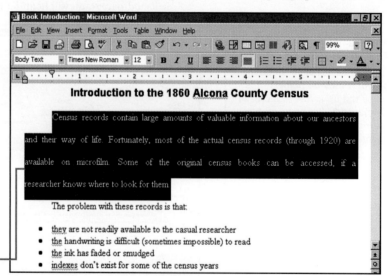

2 Double-click the **Format Painter** button. The format of the first paragraph has been attached to the Format Painter. The pointer now includes a paintbrush.

Format Painter pointer

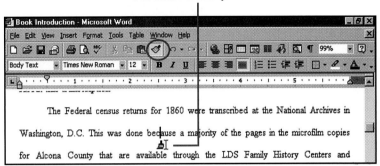

In Depth: If you click once on the Format Painter button, you can change only one paragraph before the Format Painter is turned off. By double-clicking, you have activated the Format Painter for as many uses as you want. It does not turn off until you click the Format Painter button again.

3 Use the vertical scrollbar to move the text until the two paragraphs after the **About this transcription** heading are displayed on your screen. Click anywhere in the first paragraph after the **About this transcription** heading. Notice that the first line is now indented.

The first line is now indented

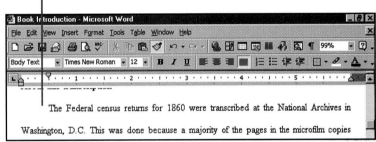

Caution: Depending on the type of format that is being copied, you may need to select the entire line, or paragraph, to apply the format. In this example, just clicking anywhere on the paragraph applies the indent to the paragraph.

4 Click anywhere in the second paragraph after the **About this transcription** heading. This paragraph now exhibits the same formatting as the original paragraph.

The first line is indented

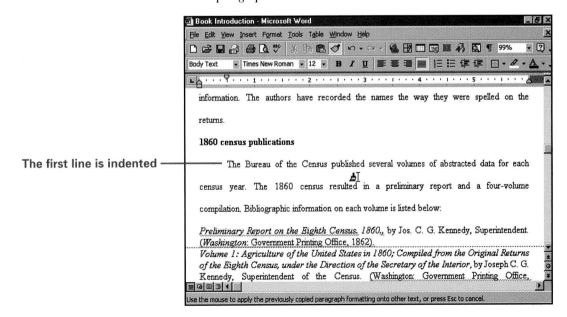

5 Scroll down and click anywhere in the first paragraph after the **1860 census publications** heading. This paragraph's first line is now indented. This is the last paragraph that needs a format change.

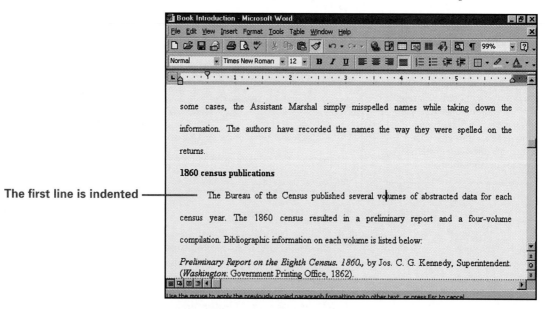

The first line is indented ——

6 Click the **Format Painter** button to turn this feature off. The pointer returns to its normal I-beam shape. Click the **Save** button to save your changes.

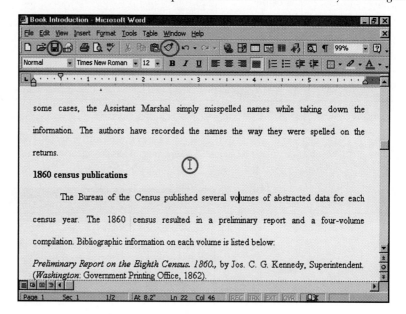

TASK 7

Creating a Hanging Indent
Why would I do this?

Some styles use a *hanging indent*, which means that the first line of the text is to the left of the rest of the text in the paragraph. For example, it is common for bibliographic references to call for the first line of a bibliographic entry to be a half-inch to the left of the rest of the entry. This is another formatting style that can be applied using the options available in the **Format**, **Paragraph** menu.

In this task, you learn to create a hanging indent.

1 With your **Book Introduction** file still active, select the last five paragraphs in the document, starting with the paragraph beginning **Preliminary Report**. These are the bibliographic entries.

Bibliographic entries ——

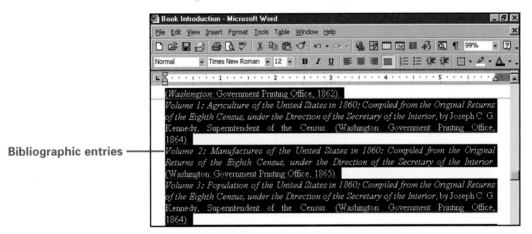

2 Select **Format**, **Paragraph** from the menu. The Paragraph dialog box opens.

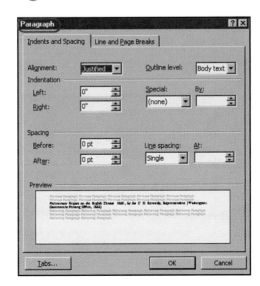

3 In the **Indentation** section, click the arrow on the right side of the **Special** drop-down list. Choose **Hanging**. The **By** box should read **0.5"**, which means that the first line will be a half-inch to the left of the rest of the paragraph. This structure is accomplished by indenting the rest of the text in each paragraph.

In Depth: If the **By** box is not set at **0.5"**, use the up or down arrows to adjust the number to that measurement. The arrows change the indent by 0.1-inch increments. In each paragraph selected, all of the lines after the first line are indented by 0.5 inches when the hanging indent is applied.

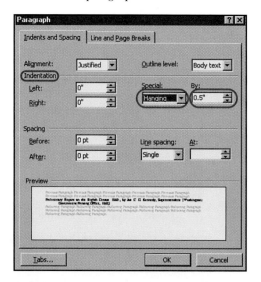

4 Click **OK**. The five bibliographic entries should now be formatted with hanging indents. Click anywhere in the document to deselect the text. Notice how much easier the entries are to read.

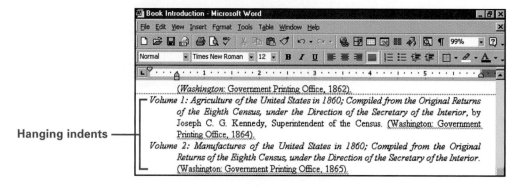

Hanging indents

5 Click the **Save** button to save your work.

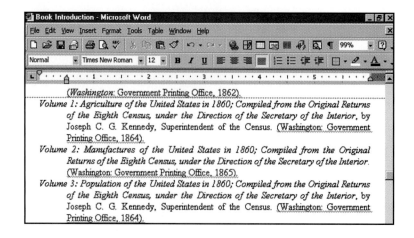

TASK 8

Adding Spaces After Paragraphs

Why would I do this?

In many cases, extra space between paragraphs makes the document easier to read. This is particularly true if the text is single-spaced. You can set up your paragraphs to add extra space automatically before or after a paragraph.

In this task, you learn how to add spacing after paragraphs.

1 With your **Book Introduction** file still active, select the last five paragraphs in the document. These are the bibliographic entries you added hanging indents to in Task 7.

Bibliography selected —

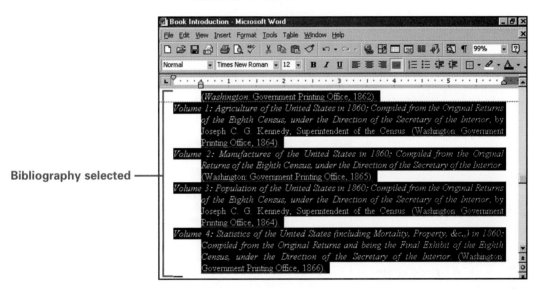

2 Select **Format**, **Paragraph** from the menu. The Paragraph dialog box is displayed.

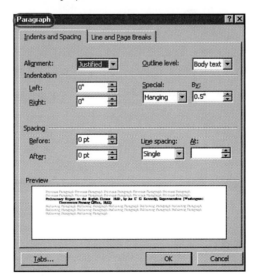

3 In the **Spacing** area of the dialog box, click the up arrow in the **After** box once, which changes the number to **6 pt**. A preview of the new look of the text is shown in the **Preview** area.

> **In Depth:** When you see **6 pt** in the **After** box, it means that space equivalent to a line of 6-point text is added after each selected paragraph. Six points of space is about the height of half a line when you are using 12-point type.

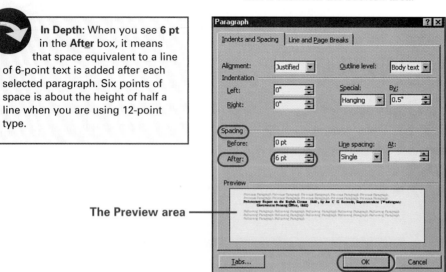

The Preview area ——

4 Click **OK** and then click anywhere in the document to deselect the text. Space is added after each selected paragraph, making the bibliographic entries even easier to read.

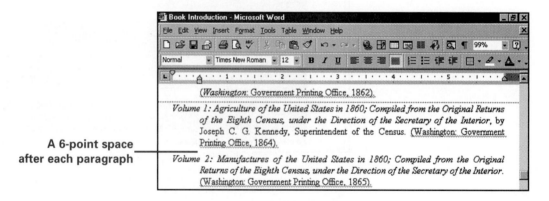

A 6-point space after each paragraph ——

5 Scroll to the top of the document and select the last item in the bulleted list.

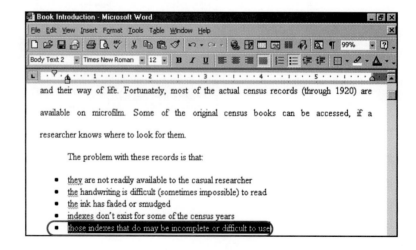

6 Select **Format**, **Paragraph** from the menu. The Paragraph dialog box opens. Click the up arrow in the **After** box twice to add **12 points** of space.

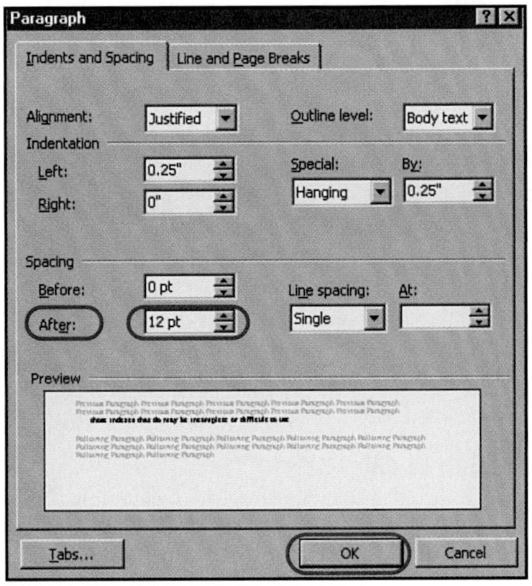

Paragraph
Indents and Spacing
Line and Page Breaks
Alignment:
Justified
Outline level:
Body text
Indentation
Left:
0.25"
Right:
0"
Special:
Hanging
By:
0.25"
Spacing
Before:
0 pt
After:
12 pt
Line spacing:
Single
At:
Preview
Tabs...
OK
Cancel

7 Click **OK** and then click anywhere in the document to deselect the text. Twelve points of space has now been added after the bulleted list. This space matches the between-paragraph spacing in the surrounding area of the document.

In Depth: You can also add space before the paragraph using the **Before** spacing option. It is a good idea, however, to be consistent and use either **Before** or **After** spacing to avoid unintended extra spacing.

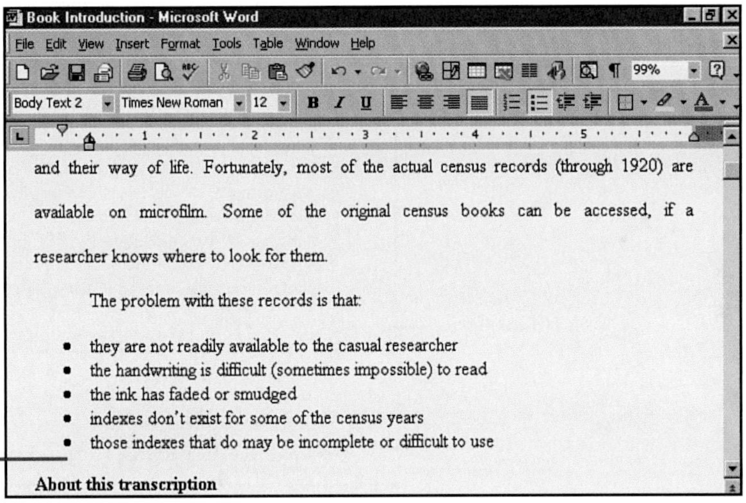

Book Introduction - Microsoft Word
File Edit View Insert Format Tools Table Window Help
Body Text 2
Times New Roman
12
99%
and their way of life. Fortunately, most of the actual census records (through 1920) are available on microfilm. Some of the original census books can be accessed, if a researcher knows where to look for them.
The problem with these records is that:
they are not readily available to the casual researcher
the handwriting is difficult (sometimes impossible) to read
the ink has faded or smudged
indexes don't exist for some of the census years
those indexes that do may be incomplete or difficult to use
About this transcription

12 points of space after the last bulleted list item

TASK 9

Working with Tabs

Why would I do this?

Tabs have become less and less important in word processing documents in favor of other indenting techniques and tables. Sometimes, however, it is necessary to know how to use tabs. For example, it is often helpful to use a tab to line up the decimals in a column of numbers with decimal points. Tabs are also the only way to put regular dots or dashes, called *leaders*, between columns. Leaders are often used to connect chapter titles with page numbers in a table of contents. If you have a line of text with some words left-aligned, other words centered, and still other words right-aligned, you might want to use tabs. Knowing how to use tabs increases your ability to create professional-looking documents.

In this task, you learn to use different kinds of tabs.

1 Place the insertion point at the end of the last item in the bulleted list. Press ⏎Enter. A new bullet point is added below the last one.

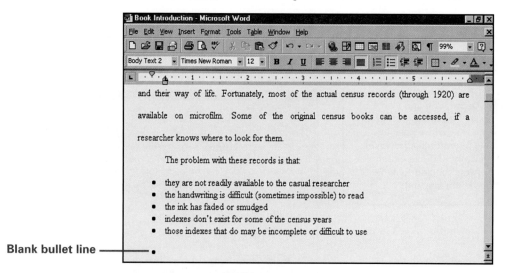

Blank bullet line ─────

2 Click the **Bullets** button to turn off the bulleted list. The new bullet is removed and the insertion point moves back to the left margin.

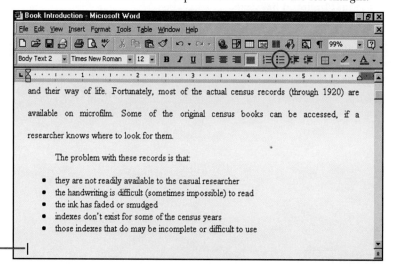

The bullet is removed ─────

3 Type **The following are the places, dates, and page numbers of the 1860 Alcona County Federal census:** and press ⟨↵Enter⟩.

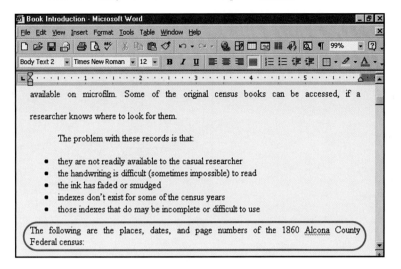

4 Select **Format**, **Tabs** from the menu. The Tabs dialog box opens. If the **Tabs** menu option is not visible when you choose the **Format** menu option, click the double-down arrow at the bottom of the drop-down menu to display the rest of the formatting options.

In Depth: The default for tabs in Word is a tab stop at every half-inch. Rather than pressing ⟨Tab⟩ several times to reach the desired stop, you should set the tabs to the needed location before entering text.

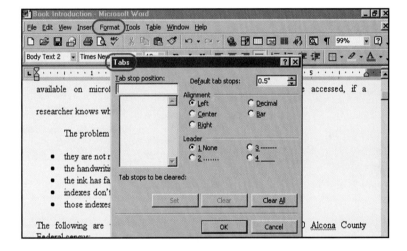

5 Type **2** in the **Tab stop position**, select **Left** in the **Alignment** area, and make sure **1 None** is selected in the **Leader** area. Click **Set** to enter the tab at the 2-inch mark.

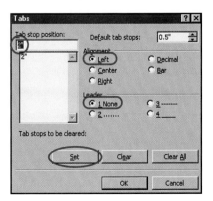

6 Type **6** in the **Tab stop position** box, select **Right** in the **Alignment** area, and select **2......** from the **Leader** area. Click **Set** to enter the tab at the 6-inch mark.

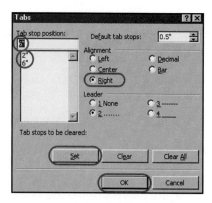

7 Click **OK**. The tabs you just added show up in the ruler at the top of the work area.

Caution: If the ruler is not showing on your screen, select **View, Ruler** from the menu.

Tab markers set at 2 inches and 6 inches

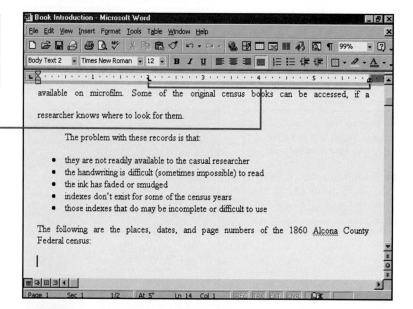

In Depth: Different types of tabs can be selected by clicking the tab marker at the left end of the horizontal ruler. When the tab you want to use is displayed, add it to the horizontal ruler by clicking on the ruler at the position where you want the tab. A tab marker will be added to the ruler. To remove a tab, click in the paragraph where you want the tab deleted. Then click the tab marker on the ruler and drag it down and off of the ruler. The tab is deleted from the selected paragraph.

8 Type **Black River** and press (Tab). This moves the insertion point to the left tab set at the 2-inch mark.

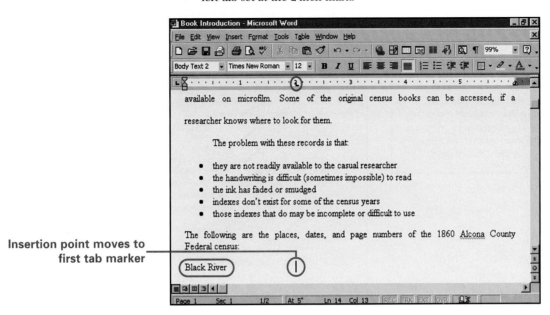

Insertion point moves to first tab marker

9 Type **June 8, 1860.** When you type the date, it moves to the right of the tab. The left tab that you set allows the left edges of the dates to line up. Press (Tab). The dot leader appears when you press (Tab).

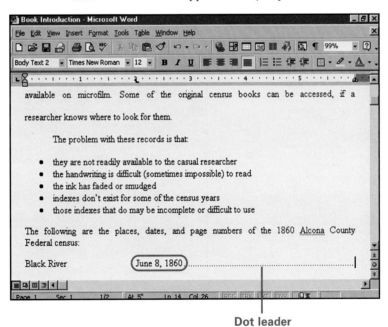

Dot leader

6

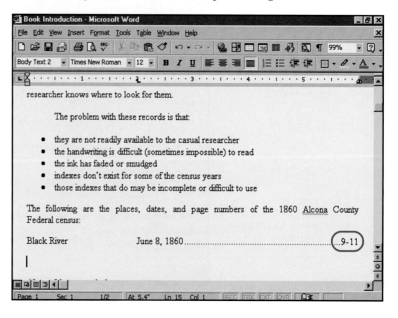

10 Type **9-11** for the page numbers, then press <kbd>⏎Enter</kbd>. Notice that because the right tab is used, the numbers move to the left as they are typed, ensuring that the numbers line up on the right side.

> **In Depth:** Another useful type of tab is the decimal tab. When you use this tab, the numbers move to the left until you press the decimal point, at which point the numbers move to the right of the decimal as you type them. This ensures that the numbers all line up on the decimal point.

11 Enter the following information using the same procedure:

Harrisville Township	**June 8-10, 1860**	**11-13**
Yewell Place	**June 11-12, 1860**	**14-15**

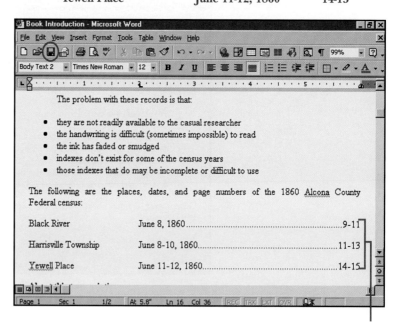

The right edges line up with the right tab marker

12 Highlight the first full paragraph (not the title) of the document, click the **Format Painter** button, and then click on the paragraph beginning with **The following are the places**. The paragraph is now double-spaced and indented.

The paragraph is now double-spaced and indented

Double-spaced

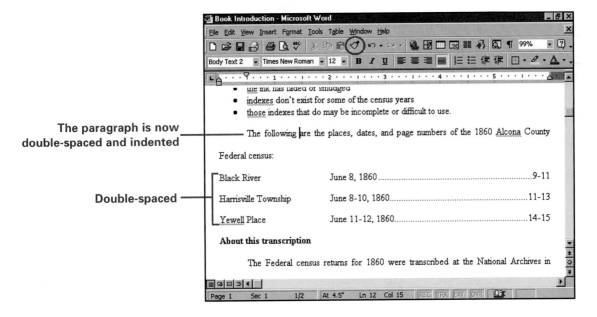

13 Select the two new lines beginning with **Black River** and **Harrisville Township**, choose **Format, Paragraph** from the menu, then use the down arrow to select **0 pt** in the **After** spacing section. Click **OK** and click anywhere in the document to deselect the text. The spacing following the paragraphs in the census information is removed. Click the **Save** button to save your work.

Spacing is reduced between paragraphs

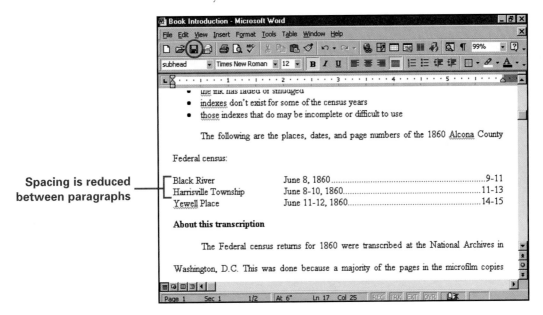

Printing Selected Text

Why would I do this?

While you are working on a document, sometimes you will want to print out only a section. Word has a feature that allows you to print selected portions of the text. This feature saves paper and enables you to print just the parts you want to use.

In this task, you learn to print only the text you have selected.

1 With your **Book Introduction** file still active, click at the end of the last paragraph of the document. Press ⏎Enter and type your name.

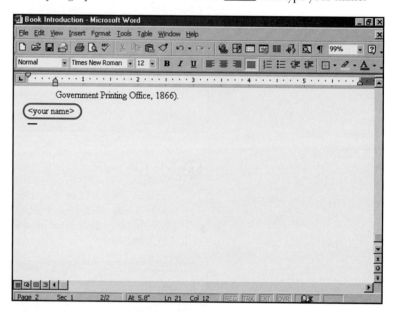

2 Select the last six paragraphs in the document. These are the five bibliographic entries, plus your name.

Selected text to be printed ———

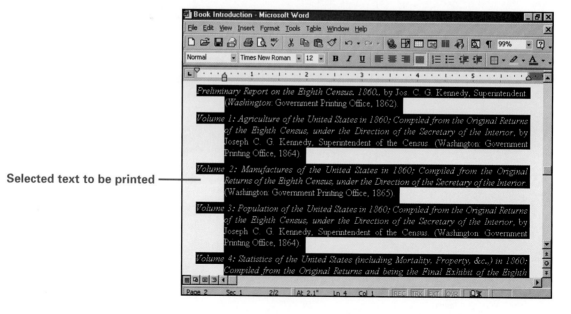

3 Select **File**, **Print** from the menu. The Print dialog box opens. Choose **Selection** from the **Page range** area.

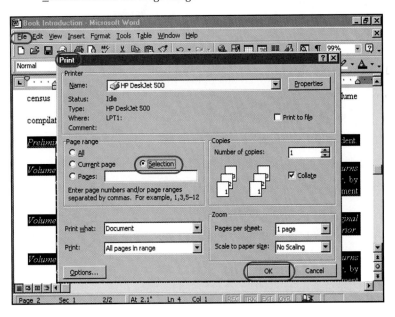

4 Click **OK**. The selected text is printed. Click anywhere in the document to deselect the text and click the **Save** button. Close the document.

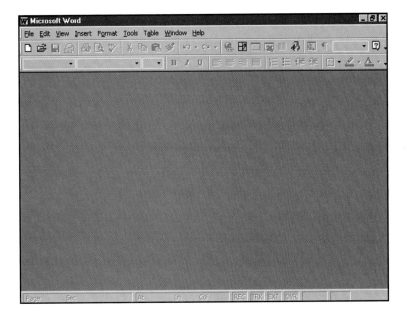

Comprehension Exercises

Comprehension exercises are designed to check your memory and understanding of the basic concepts in this lesson. You distinguish between true and false statements, identify new screen elements, and match terms with related statements. If you are uncertain of the correct answer, refer to the task number following each item (for example, T4 refers to Task 4) and review that task until you are confident that you can provide a correct response.

True-False

Circle either T or F.

T   F   **1.** When you select text and change the font, the shape of the letters changes. **(T1)**

T   F   **2.** If you change the size of the selected text to 36-point type, the text is about an inch high when it prints out. **(T1)**

T   F   **3.** If a paragraph is formatted with a hanging indent, the first line begins further to the right than the rest of the lines in the paragraph. **(T7)**

T   F   **4.** To make the letters thicker and to make them appear more important, you can select the text and then click the button on the toolbar that has a capital letter B on it. **(T1)**

T   F   **5.** A first-line indent created by pressing the Spacebar five times is the same as setting the first-line indent to 0.5 inches. **(T5)**

T   F   **6.** There is a type of tab that can be used to align a column of dollar figures so that the decimal points line up. **(T9)**

T   F   **7.** If you want to apply the formatting of one paragraph to another, select **Edit**, **Copy**, **Paste Special** from the menu. **(T6)**

T   F   **8.** If you set up a tab with a dot leader, pressing (Tab⇆) produces a series of dots between the previous text and the text at that tab. **(T9)**

T   F   **9.** The only way to place extra space between paragraphs is to press (⏎Enter) one or two extra times. **(T3)**

T   F   **10.** If you only want to print one paragraph, you can select it and then choose **File**, **Print**, **Selection**, **OK** from the menu. **(T10)**

Identifying Parts of the Word Screen

Refer to the figure and identify the numbered parts of the screen. Write the letter of the correct label in the space next to the number.

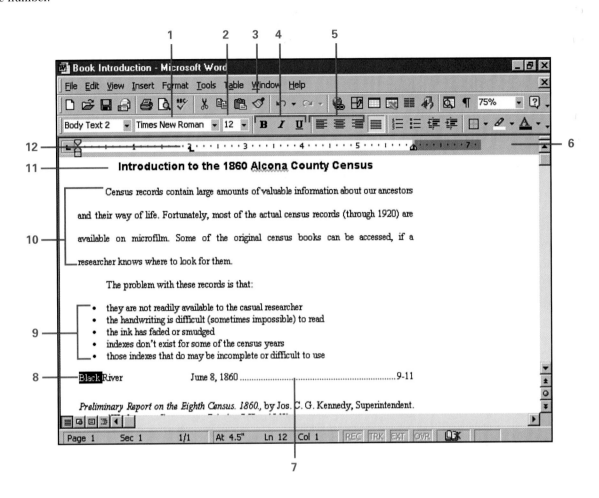

1. _____
2. _____
3. _____
4. _____
5. _____
6. _____
7. _____
8. _____
9. _____
10. _____
11. _____
12. _____

A. Bulleted list (**T4**)

B. Buttons used for adding emphasis (**T1**)

C. Buttons used for aligning text (**T2**)

D. Centered text emphasized with boldface (**T2**)

E. Dot leader (**T9**)

F. Double-spaced paragraph with the first line indented (**T5**)

G. Font size (**T1**)

H. Format Painter (**T6**)

I. Name of font (**T1**)

J. Ruler displaying tabs for currently selected line (**T9**)

K. Selected text (**T1**)

L. Tab stop (**T9**)

Matching

Match the following statements to the word or phrase that is the best match from the list. Write the letter of the matching word or phrase in the space provided next to the number.

1. **E** Rows of text preceded by round, black dots

2. **D** Automatically separates lines of text by an amount of space equal to the height of the text

3. **B** Paragraph whose first line begins to the right of the rest of the lines of text

4. **J** Paragraph whose first line of text is further to the left than the rest of the lines

5. **G** Method of printing less than a whole page of text

6. **H** A feature that fills the space between tab stops with a character such as a dash or a dot

7. **F** All of the lines of a paragraph line up at both the left and right margins

8. **I** A line of text that has the same amount of space between its first word and the left margin and its last word and the right margin

9. **A** If you use this tab, inserted text moves to the left as you type to ensure that the right side of the text stays aligned with the position of the tab

10. **C** Measurement used to describe the height of a line of text

A. Right-tab (**T9**)

B. First line indent (**T5**)

C. Point (**T1**)

D. Double-spaced (**T3**)

E. Bulleted list (**T4**)

F. Justified (**T2**)

G. File, Print, Selection (**T10**)

H. Leader (**T9**)

I. Centered (**T2**)

J. Hanging indent (**T7**)

K. Left-tab (**T9**)

Reinforcement Exercises

Reinforcement exercises are designed to reinforce the skills you have learned by applying them to a new situation. Detailed instructions are provided along with a figure, where appropriate, to illustrate the result. The Reinforcement exercises that follow should be completed sequentially. Leave the workbook open at the end of each exercise for use in the next exercise until you are specifically directed to close it.

R1—Changing the Font, Font Size, Font Style, and Paragraph Alignment

1. Launch **Word**. Open the document **Less0602** from the **Student\Lesson06** folder on the CD-ROM disc. Save it to your floppy disk as **Distance Education Technologies**.

2. Select the first two lines of the document, which make up the title.

3. Change the font to **Arial**.

4. Change the font size to **14** point.

5. Change the style to bold.

6. Change the alignment to centered.

7. Select the three lines that identify the author and date.

Show/Hide button

Selected text

Distance Education Technologies - Microsoft Word

File Edit View Insert Format Tools Table Window Help

Normal

**Affordable New Technologies in Distance Education for Adult Learners
in the
United States and the United Kingdom**

John M. Preston
Eastern Michigan University
December 1995
Edited by <Your Name>

(Note: Significant parts of the text and about half of the references have been removed to shorten this paper for more convenient editing. Not all of the references cited are contained in the reference list.)

8. Change their alignment to centered.

9. Select the line following the date. Type **Edited by \<Your Name>** (use your own name) and press **⏎Enter**. Center this line.

10. Select the section of text that you have been working on, which includes the title, the author information, the date of publication, and your name. Print this selection (see the figure).

11. Leave the document open for use in the next exercise.

R2—Using the Format Painter to Format Several Other Lines of Text

1. Click the **Show/Hide¶** button to reveal the hidden paragraph marks.

2. Select the heading **Interactive Technologies** (it follows the first long paragraph). Make sure to include the paragraph mark at the end of the line.

3. Change its alignment to centered.

4. Double-click on the **Format Painter** button on the toolbar.

5. Scroll to the bottom of page 2 to find the next heading, **Conclusion**.

6. Click on the word **Conclusion** to center it as well. If you double-click the **Format Painter** button, it remains depressed to indicate that it may be used again.

7. Scroll down and find the heading **Reference List**. Click on it to center it.

8. Click the **Format Painter** button to deselect it.

9. Leave the document open for use in the next exercise.

R3—Formatting Paragraphs

1. Scroll to the top of the document and select the paragraph that starts with **Distance education is**.

2. Choose **Format**, **Paragraph** to open the Paragraph dialog box.

3. Set the line spacing to **Double.**

4. Set the special indent to **First line** and click **OK**.

5. Double-click the **Format Painter** button on the toolbar.

6. Click in all of the following paragraphs except the headings that are underlined, the headings or titles that are centered, and the references at the end of the document.

7. Click the **Format Painter** button to turn it off.

8. Find the **Conclusion** section. Add your name in parentheses at the end of the **Conclusion** heading. Select the **Conclusion** heading and the next eight lines. Print the selected lines (see the figure).

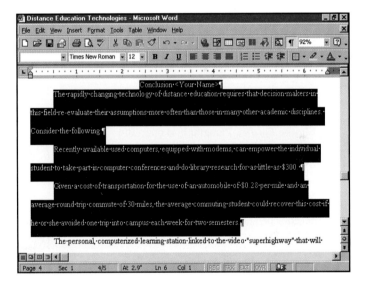

9. Leave the document open for use in the next exercise.

R4—Creating a Bulleted List

1. Locate the **Conclusion** section.

2. Select the four paragraphs that follow the phrase **Consider the following**. Since it is difficult to drag across text and scroll at the same time, click once to place the insertion point at the beginning of the first of the four paragraphs, scroll to the end of the fourth paragraph, hold (⬆Shift) and click at the end of the paragraph. This is a good method of selecting large blocks of text.

3. Click the **Bullets** button on the toolbar.

4. Click the **Decrease Indent** button on the Formatting toolbar to move the bulleted list to the left margin.

5. Add your name at the end of the last line in the bulleted list.

6. Turn off the **Show/Hide¶** button.

7. Select the text from **Consider the following** through the four paragraphs that have been changed into a bulleted list, including your name.

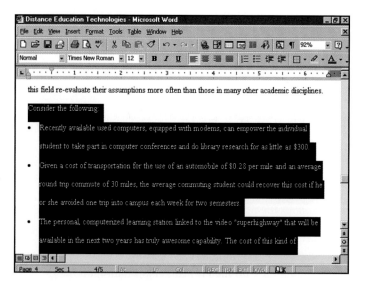

8. Print the selected text.

9. Leave the document open for use in the next exercise.

R5—Formatting a Hanging Indent and Space After Paragraphs

1. Select all of the references at the end of the document.

2. Choose **Format**, **Paragraph** to open the Paragraph dialog box.

3. Set the special indent to **Hanging**.

4. Set the line spacing to **Single**, if necessary.

5. Set the spacing after the paragraph to **6 pt** and click **OK**.

6. Type your name at the end of the Reference List.

7. Select the references portion of the text, starting with the heading **Reference List** and ending with your name. Print the selected text (see the figure).

8. Close the document and save your changes.

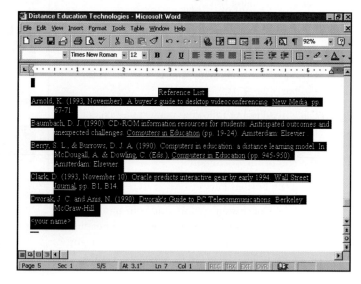

Challenge

Challenge exercises are designed to test your ability to apply your skills to new situations with less detailed instruction. These exercises also challenge you to expand your repertoire of skills by using Word commands that are similar to those you have already learned. The desired outcome is clearly defined, but you have more freedom to choose the steps needed to achieve the required result.

C1—Using the Center and Decimal Tabs, and Underlining Words in a Title

In Task 9, you created a list that used a left-aligned tab and a right-aligned tab. The decimal tab is another specialized tab that is useful for aligning numbers on a decimal point. The center tab enables you to center the title over the data.

Goal: To create a list that uses the center tab, decimal tabs, and underlining.

1. Start a new document.

2. For the first line of text, use center tabs at the 2-inch and 5-inch marks. Click the tab marker at the left end of the horizontal ruler to change the tab selection to the center tab mark. Then click on the ruler at the 2-inch mark and the 5-inch mark to set the tab locations. Now type the first line of data as shown in the figure.

3. For the remaining data, set decimal tabs at the 2-inch and 5-inch marks. Type the rest of the data as shown.

4. Select the first line of the chart and choose **Format**, **Font**. Change the **Underline style** to **Words only**.

5. Change the font of the column headings to **Arial, 14** point.

6. Change the font of the data to **Arial, 16** point.

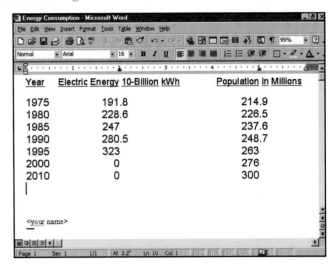

7. Add your name after the end of the list.

8. Save the document on your floppy disk as **Energy Consumption**. Print the document, and then close it.

C2—Using a Numbered List

Instead of a bulleted list, you may want to create a numbered list and choose the style of the numbers you use. In this exercise, you add numbers to paragraphs in a paper about nuclear energy.

Goal: To change paragraphs in a paper to a numbered list.

1. Locate and open the **Less0603** file in the **Student\Lesson06** folder that is on the CD-ROM disc that came with your book. Save it on your floppy disk with the name **Nuclear Energy**.

2. At the top of the page, under the By line, type **Edited by** and your name.

3. Select the first full paragraph and all the following paragraphs except the last one. Click the **Numbering** button on the formatting toolbar.

4. With the text still selected, open the **Bullets and Numbering** dialog box and format the numbers using the fourth option in the first row.

5. Save the document and leave it open for use in the next exercise.

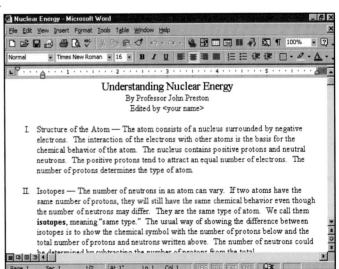

C3—Formatting Text to Subscripts and Superscripts

It is customary to use subscripts and superscripts in scientific papers and mathematical formulas. The **Format, Font** command enables you to select this type of format so you can properly represent scientific and mathematical notations.

Goal: To change characters to subscript and superscript formats.

1. Use the **Nuclear Energy** document from the previous Challenge exercise, or locate and open **Less0603** in the **Student\Lesson06** folder on the CD-ROM disc and save it on your floppy disk with the name **Nuclear Energy**.

2. If necessary, add **Edited by** and your name at the top of the page, under the By line.

3. Scroll to the bottom of the first page. Notice the subscript and superscript formats that have been used in the paragraph about chain reaction. These are notations identifying uranium and plutonium isotopes.

4. Go to the bottom of the document. Change the notations in the paragraph about breeder reactors so they match the format just examined. Select **92** in the first

notation and choose **Format**, **Font,** and click **Subscript**. Then select **238**, open the **Font** dialog box again, and click **Superscript**.

5. Repeat this process for the remaining five notations in this paragraph. You might try using the Format Painter. (Hint: You cannot do it in one step. The subscript and superscript are two different formats and have to be selected and applied or "painted" separately.)

6. Save your changes, then print the document before you close it.

Discovery

Discovery exercises are designed to help you learn how to teach yourself a new skill. In each exercise, you discover something new that is related to the topic taught in this lesson. You may be directed to use built-in wizards or some of the extensive Help features provided in Word to discover new features and learn new skills with minimum assistance from books or instructors. The required outcome demonstrates your ability to apply the new skill. Choice of topic, design of presentation, and steps of execution are determined by the learner.

D1—Changing the Size and Shape of Bullets

When you use a bulleted list, you may want to change the size or shape of the bullet to something that is more relevant to the topic, or to something that provides greater visual appeal.

In this exercise, you learn how to change the size and shape of the bullets in a bulleted list.

Locate and open the **Less0604** file that is in the **Student\Lesson06** folder on the CD-ROM disc that came with your book. Save the file on your floppy disk with the name **Case Study**. This is a list of topics about the implementation of a computer system. Select the bulleted list and open the Bullets and Numbering dialog box. Try one of the other bullet options.

Open the dialog box again and select the **Customize** button. Change the indent for the bullet position and the indent for the text position. Notice how these changes are shown in the **Preview** box. Click on the **Bullet** button and select an icon from the **Wingdings** font options. In the top row, the second icon from the right is a computer. Try this as a bullet for this list, or pick one of your own. When you are satisfied with your results, add your name to the page, print it, and save the document and close it. Open the Bullets and Numbering dialog box again and click the **Reset** button to return the bullet to its original setting.

D2—Creating a Multilevel Numbered List

Sometimes you will want to create a numbered list that has more than one level, similar to an outline.

In this Discovery exercise, you change a rough draft about a computer system implementation project into a multilevel numbered list.

Locate and open the **Less0605** file that is in the **Student\Lesson06** folder on the CD-ROM disc that came with your book. Save the file on your floppy disk with the name **Computer Implementation**. Select the body of the text. Open the Bullets and Numbering dialog box and click the **Outline Numbered** tab. Select one of the options that show a multilevel outline format, and then click the **Customize** button. Select **Level 1** and change the **Text position** box to **Indent at 0.25**. Change **Level 2** so the text will indent at 1 inch, and **Level 3** to indent at 1.5 inches. When you click **OK**, the document will be reformatted to an outline. Review the document to make sure all of it was converted to the outline. On the second title line, add **Formatted by: <your name>**. Print and save the document.

D3—Sorting a Bulleted List

Information you include in a document may need to be sorted alphabetically, by date, or by number. The **Sort** command found in the **Table** menu can be used to sort information in a bulleted list. In this Discovery exercise, you learn how to sort data in a bulleted list, first alphabetically by name, and then by date.

Open the **Less0606** file that is in the **Student\Lesson06** folder on the CD-ROM disc. Save it on your floppy disk with the name **Birthdays**. This is a listing of names and birthdays. Add your name and birthday to the bottom of the list. Select the bulleted list and open the Sort Text dialog box. Sort by **Paragraphs** and **Text**. Do a second sort, this time sorting by **Field 2** and **Date**. The list is re-sorted in date order. Print the document, save your changes, and close the file. Exit **Word**.

Lesson: 7

Formatting a Document

Introduction

In Lesson 6, you learned how to use many important Microsoft Word text and paragraph formatting tools. Word also offers a wide range of formatting options that affect the way your overall document looks when it is printed.

Margins are the spaces between the text and the edge of the paper. Word allows you to set the left, right, top, and bottom margins independently. The top and bottom margins are also used for information that can be displayed on each page of a document. These areas on the page are known as the *header* and *footer*, and can contain information such as page numbers, dates, company logos, or general text. The top and bottom margins must be large enough to contain whatever text is placed in the header or footer.

When formatting your document, you can also insert *page breaks*. If there is space at the bottom of a page for the first few lines of the next topic, but you want those lines to be at the top of the next page, you can insert a page break ahead of those lines. This feature enables you to control your document so that lines of text, images, or figures that should be displayed together can be shown on the same page. Word offers a print preview so that you can verify that the text of your document is placed on the pages exactly the way you desire.

In this lesson, you learn how to set margins, work with headers and footers, and insert page breaks.

Visual Summary

When you have completed this lesson, you will have created worksheets that look like these:

1860 & 1870 Federal Census Transcriptions
Alcona County, Michigan

Introduction

Census records contain large amounts of valuable information about our ancestors and their way of life. Fortunately, most of the actual census records (through 1920) are available on microfilm. Some of the original census books from the earlier years can be accessed, if a researcher knows where to look for them. The original books for most of the 20th century have been destroyed.

There can be several problems with early census records:

- they are not readily available to the casual researcher
- the handwriting is difficult (sometimes impossible) to read
- the ink has faded or smudged
- indexes don't exist for some of the census years
- those indexes that do exist may be incomplete or difficult to use

This and subsequent volumes will provide easy access to the Federal census information for Alcona County, Michigan. Separate books will follow for the 1880, 1900, 1910, and 1920 census records. The 1890 census was destroyed by fire.

The following are the places, dates, and census page numbers of the 1860 Alcona County census:

Black River	June 8, 1860	10-11
Harrisville Township	June 8-10, 1860	11-13
Yewell Place	June 11-12, 1860	14-15

The following are the places, dates, and census page numbers of the 1870 Alcona County census. The page numbers were reset to one at the beginning of each new location, rather than being consecutive, as in 1860.

Introduction

The names of two of the three townships were changed in the intervening decade:

Alcona Township	August 1-2, 1870	1-3
Greenbush Township	July 30, 1870	1-4
Harrisville Township	July 20-August 2, 1870	1-12

About this transcription

The census returns for 1860 were transcribed at the National Archives in Washington, D.C. This was done because a majority of the pages in the microfilm copies for Alcona County that are available through the Family History Centers of the LDS and various libraries are almost impossible to read.

The 1870 census was transcribed from microfilm copies at the University of Michigan Graduate Library. Once the transcription was completed, the results were checked against the original census records at the National Archives. Even with careful, sometimes laborious transcription, errors are bound to have occurred, particularly where the original handwriting was poor or the ink has faded.

There are other problems associated with names in these census returns. In some cases, the Assistant Marshal simply misspelled names while taking down the information. The authors have recorded the names the way they were spelled on the returns.

There are also some surnames that the enumerator spelled correctly, but which have changed over time. An example of this is the family of Robert and Mary Ann [Armstrong] Hasty, found in the 1870 census in Alcona Township. While Hasty was the correct spelling at the time, within a couple of decades the name would be 'Hastings' (which is the current spelling). Also, Mary Ann Hasty's first name is spelled 'Marty' in the 1870 census.

Non-population census schedules

Alcona Transcription   2   DRAFT

TASK 1

Setting Margins
Why would I do this?

Margins are the empty spaces around the edge of your document—both on the top and bottom and on the sides. In Word, you can control the four margin settings individually. Specific margin settings are required for particular writing styles, such as research papers that use the APA or MLA style. Increasing or decreasing one or more of the margins can also make a document look better on a page or fit on fewer pages, depending on your need. Finally, you may want to increase the left margin so you can bind the document or punch holes in it. Knowing how to work with margins helps you create professional-looking documents.

In this task, you learn to change the margins of a document.

1 Launch Word and click the **Open** button. Open **Less0701** in the **Student\Lesson07** folder on the CD-ROM disc. Save this lesson as **Full Introduction** on your floppy disk. Select **Page Width** from the **Zoom** button drop-down box, if necessary. Notice that the document is 6 inches wide.

Caution: The ruler should be visible at the top of the screen. If not, choose **View**, **Ruler** from the menu. The width of the page on the ruler shows in white. The margin area on the right is dark gray. While 6 is not shown on the ruler, you can see that the measurement from 5 to the right margin is a full inch when you compare it to the measurements showing on the ruler.

2 Select **File**, **Page Setup** from the menu. The Page Setup dialog box is displayed.

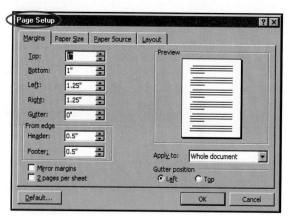

Quick Tip: You may open the Page Setup dialog box by double-clicking on the gray portion of the ruler.

3 Make sure that the **Margins** tab is selected and highlight the **Top** box if necessary. The number in this box controls the distance, in inches, from the top of the page to the top of the text on the page (excluding the header text).

In Depth: The margin settings are saved with the document. When you create a new document, the *default* margin settings are applied. The most common default margin settings are either an inch for all four sides or an inch at the top and bottom and an inch and a quarter on the left and right. You can change the default margin settings by setting new ones, and then clicking the **Default** button in the **Page Setup** dialog box. You should only do this on your own computer.

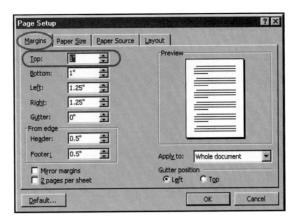

4 Leave the top margin at 1 inch, and then press Tab to move to the **Bottom** margin. Type **.75**. This leaves a three-quarter inch margin at the bottom of the document.

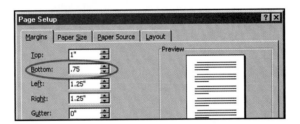

5 Press Tab to move to the **Left** margin. Type **1.5**, which leaves enough room to bind the final document.

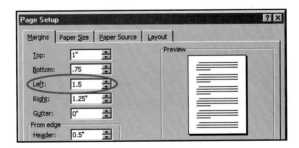

6 Press `Tab` to move to the **Right** margin. Type **.75** to make the right margin .75 inches. Make sure that the **Apply to** drop-down list says **Whole document**.

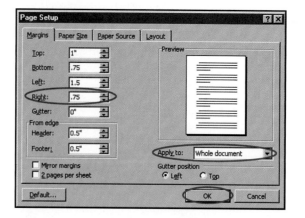

Caution: Your computer monitor may be set to a different display resolution than the one used to capture these screens. If so, the percentage shown in the Zoom box when you choose **Page Width** may differ from the example shown.

7 Click **OK**. Choose **Page Width** from the **Zoom** button drop-down list. Notice that the document is now 6.25 inches wide.

TASK 2

Inserting Page Numbers

Why would I do this?

Documents of more than two pages usually need page numbers. Page numbers help keep loose pages in order and provide easy reference for long documents. Word gives you a way to automatically insert page numbers at the top or bottom of a document. These numbers adjust themselves as necessary when you add or delete text.

In this task, you learn how to add page numbers to the document footer.

1 With your **Full Introduction** file active, choose **Insert**, **Page Numbers** from the menu. The Page Numbers dialog box is displayed.

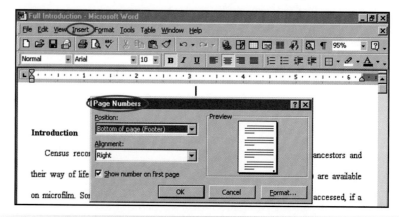

2 If necessary, select **Bottom of page (Footer)** from the Position drop-down list. This places the page number at the bottom of each page.

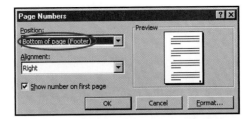

3 Select **Center** from the Alignment drop-down list.

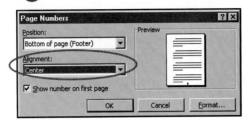

In Depth: You can center the page numbers or align them on the right or left side of the page. The other two options in the drop-down menu, inside and outside, refer to documents formatted for back-to-back printing.

4 Confirm that the **Show number on first page** option box is selected. This leaves the page number on the first page.

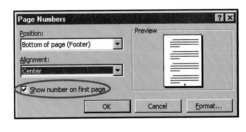

In Depth: If you plan to add other text to the header or footer, add that text before you elect to turn off the page number on the first page. Otherwise, you end up with the header or footer text on the first page only and the page numbers on every page but the first. Therefore, make certain a check mark is in the **Show number on first page** check box in this dialog box. Later, you can elect to turn off the header and footer on the first page, and the page number and other text will not show.

5 Click **OK**. The view of your document changes to the **Print Layout** view. Use the **Zoom** box to display the page in **Page Width**.

In Depth: The Print Layout view shows you the position of the document elements on the page. The edges of the page are displayed if you scroll to either side or if the Zoom is set to display a wide view of the page. The document looks like it will when it is printed, but you can edit text in this view. It is more than a preview window.

Print Layout View button —

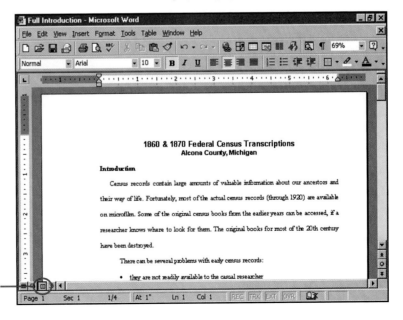

6 Scroll to the bottom of the first page. The page number is displayed in the center of the footer.

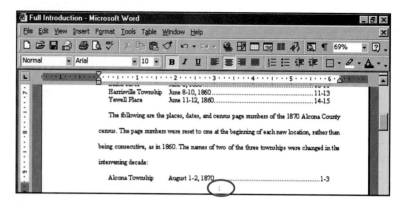

TASK *3*

Entering Text in a Header or Footer
Why would I do this?

Headers and footers are designed to display information that needs to be shown on every page of a document, with the possible exception of the first page. You can add text to the header and footer to identify your document, its author, the current version, and other relevant information.

In this task, you learn to add text to the header and footer.

1 With your **Full Introduction** file active, choose **View**, **Header and Footer** from the menu. The Page Header is displayed, with the document text shown in light gray in the background. The Header and Footer toolbar is also displayed.

Text in the header repeats on each page

Header and Footer toolbar

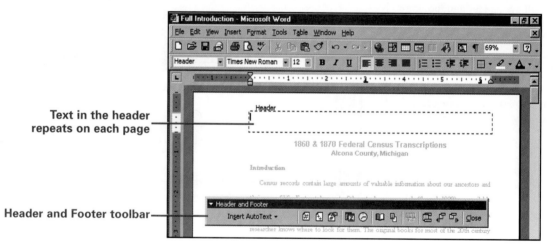

2 Type **Introduction** at the left edge of the **Header**.

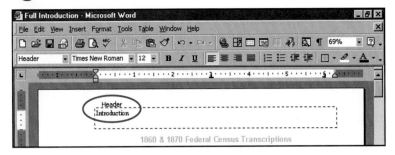

3 Click the **Switch Between Header and Footer** button on the **Header and Footer** toolbar. This takes you to the footer at the bottom of the page.

Switch Between Header and Footer button

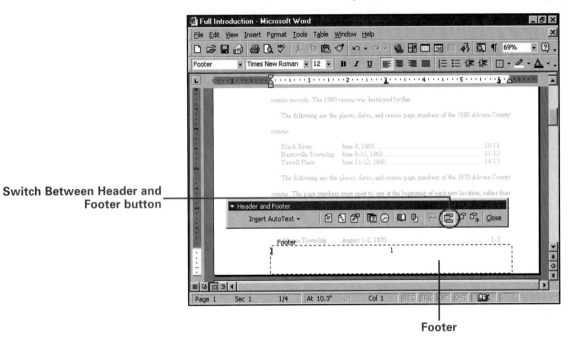

Footer

4 Type **Alcona Transcription** at the left edge of the footer.

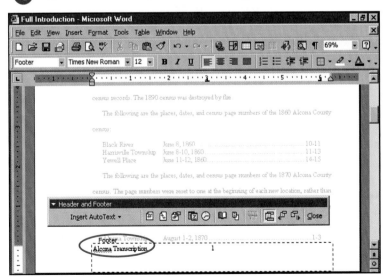

In Depth: Notice that the page number you added earlier is showing in the page footer. This number could also be added by using the page footer options showing on the toolbar.

⑤ Press `Tab` twice to move to the right tab at the right edge of the footer. The insertion point skips over the page number. Type **DRAFT**.

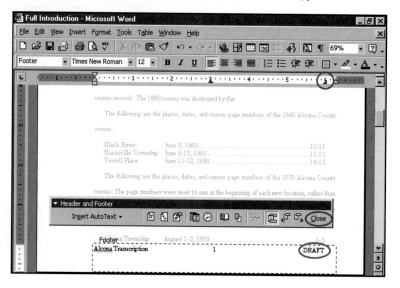

⑥ Click the **Close** button on the **Header and Footer** toolbar. Scroll downward to display the bottom of the first page and the top of the second page. Notice the footer at the bottom of page 1 and the header at the top of page 2.

Footer —————

Header —————

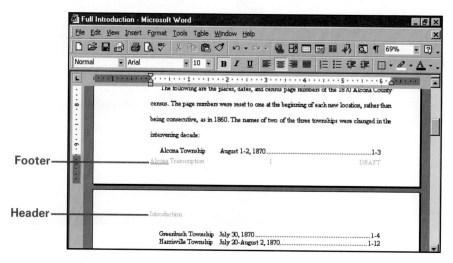

Inserting Page Breaks
Why would I do this?

You will often find that elements that should be kept together, such as lists and related data, begin on one page and finish on the next. You may be tempted to insert several blank lines to force the text onto the next page. This practice can cause problems when you make changes to the text. If you insert several blank lines, when you add or remove text you can end up with blank lines in the middle of a page. Inserting a page break is an effective way to resolve this problem. A page break enables you to edit the previous page without changing the placement of the text on the page following the break. Careful use of page breaks can help you control the layout of your document when it is printed.

In this task, you learn to insert a page break into a document.

1 With your **Full Introduction** file active, click the **Normal View** button to return to Normal view.

> **!** **Caution:** If you accidentally click the **Online Layout View** button, the view buttons are not displayed. You can change to any view by using the **View** option in the menu.

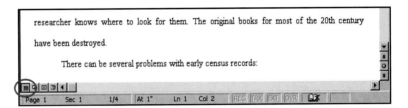

2 Scroll down until you can see the dotted line that indicates the bottom of page 1 and the top of page 2. Notice that the list of items is divided by an automatic page break. This list and its introductory sentence should be together on the same page.

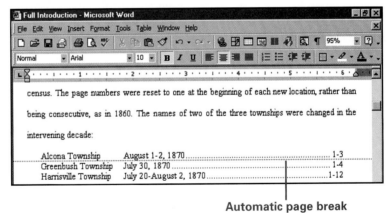

Automatic page break

3 Place the insertion point to the left of the sentence that begins **The names of ...** (see figure).

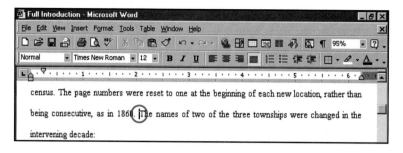

4 Select **Insert**, **Break** from the menu. The Break dialog box is displayed.

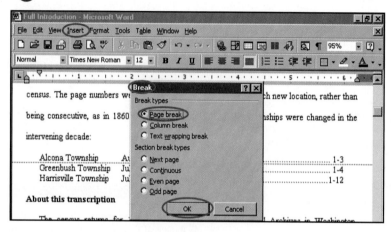

5 Select **Page break** from the Break types area of the dialog box if necessary, and then click **OK**. The new, artificial page break is marked with a dotted line that has the words **Page Break** in the middle.

Quick Tip: You can also add a page break at the insertion point by holding down Ctrl and pressing ↵Enter.

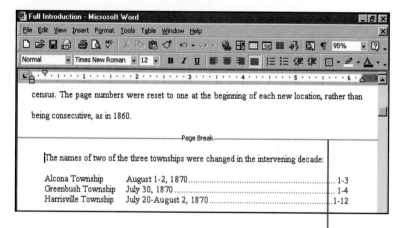

Inserted page break

6 Click the **Save** button to save your changes.

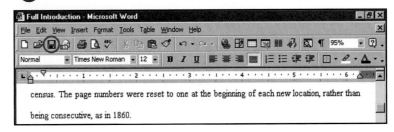

TASK 5

Using Print Preview
Why would I do this?

Inserting or removing text can have unexpected consequences, especially if you have inserted page breaks. Word gives you an easy way to look at one or more pages of your document at the same time to see how the text flows from one page to the next. *Print Preview* shows you what the layout of each page will look like when it is printed.

In this task, you learn to use Print Preview to examine the way your document will look when printed. You also learn how to turn off the header and footer information on the first page.

1 With your **Full Introduction** file active, scroll to the top of the document.

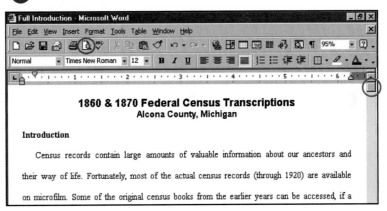

2 Click the **Print Preview** button. The first two pages of the document are displayed. The text may be difficult or impossible to read, depending on your monitor, but the layout of the page is clearly displayed.

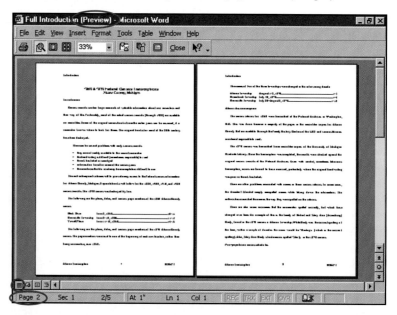

3 Position the pointer anywhere in the document. The pointer changes to a magnifying glass with a plus sign (+) in the middle.

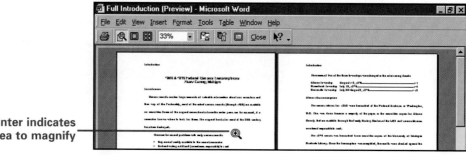

Pointer indicates area to magnify

4 Click on the page number at the bottom of page 1. You can now read the text at the bottom of the page and the footer information. Notice that the magnifying glass pointer now contains a minus sign (–).

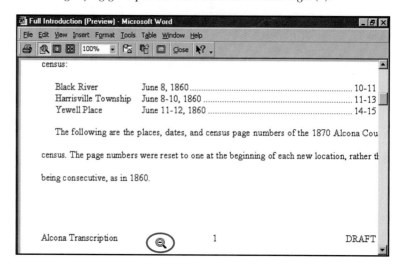

5 This footer information should not appear on the first page. Choose **File**, **Page Setup** and click the **Layout** tab in the Page Setup dialog box.

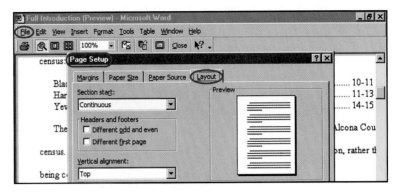

6 Click the **Different first page** check box in the Headers and footers area. This option turns the header and footer information off on the first page of the document.

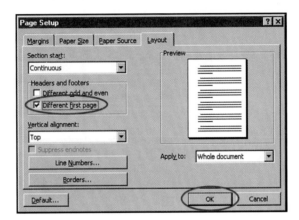

7 Click **OK**. Click the magnifying glass to fit the whole page back on the screen. Notice that no header or footer information is on the first page.

Header and footer information is not displayed on page 1

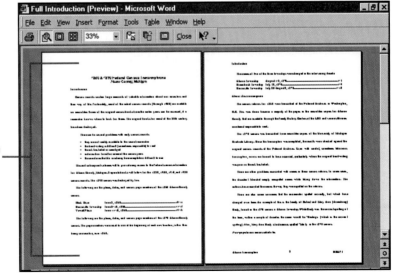

8 Click the **Multiple Pages** button on the Print Preview toolbar. Drag the pointer across the first three page icons in the first row of the menu to indicate that you want to see three pages in the same row.

Multiple Pages button —

9 Click the mouse button. Three full pages (pages 1, 2, and 3) are displayed.

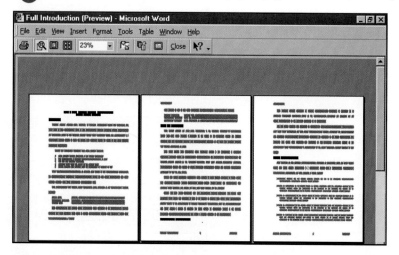

10 Scroll down to the bottom of the page using the vertical scrollbar. Pages 4 and 5 are displayed.

In Depth: You do not have to print all the pages in a document. Choose **File**, **Print**, **Pages** from the menu and enter the page numbers you want to print. The dialog box has an example that shows how to enter the page numbers.

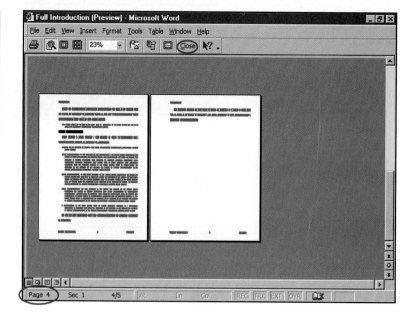

11 Click the **Close** button on the Print Preview toolbar. Click the **Save** button to save your work.

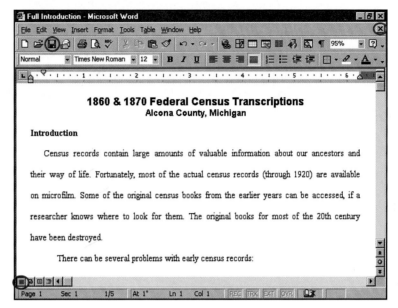

12 Click the **Close Window** button to close the document. Leave Word open for use in the following exercises.

Comprehension Exercises

Comprehension exercises are designed to check your memory and understanding of the basic concepts in this lesson. You distinguish between true and false statements, identify new screen elements, and match terms with related statements. If you are uncertain of the correct answer, refer to the task number following each item (for example, T4 refers to Task 4) and review that task until you are confident that you can provide a correct response.

True-False

Circle either T or F.

T   F   **1.** The margins may be set by using the **Format** option on the menu bar. **(T1)**

T   F   **2.** The header is placed in the top margin. **(T3)**

T   F   **3.** The text in the footer must be the same font as the text in the body of the document. **(T3)**

T   F   **4.** It is possible to enter a special date field into the header that automatically updates to the current date every time the document is used or printed. **(T4)**

T   F   **5.** If a new topic starts near the bottom of a page, it is best to insert several blank lines in front of it to force it to the top of the next page. **(T4)**

T   F   **6.** Print Preview allows you to see several pages at once so that you can see how the text flows from one page to the next. **(T5)**

T   F   **7.** If you only want to print pages 2 and 3 of a document, you can do so using the **File**, **Print**, **Pages** menu option. **(T5)**

T   F   **8.** If you use automatic page numbering, you have to use the **Recalculate Page Numbers** command when you delete or add enough text to change the previous page numbers. **(T2)**

T   F   **9.** Headers and footers appear at the top and bottom of each page (with the possible exception of the title page). **(T3)**

T   F   **10.** The left and right margins must always be the same size. **(T1)**

Identifying Parts of the Word Screen

Refer to the figure and identify the numbered parts of the screen. Write the letter of the correct label in the space next to the number.

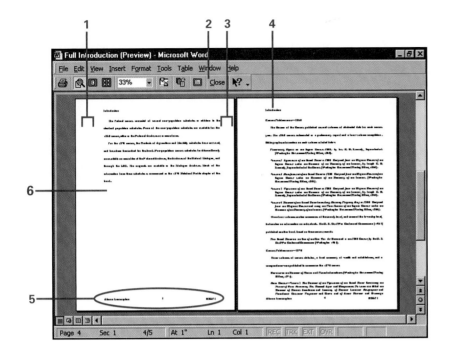

1. _____

2. _____

3. _____

4. _____

5. _____

6. _____

7. _____

8. _____

9. _____

10. _____

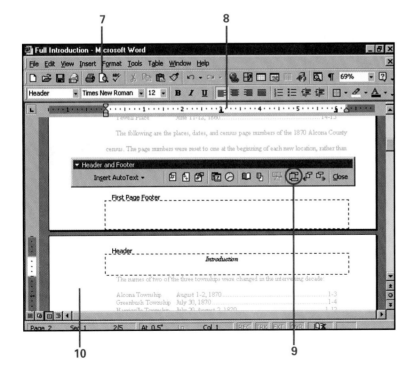

A. Text in Footer (**T3**)

B. Print Preview button (**T5**)

C. A page break has been inserted here (**T4**)

D. Left margin (**T1**)

E. Button that closes the Print Preview view (**T5**)

F. Right margin (**T1**)

G. Text in header (**T3**)

H. Print Preview view (**T5**)

I. Switch Between Header and Footer button (**T3**)

J. Ruler displaying tab markers used in the header or footer (**T3**)

Matching

Match the following statements to the word or phrase that is the best match from the list. Write the letter of the matching word or phrase in the space provided next to the number.

1. **G** Button that may be used to change the number of pages displayed in the Print Preview (**T5**)

2. **H** Displays one or more pages as they will appear when printed (**T5**)

3. **E** Contains text, page numbers, or dates that automatically print at the bottom of each page (**T3**)

4. **K** Menu commands used to display the dialog box used to set margins (**T1**)

5. **A** Automatically displays the current page number (**T2**)

6. **B** Contains text, page numbers, or dates that automatically print at the top of each page (**T3**)

7. **I** The white space between the edge of the paper and the text (**T1**)

8. **D** Forces text to the top of the next page (**T4**)

9. **F** Switches the view between the header and the footer even if they are not on the same screen (**T3**)

10. **C** A simple dotted line across the page in Normal view (**T4**)

A. Automatic page number

B. Header

C. Page break

D. Automatic page break

E. Footer

F. Switch Between Header and Footer button

G. Multiple Pages

H. Print Preview

I. Margin

J. Insert, Header and Footer

K. File, Page Setup

Reinforcement Exercises

Reinforcement exercises are designed to reinforce the skills you have learned by applying them to a new situation. Detailed instructions are provided along with a figure, where appropriate, to illustrate the result. The Reinforcement exercises that follow should be completed sequentially. Leave the workbook open at the end of each exercise for use in the next exercise until you are specifically directed to close it.

R1—Change the Margins in a Document

1. Launch Word. Open the document **Less0702** from the **Student\Lesson07** folder on the CD-ROM disc. Save it on your floppy disk as **Distance Education 2**.

2. Switch to the **Print Layout** view if necessary.

3. Select **File, Page Setup**.

4. Change the top and bottom margins to **1.0** inch.

5. Change the left margin to **1.50** inches and the right margin to **.75** inches.

6. Leave the document open for use in the next exercise.

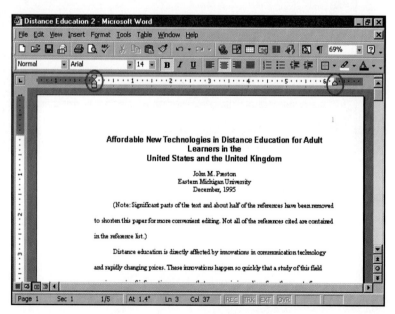

R2—Insert Page Numbers in a Document

Using the **Distance Education 2** document, insert page numbers.

1. Choose **Insert**, **Page Number** from the menu.

2. Insert page numbers on the top of the document on the right side.

3. Leave the document open for use in the next exercise.

R3—Add a Header and Footer to a Document

Using the **Distance Education 2** document, add information to the header and footer.

1. Select **View**, **Header and Footer** from the menu.

2. In the header at the left side, type **Affordable New Technologies**.

3. Switch to the footer. Use the **Insert, Date and Time** option from the menu to insert the date at the left side of the footer. Select the **November 24, 2000** format. Make sure that the **Update Automatically** option is deselected.

4. On the right side of the Footer area, type your name (use the tab, not spaces, to align your name).

5. Select your name and change the font to one of your choice. Make it bold to add emphasis. Move the tab marker over so that your name in the footer lines up with the rest of the text at the .75-inch margin.

6. Click the **Page Setup** button on the Header and Footer toolbar and select **Different First Page**. Leave the header and footer on the first page empty.

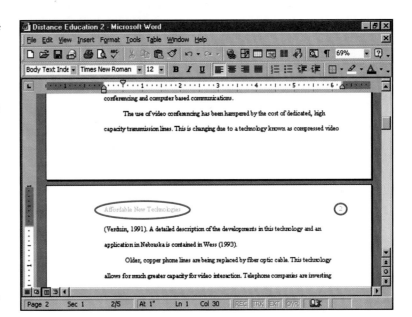

7. Save your work and leave the document open for use in the next exercise.

R4—Insert Page Breaks in a Document

Using the **Distance Education 2** document, insert page breaks at the beginning of each section.

1. Position the insertion point in front of the title **Interactive Technology** and insert a page break.

2. Add a page break before the heading **Computer-based conferencing**, so that it is on the same page as the rest of the text that follows that topic.

3. If necessary, add a page break in front of the **Conclusion** and **Reference List** sections of the paper. The paper should now have five pages.

4. Leave the document open for use in the next lesson.

R5—Use the Print Preview and Print a Range of Pages

Click the **Print Preview** button to see how the document looks.

1. Switch to Multiple Pages if necessary.

2. Verify that the header and footer areas on the first page are empty and that the remaining four pages each show information in their headers and footers.

3. Go to the Print dialog box and select pages **1** and **2** to print.

4. Save your work and close the document.

Challenge

Challenge exercises are designed to test your ability to apply your skills to new situations with less detailed instruction. These exercises also challenge you to expand your repertoire of skills by using Word commands that are similar to those you have already learned. The desired outcome is clearly defined, but you have more freedom to choose the steps needed to achieve the required result.

C1—Using a Multiple-Line Header

In this lesson, you learned how to use create headers and footers for your documents. Sometimes you may want to include more than one line of information in a header or footer. In this Challenge exercise, you create a two-line header for a group of documents that were written for a training proposal.

Goal: To create a multiple-line header in a document.

1. Locate and open the **Less0703** file that is on the CD-ROM disc that came with your book. Save it on your floppy disk as **Training Proposal**.

2. View the **Header and Footer**. In the header, tab to the center and type **Joseph A Schwartz & Associates**.

3. Press ⏎Enter to move to a second line in the **Header**. Type **A Computer Training Company**.

4. Move to the footer and enter the date at the left side. Add your name at the right side. Make sure the right tab lines up with the right margin.

5. Save the changes and leave the document open for use in the next Challenge exercise.

C2—Changing the Formatting of a Header and Adding a Line Separator

If you use the header to identify your company, as we did in the previous exercise, you may also want to change the formatting of the font to make the header stand out. Adding a line separator is a nice finishing touch to a header or footer. This sets off the header or footer area and adds a professional appearance to your document. In this Challenge exercise, you change the header font style, size, and color, and then add a border to create a line separator at the bottom of your header.

Goal: To format a header and add a separating line.

1. Use the **Training Proposal** document from the previous Challenge exercise.

2. Select the two lines of text in the header and change the font to one of your choice. Change the size of the font to **14**. If you want, use the **Font Color** button to change the color of the font.

3. Move the insertion point to the end of the second line in the header. Click the drop-down arrow next to the **Border** button. (Hint: The Border button is toward the right end of the formatting toolbar. The

ScreenTip displays the name of the currently selected option followed by the word Border.) Select **Bottom Border** from the options. It will appear as though nothing has happened. Close the Header and Footer toolbar to see the results.

4. Increase the spacing between the header and the beginning of the document by adding an empty line where necessary.

5. Save the changes, and then print and close the document.

C3—Adding a Section Break to a Document

Section breaks are often used in documents to enable you to use different headers and footers for different sections of a long document, such as chapters in a book, sections in a report, or articles in a contract. In this Challenge exercise, you will add two section breaks. The first one is used to create a separate title page, which will have a different top margin setting. The second one separates a table from the rest of the document. You are separating the table so that it can be displayed in landscape mode and expanded.

Goal: To insert section breaks in a document and change page setup formats for the different sections.

1. Launch Word. Locate and open the **Less0704** file that is on the CD-ROM disc that came with your book. Save the file as **Forms of Business** on your floppy disk.

2. Click in the empty line after the title line and choose **Insert**, **Break** from the menu. Under **Section break types**, select **Next page**. The title will move to a separate page. Click the **Show/Hide** button to see the break indicator.

3. On the new title page, add two empty lines under the title, and then type **Formatted by <your name>**.

4. Open the Page Setup dialog box. Change the top margin to **4"**, then change the **Apply to** area to **This section**.

5. Scroll down and place the insertion point on one of the empty lines just before the second title. Insert a second section break, using the **Next page** type of break.

6. Make sure your insertion point is anywhere on page 2 of the document. Open the Page Setup dialog box and change the **Orientation** to **Landscape**. (Hint: This is on the **Paper Size** page of the dialog box.) Make sure the **Apply to** area is set to **Selected sections**.

7. Use the **Print Preview** button to see the changes in your page layouts. If necessary, delete extra lines on the top of the last page to eliminate an empty fourth page.

8. Save your changes, print, and close the document.

Discovery

Discovery exercises are designed to help you learn how to teach yourself a new skill. In each exercise, you discover something new that is related to the topic taught in this lesson. You may be directed to use built-in wizards or some of the extensive Help features provided in Word to discover new features and learn new skills with minimum assistance from books or instructors. The required outcome demonstrates your ability to apply the new skill. Choice of topic, design of presentation, and steps of execution are determined by the learner.

D1—Setting Mirror and Gutter Margins, and Inserting Outside-Margin Page Numbers

If you need to create a document that is going to be printed on both sides and bound, you should use the Mirror Margins feature. This ensures that the inside margin of each page is wide enough to accommodate the binding. When a document is formatted with different inside and outside margins, you will usually place the page number for the document on the outside edge. When Mirror Margins are used, this means that the location of the outside edge alternates every other page.

In this Discovery exercise, you use Help to learn about the different margin options. Then you set Mirror Margins with a gutter for a short story and insert page numbers in the outside margin.

Locate the **Less0705** file in the **Student\Lesson07** folder on the CD-ROM disc that came with your book, and open it. Save the document on your floppy disk as **Stockton Story**. Open **Help** and look for information about page margins. In the **Overview of Page Margins** Help window, click on each of the linked topics to find out about adjusting margins, setting mirror margins, and creating a gutter margin. In the open document, select **Mirror margins** on the Page Setup dialog box. Set the margins as follows: **Top .75"**, **Bottom 1"**, **Inside 1"**, **Outside 0.8"**, **Gutter 0.25"**. Use **Print Preview** to see how the margins look. Save your changes and leave the document open for use in the next Discovery exercise.

D2—Creating a Different First Page Header

Documents that have several sections often require a different header or footer for each section. You use the Header and Footer toolbar to control the information in that area for each section of a document. In this Discovery exercise, you move the title and first paragraph about the author to the header on the first page. Because you do not want this to repeat on subsequent pages, you will create a different header for the first page of this document.

Use the file from the previous exercise, or locate and open **Less0705** on the CD-ROM disc that came with your book. Save the document on your floppy disk as **Stockton Story**. Use the Page Setup dialog box to choose **Different first page** for the headers and footers. Select the title, author, and first paragraph. Cut and paste them into the header on the first page. Indent this paragraph .5-inch from both the left and right margin. Notice that the header box is titled **First Page Header**. Now use the **Insert**, **Page Numbers** command to add page numbers to the outside margin. Make sure the **Show number on first page** check box is not checked. Go to **Print Preview** to see how the document looks. Save your changes and leave the file open for use in the next Discovery exercise.

D3—Changing Part of a Document to Two Columns

Columns are used for newslettersand other documents to make reading easier. Sometimes you will want part of the document to be in two columns and the rest to be in one column. When you change text that is already written to a two-column format, Word automatically puts in a section break. To change it back to one column, you need to put in a section break and change the layout. In this Discovery exercise, you change the body of the **Stockton Story** to a two-column layout. Then you add a section break at the end of the story and change the layout back to one column. First you use Help to learn more about columns.

Use the file from the previous exercise, or locate and open **Less0705** on the CD-ROM disc that came with your book. Save the document on your floppy disk as **Stockton Story**. Open **Help** and look for information on newspaper columns. Review the page about removing columns. Be sure to look at the definition for **Sections**. Then change the body of the document to a two-column format.

When you begin, make sure you are in **Print Layout** view. Select the body of the story (everything but the header). Use the **Columns** button to select a two-column format. Use the **Show/Hide** button to view the section break that has been inserted at the beginning of the story. Move to the end of the document, and insert a continuous section break. Then use the **Columns** button again to change the format back to one column. At the end of the document in this new section, change the font size to 20 and type **This is the conclusion of Captain Eli's Best Ear story, written by Frank Stockton, and formatted by <your name>.** This sentence should be displayed across the entire width of the page. Save your changes, print the first and last page of the document, and then close the file.

Lesson: 8

Working with Tables, Using Clip Art, and Inserting Hyperlinks

Task 1 Inserting a Table

Task 2 Entering Data into a Table

Task 3 Adding Rows to a Table

Task 4 Using the AutoFormat and AutoFit Tools

Task 5 Adding Clip Art

Task 6 Resizing Clip Art

Task 7 Wrapping Text Around an Image and Moving an Image

Task 8 Inserting a Hyperlink

Introduction

Tables are lists of data set up in a column-and-row format, somewhat like the layout of a spreadsheet. Each intersection of a row and column is called a *cell*. The cells can contain text, numbers, or graphics.

Many formatting tools are available for tables. You can line up text on the right or left sides or in the middle of cells. You can change font and font size, and use all the font formatting tools, such as bold, italic, and underline, on any text. You can also add borders and shading to the table. This formatting can be done on one or more cells at a time or on the whole table at once.

Tables can be used for many purposes. They can display numeric data, text, graphics, or a combination of the three. They are excellent for two-column tasks, such as résumés, in which the topic is on the left and the details are on the right.

Clip art can be used to enhance a document by adding visual images to create interest or illustrate a point. You can insert clip art from the Microsoft ClipArt Gallery, or you can insert images from files that you have on your computer or from the Internet. Once clip art has been inserted, you can resize it, move it, and wrap text around it.

Another useful feature of Office is the capability to insert hyperlinks to link your document to other documents, or to files created by other applications such as Microsoft Excel. You can even create a hyperlink to a Web site that is related to the topic of your document. This is particularly useful if you transmit documents to others online.

In this lesson, you learn how to set up and edit a table and use a powerful table-formatting tool. You also learn how to work with clip art and insert a hyperlink to a Web page.

Visual Summary

When you have completed this lesson, you will have created a document that looks like this:

PRESS RELEASE

TORNADO HAZARD DECREASING IN MICHIGAN

[Ypsilanti, Michigan. April 1, 1998.] The threat of injury or death from tornadoes has been decreasing in Michigan for the past four decades, a report from a noted weather and climate specialist suggests. Dr. Carl Ojala has been studying the impact of tornadoes in the U.S. for years. His latest research has focused on the state of Michigan, and his findings are startling.

The southern half of Michigan lies at the northeastern margin of "tornado alley," the nation's infamous tornado region which extends northward from Texas. For the four decades from the 1950s through the 1980s, 718 tornadoes were recorded for Michigan. In total, slightly more than one quarter of them killed 237 people, injured 3,157, and caused hundreds of millions of dollars in property damage.

The worst in Michigan's history, the June 8, 1953, Flint tornado was responsible for 116 deaths. From 1916 through 1990, this tornado ranked fourth in the U. S. in the number of fatalities. This disaster was exceeded only by the record-length "Tri-State" tornado which devastated Missouri, Illinois, and Indiana in 1925 (689 deaths), the Tupelo, Mississippi, tornado in 1936 (216 deaths), and the Woodward tornado in Texas, Oklahoma, and Kansas in 1947 (169 deaths).

Due primarily to the Flint storm and an outbreak of killer tornadoes in April 1965, Michigan is tied with Alabama for third place, after Texas and Mississippi, for total number of tornado-related fatalities from 1951 through 1990. Nevertheless, argues Ojala, the tornado hazard in Michigan has diminished in recent years. The following table, which looks at tornado casualties by decade, supports his claim:

Decade	# of Reported Tornadoes	Number of Deaths	Number of Injuries	Total Casualties
1951-1960	115	153	1,542	1,695
1961-1970	120	66	1,170	1,236
1971-1980	267	13	371	384
1981-1990	216	5	74	79
Total	**718**	**237**	**3,157**	**3,394**

Why has this dramatic decrease in deaths and injuries occurred? The first assumption, according to Ojala, was that the number or severity (or both) of tornadoes must have decreased over the four decades. A look at the total number of tornadoes partially supports this:

Decade	Weak (F=0,1)	Strong (F=2,3)	Violent (F=4,5)	Total
1951-1960	48	46	17	111
1961-1970	47	60	12	119
1971-1980	175	82	3	260
1981-1990	158	58	0	216
Total	**428**	**246**	**32**	**706**

In the decades of the 1950s and 1960s, only 235 twisters were reported, whereas during the 1970s and 1980s that number more than doubled to 483. Without doubt many tornadoes occurred but were not recorded in the earlier decades. However, in recent years few go unnoticed and, in fact, some non-tornadoes were reported as actual tornadoes. This is probably due to a combination of factors, including the development of technology such as Doppler radar, the watch and warning system and the Skywarn spotter program developed by the National Weather Service, and improved communications and increased public awareness of severe weather situations in general.

The number of severe tornadoes, on the other hand, has decreased dramatically. In the 1950s and 1960s, 29 tornadoes were determined to be severe (having an F-scale of 4 or 5), while only three were recorded in the 1970s and 1980s.

Ojala's analysis of Michigan's recent tornado history has resulted in the general finding that the tornado casualty risk in the state today is relatively minor. In fact, about nine-tenths of the deaths and three-fourths of the injuries came on four days in that 40-year span, and those four days were in the 1950s and 1960s when technology and public awareness did not approach today's levels.

TASK 1

Inserting a Table

Why would I do this?

Adding a table to a document is only one method of displaying lists of information in columns and rows. You can use tabs for many of the same functions. Tables are much easier to use than tabs, however, and they are far more powerful and flexible. After you have mastered the use of tables, you will save a great deal of time and end up with a better-looking finished product.

In this task, you learn to insert a table into a document using the Insert Table button.

1 Launch Word and click the **Open** button. Find **Less0801** in the **Student\Lesson08** folder on the CD-ROM disc and save it as **Michigan Tornadoes** on your floppy disk. Select **Page Width** from the **Zoom** button drop-down list.

2 Scroll down to the second page, then continue to scroll until you can see the paragraph that begins with the words **In the decades**. Place the insertion point at the beginning of that paragraph.

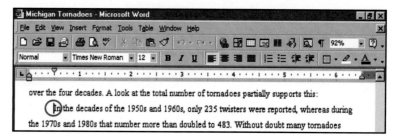

3 Click the **Insert Table** button in the Standard toolbar. A matrix is displayed that enables you to choose the number of rows and columns for your new table.

Insert Table button

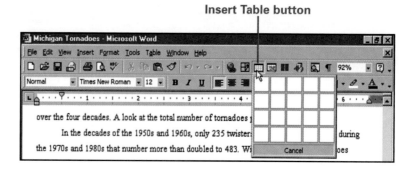

4 Move the pointer down and to the right until you have highlighted four rows and five columns. The table size appears at the bottom of the matrix.

5 columns

4 rows

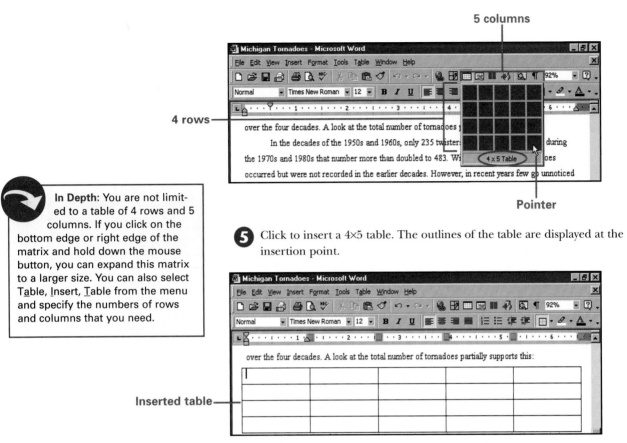

Pointer

In Depth: You are not limited to a table of 4 rows and 5 columns. If you click on the bottom edge or right edge of the matrix and hold down the mouse button, you can expand this matrix to a larger size. You can also select Table, Insert, Table from the menu and specify the numbers of rows and columns that you need.

5 Click to insert a 4×5 table. The outlines of the table are displayed at the insertion point.

Inserted table

TASK 2

Entering Data into a Table
Why would I do this?

After you have set up the rows and columns of your table, the next step is to enter data into the table cells. You can enter any kind of data you want. The most common table entries are text and numbers, but you can also enter graphics or even links to Internet sites.

In this task, you learn how to enter text and numbers into a table.

1 With the new table in the **Michigan Tornadoes** document on the screen, place the insertion point in the first cell, if necessary.

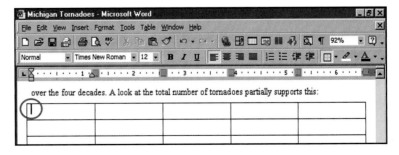

2 Type **Decade**. This is the column heading for the first column of the table. Notice that the text is left-aligned by default.

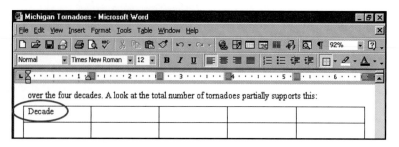

3 Press `Tab`. The insertion point moves to the second cell of the first row.

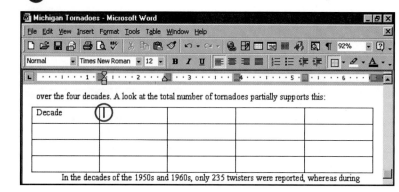

4 Type **Weak (F=0,1)** in the second cell in the top row; then type **Strong (F=2,3)** in the third cell in the top row. Finish the column headings by typing **Violent (F=4,5)** in the fourth cell and **Total** in the last cell of the first row.

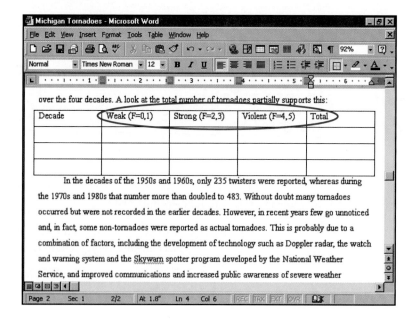

5 Fill in the next three rows with the following information:

Decade	Weak (F=0,1)	Strong (F=2,3)	Violent (F=4,5)	Total
1951-1960	48	46	17	111
1961-1970	47	60	12	119
1971-1980	175	82	3	260

> **Quick Tip:** If you need to change information in a cell, there are faster ways of moving around in the table than going across each row using (Tab⇌). You can use the mouse to click in the desired cell, or you can use the arrow keys to move up, down, left, or right one cell at a time. To move back one cell, hold down (⬆Shift) and press (Tab⇌).

TASK 3

Adding Rows to a Table
Why would I do this?

When you create a table, you may not always know ahead of time how many rows or columns you need. After a table is created, it is simple to add more rows at the end of the table. You can also add columns or rows into the middle of a table.

In this task, you learn to add rows to a table.

1 Place the insertion point to the right of the entry in the last cell in the table, if necessary.

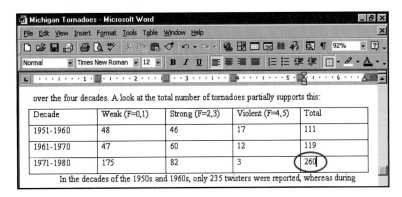

In Depth: If you want to add rows to the middle of a table, place the insertion point in the row above or below where you want the new row to appear. Then choose **Table**, **Insert**, **Rows Above** (or **Rows Below**) from the menu. Also, when you select a row or column, the appropriate insert button (**Insert Rows** or **Insert Columns**) replaces the Insert Table button on the Standard toolbar.

2 Press Tab. A new row is automatically added to the end of the table.

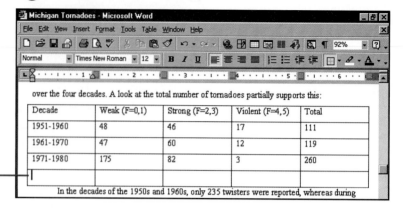

New row

3 Add the following information to the last row of your table:

Decade	Weak (F=0,1)	Strong (F=2,3)	Violent (F=4,5)	Total
1981-1990	**158**	**58**	**0**	**216**

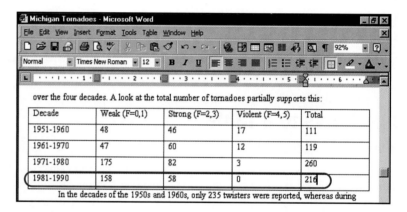

4 With the insertion point at the end of the new row, press Tab again. Another new row is added to the end of the table.

In Depth: Sometimes you want to insert a column in a table. This procedure is also relatively straightforward. To add a column, place the insertion point in a column to the right or left of where you want the new column to appear. Choose **Table**, **Insert**, **Columns to the Left** (or **Columns to the Right**) from the menu.

New row

5 Add the following data to the new row:

Decade	Weak (F=0,1)	Strong (F=2,3)	Violent (F=4,5)	Total
Total	**428**	**246**	**32**	**706**

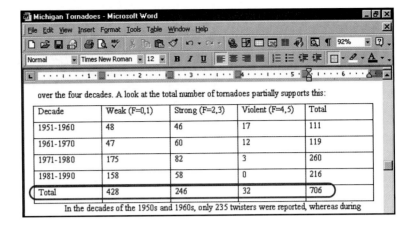

TASK 4

Using the AutoFormat and AutoFit Tools

Why would I do this?

Formatting your table can be time-consuming. The *AutoFormat* option, which enables you to choose from many different table styles, saves you a great deal of time if one of the styles fits your needs.

You may have noticed that the table you have created is wider than necessary. When you insert a table, it stretches from the left margin to the right margin. Another tool, called *AutoFit*, changes the widths of the columns.

In this task, you learn to change the format of a table using the AutoFormat option and to optimize the column widths using the AutoFit tool.

1 Confirm that the insertion point is in one of the cells in the table you have been working on.

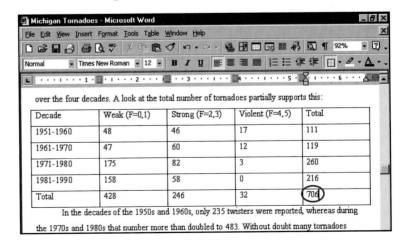

2 Choose **Table, Table AutoFormat** from the menu. The **Table AutoFormat** dialog box is displayed. Scroll down the list of table formats in the **Formats** area and click on several to see their appearance in the **Preview** box.

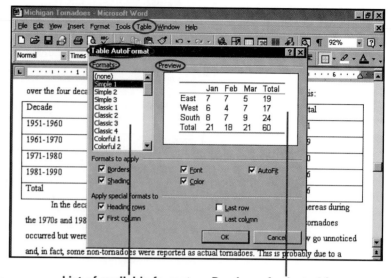

List of available formats   Preview of selected format

3 Select **Grid 8** from the **Formats** area. Click the check box for **Last row**. Notice that the last row is now boldfaced in the **Preview** area.

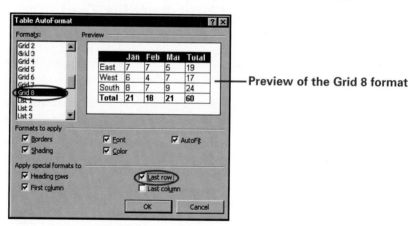

Preview of the Grid 8 format

4 Click **OK.** The table in the document now looks like the sample you saw in the **Preview** area.

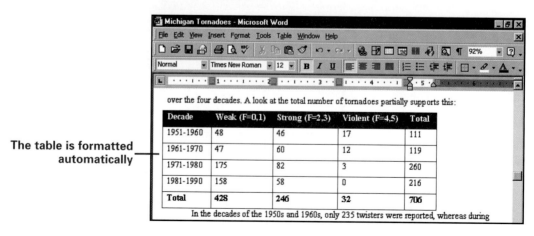

The table is formatted automatically

5 Click and drag across all the cells in the last four columns and click the **Align Right** button to line up the headings and the numbers in this table.

In Depth: Numbers are usually aligned to the right of a table cell. Words are usually left-aligned, but they are often centered when used as column headings.

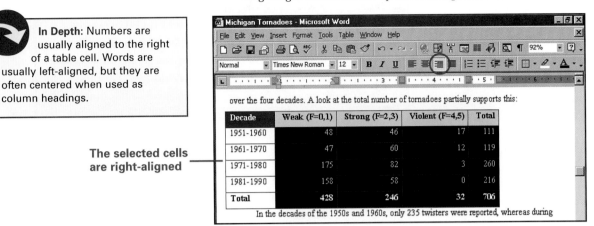

The selected cells are right-aligned

6 Choose **Table, AutoFit, AutoFit to Contents** from the menu. The AutoFit option may not appear immediately, but after a short time, it will appear with the rest of the less-used commands. Click outside the table to turn off the highlight. Notice that the columns are resized to the width of the widest element in each column, usually the column heading.

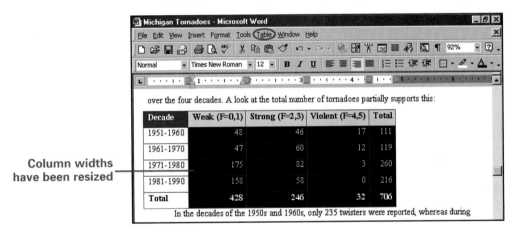

Column widths have been resized

7 To center the table, place the insertion point anywhere in the table, then choose **Table, Table Properties** from the menu. The Table Properties dialog box is displayed. Select the **Table** tab, if necessary.

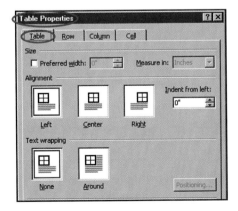

8 Click the **Center** button in the **Alignment** area.

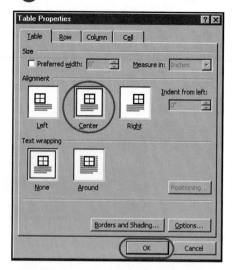

9 Click **OK.** The table is now centered between the left and right margins.

The table is centered between the margins

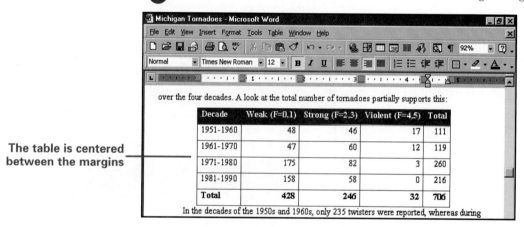

over the four decades. A look at the total number of tornadoes partially supports this:

Decade	Weak (F=0,1)	Strong (F=2,3)	Violent (F=4,5)	Total
1951-1960	48	46	17	111
1961-1970	47	60	12	119
1971-1980	175	82	3	260
1981-1990	158	58	0	216
Total	**428**	**246**	**32**	**706**

In the decades of the 1950s and 1960s, only 235 twisters were reported, whereas during

10 Scroll up to the table on page 1. Repeat all of the previous steps to format this table to match the table on page 2. Click the **Save** button to save your work.

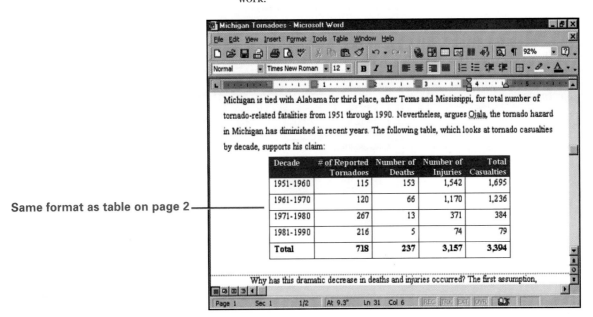

Same format as table on page 2 ⎯⎯⎯⎯⎯⎯

TASK 5

Adding Clip Art
Why would I do this?

Quite a few clip art images are included with Microsoft Office. These images cover a wide range of topics and styles, from black-and-white stick art to detailed color drawings. When you need an illustration for a flyer, poster, or brochure, you can often find one that is appropriate.

In this task, you learn how to insert a clip art image into a document.

1 Place the insertion point at the end of the first full paragraph of the **Michigan Tornadoes** document.

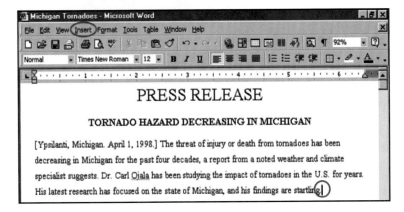

2 Select **Insert**, **Picture**, **Clip Art** from the menu. The Insert ClipArt window box is displayed. Make sure the **Pictures** tab is selected.

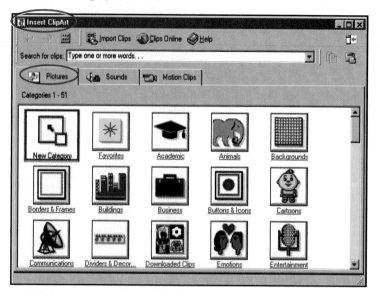

3 Scroll down until you can see the **Nature** category and click on it. Nature ClipArt images are displayed.

Summer image ———

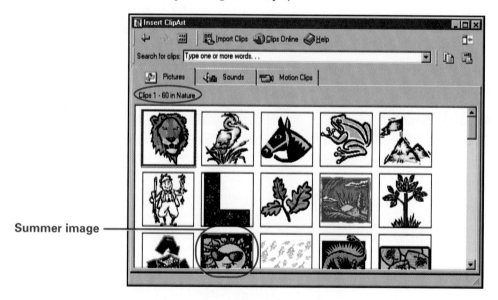

4 Click the **Summer** image. A pop-up menu is displayed.

Caution: Summer may not be available on some installations. In that case, scan through the images and pick another appropriate illustration for the report.

Insert Clip button ——

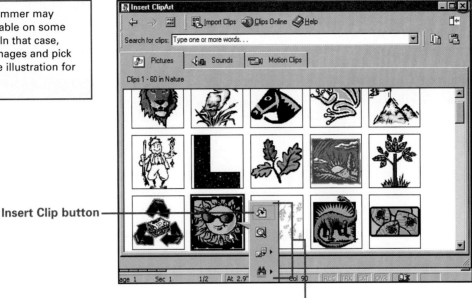

ClipArt pop-up menu

5 Click the **Insert Clip** button in the pop-up menu to place the image in the document. Click the **Close Window** button on the **Insert ClipArt** window. The image is inserted in the document, but the size and location are incorrect. Click the **Save** button to save your work.

The ClipArt image is inserted into the document ——

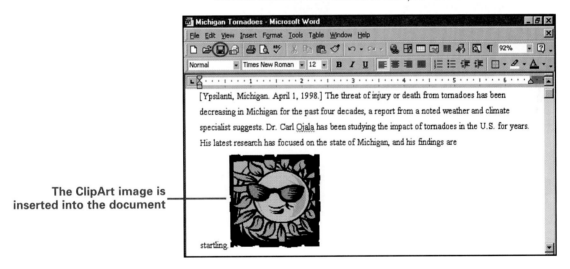

TASK 6

Resizing Clip Art
Why would I do this?

Clip art is almost never the exact size that you want when you insert it into your document, and it is seldom located exactly where you want it. Word allows you to resize and move the image so that it fits properly.

In this task, you learn to resize and move a clip art image in your document.

1 If necessary, scroll down so that you can see the bottom of the image you just inserted. Word treats the image as a large character that has been inserted at the end of this sentence.

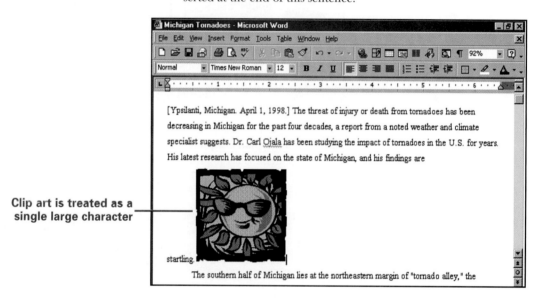

Clip art is treated as a single large character

2 Click on the clip art image of the sun. *Sizing handles* at the corners of and in the middle of the image's edges indicate that the image is selected.

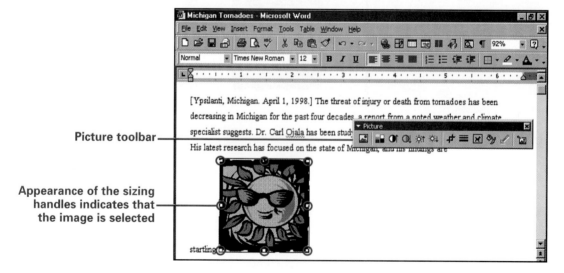

Picture toolbar

Appearance of the sizing handles indicates that the image is selected

3 Move the pointer onto the sizing handle in the lower-right corner. The pointer changes to a diagonal two-sided arrow.

In Depth: The Picture toolbar may open on your screen as shown in the figure. If this does not appear, it simply means that it has been turned off. You will not be using it in this exercise, so don't be concerned about whether it is displayed. To open or close this toolbar, choose **View**, **Toolbars** from the menu and select **Picture**.

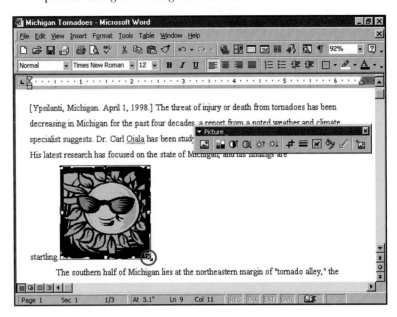

4 Click and hold down the left mouse button and drag the sizing handle up and to the left until the image is about 1.5 inches wide and then release the mouse button. Use the top ruler to determine the width of the image.

The clip art is reduced to 1.5 inches in width

Caution: If you do not see the ruler at the top of your document, select **View**, **Ruler** to turn it on.

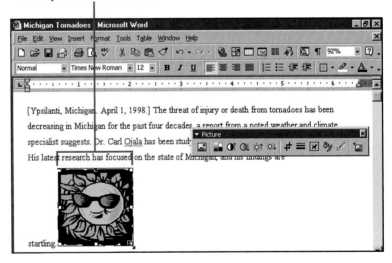

5 Click the **Save** button to save your work.

In Depth: When you first insert a clip art image, the image is placed at the insertion point. It acts just like any other character in a sentence. For instance, if you backspace over it, you delete it.

TASK 7

Wrapping Text Around an Image and Moving an Image
Why would I do this?

The clip art image is currently treated as a (very large) character in a line of text. In most cases, you want to be able to move images around freely without completely displacing nearby text. Word allows you to wrap text around images and to free up images so that they can be placed anywhere (even behind the text) without disturbing the document layout. You can also drag the image to a different location in the document.

In this task, you learn how to wrap text around an image and move it anywhere in the document.

1 Right-click the clip art to display a shortcut menu.

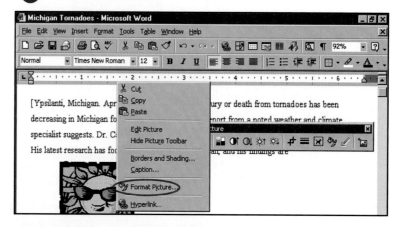

2 Click **Format Picture**. The Format Picture dialog box opens. Click the **Layout** tab to display the wrapping options.

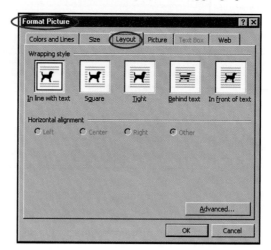

3 Click **Square** in the **Wrapping style** section. Confirm that the **Other** choice is selected for horizontal alignment.

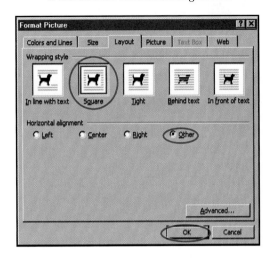

4 Click **OK**. The view automatically changes to Print Layout view. The text is wrapped around the clip art.

Text wraps around the clip art —

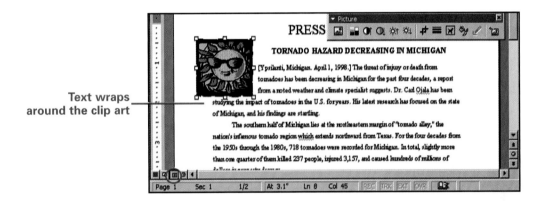

5 Place the pointer on the clip art. The pointer changes to a four-headed arrow. Click and drag the clip art to the right and place it in the paragraph as shown in the figure.

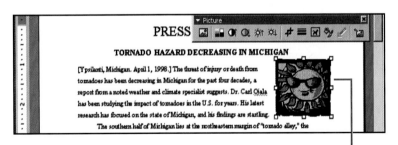

Clip art on the right side of the paragraph

TASK 8

Inserting a Hyperlink
Why would I do this?

If your document refers to another document or to a site on the Internet, the reader may want to know more about that reference. You can make it very easy for the reader to jump directly to that document or Web page by inserting a hyperlink. Hyperlinks can be used to link to other Word documents on your computer or on your computer network, and you can link to spreadsheets, presentations, and databases as well. This is a powerful way to make your document more useful to readers.

In this task, you learn how to insert a hyperlink to the National Weather Service Web site that is referred to in the **Michigan Tornadoes** paper.

1 Scroll to page 2 and locate the reference to the **National Weather Service**.

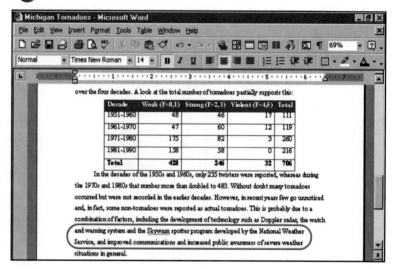

2 Select the words **National Weather Service**.

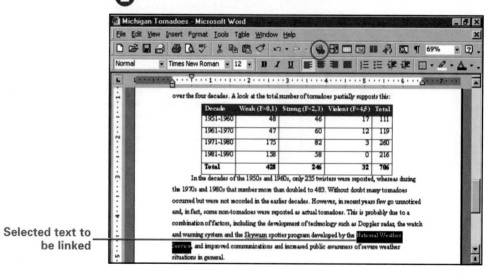

Selected text to be linked

3 Click the **Insert Hyperlink** button. The Insert Hyperlink dialog box opens.

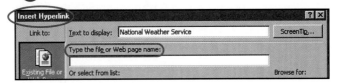

4 Locate the box labeled **Type the file or Web page name**. Enter the following Internet address: **http://www.nws.noaa.gov/**

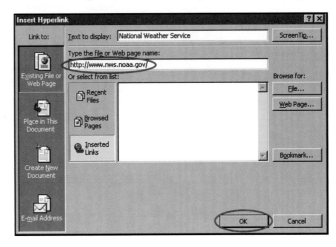

5 Click **OK**. The selected text is underlined and displayed in blue. This text is hyperlinked to the National Weather Service Web site.

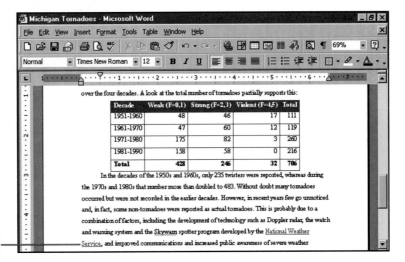

Color and underlining are used to indicate a hyperlink

6 Move the pointer onto the new hyperlink. It will turn into a small hand. A ScreenTip displays the Internet address.

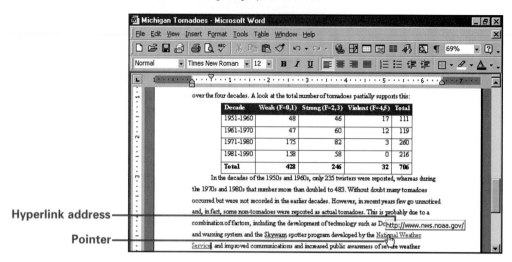

Hyperlink address ————

Pointer ————

7 If your computer is connected to the Internet, click the mouse. Your browser launches automatically and opens the National Weather Service Web site.

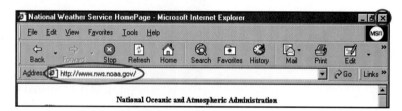

8 Close the browser. Close the **Michigan Tornadoes** document and save the changes. Leave Word open for use in the following exercises.

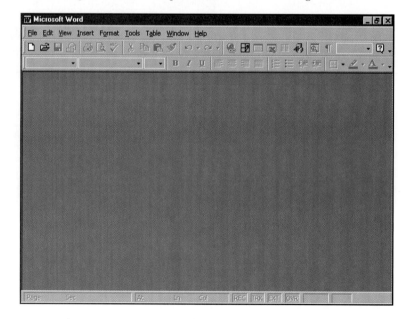

Comprehension Exercises

Comprehension exercises are designed to check your memory and understanding of the basic concepts in this lesson. You distinguish between true and false statements, identify new screen elements, and match terms with related statements. If you are uncertain of the correct answer, refer to the task number following each item (for example, T4 refers to Task 4) and review that task until you are confident that you can provide a correct response.

True-False

Circle either T or F.

T F **1.** Tables consist of rows and columns of cells that resemble a worksheet. **(T1)**

T F **2.** To create a table in a document, you enter the data, using tabs to separate the columns; select the rows and columns of data; then choose **Format**, **Table** from the menu. **(T1)**

T F **3.** When you enter text in a table, it is aligned to the left by default. **(T2)**

T F **4.** To add an extra row when you reach the last cell at the bottom of a table, press Tab⇄. **(T3)**

T F **5.** When entering data into the cells of a table, you press ↵Enter to move from one cell to the next. **(T2)**

T F **6.** A hyperlink is identified by text that is underlined and displayed in blue. **(T8)**

T F **7.** The AutoFormat and AutoFit tools provide a faster way to produce a good-looking table that fits on your page. **(T4)**

T F **8.** The clip art is placed in the document at the last position of the pointer. **(T5)**

T F **9.** If the clip art image is selected, it displays sizing handles. **(T6)**

T F **10.** When you first place a clip art image in a document, it is treated as a large character in a line of text. **(T5)**

Identifying Parts of the Word Screen

Refer to the figure and identify the numbered parts of the screen. Write the letter of the correct label in the space next to the number.

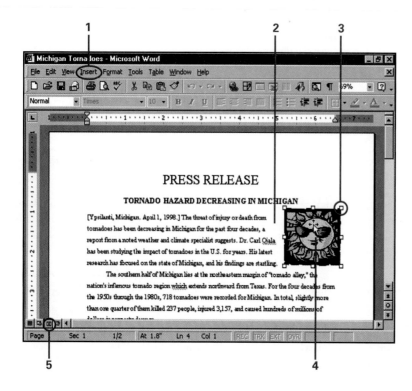

1. _____

2. _____

3. _____

4. _____

5. _____

6. _____

7. _____

8. _____

9. _____

10. _____

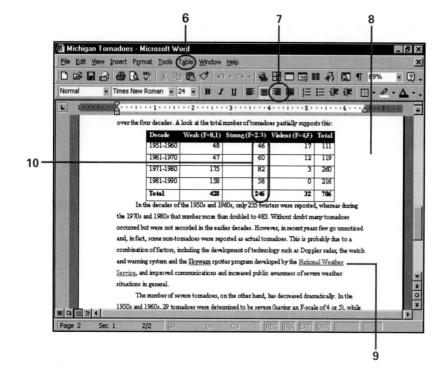

A. Sizing handle (**T6**)

B. Menu option used for adding clip art (**T5**)

C. Menu option used to add a table (**T1**)

D. Print Layout View button (**T5**)

E. Align Right button (**T4**)

F. Text wrapped around image (**T7**)

G. Right-aligned numbers (**T4**)

H. Pointer shape used to move the image (**T7**)

I. Table centered left to right (**T4**)

J. Hyperlinked text (**T8**)

Matching

Match the following statements to the word or phrase that is the best match from the list. Write the letter of the matching word or phrase in the space provided next to the number.

1. **D** Feature that automatically adjusts the width and height of the cells to accommodate the words or numbers in those cells

2. **B** Button that adds a table to the document

3. **A** Key you can press to add another row to the table if the insertion point is in the lower-right cell (the last cell in the table)

4. **I** A connection between words in your document and other files or Web sites on the Internet

5. **E** Markers that indicate an image is selected

6. **J** Option allowing images and text to share the same lines even if the image is taller than one line of text

7. **C** Feature that automatically changes the borders, shading, and column widths of a table

8. **F** Alignment typically used for numbers

9. **G** Alignment typically used for words that are column headings

10. **H** Menu options that open a dialog box used to center the table

A. Tab⇥ (**T3**)

B. Insert Table (**T1**)

C. AutoFormat (**T4**)

D. AutoFit (**T4**)

E. Sizing handles (**T6**)

F. Right-align (**T4**)

G. Center-align (**T4**)

H. Table, Properties (**T4**)

I. Hyperlink (**T8**)

J. Wrapping style (**T7**)

Reinforcement Exercises

Reinforcement exercises are designed to reinforce the skills you have learned by applying them to a new situation. Detailed instructions are provided along with a figure, where appropriate, to illustrate the result. The Reinforcement exercises that follow should be completed sequentially. Leave the workbook open at the end of each exercise for use in the next exercise until you are specifically directed to close it.

R1—Insert a Table into a Document

1. Launch Word and click the **Open** button. Find **Less0802** in the **Student\Lesson08** folder on the CD-ROM disc and save it as **Lightning Strikes** on your floppy disk.

2. Type your name below the title in the space provided.

3. Scroll to the bottom of the second paragraph. Click in the blank space that has been left below the second paragraph.

4. Choose **Table**, **Insert**, **Table** from the menu.

5. Choose a table that has three columns and nine rows. Do not use the AutoFormat feature. Click **OK**.

6. Start at the upper-left cell and enter the following data:

Location	Number	Percent of Total
Playground/Ballpark	23	28.4
Under trees	19	23.4
Golfing	10	12.3
Water-related	8	9.9
Farm equipment	2	2.5
Telephone	2	2.5
Radio equipment	1	1.2
Other locations	16	19.8

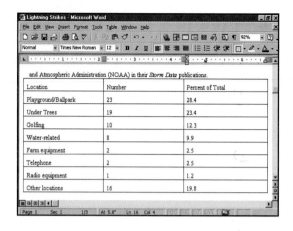

7. Leave the document open for use in the next exercise.

R2—Add a Row to a Table

1. Make sure the insertion point is located in the last cell in the bottom row of the table that was inserted in the previous exercise.

2. Press the (Tab) key to insert another row at the bottom of the table.

3. Add the following summary data to the three cells in the newly created row: **Totals, 81, 100.0**

4. Leave the document open for use in the next exercise.

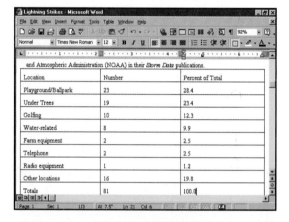

R3—Using AutoFit to Adjust Column Widths, Then Centering the Table

1. Make sure the insertion point is located somewhere in the table, and choose **Table**, **Select**, **Table** from the menu.

2. Choose **Table**, **AutoFit**, **AutoFit to Contents** from the menu.

3. Choose **Table**, **Table Properties** from the menu.

4. Click the **Table** tab if necessary, select the **Center** option, and then click **OK** to center the table.

5. Leave the document open for use in the next exercise.

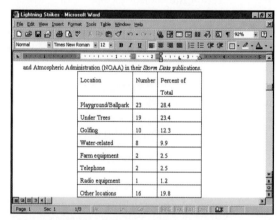

R4—Use AutoFormat to Apply a Predetermined Format to a Table

1. Click anywhere in the second table in the document.

2. Choose **Table**, **Table AutoFormat** from the menu.

3. Select **Simple 2** from the list of formatting designs.

4. Do not change any of the default settings. Click **OK**.

5. Select the numbers and click the **Align Right** button.

6. Leave the document open for use in the next exercise.

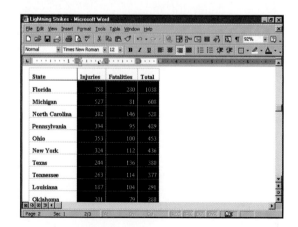

R5—Insert a Hyperlink to the National Weather Service

1. Scroll to the last paragraph at the end of the document and select **National Weather Service**.

2. Select these three words and insert a hyperlink to http://www.nws.noaa.gov/

3. Test the link. Close the browser after you have confirmed that the link works. Close the document and save your changes.

Challenge

Challenge exercises are designed to test your ability to apply your skills to new situations with less detailed instruction. These exercises also challenge you to expand your repertoire of skills by using Word commands that are similar to those you have already learned. The desired outcome is clearly defined, but you have more freedom to choose the steps needed to achieve the required result.

C1—Merging Cells in a Table

In this lesson, you learned many of the skills needed to work with tables. Some table designs have several topics that can be grouped together under one heading. To create a heading that covers multiple columns, you merge selected cells into one cell. This enables you to have two heading levels in a table. In this Challenge exercise, you add a row at the top of a table, merge cells, and add headings for a group of columns.

Goal: To create headings for a table by merging cells.

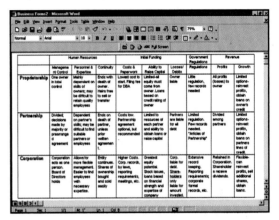

1. Locate and open the **Less0803** file in the **Student\Lesson08** folder on the CD-ROM disc that came with your book. Save it on your floppy disk as **Business Forms2**.

2. Click in the first row of the table and select **T**able, **I**nsert, Rows **A**bove.

3. Select the second, third, and fourth cell of the new empty row. Click the right mouse button and select **M**erge Cells from the shortcut menu.

4. Repeat this process to merge the next three cells, and then to merge the last two cells. Not counting the first column, you should now have four cells for a group heading in the first row.

5. Starting in the first merged cell and continuing across the row, type the following four headings:

Human Resources, Initial Funding, Government Regulations, Revenue.

6. Save your changes and leave this file open for use in the next Challenge exercise.

C2—Using Other Cell Alignment Options

You can align text vertically at the top, center, or bottom of a cell. In this Challenge exercise, you explore some of these options and change the alignment on the first row and column of the **Business Forms2** table.

Goal: To use other cell alignment options in a table.

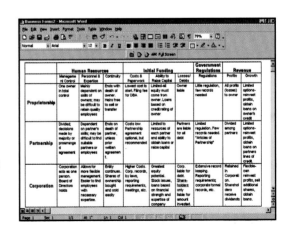

1. Use the **Business Forms2** document from the previous Challenge exercise. If you have not completed that exercise, go back and do it now.

2. Select the first row of headings and change the **font to Arial, 12 point, bold**. (Hint: This document uses a landscape orientation, therefore you may find it easier to work with if you change the **Zoom to 50%**.)

3. Click and drag the line between **Government Regulations** and **Revenue** to decrease the column width and force **Government Regulations** to display on two lines.

4. Select the four group headings and right-click. Point to **Cell Alignment** on the shortcut menu to display the alignment options. Select the option in the middle of the bottom row.

5. Select the three row headings in the first column. Right-click on them and point to **Cell Alignment** to display the alignment options. Select the middle option in the second row.

6. Save your changes and leave this file open for use in the next Challenge exercise.

C3—Aligning Text Vertically Within a Cell

In addition to changing the horizontal alignment of text within a cell, you can also display text vertically. This is useful to save space or to create a group heading similar to the one used at the top of the **Business Forms2** table. In this Challenge exercise, you change the alignment of the text to vertical.

Goal: To display text vertically in a cell.

1. Use the **Business Forms2** document from the previous Challenge exercise, or locate and open the **Less0803** file in the **Student\Lesson08** folder on the CD-ROM disc that came with your book and save it on your floppy disk as **Business Forms2**.

2. Select the three row headings in the first column of the table.

3. Right-click the mouse and select **Text Direction** from the shortcut menu. Select the vertical orientation that is displayed on the left. Notice that the option is displayed in the **Preview** portion of the dialog box. Click **OK**.

4. Click and drag the line between **Partnership** and **Proprietorship** to adjust the row height so the first heading is displayed on one line.

5. Select the table and use the **AutoFit to Contents** option to readjust the column and row sizes.

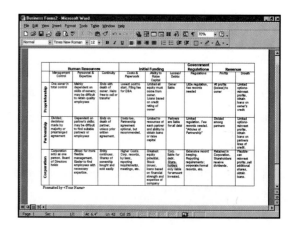

6. At the end of the document, outside the table, type **Formatted by <your name>**.

7. Save your changes, print the document, then close the file.

C4—Changing Clip Art to a Watermark Image

In this lesson, you learned how to insert clip art into a document. You have many options when working with clip art, one of which is to change the image to a watermark. This fades the image and enables it to be used in the background with text in the foreground. To make a clip art image into a watermark, it first needs to be inserted in a header.

Goal: To add clip art and change it to a watermark image.

1. Locate **Less0804** in the **Student\Lesson08** folder on your CD-ROM disc. Save it on your floppy disk as **Field Trip**.

2. Choose **View, Header and Footer**.

3. With the insertion point in the header, insert the clip art image of a wading bird found with the **Animals** clips.

4. Select the image and choose **Format, Picture** and select **Behind text** on the **Layout** page.

5. Click the **Picture** tab and change the **Color** box under **Image control** to **Watermark**. Click **OK**.

6. Resize and move the image to a location in the middle of the page that you like. The text should show on top of the image.

7. Add your name to the footer area.

8. Print the document, save your changes, and close the document.

Bird Sanctuary Field Trip
- Look for migrating finches
- Spot red-tailed hawks
- Observe nesting marsh birds
- Saturday, October 23rd
- 6:30 AM till dawn
- Hidden Lakes Marsh on N. Territorial Road
- Bring binoculars and camera
- Wear boots and warm clothes
- Call Joann Jacobs at 555 7654 for more information
- BYOC (Bring your own caffeine)

Discovery

Discovery exercises are designed to help you learn how to teach yourself a new skill. In each exercise, you discover something new that is related to the topic taught in this lesson. You may be directed to use built-in wizards or some of the extensive Help features provided in Word to discover new features and learn new skills with minimum assistance from books or instructors. The required outcome demonstrates your ability to apply the new skill. Choice of topic, design of presentation, and steps of execution are determined by the learner.

D1—Change Text to a Table

You may find that text in a document would work better if it were in a table. Word provides a table command that converts text to a table or a table to text.

In this Discovery exercise, you convert a text file to a table.

Locate and open the **Less0805** file in the **Student\Lesson08** folder on the CD-ROM disc that came with your book. Save the document on your floppy disk as **January Sales**. Select everything but the main title. This will include all the text from the **Date** heading through the end of the data. Choose **Table, Convert, Text to Table**. The **Convert Text to Table** dialog box opens and displays how many columns it is detecting. This may or may not agree with the number you are seeing in the data. It is best to accept the suggested number and then modify the table as needed. If this does not work, you can always click **Undo** and start over again. Notice that you can convert data that has been separated by tabs, paragraph marks, commas, or some other notation. The program has correctly identified the delimiter in this data to be tabs. Click **OK** to convert the text to a table. Format the table so numbers and dates are aligned on the right, headings are centered, and columns are wide enough for the data without wrapping words. Eliminate the extra column. Save your changes and leave the document open for use in the next Discovery exercise.

D2—Using a Formula in a Table

When you have a table of data that includes a column of numbers, you may need to use the **Table, Formula** command to calculate a total. While using formulas in a table of data in Word is not as foolproof as using formulas in Excel, it is a handy tool and is better than adding the figures separately on a calculator. In this Discovery exercise, you will find a total for the **Amount** and **Points** columns in the **January Sales** document.

Use the **January Sales** document from the previous exercise. Add a row to the end of the table. Click the empty cell at the bottom of the **Amount** column. Choose **Table, Formula**. The Formula dialog box opens and displays **=SUM(ABOVE)** in the **Formula** box. Use the down arrow at the end of the **Number format** box to select the format for dollars. A total of **$983,600.00** is displayed. Repeat this procedure to add a total at the bottom of the **Points** column. The total should be **9303.3**. Add your name below the table. Save your changes, print the document, then close the file.

D3—Wrap Text Around a Table

In this lesson, you learned how to wrap text around a clip art image. You can also wrap text around a table. In this Discovery exercise, you wrap text around the table that is included in the **Armstrong Memo** document.

Locate and open the **Less0806** file in the **Student\Lesson08** folder on the CD-ROM disc that came with your book and save it on your floppy disk with the name **Armstrong Memo**. Move the insertion point so it is in the table. Choose **Table, Table Properties**. Select the **Table** tab and change the **Text wrapping** option to **Around**. Then select either the **Left** or **Right** alignment. Depending on which side you selected, you may need to add or remove a paragraph mark to align the top of the table and the top of the text. Add your name to the bottom of the document. Save your changes, print the memo, and close the file.

D4—Getting Clip Art from the Online Gallery

There are plenty of other sources of clip art and pictures available on the Internet. Open the **Michigan Tornadoes** document that you worked on in this lesson and scroll to the bottom of the document. Insert a picture from the Internet. (Hint: When the **Insert Clip Art** dialog box opens, choose **Clips Online**. If your computer is connected to the Internet, you will be connected to Microsoft's online gallery.) Locate the map of Michigan and insert it. Resize it to a more appropriate size, and format it to wrap text around it. If you're not connected to the Internet, don't attempt this exercise.

Introduction to Excel

What Is Excel?

Computers were first designed for the purpose of calculating large quantities of numerical information. In fact, people who had the job of summing columns of numbers for statistical charts were known as computers. The form they used to record the numbers was called a spreadsheet, which is a tabular form that is divided into vertical columns and horizontal rows. Accountants use spreadsheets to manually keep track of financial data. The first electronic spreadsheet program written for the personal computer was called VisiCalc. It was introduced in 1979 by Bob Frankston and Dan Bricklin and is considered by many in the computer industry as the single most important reason why personal computers gained acceptance in the business world.

Microsoft Excel is a popular electronic spreadsheet program designed for the purpose of recording, calculating, and graphing numerical data. In Excel, a book of spreadsheets is referred to as a workbook and can be compared to an accounting ledger book that is bound and has many pages. When you open Excel, you open a workbook that can consist of up to 255 worksheets. A tab at the bottom of the window identifies each worksheet, which is also referred to as a sheet. The tab for each sheet is labeled with the word Sheet and the number of the sheet. Only three sheets show when you open Excel, but you can easily add sheets when needed. Each worksheet consists of 256 columns and 16,384 rows. You see only a fraction of the available columns and rows on the screen and will learn to use the scrollbar, scroll arrows, and keyboard to move around in a worksheet.

The value of an electronic spreadsheet program, such as Excel, is its capability to perform calculations rapidly and to recalculate formulas when the data changes. This saves an enormous amount of time, reduces the risk of errors, and provides the opportunity to examine scenarios for the future. The capability to consider the impact of changes in numerical assumptions helps decision-makers examine numerous options to find the best plan for the future.

Spreadsheet programs are widely used in a variety of formats throughout business and industry. To use a spreadsheet program successfully, you need to understand the basic concepts of how the program works. You need to know what features are available and the methods used to enter data, write formulas, and create charts. These tools will assist you in your career development and in tracking personal information. They can help you make purchase decisions for a car or a home. You can use them to record information for taxes, investments, or retirement. On the whole, the ability to use a spreadsheet program is a valuable skill to have.

Lesson: 9

The Basics of Excel

Introduction

Spreadsheets are used for a variety of information that benefits from being displayed in a grid of columns and rows. Traditionally, spreadsheets have been used for financial data, but they can also be used for schedules, inventories, and other information.

This lesson is designed to provide you with the basic skills you need to create a simple spreadsheet, print it, and save it. In Excel, spreadsheets are called worksheets. A workbook may contain several worksheets.

Visual Summary

When you have completed this lesson, you will have created a worksheet that looks like one below and you will have learned to use Help.

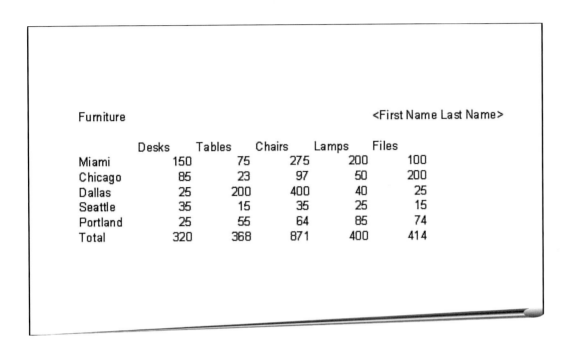

Furniture					<First Name Last Name>
	Desks	Tables	Chairs	Lamps	Files
Miami	150	75	275	200	100
Chicago	85	23	97	50	200
Dallas	25	200	400	40	25
Seattle	35	15	35	25	15
Portland	25	55	64	85	74
Total	320	368	871	400	414

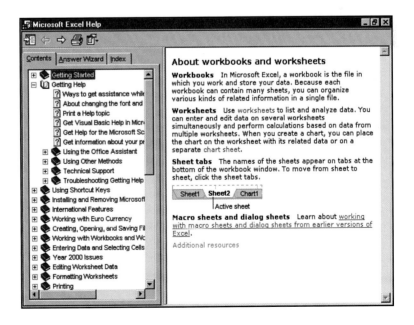

TASK 1

Navigating a Workbook
Why would I do this?

To understand how to use Excel, you first need to have a basic understanding of how Excel is structured. An Excel file is a *workbook* that consists of several *worksheets* identified by tabs at the bottom of the window. Each of these worksheets is divided into rows and columns; their intersections form a grid of cells. There are many more rows and columns available than will show in the window. To work in Excel, you need to know how to navigate in a worksheet to see different rows and columns.

In this task, you will learn how to select a *sheet* and scroll it to display additional rows and columns.

1 Launch **Excel**. The program displays a set of empty worksheets. The sheets are designated with tabs near the bottom of the window.

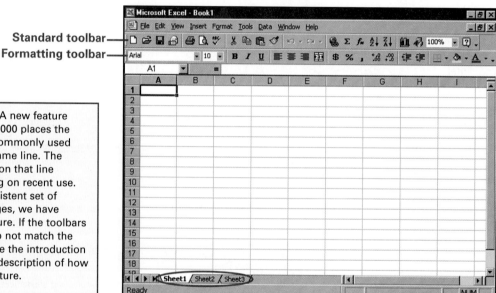

In Depth: A new feature of Office 2000 places the two most commonly used toolbars on the same line. The buttons showing on that line change depending on recent use. To provide a consistent set of instructional images, we have disabled this feature. If the toolbars on your screen do not match the figures shown, see the introduction to the book for a description of how to disable this feature.

2 Move the pointer to the tab labeled **Sheet2** at the bottom of the window. Click on the tab. A second empty sheet is displayed.

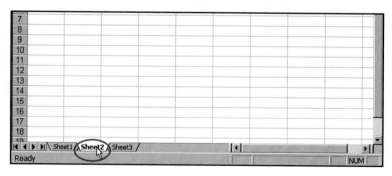

3 Click the **Sheet1** tab to return to the *default* sheet.

4 Click once on the down arrow at the bottom of the **vertical scrollbar**. Row 1 disappears, and a previously hidden row appears at the bottom of the screen.

Row 1 is off the screen—

Vertical scrollbar—

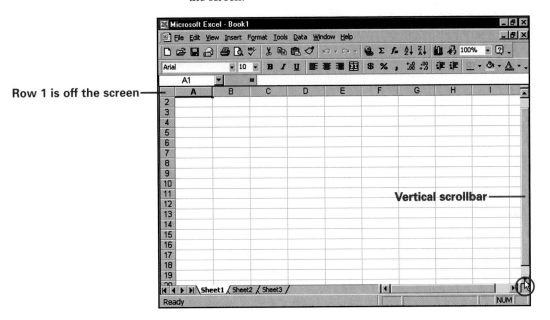

5 Click the same **down arrow** and hold down the mouse button. The rows will scroll by rapidly. Release the mouse button.

In Depth: The number of columns and rows shown on a screen depends on the display settings and the Zoom. If your screen displays more rows and columns than the illustrations in this book, do not be concerned.

In general, the left mouse button is used for more operations than the right button. Unless otherwise stated, all mouse operations will assume the use of the left mouse button.

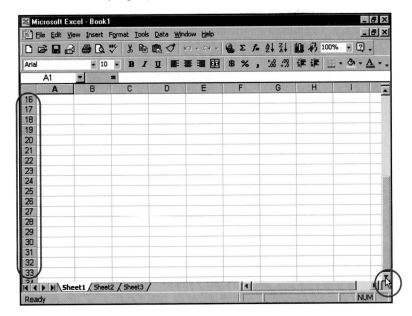

6 Click the up arrow at the top of the **vertical scrollbar**, and hold the button until row **1** appears. Release the button.

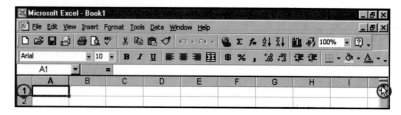

7 Click once on the right arrow on the **horizontal scrollbar**. Column A will scroll off the screen and the next column to the right will appear.

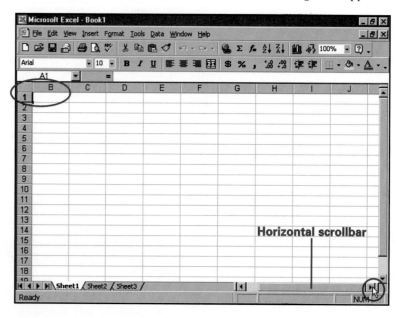

Horizontal scrollbar

8 Click once on the left arrow on the **horizontal scrollbar**. The sheet will scroll to the right and column A will reappear.

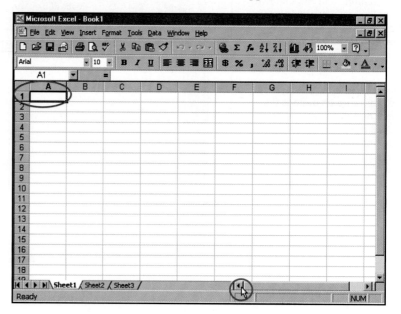

TASK 2

Selecting Individual Cells
Why would I do this?

You must *select a cell* before you can enter text, numbers, or formulas. If a cell is selected, it will have a dark border around it.

In this task, you learn how to move the selection from one cell to another on a worksheet.

1 Use the mouse to move the pointer to the cell that is in column **B** and row **2** (this cell can be referred to as cell **B2**). Notice that the cell selection does not move with the pointer.

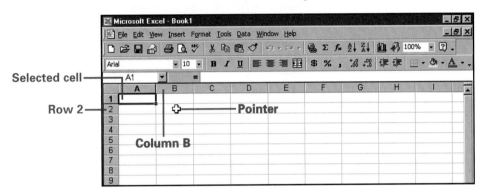

Caution: Moving the pointer to a cell does not select it. If you start typing without actually moving the selection, your text or number will be placed in whatever cell is currently selected.

2 Click the **left mouse button**. Notice that the border of the cell changes to a darker line. The column and row *headings* become boldface and the address of the cell (B2) appears in the Name box.

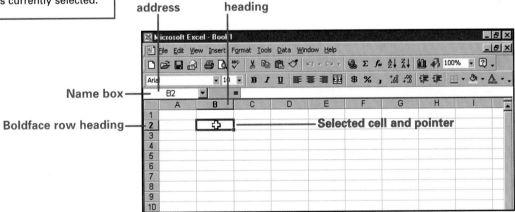

3 Press the up arrow on your keyboard once. Notice that the selection moves to cell **B1**.

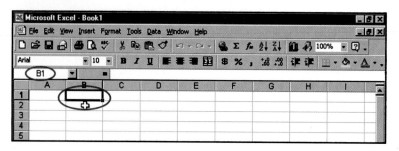

4 Press ⟨Tab⟩ three times. The selection moves one cell to the right each time you press this key.

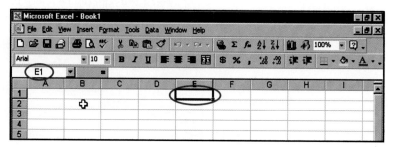

5 Press the ⟨Enter⟩ key. The selection drops to the next row and returns to the cell below **B1**.

In Depth: If you use ⟨Tab⟩ to move the selection to the right and ⟨Enter⟩ to drop down a row and return to the original column, it makes it easier to enter multiple rows of data.

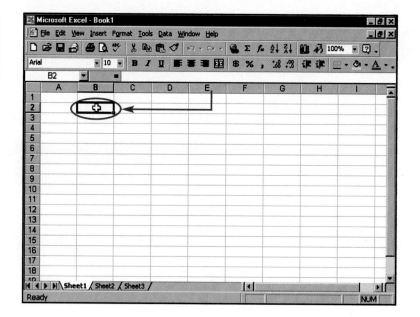

Entering Text and Numbers into Cells
Why would I do this?

Text is entered into cells to provide labels and other information for users of the sheet. Numbers are used in calculations and formulas. A cell may contain text or numbers, but not both. Once the numbers have been entered into the cells, you can manipulate the numbers, perform calculations, and use the numbers to visually portray a trend by creating a chart.

In this task, you learn how to enter text and numbers in cells.

1 Move the pointer to cell **A1** and click the left mouse button to select the cell.

In Depth: If numbers are used as labels or mixed with text, as in a street address, they are treated as text.

2 Type the word **Stock** and press ⏎Enter.

In Depth: The direction that the selection moves when you press ⏎Enter can be changed. The setting is found under **Tools, Options, Edit, Move selection after Enter.**

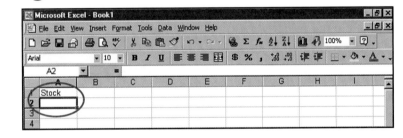

3 Select cell **A3**. This will be the upper-left corner of the table of data. It is left blank.

In Depth: This cell is not used in this table, but you start here so that the selection will return to this column when you press ⏎Enter at the end of the row of cells.

4 Press Tab⇄. This moves the selection to cell **B3**.

5 Type **Desks** and press Tab⇄. The text is entered and the selection moves to cell **C3**.

6 Type **Tables** and press Tab⇄. Repeat this process to enter **Chairs** and **Lamps** in cells **D3** and **E3**.

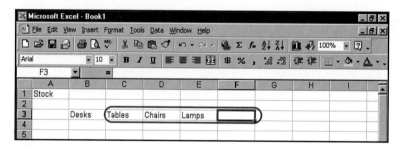

7 Type **Files** in **F3**, but press ↵Enter instead of Tab⇄. The selection automatically returns to cell **A4** to start the next row.

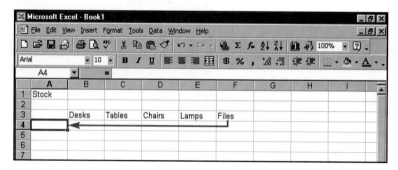

8 Type **Miami** in cell **A4** and press `Tab↹`.

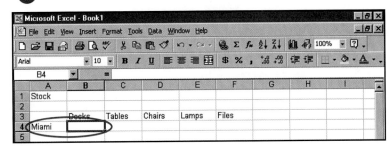

9 Refer to the figure and use this method to fill out the table with the following information:

	Desks	Tables	Chairs	Lamps	Files
Miami	150	75	275	200	100
Chicago	85	23	97	50	200
Dallas	25	200	400	40	25
Seattle	35	15	35	25	15
Portland	25	55	64	85	74

Caution: When you use `Tab↹` to enter values in adjacent cells, Excel remembers the starting point of the series and returns to that column when you press `↵Enter`. Interrupting the pattern, for instance to correct an error, sets a new starting point. Therefore, if you make mistakes entering the text or the numbers, leave them for now. You will learn how to fix mistakes in the next task.

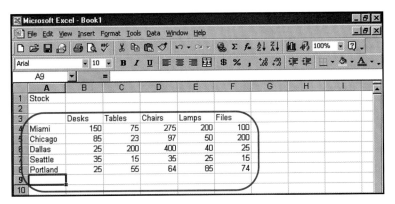

10 Select cell **F1** and type your last name. Press `↵Enter`. If your name is too long to fit in the cell, enter it anyway. You will learn how to deal with this in Lesson 10.

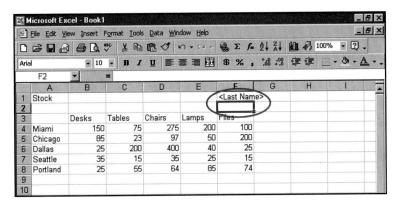

TASK 4

Fixing Simple Typing Errors
Why would I do this?

It is possible to make mistakes when entering data. Also, information may change and need to be adjusted. The power of using an electronic spreadsheet is in the ability to easily change information and have formulas recalculated.

In this task, you learn how to edit the contents of the cells.

1 Select cell **A9** and type the incorrectly spelled word **Totle** in the cell. Do not press the ↵Enter or Tab⇄ key yet. Notice that a vertical line marks the position where text is entered. This line is called the insertion point.

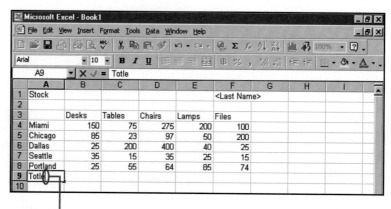

Insertion point

2 Press ←Backspace twice. The insertion point moves to the left, erasing the last two letters.

> **In Depth:** You can move the insertion point within the text by using the right and left arrow keys on the keyboard. ←Backspace deletes characters to the left of the insertion point and Del deletes letters to the right of the insertion point.

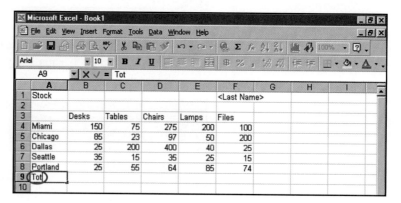

3 Type **al** and press Tab⇥.

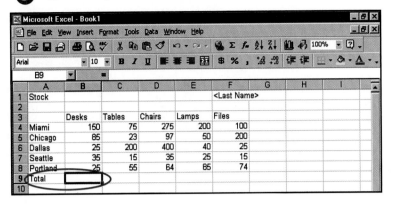

4 To replace an entire entry, just type over it. Select cell **A1**, type **Furniture** and press ↵Enter. The word **Stock** is replaced with **Furniture**.

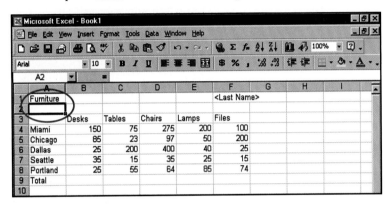

5 If you change your mind you may undo your action. Click the **Undo** button on the Standard toolbar.

Undo button   Redo button

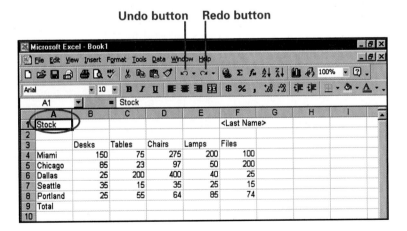

6 Click the **Redo** button to change the cell back to **Furniture**.

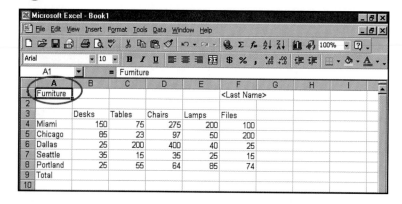

Caution: If you are using the feature that places the Standard and Formatting toolbars on the same line, you may not see the Undo button if it has not been used recently. If that is the case, locate the **More Buttons** button for the Standard toolbar and click on it to display the rest of the buttons on the Standard toolbar. Do not use the **More Buttons** button at the far right. That one refers to the additional buttons on the Formatting toolbar.

7 You can also edit the contents of a cell. Move the pointer to cell **F1**. Double-click the left mouse button to place the insertion point in the text within the cell.

Double-click cell to edit contents

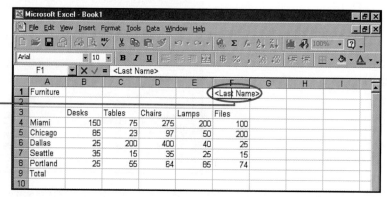

8 Use the left arrow on the keyboard to position the insertion point to the left of your last name and type in your first name and a space. Press ↵Enter to finish.

Caution: You may have trouble double-clicking. The most common problem is caused by the mouse rolling slightly between clicks. Rest the heel of your hand on the table so the mouse is less likely to roll. It may take a little practice. If this is frustrating you, click the cell once and the contents will appear in the *Formula bar*. Click once on the text in the Formula bar and edit it there.

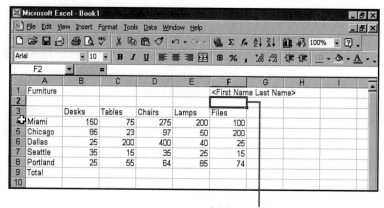

Add your first name

TASK 5

Summing a Column of Numbers
Why would I do this?

The purpose of most worksheets is to make *calculations* based on the data you have entered. The simplest and most commonly used calculation is the sum calculation. It is used so often, in fact, that Excel has a built-in AutoSum button.

In this task, you learn how to sum columns of numbers using AutoSum.

1 Select cell B9.

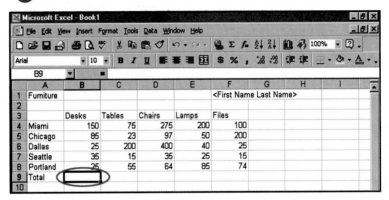

2 Click the **AutoSum** button located on the *Standard toolbar*. Several things will happen. A formula, **=SUM(B4:B8)**, will appear in cell B9 and in the Formula bar. Also, a moving dashed line called a *marquee* will surround the group of cells being summed.

AutoSum button

> **In Depth:** Excel guesses which group of numbers you want to sum. If it is not the correct group, you can edit the formula just as you edit text. In the formula above, B4:B8 refers to all of the cells in a rectangle that starts with B4 and ends with B8. If you wanted to add up a different range of cells, you would edit the formula and put in different cell addresses. You will learn more about such formulas in later lessons.

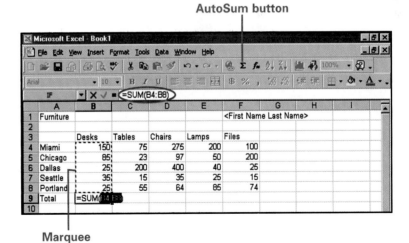

Marquee

3 Press Tab⇄ to activate the formula. The sum is the total number of desks on hand in the various locations.

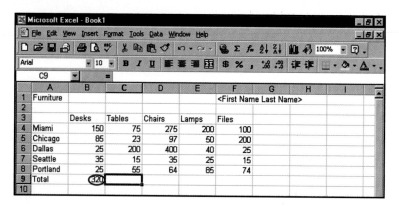

4 Repeat this process for each of the remaining columns. If the Office Assistant appears, right-click on it and choose **Hide** from the shortcut menu.

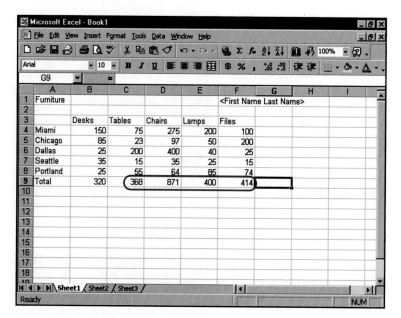

Saving a Workbook, Printing and Closing a Worksheet
Why would I do this?

A computer has a short-term memory that forgets when the power is turned off or interrupted. In order to record your spreadsheet for later use, you will need to make a more permanent copy of it. One way to do this is to save a copy magnetically on a disk.

Even in an age of digital communications, there are still advantages to recording data on paper. A paper copy is lightweight, portable, and compatible with older storage systems. It is often easier to review several pages of data simultaneously and share the information with others who do not have a computer.

In this task, you will learn how to print a worksheet and save the workbook on disk.

1 Click the **Save** button on the Standard toolbar. The Save As dialog box will appear with a suggested filename already highlighted in the File name box.

In Depth: The conventions of this book assume that the file extensions for *registered programs* have been hidden. If this is not the case in your computer setup, you will see an .xls extension added to your Excel filenames. File extensions can be turned on or off in Windows Explorer under **View**, **Options**.

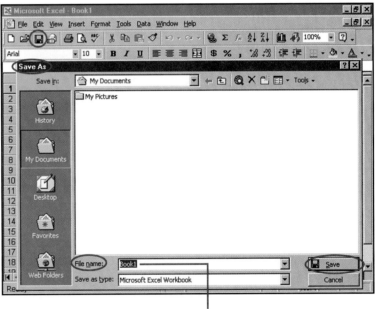

Suggested filename

② Type **Basic Skills** to replace the highlighted text in the **File name** box. Do not press ⏎Enter yet.

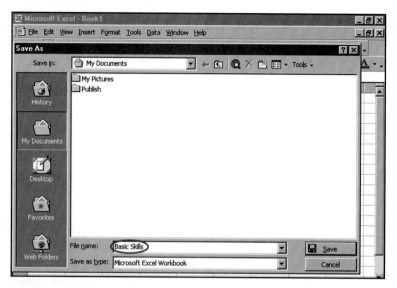

> **Caution:** A dialog box has buttons in it that you can click on to produce certain actions. Often, one of the buttons is indicated as the default choice by a darker and thicker border. In this case, the **Save** button is the default. If you press the ⏎Enter key after typing in the name of the file, it will save the file in whatever folder or disk is currently selected. If you do this by mistake, click **File**, **Save As**. This will open the Save As dialog box and you can now select the folder where this file should be saved.

③ Place a 3 1/2 - inch floppy disk in drive A:. Ask your instructor for assistance if necessary. Click the down arrow at the right side of the **Save in** box. A diagram of your computer's disk drives will appear.

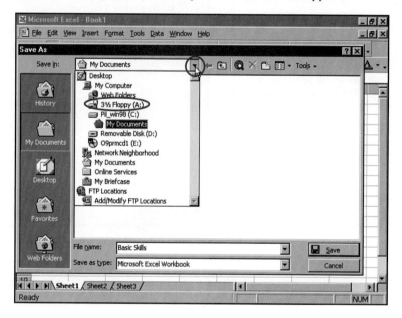

4 Click the **3 1/2 Floppy (A:)** drive. If your class is using another disk drive, follow your instructor's directions.

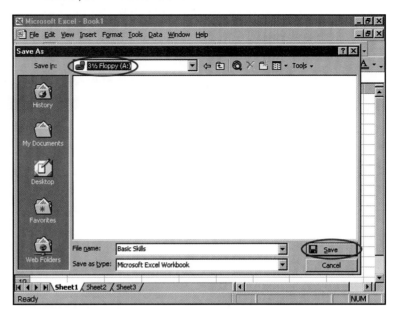

5 Click **Save**. A copy of the workbook will be saved on your floppy disk. The pointer will turn into an hourglass while the file is being saved and an indicator displays in the status bar.

Indicates computer is busy ——

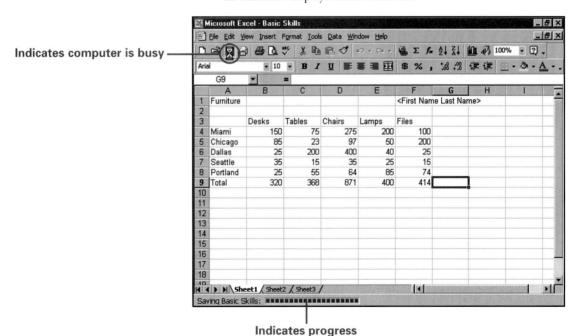

Indicates progress

6 Check to make sure that your printer is connected and turned on. Click the **Print** button on the Standard toolbar. The current worksheet will be sent to the printer.

Print button

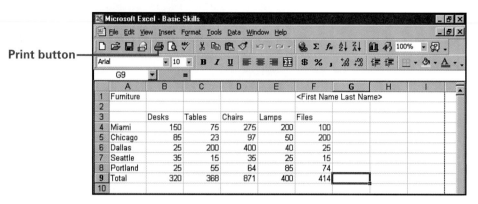

7 Move the pointer onto the **Close Window** button on the Menu bar.

Close Window   Close

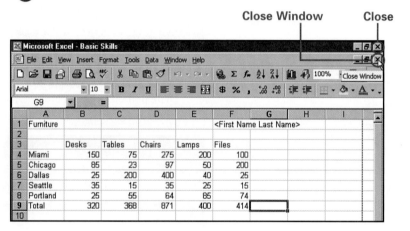

Caution: If you click the **Close** button on the title bar, the Excel program will close along with any open workbooks. This is not a big problem, because you will not lose your work. Simply launch Excel again if you intended to leave it open.

8 Click the **Close Window** button on the menu bar. The workbook closes, but Excel stays open. If you have made any changes to the workbook since the last time it was saved, you will be prompted to save it.

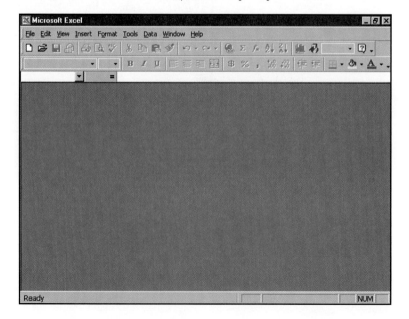

Comprehension Exercises

Comprehension exercises are designed to check your memory and understanding of the basic concepts in this lesson. You distinguish between true and false statements, identify new screen elements, and match terms with related statements. If you are uncertain of the correct answer, refer to the task number following each item (for example, T4 refers to Task 4) and review that task until you are confident that you can provide a correct response.

True-False

Circle either T or F.

T   F   **1.** The scrollbar at the right of the screen is the vertical scrollbar. **(T1)**

T   F   **2.** Workbook and worksheet are the same thing. The words may be used interchangeably. **(T1)**

T   F   **3.** The cells that are visible on the screen when you first open Excel are the only ones available. **(T1)**

T   F   **4.** The vertical scrollbar and its arrows can be used to rapidly scroll through the sheet or scroll one row at a time. **(T1)**

T   F   **5.** A cell in column C and row 2 would be referred to as cell 2C. **(T2)**

T   F   **6.** A selected cell has a darker border than the other cells. **(T2)**

T   F   **7.** When you press ⏎Enter, the selection will always move to the cell below it. This is a basic feature of Excel that cannot be changed. **(T3)**

T   F   **8.** Text and numbers should be placed in the same cell together to save space. **(T3)**

T   F   **9.** Clicking on the AutoSum button will place a formula in the currently selected cell that will automatically add up the nearest row or column of numbers. **(T5)**

T   F   **10.** If you make entries into a row of cells by pressing the Tab⇥ key between entries, pressing the ⏎Enter key after the last entry will cause the selection to move to the cell below the last entry. **(T3)**

Identifying Parts of the Excel Screen

Refer to the figure and identify the numbered parts of the screen. Write the letter of the correct label in the space next to the number.

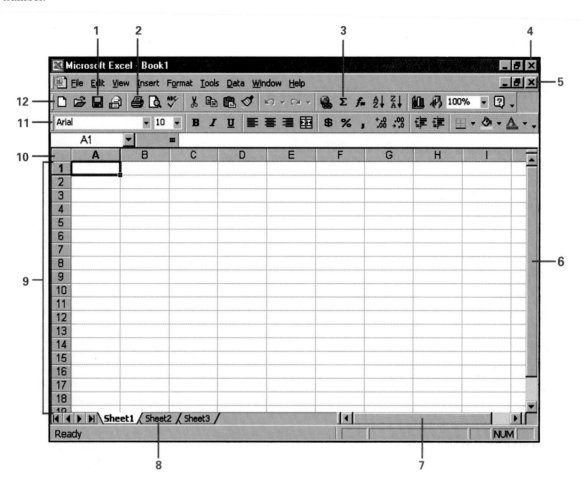

1. _____

2. _____

3. _____

4. _____

5. _____

6. _____

7. _____

8. _____

9. _____

10. _____

11. _____

12. _____

A. Tabs to identify sheets (T1)

B. Column headings (T2)

C. Row headings (T2)

D. Vertical scrollbar (T1)

E. Horizontal scrollbar (T1)

F. Save button (T6)

G. Print button (T6)

H. Close button for Excel (T6)

I. Close Window button for the workbook (T6)

J. AutoSum button (T5)

K. Standard toolbar (T1)

L. Formatting toolbar (T1)

Matching

Match the statements below to the word or phrase that is the best match from the list. Write the letter of the matching word or phrase in the space provided next to the number.

1. ___ A tab at the bottom of the second worksheet in a workbook (**T1**)

2. ___ Automatically adds up the numbers in nearby cells (**T5**)

3. ___ Method used to begin editing existing text or numbers in a cell (**T4**)

4. ___ May be the Close button or the Close Window button (**T6**)

5. ___ Button that looks like a 3 1/2" floppy disk (**T6**)

6. ___ The cell in row 3, column D (**T2**)

7. ___ May be used to erase to the left of the insertion point (**T4**)

8. ___ May be used to finish the process of placing a number or text into a cell and move downward to the next cell (**T3**)

9. ___ May be used to move the selection to the right (**T2**)

10. ___ Numbers that appear along the left side of the sheet (**T2**)

A. Move pointer to cell and double-click

B. Save

C. 3D

D. ↵Enter

E. AutoSum button

F. ←Backspace

G. Tab↹

H. Sheet2

I. Button with an X in it

J. D3

K. Row headings

Reinforcement Exercises

Reinforcement exercises are designed to reinforce the skills you have learned by applying them to a new situation. Detailed instructions are provided along with a figure, where appropriate, to illustrate the final result. The Reinforcement exercises that follow should be completed sequentially. Leave the workbook open at the end of each exercise for use in the next exercise until you are specifically directed to close it.

R1—Creating a Worksheet to Show Income for January

1. Launch **Excel**.

2. Enter **January** in cell **A1**.

3. Enter your name in cell **F1**.

4. Enter the following data in the cells as shown in the figure:

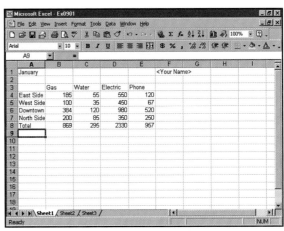

	Gas	Water	Electric	Phone
East Side	185	55	550	120
West Side	100	35	450	67
Downtown	384	120	980	520
North Side	200	85	350	250
Total				

5. Use **AutoSum** at the bottom of each column.

6. Print **Sheet1**.

7. Save the workbook on your floppy disk. Use **Ex0901** for its name.

8. Leave the workbook open for use in the next exercise.

R2—Using Another Sheet

1. Click the **Sheet2** tab to select the second sheet of the **Ex0901** workbook.

2. Enter **February** in cell **A1**.

3. Place your name in cell **E1**.

4. Enter the following text and numbers as shown in the figure:

	Gas	Water	Electric	Phone
East Side	168	57	500	130
West Side	95	38	480	85
Downtown	350	115	900	650
North Side	185	80	360	300
Total				

5. Use the **AutoSum** button to calculate the sum of the column of numbers.

6. Print the sheet.

7. Click the **Save** button on the Standard toolbar to save your changes. (You will not need to give it a name

again. It will automatically update the existing file on your disk.)

8. Leave the workbook open for use in the next exercise.

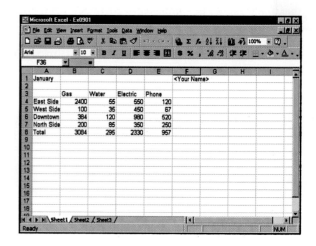

R3—Editing a Worksheet

1. Click the **Sheet1** tab to select **Sheet1**.

2. Edit cell **B4** to read **2400**. (If you have used the AutoSum button correctly, the sum of the column B will be automatically updated.)

3. Click the **Save** button to save the change.

4. Print **Sheet1**.

5. Leave the workbook open for use in the next exercise.

R4—Closing and Exiting Excel

1. Click the **Close Window** button to close the workbook. (If you have any unsaved work, the program will always prompt you to save your changes before it closes the workbook.

2. Click the **Close** button to close the Excel program.

Challenge

Challenge exercises are designed to test your ability to apply your skills to new situations with less detailed instruction. These exercises also challenge you to expand your repertoire of skills by using Excel commands that are similar to those you have already learned. The desired outcome is clearly defined, but you have more freedom to choose the steps needed to achieve the required result.

C1—Create a Monthly Income and Expense Sheet

Sometimes it is not obvious where your money is going. You can use Excel to take a look at the amount of money coming in and compare it to your expenses. Since many expenses occur on a monthly basis, it is useful to compare them to monthly income.

Goal: Create a worksheet that looks like the figure. Use the **AutoSum** feature to add the incomes and expenses, and then print the worksheet.

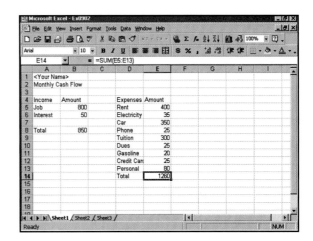

Use the following guidelines:

1. Launch **Excel**. Place your name in cell **A1**.

2. Refer to the figure and set up two columns to list the type and amount of monthly income you have and two more columns to list the type and amount of monthly expenses. Fill in all four columns with types and amounts of income and expenses. Use your own numbers. Change the types of incomes or expenses as needed to match your incomes and expenses.

3. Use **AutoSum** to sum the amount of income in the cell at the bottom of the column of income amounts and the amount of expenses at the bottom of the column of expenses.

4. Save the workbook on your floppy disk as **Ex0902**.

5. Print the worksheet. Leave the workbook open for use in the next exercise.

C2—Find Present Balance of a Checkbook

If the total income matches or exceeds the total expenses for a month, you may still run out of money in your checking account, depending on when the deposits are made and the checks are written.

Goal: Create a worksheet that resembles a check register as shown in the figure. Enter the deposits as positive numbers and check amounts as negative numbers. Sum the starting balance, deposits, and check amounts using the **AutoSum** feature.

1. Select **Sheet2**. Set up a three-column system for calculating your checkbook balance as shown in the figure.

2. Enter your own starting deposits and check amounts. The deposits should be positive numbers and the check amounts should be negative numbers (there are two negative signs on most keyboards, one at the upper-right corner of the number keypad, and the other two keys to the left of (◆Backspace)).

3. Use the **AutoSum** feature to display the balance at the bottom of the column.

4. Look at the deposits and the check amounts. Estimate what the balance should be to within ten dollars. Does the final balance agree with your estimate? If so, it is probably right. Always do a quick check of your spreadsheet to make sure that it makes sense.

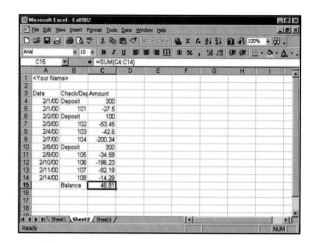

5. Save the workbook. Print **Sheet2**.

6. Close the workbook, but do not close Excel.

C3—Open a New Workbook and Close It Without Saving Changes

Excel will open a new workbook when it is launched. If you want to open a new workbook without closing and re-launching Excel, you can do so by clicking the **New** button.

Goal: Open a workbook without closing and re-launching Excel.

1. Click the **New** button on the Standard toolbar.

2. Enter your name in cell **A1** of **Sheet1**.

3. Print the sheet.

4. Close the workbook. Do not save the changes.

Discovery

Discovery exercises are designed to help you learn how to teach yourself a new skill. In each exercise, you discover something new that is related to the topic taught in this lesson. You may be directed to use built-in wizards or some of the extensive Help features provided in Excel to discover new features and learn new skills with minimum assistance from books or instructors. The required outcome demonstrates your ability to apply the new skill. You determine the choice of topic, worksheet design, and steps of execution.

D1—Use Pre-written Spreadsheet Templates

If you use the menu option for opening a new worksheet, you will have the opportunity to open one of several pre-written worksheets that have been set up to accomplish specific tasks.

Goal: Explore the available pre-written worksheets.

1. Click **File** on the menu bar. Hold the mouse on this selection for several seconds until the complete menu displays.

2. Click **New**. The New dialog box appears.

3. Click the **Spreadsheet Solutions** tab.

4. Select one of the solutions listed. If they have not been installed, check with your instructor. If you have a set of Office 2000 CD-ROM discs, you will be prompted to insert the first CD.

5. These workbooks contain automated features called macros and are fairly complex. Your objective at this time is to just take a look to see what is available.

6. Close the workbook(s) and close Excel.

Lesson: 10

Formatting the Worksheet

Introduction

There are a variety of formatting techniques that can be used to improve the appearance of a worksheet. Formatting your worksheet can also make it easier to read. This is especially important for worksheets that are used by others.

In this lesson, you learn how to work with existing worksheets to improve their appearance, make them easier to read, and give them a professional look.

Visual Summary

When you have completed this entire lesson, you will have a worksheet that looks like this:

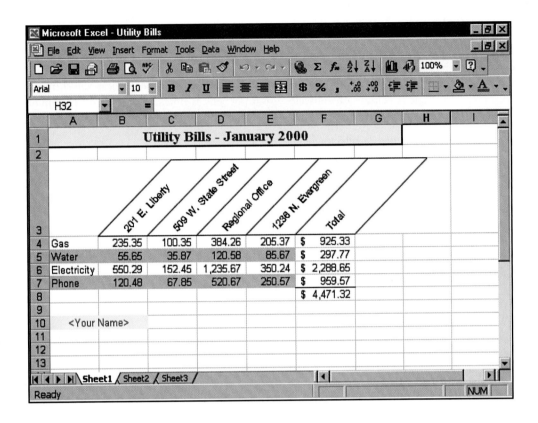

TASK *1*

Selecting Groups of Cells

Why would I do this?

To change the formatting of a cell, the cell must be selected. It is common to want to change the formatting of groups of cells, so it is preferable to select the entire group and format all of them at the same time. You can select the entire sheet, an entire row or column, a rectangle of cells, or unconnected groups of cells. By formatting the entire group of cells, you help ensure that the same formatting is applied.

In this task, you learn different techniques for selecting a group of cells.

1 Launch **Excel** and click the **Open** button. Find **Less1001** in the **Student\Lesson10** folder on the CD-ROM disc and open it. Save it as **Utility Bills** on your floppy disk.

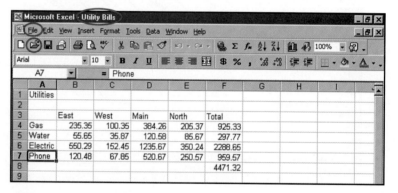

2 Click the **Select All** button in the upper-left corner of the sheet. The entire worksheet is selected.

Select All button —

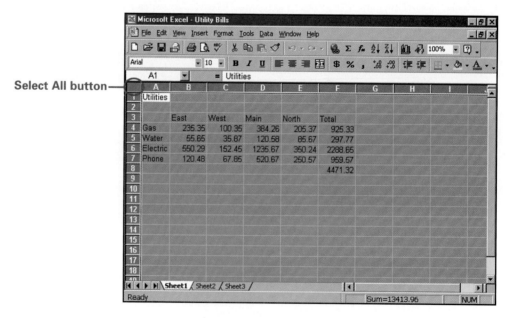

3 Click the heading of column **F**. The entire column of totals is selected.

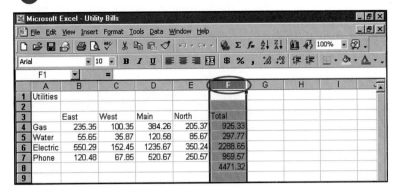

4 Click the heading for row **5**. The entire row pertaining to water bills is selected.

Notice that the first cell of the group is always the opposite highlight of the rest of the selected cells. It is still one of the selected group.

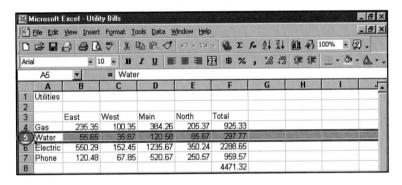

5 Position the pointer over cell **B4**. Click and drag a rectangular selection area to cell **E7**; then release the mouse button. This selects the actual bills.

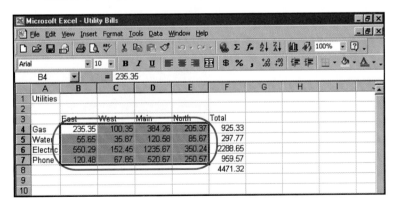

6 Selecting two groups of cells that are not next to each other is a two-step process. First, select cells **B4** through **B7** and release the mouse button.

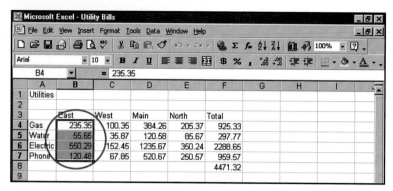

7 Hold down Ctrl and select cells **E4** through **E7**. Release the mouse button and Ctrl. Both sets of cells are selected.

This is a useful skill that can be applied in a later lesson when you chart content of cells that are not next to each other.

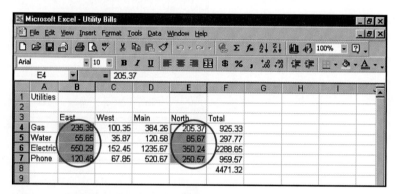

8 Click cell **B1** to select it. Use the vertical scrollbar to scroll down so that you can see cell **B30**.

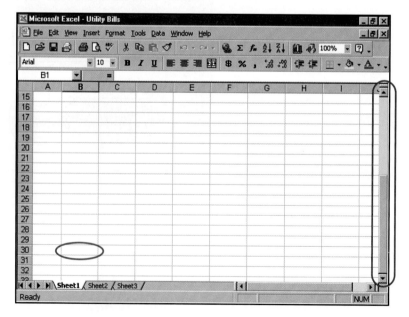

9 Hold down ⦗⬆Shift⦘ and click cell **B30**. This selects all of the cells between **B1** and **B30**.

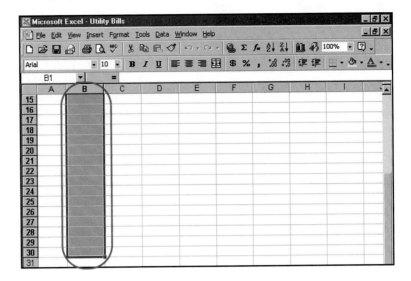

Caution: If you try to select a large group of cells that extends beyond the edge of the screen by using the click-and-drag method, you may find that the screen scrolls by so fast that you are hundreds of rows or columns beyond your intended destination. Scroll back to the beginning of the group and try it again using ⦗⬆Shift⦘ as described in steps 8-10.

10 Scroll back to the top of the sheet. This method is useful when you are selecting a group of cells that are so far apart that you have to use the scrollbar to find the other end of the group.

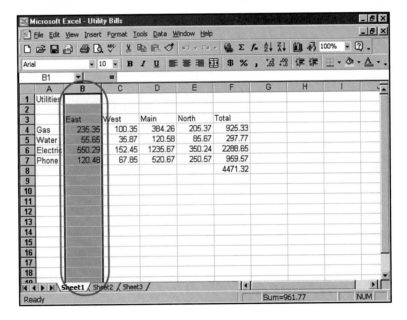

Quick Tip: If you want to select a long range of cells without taking your hands off the keyboard, hold down the ⦗⬆Shift⦘ key, and then use the arrow keys on the keyboard to select the range.

TASK 2

Formatting Large Numbers, Currency, Decimal Places, and Dates
Why would I do this?

Most numbers greater than 999 should have commas inserted to make them easier to read. In some cases, numbers represent money and should have commas and dollar signs. Many numbers have decimal components and you have to decide how many places to display. Excel allows you to format numbers the way you want them to be displayed. You also need to know how to handle dates.

In this task, you learn how to apply different types of numerical formats.

1 Select the cells from **B4** through **E7** and click the **Comma Style** button. Notice the electricity bill for the Main office in cell D6 is now displayed with a comma.

Comma Style button

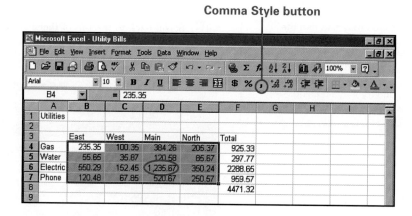

2 Select cells from **F4** through **F8** and click the **Currency Style** button. A dollar sign is added to the left side of the cell, and commas are inserted in numbers that are greater than 999. Leave this range selected for the next step.

Currency Style button

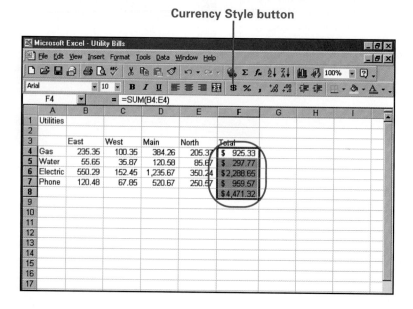

3 Click once on the **Decrease Decimal** button. Notice that the numbers are displayed with one fewer decimal place.

Decrease Decimal button

In Depth: The display of a number in a cell may be rounded off; however, Excel shows the full number in the formula bar and uses it in calculations. If the number that needs to be rounded ends in a 5, Excel rounds up. Numbers 0 through 4 are rounded down, and numbers 5 through 9 are rounded up.

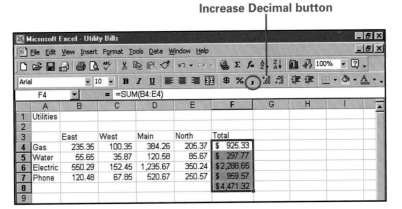

Display Rounded down   Display Rounded up

4 Click the **Increase Decimal** button once to display two decimal places.

Increase Decimal button

Caution: Rounding the display does not change the actual number in the cell or any cell that depends upon it. If you use the Decrease Decimal button to change the display so that it does not show any of the decimal places in cells F4 through F8, the rounded numbers do not appear to add correctly to the sum in cell F8.

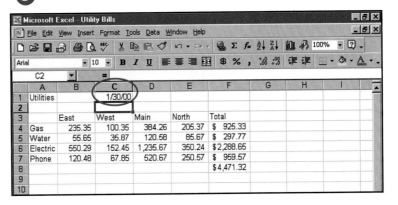

5 Select cell **C1**, type **1/30/00**, and press ↵Enter.

6 Select cell **C1** again. Choose **Format** from the menu, then choose **Cells**. The Format Cells dialog box is displayed. Click the **Number** tab if necessary.

Quick Tip: Commonly used menu items can be accessed quickly by clicking on an object using the right mouse button. A shortcut menu opens containing options that are relevant to the object. At step 6 you could have right-clicked cell C1 and chosen Format Cells from the shortcut menu.

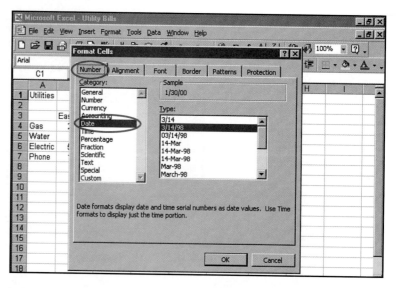

7 Click **Date** if necessary to select it. Click the example **Mar-98** in the **Type** box.

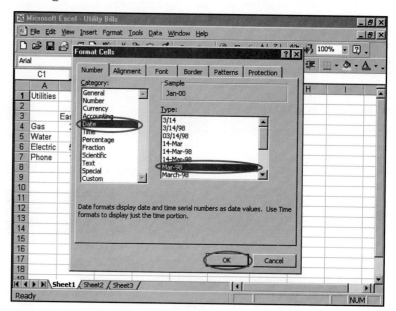

8 Click **OK.** The date now shows just the month and year. Notice the actual content of the cell is displayed in the formula bar.

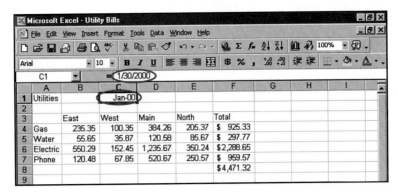

9 With cell **C1** still selected, choose **Edit, Clear, Formats.** The number **36555** appears.

> **In Depth:** Excel thinks of dates in terms of the number of days from a fixed date in the past. When you remove the formatting from the cell, it displays the number that it is actually using. This makes it possible to subtract one date from another to determine the number of days between two dates.

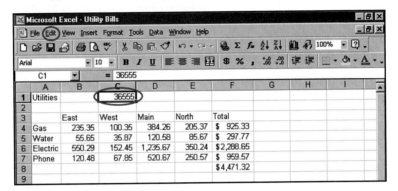

10 Choose **Edit, Clear, All.** The date is removed.

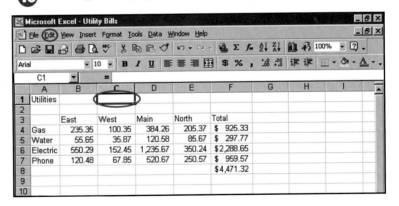

TASK *3*

Adjusting Columns and Cells for Long Text or Numbers
Why would I do this?

Text and numbers entered into a cell are often longer than the cell width. If the cell to the right contains an entry, the text in the left cell is cut off. If a number is too long, Excel displays a string of # signs.

In this task, you learn how to change column widths to accommodate entries, wrap text onto several lines within a cell, and center titles across several columns.

1 Select cell **A6** and type **Electricity**. Press the ⏎Enter key. Notice that word is cut off.

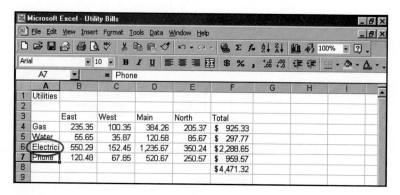

2 Move the pointer to the line that separates the headings for columns **A** and **B**. The mouse pointer turns into a double-sided black arrow.

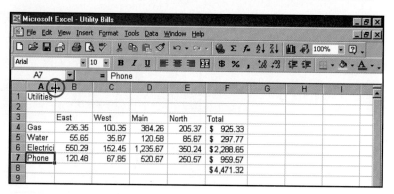

③ Double-click the line. The width of the column automatically adjusts to fit the longest word in any of the cells in column A.

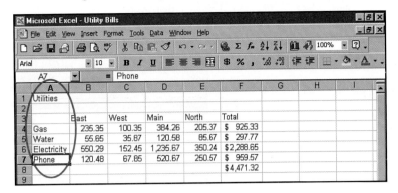

④ Select cell **A1** and type **Utility Bills - January 2000**. Press ⏎Enter. Notice that the text overlaps the cells to the right because they are empty.

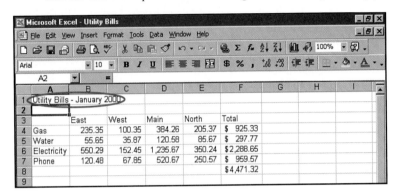

⑤ Select cells **A1** through **G1**. Click the **Merge and Center** button. The selected cells display the text as if they were one cell, and the long title is centered. The text is centered across one more column than necessary to accommodate a change that will be made in a later task.

Merge and Center button

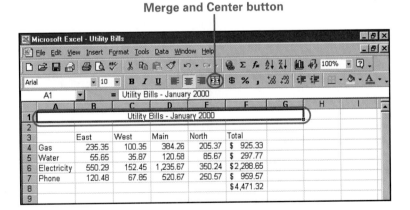

6 Select cell **D6**, type **7000** and press ↵Enter. Notice that the size of the final total in cell F8 exceeds the available cell space. A series of # signs is displayed.

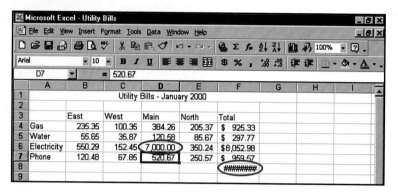

7 Double-click the line between the headings for columns **F** and **G**. The width of column F adjusts to display the larger number.

In Depth: If you want to make sure that the column is wide enough to handle future entries, there is another way you can make the column wider: Click and drag the line between the headings to the right to widen the column.

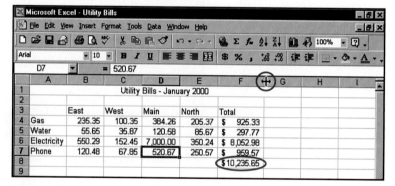

8 Select cell **D6**, type **1235.67** and press ↵Enter to replace the entry with a more realistic number.

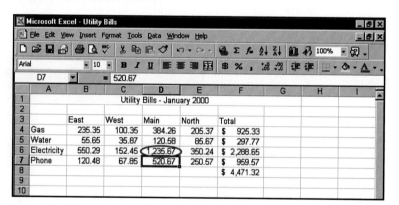

9 Click the **Save** button to save the changes made up to this point.

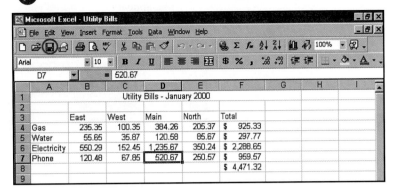

TASK 4

Aligning Text in a Cell
Why would I do this?

If text is used to label a row or column, you may find that it looks better if the text is centered in or aligned with the right side of the cell. If the text used as a column label is much longer than the numbers in the column, you may want to increase the height of the row and wrap the text in the cell. Another way to handle long column labels is to slant the cells at an angle.

In this task, you learn how to align long text labels.

1 Select cell **B3** and type **201 E. Liberty**. Press ⟨Tab⟩ and type **509 W. State Street**. Press ⟨Tab⟩ and type **Regional Office**. Press ⟨Tab⟩ and type **1236 N. Evergreen**. Press ⟨Enter⟩.

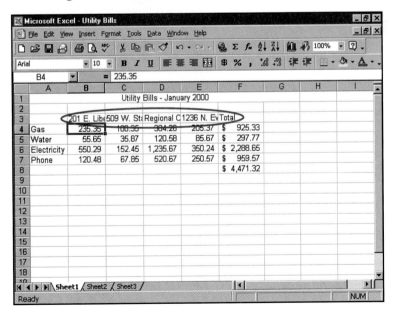

2 Select cells **B3** through **F3**. Click **Format**, **Cells**. The Format Cells dialog box appears. Click the **Alignment** tab, if it is not already selected.

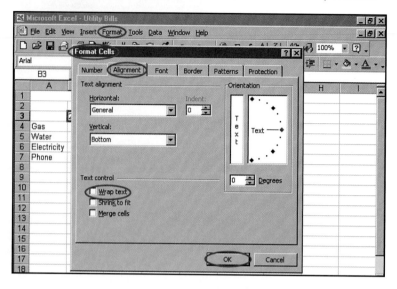

3 Click the **Wrap text** check box. Click **OK**. The height of the row increases and the text wraps within the cells just as if it were a word processing document.

Caution: Excel's word wrapping feature does not have an automatic hyphenation feature and is not as smart as a word processor when it comes to estimating where to break words. Check your work when you use the Wrap text feature.

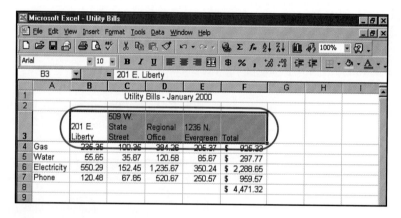

4 Click the **Undo** button to remove the **Wrap text** feature. There is another way to handle this type of column label.

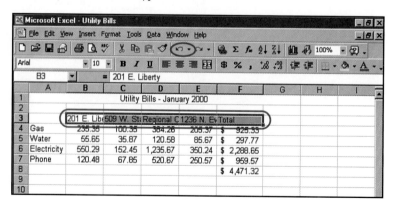

5 Make sure that cells **B3** to **F3** are still selected and click **Format, Cells**. The Format Cells dialog box appears.

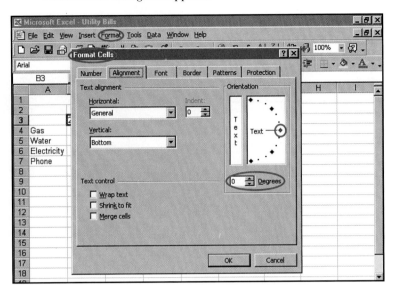

6 Click and drag the small red diamond in the **Orientation** window upward until the **Degrees** box reads 45.

> ✔ **Quick Tip:** You can also type the angle in the **Degrees** box or use the small arrows in the **Degrees** box to change the angle.

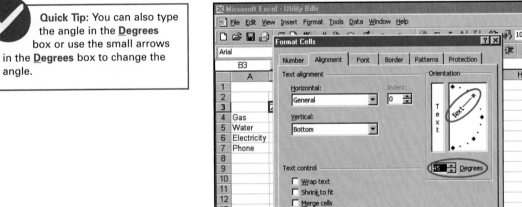

7 Click the down arrow next to the **Horizontal** box. Click **Center**. This centers the text in the cell.

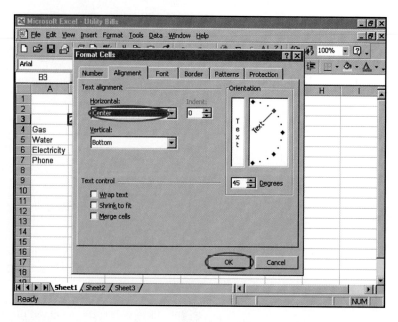

8 Click **OK.** The text in cells **B3** to **F3** is displayed at an angle.

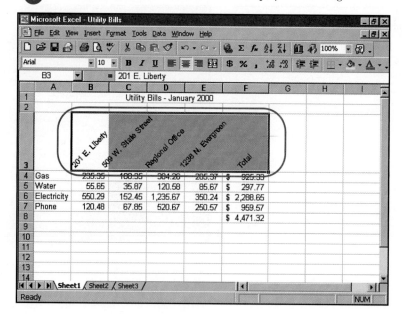

TASK 5

Changing the Font, Size, and Emphasis of Text
Why would I do this?

You may want to emphasize titles and important words by making them larger and by using a different font. This helps improve the overall appearance of your worksheet. You can draw attention to key numbers by adding emphasis to those numbers.

In this task, you learn how to change the point size of a title and change a font from Arial to Times New Roman. You also add emphasis by using boldface or italicized versions of the font.

1 Click anywhere on the title to select it. Click the down arrow next to the **Font** box. Scroll down and click **Times New Roman**. The font of the title changes.

Times New Roman font

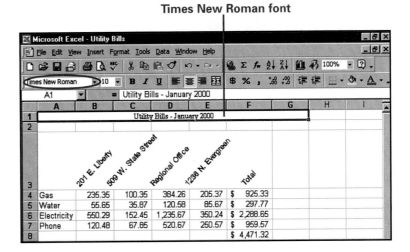

2 Click the down arrow next to the **Font Size** box. Click **14**. The size of the title changes to 14 point.

Font Size

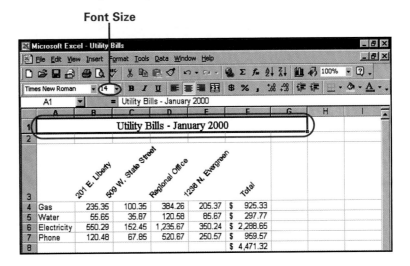

3 Click the **Bold** button.

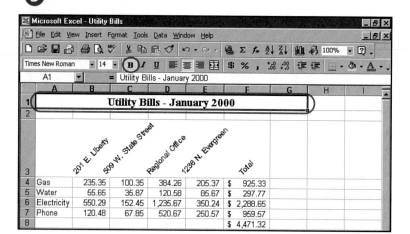

TASK 6

Adding Lines, Borders, Colors, and Shading

Why would I do this?

You may want to separate a column's total from the preceding numbers or add shading and borders to assist the reader in following a row of numbers across a complex page. Color, if used carefully, can add a special emphasis. Unless you have a color printer, use of colors on printed documents can be a hindrance rather than a help. It is important to use colors judiciously.

In this task, you learn how to add borders and shading to various parts of the worksheet.

1 Make sure that the title is still selected from the previous task. Click the down arrow next to the **Borders** button.

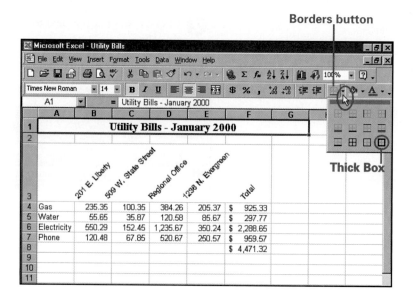

2 Click the **Thick Box Border** option at the right side of the bottom row. Select cells **B3** to **F3**. Click the down arrow next to the **Borders** button.

Thick box border —

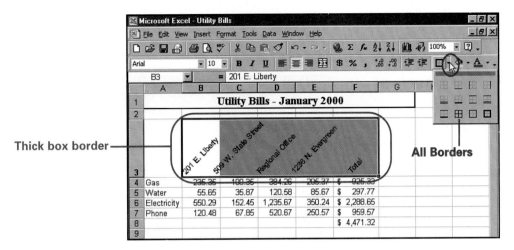

All Borders

3 Click the **All Borders** option that is the second box from the left in the bottom row. Select cell **F7**. Click the down arrow next to the **Borders** button.

All Borders options applied to text at an angle

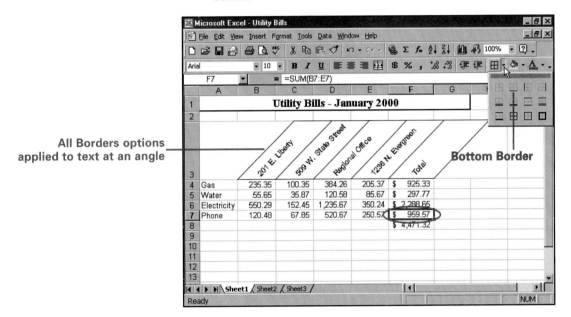

Bottom Border

4 Click the **Bottom Border** option that is second from the left in the top row. Select cells **A5** through **E5** and cells **A7** through **E7** (remember to use Ctrl to select the second group of cells). Click the down arrow next to the **Fill Color** button.

Fill Color button

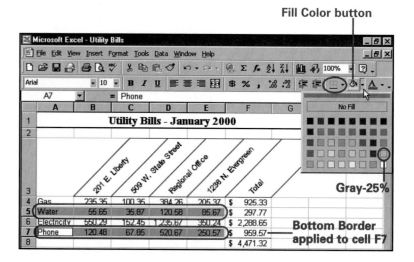

Gray-25%

Bottom Border applied to cell F7

5 Click the **Gray-25%** button. The selected cells are shaded. (To see the gray, deselect the shaded cells by clicking in any other cell.)

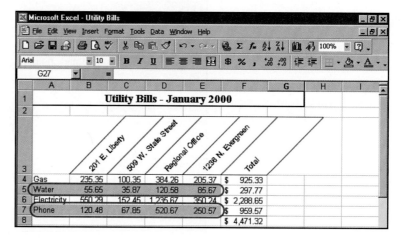

6 Select the title again. Click the down arrow next to the **Fill Color** button and click the **Light Turquoise** option. This changes the background (fill color) to a light turquoise color on the screen.

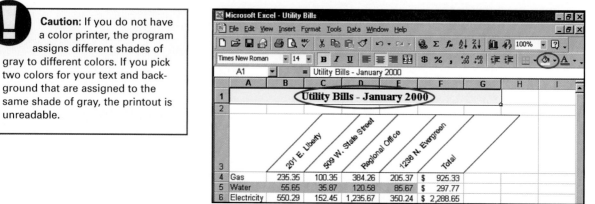

7 With the title still selected, click the down arrow next to the **Font Color** button.

Font Color button

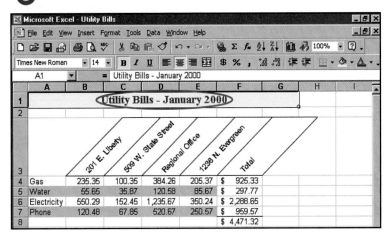

Quick Tip: The Font Color, Fill Color, and Borders buttons on the Formatting toolbar display the most recent choice. If you want to use the type of emphasis that is displayed on the button, you can apply it by clicking once on the button without using the drop-down menu.

8 Click the **Dark Red** option.

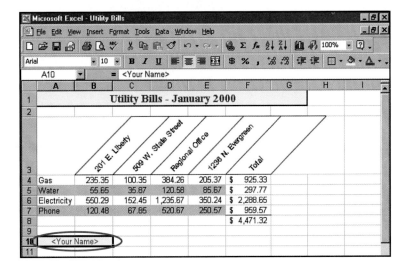

9 Select cell **A10** and type your name. Change the font, font size, border, background color, and font color to something you like. Merge across two or more cells if your name exceeds the current column width.

10 Click the **Print** button to print a copy.

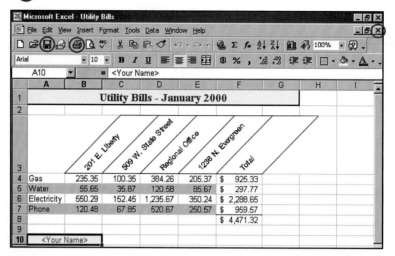

11 Click the **Close Window** button to close the workbook. A dialog box warns you that you have not saved the changes that you have made.

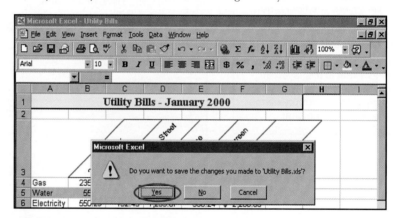

12 Click **Yes**. The workbook closes, leaving the Excel program active.

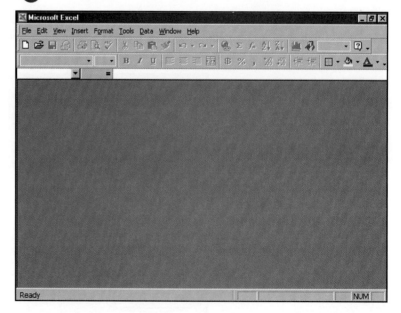

Comprehension Exercises

Comprehension exercises are designed to check your memory and understanding of the basic concepts in this lesson. You distinguish between true and false statements, identify new screen elements, and match terms with related statements. If you are uncertain of the correct answer, refer to the task number following each item (for example, T4 refers to Task 4) and review that task until you are confident that you can provide a correct response.

True-False

Circle either T or F.

T   F   **1.**   If a number is too long to fit in a cell, it will extend into the cell to the right. **(T3)**

T   F   **2.**   You can select all of the cells in a row by clicking on the row heading. **(T1)**

T   F   **3.**   All the cells in a selection must be touching each other; separate groups of cells cannot be selected at the same time. **(T1)**

T   F   **4.**   If you select a group of cells and click the **Comma Style** button, all of the numbers in those cells are displayed with a comma placed between every two numbers. **(T1)**

T   F   **5.**   If a selected cell contains the number 5.25 and you click the **Decrease Decimal** button, the number 5.2 is displayed. **(T1)**

T   F   **6.**   If a cell displays a row of # signs, it means that you made a mistake in writing a formula. **(T3)**

T   F   **7.**   One way to handle long labels is to use the **Wrap text** option. **(T4)**

T   F   **8.**   A 16-point character is larger than an 8-point character. **(T5)**

T   F   **9.**   If you have a printer with only one color of ink, it does not matter what colors you choose for text and background. **(T6)**

T   F   **10.**   It is possible to print long column labels at an angle. **(T4)**

Identifying Parts of the Excel Screen

Refer to the figure and identify the numbered parts of the screen. Write the letter of the correct label in the space next to the number.

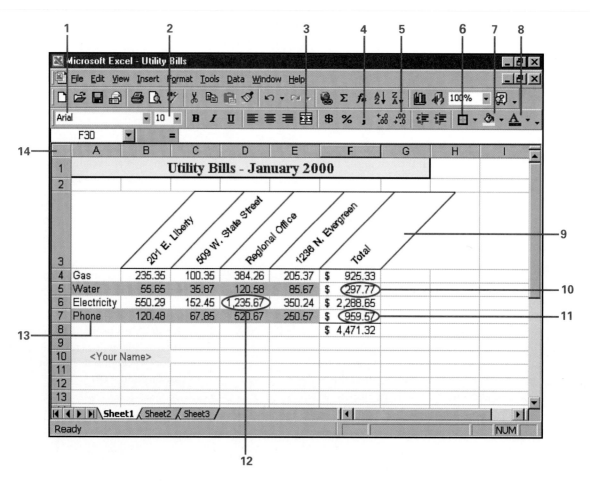

1. _____ **A.** Text aligned at an angle (**T3**)

2. _____ **B.** Cells displaying a gray fill color (**T6**)

3. _____ **C.** Select All button (**T1**)

4. _____ **D.** Example of Comma Style (**T2**)

5. _____ **E.** Example of Currency Style (without border) (**T2**)

6. _____ **F.** Comma Style button (**T2**)

7. _____ **G.** Decrease Decimal button (**T2**)

8. _____ **H.** Merge and Center button (**T3**)

9. _____ **I.** Borders button (**T6**)

10. _____ **J.** Font Size (**T5**)

11. _____ **K.** Font Name (**T5**)

12. _____ **L.** Fill Color button (**T6**)

13. _____ **M.** Font Color button (**T5**)

14. _____ **N.** Cell with a bottom border (**T6**)

Matching

Match the statements below to the word or phrase that is the best match from the list. Write the letter of the matching word or phrase in the space provided next to the number.

1. ___ Text that is used as a title may occupy several cells using this feature (**T1**)

2. ___ Used to select a group of cells that is not touching the first group (**T1**)

3. ___ Method used to automatically adjust the width of a column to accommodate the widest cell entry (**T3**)

4. ___ Method used to manually change the width of a column (**T3**)

5. ___ Button that inserts dollar signs (**T2**)

6. ___ Symbols that indicate that a number is too long to fit in a cell (**T3**)

7. ___ Method for displaying column labels at a slant (**T3**)

8. ___ Setting that forces long text entries to fit within the available column width by increasing the row height and displaying the text on several lines within the cell (**T3**)

9. ___ A font (**T5**)

10. ___ A border style (**T5**)

A. Move pointer to the line between column headings and double-click

B. Save

C. Currency Style

D. Ctrl

E. #######

F. Click and drag the small red diamond in the Orientation box to the desired angle of slant

G. Click and drag the line between column headings

H. Wrap text

I. Merge and Center

J. Arial

K. Thick box

Reinforcement Exercises

Reinforcement exercises are designed to reinforce the skills you have learned by applying them to a new situation. Detailed instructions are provided along with a figure, where appropriate, to illustrate the final result. The Reinforcement exercises that follow should be completed sequentially. Leave the workbook open at the end of each exercise for use in the next exercise until you are specifically directed to close it.

Open **Less1002** and save it as **Comparison** on your floppy disk for use in the following exercises.

R1—Applying Formats to an Existing Worksheet

1. Select **Sheet1**, if necessary.

2. Enter your name in cell **F17**.

3. Format **Sheet1** to match the figure. See the steps below for more detail.

4. Use the **Merge and Center** feature to center the main title across columns **A** through **F**. Center the subtitle **All Metal** across **C2** and **D2** and the subtitle **Glass and Metal** across cells **E2** and **F2**.

5. Center and wrap the text in cells **B3** through **F3**.

6. Center data in all cells from **B4** through **F13**.

7. Select both groups of shaded cells and choose a fill color of **Gray-25%**.

8. Select cells **A1, A4, A7, A11, A14, A15,** and **A16**. Make them **Bold**.

9. Select **D15** and **F15** and format the numbers to display currency with no decimals.

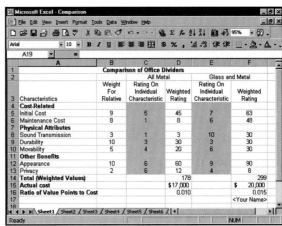

10. Select **D16** and **F16** and format the numbers to display only three decimal places.

11. Adjust the column widths, print the sheet, and save the workbook.

R2—Adding Border Lines and Colors

1. Select **Sheet2**. Enter your name in cell **F19**.

2. Add border lines and colors to match the figure. (The status bar has been turned off to display the entire sheet in the figure—you may have to scroll to see the last line on your screen.) See the steps below for more information.

3. Place a **Thick Box** border around the title and the two ratio numbers in cells **D15** and **F15**.

4. Add a **Bottom Border** to the cells in rows **3**, **6**, and **10** in columns **A** through **F** only. (Do not use the row heading to select the row.)

5. Add a **Bottom Double Border** to the bottom of cells **D12** and **F12**.

6. Change the **Fill Color** of the title to **Turquoise** and change the **Font Color** to **Dark Red**.

7. Change the orientation of the column labels in cells **B2** through **F2** to a **45** degree angle. Select the **All Borders** option that shows all lines. (Your text may wrap differently than is shown in the figure.)

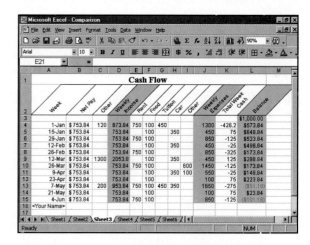

8. Drag the line between the row headings for rows **2** and **3** to increase the height of row **2** to show the labels correctly.

9. Adjust the column widths, print the sheet, and save the workbook.

R3—Editing a Worksheet

1. Select **Sheet3**.

2. Enter your name in cell **A16**.

3. Format the sheet to match the figure. Make sure you change font size and style, merge and center, center text, fill color, align text, and add borders. Remember to adjust the columns to fit to the data. See the steps below for further details.

4. Merge the title in cell **A1** across the cells **A1** through **L1**. Change its font to **Times New Roman**, **16** point, and make it **Bold**.

5. Select cells **A2** through **L2**. Format the cells to wrap text, centered, and display the text at a **45** degree angle. Use the **All Borders** option and center them.

6. Drag the boundary between rows **2** and **3** to adjust the height. Select the column headings, **A** through **L**, and double-click on one of the boundaries between columns to adjust all of the widths at once.

7. Apply a **Gray-25%** fill color to the cells in columns **D**, **J**, and **L**.

8. Format cells **B4** through **B15** as currency.

9. Save the workbook and print the sheet.

10. Close the file.

Challenge

Challenge exercises are designed to test your ability to apply your skills to new situations with less detailed instruction. These exercises also challenge you to expand your repertoire of skills by using Excel commands that are similar to those you have already learned. The desired outcome is clearly defined, but you have more freedom to choose the steps needed to achieve the required result.

C1—Use Borders and Remove Gridlines to Format a Table

If a table of data is to be distributed to several people, it is useful to use formatting tools to organize the cells into functional groups. In this example, several people in the office have been asked to evaluate and compare two room divider systems using a weighted scale.

Goal: Format the worksheet that is provided to look like the example in the figure.

Use the following guidelines:

1. Use the **Comparison** file created in the Reinforcement exercises or open **Less1002** and save it on your floppy disk as **Comparison**. Select **Sheet4**.

2. Center the text in cells **B2** through **F2**.

3. Use **Tools**, **Options**, **View**, **Gridlines** to turn off the gridlines on the screen.

4. Use **Borders** to add the lines shown.

5. Print the worksheet. Leave the workbook open for use in the next exercise.

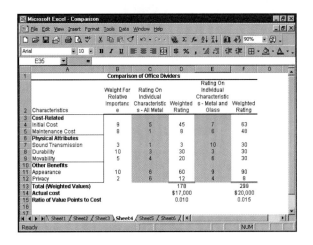

C2—Align Text Displayed at an Angle

When you display a column heading at a 45-degree angle, it is unclear which direction is indicated by the horizontal or vertical controls. Use **Sheet5** of the Comparison workbook.

Goal: Change the column headings of the **Sheet5** to align at a 45-degree angle. Adjust the height of the row so that the text wraps as shown. Add borders and set the vertical and horizontal alignments to match the figure.

1. Select cells **B2** through **F2** and align the text at **45** degrees.

2. Use the **All Borders** option that looks like a window with four panes.

3. Drag the line between row headings **2** and **3** to adjust the height of the row so that none of the text wraps to more than two lines and no words are wrapped incorrectly.

4. In the Format Cells dialog box, you can change the vertical alignment as well as the horizontal alignment of the text. Experiment with the **Horizontal** and **Vertical** alignment options to find the combination that matches the figure. Observe what the effect of each option is on the placement of the text in the cell.

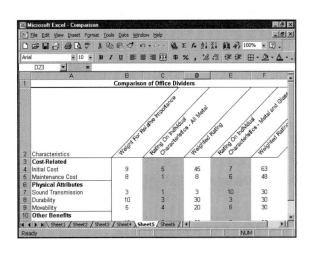

5. Save the workbook. Print the sheet.

C3—Use Help to Learn More About Working with Dates

Computers work with dates and times as if they were numbers, which allows you to subtract one date (or time) from another.

Goal: Open the **Office Assistant** and use it to find out how Excel works with dates. Print the **Help** page. Experiment with sample figures.

1. Click the **Office Assistant** or click the **Microsoft Excel Help** button to open the Assistant's dialog box.

2. Type the following question: **How does Excel subtract one date from another?** Click the **Search** button.

3. Click **How Microsoft Excel stores dates and times**. The Microsoft Excel Help window opens.

4. Read the topic and print a copy.

5. Close the workbook.

Discovery

Discovery exercises are designed to help you learn how to teach yourself a new skill. In each exercise, you discover something new that is related to the topic taught in this lesson. You may be directed to use built-in wizards or some of the extensive Help features provided in Excel to discover new features and learn new skills with minimum assistance from books or instructors. The required outcome demonstrates your ability to apply the new skill. You determine the choice of topic, worksheet design, and steps of execution.

D1—Explore Some Effects of the Year 2000 Problem

Representing the year in a date with only two digits creates problems because the computer is forced to guess the century in which it belongs.

Goal: Determine how to work with the century assumptions built into Excel 2000 so that you know when you must use four digits to represent the year in a date.

1. Open **Less1003** from the **Student\Lesson10** folder on your CD-ROM disc and save it on your floppy disk as **Year2000**. Place your name in cell **A1**.

2. In cell **B3**, type a date of birth from the Twenties such as **5/20/28**. In cell **C3**, type today's date. Notice the calculation in cell **D3** displays a negative number because it assumed you meant **2028** rather than **1928**.

3. Type the date in again, but specify the year using four digits.

4. Refer to Excel's Help on this matter and write a directive that you might send out to your staff telling them when to use four digits for the year when entering numbers into Excel worksheets. Enter the message in cell **A6**.

5. Widen column **A** to about four times its current width and format the text in cell **A6** to wrap.

6. Leave the page open for use in the next Discovery exercise.

D2—Use Help to Learn About Conditional Formatting

You can use formatting to draw attention to errors or unusual results. Use the **Year2000** file that was created in the previous exercise or open **Less1003** and save it as **Year2000** on your floppy disk.

Goal: Use Help to learn about conditional formatting. Format cell **D3** in the **Year2000** worksheet so that the number is displayed in red, boldface type whenever the number is negative.

1. Search Help for information about conditional formatting.

2. Format cell **D3** as described above.

3. Enter the date 1/1/25 in cell **B3** that is supposed to be from the year 1925. The value in cell **D3**, which should be a negative number, is displayed as described.

4. Print the page.

5. Leave the page open for use in the next Discovery exercise.

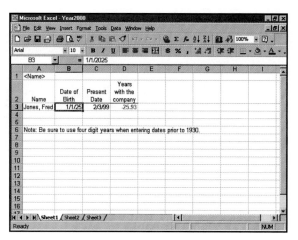

D3—Protect Cells from Unintentional Change

The formula in cell D3 will be lost if someone accidentally enters a value in the cell. Similarly, you do not want others to change the column headings or message you have chosen. To prevent users from overwriting formulas or making unauthorized changes, you can limit the cells they can write in by unlocking those cells and then protecting the rest of the sheet. Use the **Year2000** file that was created in the previous exercise or open **Less1003** from the **Student\Lesson10** folder and save it as **Year2000** on your floppy disk.

Goal: Unlock cells **B3** and **C3**, then protect the rest of the sheet so that users can only change values in cells **B3** and **C3**.

1. Select cells **B3** and **C3**. Choose **Format**, **Cells and Protection**. Unlock the cells.

2. Use the **Tools** menu to protect the sheet. Do not use a password.

3. Try to make changes to any other part of the sheet and observe the error message.

4. Save the changes you have made.

5. Close the workbook and close Excel.

Lesson: 11

Editing Cell Contents and Adding Sheets

Introduction

In Lesson 9, you learned some simple rules about editing cells and making corrections. In this lesson, you will expand on those basic skills by learning other techniques for editing cells. You will also learn how to insert and delete rows and columns in your worksheet. There are a number of automated features that come with Excel 2000, and you will learn how to use these tools. To use a worksheet effectively and easily, not only do you need to know how to edit cells, but you can benefit from knowing how to take advantage of the automated features to help you work more efficiently.

Visual Summary

When you have completed this entire lesson, you will have edited a worksheet that looks like this:

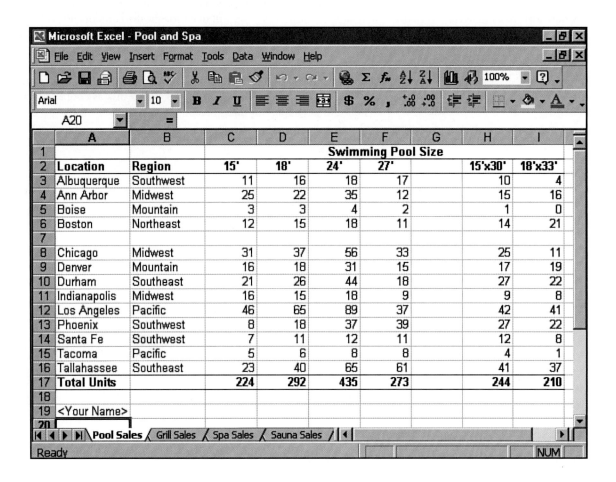

TASK 1

Changing Numbers and Editing Text
Why would I do this?

When you enter a lot of data into a worksheet, you will sometimes make errors. There will also be times when you enter data or labels correctly, but decide to change them later. In either case, you will need to edit the contents of a cell.

In this task, you change data in one cell and edit text in another.

1 Launch **Excel**, open **Less1101** from the **Student\Lesson11** folder on your CD-ROM disc, and save the file on your floppy disk as **Pool and Spa**. The new title will appear in the title bar.

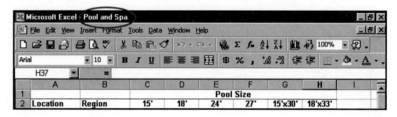

2 Select cell **F8**, type **33** and press ↵Enter. The new number replaces the old one, and the sum at the bottom of the column is recalculated.

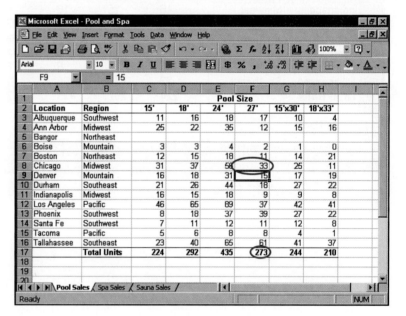

3 Select cell **C1**, which has been merged and centered over six columns. Notice that the contents of the cell are shown both in the cell and in the formula bar. The cell location is also shown in the **Name** box.

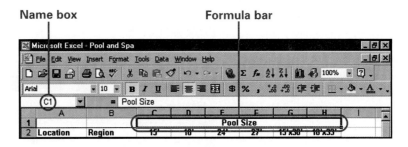

4 Move the pointer to the left of the word **Pool** in the formula bar and double-click to position the insertion point. Type **Swimming**, then press [Spacebar], [←Enter]. The contents of cell C1 reflect the change you made.

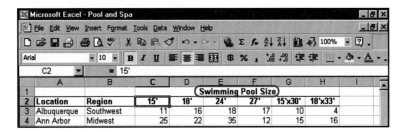

TASK *2*

Inserting and Deleting Rows and Columns
Why would I do this?

If your worksheet lists items in a particular order, it would not be ideal to add a new item at the bottom of the list if it did not belong there. Similarly, if you deleted the contents of a row or column, it would not look right to leave the row or column empty. Excel can insert or delete rows or columns in a worksheet and automatically move the rest of the data. It will also revise any formulas that are affected by the change.

In this task, you insert and delete rows and columns.

1 Click on the row heading for row **5** to select the entire row.

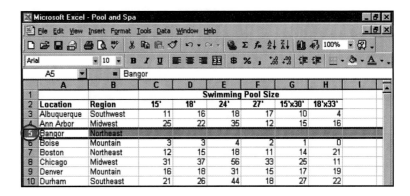

② Choose **Edit**, **Delete**. The entry for Bangor disappears and the entry for Boise has now moved up to row **5**.

Caution: It would seem that you should be able to delete a row by highlighting it and pressing the Del key. This will remove the contents of the cells, but will not delete the row.

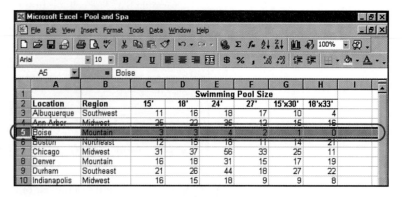

In Depth: To insert more than one row at a time, select more than one cell vertically, then choose **Insert**, **Rows**. The number of new rows equals the number of cells selected. You may also insert or delete rows using Ctrl and the ⊞ or ⊟ keys.

③ Select any cell in row **7**, then choose **Insert**, **Rows**. The contents of row 7, and all the rows below it, moves down one row.

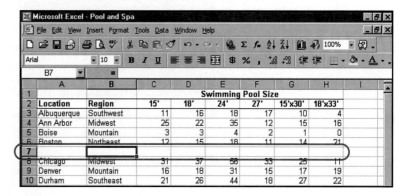

④ Select any cell in column **G**, then choose **Insert**, **Columns**. The contents of column G, and all columns to the right of it, are moved to the right.

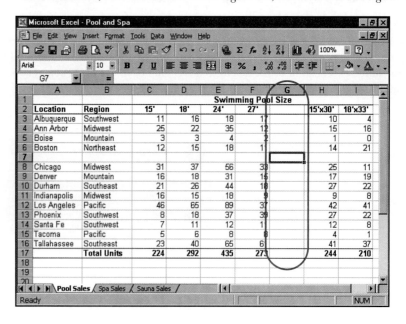

TASK 3

Inserting and Moving Sheets
Why would I do this?

Separate sheets may be used to track different items, months, or other related topics. If you designate a separate sheet for each purpose, it may be necessary to add new sheets. Once you add a new sheet, you may want it to appear in a different order relative to the other sheets.

In this task, you learn how to insert a new worksheet and then move it.

1 Choose **Insert**, **Worksheet**. A new worksheet will appear named **Sheet1**.

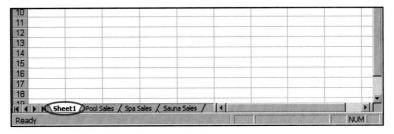

2 Double-click on the **Sheet1** tab, then type **Grill Sales**. The sheet tab is now renamed.

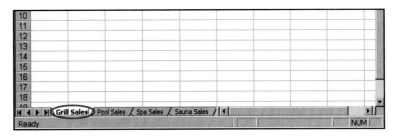

3 Click on the tab labeled **Grill Sales** and continue to hold the mouse button. Drag the mouse to the right. The pointer displays a small sheet, and a small arrow indicates where the sheet will be placed when you release the mouse.

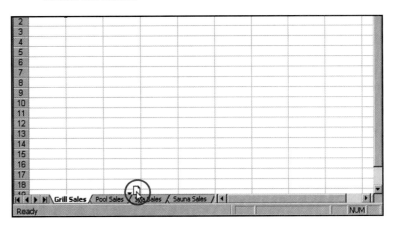

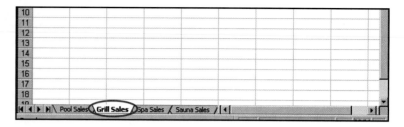

4 Move the pointer to the right of the **Pool Sales** tab and release the mouse. The **Grill Sales** sheet has been moved.

TASK 4

Removing Cell Content and Formatting

Why would I do this?

When you use Del to delete the contents of a cell, the contents are removed. Any formatting that has been added, such as decimal places, currency, and character formatting, remains. If you enter data into what appears to be a blank cell, you will find that the formatting will be applied. Sometimes this is beneficial and sometimes it is not. There are ways you can delete the content, the formatting of cells, or both at the same time.

In this task, you delete the contents of a cell and remove the formatting.

1 Click on the **Pool Sales** sheet tab. Select cell **A17**, type **Total Units** and press Enter. Notice that the text is bold, even though you did not format it.

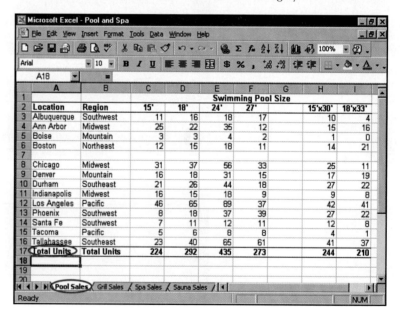

2 Select cell **B17** and press Ⓓⓔⓛ. Select another cell so that you can see cell **B17** when it is not selected. The contents of the cell are deleted, but the top and bottom border lines remain.

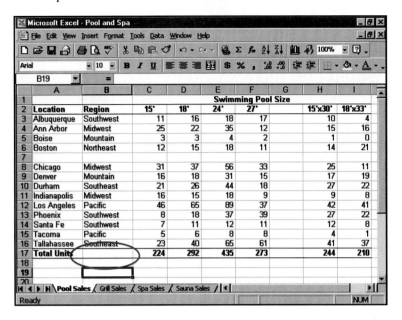

3 Select cell **B17** again. Choose **Edit**, **Clear**, **Formats**. Select another cell to reveal the change to cell **B17**. The formatting, including the text formatting and the border lines, is gone.

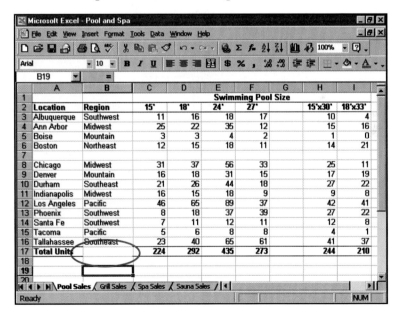

TASK 5

Undoing and Redoing Previous Steps
Why would I do this?

Occasionally, you will begin a procedure and decide that you want to do it differently. You may also make major changes to the worksheet by mistake. Excel gives you a way to undo and redo previous procedures.

In this task, you learn to use the Undo and Redo buttons to change a sequence of actions.

1 Select cell **A19**, type your name, and press ↵Enter. Click the **Undo** button. The program removes your name, undoing the last action you took.

Undo button ─

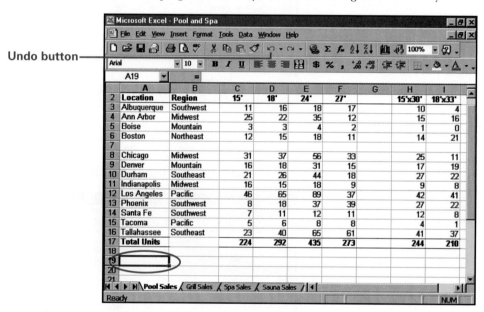

2 Click the **Undo** button repeatedly to undo the last few steps of the previous task. Stop when cell B17 has its formatting restored and the text replaced.

3 Click the **Redo** button. This reverses the last undo, removing the text, but leaving the top and bottom border lines.

Redo button

In Depth: If you click the drop-down arrow next to the **Undo** or **Redo** button, a list of the previous actions will display. If you select one of the actions from the list, it will have the same effect as clicking the button repeatedly to get down to that item on the list. You cannot undo a single item from the list except the one at the top of the list.

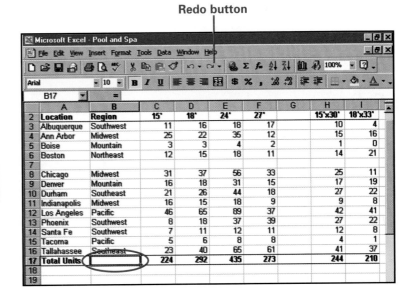

4 Enter your name into cell A19.

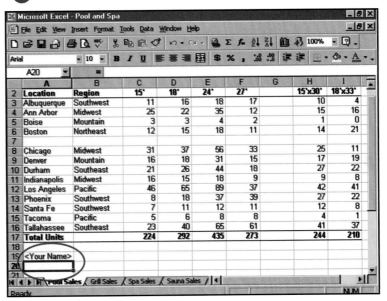

5 Click the **Close Window** button to close the workbook. Leave Excel open for use in the following exercises.

Comprehension Exercises

Comprehension exercises are designed to check your memory and understanding of the basic concepts in this lesson. You distinguish between true and false statements, identify new screen elements, and match terms with related statements. If you are uncertain of the correct answer, refer to the task number following each item (for example, T4 refers to Task 4) and review that task until you are confident that you can provide a correct response.

True-False

Circle either T or F.

T F **1.** One way to change a number in a cell is to select the cell and type the new number. **(T1)**

T F **2.** One way to insert a row is to select the entire row by clicking on the row heading and then inserting a row. **(T2)**

T F **3.** When you select a cell, the contents are shown both in the cell and in a box on the Formula bar near the top of the screen. **(T1)**

T F **4.** The cell location is shown in the **Name** box (if no other name has been assigned). **(T1)**

T F **5.** To rename a sheet tab, double-click on the tab and type the new name. **(T3)**

T F **6.** When you use Del to remove the contents of a cell, you remove both the contents and the formatting. **(T4)**

T F **7.** You can only undo one previous step. **(T5)**

T F **8.** The sequence of sheets can be changed by clicking and dragging the sheet tab. **(T3)**

T F **9.** Sheet tabs are given names when they are created that indicate the sequence in which they were created. These names cannot be changed. **(T3)**

T F **10.** If you select a cell in a column and insert a new column, the contents of that column are erased. **(T2)**

Identifying Parts of the Excel Screen

Refer to the figure and identify the numbered parts of the screen. Write the letter of the correct label in the space next to the number.

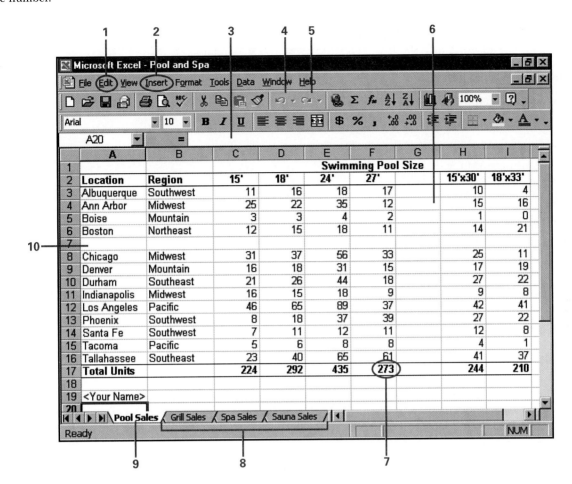

1. _____   **A.** Sheet tabs (**T3**)

2. _____   **B.** Menu option used to clear formatting (**T4**)

3. _____   **C.** Undo button (**T5**)

4. _____   **D.** Inserted column (**T2**)

5. _____   **E.** Redo button (**T5**)

6. _____   **F.** Inserted row (**T2**)

7. _____   **G.** Formula bar (**T1**)

8. _____   **H.** Cell with formula that automatically updates if a number in the column above it is changed (**T1**)

9. _____

10. _____   **I.** Menu option used to add rows, columns, and sheets (**T5**)

J. Current sheet tab (**T3**)

Matching

Match the statements below to the word or phrase that is the best match from the list. Write the letter of the matching word or phrase in the space provided next to the number.

1. ___ Shows the cell that is selected **(T1)**

2. ___ Removes just the cell contents **(T4)**

3. ___ Reverses the last action **(T5)**

4. ___ Method used to rearrange sheets **(T3)**

5. ___ Action that may be used to begin editing the contents of a cell **(T1)**

6. ___ Shows the names of the worksheets available in the workbook **(T3)**

7. ___ The second place, besides the cell itself, where the cell contents are shown **(T1)**

8. ___ Sequence of commands that removes both contents and formatting of a cell **(T1)**

9. ___ Contains several worksheets **(T2)**

10. ___ Reverses a previous Undo action **(T5)**

A. Sheet tabs

B. Click and drag

C. Double-click

D. Formula bar

E. Edit, Clear, All

F. Del

G. Workbook

H. Name box

I. Font Size box

J. Undo

K. Redo

Reinforcement Exercises

Reinforcement exercises are designed to reinforce the skills you have learned by applying them to a new situation. Detailed instructions are provided along with a figure, where appropriate, to illustrate the final result. The Reinforcement exercises that follow should be completed sequentially. Leave the workbook open at the end of each exercise for use in the next exercise until you are specifically directed to close it.

Open **Less1102** from the **Student\Lesson11** folder on your CD-ROM disc and save it as **Ex1101** on your floppy disk for use in the following exercises.

R1—Editing Text and Numbers and Using Automatic Entries

1. Select **Sheet1**.

2. Enter your name in cell **A17**.

3. Change the sheet tab name to **Books**.

4. Modify the **Books** worksheet to match the figure. See the steps below for more detail.

5. Change the year in cell **C7** to **1910**.

6. Edit the names of the authors in cells **A7** and **A9**. In cell **A7**, replace **H.** (the middle initial) with **Harding**. In cell **A9**, add a middle name of **Salisbury** between Edward and Field.

7. Center and boldface the column headings in row **1**. Choose a background of **Grey-25%**, and put a thin line border on the bottom of the row.

8. Click on another cell to deselect the heading cells. Run the **Spelling Checker** program and correct the misspelled words. Don't worry about unrecognized

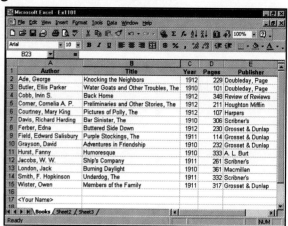

author or publisher names. You may need to move the Spelling Checker window to see the word it has found.

9. Print the worksheet and save the workbook.

R2—Adding Columns and Rows

1. Select **Sheet2**.

2. Enter your name in cell **F19**.

3. Change the sheet tab name to **Occupations**.

4. Modify the **Occupations** worksheet to match the figure. See the steps below for more detail.

5. Insert a new row 1. Type **Alcona County, Michigan Occupations** into cell **A1**.

6. Merge and center the title between cells **A1** and **D1**. Boldface the title and increase the font size to **14** point.

7. Add a bottom border to cells **B2** through **D2**.

8. Insert a new column **B**. Adjust the column width to match columns **C** through **E**.

9. Add the year **1860** to the cell **B2**. Make sure the formatting of the new year matches the other three years. Fill in the numbers in column **B** to match the figure. They are Farming, **6**; General Labor, **18**; Lumbering, **4**; Skilled Trades, **2**; and Fishing, **47**.

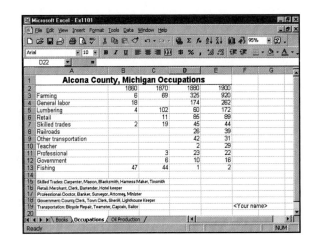

10. Save the workbook and print the worksheet.

R3—Adding Columns, Totals, and Formatting

1. Select **Sheet3**.

2. Enter your name in cell **A18**.

3. Change the sheet tab name to **Oil Production**.

4. Modify the **Oil Production** worksheet to match the figure. See the steps below for more detail.

5. Merge and center the titles in row **1** and then row **2**.

6. Boldface the main title in row **1** and change the font size to **14** point. Change the title in row **2** to **11** point.

7. Center and boldface the column labels, then add a bottom border.

8. Add a new column between the USSR and the USA. Add the **Saudi Arabia** data from the figure. Make sure the column label is formatted the same as the other column labels. The numbers are: **7.60**, **8.48**, **7.08**, **8.58**, **9.25**, **8.30**, **9.53**, **9.90**, **9.81**, **6.47**, **5.09**, and **4.67**.

9. Center the row labels (the years in column **A**).

10. Add totals to the columns as shown in the figure. Add a bottom border to cells **B15** through **E15**. Also, give the totals row a label: **Totals**. Boldface the totals.

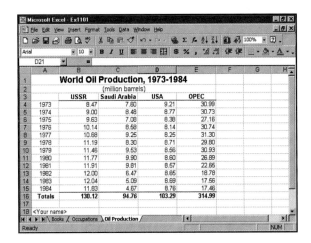

11. Format all of the numbers (except the years) so they show two decimal places.

12. Save the workbook; leave the workbook and Excel open for use in the following exercises.

Challenge

Challenge exercises are designed to test your ability to apply your skills to new situations with less detailed instruction. These exercises also challenge you to expand your repertoire of skills by using Excel commands that are similar to those you have already learned. The desired outcome is clearly defined, but you have more freedom to choose the steps needed to achieve the required result.

The following Challenge exercises use the file Ex1101 that was created in the previous Reinforcement exercises. If you have not done those exercises, you may open **Less1102** from your CD-ROM disc in the **Student\Lesson11** folder and save it as **Ex1101**.

C1—Copying a Sheet and Moving It

To manage a workbook effectively, you need to be able to add, delete, rename, and rearrange the sheets.

Goal: Make a copy of the **Books** sheet and place it at the end of the list of sheets. Rename the sheet and then move it to second place in the list.

Use the following guidelines:

1. Open **Ex1101** and right-click on the **Books** sheet tab.

2. Use the shortcut menu to create a copy and move it to the end of the list.

3. Double-click the name of the new sheet to select it and change the name to **Columns**.

4. Point at the **Columns** tab. Click and drag the tab to a position between the **Books** and **Occupations** tabs.

5. Save the workbook. Leave the workbook open for use in the next exercise.

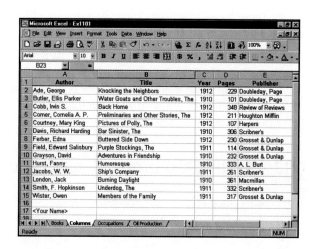

C2—Hiding and Unhiding Columns

Use the **Columns** sheet created in Challenge exercise 1.

If your worksheet has numerous columns, it is difficult to manage the display and printouts. It is often useful to hide certain columns so that printouts only display the needed columns.

Goal: Learn how to hide selected columns so that they do not display on the screen or on a printout. Also, learn how to unhide columns.

1. Select columns **C** and **D**.

2. Use the **Format** menu to hide the columns.

3. Select the columns on either side of the hidden columns, columns **B** and **E**, and use the **Format** menu to unhide the columns.

4. Select columns **C** and **E** (hold Ctrl before you click the second column heading).

5. Hide both columns.

6. Print the worksheet.

7. Save the workbook. Leave the workbook open for use in the next exercise.

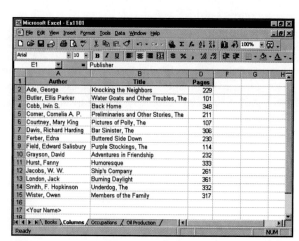

C3—Freezing Panes

If a worksheet consists of long columns or rows, you may have to scroll to see the desired cell. This action may cause the row or column labels to scroll off the screen. You can prevent this by selecting a cell and freezing the rows above it and the columns to the left of it. This feature is called *Freeze Panes*.

Goal: Freeze the columns and rows that contain the labels for the **Oil Production** table.

1. Open the **Ex1101** file and choose the **Oil Production** sheet.

2. Select cell **B4**.

3. Select **Window, Freeze Panes**.

4. Scroll vertically and horizontally to observe the effect.

5. Leave the workbook open for use in the Discovery exercises.

Discovery

Discovery exercises are designed to help you learn how to teach yourself a new skill. In each exercise, you discover something new that is related to the topic taught in this lesson. You may be directed to use built-in wizards or some of the extensive Help features provided in Excel to discover new features and learn new skills with minimum assistance from books or instructors. The required outcome demonstrates your ability to apply the new skill. You determine the choice of topic, worksheet design, and steps of execution.

D1—Using Named Ranges

Cell references are hard to remember or relate to specific totals or ranges. You can apply your own names to cells or cell ranges. These names may be used to find the desired cell or range, or they may be used in formulas as substitutes for cell references.

Goal: Name the cells that contain oil production totals and name the range of OPEC production from 1980 to 1984.

1. Open **Ex1101** and select the **Oil Production** sheet (if you have not yet created this file, open **Less1102** and save it as **Ex1101**).

2. Select cell **B16** (total USSR oil production).

3. Locate the **Name** box. It is at the left end of the formula bar and displays the name of the currently selected cell. Click the name of the cell, **B16**, to select it.

4. Type the following cell name: **USSR_total**. (Spaces are not allowed in range names so an underline character has been used to simulate the appearance of a space.)

5. Use this method to name the totals in cells **C16, D16,** and **E16** as **Saudi_total, USA_total,** and **OPEC_total**, respectively.

6. Select cells **E11** through **E15**. Use the same method to name this range of cells **OPEC_in_the_early_80s**.

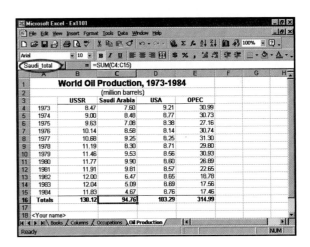

7. Click the list arrow next to the **Name** box. Pick a name from the list. Notice the selection is moved to that cell. This method may be used as a fast way to move around large worksheets.

8. Leave the workbook open for use in the next Discovery exercise.

D2—Inserting Comments

You can communicate thoughts or comments to yourself or others by inserting comments into the cells. Excel allows you to create a pop-up comment and attach it to a cell so that it appears when you move the pointer onto the cell. Cells with comments are denoted by a small red triangle in the corner that does not print.

Goal: Insert comments into cells.

1. Open Ex1101, if necessary, and select the Oil Production sheet.

2. Search for Help on how to add a comment to a cell. Read the instructions.

3. Add the comment Notice the dramatic decrease to cell C13.

4. Move your pointer onto the cell. Notice the username is included. This name is taken from the Office registration.

5. Use the Tools, Options menu to find the username and change it to your own.

6. Insert a second comment. Notice the name displayed reflects the new username. Change the username back if you are not the sole operator of the computer.

7. Save the workbook and close it.

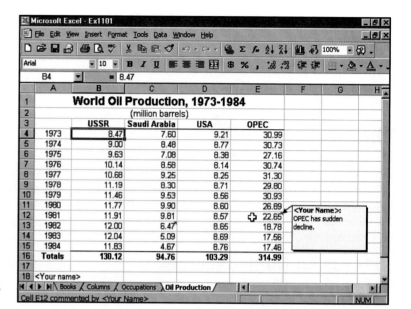

Lesson: 12

Filling, Copying, and Printing

Introduction

There are many instances where you need to *fill* in a series of dates or times as row or column labels. You may also find occasions where the same text must be entered into numerous cells. Excel has powerful tools that help you with these tasks and can improve your efficiency. In this lesson, you learn how to fill sequences of labels and how to copy cell contents in order to produce a work schedule for several part-time employees. Finally, you learn how to change the orientation of the page to print out sheets that are wider than they are tall.

Visual Summary

When you have completed this entire lesson, you will have created a worksheet that looks like this:

4/23/99

Schedule for Jan 6 to Jan 12							
	Monday	Tuesday	Wednesday	Thursday	Friday	Saturday	Sunday
8:00 AM	Bill	Bill	Angi	Bill	Grace	Scott	Scott
8:30 AM	Bill	Bill	Angi	Bill	Grace	Scott	Scott
9:00 AM	Bill	Bill	Angi	Bill	Grace	Scott	Scott
9:30 AM	Bill	Bill	Angi	Bill	Grace	Scott	Scott
10:00 AM	Bill	Bill	Angi	Bill	Grace	Scott	Scott
10:30 AM	Bill	Bill	Angi	Bill	Grace	Scott	Scott
11:00 AM	Bill	Bill	Angi	Bill	Grace	Scott	Scott
11:30 AM	Bill	Bill	Angi	Bill	Grace	Scott	Scott
12:00 PM	Bill	Bill	Angi	Bill	Grace	Scott	Scott
12:30 PM	Bill	Bill	Angi	Bill	Grace	Scott	Scott
1:00 PM	Bill	Bill	Angi	Bill	Grace	Scott	Scott
1:30 PM	Bill	Bill	Angi	Bill	Grace	Scott	Scott
2:00 PM	Derek	Alexis	Alexis	Grace	Derek	Angi	Scott
2:30 PM	Derek	Alexis	Alexis	Grace	Derek	Angi	Scott
3:00 PM	Derek	Alexis	Alexis	Grace	Derek	Angi	Scott
3:30 PM	Derek	Alexis	Alexis	Grace	Derek	Angi	Scott
4:00 PM	Derek	Alexis	Alexis	Grace	Derek	Angi	Scott
4:30 PM	Derek	Alexis	Alexis	Grace	Derek	Angi	Scott
5:00 PM	Derek	Alexis	Alexis	Grace	Derek	Angi	Scott
5:30 PM	Derek	Alexis	Alexis	Grace	Derek	Angi	Scott
6:00 PM	Derek	Alexis	Alexis	Grace	Derek	Angi	Scott
6:30 PM	Derek	Alexis	Alexis	Grace	Derek	Angi	Scott
7:00 PM	Derek	Alexis	Alexis	Grace	Derek	Angi	Scott
7:30 PM	Derek	Alexis	Alexis	Grace	Derek	Angi	Scott
8:00 PM	Derek	Alexis	Alexis	Grace	Derek	Angi	Scott
8:30 PM	Derek	Alexis	Alexis	Grace	Derek	Angi	Scott
9:00 PM	Derek	Alexis	Alexis	Grace	Derek	Angi	Scott

TASK 1

Creating Sequential Labels
Why would I do this?

Many worksheets use days of the week, months of the year, fiscal quarters, or other sequences of labels as column or row headings. Excel recognizes text that begins such sequences and assists you in entering them. This feature of Excel improves your efficiency in creating your worksheet.

In this task, you learn how to create sequential labels.

1 Launch **Excel** and open **Less1201** from the **Student\Lesson12** folder on the CD-ROM disc that came with this book and save it as **Work Schedule** on your floppy disk.

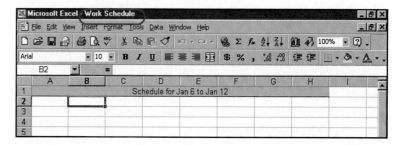

2 Select cell **B2**, type **Monday**, and press Tab.

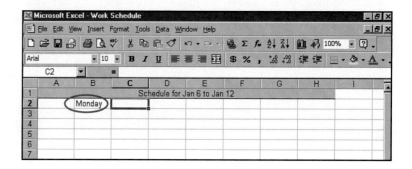

3 Select cell **B2** again. Move the pointer to the small black square at the lower-right corner of the cell, called a *fill handle*. The pointer changes to a black plus sign.

Fill handle

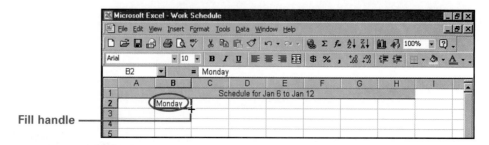

4 Click and drag the fill handle to the right to cell **H2**. Notice that the name of the next day in the sequence is displayed in a ScreenTip as you drag.

ScreenTip —

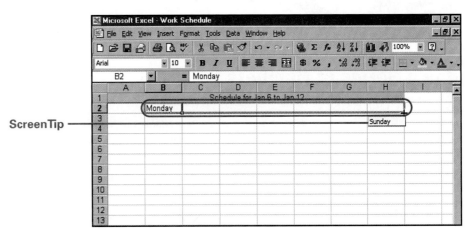

5 Release the mouse button. The sequence of days is filled in.

In Depth: There are several interesting options available when you fill cells with dates or numbers. Hold down the right mouse button rather than the left when you drag the fill handle and you get a shortcut menu of options. One option is to fill weekdays, excluding weekend days. Other choices include filling months or years, and numeric series using growth, linear, or specific trends. These options are explored in the end-of-lesson exercises.

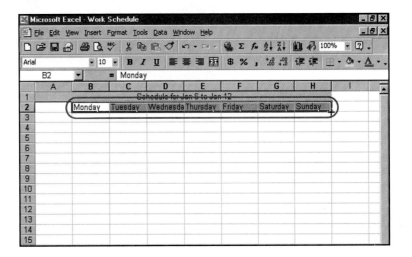

6 Click the **Save** button. The workbook is saved on your floppy disk.

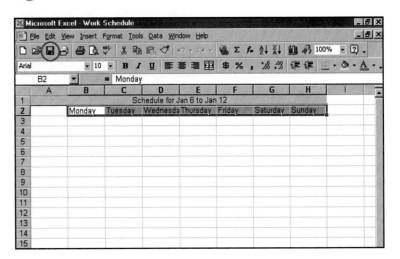

TASK 2

Creating a Series of Numbers
Why would I do this?

Normally, numbers in a worksheet are entered in order to make calculations, which is why they are entered in separate cells. Sometimes you use numbers to represent dates or times as the labels for rows or columns. Excel is able to recognize when date formats such as 9/5 or 9-5-00 are entered in a cell. You can choose how to format dates or times.

In this task, you learn how to create a series of times as row labels. You also learn how to set both common and custom intervals.

1 Select cell **A3**, type **8:00**, and press ⏎Enter.

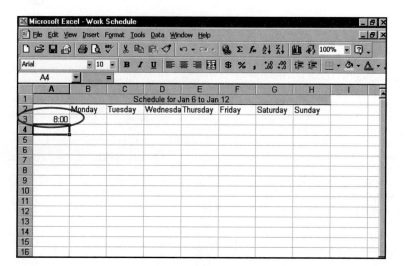

2 Select cell **A3** again. Click and drag the fill handle down to cell **A10**.

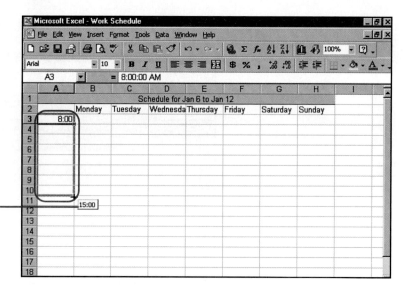

ScreenTip displays series value using a 24-hour format

3 Release the mouse button. Notice that the sequence of times increases by one hour and each time is displayed using a 24-hour format.

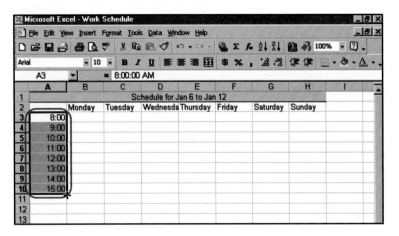

4 Click the **Undo** button. The fill is undone.

This company schedules its part-time workers on the half hour. In order to establish this half-hour pattern, you need to enter data in at least two cells before applying the fill.

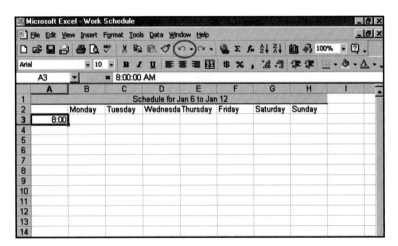

5 Select cell A4, type **8:30**, and press **⏎Enter**.

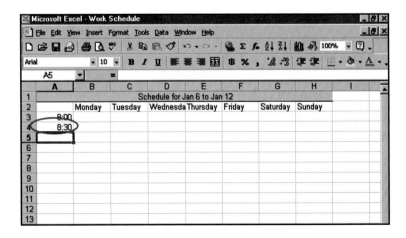

12

6 Select cells A3 and A4.

Caution: Remember, since the first cell of a selected group does not change background color, cell A3 may not look to be selected. The thick line border encloses both cells if they are both selected.

It is important that both cells are selected to indicate what interval to use to create the rest of the series.

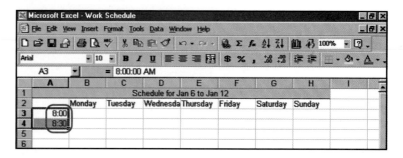

7 Click and drag the fill handle down to cell **A18**.

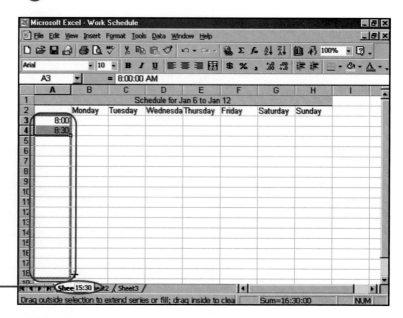

ScreenTip displays series value using 24-hour format

8 Release the mouse button. The sequence is filled in half-hour increments.

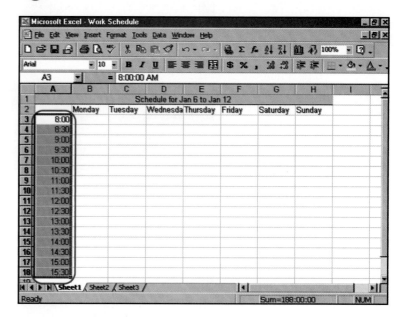

9 Use the vertical scrollbar to scroll down to show rows 18 through 30.

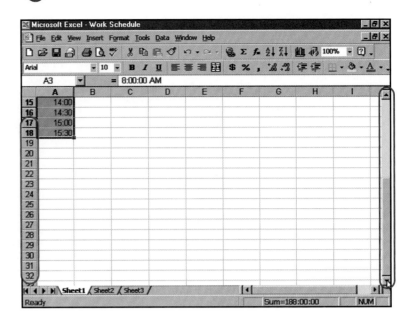

10 Click and drag the fill handle down to cell **A29**. Release the mouse and the sequence is extended.

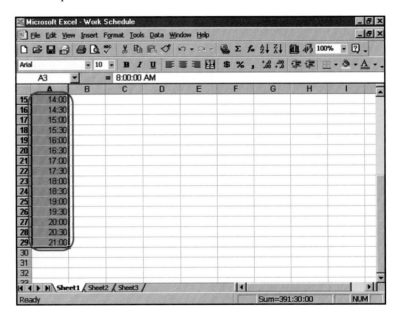

11 With cells **A3** through **A29** still selected, choose **Format, Cells** to open the Format Cells dialog box. Click the **Number** tab, if necessary.

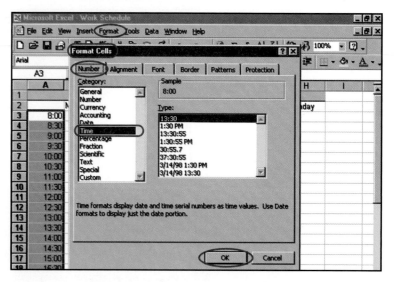

12 Click the **1:30 PM** sample format and click **OK**.

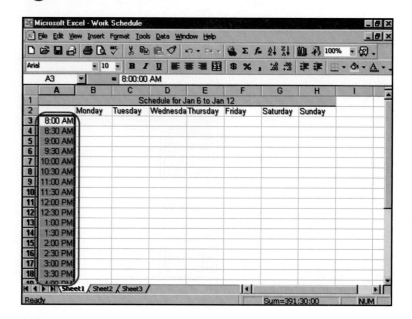

Freezing Panes and Changing Zoom
Why would I do this?

When rows and columns are too long to be viewed on the screen in their entirety, you have to scroll the window in order to see cells at the end of the row or column. Unfortunately, when you get to the cell, the row or column label is no longer visible, so you may easily mistake one row or column for another.

In this task, you learn how to change the magnification of the view so that you can see larger areas of the worksheet. You also learn how to freeze the row and/or column labels so they stay visible while you scroll.

1 Select cell **A1**. This step is not required, but ensures that the upper-left part of the sheet remains visible when you change the magnification.

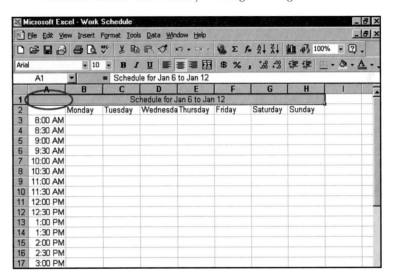

2 Click on the down arrow next to the **Zoom** box on the Standard toolbar. A list of magnification percentages is displayed.

List of Zoom options —

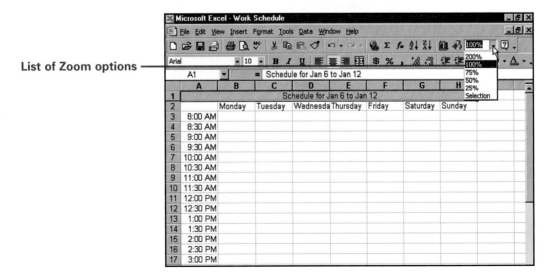

3 Click **75%**. All of the screen components are displayed at 3/4 size so more information fits on the screen.

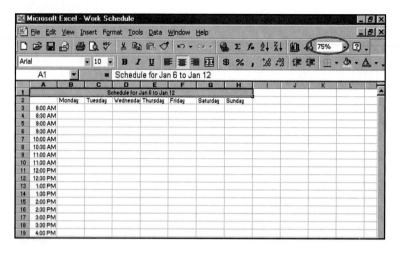

4 Click the down arrow next to the **Zoom** box and click on **100%** to return to normal magnification.

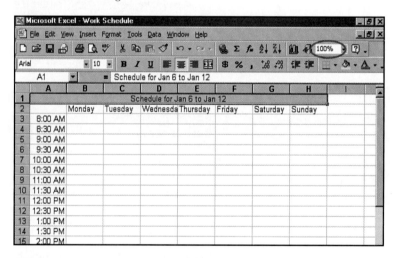

5 Click cell **B3**. Notice that this cell is below rows 1 and 2 and to the right of column A. We want to freeze the two rows above and the column to the left of B3.

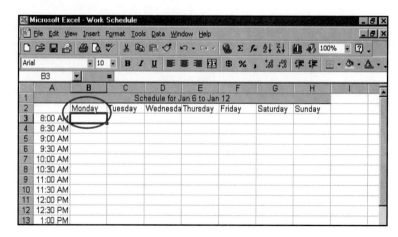

6 Choose **Window, Freeze Panes**. The rows above the selected cell (rows 1 and 2) and the columns to the left of the selected cell (column A) remain on the screen, regardless of how far to the right or bottom you may scroll.

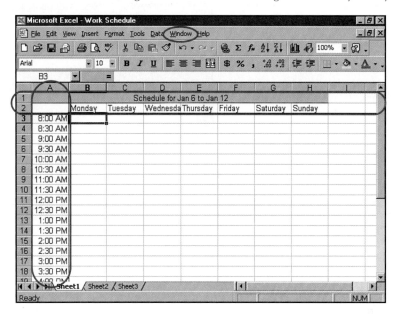

7 Scroll down until row **14** follows row **2**. Notice that rows 1 and 2 remain on the screen.

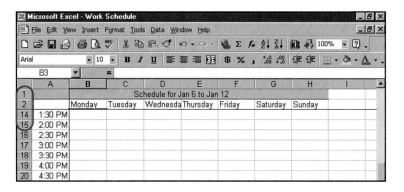

8 Scroll to the right until column **D** is next to column **A**. Notice that column A remains on the screen.

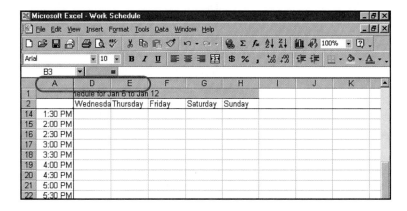

9 Choose **Window, Unfreeze Panes**. Columns B and C and rows 3 through 13 return to view.

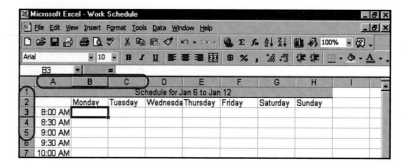

TASK 4

Copying Cell Contents

Why would I do this?

Some worksheets require the display of the same data in many cells. For example, a business that is open from 8 a.m. to 9 p.m., Monday through Sunday, uses six different part-time employees. If you wanted to post a work schedule for these employees, you would have to fill out a table with more than 200 cells.

In this task, you learn how to use the fill, copy, and paste techniques to fill out a form with repetitive data.

1 Select cell **B3**, type **Bill**, and press Enter.

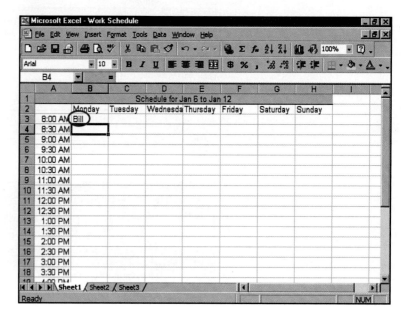

2 Select cell **B3** again. Click and drag the fill handle down to cell **B14**. Release the mouse button. Bill's name is filled into the cells from **B4** to **B14**.

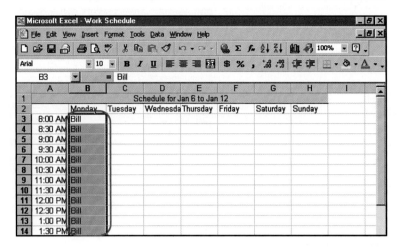

3 Click and drag the fill handle to the right to cell **C14**. Release the mouse button. The cells to the right are filled with Bill's name.

Caution: If a custom list that starts with Bill has already been created on your computer, you may see the custom list rather than Bill's name. If this occurs, you can either use the copy and paste method or delete the custom list by choosing **Tools**, **Options**, **Custom Lists**.

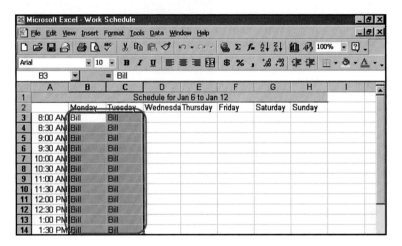

4 Click cell **B3** again to select a cell that contains Bill's name. Click the Copy button on the Standard toolbar.

Copy button

Marquee around cell selected for copying

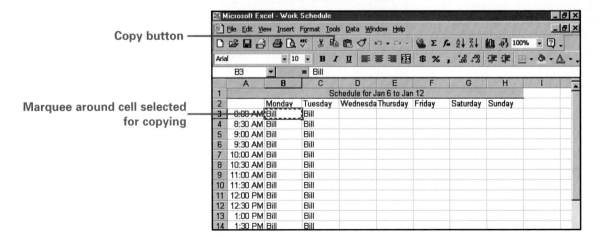

5 Select cells **E3** through **E14**.

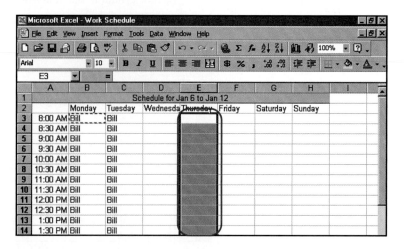

6 Click the **Paste** button on the standard toolbar. Bill's name fills into the entire cell range.

Paste button ———

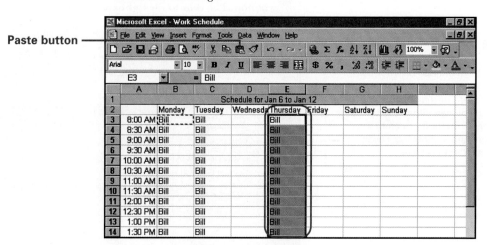

7 Use the fill and copy techniques described above to fill out the rest of the schedule. Click the **Save** button to save your work.

In Depth: The figure is shown at 85% percent Zoom and the view is set to Full Screen to show the whole work schedule. You do not have to make these changes.

This figure has been altered to display the full table ————

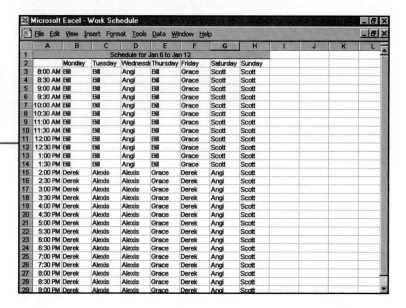

TASK 5

Selecting a Range of Cells to Print and Previewing the Printout
Why would I do this?

If a worksheet is too large to fit on one page or for some other reason you do not want to print an entire sheet, you may select a portion of the sheet to print. It is useful to first preview the printout on the screen to catch errors in layout and formatting, such as a column printing on a page by itself. You can make the needed adjustments and save time and paper by not printing mistakes.

In this task, you learn how to print part of the work schedule and to preview it before printing.

1 Scroll down to display rows **15** through **29**. Select the cells from **A15** through **H29**. This includes the row labels and all of the work scheduled after 2 p.m.

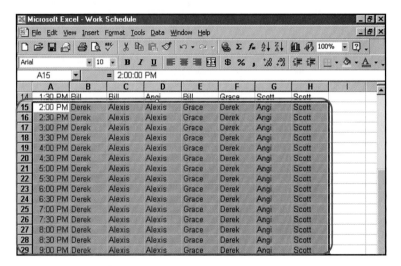

2 Choose File, Print, Selection.

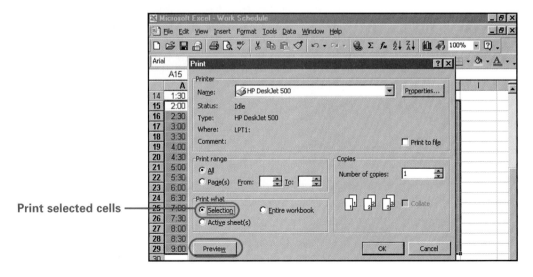

Print selected cells ———

3 Click the **Preview** button. The page is displayed as it will look when printed.

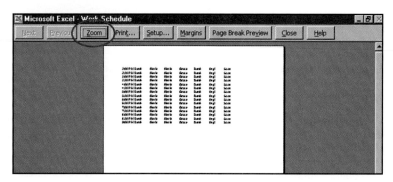

4 Click the **Zoom box** to switch the magnification. Notice that the column labels in rows 1 and 2 are not shown, because they were not part of the print area selected.

In Depth: There is an option in the Page Setup dialog box under the Sheet tab that will allow you to specify rows to print at the top of each page.

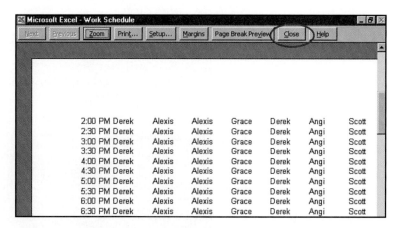

5 Click on the **Close** button on the Print Preview toolbar. The worksheet now has a vertical dotted line to indicate how many columns fit on the page.

Quick Tip: You can also preview the printed pages by clicking the **Print Preview** button.

Print Preview button —

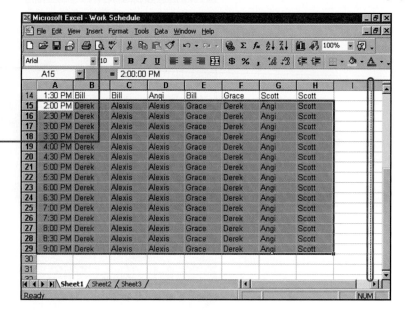

TASK 6

Using Page Setup to Enhance a Printout
Why would I do this?

There are several options you can use to improve the appearance and readability of your printed worksheets. Sometimes a worksheet has many columns, and the page orientation needs to be changed to accommodate all the information. It is also useful to add information in a header that you want repeated on each page of the printed worksheet. This may include the current date, the name of the file, or your name. Lastly, to give your work a professional appearance, the columns of data can be centered on the page.

In this task, you learn how to change the orientation of the page to handle wider worksheets, center data on the page, and add your name and an automatic date to a header.

1 Choose **File**, **Page Setup**. The Page Setup dialog box opens. Click the **Page** tab, if it is not already selected.

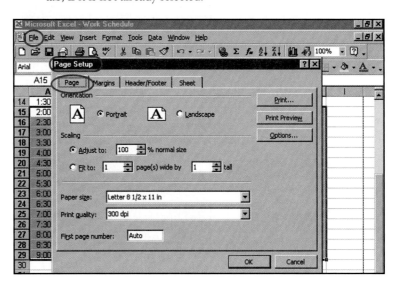

2 Click the **Landscape** option. This option is useful when printing worksheets that have many columns.

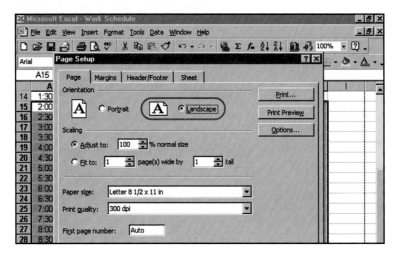

3 Click the **Margins** tab.

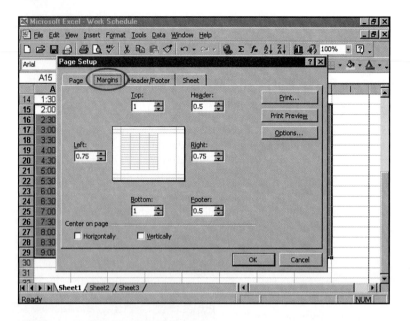

4 Click the **Horizontally** option under **Center on page** at the bottom left of the dialog box. The sample layout in the middle of the window shows how the data will be centered on the page.

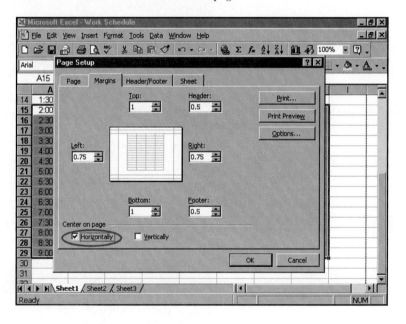

5 Click the **Header/Footer** tab. The Header/Footer page opens. Headers appear at the top and footers appear at the bottom of each page of a printout.

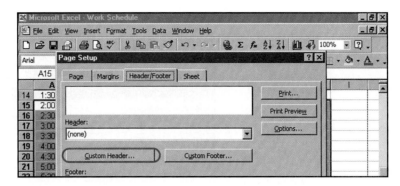

6 Click the **Custom Header** button. The Header dialog box opens. The header is divided into the **Left section**, the **Center section**, and the **Right section**.

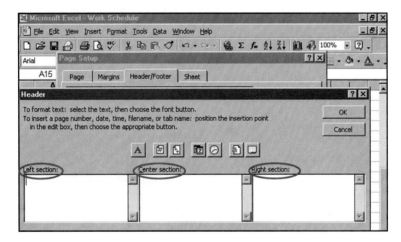

7 Move the pointer to the **Center section** and click. The insertion point appears, centered. Type your name.

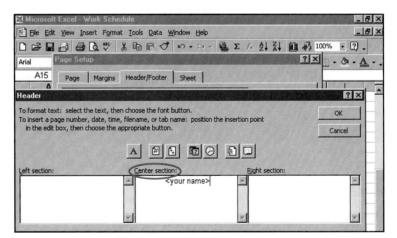

8 Press the ⌨Tab⇄ key to move to the **Right section**. Click the **Date** button. &[Date] is placed at the right margin. &[Date] is replaced by the current date each time the sheet is printed.

Code used to determine and display the current date

Date button

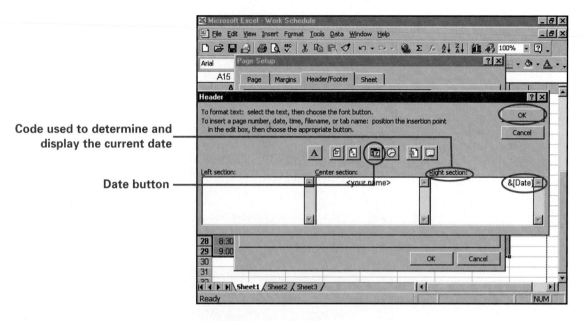

9 Click the **OK** button in the Header dialog box. The sample displays your name in the **Center section** of the header and the current date in the **Right section**.

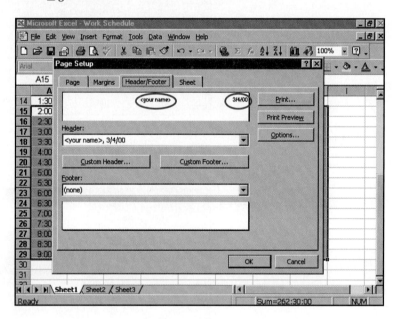

10 Click the **Sheet** tab. The Sheet page opens.

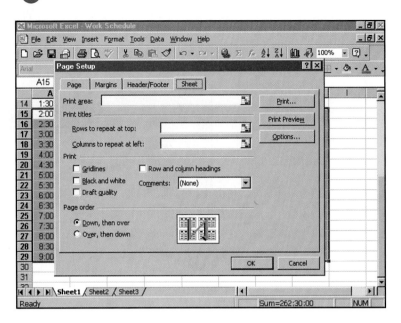

11 Click the **Gridlines** option to print the *gridlines* that outline the cells and make it easier to follow rows and columns.

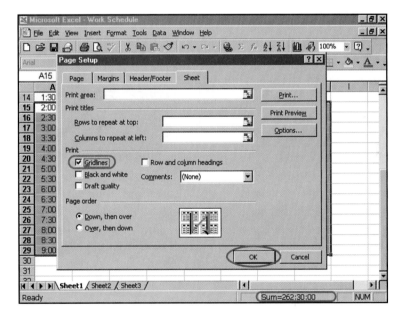

12 Click **OK**. The Page Setup dialog box closes. Scroll to the top of the page and widen column D to display all of the heading.

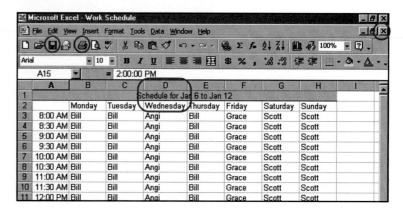

13 Click the **Print** button. Your table prints with your name and the current date in the header. Save your changes and close the workbook. Leave Excel open for use in the following exercises.

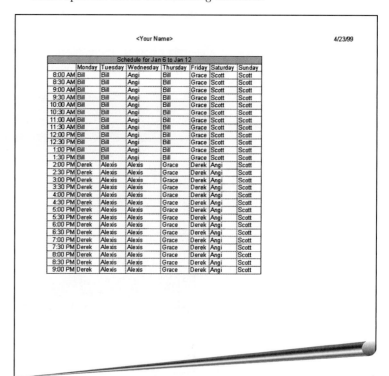

Comprehension Exercises

Comprehension exercises are designed to check your memory and understanding of the basic concepts in this lesson. You distinguish between true and false statements, identify new screen elements, and match terms with related statements. If you are uncertain of the correct answer, refer to the task number following each item (for example, T4 refers to Task 4) and review that task until you are confident that you can provide a correct response.

True-False

Circle either T or F.

T F **1.** If you select cell B4 and freeze the panes, rows 1 through 3 would be frozen, as well as column A. **(T3)**

T F **2.** The fill handle is located in the lower-left corner of the selected cell. **(T1)**

T F **3.** If you select a cell that contains the word "Jane" and drag the fill handle to an adjacent cell, the adjacent cell would contain the word "Jane". **(T4)**

T F **4.** To print a range of cells, select the range and then click the **Print** button on the toolbar. **(T5)**

T F **5.** If you select a Zoom percentage of 75%, you can see more cells on the screen. **(T3)**

T F **6.** The **Copy** button on the Standard toolbar looks like a small clipboard with a page in front of it. **(T4)**

T F **7.** The Preview window has a **Zoom box**, but it only toggles back and forth between two sizes. **(T5)**

T F **8.** If you had a worksheet that was wider (columns) than it was long (rows), you would use the Portrait page orientation. **(T6)**

T F **9.** You can use the Zoom setting to change the size of the table when it is printed. **(T3)**

T F **10.** It is better to print several copies of the worksheet as you create it to make sure the final copy is error free. **(T5)**

Identifying Parts of the Excel Screen

Refer to the figure and identify the numbered parts of the screen. Write the letter of the correct label in the space next to the number.

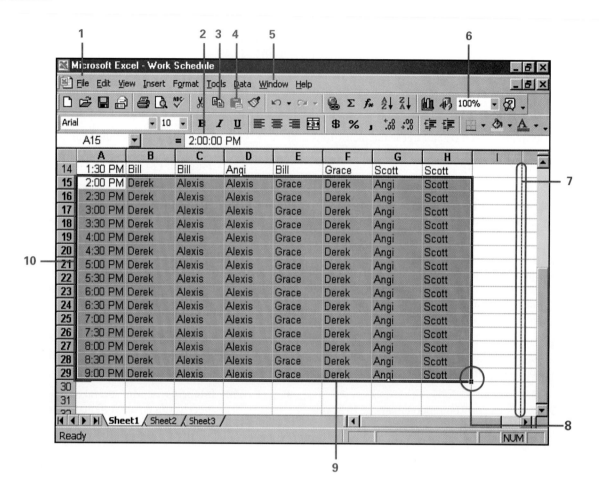

1. _____   **A.** Fill handle (T1)

2. _____   **B.** Copy button (T4)

3. _____   **C.** Paste button (T4)

4. _____   **D.** Zoom box (T3)

5. _____   **E.** Freeze Panes option found here (T3)

6. _____   **F.** Indicates the last column that fits on the page (T5)

7. _____   **G.** Selected area (T5)

8. _____   **H.** Page Setup options found here (T6)

9. _____   **I.** An example of a 12-hour time format (T2)

10. _____   **J.** Repeating series at half-hour intervals (T2)

Matching

Match the statements below to the word or phrase that is the best match from the list. Write the letter of the matching word or phrase in the space provided next to the number.

1. ___ An example of a first label in a sequence (T1)

2. ___ Values that can be used to fill a column or row with times that are separated by fifteen minute increments (T2)

3. ___ Small box at the lower-right corner of a selected cell (T4)

4. ___ The method used to fill the cells in two non-adjacent columns with the same word (T4)

5. ___ The method used to keep the first row and column visible on the screen even when you scroll (T3)

6. ___ To select a range of cells to print, you would do this (T5)

7. ___ The page orientation used to print worksheets that are longer (more rows) than they are wide (T6)

8. ___ The lines between the cells on a worksheet (T6)

9. ___ The option in the Page Setup window that allows you to center the data left to right (T6)

10. ___ The button that changes the size of cells and their contents on the screen but not on the printout (T3)

A. Portrait

B. Gridlines

C. Freeze Panes

D. Zoom

E. Copy and paste

F. Center horizontally

G. Select the range and use **File**, **Print**, **Selection**

H. Center vertically

I. Fill handle

J. January

K. 9:00, 9:15

Reinforcement Exercises

Reinforcement exercises are designed to reinforce the skills you have learned by applying them to a new situation. Detailed instructions are provided along with a figure, where appropriate, to illustrate the final result. The Reinforcement exercises that follow should be completed sequentially. Leave the workbook open at the end of each exercise for use in the next exercise until you are specifically directed to close it.

Open **Less1202** from the **Student\Lesson12** folder on the CD-ROM disc and save it as **Ex1201** on your floppy disk for use in the following exercises.

R1—Create a Sheet to Track Leases

In this exercise, you create a lease report worksheet for a small office building.

1. Select **Sheet1**. Rename the tab at the bottom **Leases**.

2. Refer to the figure and fill in the sheet. Check the following steps to make sure that you have completed all of the required steps.

3. Fill in the months in column **A**.

4. Select the first two office numbers in cells **B3** and **C3**, then fill in the column labels up to **120** in column **L**.

5. Type **Armstrong** in cell **B4**. Copy the name into the cells as shown for offices **100**, **102**, and **104**. (Try the **Fill** method, just to see what happens.)

6. Use **Fill** and/or **Copy** to put **Tax** (a tax accounting firm) in office **104** from **July** to **December** and in offices **108** through **118**. Place **Arch** (an architectural firm) in **106** and **Admin** (administrative staff) in **120**.

7. Adjust column widths, if necessary, to show all data.

8. Center the headers in row **3**.

9. Change the page orientation to **Landscape**.

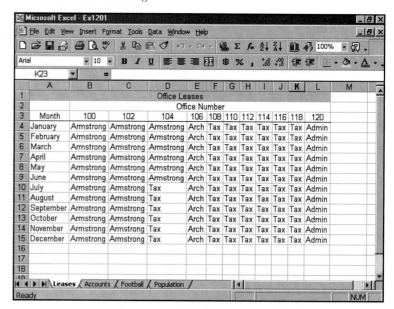

10. Place your name in the center of the header.

11. Save the workbook.

12. Preview and print the sheet.

R2—Create a Sheet to Track Time

In this exercise, you create a sheet to track time spent on several different accounts during the work week.

1. Select **Sheet2**. Rename the sheet tab at the bottom **Accounts**. Change the **Zoom** to **75%**.

2. Fill in the days of the week (weekdays only) and the dates as shown in the figure. See the steps below for additional information.

3. Select cell **A4**.

4. Click the fill handle with the right mouse button and drag to cell **A23**. Release the mouse button.

5. Select **Fill Weekdays** from the shortcut menu. Make sure that there are no Saturdays or Sundays.

6. Select cell **B4**. Repeat the same process to fill in the dates for the weekdays. Notice how the program displays the year 2000.

7. Add your name to the left side of the footer.

8. Save the workbook. Preview and print the sheet.

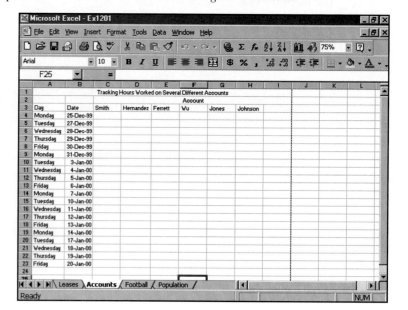

R3—Create a Schedule

In this exercise, you create a schedule for a once-a-week activity.

1. Select **Sheet3**.

2. Change the name on the tab from **Sheet3** to **Football**.

3. Fill in the dates to match the figure. Refer to the steps below for additional information.

4. Select the dates in cells **A3** and **A4**. Drag the fill handle down to cell **A14**.

5. Repeat this process for the games in column **C**.

6. Add your name in the left side of the header.

7. Save the workbook. Preview and print the sheet.

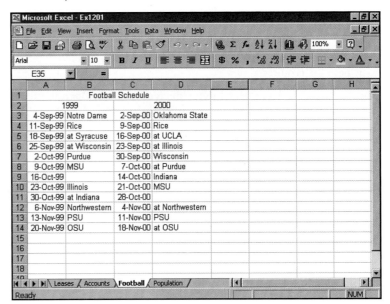

R4—Project a Population Growth

In this exercise, you project a population growth of 1 percent per year for the United States for 20 years.

1. Select **Sheet4**.

2. Change the name on the tab from **Sheet4** to **Population**.

3. Fill in a sequence of years from **1997** to **2017** in column **A**. Refer to the figure for guidance. All the years do not show in the figure, but it provides a general idea of the layout of the worksheet.

4. Select cell **B3**, which shows the 1997 population of the United States in millions of people.

5. Use the right mouse button to drag the fill handle to cell **B23**. Release the mouse button.

6. When the shortcut menu appears, choose **Series** (not Fill Series).

7. In the **Series** window, choose **Growth** and set the **Step Value** to **1.01**. This causes the value in each cell to be 1 percent larger than the preceding value. Click **OK**. (The value in the year 2017 will be over 300 million.)

8. Format the population cells to show two decimal places.

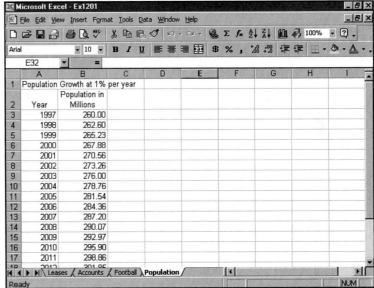

9. Add your name in the left side of the header.

10. Save the workbook. Preview and print the sheet.

11. Close the workbook.

Challenge

Challenge exercises are designed to test your ability to apply your skills to new situations with less detailed instruction. These exercises also challenge you to expand your repertoire of skills by using Excel commands that are similar to those you have already learned. The desired outcome is clearly defined, but you have more freedom to choose the steps needed to achieve the required result.

The following Challenge exercises use the file **Less1203**. Open this file from the CD-ROM disc in the **Student\Lesson12** folder and save it on your floppy disk as **Ex1202**.

C1—Customize a Fill List

Excel recognizes several common sequences of names. You may want to create your own. For example, if your company works six days a week (closed Sunday) you may want to fill in a sequence of days that does not include Sundays. In this example, three friends decide to buy a car together and take turns paying the car payment. Their names will appear many times, in the same sequence. If you create a custom list, you can fill in a column of names using the fill handle.

Goal: Create a custom list of three names that can be used to fill in the column that shows whose turn it is to pay the loan.

This worksheet contains formulas that you learn about in later lessons. It has also been protected so that you will not accidentally overwrite those formulas (see Discovery exercise 3 in Lesson 10).

Use the following guidelines:

1. Select the **Car Payment** sheet, if necessary.

2. Enter the names **Jack**, **Bill**, and **Mary** in cells **E4**, **E5**, and **E6**, respectively. Select these three cells.

3. Choose **Tools**, **Options**, **Custom Lists**, **Import**. Your list of entries is displayed. Click **OK**.

4. Fill in the rest of the names in column **E**. The three names should repeat so that each person is responsible for a payment every third month.

5. Save the workbook. Leave the workbook open for use in the next exercise.

C2—Use Header and Footer Options

There are several built-in options for headers and footers. In this exercise, you print the Car Payment sheets using a built-in header and footer.

Goal: Print a two-page worksheet using one of the built-in headers and footers.

Use the following guidelines:

1. Use the workbook **Ex1202** that was created in the previous exercise. If you do not have this file, open **Less1203** from the **Student\Lesson12** folder on the CD-ROM disc and save it as **Ex1202**.

2. Choose **File**, **Page Setup**, **Header/Footer**.

3. Click the list arrow at the right end of the **Header** box. Select the built-in header that begins **Prepared by**....

4. Use a similar method to select a built-in footer.

5. Preview the printout. Print the first page.

6. Save the workbook. Leave the workbook open for use in the next exercise.

C3—Include Row and Column Labels for Multiple Sheet Printouts

If a worksheet is too large to print on one sheet, the data prints on additional sheets, but the row and column labels do not. You can end up with sheets of data that have no labels and are hard to identify. It is possible to specify rows or columns that print on every page in order to provide labels for pages beyond the first page.

Goal: Specify that the first three rows of the Car Payment sheet print on all pages.

1. Use the workbook **Ex1202** that was created in exercise C1. If you do not have this file, open **Less1203** from the **Student\Lesson 12** folder on the CD-ROM disc and save it as **Ex1202**.

2. Select **File**, **Page Setup**, **Sheet**.

3. Click the **Rows to repeat at top** box.

4. Click the **Collapse Dialog Box** button at the right of the box and drag down the first three rows. Click the

   Expand Dialog Box button. The **Rows to repeat at top** box should indicate the first three rows with the code **$1:$3**.

5. Preview the second page of the printout to confirm that the first three rows print there as well.

6. Print both pages of the sheet.

7. Save the workbook and close it.

Discovery

Discovery exercises are designed to help you learn how to teach yourself a new skill. In each exercise, you discover something new that is related to the topic taught in this lesson. You may be directed to use built-in wizards or some of the extensive Help features provided in Excel to discover new features and learn new skills with minimum assistance from books or instructors. The required outcome demonstrates your ability to apply the new skill. You determine the choice of topic, worksheet design, and steps of execution.

D1—Use Keyboard Shortcuts

If you have to do a lot of cutting, copying, and pasting, it is time consuming to take your hand off the keyboard and use a mouse to click a button on a toolbar or select an option from a menu. You may also need to cut, copy, or paste when a dialog box is open and the toolbars and menus are not available. At times like these, you can use the [Ctrl] key plus a keyboard letter to perform the task.

Some tasks require that you use menu options, but it would still be faster to use the keyboard to make the selection. In these cases, you can hold the [Alt] key and press the key that is underlined (the hotkey) in the menu option to choose that option.

When you are done specifying your selections in a dialog box or window, you may need to choose a button such as **OK**, **Next**, or **Finish**. If a button has a bold outline, it can be selected by pressing [↵Enter].

Goal: Learn how to use the [Ctrl] key with another key to perform functions, the [Alt] key to select menu options, the [⇧Shift] key with arrow keys to select cells, and [↵Enter] to push buttons.

1. Open **Less1204** from the **Student\Lesson12** folder on the CD-ROM disc and save it as **Ex1203**. Select the **Keyboard** sheet, if necessary.

2. Use the Office Assistant to find the quick reference to keyboard shortcuts. Print out the Help page titled **Keys for editing data**.

3. Use the arrow keys to move the selection to cell **A1**. Press [⇧Shift] and use the down arrow to select cells **A1** through **A12**.

4. Press [Ctrl] and **C** to copy the contents of the cells.

5. Use the arrow key to move the selection to cell **C1**. Press [Ctrl] and **V** to paste the selection.

6. Cut **Wednesday** out of cell **C3** and paste it into cell **E3** (use [Ctrl] and **X** to cut).

7. Copy **Wednesday** and paste it into cells **E4** through **E12**.

8. Use the ⬆Shift and arrow keys to select cells **A1** through **E12**.

9. Notice that the **Format** menu option has an underlined letter **o** (this is called a hotkey). Hold the Alt key and press the **o** key. Type the letter **e** in C**e**lls to open the Format Cells dialog window.

10. Use the arrow keys on the keyboard to select the **Font** tab. Use a combination of arrow keys, Tab↹ key, and the Alt plus a hotkey to choose **Bold Italic** and 14 points as shown in the figure.

11. Notice that the **OK** button at the bottom of the window has a bold outline. Press ↵Enter to push the **OK** button. Cells A1 through E12 are formatted as described.

12. Use these keyboard methods to format cell **A1** as **Book Antigua, Bold, 16 points** as shown in the figure.

13. Save the workbook. Leave the workbook open for use in the next exercise.

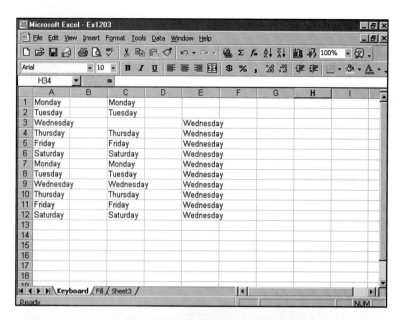

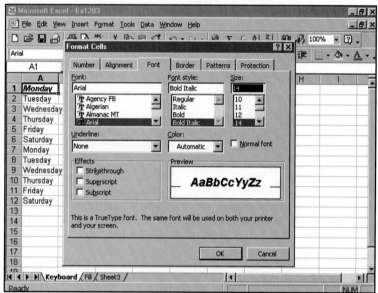

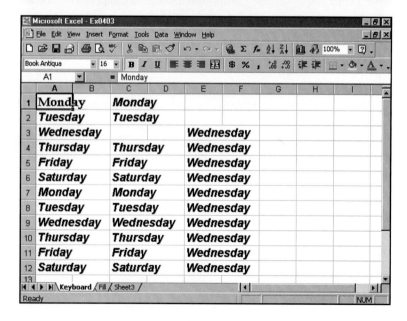

D2—Advanced Fill Options

The right mouse button can be used with the fill handle to provide several useful options.

Goal: Use the fill handle with the right mouse button to fill in the columns as shown in the figure. Use the Series option for the last two and experiment with the step feature to determine how to produce a linear and a growth series.

1. Use **Ex1203** from the previous Discovery exercise. If you did not do that exercise, open **Less1204** from the **Student\Lesson12** folder on the CD-ROM disc and save it as **Ex1203**. Select the **Fill** sheet.

2. Fill in the columns as shown. The last column uses a **2%** growth factor.

3. Save the workbook. Leave it open for use in the next exercise.

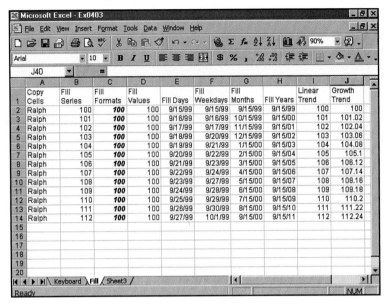

D3—Set Print Area and Print Preview

If you click the **Print** button on the toolbar, the entire sheet is printed. You can specify a different default range that will be printed automatically. The range is called the print area. If you want to print a small range within a single sheet, use **File**, **Print Area**, **Set Print Area** option. If you want to control the areas printed together in a multipage printout, you need to know how to use the **Page Break Preview** option.

1. Use **Ex1203** from the previous Discovery exercise. If you did not do that exercise, open **Less1204** from the **Student\Lesson 12** folder on the CD-ROM disc and save it as **Ex1203**. Select the **Fill** sheet.

2. Use the first method mentioned above to set the print area to cells **C1** through **C14**. Click the **Print** button on the toolbar and print that range automatically.

3. Use Help to learn about setting the print areas with the **Page Break Preview** option. Print the sheet on two pages where the second page has the **Linear Growth** and **Growth Trend** columns and the other columns are on the first page.

4. Save the workbook and close it.

Lesson: 13

Making the Computer Do the Math

Introduction

Excel is at your command, whether you need to do basic arithmetic or advanced statistics. Once you set up a worksheet, you can change the numbers many times to see how those changes affect the "bottom line." When you change a number in a worksheet, all the formulas that use that number are immediately recalculated.

In this lesson, you work on three worksheets. The first worksheet shows you how to perform basic math calculations using Excel. The next worksheet shows you how to use the Fill operation with a formula and how to use absolute and relative cell references. In the third worksheet, you learn how to use the Paste Function dialog box to calculate a monthly payment on a car or house loan. You also calculate the total amount you will pay for the loan.

Visual Summary

When you have completed this entire lesson, you will have created three worksheets that look like these:

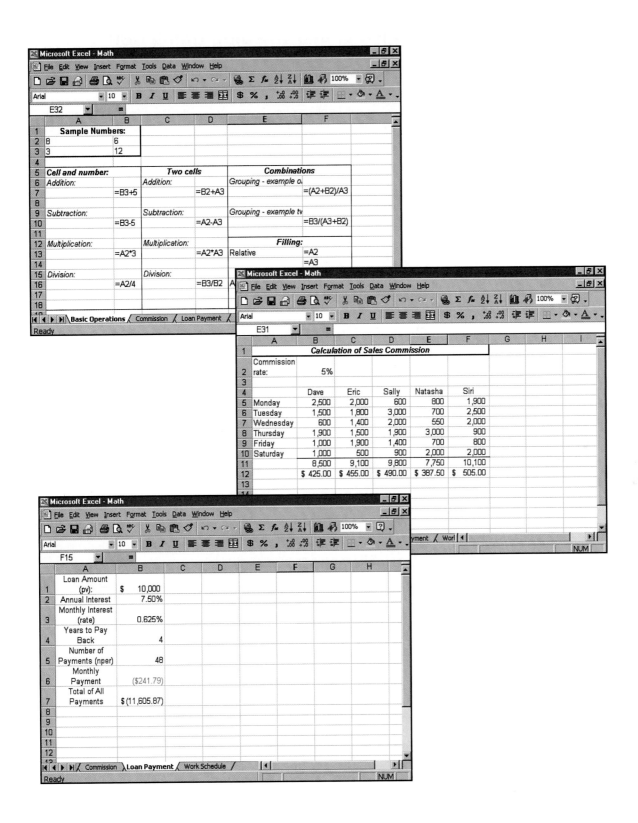

TASK *1*

Adding, Subtracting, Multiplying, and Dividing Using Cell References and Numbers

Why would I do this?

Worksheets have been used in paper form for years as a means of keeping track of financial data. The value of using an electronic worksheet program such as Excel is its capability to quickly make mathematical calculations. Before the era of computers, people were employed to calculate rows and columns of numbers for use in navigational charts or other types of computational charts. The job title for the people who performed these calculations was Computer. In today's world, electronic computers keep track of financial data and perform mathematical computations. Computers are faster and more accurate than people for these kinds of tasks.

When you use Excel to perform a mathematical operation, it needs to be done in a way that is similar to ordinary math, but with a few special rules. For example, all formulas must begin with an equal sign (=), and you use cell names in the formulas.

In this lesson, you practice applying the basic formula rules in Excel. The sheet you produce serves as a convenient reference for later use.

1 Open **Less1301** from the **Student\Lesson13** folder on the CD-ROM disc that came with this book. Save it as **Math** on your floppy disk.

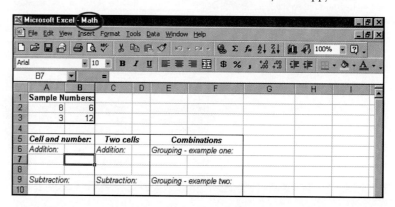

2 Select cell **B7** and type **=B3+5** in the cell. This formula adds the contents of cell B3 and the number 5.

Enter button on the formula bar ⎯

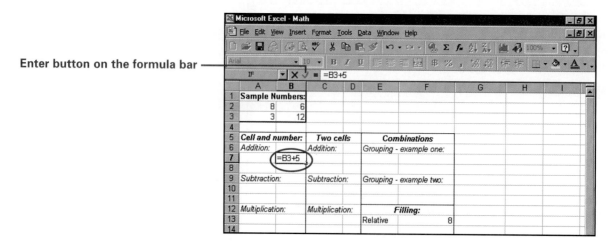

3 Click the **Enter** button on the formula bar. Notice that the cell B3 contains the number 12, and cell B7 displays the result of adding 5 to the contents of B3.

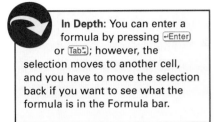

In Depth: You can enter a formula by pressing ⏎Enter or Tab↹; however, the selection moves to another cell, and you have to move the selection back if you want to see what the formula is in the Formula bar.

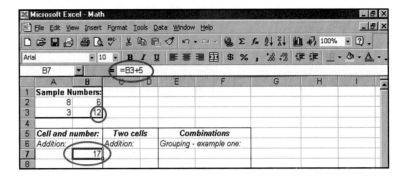

4 Select cell **B10** and type **=B3-5**. Determine what you think the answer should be before you proceed. In this case, you subtract 5 from the contents of cell B3. Click the **Enter** button on the formula bar. If you anticipated a different answer, take the time to figure out why.

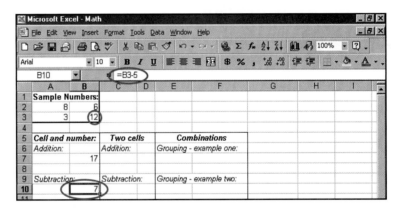

5 Select cell **B13**, type **=A2*3**, determine what you think the answer should be, and click the **Enter** button on the formula bar. Excel uses the asterisk to indicate multiplication.

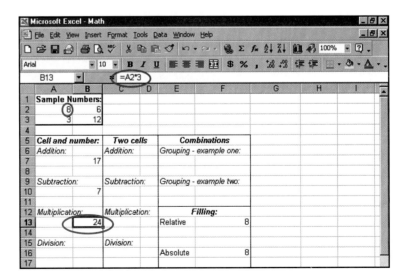

6 Select cell **B16**, type **=A2/4**, anticipate the answer, and click the **Enter** button on the formula bar. Excel uses the slash to indicate division.

Caution: There are two slash keys. The forward slash (/) is used to indicate division in Excel formulas. If you use the backslash (\) by mistake, Excel displays **#NAME?** to indicate that it does not recognize your entry as a formula, but thinks it is a misspelled cell name.

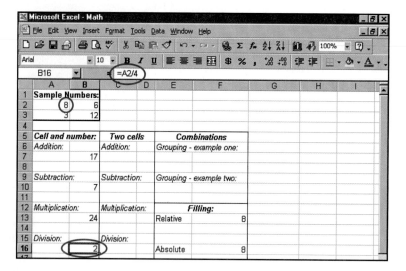

TASK 2

Using Formulas with More Than One Cell Reference
Why would I do this?

When writing a *formula*, an equation used to calculate values in a cell, it is common to refer to numbers entered in more than one cell on your spreadsheet. For example, if you want to know the profit for your business, you subtract expenses from income. If you want to know the percent increase in sales, you use numbers entered for two different sales periods to make that calculation.

In this task, you learn to use numbers from more than one cell to make calculations.

1 Select cell **D7**, type **=A2+A3**, estimate the answer, and click the **Enter** button on the formula bar. In this case, the formula adds the numbers in cells A2 and A3.

Quick Tip: After typing an equal sign to begin the formula, you can point to a cell and click to enter its name in the formula. You can then type the math symbol you want to use before you point and click on the next cell you want in the formula. When this method is used, a marquee outlines the cell that has been selected. This method is preferable if you are writing a formula and the cell you want is off the screen where you cannot see the cell reference.

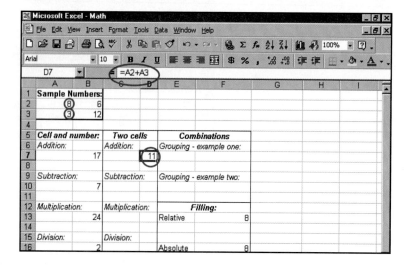

2 Select cell **D10**, type **=A2-A3**, estimate the answer, and then click the **Enter** button on the formula bar. This formula tells the program to take the number in cell A2 and subtract the number in cell A3.

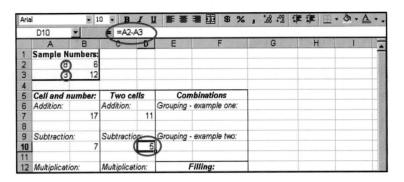

3 Select cell **D13**, type **=A2*A3**, determine what the answer should be if the numbers in these cells were multiplied together, and click the **Enter** button on the formula bar. In this case, you told the program to multiply the number in cell A2 by the number in cell A3.

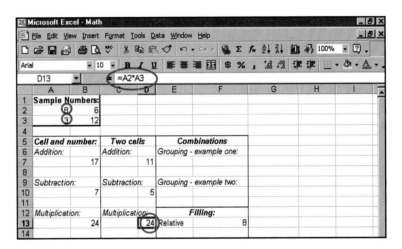

4 Select cell **D16**, type **=B3/B2**, estimate the answer, and click the **Enter** button on the formula bar. In this case, you told the program to take the number in cell B3 and divide by the number in cell B2.

Quick Tip: If you make a mistake and want to start over, click the **Cancel** button ⊠ next to the **Enter** button on the formula bar.

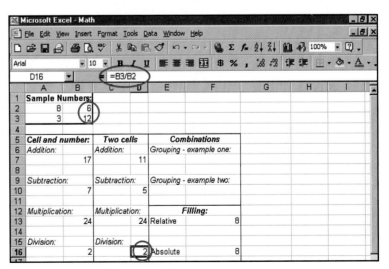

5 Select cell **A2**, and then choose **Tools**, **Auditing**, **Trace Dependents**. (You may need to click the double arrow at the bottom of the menu to reveal the Auditing option.) Arrows are drawn on the screen to show which cells contain formulas that depend on cell A2.

Arrows indicate dependent cells ————

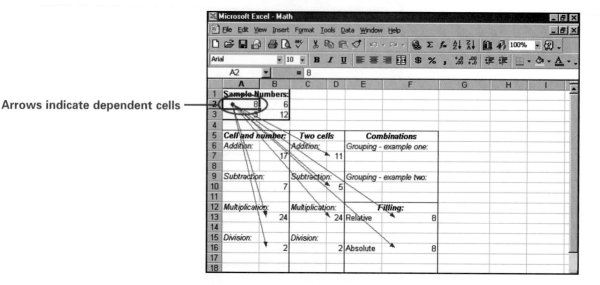

6 Choose **Tools**, **Auditing**, **Remove All Arrows**. The arrows are removed.

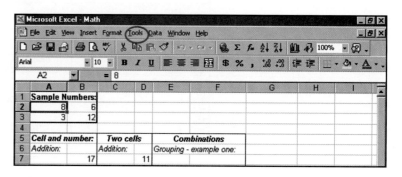

7 Double-click on cell **D7**. The formula is displayed in the cell and in the formula bar. The cell references in the formula and the cells to which they refer change to matching colors. An insertion mark is placed in the formula.

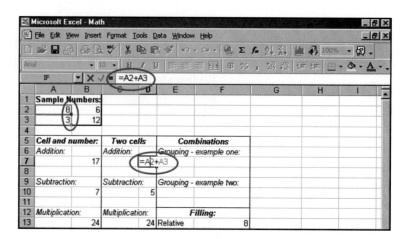

8 Edit the formula the way you would ordinary text. Change it to **=B2+A3**. Click the **Enter** button on the formula bar to finish the change.

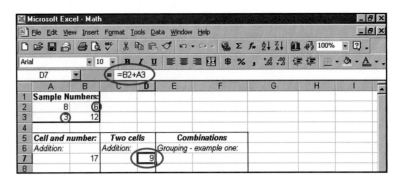

TASK 3

Combining Operations and Filling Cells with Formulas
Why would I do this?

You may want to add the contents of several cells together and then divide by the contents of another cell. To do this, use parentheses to group operations together to make sure they are done first.

If the same formula is to be used in several cells, it may be filled into those cells using the fill handle. Sometimes you want cell references to change to adapt to the new position they are in; for example, you may have a formula that totals the cells above it and want to copy this formula across several cells. In each case, you want the formula to add up the column of cells directly above the formula. This is called a *relative reference*. In other cases, you want the cell reference to always refer to a specific cell. This is called an *absolute reference*.

In this task, you will learn how to group operations in a formula, and how to fill formulas using relative and absolute cell references.

1 Select cell **F7**, and then type **=(A2+B2)/A3**. Estimate what the result should be if you add the contents of cells A2 and B2 and then divide by the number in cell A3 (it is not a whole number). Click the **Enter** button on the formula bar to confirm your estimate. Notice that the numbers in cells A2 and B2 (8 and 6) are added first and then divided by the number in cell A3 (3).

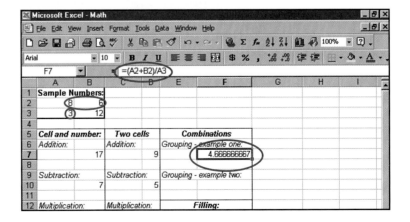

2 Select cell **F10**, and then type **=B3/(A3+B2)**. Estimate what the answer will be if the number in cell B3 is divided by the sum of the numbers in cells A3 and B2. Click the **Enter** button on the formula bar to confirm your estimate.

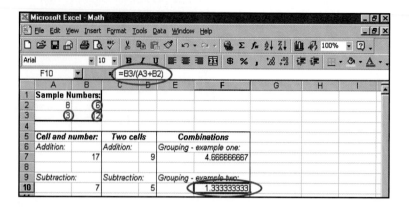

3 Select cell **F13**. Look at the formula in the formula bar. It shows that the formula simply equals the value of cell A2.

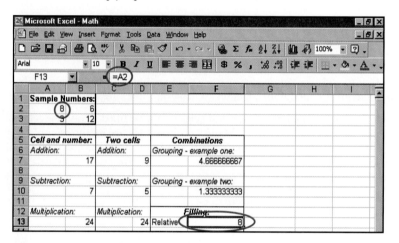

4 Click and drag the fill handle down to cell **F14**. Release the mouse button. Notice that cell F14 displays the number 3, which is the value in cell A3.

Fill handle ——

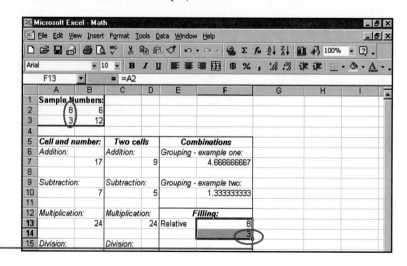

5 Select cell **F14**. Notice that the formula changed and it now equals the value in cell A3. The formulas in cells F13 and F14 both refer to a cell that is eleven rows up and five columns to the left.

In Depth: When you fill a formula from one cell to another, Excel uses a relative cell reference. In this example, Excel used A3 to fill cell F14. Cell F14 is one position below F13, and cell A3 is one position below A2. Excel uses the relative position of the cell that is being referenced to determine the location of the next value to place in the new cell. This is the default method that Excel uses to fill a formula from one cell to another.

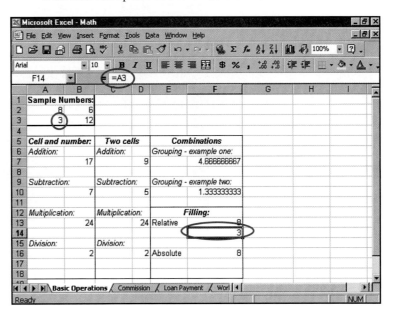

6 Select cell **F16**. Look at the formula in the formula bar. In this case, a $ has been placed to the left of the column and row identifiers to indicate that the cell reference will not change when it is copied.

In Depth: The dollar sign ($) that is used as a code to prevent the reference from changing has nothing to do with currency. It is a symbol that was used in the earliest spreadsheets for this purpose and has been used ever since.

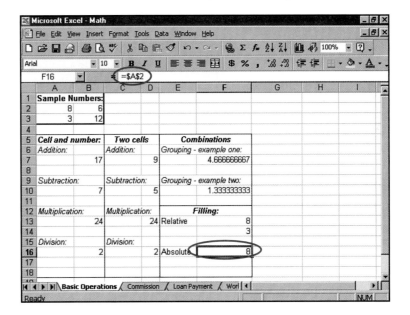

7 Use the fill handle to fill this formula into cell **F17**. Notice that F17 also displays the contents of cell A2.

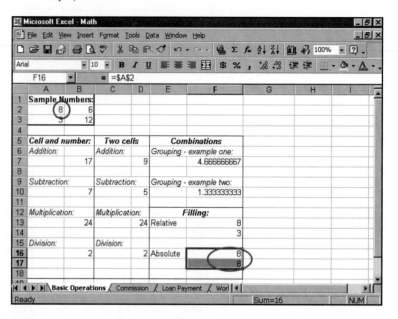

8 Select cell **F17**. Look at the formula in the formula bar. Notice that it did not change when the formula was filled into the cell. This type of cell reference (with the $ sign) is called an absolute reference. Use an absolute reference when you want to ensure that the formula always refers to a specific cell.

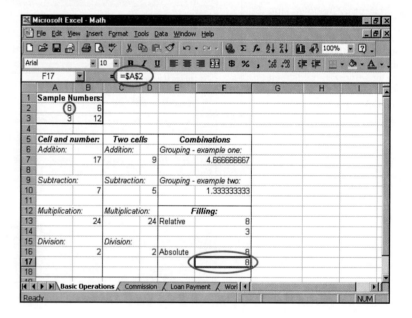

9 Press Ctrl+` (the accent grave mark found on the key to the left of the 1 key). The formulas for each cell are displayed.

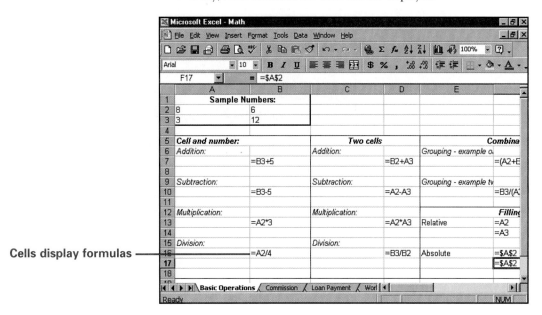

Cells display formulas ——

10 Add your name to the header **Center section**, using the Page Setup dialog box (refer to Lesson 12, Task 6). Print the worksheet.

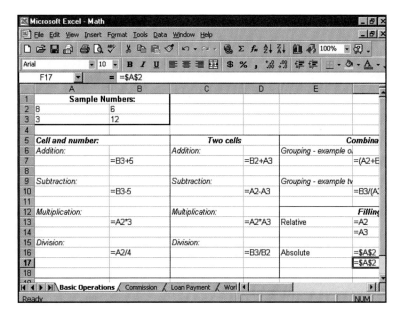

11 Press Ctrl+` to return the worksheet to Normal view showing numbers. Save your workbook.

TASK 4

Filling Cells with Relative and Absolute Formulas
Why would I do this?

The ability to fill formulas into adjacent cells greatly increases the speed at which a worksheet can be created.

In this task, you learn how to fill cells using both relative and absolute formulas.

1 Click the **Commission** tab to switch to the **Commission** sheet and select cell **B11**, if necessary. Notice that it contains a formula that adds the contents of cells B5 through B10, which are directly above B11.

In Depth: Two cell names separated by a colon indicate a rectangular shaped group of cells where the two cells are at opposite corners of the block of cells.

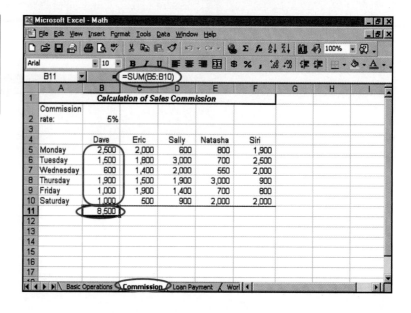

2 Drag the fill handle to the right to cell **F11** and release the mouse. The formula is filled into cells C11 through F11.

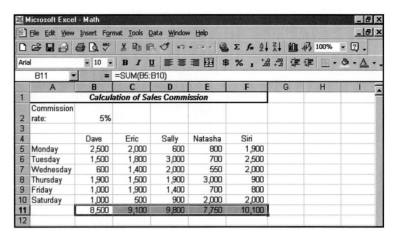

3 Click on cell **D11**, and you see that the formula changed to add the six cells in the column above cell D11. This shows how the use of the fill handle results in a relative reference.

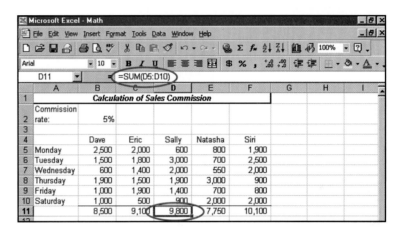

4 Select cell **B12** type =**B11*$B$2**, and then click the **Enter** button on the formula bar. This formula multiplies the sum of Dave's sales in cell B11 by the commission rate in cell B2. The reference to B11 is relative, and the reference to B2 is absolute.

Absolute reference to cell B2 —

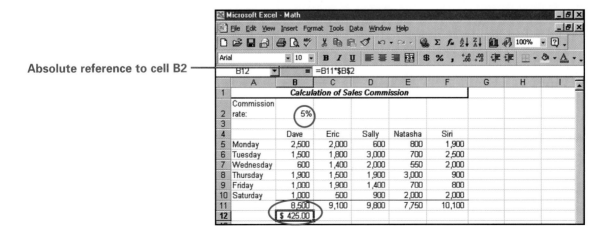

5 Drag the fill handle to the right to cell **F12** and release the mouse button. The formula is filled in.

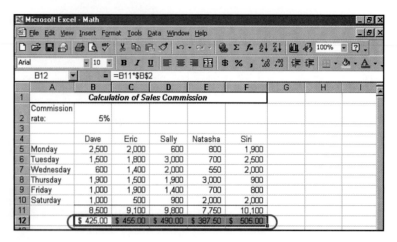

6 Click on cell **D12** and look at the formula bar. The relative reference changed so that it refers to the sum of Sally's sales in cell D11, but the absolute reference to the commission rate in cell B2 did not change.

Relative cell reference changed   Absolute cell reference did not change

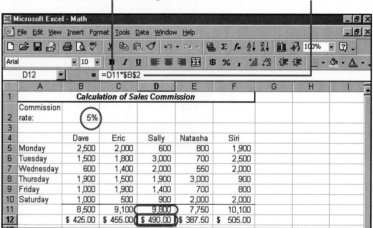

7 Add your name to the sheet header. Save your work and print the worksheet.

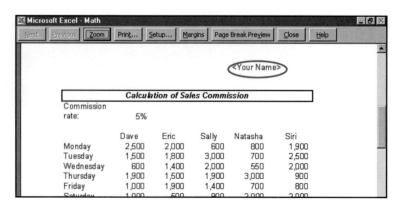

TASK 5

Applying Basic Formulas to a Loan Repayment
Why would I do this?

When you borrow money for a car or a house, the loan repayment is based on several factors, such as interest rate, time to repay, and the loan amount. With Excel, you can set up a worksheet to calculate your monthly payments based on these factors, and then change the value of the factors to match whatever loan terms you are quoted by a bank or other lender.

In this task, you learn how to set up a worksheet to calculate total monthly payments.

1 Click on the **Loan Payment** tab to switch to the **Loan Payment** sheet. Notice that column A is used for labels and column B is used for formulas.

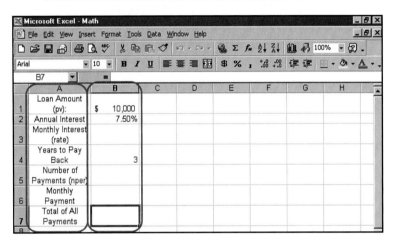

2 Select cell **B3**, type **=B2/12**, and click the **Enter** button on the formula bar. This formula takes the annual interest rate in cell B2 and divides by 12 to calculate the monthly interest rate.

In Depth: To calculate the monthly payment, the formula requires the number of months and the interest rate per month. Most loan interest rates are given as Annual Percentage Rate, or *APR*. If the payment is made every month, the formula needs to use one-twelfth of the annual interest rate to calculate the interest cost per month.

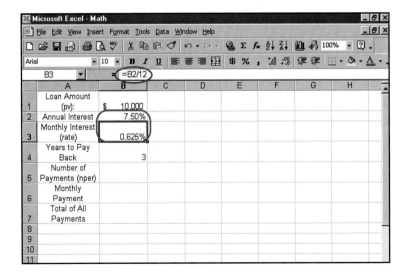

3 Select cell **B5**, type **=B4*12**, and click the **Enter** button on the formula bar. This formula calculates the number of months over which the loan is repaid.

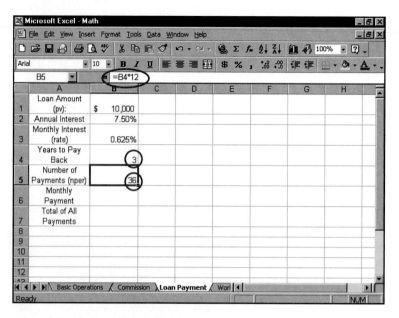

4 Select cell **B7**, type **=B5*B6**, and click the **Enter** button on the formula bar. This formula multiplies the number of payments in cell B5 times the amount of the payment in B6. In this case, no number is displayed in the cell because cell B6 is still empty, and the cell has been formatted to show a dollar sign and a dash when the value is zero.

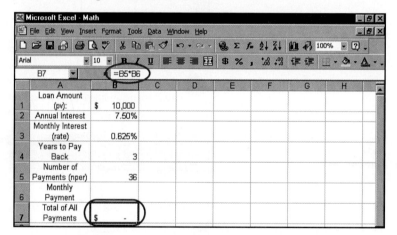

Using Built-in Financial Formulas

Why would I do this?

When you take out a loan, you usually rely on someone else to tell you how much the payment will be. To shop around for the best rate or terms, it is helpful to see the effect of different loan terms that may be quoted to you. In the previous task, the factors used to calculate a loan were outlined.

In this task, you learn how to use one of Excel's built-in financial formulas to calculate the monthly payment.

1 Select cell **B6**. Click the **Paste Function** button on the Standard toolbar. (If the Office Assistant appears, select **No, don't provide help now**.) The Paste Function dialog box opens.

Paste Function button —

In Depth: The first choice, **Most Recently Used**, displays a list of recently used functions in the box to the right. This list is different for each computer because it is based on personal use.

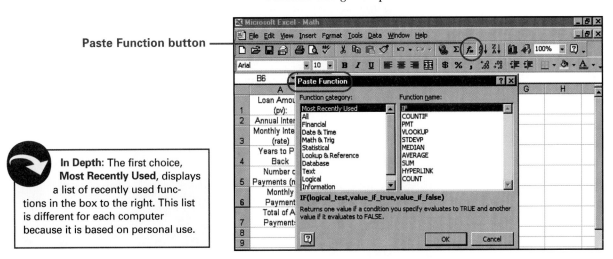

2 Click on the **Financial** option in the **Function category** box. A list of built-in financial formulas appears in the Function name box.

Financial functions —

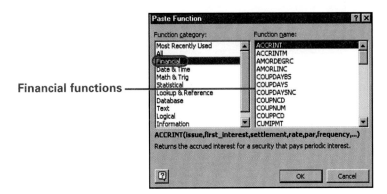

3 Scroll down, if necessary, and click on the **PMT** function. The name of the function and the values it requires are displayed. These values are called *arguments*. This function is used to calculate loan payments.

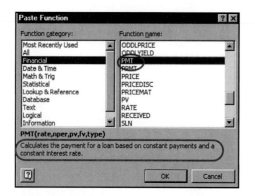

4 Click **OK**. The Formula palette, a wizard dialog box opens. You use the wizard to identify the cells that contain values, or arguments, that the payment function requires. The first three arguments are required, and their names are in boldface type. The last two are optional, and their names are in normal type.

Collapse Dialog Box button

Required arguments

Optional arguments

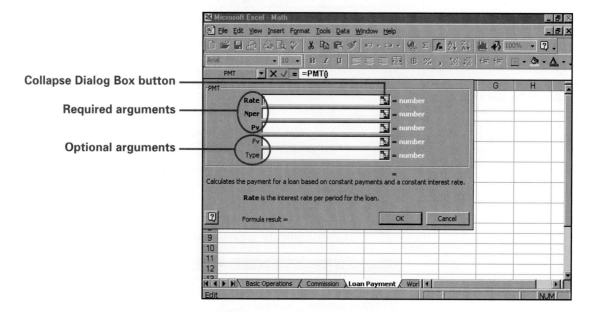

In Depth: Wizards usually consist of a series of questions that guide you through the creation of a formula or a chart. Wizards are used in Excel to help with a number of different processes. These include a Help Wizard known as the Office Assistant, a Chart Wizard used for creating charts, and the wizards in Paste Function that help create complex formulas such as a payment formula. When you are working on a formula, you can click the equal sign on the formula bar to open the Formula palette, which displays current information about the formula you are using.

5 Click the **Collapse Dialog Box** button at the right end of the **Rate** box.

In Depth: If the Collapse Dialog Box obscures the range of cells that you want to select, expand the dialog box, drag it to another location, and then collapse it.

Collapsed dialog box showing only the Rate box

Results of the calculation will appear here

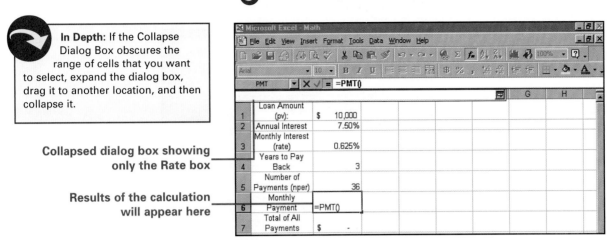

6 Click cell **B3**. This cell reference is entered into the formula as the first argument.

Expand Dialog Box button

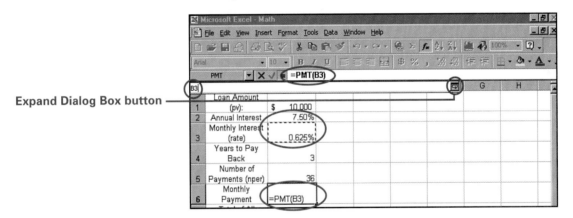

7 Click the **Expand Dialog Box** button to restore the dialog box. The cell reference is displayed in the **Rate** box.

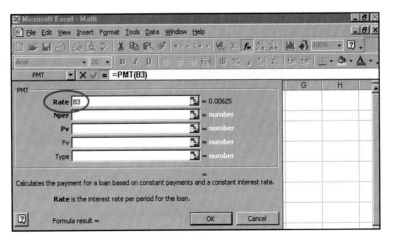

8 Press `Tab⇄` to move to the **Nper** box. The message at the bottom of the box explains that this is the total number of loan payments.

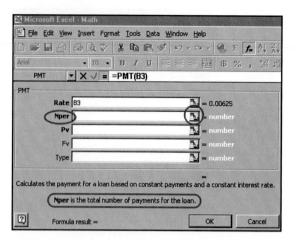

9 Click the **Collapse Dialog Box** button at the right side of the **Nper** box, click on cell **B5**, and click the **Expand Dialog Box** button. The reference to cell B5 is added as the second argument to the formula.

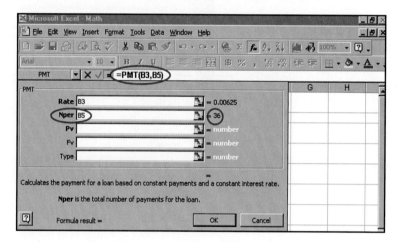

10 Press `Tab⇄` to move to the **Pv** box. This argument is used to identify the present value of the loan, or the amount you want to borrow.

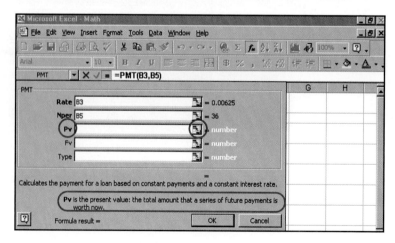

11 Click the **Collapse Dialog Box** button, click on cell **B1**, and click the **Expand Dialog Box** button. The reference to cell B1 is added as the third argument to the formula. The formula now has enough information to calculate the payment. The result is displayed at the bottom of the dialog box.

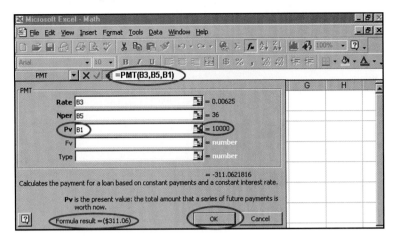

12 Click **OK**. The calculated payment is displayed. The currency format that has been chosen for this cell displays negative numbers in red, enclosed by parentheses. (If the loan amount is entered as a positive number, the payment is negative.) Notice that cell B7 now shows the total amount of all payments.

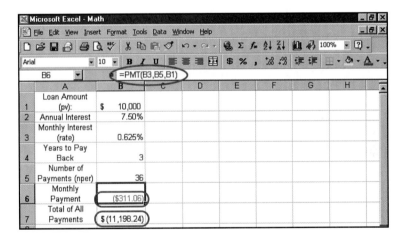

13 Add your name to the center of the sheet header, save your work, preview the printout, and then print the sheet.

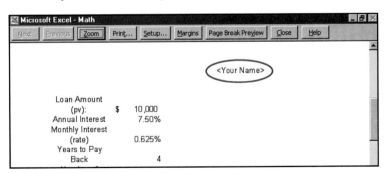

Comprehension Exercises

Comprehension exercises are designed to check your memory and understanding of the basic concepts in this lesson. You distinguish between true and false statements, identify new screen elements, and match terms with related statements. If you are uncertain of the correct answer, refer to the task number following each item (for example, T4 refers to Task 4) and review that task until you are confident that you can provide a correct response.

True-False

Circle either T or F.

T F **1.** You can only use one cell reference in a formula. **(T2)**

T F **2.** Math operations that are grouped inside parentheses are calculated first in a formula. **(T3)**

T F **3.** When you use the fill handle to copy a formula that sums a column, Excel assumes an absolute reference to the numbers in the original column. **(T3)**

T F **4.** To designate a cell reference as absolute, place a $ to the left of both the column and row identifiers. **(T4)**

T F **5.** To view the formulas used in an Excel worksheet, press Ctrl+`, which is the key to the left of the 1 key. **(T3)**

T F **6.** The loan payment formula uses an annual interest rate and the number of years of the loan to calculate the monthly payment amount. **(T6)**

T F **7.** The Paste Function button on the Standard toolbar opens a wizard that can be used to enter formulas for making a variety of financial calculations. **(T6)**

T F **8.** A relative reference is a cell reference that will change when the formula is copied, moved, or filled. **(T4)**

T F **9.** A quick way to format a cell to display currency is to use dollar signs in the name of the cell. **(T4)**

T F **10.** When you change a number in a cell, it automatically changes the results of every formula that uses that cell. **(Introduction)**

Identifying Parts of the Excel Screen

Refer to the figure and identify the numbered parts of the screen. Write the letter of the correct label in the space next to the number.

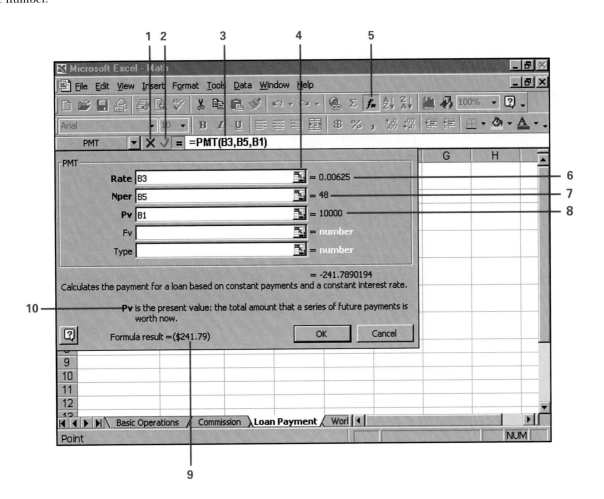

1. _____
2. _____
3. _____
4. _____
5. _____
6. _____
7. _____
8. _____
9. _____
10. _____

A. Paste Function (**T6**)

B. Enter button (**T1**)

C. Projected payment amount (**T6**)

D. Interest rate per loan period (**T6**)

E. Amount of money that is borrowed (**T6**)

F. Number of payments in a loan (**T6**)

G. Collapse Dialog Box button (**T6**)

H. Formula with arguments (**T6**)

I. Description of the selected argument (**T2**)

J. Cancel button (**T2**)

Matching

Match the statements below to the word or phrase that is the best match from the list. Write the letter of the matching word or phrase in the space provided next to the number.

1. ___ Symbol used to represent division (**T1**)

2. ___ Term used for numbers or words that are used by a function to perform a calculation or operation (**T6**)

3. ___ Symbol used to represent multiplication (**T1**)

4. ___ Enter button on the formula bar (**T1**)

5. ___ An example of a relative cell reference (**T3**)

6. ___ Used to begin every formula (**T1**)

7. ___ Name of the character that is used to reveal the formulas in the cells (it resembles an apostrophe) (**T3**)

8. ___ An example of an absolute cell reference (**T4**)

9. ___ A cell reference that will change when copied or filled (**T4**)

10. ___ Used to group math operations (**T3**)

A. $B$3

B. ( )

C. B3

D. =

E. Accent grave

F. ✔

G. Relative reference

H. Arguments

I. APR

J. /

K. *

Reinforcement Exercises

Reinforcement exercises are designed to reinforce the skills you have learned by applying them to a new situation. Detailed instructions are provided along with a figure, where appropriate, to illustrate the final result. The Reinforcement exercises that follow should be completed sequentially. Leave the workbook open at the end of each exercise for use in the next exercise until you are specifically directed to close it.

Open **Less1302** from the **Student\Lesson13** folder on the CD-ROM disc that came with your book, and save it as **Ex1301** on your floppy disk for use in the following exercises.

R1—Using Basic Excel Formulas

1. Select **Sheet1** and change the sheet tab name to **Patio Division**.

2. Modify the **Patio Furniture Division** worksheet to match the figure. See the steps below for more details. (The sheet zoom is set at 80 percent to provide a full view of the worksheet.)

3. To calculate the total cost of each item, select cell **D3** and enter **=B3*C3**. Adjust the column width as necessary.

4. Use the fill handle to copy the formula in **D3** to cells **D4** through **D9**. Format the values in this column to be currency with no decimals. Adjust the column width as shown in the figure.

5. To calculate the retail value, select cell **F3** and enter **=B3*E3**.

	A	B	C	D	E	F	G	H
1				Patio Furniture Division				
2	Inventory	Quantity	Average Cost	Total Cost	Retail Price	Retail Value	Percent Mark Up	Percent Contributio
3	Table Umbrellas	2000	$ 22.70	$ 45,400	$ 45.00	$ 90,000	98%	10.31%
4	Patio Chairs	5000	$ 35.00	$ 175,000	$ 65.00	$ 325,000	86%	37.23%
5	Patio Tables	1000	$ 48.00	$ 48,000	$ 120.00	$ 120,000	150%	13.75%
6	Side Tables	2000	$ 19.25	$ 38,500	$ 33.00	$ 66,000	71%	7.56%
7	Grills	1500	$ 38.50	$ 57,750	$ 89.00	$ 133,500	131%	15.29%
8	Citronella Torches	5000	$ 2.50	$ 12,500	$ 12.50	$ 62,500	400%	7.16%
9	Lounge Chairs	3450	$ 5.00	$ 17,250	$ 22.00	$ 75,900	340%	8.70%
10				$ 394,400		$ 872,900		100.00%

Microsoft Excel - Ex1301

H10 = =SUM(H3:H9)

6. Use the fill handle to copy the formula in **F3** to cells **F4** through **F9**. Format the values in this column as currency with no decimals.

7. Place a bottom border in cells **D9** and **F9**. Use the **AutoSum** button to place a sum function in cells **D10** and **F10** to add the numbers in the column above.

8. To calculate the percent markup, select cell **G3** and enter =**(E3-C3)/C3**. Fill the formula to the other cells in the column. Format the values in this column as percentages with no decimals (use the % button on the Formatting toolbar).

9. To calculate the percent contribution, select cell **H3** and type =**F3/$F$10**. Fill the formula to the other cells in the column. Format the values in this column as percentages with two decimals.

10. Place a bottom border in cell **H9** and sum the column in cell **H10**.

11. Add your name to the sheet header and choose **Landscape** orientation.

12. Preview and print the sheet.

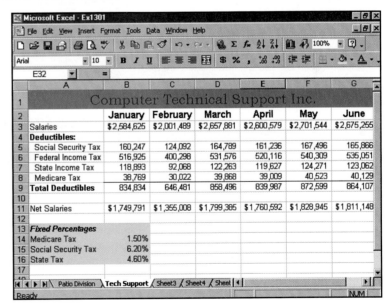

<Your Name>

Patio Furniture Division

Inventory	Quantity	Average Cost	Total Cost	Retail Price	Retail Value	Percent Mark Up	Percent Contribution
Table Umbrellas	2000	22.7	=B3*C3	45	=B3*E3	=(E3-C3)/C3	=F3/$F$10
Patio Chairs	5000	35	=B4*C4	65	=B4*E4	=(E4-C4)/C4	=F4/$F$10
Patio Tables	1000	48	=B5*C5	120	=B5*E5	=(E5-C5)/C5	=F5/$F$10
Side Tables	2000	19.25	=B6*C6	33	=B6*E6	=(E6-C6)/C6	=F6/$F$10
Grills	1500	38.5	=B7*C7	89	=B7*E7	=(E7-C7)/C7	=F7/$F$10
Citronella Torches	5000	2.5	=B8*C8	12.5	=B8*E8	=(E8-C8)/C8	=F8/$F$10
Lounge Chairs	3450	5	=B9*C9	22	=B9*E9	=(E9-C9)/C9	=F9/$F$10
			=SUM(D3:D9)		=SUM(F3:F9)		=SUM(H3:H9)

13. Change the worksheet to show the formulas. Adjust the columns and wrap the column headings so that the worksheet will print on one page. Print the sheet showing the formulas.

14. Change the worksheet back to show the values rather than the formulas and use the **Undo** button to restore the previous column widths.

R2—Using Absolute and Relative Reference

1. Select **Sheet2** and change the sheet tab name to **Tech Support**.

2. Modify the **Computer Technical Support Inc.** worksheet to match the figure. See the steps that follow for more detail.

3. Select cell **B5** and enter =**B3*$B$15**. Use the fill handle to copy the formula to the right to cell **G5**. With the cells still selected, use the **Comma Style** button to format the cells, if needed, and then decrease the decimals to show no decimals.

4. Select cell **B6** and type =**B3*.20**. Use the fill handle to copy the formula to the right to cell **G6**. Format row **6** the same as row **5**.

5. Select cell **B7** and type **=B3*$B$16**. Use the fill handle to copy the formula to the right to cell **G7**. Format row **7** the same as rows **5** and **6**.

6. Select cell **B8**. Write a formula that will multiply the salaries by an absolute reference to the Medicare tax percent (refer to the **Fixed Percentages** table in the figure). Use the same format for these cells. Use the fill handle to copy the formula to the right to cell **G8**.

7. Add a bottom border to the figures in row **8** and sum the deductibles in each column in row **9**. Notice that the empty cell in row **4** prevents the AutoSum unction from accidentally selecting the salaries in row **3**.

8. Calculate the net salary figures by writing a formula in cell **B11** that takes the salaries for the month and subtracts the deductibles for the month. Copy the formula to cell **G11**.

9. Check the results of your formulas against the figure to be sure they are working properly. Change the state tax to **6%**. The worksheet is recalculated.

10. Add your name to the sheet header. Change the orientation to **Landscape** and print a copy of the worksheet. Save your work.

R3—Calculating a House Payment and Amortization Schedule for a 5-Year Balloon Mortgage

In this exercise, you use the PMT function to calculate a house payment. Then you use Excel's capability to copy relative and absolute cell references to calculate a list of payments and balances for each month. You also learn how to use this table of payments to determine how much you would need to refinance if you select a common form of loan known as a 5-year balloon mortgage.

1. Select **Sheet3** and change the sheet tab name to **Mortgage**.

2. Modify the **Mortgage** worksheet to match the figure. See the steps below for more detail.

3. Select cell **B5** and write a formula to determine the monthly interest rate. Format it as a percent showing three decimal places.

4. Select cell **B7** and write a formula to determine the number of monthly payments over the term of the loan.

5. Select cell **B8** and use the **Paste Function** to insert the payment formula for the mortgage. Select the appropriate arguments for the formula.

6. Select cells **D5** and **D6** and fill the date column for five years. The last date should be 1/1/03 in row 64.

7. Select cells **E6** through **G6**. Drag these three cells to the bottom of the date column to complete the amortization schedule. Look in cell **G64**. If you need to refinance the home loan in five years, you will need to borrow $118,688.88 (and pay closing costs again).

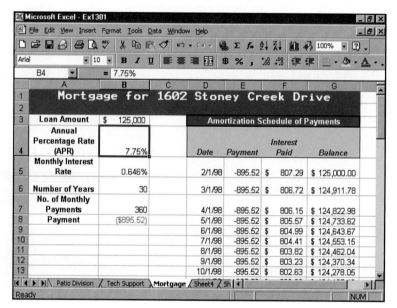

8. Change the Annual Percentage Rate (APR) to **8%**.

9. Add your name to the sheet header, set the first four rows to repeat on the second page (see Lesson 12, Challenge exercise C3), and print a copy of the worksheet (two pages).

10. Save the workbook and close it.

Challenge

Challenge exercises are designed to test your ability to apply your skills to new situations with less detailed instruction. These exercises also challenge you to expand your repertoire of skills by using Excel commands that are similar to those you have already learned. The desired outcome is clearly defined, but you have more freedom to choose the steps needed to achieve the required result.

The following Challenge exercises use the file **Ex1302**. Open **Less1303** from the **Student\Lesson13** folder on your CD-ROM disc and save it as **Ex1302** on your floppy disk.

C1—Using Goal Seek

Sometimes you know what the answer needs to be, but you do not know how to get there. If you have a worksheet set up to calculate an answer based on one or more cells, you can use an Excel tool named Goal Seek that will try different numbers in the cell you select until the answer in another cell matches the value you set.

Goal: Use the Goal Seek tool to determine the value in one cell that will produce the desired result in another cell.

Use the following guidelines:

1. Open **Ex1302** and select the **Goal Seek** sheet tab.

2. Select **Tools**, **Goal Seek** from the menu.

3. Use the Goal Seek dialog box to set cell **B6** to **600** by changing the annual interest rate in cell **B2**. The resulting Annual Interest Rate is 7.02%.

4. Use this method to determine how big a loan you can afford (**Loan Amount**) on a five-year car loan at an Annual Interest Rate of 8.5 percent if the

most you can afford for a monthly car payment is $350. See the step below for more detail.

5. Change cell **B2** to **8.5%**. Change cell **B4** to 5. Use **Goal Seek** to find out what loan amount will yield a payment of $350. (The sheet is protected so that you do not accidentally overwrite the formulas.)

6. Save the workbook. Leave the workbook open for use in the next exercise.

C2—Percentage Increases or Decreases

Prices are often determined by marking up a wholesale price by a certain percentage. When those items go on sale, the price is reduced by a certain percentage.

In this exercise, you will see how formulas are used to increase or decrease a price by a given percentage. In general, if you want to increase a value by 40 percent, you multiply the value by **(1+40%)**. If you want to decrease the price by 20 percent, you multiply by **(1-20%)**. An example is provided to show how a merchant starts with a wholesale price for a pair of boots, increases the price by 40 percent to get the retail price, decreases the retail price by 20 percent for a sale, and then figures out the gross profit and percent profit.

Goal: Learn how to calculate percentage increases and decreases.

1. Open the file **Ex1302** and select the **Percent** sheet.

2. Look at the formula in cell **C2**. Notice how the retail price for the boots was calculated by multiplying the wholesale price in cell **B2** by **(1+40%)**.

3. Enter a similar formula in cell **C3** that calculates a retail price for gloves at a 50 percent increase over the wholesale price.

4. Observe the formula in cell **D2** to see how the sale price for boots was determined by multiplying the retail price by **(1-20%)**.

5. Enter a similar formula in cell **D3** to calculate the sale price for gloves if their price is reduced by 30 percent.

6. Fill the formulas in cells **E2** and **F2** into cells **E3** and **F3**, respectively. The percent profit on the gloves will be 5 percent if you have written the formulas correctly.

7. Enter two similar formulas for the hats. Use an increase of 120 percent to determine the retail price and then determine the sale price for a 50-percent-off sale. Fill the gross profit and percent profit formulas into cells **E4** and **F4**.

8. Save the workbook. Leave the workbook open for use in the next exercise.

C3—Statistics: Average, Median, and Standard Deviation

When we describe a set of numbers, such as the income of a certain group, we often use terms such as average or median. We can use Excel to compute these numbers and see how they describe a set of numbers. Average and median are two ways of describing where the "center" of a set of numbers is. They do not describe whether the numbers are all close to that central number or if they vary greatly. The statistic that describes this type of variation is the standard deviation.

In this exercise, you look at the monthly rainfall in Buffalo and Seattle.

Goal: Use Excel's statistical functions to compare the average, median, and standard deviation of rainfall.

1. Open the file **Ex1302** and select the **Stats** sheet. Notice that both cities have almost the same total annual rainfall. Look at the rainfall for each month of the year—it is apparent that the rainfall in Seattle varies much more from month to month.

2. Paste the **Average** function in cell **B16** (it is one of the Statistics functions). Use cells **B3:B14**; do not include the total in cell **B15**. Use the same method to find the average rainfall in Seattle.

3. The median of a set of numbers is the value that has as many values above it as below it. Find the median rainfall for each city and place it in the table.

4. To see how much the numbers vary from the average, find the standard deviation of the rainfall for both cities. Use the **STDEVP** function. About 2/3 of the values will be within this range of the average. A small standard deviation means that the numbers are closely grouped around the average. Does the city with the smaller standard deviation have about the same amount of rain each month? If so, you have done the assignment correctly.

5. Save the workbook and close it.

Discovery

Discovery exercises are designed to help you learn how to teach yourself a new skill. In each exercise, you discover something new that is related to the topic taught in this lesson. You may be directed to use built-in wizards or some of the extensive Help features provided in Excel to discover new features and learn new skills with minimum assistance from books or instructors. The required outcome demonstrates your ability to apply the new skill. You determine the choice of topic, worksheet design, and steps of execution.

The following Discovery exercises use the file **Less1304**. Open **Less1304** from the **Student\Lesson13** folder on your CD-ROM disc and save it on your floppy disk as **Ex1303**.

D1—Vlookup

If you are providing a quotation for a job, the price often depends on the cost of parts and labor. These costs vary depending on the item and the quantity purchased. It can be very time-consuming to look up information in tables to include in your calculations. Excel has two functions that are designed to look up values in a table, column, or array. These are called Vlookup and Hlookup. Vlookup is used to look up values in a vertical column and Hlookup is used to look up values in a horizontal row. In this exercise, you will learn how to use the Vlookup function.

To use the Vlookup function to find the correct value in a table and use it in a calculation, follow these steps:

1. Select the **Lookup** sheet, if necessary.

2. Use Help to find the description of the **Vlookup** function. Read the description and examine the example in cell **C4**. There are three arguments included in this formula. The first defines the value that is looked up in a table. The second argument defines the table or range of cells that should be examined. The third is the column that should be used to locate the matching value. Each column in the defined table is identified with a number: 1, 2, 3, and so on. (Note: The values in the first column of a table that is used with this function must be sorted in increasing order.)

3. Test the function by changing values in cells **A4** and **B4**. Use one of the codes from column **1** of the **Quantity Charge** table for cell **A4**, and either a 2 or 3 for cell B4. The number in cell B4 indicates whether column 2 or 3 of the Quantity Charge table should be used to look up the value that matches the code in cell A4.

4. Find the **Multi-Color Charge** table. Paste the **Vlookup** function into cell **C18** and select the arguments so that it will find the correct charge for additional shirt colors and display it in cell C18.

5. Test the function by trying different numbers in cells **A18** and **B18**.

6. Save the workbook and leave it open for use in the next Discovery exercise.

D2—Frequency Distribution

This exercise requires the Analysis ToolPak Add-in. Open the **Tools** menu to determine if you have the **Data Analysis** option. If not, select **Tools**, **Add-Ins**, **Analysis ToolPak**. If you plan to do the Solver exercise, D3, select the Solver Add-in. You may need your Office 2000 CD-ROM disc, or ask your lab administrator to install these features.

If you are trying to determine how many of each kind of number you have in a group, you want to know the frequency distribution. For example, 25 people have answered a question that has five possible answers numbered 1 through 5, and you would like to know how many people chose each answer.

Excel provides two options for determining the frequency distribution. There is a Frequency Distribution function that can be found by using the Paste Function button. The other is part of the Histogram tool in the Analysis ToolPak. The Histogram tool is much easier.

Goal: Learn how to use the Histogram tool to determine the number of people answering each option for a question.

1. Open **Ex1303** and select the **Frequency** sheet.

2. Search for Help on the Histogram analysis tool.

3. Look at the example analysis that was done on the first question.

4. Use the Histogram analysis tool to produce a similar analysis of the second question. Select cell **Y14** as the output cell that will be used as the upper-left corner of the output range.

5. Save the workbook and leave it open for use in the next exercise.

D3—Solver

Solver is similar to Goal Seek, but it has more options. It can change more than one input cell, and you can specify constraints on several cells. You can have it determine the inputs to produce a match, a maximum, or a minimum value.

A classic physics problem is to determine how high a projectile will go if it is shot straight up at a given initial speed. The formula is $H = -16T^2 + ST$. This formula can be written in Excel as **=–16*(time cell reference)^2+(speed cell reference)*(time cell reference)**. In the example sheet used for this exercise, the formula is =–16*B3^2+B4*B3. You can solve this problem in two ways. You could use differential calculus to find the derivative, set it equal to zero, solve for T, and then plug the value of T into the original formula. A second way would be to try increasing values of time in the formula until the value of the height stopped increasing and started decreasing. To account for the time down to the nearest tenth of a second, you would have to do the formula many times.

The Solver works by trying different values in the formula, subject to the constraints you have imposed, until the target cell matches the value you have chosen or is a maximum or minimum if you have selected either of those options.

Goal: Use the Solver tool to find the maximum height to which a projectile will rise given an initial speed.

1. Open **Ex1303** and select the **Solver** sheet.

2. Search for Help on guidelines for using the Solver.

3. Use the Solver to determine the maximum value for the formula in cell **B5** by changing the time values in cell **B3**.

4. Keep the Solver solution.

5. Save the workbook and close it.

Lesson: 14

Understanding the Numbers Using a Chart

Introduction

People process information in several different ways. Most of us recognize trends more readily if a line or a series of columns of differing heights represents them. We also recognize how one member of a group compares to the others if they are represented by slices of a pie chart.

This lesson is designed to provide you with the basic skills you need to create a variety of charts to represent your numerical data graphically. Excel's Chart Wizard guides you through the necessary steps.

Visual Summary

When you have completed this lesson, you will have created charts that look like these:

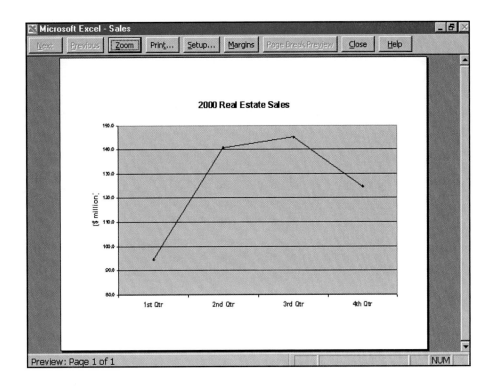

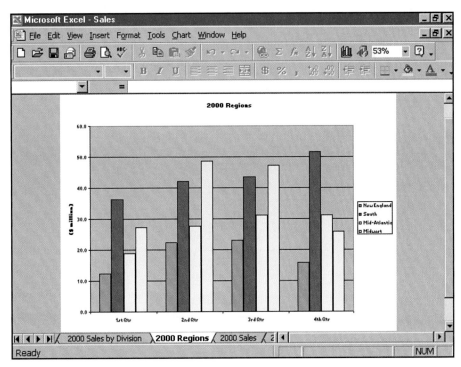

TASK 1

Creating a Chart to Show a Trend

Why would I do this?

It is sometimes easier to analyze numbers when looking at a visual representation. A picture or *chart* helps, and some types are better than others for specific purposes. For instance, when you want to show a trend (change over time), a *line chart* is usually most effective.

In this task, you learn how to create a line chart to show the trend in sales for a real estate firm.

1 Launch **Excel**. Open **Less1401** from the **Student\Lesson14** folder on the CD-ROM disc that came with this book, and save the file on your floppy disk as **Sales**. The new title appears in the title bar.

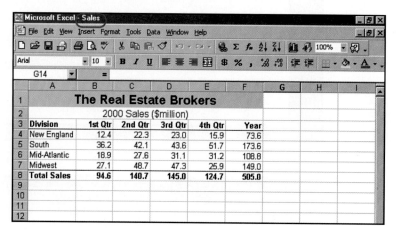

2 Move the pointer to cell **A3**. Click and drag to select cells **A3** through **E3**, and then release the mouse button. Hold down Ctrl and select cells **A8** through **E8**.

3 Click the **Chart Wizard** button. The first Chart Wizard dialog box is displayed. (If the Office Assistant opens, right-click it and choose **Hide** to close it.) Click **Line** in the **Chart type** area, and observe that the default chart sub-type is a line with data markers. Each chart type has several variations you can use to display the data.

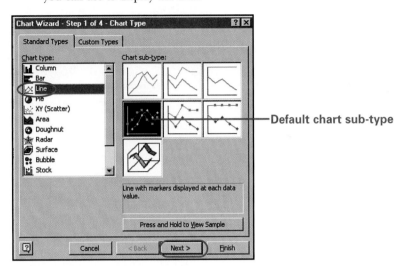

—Default chart sub-type

4 Click **Next**. The second Chart Wizard dialog box is displayed. Make sure **Rows** is selected from the **Series in** area.

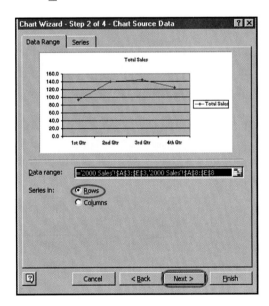

5 Click **Next**. The third Chart Wizard dialog box is displayed. Click the **Titles** tab, if necessary. Type **2000 Real Estate Sales** in the **Chart title** box. Type **($ million)** in the **Value (Y) axis** box.

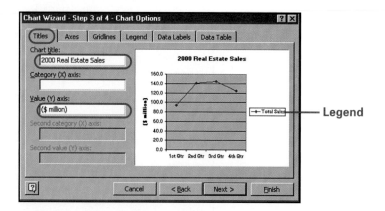

— Legend

6 Click the **Legend** tab. A *legend* is a list that identifies a pattern or color used in an Excel chart. Click the **Show legend** box to turn off the legend.

In Depth: The first three Chart Wizard dialog boxes contain multiple tabs. These tabs let you control such things as the chart scale, whether to show vertical or horizontal gridlines, and how to label the data points.

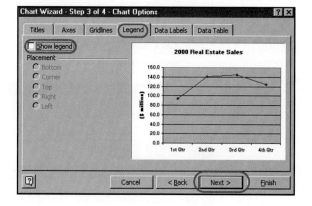

7 Click **Next**. The fourth Chart Wizard dialog box is displayed. Click **As new sheet** to select it and type **2000 Sales Chart** in the adjacent box.

8 Click **Finish**. The chart is shown full-size on its own sheet. Click the **Save** button to save your work. If the Chart toolbar appears, close it.

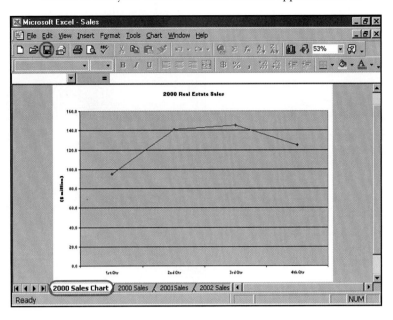

TASK 2

Creating a Chart to Show Contributions to a Whole

Why would I do this?

In the previous task, you took a set of data and created a line chart to show a trend over time. You may find that it is often beneficial to graphically represent the contribution of various elements to the whole. The best way to illustrate parts of a whole is to use a *pie chart*.

In this task, you learn how to create a pie chart that shows the contribution each region made to the total sales amount for the year.

1 Click the **2000 Sales** sheet tab. Select cells **A3** through **A7**. Hold down Ctrl and select cells **F3** through **F7**.

> **Caution:** When you create a pie chart, you want to show the contribution each part makes to the whole. A common mistake when building a chart from a worksheet that contains totals is to include the totals with the data. Doing this would defeat the purpose of a pie chart, since the total figure would appear to be a piece of the pie rather than the sum of the parts.

Division	1st Qtr	2nd Qtr	3rd Qtr	4th Qtr	Year
New England	12.4	22.3	23.0	15.9	73.6
South	36.2	42.1	43.6	51.7	173.6
Mid-Atlantic	18.9	27.6	31.1	31.2	108.8
Midwest	27.1	48.7	47.3	25.9	149.0
Total Sales	94.6	140.7	145.0	124.7	505.0

2 Click the **Chart Wizard** button. The first Chart Wizard dialog box is displayed. Click **Pie** in the **Chart type** area, and select **Pie** in the **Chart sub-type** area.

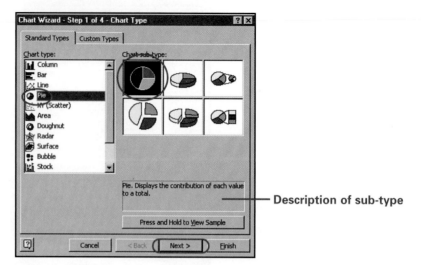

Description of sub-type

3 Click Next. The second Chart Wizard dialog box is displayed. Make sure **Columns** is selected from the **Series in** area, because the data you are charting is in a column.

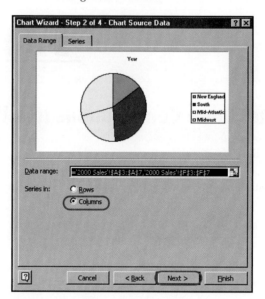

4 Click **Next**. The third Chart Wizard dialog box is displayed. Click the **Titles** tab, if it is not already selected. Type **2000 Sales by Region** in the **Chart title** box.

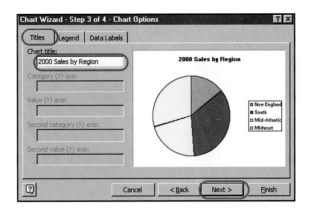

5 Click **Next**. The fourth Chart Wizard dialog box is displayed. Select **As new sheet** and type **2000 Sales by Division** in the adjacent box.

In Depth: In this example, the company is divided into four operating divisions that are based on geographical regions. The terms division and region are used interchangeably.

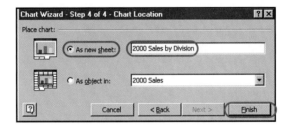

6 Click **Finish**. The chart is placed on its own sheet. (You learn how to change the size of the title and legend in a later task.) Save your work.

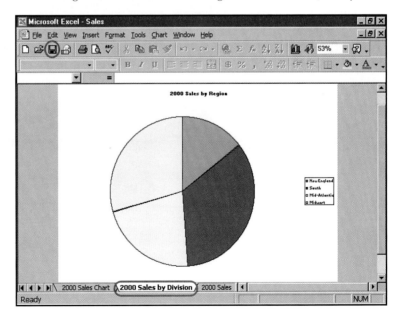

TASK 3

Creating a Chart to Make Comparisons

Why would I do this?

Perhaps the most common use for a chart is to make comparisons. For example, you might want to compare oil production by country over a series of years. To illustrate this type of comparison, a *column chart* (with vertical bars) or *bar chart* (with horizontal bars) is most often used.

In this task, you learn how to create a column chart that compares a company's regional sales for each quarter in 2000.

1 Click the **2000 Sales** sheet tab. Select cells **A3** through **E7**.

In Depth: It is important that you do not include the total rows or columns when doing a comparison chart. If you included these figures, it would distort the chart, since the totals would be compared to regional and quarterly sales amounts.

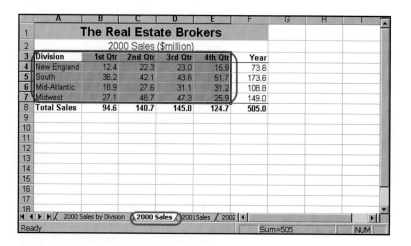

2 Click the **Chart Wizard** button. The first Chart Wizard dialog box is displayed. Click **Column** in the **Chart type** area, and accept the **Clustered Column** option in the **Chart sub-type** area.

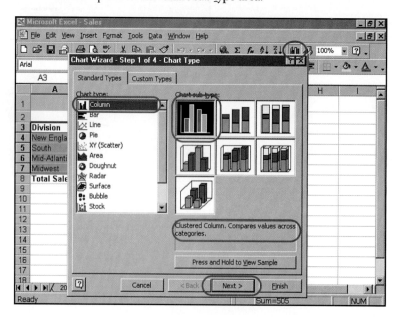

3 Click **Next**. The second Chart Wizard dialog box is displayed. Make sure **Rows** is selected from the **Series in** area. This keeps all of the sales figures from each quarter together.

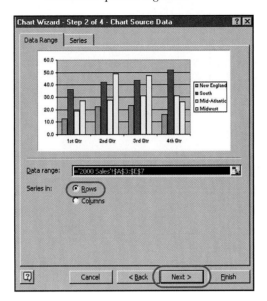

4 Click **Next**. The third Chart Wizard dialog box is displayed. Type **2000 Regions** in the **Chart title** box. Type **($ million)** in the **Value (Y) axis** box.

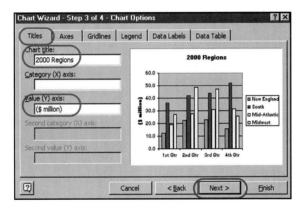

5 Click **Next**. Select **As new sheet** and type **2000 Regions** in the adjacent box.

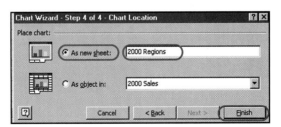

6 Click **Finish**. The chart is on its own sheet. Save your work.

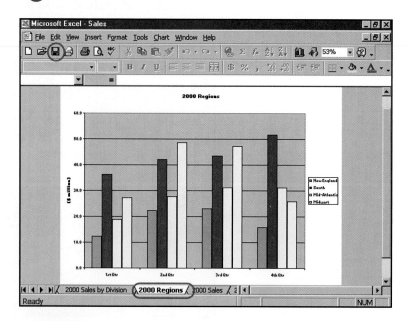

TASK 4

Editing the Elements of a Chart

Why would I do this?

When you create a chart in Excel, the proportions of the various elements often need to be adjusted. For example, the text on the axes, titles, and legends on the charts is too small. There are many options for customizing your charts in Excel, and they are easy to use.

In this task, you make changes to the 2000 Sales Chart to make it easier to read and to emphasize the variation from one quarter to the next.

1 Click the **2000 Sales Chart** sheet tab. Right-click on the title, **2000 Real Estate Sales**. A shortcut menu appears.

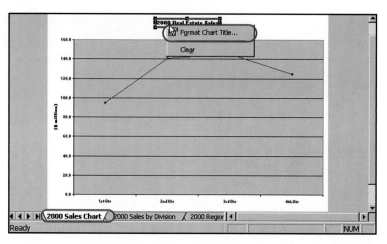

2 Select **Format Chart Title** from the shortcut menu and click the **Font** tab in the Format Chart Title dialog box. Scroll down the list of available font sizes and select **18**.

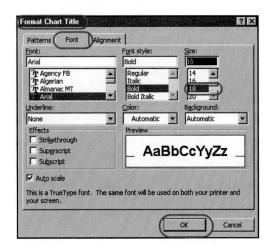

3 Click **OK**. The title is now much easier to read.

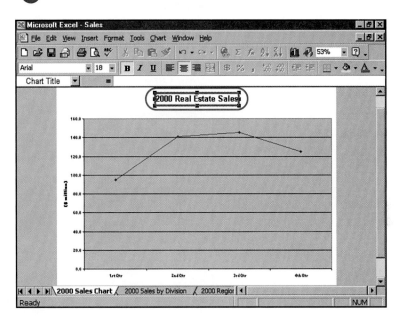

4 Right-click on the value (Y) axis label, (**$ million**), and choose **Format Axis Title** from the shortcut menu. Change the size of the font to **14** point.

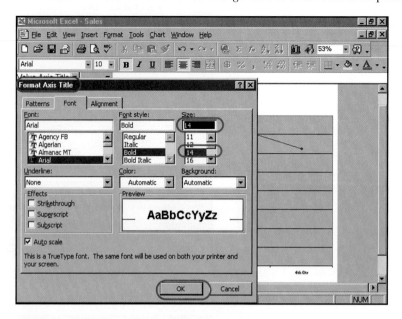

5 Click **OK**. Use this procedure to change the size of the category (X) axis labels to **14** point.

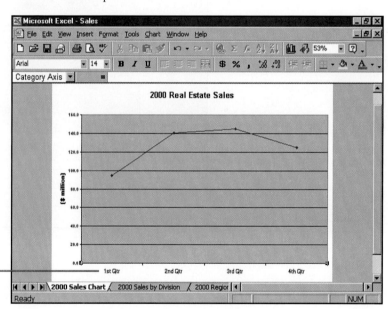

Category (X) axis labels displayed
using 14 point font

6 Move the pointer onto the numbers on the value (Y) axis. The ScreenTip Value Axis is displayed.

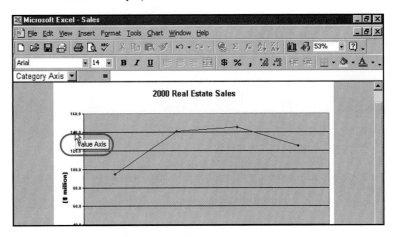

7 Right-click and select **Format Axis** from the shortcut menu. Click the **Scale** tab. Change the **Minimum** value to **80**.

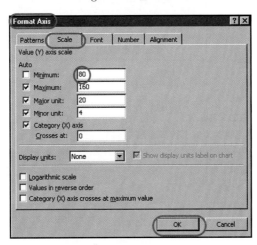

8 Click **OK**. Notice the new scale exaggerates the difference in the values. Save the changes you have made.

Differences are exaggerated ———

New scale starts at 80 ———

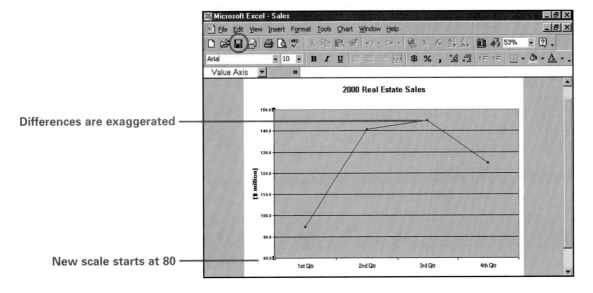

TASK 5

Printing a Chart

Why would I do this?

Many spreadsheets are created for the sole purpose of generating one or more charts. These charts might be printed on paper to be included in a report or on overhead transparencies to be used as part of a presentation.

In this task, you learn how to print a chart.

1 Click the **2000 Regions** sheet tab. This sheet contains a column chart comparing sales by region.

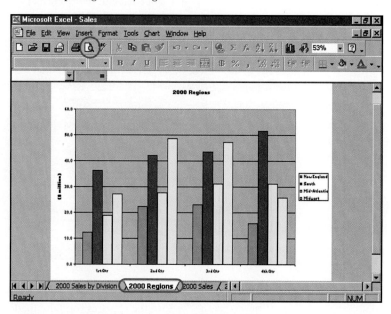

2 Click the **Print Preview** button.

In Depth: If your computer is connected to a color printer, the preview is in color and the chart will print in color. If not, the preview will not be in color.

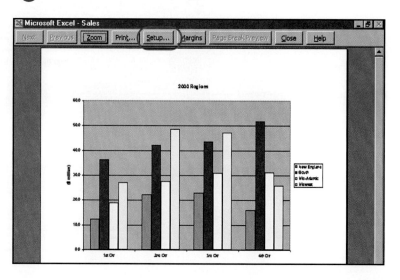

3 Click **Setup**. Click the **Header/Footer** tab if necessary. Click **Custom Header** and type your name in the **Left section** of the header.

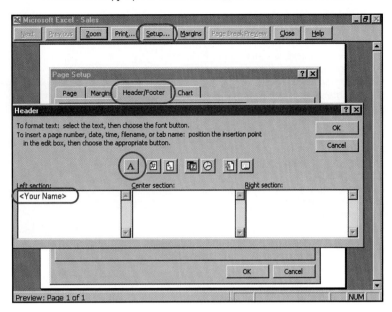

4 Click the **Font** button and change the size of the font to **14** point and the **Font** style to **Bold Italic**.

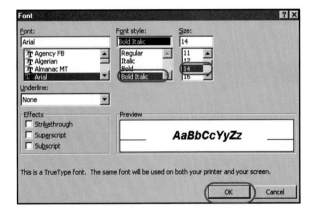

5 Click **OK** to return to the Header dialog box. Click **OK** to return to the **Page Setup** dialog box. Click **OK** to return to the **Print Preview**.

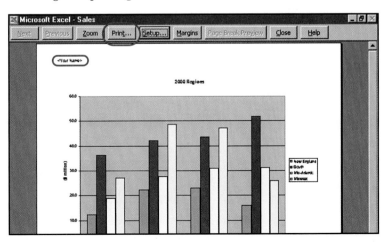

6 Click the **Print** button to print the chart. Click **OK** in the Print dialog box. Close the workbook and save the changes.

Caution: If you plan to create transparencies from your charts, there are several problems you should know about. If you plan to print the transparency directly from your printer, you must use a transparency that is designed for your type of printer. Colors seldom look as dark or saturated as onscreen or on paper. If your office has transparencies that work with your copier, you would be wise to print the charts on regular paper and then use the copier to transfer them to transparencies. Transparency material is expensive, and you usually have to buy an entire box. Preview your work and print samples on paper to avoid costly reprints. Transparencies often jam when you try to feed several through the printer or copier.

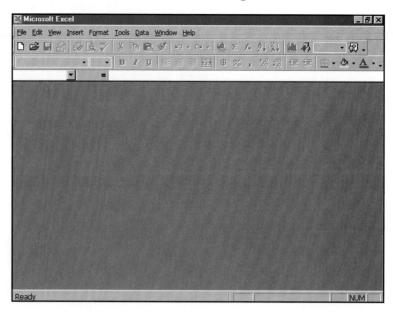

Comprehension Exercises

Comprehension questions are designed to check your memory and understanding of the basic concepts in this lesson. You distinguish between true and false statements, identify new screen elements, and match terms with related statements. If you are uncertain of the correct answer, refer to the task number following each question (for example, T4 refers to Task 4) and review that task until you are confident that you can provide a correct response.

True-False

Circle either T or F.

T F **1.** The Chart Wizard walks you through the creation of a chart. **(T1)**

T F **2.** Pie charts are used to show trends. **(T1)**

T F **3.** If the printer you use is a color printer, the print preview will be in color. **(T5)**

T F **4.** When selecting data to chart, always include the row and column totals. **(T2)**

T F **5.** When you right-click on a chart title, it automatically sizes the font to produce a title that spans 3/4 of the printed page. **(T4)**

T F **6.** Column charts and bar charts are both used to illustrate data that shows comparisons. **(T3)**

T F **7.** When you increase the font size of the Y-axis, the size of the plot area remains the same. **(T4)**

T F **8.** One of the choices you can make in the Chart Wizard is whether you want your chart to be on the same worksheet as the data or on its own sheet. **(T1)**

T F **9.** Once a line chart is created, the Y-axis scale must always start at zero. **(T4)**

T F **10.** Right-clicking on a chart element will call up a shortcut menu that allows you to make changes. **(T4)**

Identifying Parts of the Excel Screen

Refer to the figure and identify the numbered parts of the screen. Write the letter of the correct label in the space next to the number.

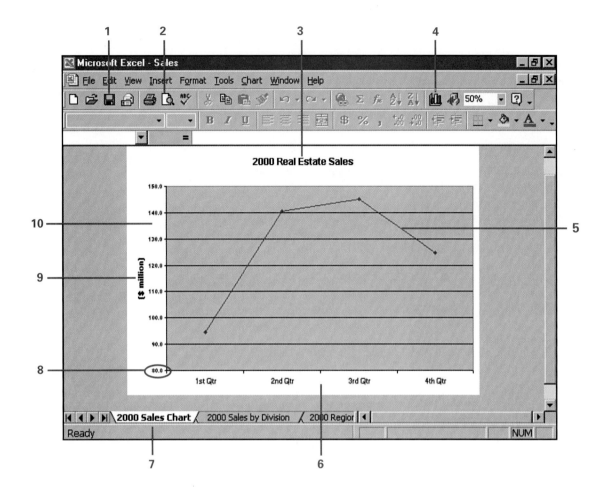

1. _____   **A.** Save button (**T1**)

2. _____   **B.** Category (X) axis (**T4**)

3. _____   **C.** Print Preview button (**T5**)

4. _____   **D.** Value (Y) axis (**T4**)

5. _____   **E.** Value (Y) axis title (**T4**)

6. _____   **F.** Chart Wizard button (**T1**)

7. _____   **G.** Sheet tab (**T2**)

8. _____   **H.** Chart title (**T1**)

9. _____   **I.** Minimum scale value (**T4**)

10. _____   **J.** Line connecting data points (**T1**)

Matching

Match the statements below to the word or phrase that is the best match from the list. Write the letter of the matching word or phrase in the space provided next to the number.

1. ___ A chart type used to make comparisons (T3)

2. ___ Displays chart as it will look when printed (T5)

3. ___ Where you can add a header to the printout (T5)

4. ___ A chart type used to show trends over time (T1)

5. ___ The chart axis at the bottom of the chart (T4)

6. ___ The chart axis at the left side of the chart (T4)

7. ___ Prints at the top of a chart (T5)

8. ___ A list that identifies a pattern or color used in an Excel worksheet chart (T1)

9. ___ A chart type used to show contributions to a whole (T2)

10. ___ A way to choose chart elements (T4)

A. Legend

B. Right-click

C. Column chart

D. Category (X) axis

E. Value (Y) axis

F. Page Setup dialog box

G. Print Preview button

H. Line chart

I. Header

J. Sub-type

K. Pie chart

Reinforcement Exercises

Reinforcement exercises are designed to reinforce the skills you have learned by applying them to a new situation. Detailed instructions are provided along with a figure, where appropriate, to illustrate the final result. The Reinforcement exercises that follow should be completed sequentially. Leave the workbook open at the end of each exercise for use in the next exercise until you are specifically directed to close it.

Open **Less1402** from the **Student\Lesson14** folder on your CD-ROM disc and save it as **Ex1401** on your floppy disk for use in the following exercises.

R1—Create and Print a Pie Chart

1. Change the **Sheet1** tab name to **Casualties**.

2. Create a 3-D pie chart showing how each decade has contributed to the total number of casualties. See the following steps for more detail.

3. Select cells **A2** through **A6** and cells **E2** through **E6**.

4. In the first dialog box, click the **Chart Wizard** button. Choose the **Pie** chart type, then choose the **Pie with a 3-D visual effect** chart sub-type (the middle choice on the top row). In the second dialog box, choose **Columns**, if necessary.

5. In the third dialog box, change the title to **Michigan Tornado Casualties by Decade**.

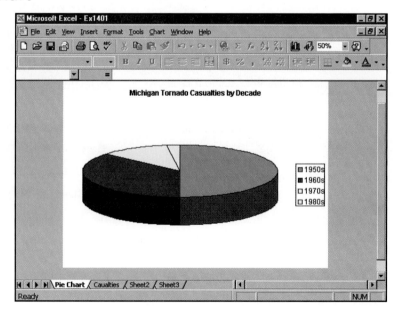

6. In the fourth dialog box, choose to save the chart as a new sheet named **Pie Chart**. Save your work.

7. Change size of the font in the title and the legend to **18** point.

8. Add your name to the header using **Bold**, **Italic**, 12 point font. Preview and print the chart.

R2—Create and Print a Column Chart

1. Select the **Casualties** sheet.

2. Create a column chart to compare the number of tornadoes in each decade. See the following steps for more detail.

3. Select cells **A2** through **B6**.

4. Click the **Chart Wizard** button. Choose the **Column** chart type, then choose the **Clustered column with a 3-D visual effect** chart sub-type (the first choice in the second row).

5. View a sample of the chart and compare it to the figure.

6. Change the title to **Michigan Tornadoes by Decade**.

7. In the fourth dialog box, place the chart on a new sheet named **Column Chart**.

8. Change the size of the title font to **18** point. Select and delete the legend. Change the size of the X and Y axis labels to **12** point.

9. Add your name to the footer in the lower left. Print the chart.

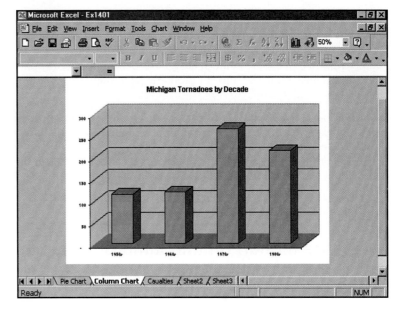

R3—Show a Trend with a Line Chart

1. Select the **Casualties** tab.

2. Create a chart to show the trend in total casualties. See the steps below for more detail.

3. Select cells **A2** through **A6** and cells **E2** through **E6**.

4. Click the **Chart Wizard** button and select the **Line** chart type and **3-D Line** as the sub-type.

5. Change the title to **Tornado Casualties in Michigan**.

6. Save as a new sheet with the name **Line Chart**.

7. Delete the legend. Change the size of the font in the title to **18** point.

8. Add your name to the header in the upper left. Preview and print the chart. Close the workbook.

Challenge

Challenge exercises are designed to test your ability to apply your skills to new situations with less detailed instruction. These exercises also challenge you to expand your repertoire of skills by using Excel commands that are similar to those you have already learned. The desired outcome is clearly defined, but you have more freedom to choose the steps needed to achieve the required result.

In these Challenge exercises, you work with data concerning the consumption of energy compared to gross national product (GNP) for sixteen countries around the world. You will use Excel's charting capability to determine if the amount of energy that a person uses is proportional to the amount of goods they produce. In other words, if a person in an affluent country consumes ten times as much energy as a person in a poor country, do they produce ten times as much? If the amount of goods produced is directly proportional to the energy consumed, a line chart of the data should be a fairly straight line.

In these exercises, you examine this data to see if such a relationship exists, using some of the advanced Excel charting tools. First, you create a simple chart that displays the energy used per person for each country and save it as an object in the worksheet. Then you create a line chart of the energy consumption and GNP as a first attempt to show data with unequal category axis intervals. Finally, you create a chart of the data to show the relationship between energy consumption and GNP using an X-Y scatter chart.

Open **Less1403** from the **Student\Lesson14** folder on the CD-ROM disc and save it on your floppy disk as **Ex1402**. This file is used for both Challenge and Discovery exercises.

C1—Place a Chart on the Same Sheet as the Data

If a chart is small, it may be placed on the same sheet as the rest of the data. In this example, you will chart the energy used per person by country, then save it on the same sheet as the data.

Goal: Create a column chart that displays the country and the energy used per capita and place it on Sheet1 with the data. Adjust the font size of the category labels so they all display.

Use the following guidelines:

1. Open **Ex1402** and select **Sheet1**.

2. Select the data (and headings) in the **Country** and **Energy** columns.

3. Create a column chart and save it as an object in **Sheet1**.

4. Notice that all the country names do not fit on the X axis. Double-click on one of the country names on the chart and change the font size to **8** point.

5. Deselect the chart and change the **Zoom** to **50%**.

6. Change the **Page Setup** to **Landscape** orientation.

7. Move the chart to a place below the data and drag one of its handles to stretch the chart to display all the names. Work with the Print Preview option to make sure the chart will fit on one page and all the country names will print.

8. Add your name to the header. Print the page with the chart. Change the Zoom back to 100%.

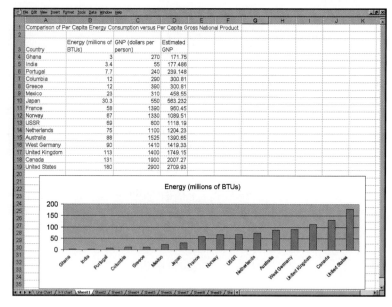

9. Save the workbook. Leave the workbook open for use in the next exercise.

C2—Chart Data with Unequally Spaced Category Values Using a Line Chart

If the value on the value (Y) axis is supposed to depend on its corresponding value on the category (X) axis, it is important that the numeric intervals between the values on the category (X) axis are equal. If you use a line chart, the data in the left-most column is automatically placed along the category axis, spaced at even intervals, even if the values between the data points are not equal. The result is a chart where it is not easy to determine if a proportional or "straight line" relationship exists. In this exercise, you chart the energy used per capita compared to the GNP per capita using a line chart so you can see what the problem looks like. In the next exercise, you will use an X-Y chart so you can compare the two types of graphs.

Use **Ex1402** that was opened in the previous exercise.

Goal: Chart related data using a line chart.

1. Select the data and column heading for GNP (cells **C3** through **C19**).

2. Create a line chart like the one in the figure. See the steps below for more detailed instruction.

3. In the second dialog box of the Chart Wizard, select the **Series** tab.

4. Click the **Collapse dialog box** button on the **Category (X) axis labels** box and select the data in the **Country** and **Energy** columns (**A4** through **B19**; do not include the column labels).

5. Create the chart on its own sheet named **Line Chart**.

6. Add your name to the page header. Print the chart. Save the workbook.

7. Examine the chart. The values along the category (X) axis are evenly spaced even though they do not represent equal intervals. For example, Columbia and Greece both use 12 BTUs per person, but these two points are displayed at different locations along the horizontal or category (X) axis. Obviously, a graph with two data points of the same value in two different locations creates a misleading picture. It is not a good idea to use a line

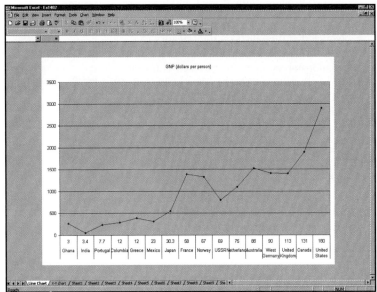

chart to represent data where the value shown on the value (Y) axis depends on the number shown on the category (X) axis unless the interval between the values on the category (X) axis are already equally spaced. Do the next exercise to see how this example data should be charted.

C3—Chart Related Data Using the X-Y Chart

If you are charting two columns of numbers where the second column is dependent on (or related to) the first column, you should use an X-Y chart, sometimes called a scatter chart. The data points are scattered on the chart to indicate each intersection of the X and Y coordinates, and the intervals on the category (X) axis are forced to be equal.

When plotting real-life data, you seldom get an exact relationship. You look to see if the points represent a general trend, such as a straight line or a curve. In our example, the energy used per person is displayed on the category (X) axis and the GNP per person is displayed on the value (Y) axis.

Use the file **Less1403,** that was created in a previous exercise and saved as **Ex1402**.

Goal: Represent the per capita Gross National Product as it relates to the amount of energy used per person.

1. Open **Sheet1**. Select the **Energy** and **GNP** columns (cells **B3** through **C19**). Chart the Energy and GNP data using an X-Y scatter chart as shown.

2. Use a chart title of **GNP per Energy Used**, **Millions of BTUs** for the X-axis title, and **Dollars** for the Y-axis title.

3. Do not show the legend.

4. Save the chart on its own sheet named **X-Y chart**.

5. Add your name to the header and print the chart.

6. Notice that the values on the category (X) axis have evenly spaced intervals and the relationship between the two factors appears to be more linear. The two data points with 12 BTUs are at the location on the category (X) axis and vary slightly on the value (Y) axis because of a difference in GNP.

Leave the workbook open for use in the Discovery exercises.

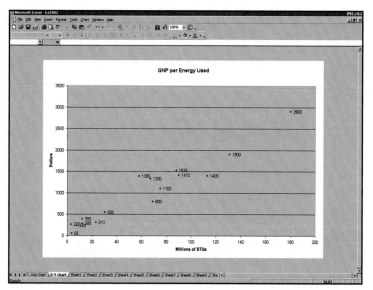

Discovery

Discovery exercises are designed to help you learn how to teach yourself a new skill. In each exercise, you discover something new that is related to the topic taught in this lesson. You may be directed to use built-in wizards or some of the extensive Help features provided in Excel to discover new features and learn new skills with minimum assistance from books or instructors. The required outcome demonstrates your ability to apply the new skill. You determine the choice of topic, worksheet design, and steps of execution.

These Discovery exercises continue the exploration of using advanced Excel charting concepts and statistical analysis. The exercises use the X-Y chart that was created in Challenge exercise 3. These exercises should be completed in order as presented. In the first exercise, you add data labels to the X-Y chart. In the second exercise, you add a trend line to the chart and determine how much the GNP per person depends on the energy consumed per person. In the last exercise, you use the trend line formula to estimate the GNP for the countries listed in the worksheet.

D1—Add Data Labels to an X-Y Chart

You can add information to a chart using the short-cut menu that displays when you right-click on a data point on the chart.

Goal: Use the shortcut menu to display the Y-axis value next to each data point on an X-Y chart.

1. Select the X-Y chart sheet that you created in C3 and right-click on one of the chart's data points.

2. Format the data series so that the data labels show.

3. Leave the workbook open for use in the next Discovery exercise.

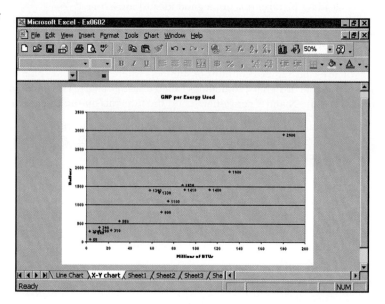

D2—Add a Trend Line to an X-Y Chart

If there is a linear relationship between the values displayed on the category (X) axis and those on the Y-axis of an X-Y chart, the data points will be close to a straight line. Excel can calculate the straight line that is the best fit to the data points and add it to the chart.

The method of determining the formula for the best-fitting straight line is called a *linear regression analysis*. The degree of fit is represented by the R^2 value. A perfect fit would have an R^2 value equal to 1.

Goal: Add the trend line to the X-Y chart that is the best fit to the data. Use the R^2 value to determine if the best fit is a straight line or one of the other shapes.

1. Select the **X-Y chart** sheet.

2. Right-click on one of the data points and add a trend line.

3. Choose one of the six types of trend lines. Click the **Options** tab and choose to display the R-squared value.

4. Look at the trend line and its R-squared value, and then delete the trend line.

5. Try each of the trend lines and decide which one is the best fit (has the highest value of R-squared).

6. Once you determine which trend line is the best fit, add it to the data and display the R-squared value on the chart.

7. Save the workbook and leave it open for use in the next exercise.

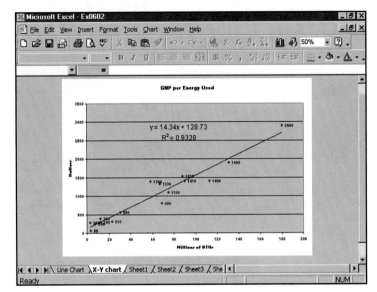

D3—Use the Trend Line Formula to Estimate Values

Excel displays the formula for the line that you select. You can use this formula to estimate new values or determine how much a given point differs from the trend line. For this example, we will use the straight trend line to keep the formula as simple as possible.

Goal: Determine the formula for the straight trend line and use it to generate a new column of estimated GNP values.

1. Select the **X-Y chart** sheet. Use the shortcut menu to add a linear trend line to the data points. Set the option to display the equation on the chart.

2. Right-click on the formula and change its font size to **18** point. Drag the formula to a clear space on the chart.

3. Select **Sheet1**. Rewrite this formula so that you can use it in cell **D4** to estimate the GNP based on the value in cell **B4**. Use a cell reference in place of X in the formula. (The estimated value for Ghana will be 171.75. Ghana's GNP per energy used, 270, is much higher than the estimate.)

4. Fill this formula into the cells below to create a new column of estimated GNP for each country.

5. Print **Sheet1**.

6. Save the workbook and close it.

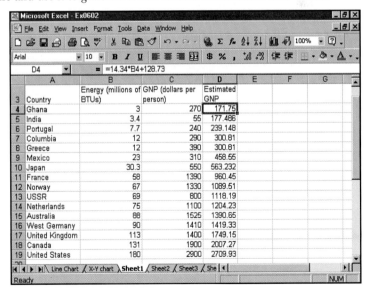

Introduction to Access

What Is Access?

Access is a database management program that allows you to store, retrieve, analyze, and print information. It is a system for managing large amounts of data. A simple example of a database is an address book or a card file system listing people's names, addresses, and phone numbers. Access enables you to develop databases that can manage thousands of pieces of related data in an organized, efficient, and accurate manner.

How Does Access Work?

To begin to use Access, there are a number of terms that you need to understand. An Access database consists of *tables, queries, forms, reports, pages, macros,* and *modules,* known generally as *objects.* These objects work together to store, search, input, report, and automate the data. The objects of the database are viewed from the *Database window,* which is the window that opens when you open a database.

Tables are the foundation of the database because they store the data. A database table is made up of columns and rows of information, similar to a spreadsheet. The columns contain *fields,* which are types of information, such as first name or last name. Rows contain *records,* which represent all of the related information about a single person, event, or transaction. For example, in a phone book, the columns would consist of fields such as first name, last name, street address, city, state, zip code, and phone number. The rows would contain all the specific information about each individual.

Queries are used to sort, search, and limit the data to just those records that you need to see. Queries are designed to question the data that is contained in the tables. They can be based on one or more tables and can be used to create new fields that are calculated from other fields. Queries are based on the current information in a table and can be used to revise and analyze data.

Forms are generally used to input or edit data, or to view one record at a time. They can be based on a table or on a query. Forms are interactive with a table because they can be used to view the information in the table or to update the information in a table.

Reports are used to summarize information for printing and presentation of the data. Reports can be based on tables or on queries. They report information based on the current data in the tables, but cannot be used to change the information in a table or a query.

Pages are data access pages that are created for a database. A data access page is a Web page that can be used to add, edit, view, or manipulate data. These pages are similar to forms used for entering and viewing data, or reports used for grouping and presenting data. Pages are created to take advantage of the ability to share database information in a Web environment.

Macros are used to automate existing Access commands. Macros are often a series of commands that may be attached to buttons on forms, tables, or queries.

Modules are programs in the Visual Basic programming language that are used to customize the database for special needs.

Together, these seven objects make up an Access database. The objects of the database are viewed from the Database window.

Why Use a Database?

One of the main advantages of using an electronic database is its capability to search and sort the data and find information quickly. As a database designer, your job is to set up the tables and queries so information can be retrieved that is useful and helpful to the end user. When designing a database, it is usually best to start with the desired outcomes in order to determine the information that needs to be included in the database.

Once the database has been designed and the data entered, you will want to be able to retrieve information from the database. Queries and form filters can be used to retrieve records that meet certain conditions, such as all of your friends who live in Florida. Queries can also be used to calculate values based on other fields or to analyze data.

Databases are also used to print or present information. Access uses a number of wizard tools that help to design reports that can summarize data based on groups you select.

A relational database such as Access can help you organize, maintain, update, retrieve, and analyze data. It is designed to reduce repetition of data, reduce errors, and save storage space.

The approach used in the Access lessons emphasizes the coordination of tables, forms, queries, and reports so you understand their interaction. In the first lesson, you create a database, establish the basic structure of the database table, and create a form and a report. This gives you an overview of a database and three of the main objects in a database. In later lessons, objects in the database are examined in more detail.

Lesson: 15

Create a Customized Database

Introduction

There are three ways to use Access once it is launched. You can use the Database Wizard, open an existing database file, or create a new database. In this lesson, you create a new database by creating and defining a set of fields for a personnel file for the Armstrong Pool, Spa, and Sauna Co. Normally, you would spend time thinking about how the database would be used, what information was needed, and what kinds of reports you would need to produce. Like any other computer application, a database is only as useful as the information that it contains. Once you decide on the information you need in your database, you create it by designing tables and adding records.

In this lesson, you create a database and personnel table for a company. You enter records, create and modify a form, and create and print a report.

Visual Summary

When you have finished this entire lesson, you will have created a database report that looks like this:

Personnel File by Department

Department	Last Name	First Name	Social Security Number	Telephone	Hourly Pay	Employed
Sales						
	Dent	Arthur	323232322	(313) 941-0000	$9.00	10/1/90
	Johnson	Deborah D.	111223333	(313) 555-1234	$9.50	5/25/95
	Johnson	John J.	123456789	(313) 555-1234	$9.50	5/25/95
	Prefect	Ford	232323233	(313) 461-0000	$9.00	10/1/90
Service						
	Robinson	Robert R.	987654321	(313) 487-0000	$12.80	1/2/89
Stock						
	Abercrombie	Aaron A	222554444	(810) 437-0000	$5.00	6/12/97
	Wilson	Wendy W.	221212211	(313) 769-0000	$5.00	7/17/97

Thursday, May 06, 1999

Page 1 of 1

TASK 1

Creating a New Database Using the Blank Database Option
Why would I do this?

In most situations, you will use the blank database option to create your database rather than using the Database Wizard. The blank database enables you to define the field name, data type, and size. You can also add a description if you want. The blank database is the most flexible approach because you can easily create the fields that you need for your business.

In this task, you create a database to manage the personnel records for the Armstrong Pool, Spa, and Sauna Co. You launch Access, choose Blank Database, give the database a name, and choose where to store the file. Unlike other applications, when you create a database, the first action you take is to name the database and designate where you will be saving the file. Only after the file has been created and saved can you actually begin to use the database.

1 Launch **Access**. The Microsoft Access dialog box opens and enables you to **Open an existing file**, or to create a new database using the **Access database wizards, pages, and projects** or the **Blank Access database** option.

2 Click the **Blank Access database** option, if necessary, and click **OK**. The **File New Database** dialog box is displayed. In the **Save in** box, choose where you want to save your file. Type **Armstrong Personnel** in the **File name** box.

— **Create button**

3 Click **Create**. The Database window opens. The name of the database shows in the title bar of the Database window. The Tables object button is selected on the left side of the Database window, and you are given three table-creation options. At this time, no objects have been created for this database. Leave the database open and continue to the next task.

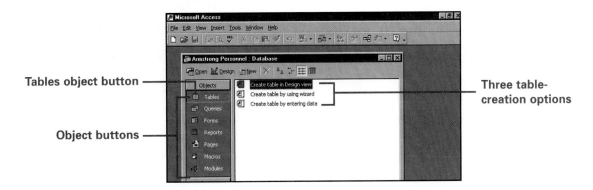

Tables object button

Object buttons

Three table-creation options

TASK 2

Creating a Table and Defining Its Fields
Why would I do this?

Once you have opened a new blank database, the next thing you must do is create a table. Tables are key to good database design. In a business, you might need to collect information about the customers you serve, the vendors you buy from, and your employees. While each group is related to your business, and there is interaction between the groups, they are each distinct and separate from each other. One you sell to, another you buy from, and the third group you employ. Therefore, you would create a separate table for information that would be maintained on each group. Each table should contain only the information that is directly related to the specific kind of data you are collecting. You decide what information you need to collect about each group of data, and then decide on the categories, or names, for each piece of data. For example, in a phone book, you might include first name, last name, street address, city, state, postal code, and phone number as categories of data to include in a phone book table. In this manner, you define the content of your data by establishing the fields to include in each table.

In this task, you create a table in Design view, assigning each field a name, *data type*, and description. Your field names will be displayed as column headings in the table, the data type tells the computer what type of data will be entered, and the description appears on the status line of the table to aid in entering data.

1 With the **Tables** object selected, choose **Create table in Design view**, if necessary.

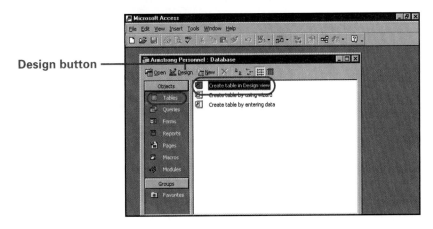

Design button

2 Click the **Design** button on the dialog box toolbar. The table Design view window opens. It contains three columns—Field Name, Data Type, and Description. There is also an area at the bottom of the dialog box where you can modify the Field Properties.

Field Name column   **Data Type column**   **Description column**

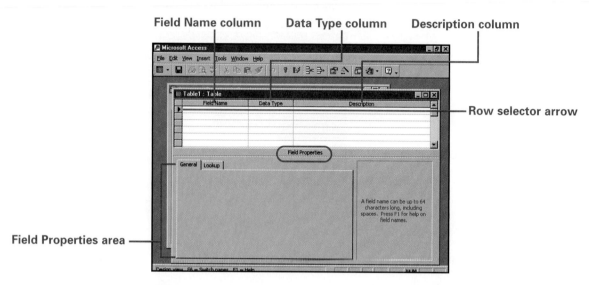

Row selector arrow

Field Properties area

3 With the insertion point in the first **Field Name** box, type **Last Name** and press ↵Enter. The first field name is entered and the insertion point jumps to the Data Type column. The default data type value, **Text**, is displayed.

In Depth: Once you have entered a field name and moved to the Data Type column, the Field Properties section becomes available. Each field has associated properties, such as field size and format. The types of properties that are available will depend on the data type that is selected. Field properties are optional tools that can be used to help control or restrict a field, or to improve its function in a table.

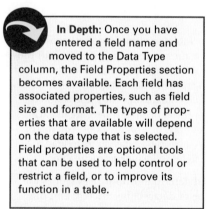

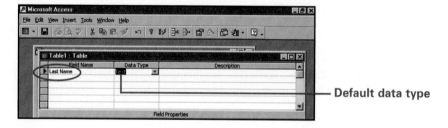

Default data type

4 Because the first field will be text, press ↵Enter to accept the default **Text** data type and move the insertion point to the Description box. Type **Employee's last name** in the **Description** box and press ↵Enter. The insertion point jumps to the next Field Name box and the row selector moves to the second field.

Row selector column

Arrow indicates the currently selected row

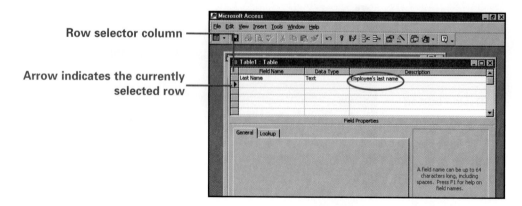

5 In the second field, type **First Name**, accept the **Text** data type, and type **Employee's first name and middle initial**. Press ↵Enter to move to the third field.

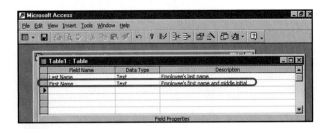

6 Type **Age** for the third field, then press ↵Enter. Click the arrow on the **Data Type** drop-down list box to reveal all of the data types.

Maximize button

Data Type drop-down list box

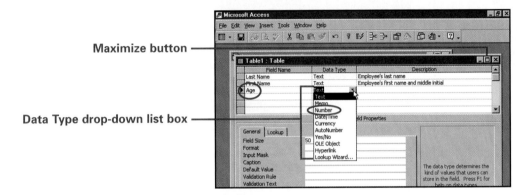

7 Select the **Number** data type; then fill in the rest of the fields as shown in the figure. If your screen does not have enough room, click the **Maximize** button to maximize the design window.

View button

8 Click the **View** button on the Standard toolbar to go to the **Datasheet** view. A dialog box prompts you to save the table.

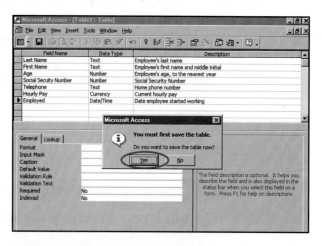

Caution: If you click the drop-down arrow on the right side of the **View** button, you will be given a choice of views. Choose **Datasheet View**. If you click directly on the **View** button, it will change automatically to the view represented by the icon that is displayed on the button. In most cases, clicking on the button will move you between a view of the design of an object and the view that shows that data in its most common form for that object. For example, in a table, the View button moves you between the Design view and the Datasheet view. In a form, the View button moves you between the Design view and the Form view. The View button is used in this book as the quickest and easiest way to switch between different views of the same object.

9 Click **Yes**. The Save As dialog box opens. Type **Personnel File** in the **Table Name** box.

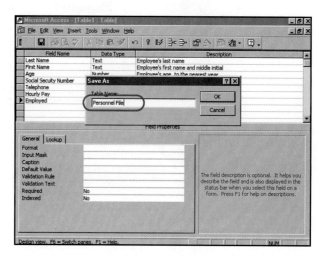

10 Click **OK**. A dialog box warns you that you haven't selected a primary key and asks if you want to create one.

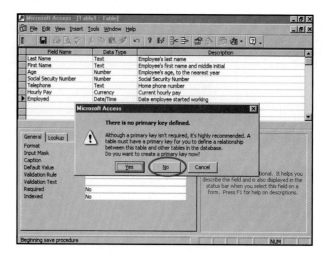

11 Click **No**. You will deal with the primary key later. The table is now displayed in Datasheet view and is ready to accept data. Click the **Maximize** button, if necessary, to give you the full screen to work in. Notice the field names are shown as column headings, and the description of the field shows in the status bar. Leave the window open and continue to the next task.

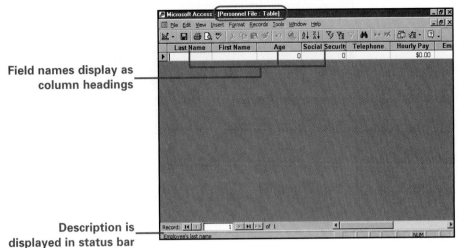

Field names display as column headings

Description is displayed in status bar

TASK 3

Entering Records into a Table and a Form
Why would I do this?

The main function of a database is to provide a source of information about a topic. Data can be entered into the computer in three different ways: it can be imported from another source, it can be captured from a Web site, and it can be entered at the keyboard. With customized databases, this last method is the most common. Records can be entered directly in a table or by using a form.

In this task, you learn how to enter data directly into the table and also into a form.

1 With the insertion point in the **Last Name** field, type **Johnson** and press (←Enter). The insertion point moves to the First Name field. Notice that the description you entered when you created the field appears in the status bar. Also note that the record selector looks like a pencil, meaning that the record is being edited but has not yet been saved. Lastly, note that when you enter the first piece of data, a new empty record is displayed with an asterisk for the record selector.

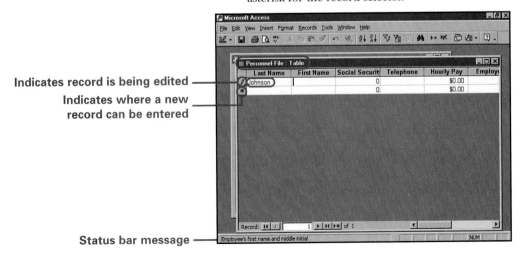

Indicates record is being edited

Indicates where a new record can be entered

Status bar message

2 Type **John J.** in the **First Name** field and press ↵Enter.

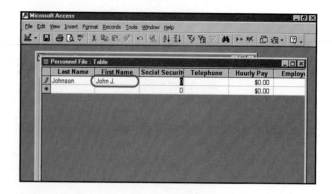

3 Enter **32** for the age, **123456789** (no dashes) for the Social Security number, **(313)555-1234** for the telephone number, **9.50** for the hourly pay, and **5/25/95** for the date employed. Press ↵Enter after each entry. When you press ↵Enter after the last field, the record is saved and the insertion point moves to the first field of the new record.

Quick Tip: You can also press Tab⇄ to move from one field to the next in the Datasheet view or from one column to the next in the Design view of the table. As you move from one field to the next, the display scrolls as needed to show the insertion point.

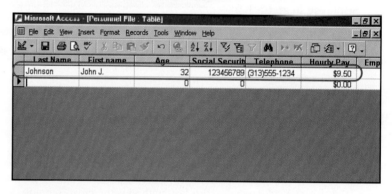

4 Fill in the next record as follows:

Last Name	Robinson
First Name	Robert R.
Age	47
Social Security Number	987654321
Telephone	(313)487-0000
Hourly Pay	12.80
Employed	1/2/89

A form can be created automatically that will display all the fields for one record. This *AutoForm* is a good tool to use for entering data.

New Object down arrow —

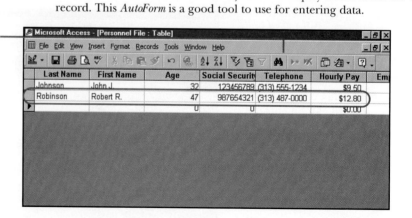

5 Click the down arrow next to the **New Object** button and select **AutoForm** from the list. An AutoForm is created. Notice that the form places all of the fields in one vertical column. Using a form to enter records can be easier because all of the fields are visible on the screen and you see only one record at a time.

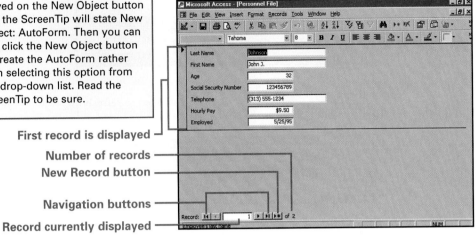

First record is displayed

Number of records

New Record button

Navigation buttons

Record currently displayed

6 Click the **New Record** button on either the **Standard** toolbar or at the right end of the navigation buttons to move to an empty record. Use the AutoForm to enter the next four records listed below. Press Tab or Enter to move from field to field. After the last record is entered, the status bar will show that six records have been entered.

Last Name	Johnson	Abercrombie	Prefect	Dent
First Name	Deborah D.	Aaron A.	Ford	Arthur
Age	30	16	34	28
SSN	111223333	222334444	232323233	323232322
Telephone	(313)555-1234	(810)437-0000	(313)461-0000	(313)941-0000
Hourly Pay	9.50	6.25	9.00	9.00
Employed	5/25/95	6/12/97	10/1/90	10/1/90

New Record button

New Record button

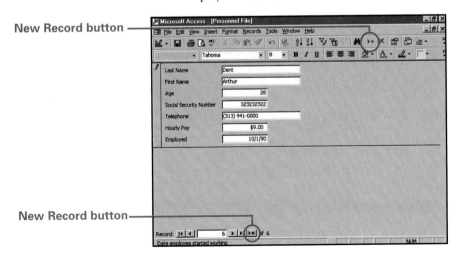

7 Click the **Close Window** button to close the AutoForm. When it asks if you want to save the form, choose **No**. The table datasheet that was opened when you created the AutoForm is now visible; however, only the first two records are displayed.

Only two records are displayed ⎯

8 To see the rest of the records, you need to refresh the window. Click the **View** button to change to **Design** view.

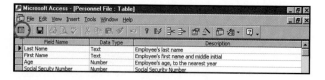

9 Click the **View** button again to return to the **Datasheet** view. Now you can see all of the records you have entered.

Records added using the Autoform

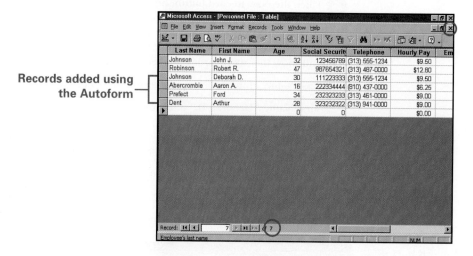

10 Click the **Close Window** button. The Tables object window now shows the Personnel File table.

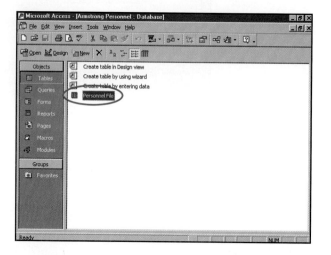

15

Adding and Deleting Fields

Why would I do this?

Prior planning is critical when designing a customized database. This helps to avoid problems at a later date. No matter how well you plan, however, there will be times when you need to add new fields to your database. You may also discover that some fields are extraneous and need to be removed.

You can modify a table by adding new fields and deleting others. When you make changes to the design of a table after records have been entered, Access gives you warning messages that the changes may affect your data. For this reason, it is recommended that you back up your file before you begin. If you know the content of your data, you will be able to judge the impact of the warnings. Be aware of the following:

- If you delete a field, all of the data in that field will be deleted as well.

- If you delete a field from a table, it must also be removed from other objects. If you forget and do not remove the deleted field, any query that uses the field will not work, and forms or reports will display an error message.

- If you rename a field in a table, the field also needs to be renamed in any object that uses that field.

- If you resize a field to a smaller size, Access will warn you that data may be lost because it may not fit in the new smaller field.

- If you change a field's data type, Access will try to convert the data in that field. If there are data mismatches, you will lose some of your data.

In this task, you learn how to add and delete fields and have the opportunity to see some of these warnings.

1 Click the **Personnel File** table to select it and click the **Design** button to go to **Design** view. Because there is some question about whether it is legal to keep an employee's age, you will delete the **Age** field.

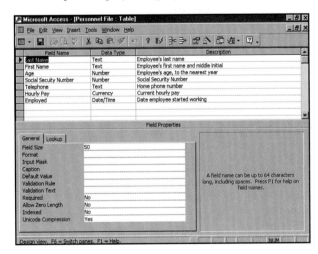

② Click the **row selector** to the left of the **Age** field. The entire row is selected.

Clicking the Row Selector
selects the entire row

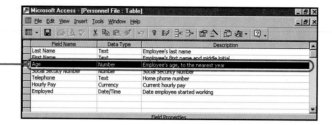

③ Press Del. A dialog box warns you that the deletion will be permanent, and asks if you want to delete the field(s).

Caution: When you delete a field, the deletion is final and all of the data in that field is lost. The Undo button will not work for this type of action.

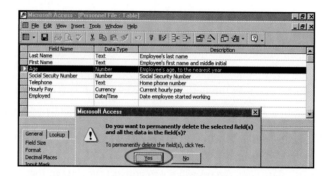

④ Click **Yes**. To add another field, place the insertion point in the **Field Name** box of the first blank row. Type **Department** as the new field name, accept the **Text** data type, and leave the **Description** area blank.

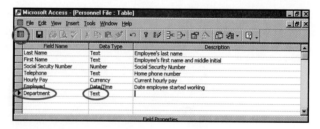

⑤ Click the **View** button to change to **Datasheet** view. A dialog box opens and prompts you to save the table.

Caution: Anytime you change the structure of a database object, such as the change you made to the **Personnel File** table in Step 4, you must save the change when it is made. You must save your changes before you go to Datasheet view or they will be lost.

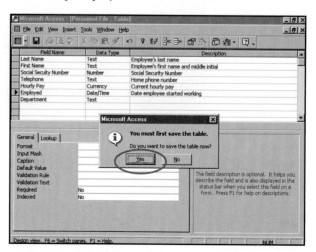

6 Click **Yes** to save your changes. The datasheet no longer contains an Age field, but does show the Department field on the right.

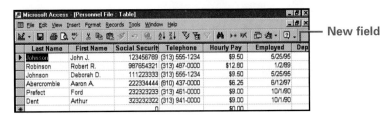

New field

7 Use the horizontal scrollbar to move to the right, and then fill in the **Department** field as shown. Use the ↓ to move from one record in this field to the next.

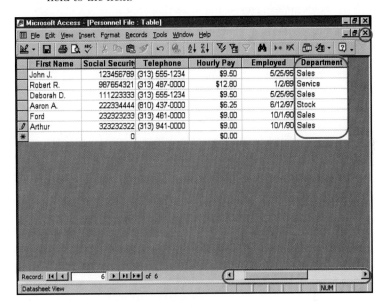

8 Click the **Close Window** button to close the table.

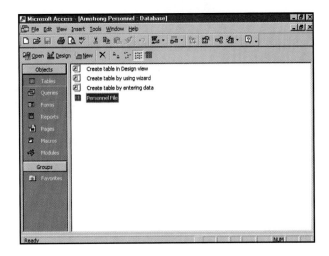

TASK 5

Creating a Form Using the Form Wizard
Why would I do this?

In small databases, where all of the fields can be seen on the screen, you can easily enter records in the table Datasheet view. With larger databases, scrolling back and forth to view a field becomes tedious; in that case, a form is helpful. Forms enable you to place more fields on the screen at a time. You can see more information about a record, and unlike the Datasheet view, you can view one record at a time. In Task 3, you created a form using the AutoForm option. This form is created based on the open or selected table. When you use the AutoForm, you do not have the opportunity to modify the order in which the fields appear, choose the fields that appear, or select a style or background.

In this task, you learn how to use the Form Wizard to create a form. Using the Wizard enables you to arrange fields in a different order, select only those fields that you want to use, and select a background and style for the form. This task is designed to introduce you to the Form Wizard so you can see the different options that are available. While the form you will create is similar to the AutoForm, the process used is different. This form will be used in the next task to show you how to modify a form design.

1 Click the **Forms** object button. The Forms window shows that no forms exist in the **Armstrong Personnel** database. There are, however, two ways shown to create a new form.

New button

Forms object button

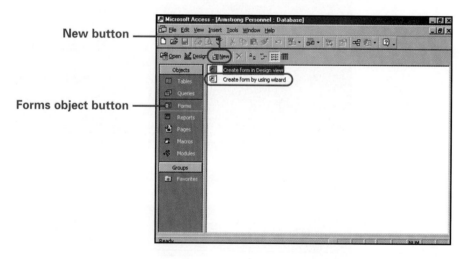

2 Select **Create form by using wizard**, and then click the **New** button. The New Form dialog box is displayed. Click **Form Wizard**, then select **Personnel File** from the drop-down menu.

In Depth: You could use the AutoForm: Columnar option to create the same form you will create here with the Form Wizard. The Form Wizard, however, gives you much more control over the choice of fields and the color and design of the form background.

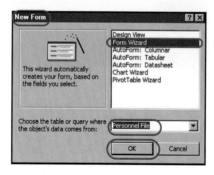

3 Click **OK** to activate the **Form Wizard**. The first Form Wizard dialog box enables you to select the fields you want to display in your form. Highlight the **Last Name** field in the **Available Fields** box, if necessary, and click the **Add Field** button to move it to the **Selected Fields** box.

Add Field button ⎯

Add All Fields button ⎯
Remove Field button ⎯

Remove All Fields button ⎯

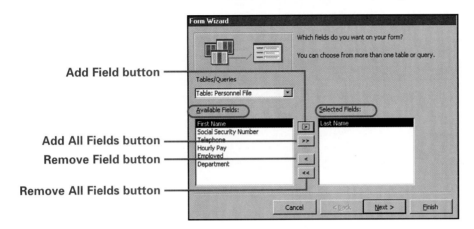

4 Click the **Add All Fields** button to place the rest of the fields in the **Selected Fields** box.

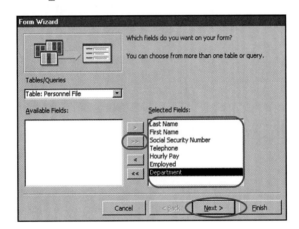

5 Click **Next**. The second Form Wizard dialog box prompts you to structure the form. Choose **Columnar**, if necessary, for the layout of the form. This will display each record in a single column as shown in the preview at the left side of the dialog box.

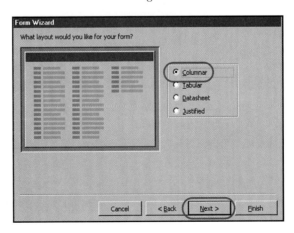

6 Click **Next**. The third Form Wizard dialog box prompts you to select a background style. Choose **Standard**, if necessary. A preview is shown on the left side of the dialog box.

Preview box ——

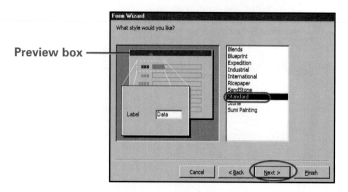

7 Click **Next**. The fourth (and final) Form Wizard dialog box prompts you to name the form. Type **Personnel File Input Form**. Make sure that the **Open the form to view or enter information** option is selected.

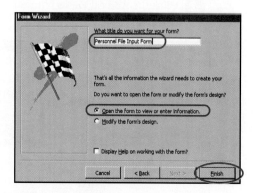

8 Click **Finish**. Access generates the columnar form with the fields and background you selected. If your form is not maximized, click the **Maximize** button. Leave the form open and continue with the next task.

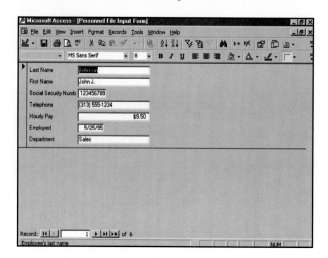

TASK **6**

Arranging Text and Label Fields in a Form and Adding a Label
Why would I do this?

When you use the Form Wizard or AutoForm, Access arranges the data labels and the data boxes in a preset order. There will be many times when you would like to rearrange the fields to match the layout of a paper form. With practice, you can design an Access form to look exactly like a printed form.

In this task, you will learn how to move around in a form and change the layout of the text and label boxes.

1 Click the **View** button to move to **Design** view. The form design window is displayed, along with the *Toolbox*. (Note: If the Toolbox is not displayed on your screen, click the **Toolbox** button on the Standard toolbar.) The field list box may also be displayed. All of the fields that contain data are shown in the Detail section of the form.

> **Caution:** The Toolbox may be docked at the bottom of your screen as shown in the figure. However, sometimes the Toolbox is displayed as a floating toolbar and its location interferes with the work you need to do. If this is the case, click the Toolbox title bar and drag the Toolbox to the bottom of the screen. When the outline of the Toolbox is a long rectangle, release the mouse button and the Toolbox will dock at the bottom of your screen.

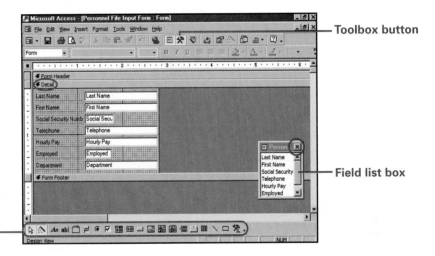

Toolbox button

Field list box

Toolbox

2 You will not be using the field list, so click the **Close** button to close this list. Click and drag the **First Name** field to the right of its current location, as shown in the figure.

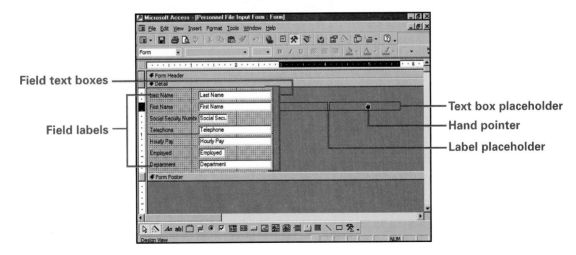

Field text boxes

Field labels

Text box placeholder

Hand pointer

Label placeholder

3 Release the mouse button. The First Name field is now on the right half of the screen. The Detail work area automatically increases to accept the new field location. The sizing handles around the text box indicate that this field is still selected.

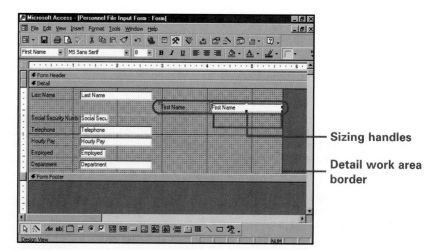

— Sizing handles

— Detail work area border

4 Drag the other fields to match the illustration.

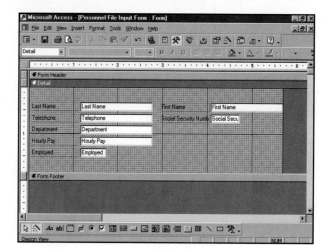

Caution: To begin drawing, click the mouse above the **Last Name** field and drag down and to the right above the **First Name** field. Do not release the mouse until you have finished drawing the new box for the label. If you release the mouse too soon, click outside the undersized label and repeat the process.

5 Click the **Label** button on the Toolbox toolbar. When you move the pointer to the **Detail** area, it changes to a crosshair with the letter **A** attached. Circle and drag to draw a box for the label as shown in the figure.

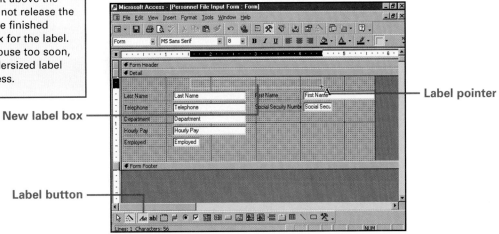

Label pointer

New label box

Label button

6 Type **Armstrong Pool, Spa, and Sauna Co.** in the box and press ↵Enter. Sizing handles surround the outer edge, showing that the label is selected.

Sizing handles indicate a control is selected

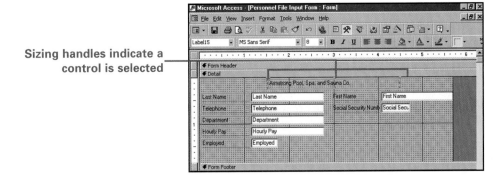

In Depth: If the formatted label no longer fits in the box, adjust the size of the box by clicking on a sizing handle and then stretching the box to enlarge it. You may need to increase both the length and the height of the box.

7 Click the **Bold** button and then the **Center** button on the Formatting toolbar. In the **Font** box, change the font to **Arial**, if necessary. Use the **Font Size** box to increase the font size to **12** point.

Font box

Font Size box

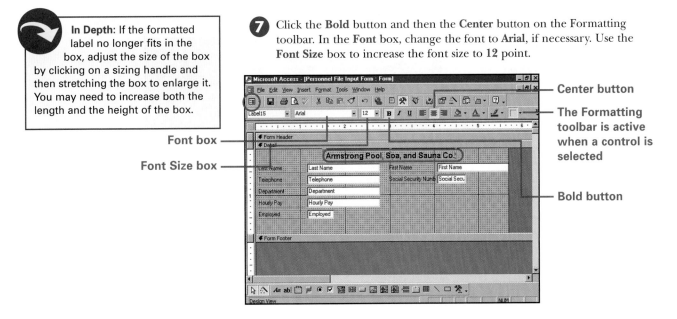

Center button

The Formatting toolbar is active when a control is selected

Bold button

8 Click the **View** button to return to **Form** view. Notice the effect of your changes. Leave the form open and continue with the next task.

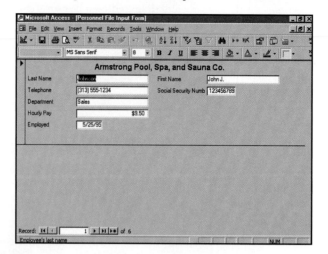

TASK 7

Setting the Tab Order in a Form

Why would I do this?

The layout of your newly modified form may make great sense now, but when you start entering data, you will find that the insertion point moves from field to field in the same order that the fields were entered in the table. The order the insertion point follows in moving from field to field is called the *tab order*. By changing the tab order to match the new layout of the form, you make it easier to enter data.

In this task, you learn how to change the tab order to match the design of your form.

1 Click the **New Record** button.

New Record button ——

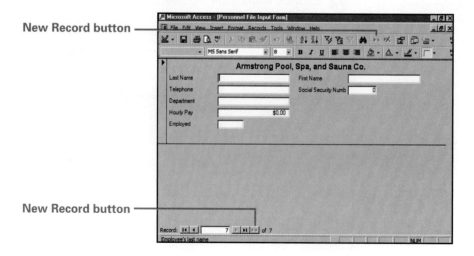

New Record button ——

2 Type **Wilson** in the **Last Name** field and press ↵Enter. Type **Wendy W.** in the **First Name** field and press ↵Enter. Notice that the insertion point jumps to the Social Security Number field, which was the third field you entered when you created the table.

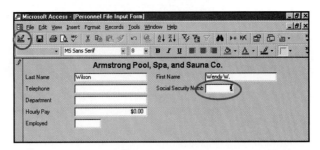

3 Click the **View** button to move to **Design** view. Choose **View**, **Tab Order** from the menu. (You may have to expand the **View** menu to see the **Tab Order** option.) The Tab Order dialog box opens with Social Security number shown as the third field. The last three fields are also out of order.

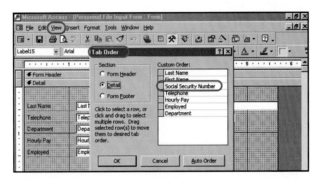

4 Click the **Auto Order** button. The order of data entry automatically changes to match the fields, so it will go from left to right and top to bottom.

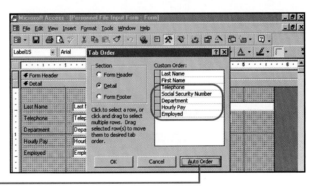

In Depth: There will be times when the automatic order will not fit your needs. To change the tab order manually, click the selector box to the left of the field name that you want to move. Release the mouse button, and then click the selector box for that field again and drag the field up or down.

Auto Order button —

5 Click **OK**, then click the **View** button to change to **Form** view. Click the **Last Record** button to return to the record you were adding. Finish filling in the information as shown.

Print Preview button ——

Last Record button ——

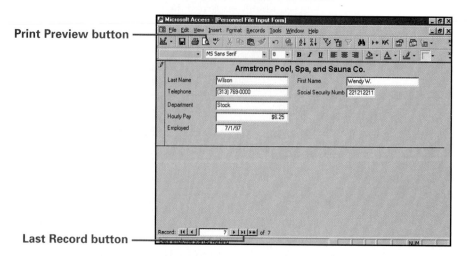

6 Click the **Print Preview** button. The form you created is displayed in a Print Preview window. Click the **Print** button to print the forms.

Print button ——

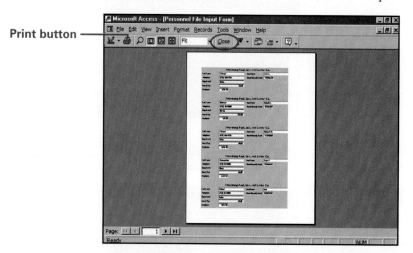

7 Click the **Close** button on the toolbar to return to **Form** view.

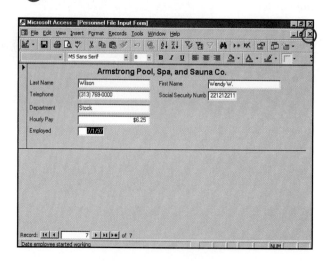

8 Click the **Close Window** button to close the form and move to the Database window. Save your changes when prompted.

TASK 8

Creating a Report Using the Report Wizard
Why would I do this?

When you have spent a great deal of time creating a database structure and entering data, you will want to print the information. A report gives you the flexibility to print the records and fields you select. You can also sort and group the records in a number of ways. The Access Report Wizard helps you create a customized report that includes the fields you want, grouped and sorted in the manner you select. Reports, like forms, can be modified once they have been created.

In this task, you will create a report, based on the Personnel File table, that is grouped by department and sorted on last and then first name.

1 Select the **Reports** object button. No reports are shown because none have been created in this database. There are, however, two available methods to create a report.

Reports object button ——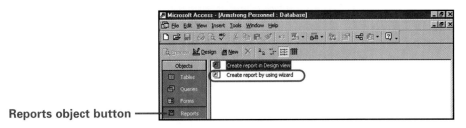

2 Double-click the **Create report by using wizard** option. The Report Wizard dialog box opens. Select the **Personnel File** table from the drop-down box.

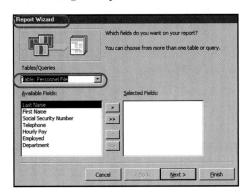

3 Click the **Add All Fields** button to move all of the fields from the **Available Fields** box to the **Selected Fields** box.

Add All Fields button —

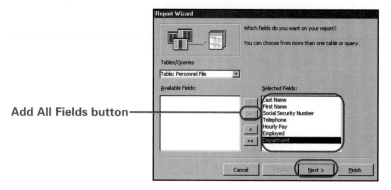

4 Click **Next**. The second Report Wizard dialog box enables you to group data. Select the **Department** field and click the **Add Field** button. The preview area shows that the other fields will be grouped on the Department field.

Preview area —

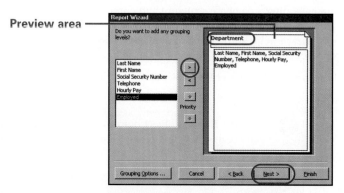

5 Click **Next**. The third Report Wizard dialog box enables you to sort data. You can sort on up to four fields. Select the **Last Name** field in the first sort drop-down box. Select the **First Name** field in the second drop-down box.

In Depth: The buttons to the right of the sort boxes enable you to sort in either ascending (A-to-Z or 1-to-10) or descending (Z-to-A or 10-to-1) order. The buttons toggle back and forth between ascending and descending order.

Click this arrow to
see the list of fields

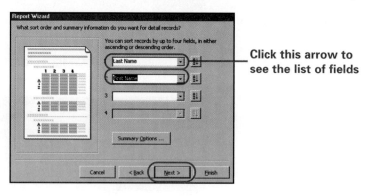

6 Click **Next**. The fourth Report Wizard dialog box enables you to choose the report layout. Select **Stepped** as the layout and **Landscape** for the print orientation to print the report horizontally.

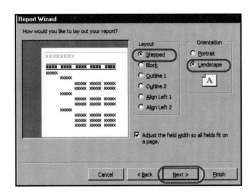

7 Click **Next**. The fifth Report Wizard dialog box enables you to choose the report design. Select **Soft Gray**, if it is not already selected. A preview of the design is shown in the preview area.

Design preview —

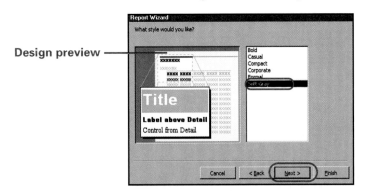

8 Click **Next**. The sixth Report Wizard dialog box asks for a report name. Name the report **Personnel File by Department**.

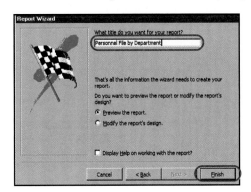

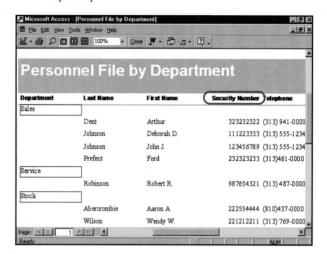

⑨ Click **Finish**. A Report Preview is displayed. Notice that the form looks quite good, but still needs a little editing, because some of the field names are cut off and the spacing of the columns needs improvement. Leave the report open for the next task.

TASK 9

Modifying and Printing a Report

Why would I do this?

The Report Wizard is an excellent tool to create the overall structure of a report. Often, however, the report may need some modifications to align fields under headings properly, or to show the full field name. In the report that was just created, the column heading for Social Security Number was cut off on the left and only shows "Security Number". Spacing between the columns is uneven, and the report would look better if the spacing was more evenly distributed. Once the report looks the way you want, it is easy to print a copy.

In this task, you learn a few techniques for modifying a report. The techniques used are similar to the ones used in Task 6 when you changed the design of the Personnel File Input Form. After modifying the report, you will print it.

❶ Click the **View** button to view to move to the **Report Design** window. If necessary, close the **field list** box, and double-click the title bar of the **Toolbox** to dock it at the bottom of the window.

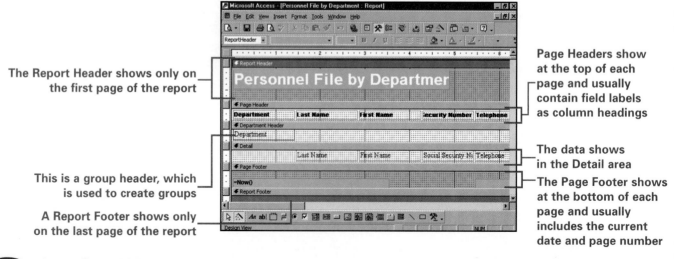

The Report Header shows only on the first page of the report

Page Headers show at the top of each page and usually contain field labels as column headings

This is a group header, which is used to create groups

The data shows in the Detail area

A Report Footer shows only on the last page of the report

The Page Footer shows at the bottom of each page and usually includes the current date and page number

2 Click the **First Name** label in the **Page Header** to select it. Sizing handles are displayed around the edges of the label.

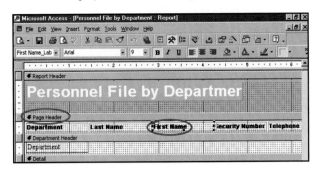

3 Hold down ⬆Shift and click the **First Name** text box in the **Detail** section to select it. Both the label and the text box are now selected and can be modified together.

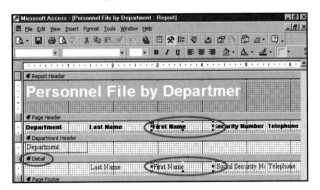

4 Point to the handle in the middle of the right end of the **First Name** text box. When the pointer turns into a double-headed arrow, click and drag the end of the box to the left to shorten the length of the box as shown in the figure. Now there is room to lengthen the size of the Social Security Number label.

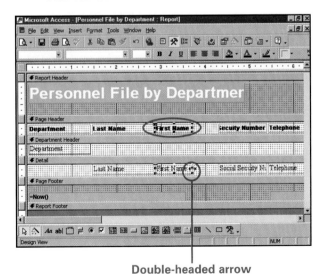

Double-headed arrow

5 Click the **Social Security Number** label to select it. Hold down ⬆Shift and click the **Social Security Number** text box to select it.

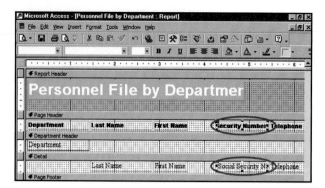

6 Point to the handle in the middle of the left end of the **Security Number** label. Click and drag the end of the box to the left to lengthen it as shown in the figure.

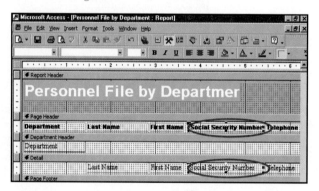

7 With both the label and text box still selected, click the **Center** alignment button on the Formatting toolbar. This centers the numbers under the label in the report.

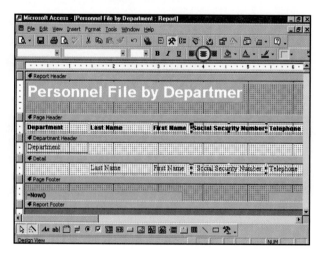

8 Click on the title in the **Report Header** area. Click and drag a sizing handle on the right side of the title until the whole title can be seen.

9 Click the **View** button to see the effect of your changes. Scroll to the right and notice that the **Hourly Pay** and **Employed** fields are too close together.

10 Click the **View** button to return to Design view. Use the horizontal scrollbar to scroll to the right; then click the **Hourly Pay** label, hold down ◆Shift) and click the **Hourly Pay** text box.

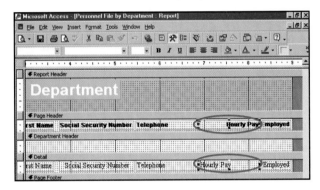

In Depth: In some cases, you will have columns of numbers with much wider multiple-word labels. One solution to this problem is to expand the size of the Page Header area and change the shape of the labels. Select a long label; then use the sizing handle on the bottom to increase the depth of the label, and use the sizing handle on the right side to decrease the width of the label. The text in the label will then wrap onto two lines. You can also decrease the font size of labels to reduce their width.

11 Point to the handle on the right end of the **Hourly Pay** label. Click and drag the end of the box to the left to shorten both the label and text box as shown in the figure.

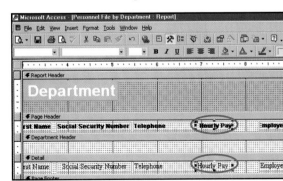

12 Click the **View** button to see the effect of your changes. The mouse pointer is in the shape of a magnifying glass. Click the report to see a full-page view of the report. The columns are more evenly spaced now, and the column headings are fully displayed. If necessary, adjust the width of the **Employed** field so the title is fully displayed.

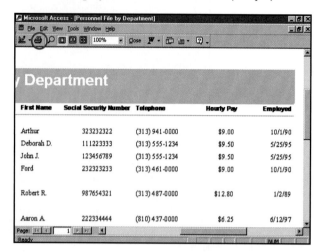

13 Click the **Print** button to print a copy of the report.

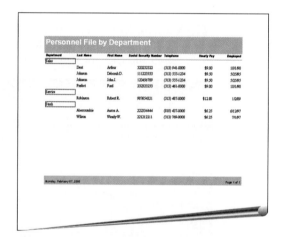

14 Click the **Close** button in the center of the toolbar to return to Design view of the report.

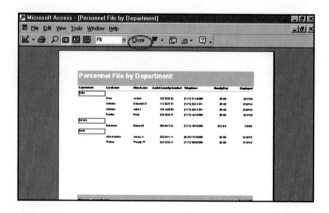

15 Click the **Close Window** button and save the changes when prompted. The Report tab of the Database window shows the title of the report you created. If you are through working, close the database and close Access.

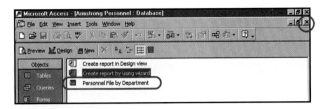

Comprehension Exercises

Comprehension exercises are designed to check your memory and understanding of the basic concepts in this lesson. You distinguish between true and false statements, identify new screen elements, and match terms with related statements. If you are uncertain of the correct answer, refer to the task number following each item (for example, T4 refers to Task 4) and review that task until you are confident that you can provide a correct response.

True-False

Circle either T or F.

T F **1.** To create a customized Access database, you need to launch Access, choose **B**lank **Database**, name the file, and select a file location. (**T1**)

T F **2.** Once you have created a new database, the first thing you have to do is to create a form for data entry. (**T2**)

T F **3.** When creating a table in Design view, whatever you type in the Description column will appear in the Datasheet title bar. (**T2**)

T F **4.** When you make changes in the structure of a table, you need to save the table in order for your changes to take effect. (**T4**)

T F **5.** The first step in deleting a field is to click on the field's row selector. (**T4**)

T F **6.** If you delete a field, you can recover the data by using the **Undo** button. (**T4**)

T F **7.** Data that you enter into a form or table is saved automatically. (**T3**)

T F **8.** You can see only one record at a time in a Columnar form. (**T5**)

T F **9.** The **AutoForm: Columnar** option gives you more control than the Form Wizard when creating a new form. (**T5**)

T F **10.** In a report, you can sort records on up to four fields. (**T8**)

Identifying Parts of the Access Screens

Refer to the figures and identify the numbered parts of the screens. Write the letter of the correct label in the space next to the number.

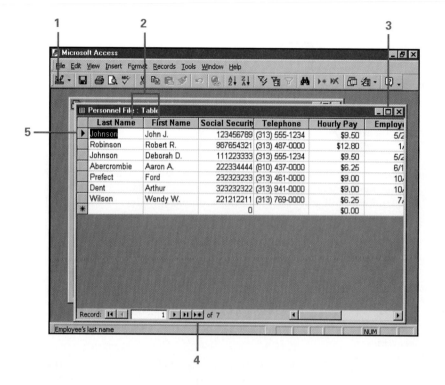

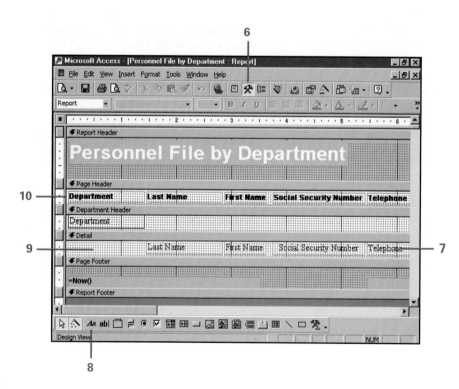

1. _____

2. _____

3. _____

4. _____

5. _____

6. _____

7. _____

8. _____

9. _____

10. _____

A. Label button (**T6**)

B. Toolbox button (**T6**)

C. View button (**T2**)

D. Field name (**T2**)

E. Maximize button (**T2**)

F. New Record button (**T3**)

G. Detail area (**T6**)

H. Text box (**T6**)

I. Label (**T6**)

J. Record selector (**T3**)

Matching

Match the statements below to the word or phrase that is the best match from the list. Write the letter of the matching word or phrase in the space provided next to the number.

1. ___ A toolbar of Access design tools

2. ___ Option that enables you to create a customized database

3. ___ Sets the tab order from left to right and top to bottom

4. ___ Indicates you are editing a record that isn't saved yet

5. ___ The shape of the pointer when you are moving a text box on a form

6. ___ Indicates that a text box or label is selected

7. ___ Indicates an empty record

8. ___ Horizontal report orientation

9. ___ The shape of the pointer when you are drawing a label

10. ___ Where the data is shown on a form

A. Hand pointer (**T6**)

B. Asterisk record selector (**T3**)

C. Text box (**T6**)

D. Toolbox (**T6**)

E. Crosshair pointer with an attached A (**T6**)

F. Blank Access database (**T1**)

G. Sizing handles (**T6**)

H. Auto Order (**T7**)

I. Pencil record selector (**T3**)

J. Portrait (**T8**)

K. Landscape (**T8**)

Reinforcement Exercises

Reinforcement exercises are designed to reinforce the skills you have learned by applying them to a new situation. Detailed instructions are provided along with a figure, where appropriate, to illustrate the final result. The Reinforcement exercises that follow should be completed sequentially. Leave the database open at the end of each exercise for use in the next exercise until you are specifically directed to close it.

R1—Creating a Database and a Table

1. Launch **Access**. Choose the **Blank Database** option. Name the new database **Ex1601** and save it on your floppy disk, or wherever you are saving your files.

2. Use the skills you have learned in this lesson to create the **Pool Parts Inventory** table as shown in the figure. See the steps below for more detail.

3. Click the **New** button.

4. Select **Design** view from the **New Table** dialog box.

5. Enter the fields as shown in the figure.

6. Click the **View** button to move to **Datasheet** view. Save the table as **Pool Parts Inventory**.

7. Let Access create a **primary key** for you.

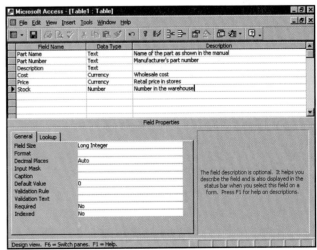

R2—Entering Records into the Inventory Table

1. Make sure you are in Datasheet view of the **Pool Parts Inventory** table.

2. Use the skills you have learned in this lesson to enter the data into the table as shown in the figure. See the steps below for more detail. You can create an AutoForm to enter the data if you prefer. (Note: The widths of the columns in this table have been resized to show all of the fields.)

3. Enter the data for each field as shown. Press (Tab⇆) or (↵Enter) after each entry and at the end of each record. (Tab to the **Part Name** field and begin to enter the data. The AutoNumber will be completed automatically by the program when you begin to enter a record.)

4. Choose **File**, **Page Setup** and choose **Landscape** orientation from the **Page** tab.

5. Choose **File**, **Print** to print a copy of the table.

R3—Adding and Deleting Fields

1. Click the **View** button to return to **Design** view. Because this information is to be printed for a customer price list, you will remove the **Cost** field. You will also add a **Sale Price** field.

2. Use the skills you have learned in this lesson to modify the **Pool Parts Inventory** table as shown in the figure. See the steps below for more detail.

3. In the Design view of the table, click the **Row Selector** for the **Cost** field and press (Del). Agree to permanently lose the data.

4. Move the insertion point to the first blank row and type **Sale Price**. Choose the **Currency** data type. Type **10% off** in the Description area.

5. Click the **View** button to move back to the **Datasheet** view. Save the changes to the table.

6. Fill in the **Sale Price** field as shown.

7. Choose **File**, **Print** and print a copy of the table in landscape orientation. Close the table.

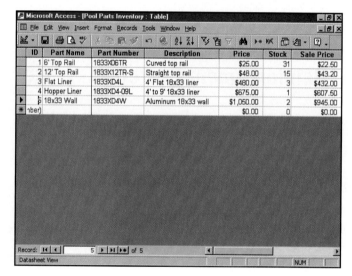

R4—Creating a Report Using the Report Wizard

1. Click the **Reports** object button.

2. Use the skills you have learned in this lesson to create the **Pool Parts Inventory Report** as shown in the figure. See the steps below for more detail.

3. Double-click the **Create report by using wizard** option.

4. Select all of the fields.

5. Do not group on any of the fields.

6. Sort by **Part Name**.

7. Select a **Tabular** report printed in the **Landscape** orientation.

8. Select the **Corporate** style.

9. Name the report **Pool Parts Inventory Report**.

10. Preview the report, then print it.

11. Close the report and return to the Database window.

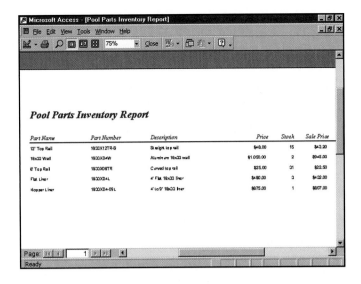

R5—Create and Modify a Form

1. Click the **Forms** object button.

2. Use the skills you have learned in this lesson to create the **Pool Parts Inventory Input Form** as shown in the figure. See the steps below for more detail.

3. Click **New**. Select the **AutoForm: Columnar** and the **Pool Parts Inventory** table. (Note: You may have a different background to your form.)

4. Click the **View** button to change to **Design** view. (Note: If necessary, click the **Maximize** button to enlarge the view.)

5. Rearrange the fields as shown. Choose **View, Tab Order, Auto Order** to reset the order of entry.

6. Return to **Form** view. Save the form as **Pool Parts Inventory Input Form**. Print a copy of the current record (record 1) only.

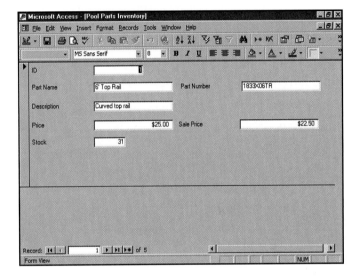

Challenge

Challenge exercises are designed to test your ability to apply your skills to new situations with less detailed instruction. These exercises also challenge you to expand your repertoire of skills by using Access commands that are similar to those you have already learned. The desired outcome is clearly defined, but you have more freedom to choose the steps needed to achieve the required result.

The following Challenge exercises use the file **Ex1501** that was created in the previous Reinforcement exercises. If you have not done those exercises, do them now.

C1—Modify the Tab Order of a Form

1. Open the **Pool Parts Inventory Input** form in Design view.

2. Choose **View**, **Ta<u>b</u> Order**. Read the directions on the **Tab Order** window. Change the **Custom Order** so that the tab order is **ID**, **Part Name**, **Description**, **Part Number**, **Price**, **Sale Price**, and **Stock**.

3. Switch to **Form** view and press Tab⇄ repeatedly to see if the insertion point jumps from one text box to the next in the order specified.

4. Save the form.

5. Choose **File**, **Print** and the **Selected Record(s)** option to print one record only.

6. Close the form. Leave the database open for use in the next exercise.

C2—Add a Memo Field to the Table

A memo field is similar to a text field, but it is designed to allow you to put in several sentences and comments.

Goal: Add a memo field to the **Pool Parts Inventory** table and use it to store a comment about one of the parts.

1. Open the **Pool Parts Inventory** table in Design view.

2. Add another field to the list named **Comments**. Select **Memo** as the data type. Save the change.

3. Switch to the **Datasheet** view and type the following comment about the **Flat Liner**:

This item is on back order and is not expected to be available until late June.

4. Close the table and leave the database open for use in the next exercise.

C3—Add a Memo Field to the Form

Forms that are based on a table are not automatically updated if you add a field to the table.

Goal: Add the **Comments** field to the **Pool Parts Inventory Input** form.

1. Open the **Pool Parts Inventory Input** form in Design view.

2. Drag the bottom edge of the **Detail** section downward to enlarge the section.

3. If the **field list** box is not displayed, locate and click the **Field List** button on the Standard toolbar to open it.

4. Drag the **Comments** field from the **field list** box onto the form design and place it under the **Sale Price** text box. Release the mouse.

5. Adjust the size and position of the field to match the figure.

6. Switch to **Form** view and scroll to record 3. The comment that you entered in the previous exercise displays in the memo field.

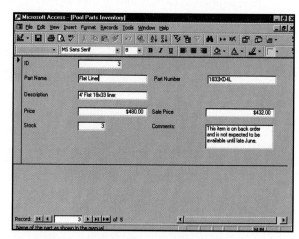

7. Save the changes to the form and close it. Leave the database open for use in the Discovery exercises.

Discovery

Discovery exercises are designed to help you learn how to teach yourself a new skill. In each exercise, you discover something new that is related to the topic taught in this lesson. You may be directed to use built-in wizards or some of the extensive Help features provided in Access to discover new features and learn new skills with minimum assistance from books or instructors. The required outcome demonstrates your ability to apply the new skill. You determine the choice of topic, worksheet design, and steps of execution.

The following Discovery exercises use the file **Ex1501** that was created in the previous Reinforcement exercises. If you have not done those exercises, do them now.

D1—Hide and Unhide Columns

Tables may contain columns that you do not want to print or display. You can hide columns without losing the data they contain.

Goal: Hide the **ID**, **Sale Price**, and **Comments** columns in the **Pool Parts Inventory** table.

1. Use Help to find information about hiding columns in a datasheet. Read this information.

2. Hide the **ID** and **Sale Price** columns in the **Pool Parts Inventory** table and hide the **Comments** column if it is present.

3. Print the table.

4. Unhide the **Sale Price** and **Comments** columns.

5. Use the **Print Preview** button to see how the table will print. If necessary, change **Page Setup** to landscape, and expand the column width. Then print the table again.

6. Save the changes to the table and leave the database open for use in the next Discovery exercise.

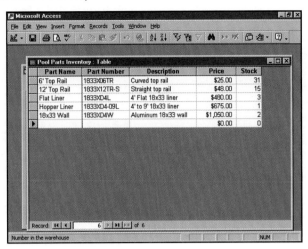

D2—Calculating Values in a Report

You can write formulas and use functions such as **Sum** in a report if the formula is placed in a text box. Field names must be enclosed in square brackets: []. For example, if you want to display the sum of the number of stock items in the report header, you can place the formula **=Sum([Stock])** in a text box in the report header.

Extra text boxes can be created using the **Text Box** button in the **Toolbox.**

Goal: Display the sum of the number of stock items in the report header as shown.

1. Open the **Pool Parts Inventory Report** in Design view, and open the **Toolbox** if necessary.

2. Click the **Text Box** button. Click and drag to place a text box in the **Report Header**. Enter a formula in the text box to sum the stock items. Edit the label. (Test your design as necessary by switching to **Print Preview**.)

3. Move and resize the field text and label boxes in the **Page Header** and **Detail** sections for the Price and Stock fields.

4. Print the report.

5. Save the changes in the database and close it.

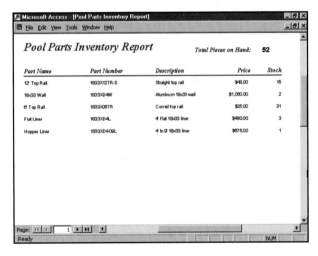

D3—Compacting Files

When you create a new database, the program reserves space for many features that you do not use. Compacting the databases you create removes that reserved space and allows you to put more assignments on a floppy disk.

Goal: Compact the database file **Armstrong's Personnel** that you created in this form.

1. Use **Help** to look up how to compact a database and how to rename a database.

2. Follow the **Compact an Access database or Access project that is not open** directions to compact **Armstrong's Personnel** and save it as **Ex1501b**.

3. Turn on the **Details** view in the Access Open window or in Windows Explorer or My Computer and compare the sizes of the two databases. The compacted database is almost half the size of the original.

4. Test the compacted version.

Lesson: 16

Modify the Structure of an Existing Database

Introduction

When you create a database, there are many modifications you can make so that the database is easier to read and more useful for the end-user. One reason you would make these changes is to help reduce errors and improve data integrity. There are a number of field property changes you can make to improve the data-entry process. You can apply an input mask to format a field so that it looks like the information you are entering. You can make common values appear in a field automatically, and you can create lists of common field entries so that the user does not have to type the same information over and over.

In this lesson, you change some of the properties in a table, and add a combo box and a list box to a form.

Visual Summary

When you have completed this entire lesson, you will have created a form in a database that looks like this:

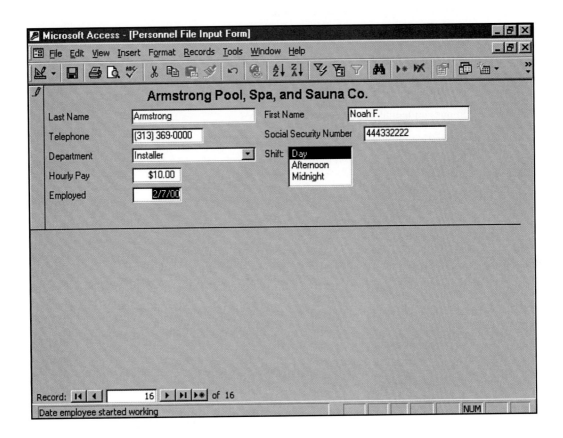

TASK 1

Changing the Data Type of a Field

Why would I do this?

There are ten data type options available when you create a table. You have been introduced to four of these. The other data types include the following:

- *Memo*   Used for lengthy text and numbers, such as comments or descriptions
- *AutoNumber*   Unique sequential numbers incremented by 1
- *Yes/No*   Either/or condition, Yes/No, True/False, On/Off
- *OLE Object*   Uses the object linking and embedding protocol to display objects such as spreadsheets, pictures, or sounds
- *Hyperlink*   Stores hyperlinks, which are highlighted text that can connect you to a file or a Web page
- *Lookup Wizard*   Creates a field that enables you to choose a value from another table or from a list

If you plan your database carefully, you should not have to change a field data type very often. If you create enough databases, however, you will eventually need to modify the data type. One reason you might need to change a data type is to use the Input Mask Wizard to apply an input mask. An *input mask* applies a format to a field so that it is spaced and formatted in a specific manner. Examples of data that benefit from the use of an input mask include telephone numbers, Social Security numbers, and dates.

In this task, you will change a number field to a text field so that you can add an input mask to the field.

1 Launch **Access**, select **Open an existing file** from the Microsoft Access dialog box, and click **OK**. The Open dialog box is displayed.

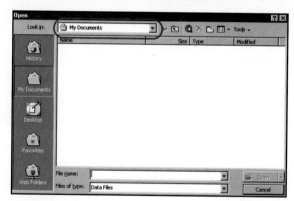

2 Find **Less1601** in the **Student\Lesson16** folder on your CD-ROM disc. Right-click **Less1601** and select **Send To, 3 1/2 Floppy (A)** from the shortcut menu. Change the **Look in** box to **3 1/2 Floppy (A:)**.

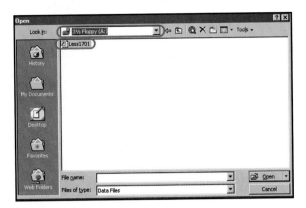

3 Right-click **Less1601** and select **Properties** from the shortcut menu. Deselect the **Read-only** property.

Selected file ——

Read-only property ——

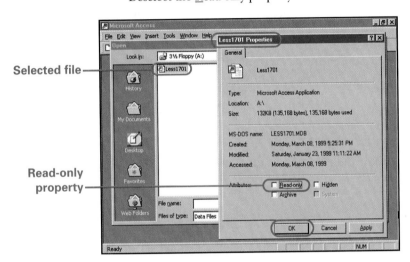

! Caution: Access does not offer a Save As option for the entire database, so you cannot open the file and save it with another name. Therefore, before you open it, you need to change the read-only property so that you can make changes to the database. You can move an Access file, remove the read-only property, and rename the file in the Open dialog box as done in the previous steps. These steps can also be completed using Windows Explorer or My Computer. Review the instructions in Lesson 2 if you prefer to use Windows Explorer. For each database file that you open in this section of the book, you will need to complete these steps.

4 Click **OK**. Right-click the file again and choose **Rename**. Type **Armstrong Personnel Information** and press <u>Enter</u> to change the name of the file. Click the **Open** button to open the file.

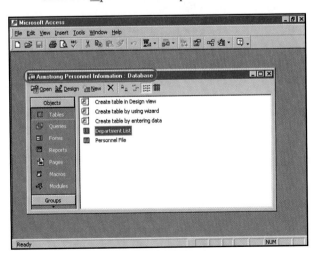

5 Select the **Personnel File** table and click the **Design** button to open the file in Design view.

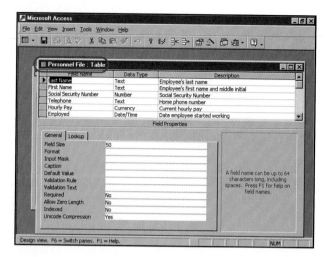

6 Place the insertion point in the **Data Type** column of the **Social Security Number** row. Click the down arrow to open the **Data Type** list box.

Data Type list box

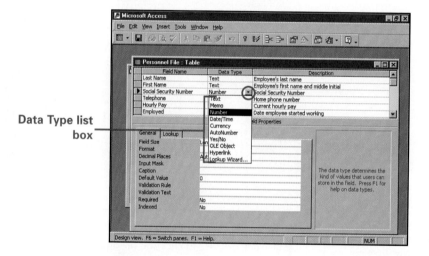

7 Choose the **Text** option from the **Data Type** list box.

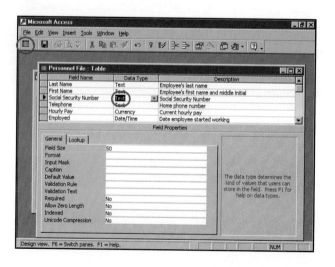

8 Click the **View** button to switch to **Datasheet** view. You are prompted to save the changes to the table.

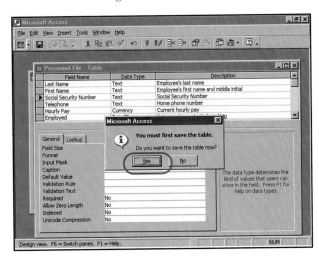

9 Click **Yes** to save your table. Notice that the numbers in the Social Security Number field are left-aligned now that you have designated them as a Text data type.

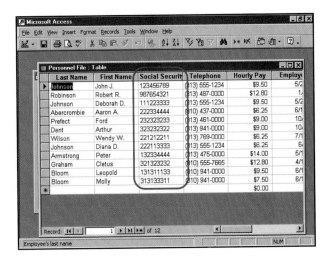

Adding Input Masks to Aid Data Entry
Why would I do this?

Many types of information, such as telephone numbers, Social Security numbers, and dates, include dashes and parentheses as part of their structure. In Lesson 15, the table you designed did not contain this formatting. Entering data is much easier when the format needed has already been applied to the field structure in the table. The Input Mask Wizard is an easy tool to use to apply this type of formatting to selected fields. Input masks are primarily used in Text and Date/Time fields, but can be manually applied to Number or Currency fields.

In this task, you learn how to use the Input Mask Wizard to create a formatting structure for the Social Security Number field.

1 Click the **View** button to switch to **Design** view. Click anywhere in the **Social Security Number** field to select it.

Row selector arrow
indicates that this
is the selected field

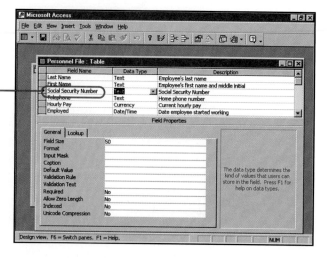

2 In the **Field Properties** section, click in the **Input Mask** box. A Build button is displayed on the right edge of the box.

Build button

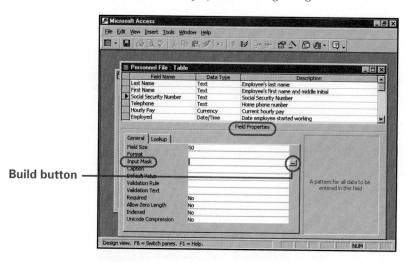

3 Click the **Build** button. The first Input Mask Wizard dialog box opens. Select the **Social Security Number** option.

Caution: If your system was set up with a standard installation, you will be prompted to insert the original Access (or Microsoft Office) CD-ROM disc. Consult with your instructor for further direction. If you are unable to install the wizard, continue reading this task and you can manually enter the necessary coding. See the In Depth note next to step 6 for further instructions.

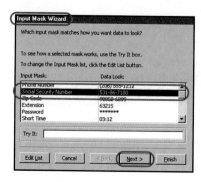

4 Click **Next**. The second Input Mask Wizard dialog box opens. Accept the underscore as the placeholder.

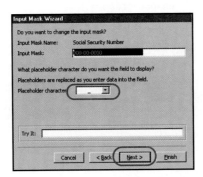

5 Click **Next**. The third Input Mask Wizard dialog box opens. Choose to store the data without the dashes. This will take less storage space, but the dashes will still be displayed.

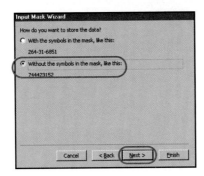

6 Click **Next**. The last Input Mask Wizard dialog box opens. It requires no input. Click **Finish** to close the Input Mask Wizard. The input mask is shown in the Input Mask box.

In Depth: You can manually enter an input mask if you know the proper coding. If you were unable to use the Input Mask Wizard, enter the coding you see in the figure on the Input Mask line for the Social Security Number field (000-00-0000;;_).

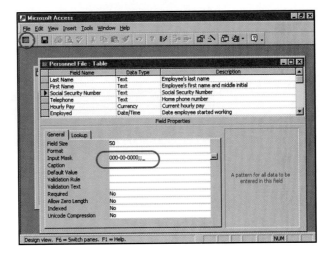

7 Click the **View** button to switch to **Datasheet** view. Save changes when prompted. Notice that all the Social Security numbers have dashes in the proper locations.

> **Caution:** When you add an input mask to a field in a table that is already used as the basis for a form or record, the input mask will not affect the appearance of the field in either the form or the report. You will need to add an input mask to each object.

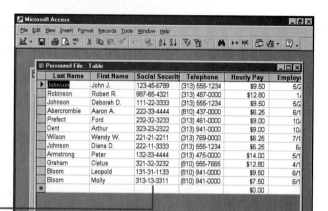

All of the Social Security numbers have dashes

TASK 3

Setting Default Values
Why would I do this?

Default values are values that are entered into a field as soon as you start editing a record. For example, if most of your employees hire in at $7.50 an hour, you can have the program automatically put that number in the Hourly Pay field every time a new employee record is created. Using a default value can save time in entering data if there will be few exceptions to the default. It also ensures that a field is not left blank.

In this task, you add the current date to the Employed field, because the only new records you will be adding will be for new employees.

1 Click the **View** button to move to **Design** view. Click anywhere in the **Employed** field.

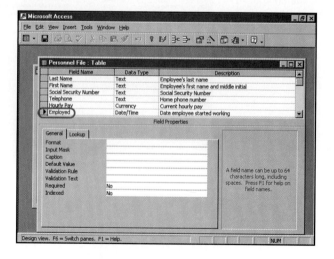

2 In the **Field Properties** area, click in the **Default Value** box.

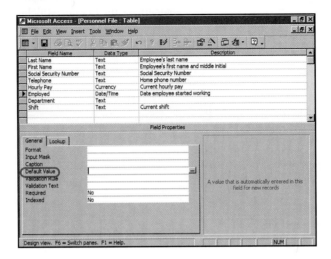

3 Type **Date()** in the **Default Value** box. This is the code necessary to use the current date as the default value.

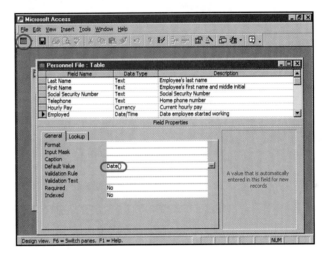

4 Click the **View** button to switch to the table **Datasheet** view. Save changes when prompted. Click the **Maximize** button to see more of the datasheet. Notice that the default date already appears in the Employed field of the empty record at the bottom of the table.

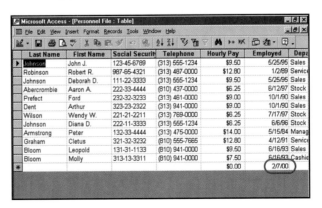

5 Notice that several of the columns are too wide and not all of the columns are shown on the screen. Move the pointer to the right edge of the **field selector** for the **Employed** field. The pointer changes to a two-sided arrow.

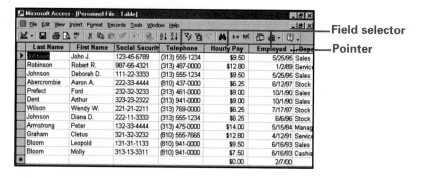

— Field selector

— Pointer

6 Click and drag the right edge of the **field selector** until the column width is just large enough to show the **Employed** label. It may take more than one try.

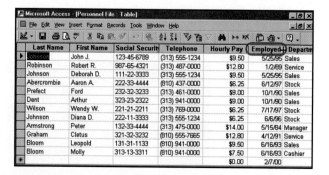

7 Change the column widths of the other columns as shown in the figure. In some cases, part of the field name in the field selector will be hidden. That's all right. The objective is to view all the record data without scrolling.

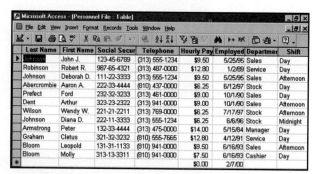

Quick Tip: You can automatically adjust a column width by double-clicking the right edge of the field selector, which will adjust the column width to the widest item in the column (which is often the field name). You can also adjust more than one field at a time by clicking in the middle of a field selector and dragging to the right or left to select multiple columns. You can double-click on the right edge of any one of the selected columns to automatically adjust all of them at once.

8 Add another record with the following data as shown: **Hawkin**; **Charity**; **123112233**; **(313) 753-0000**; **6.25**; (accept the current date); **Stock**; **Day**. Watch how the structure of the Social Security number is displayed as you enter the number.

Current date is accepted as the default value —

Social Security number is formatted automatically —

New record —

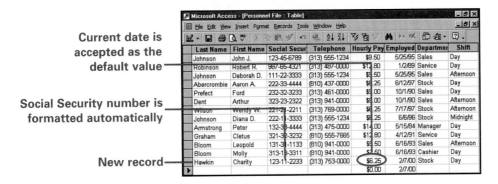

TASK 4

Assigning a Primary Key Field
Why would I do this?

Primary key fields are fields that are used to speed up sorting and finding data in a large table and to link tables together. A primary key field must contain unique data for each record—that is, there can be no duplication in that field from one record to the next. Some tables use sequential numbers, known as counters, as primary keys. Others use fields that are naturally unique, such as Social Security numbers or employee identification numbers.

In this task, you learn how to designate the Social Security Number field as your primary key field.

1 With the **Personnel File** table still selected, click the **Design** button to move to Design view. Click anywhere in the **Social Security Number** field.

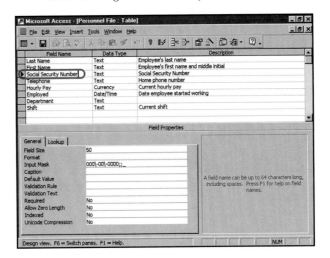

2 Click the **Primary Key** button on the toolbar. A key symbol is placed in the row selector column to the left of the field name.

Primary Key button →

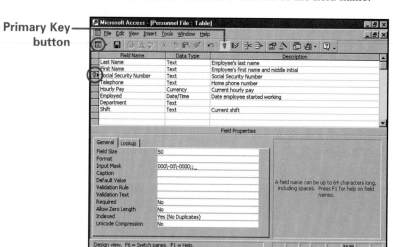

3 Click the **View** button to move to **Datasheet** view. Save changes when prompted. Notice that the table has now been sorted in order of Social Security number.

In Depth: By definition, the data in the primary key field has to be unique. Therefore, if you try to enter a duplicate primary key, Access displays a warning message that it could not enter the record because it would create a duplicate. To continue, acknowledge the warning box and press Esc to remove the entry you are trying to make. Determine what is being duplicated and then try again to enter the record.

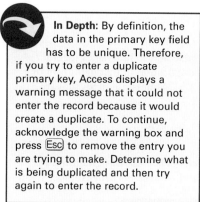

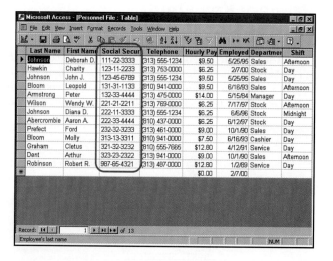

4 Click the **Close Window** button to close the table and return to the database window.

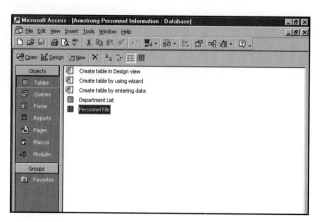

TASK 5

Adding a List Box to a Form

Why would I do this?

When there are only a few possible values for a field, a list box makes it easy to select the correct entry. By clicking on one of the items in a list box, you also ensure that the entry will be spelled correctly. List boxes have certain restrictions. The entries shown in the box are the only possible entries; nothing else can be entered into that field. Also, the list box remains on the screen at all times.

In this task, you add a list box to the Shift field, a field which has only three possible values.

1 Click the **Forms** object button and select **Personnel File Input Form**.

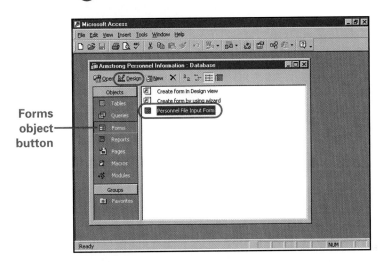

2 Click the **Design** button to open the form in Design view. If necessary, move the toolbox and close the field list so they don't interfere with any of the fields. Click the text box in the **Shift** field to select it.

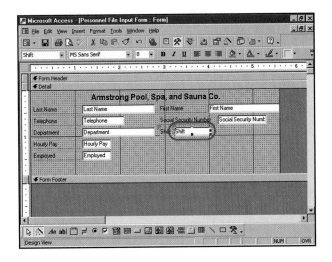

Caution: If the List Box option is not available from the menu, it means you selected the label instead of the text box for the Shift field. Click the **Shift** field text box and try again.

3 Choose F**o**rmat, **C**hange To, **L**ist Box from the menu. (The Change To command might not be immediately available in the F**o**rmat menu; wait a moment for the menu to expand.) A list box replaces the text box. Click and drag the bottom handle on the box and reduce the size as shown in the figure so that three lines of text will fit.

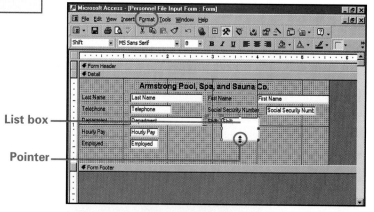

List box —

Pointer —

4 Click the **Properties** button on the Form Design toolbar. The List Box: Shift properties dialog box is displayed.

Caution: It is important that the Properties dialog box is titled List Box: Shift. This indicates that the properties sheet displayed is for the list box you just created for the Shift field. If the box has any other title, it means that you clicked the mouse in another part of your screen before clicking the Properties button. If this happens, click the title bar of the Properties dialog box and drag the box to another part of the screen until you can see the list box. Then click the **Shift** list box and the Properties dialog box will change to the properties sheet for the selected field.

Properties button

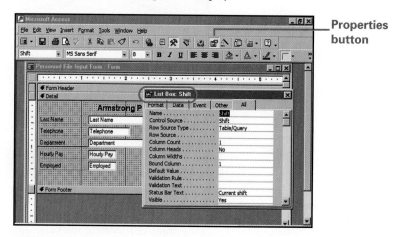

5 Select the All tab if necessary, and then click in the **Row Source Type** box. Click the down arrow at the right of the box and select **Value List**.

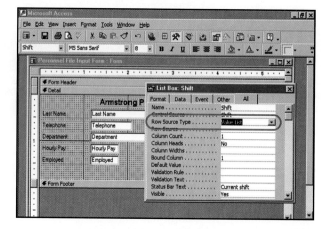

6 Click in the **Row Source** box. Type the three possible entries exactly as shown (with semicolons and no spaces): **Day;Afternoon;Midnight**. Make sure you include the semicolons between each item. These three items will appear in the list box.

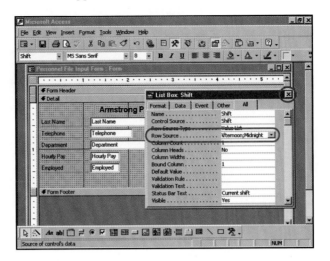

7 Click the **Close** button to close the List Box: Shift properties box. The list box does not show the individual items in Design view.

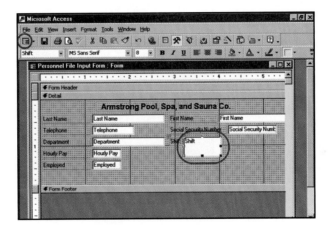

8 Click the **View** button to switch to **Form** view. You should be able to see all three items in the list box.

> **Caution:** If the list box has a scrollbar on the right and does not show all the items, it means that you made the box too small. Return to **Design** view, select the list box, and resize it using the middle handle on the bottom edge of the box.

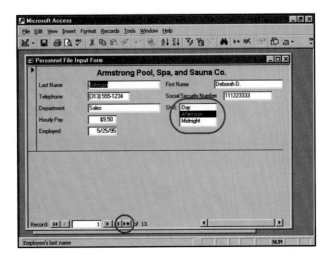

9 Click the **New Record** button to add a new record. Notice that none of the items in the list box is selected.

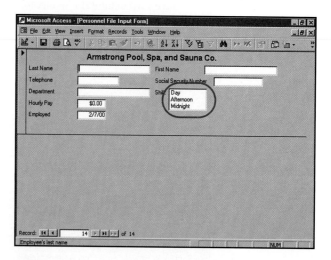

10 Enter the information for the new record as shown in the figure. When you reach the **Shift** field, click **Day** to select the Day shift. Accept the default value of the current date for the Employed field.

In Depth: Remember that the current date will show automatically in the Employed date field because of the default property that was set for this field. The Social Security number is not formatted in the form, however, because the input mask was added to the table after the form had been created and you have not added the input mask formatting to the form.

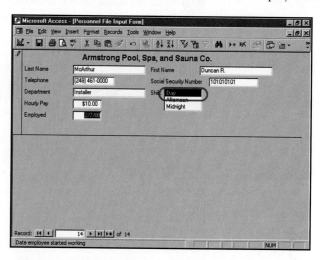

11 Click the **Save** button to save the changes made to the form. Leave the form open and continue to the next task.

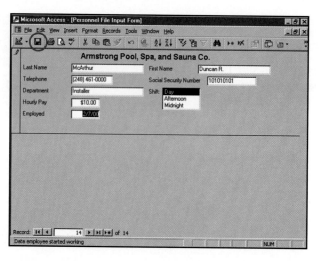

TASK 6

Adding a Combo Box to a Form

Why would I do this?

A list box is handy in some cases, but in others, a *combo box* is far more useful. A combo box is similar to a list box in that it helps in the data entry process. A list of items is presented from which the correct data can be selected. However, a combo box uses a drop-down list, so it takes up less space on the screen. You can also enter items not found in the data source, whereas the list box restricts you to the items in the list.

In this task, you learn how to add a combo box to the Department field. Instead of typing the items, you will use another table as the data source.

1 Click the **View** button to switch to **Design** view of the **Personnel File Input Form**.

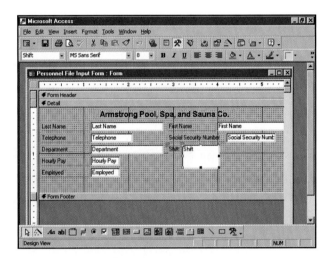

2 Click the text box of the **Department** field to select it.

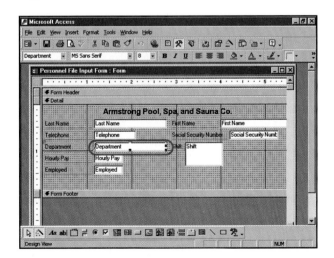

3 Choose **F**ormat, **C**hange To, **C**ombo Box. The text box changes to a combo box and a down arrow is displayed on the right side of the box.

Caution: If the Combo Box option is not available from the menu, it means you selected the label instead of the text box for the Department field. Click the **Department** field text box and try again.

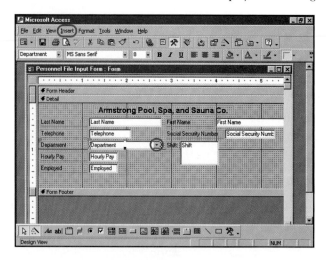

4 Click the **Properties** button. The Combo Box: Department properties dialog box is displayed. **Table/Query** is the default choice for the **Row Source Type**.

In Depth: When you created the list box in the previous task, you selected the Value List option in the Row Source Type box. This allowed you to type a list of values. In this case, you will accept the default choice to use the Table/Query option in the Row Source Type box, because you will be using a table as the source of the list for the combo box. You could, however, use one of the other options for the Row Source Type with a combo box.

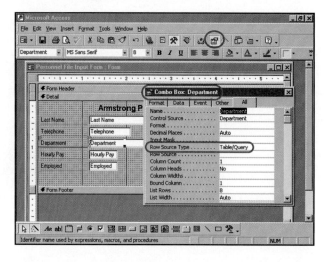

5 Click in the **Row Source** box. Click the down arrow to display the tables and queries available as data sources. Select **Department List**.

In Depth: The Department List is a table that has just one field. This field lists all five of the current departments in the company. You will see the departments listed when you move to Form view to test the combo box.

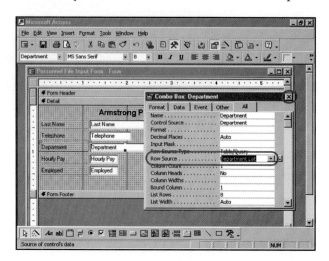

16

6 Click the **Close** button to close the Combo Box: Department properties dialog box. The combo box does not show the department list in Design view.

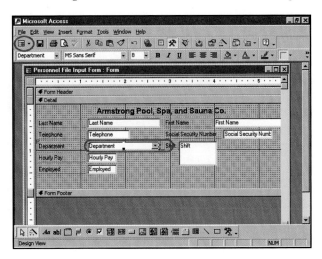

7 Click the **View** button to move to **Form** view. Notice that the Department field has a down arrow on the right side of the text box.

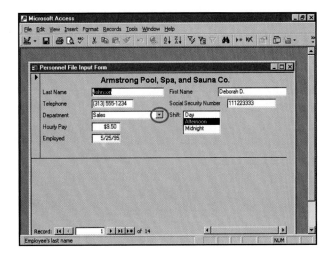

8 Click the **New Record** button to add a new record. Notice that the combo box is empty.

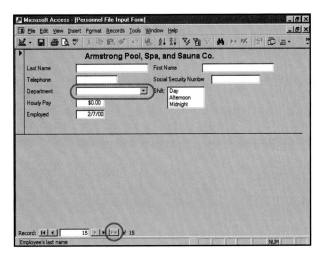

9 Enter the information for the new record as shown in the figure. When you get to the **Department** field, click the down arrow to view the available items.

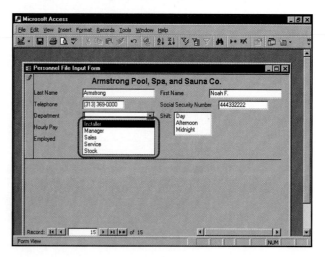

10 Select **Installer** from the combo box, and then finish filling in the record as shown. Accept the current date as provided in the **Employed** box.

Quick Tip: A quick way to select items from a combo box or a list box is to type the first letter of the option you want. The program will choose the option based on the first letters that are typed. When you see your choice in the field text box, you can press ↵Enter to select it and move to the next field.

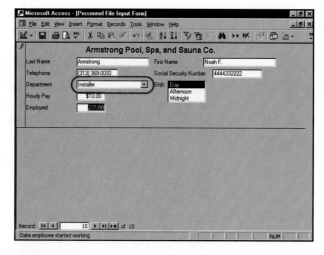

11 Click the **Save** button to save the changes made to the form, and then close the form. Close the database and close Access if you are finished working.

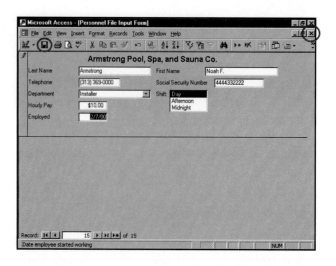

Comprehension Exercises

Comprehension exercises are designed to check your memory and understanding of the basic concepts in this lesson. You distinguish between true and false statements, identify new screen elements, and match terms with related statements. If you are uncertain of the correct answer, refer to the task number following each item (for example, T4 refers to Task 4) and review that task until you are confident that you can provide a correct response.

True-False

Circle either T or F.

T   F   **1.** Input masks are used to apply specific formats to text fields. **(T2)**

T   F   **2.** Default values work only with fields that have a Number data type. **(T3)**

T   F   **3.** An input mask added to a field in a table will also appear in previously created forms or reports that include that field. **(T2)**

T   F   **4.** Assigning a primary key can help speed up searching or sorting. **(T4)**

T   F   **5.** You can automatically adjust a column width in Datasheet view by double-clicking the right edge of the field selector. **(T4)**

T   F   **6.** If the entry you are looking for is not in the list box, you can always type a new item. **(T5)**

T   F   **7.** A combo box gives you a list to choose from and also allows you to type a new entry. **(T6)**

T   F   **8.** A Memo data type can be used for lengthy comments or descriptions. **(T1)**

T   F   **9.** A list box shows the list on the form, whereas a combo box uses a drop-down list. **(T6)**

T   F   **10.** A primary key field cannot contain duplicate entries. **(T4)**

Identifying Parts of the Access Screens

Refer to the figures and identify the numbered parts of the screens. Write the letter of the correct label in the space next to the number.

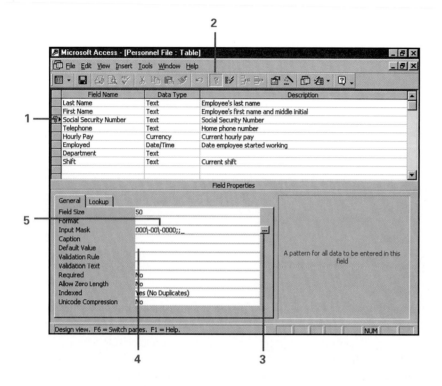

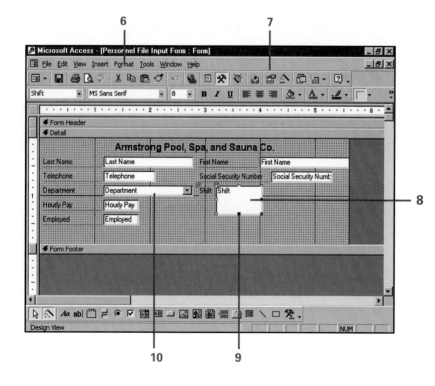

1. _____

2. _____

3. _____

4. _____

5. _____

6. _____

7. _____

8. _____

9. _____

10. _____

A. Primary Key button (**T4**)

B. Build button (**T2**)

C. Properties button (**T6**)

D. Combo box

E. Primary Key indicator (**T4**)

F. Input Mask field property (**T2**)

G. Default Value property box (**T3**)

H. Used to change the shape of a control (**T5**)

I. Used to change a text box to a combo box (**T6**)

J. List box (**T5**)

Matching

Match the statements below to the word or phrase that is the best match from the list. Write the letter of the matching word or phrase in the space provided next to the number.

1. ___ Where the items for a list box or combo box come from

2. ___ A data type used for an either/or condition

3. ___ Values will automatically be filled in when a new record is added, unless overwritten

4. ___ Applies special format structure for phone numbers, zip codes, and so on

5. ___ Displays the current date

6. ___ A field containing unique values

7. ___ A data type used to insert pictures, spreadsheets, and other objects

8. ___ A data type used for large quantities of data

9. ___ The label area at the top of the column in a table

10. ___ In a form, creates a drop-down list of possible data for a field

A. Primary key (T4)

B. OLE object (T1)

C. Field selector (T4)

D. Memo (T1)

E. Row Source (T5)

F. Input mask (T2)

G. Default (T3)

H. Date()(T3)

I. Combo box (T6)

J. Yes/No (T1)

K. Hyperlink (T8)

Reinforcement Exercises

Reinforcement exercises are designed to reinforce the skills you have learned by applying them to a new situation. Detailed instructions are provided along with a figure, where appropriate, to illustrate the final result. The Reinforcement exercises that follow should be completed sequentially. Leave the database open at the end of each exercise for use in the next exercise until you are specifically directed to close it.

Access works with files differently from other Office applications. You cannot open a database and save it as another filename. You must copy the file from the CD-ROM disc to your floppy disk, remove the read-only property, and then rename it. If you are familiar with Windows Explorer or My Computer, you may use either of these programs to copy and rename files. You can also copy a file from the CD-ROM disc to your floppy disk in drive A:\ using shortcut menus within Access.

Use the following two-step method to copy, remove the read-only property, and rename the file that is used in these exercises.

1. Launch **Access**, select **Open an existing file** from the Microsoft Access dialog box, and click **OK**. Find and highlight **Less1602** from in the **Student\Lesson16** folder on your CD-ROM disc. Click the right mouse button, select **Send To**, and choose **3 1/2 Floppy (A)**. (Note: You may have run out of space on your first floppy disk. Insert a new, formatted disk and try again.)

2. Select drive **A** in the **Look in** box, and then right-click on **Less1602** and select **Properties**. Deselect **Read-only**, and then click **OK**. Right-click **Less1602** again and select **Rename**. Change the name of the file to **EX1601**. Select the file and click the **Open** button. This is a slightly expanded version of the exercises you worked on in Lesson 15.

R1—Add Input Masks to a Table

1. Use the skills you have learned in this lesson to create input masks for the **Phone** and **Zip** fields. See the steps below for more detail. (Note: The widths of the columns in this table have been resized to show all the fields you will be working on.)

2. Make sure the **Table** object button is selected.

3. Select the **Design** view option for the **Parts Suppliers** table.

4. Select the **Zip** field. Click in the **Input Mask** box in the **Field Properties** area.

5. Click the **Build** button and choose the preset **Zip Code** option. Store the **Zip** field information without the symbols.

6. Scroll down and select the **Phone** field. Click in the **Input Mask** box in the **Field Properties** area.

7. Click the **Build** button and choose the preset **Phone Number** option (save the table when prompted). Store the **Phone** field information without the symbols.

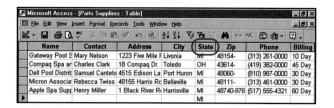

R2—Add a Default Value to a Table

1. Use the skills you have learned in this lesson to add a default value for the state field. See the steps that follow for more detail.

2. Select the **State** field. Click in the **Default Value** box and type **MI** (most of the suppliers will be from Michigan). Save your changes.

3. Switch to **Datasheet** view and save your changes when prompted. Enter the following new record using the input masks and default value you just created: **Apple Spa Supplies; Henry Miller; 1 Black River Rd.; Harrisville; MI; 487409764; 5175554321; 60 Day**.

4. Adjust the column widths to show all the data. Choose **File**, **Page Setup** and click the **Page** tab. Select the **Landscape** orientation option.

5. Choose **File**, **Print** and print the table. Save the changes to the layout of the table. Close the table.

R3—Assign a Primary Key and Adjust Column Widths

1. Open the **Pool Parts Inventory** table in **Design** view.

2. Use the skills you have learned in this lesson to add a primary key to this table. See the steps that follow for more detail.

3. Click anywhere in the **Part Number** field. (Note: This field will be used as a primary key because each part number is unique.)

4. Click the **Primary Key** button.

5. Move to **Datasheet** view. Save your changes when prompted.

6. Resize the columns as shown.

7. Print a copy of the table in **Landscape** orientation, and then close it. Save your changes when prompted.

R4—Add a List Box to a Form

1. Click the **Forms** object button. Open the **Parts Suppliers Input Form** in **Design** view.

2. Use the skills you have learned in this lesson to add a list box to the **Billing** field.

3. Click in the text box of the **Billing** field.

4. Choose **Format**, **Change To**, **List Box**.

5. Click the **Properties** button on the Form Design toolbar. Choose **Value List** from the **Row Source Type** drop-down menu.

6. In the **Row Source** box, type the following entries exactly as shown: **10 Day;30 Day;45 Day;60 Day**.

7. Close the List Box: Billing properties dialog box and move to **Form** view.

8. Switch back to **Design** view and resize the list box as necessary.

9. Switch to **Form** view, and move to record 5. Choose **File**, **Print**, and click the **Selected Record(s)** option button to print only the current record. Close the form and save your changes when prompted.

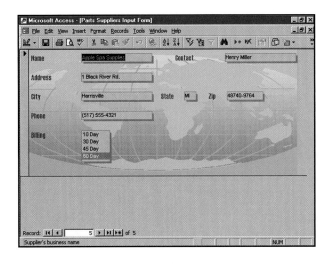

R5—Add a Combo Box to a Form

1. Open the **Pool Parts Inventory Input Form** in **Design** view.

2. Use the skills you have learned in this lesson to add a combo box to the **Distributor** field.

3. Click in the text box of the **Distributor** field.

4. Choose **Format**, **Change To**, **Combo Box**.

5. Click the **Properties** button on the Form Design toolbar. Choose **Table/Query** from the **Row Source Type** drop-down menu.

6. In the **Row Source** box, select the **Parts Suppliers** table. The combo box will read the information in the first field in that table.

7. Close the Combo Box: Distributor properties dialog box and switch to **Form** view.

8. Switch back to **Design** view and resize the combo box, if necessary.

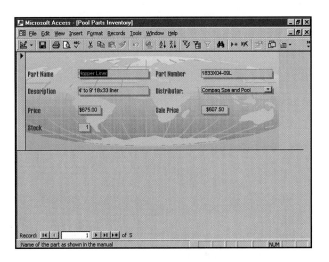

9. Choose **File**, **Print** and click the **Selected Record(s)** option button to print only the current record. Close the form and save your changes when prompted.

Challenge

Challenge exercises are designed to test your ability to apply your skills to new situations with less detailed instruction. These exercises also challenge you to expand your repertoire of skills by using Access commands that are similar to those you have already learned. The desired outcome is clearly defined, but you have more freedom to choose the steps needed to achieve the required result.

The following Challenge exercises use the file **EX1601** that was used in the previous Reinforcement exercises. If you have not done those exercises, follow the directions that precede the Reinforcement exercises to copy and rename the file.

C1—Simple Validation Rule

Sometimes people enter numbers that are not possible or have meanings that are not shared with everyone else. For example, someone might enter a negative number into the Stock field to indicate that an item has been promised or is on back order. If those using the database have not agreed upon this method, it could cause problems.

Goal: Use a validation rule to prevent the entry of negative numbers by requiring that the entry be greater than or equal to zero.

1. Open the **Pool Parts Inventory** table in Design view and select the **Stock** field.

2. Find the Validation Rule box in the Field Properties pane. Enter the rule **>=0** in the **Validation Rule** box.

3. Select the **Validation Text** box and enter a message that appears when the rule is violated, **Stock numbers must be greater than or equal to zero.**

4. Save the change in table design and switch to the **Datasheet** view. (The warning about data integrity rules is a standard warning whenever validation rules are added. Choose **Yes** to test existing data. Negative

quantities don't exist, so that won't be a problem.) Try to change one of the **Stock** numbers to a negative number. Your error message appears.

5. Click **OK** to close the error message window and press (Esc) to remove the negative entry.

6. Close the table and open the **Pool Parts Inventory Input Form**. Try changing a **Stock** number to a negative value. Does the validation rule work in the form?

7. Close the form. Leave the database open for use in the next exercise.

C2—Indexing a Field

If the table does not have a primary key or indexed field, the records will display in the order in which they were entered. If you want the records to display in order based on a field that may involve duplicate numbers, you cannot choose that field to be the primary key. You can choose to index on that field and allow duplicates.

Goal: Index the **Parts Suppliers** table on the Zip field.

1. Open the **Parts Suppliers** table in **Design** view.

2. Choose the **Zip** field and change its **Indexed** property to **Yes (Duplicates OK)**.

3. Save the change and switch to the **Datasheet** view. The records are sorted by Zip.

4. Close the table and leave the database open for use in the next exercise.

C3—Rearranging Columns in a Table Display

The Datasheet view normally displays the fields in the same order that they occur in the table design. You can rearrange the order of display without changing the table design.

Goal: Move the Phone number field to follow the Name field in the Datasheet view of the **Parts Suppliers** table.

1. Open the **Parts Suppliers** table in **Datasheet** view.

2. Click the column heading for the **Phone** field. The entire column is selected. Release the mouse button.

3. Point to the **Phone** column heading and click and drag it to the left. Notice a dark vertical line indicates where it will be placed when you release the mouse button. Place the phone column to the right of the **Name** field.

4. Save the change to the table layout. Switch to the **Design** view of the table. Notice that the Phone field has not moved.

5. Leave the database open for use in the Discovery exercises.

Discovery

Discovery exercises are designed to help you learn how to teach yourself a new skill. In each exercise, you discover something new that is related to the topic taught in this lesson. You may be directed to use built-in wizards or some of the extensive Help features provided in Access to discover new features and learn new skills with minimum assistance from books or instructors. The required outcome demonstrates your ability to apply the new skill. You determine the choice of topic, database design, and steps of execution.

The following Discovery exercises use the file **EX1601** that was used in the previous exercises. If you have not completed those exercises, follow the directions that precede the Reinforcement exercises to copy and rename the file.

D1—Required Entry

You can require that certain fields contain an entry.

Goal: Require that all records have a description and learn what effect this has on existing records that do not have a description.

1. Use Help to find information on the **Required** property. Read this information.

2. Open the **Pool Parts Inventory** table in **Datasheet** view.

3. Delete the description for the **Curved top rail**. Save the change.

4. Change the **Required** property of the **Description** field to **Yes**. Save the change. Read the warning and proceed.

5. Switch to **Datasheet** view and enter the missing description, **Curved top rail**.

6. Try to delete one of the other descriptions. Read the message. Press Esc to remove the attempted change.

7. Close the table and leave the database open for use in the next Discovery exercise.

D2—Lookup Boxes in the Table Datasheet View

If you prefer to enter data in the table's Datasheet view, you can add combo boxes to the cells in this view. One of the options in the Data Type list is a Lookup Wizard. This wizard can be used to create a combo box on a particular field. It changes the field properties to include a lookup list. You can also set the control for a lookup field property by clicking the Lookup tab in the Design view window of the table.

Goal: Use the Lookup field property to add a combo box to the Distributor field of the **Pool Parts Inventory** table.

1. Use Help to search for information on the **Lookup Wizard**. Read the topics titled: **Create a Lookup list field in Design view**, and **Create a value list field in Design view**. Then search for information on **Display Control Property**.

2. Use the information you have read to add a lookup list to the **Pool Parts Inventory** table that looks up the distributor's name from the **Parts Suppliers** table.

3. Open the **Pool Parts Inventory** table in Design view and select the **Distributor** field.

4. Click the **Lookup** tab in the **Field Properties** pane and change the properties so that a combo box is added to this field that looks up values in the **Parts Suppliers** table.

5. Save the change. Switch to the **Datasheet** view and select one of the cells in the **Distributor** column. Confirm that a combo box displays the distributors.

6. Close the table and leave the database open for use in the next exercise.

D3—Add a Header and Footer to a Form

Page headers or page footers can be added to a form to supply additional information such as the date and time the form was printed. You can also insert a page break so that you can print forms one to a page.

Goal: To modify the **Parts Suppliers Input Form** to include information in a header and footer, and add a page break.

1. Use **Help** to look for information about adding headers and footers to a form. Use the Help, Index feature to search for information about adding a page number and a page break.

2. Open the **Parts Suppliers Input Form** in **Design** view.

3. Open a page header/footer and insert a simple page number on the right-hand side of the page footer.

4. Insert the full date and time on the right side of the page header. (Hint: You have to move the date and time box from the form header to the page header.)

5. Add a label box to the left side of the page header area and add the company name **Armstrong Pool, Spa, and Sauna Co.** Change the font size to 14 point. Adjust the size of the page header area and label box as necessary.

6. Place a page break just under the **Billing** list box.

7. Examine the form using **Print Preview**. Print one record. Close the form and save your changes when prompted. Close the database.

Lesson: 17

Extract Useful Information from Large Databases

Introduction

Extracting information from databases is crucial in many types of research. Recent natural events such as hurricanes, earthquakes, floods, and tornadoes can be placed in perspective by studying the frequency and severity of such disasters over long periods of time. One natural disaster is almost unique to the United States. For every 1000 tornadoes in the world, 953 of them occur in the United States (Australia is in second place with 30). Each year, news services are filled with stories about tornadoes. We are fascinated by their power and fearful of their destructiveness. Scientists have collected the data that is provided with this lesson in order to study it and understand this force of nature that is part of our lives.

In this lesson, you learn how to work with a database that contains data about all of the tornadoes occurring in the United States from 1986 through 1995. This database has nearly 11,000 records, but with the skills you learn in this lesson, you will be able to find the answers to questions such as, "Which states have the most tornadoes?" or "Where have the biggest tornadoes occurred?" and "How many people have been injured or killed by tornadoes in my county?" This is an example of how scientists conduct such research. Because you are working with real data, you have the opportunity to ask your own questions, discover new relationships, and experience the excitement of doing real research!

In this lesson, you learn how to use form filters and how to create queries.

Visual Summary

When you have completed this lesson, you will have created several filters and saved a query that looks like this:

	Path Width		2/7/00

Year	Killed	Injured	Path Width (ft)
95	5	60	2110
95	3	32	3000
95	3	24	900
95	3	6	2100
95	3	5	750
95	2	11	2640
95	2	1	300
95	1	70	2110
95	1	55	3900
95	1	20	1320
95	1	12	600
95	1	3	450
95	1	3	510
95	1	1	150
95	1	0	60
95	1	0	90
95	0	122	120
95	0	46	2640
95	0	36	450
95	0	28	220
95	0	23	2640
95	0	22	150
95	0	22	600
95	0	20	300
95	0	17	360
95	0	13	220
95	0	12	1500
95	0	12	1500
95	0	11	60
95	0	10	60
95	0	9	1200
95	0	8	210
95	0	8	300
95	0	8	300
95	0	8	600
95	0	8	90
95	0	7	600
95	0	6	980
95	0	6	2640
95	0	6	240
95	0	5	90
95	0	5	1050
95	0	5	30
95	0	5	900
95	0	5	750
95	0	5	220

Page 1

TASK *1*

Moving Between Records and Columns of a Table

Why would I do this?

When you are dealing with a large database, it is important to know how to navigate the records. Simply scrolling through thousands of records looking for what you want will not work well. It is also important to examine the data to understand the kind of information contained in each field. There are some techniques that can be used to move quickly from the beginning to the end of data, and to have columns shift to appear next to each other for easy comparison.

In this task, you learn how to freeze selected columns and how to move to the last record and then the first record in the table. Before you begin, make sure you use an empty floppy disk for this lesson. If you need to reformat a disk, review Lesson 2.

❶ Launch **Access**, select **Open an existing file** from the **Microsoft Access** dialog box, and click **OK**. Locate **Less1701** from the **Student\Lesson17** folder on your CD-ROM disc. Right-click the file and select **Send To**; then choose **3 1/2 Floppy (A:)**.

> **⚠ Caution:** You will need to use a new floppy disk in drive A:, since the **Less1701** database is nearly 1.3 megabytes— close to the 1.44 megabyte capacity of a disk.

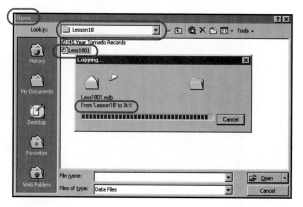

❷ Move to drive **A:**, then right-click on **Less1701** and select **Properties**. Deselect the **Read-only** attribute. Right-click again and choose **Rename**. Change the name of the file to **10 Year Tornado Records**.

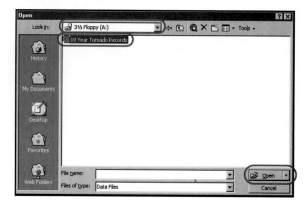

3 Click the **Open** button to open the file, click the **Tables** object button, if necessary, and select **Tornadoes**.

4 Click the **Open** button. The **Tornadoes** table opens and displays the records. The first column is a sequential number that is used as the key field, and the second column is the last two digits of the year of the tornado.

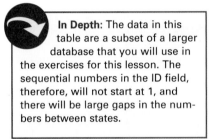

In Depth: The data in this table are a subset of a larger database that you will use in the exercises for this lesson. The sequential numbers in the ID field, therefore, will not start at 1, and there will be large gaps in the numbers between states.

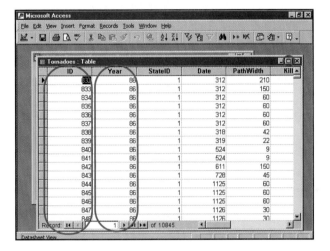

5 Click the **Maximize** button, then use the horizontal scrollbar to scroll the view all the way to the right. The last column contains a code that identifies the county. The first two digits in the code are the state code, and the last three digits are the county code. (Note: State code 1 is Alabama.)

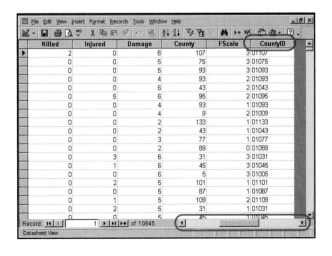

6 Scroll all the way back to the left. Right-click the **StateID** field selector to select this column and open a shortcut menu.

StateID field selector

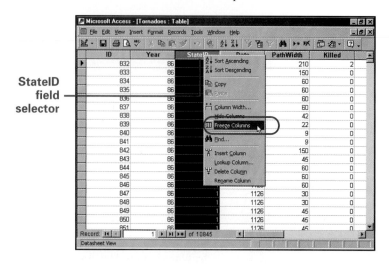

7 Click **Freeze Columns**. Notice that the column is automatically moved to the far left.

The StateID field is moved to the first column

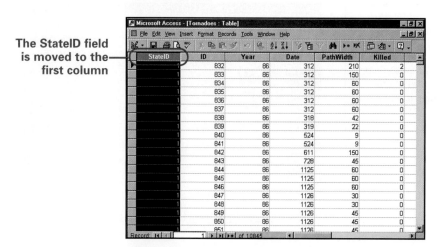

8 Scroll to the right until there are only six columns displayed. Right-click the **County** heading to select this column and to open the shortcut menu. Notice that the StateID field remains on the screen.

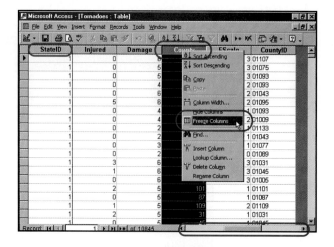

9 Click **Freeze Columns**. The County column moves to the left and is now next to the StateID column. Click anywhere in the datasheet to turn the highlight off.

The CountyID field is moved to the second column

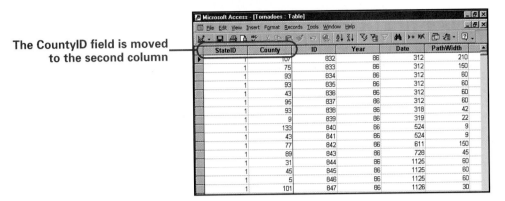

10 Scroll to the right until there are only three columns displayed: **StateID**, **County**, and **CountyID**. Notice how much easier it is to compare the three columns using the Freeze Columns feature. You can now verify that the **CountyID** field is a combination of the **StateID** and **County** numbers.

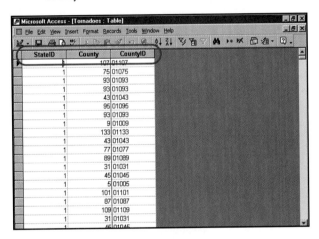

11 Click the **Last Record** button and scroll to the right until only three columns show. Notice that the StateID code is 56. The codes used in this database skip some numbers and include some U.S. territories, so the last state (Wyoming) is not number 50.

Last Record button

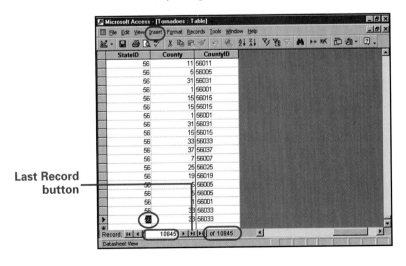

12 Choose **Format, Unfreeze All Columns** to remove the freeze. Notice that the StateID and County columns are still located at the left.

In Depth: The effect of freezing the StateID and County fields is that the columns have been temporarily moved to the left. The Unfreeze All Columns action removes the freeze, but does not immediately move the columns back to their original position. If you close the table without saving these changes to the layout, the columns will appear in their original location the next time you open the table. However, you can save these changes to the layout for the next time the table is opened. Saving the changes to the layout does not affect the original organization of the fields in the table design.

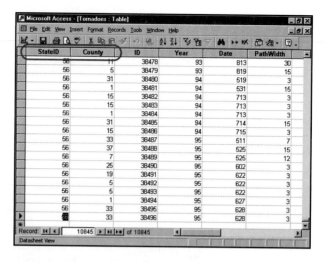

13 Click the **First Record** button to move to the beginning of the table. Click the **Save** button to save the changes in layout.

First Record
button

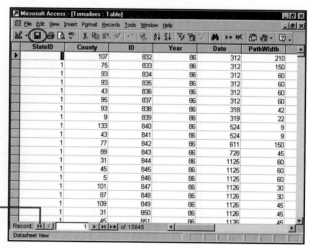

Finding Records

Why would I do this?

Sometimes it is not necessary to use a filter or write a query to find the information you need. You may need to locate a particular record to change some information. For instance, in a personnel database you may need to change an employee's address, marital status, or pay rate. In this case, you want to find one record and make the necessary changes. Other times, you may want to find a particular record or do a quick search to see if the database contains a record. When you are looking for one particular record, often the quickest way to find it is to use the Find feature.

In this task, you learn how to use the Find feature to determine how many tornadoes have occurred in the United States on Halloween.

1 Click in the first record in the **Date** column, then click the **Find** button on the **Table Datasheet** toolbar. The Find and Replace dialog box opens.

Find button —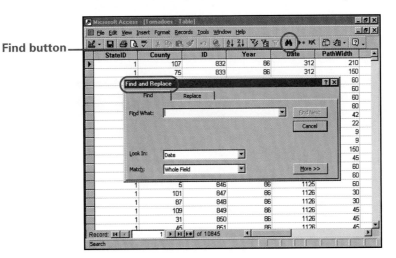

2 Make sure that the **Date** field appears in the **Look In** box and the **Match** box displays **Whole Field**.

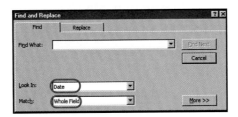

3 Click the **Find What** box and type **1031**. This is the date (October 31) of Halloween. If there is a previous entry in the **Find What** box, delete the entry and type in the date.

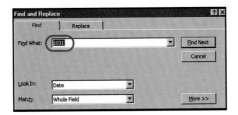

4 Click **Find Next**. The first record in the table that has a date of 1031 is record number 3138. It occurred in Indiana (state code 18).

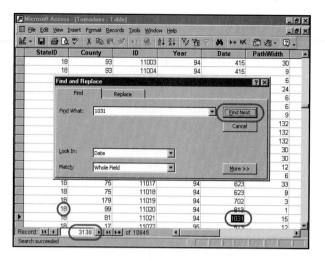

5 Click **Find Next**. Notice how quickly the program scans the records to find the next occurrence in record number 9733. This tornado occurred in Texas (state code 48).

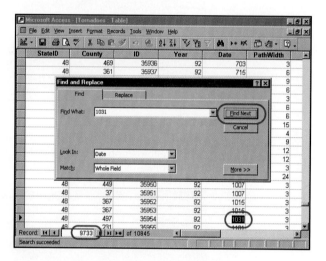

6 Click **Find Next** again. You will see a message stating that Access is finished searching. There are no more records to find. You have determined that there have been only two tornadoes on Halloween in the United States from 1986 to 1995.

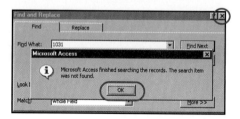

7 Click **OK** to close the dialog box. Click the **Close** button on the **Find and Replace** dialog box. The table will remain open at the last record that was found.

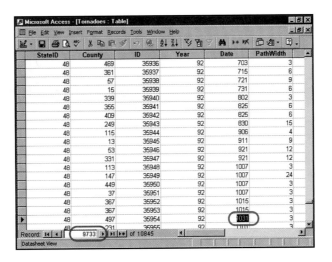

TASK 3

Sorting and Indexing Records

Why would I do this?

In this table, the records are arranged by date of occurrence, but you have the option of sorting the records by any of the other fields as well. Sorting tools are available that can be used to sort a database on one particular field. Sometimes, however, it is helpful to index a database before it is sorted. An index can speed up the sorting process on very large databases.

In this task, you learn how to sort the records by the FScale field in descending order. The numbers in this field indicate the intensity of the tornado, where higher numbers indicate more violent tornadoes. You also learn how to index a field to increase sorting speed.

1 Scroll to the right and click anywhere in the **FScale** column.

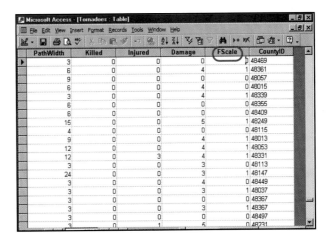

2 Click the **Sort Descending** button. After a few seconds, the records will be reorganized with the contents of the FScale field displayed in descending order.

Sort Descending button—

The table is sorted in descending order on the FScale field—

In Depth: The time it takes to sort depends on your computer's processor speed. A Pentium-class processor operating at 133 megahertz takes one or two seconds to sort this table, while a faster processor will take less time.

3 A few seconds' delay is usually not a problem, but if you have a table with millions of records, the delay can affect your productivity. Click the **View** button to switch to **Design** view.

4 Scroll down the list of fields, if necessary, and click the **FScale** row selector. The field properties for the FScale field are displayed.

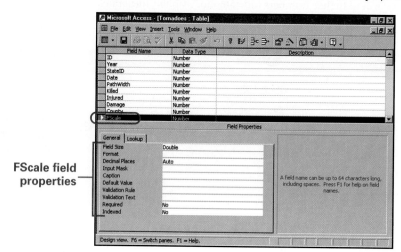

FScale field properties—

5 Click the **Indexed** box. A list arrow appears at the right end of the box.

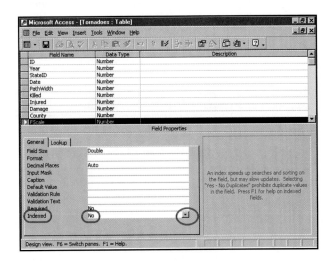

In Depth: The program calculates the order of the records if they are sorted by this field and stores this calculation for later use. If you decide to sort on this field again, it will not have to calculate the proper order, so the display will be updated much more quickly. The order will have to be recalculated whenever a record is added or deleted, however, so it is better to wait until most of the records have been entered before you index the fields.

6 Click the list arrow and select **Yes (Duplicates OK)** from the drop-down menu. Notice that Help for the Indexed property is displayed on the right side of the Field Properties area.

Help for the selected field property

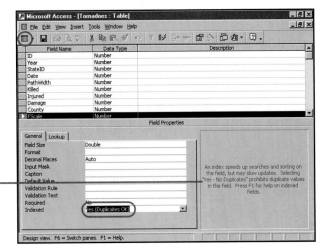

7 Click the **View** button, and then click **Yes** to save the change. The table is displayed in Datasheet view.

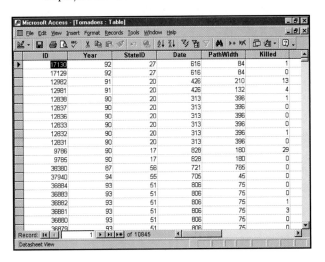

8 Scroll to the right, click anywhere in the **CountyID** column, then click the **Sort Descending** button. Observe how long it takes to sort the table.

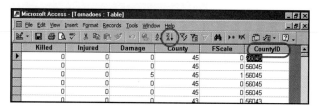

9 Click anywhere in the **FScale** column and click the **Sort Descending** button. It takes slightly less time to sort the 10,000 records on a field that is indexed. You will find that faster sorting time on indexed fields is most noticeable on very large tables or on slower computers.

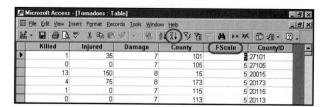

10 Scroll to the left and click anywhere in the **ID** column. Click the **Sort Ascending** button. This will return the table to its original organization.

Sort Ascending button

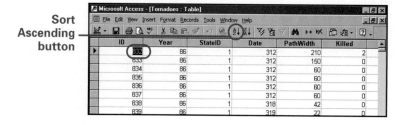

TASK 4

Using a Form to Define a Filter

Why would I do this?

There will be times when you want to view only a few of the many records in a database. To show only the records you are interested in viewing, you can create a *filter* that will specify the *criteria* that will allow only certain records to be displayed. Using a form filter is a simple way to limit records based on criteria. Generally, if you want to be able to look at your data with the same filter over and over, it is best to create a query that can be saved. Form filters are not usually saved, but can provide a quick method for searching your data. Filters also provide a good introduction to some of the concepts you will learn in Task 5 when you create a query. Form filters use the same logical and/or operators as queries, but may seem more intuitive in this format.

In this task, you learn how to use a form to create a filter. You will use it first to restrict the records to those from a particular year. Then you learn how to create more complex filters.

1 Click the list arrow next to the **New Object** button.

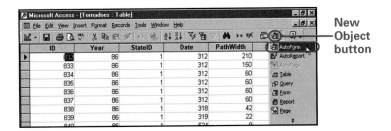

New Object button

2 Click **AutoForm** and click **Yes** to save the previous changes. The program will create a simple form that displays the fields in the Tornadoes table.

Filter By Form button

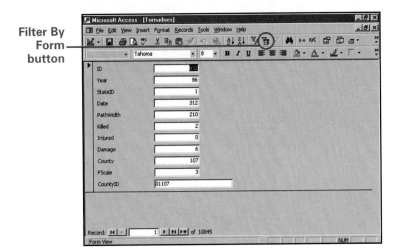

3 Click the **Filter by Form** button. The form is cleared of entries and may be used to enter data.

In Depth: Each field box in the form displays a list arrow when the box is selected. This list enables you to select either all the records that have no entry (Is Null) for the field or all the records that do have an entry (Is Not Null) for the field.

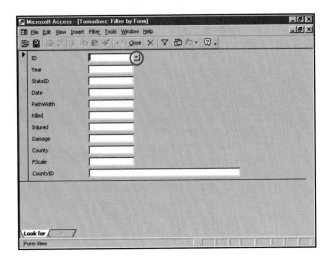

4 Click in the **Year** field box and type **92**.

Apply Filter button

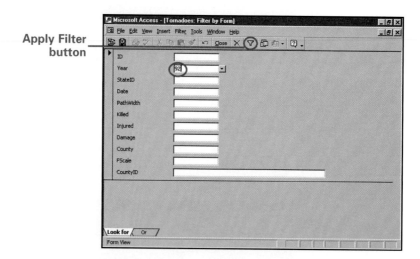

5 Click the **Apply Filter** button. Notice that there were 1,404 tornadoes in 1992.

In Depth: Notice that the ScreenTip for the Apply Filter button now says Remove Filter. This is a toggle button that will apply and remove the filter that has been created. Also notice that FLTR is highlighted on the status bar, which indicates that a filter is currently applied to the data.

The Apply Filter button is now a Remove Filter button

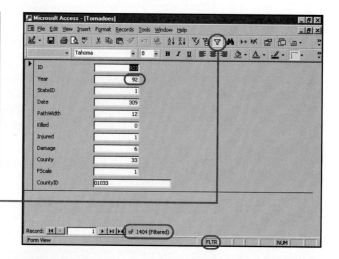

6 Click the **Filter by Form** button again. Click in the **FScale** field box and type **5**. Notice that the year is still displayed.

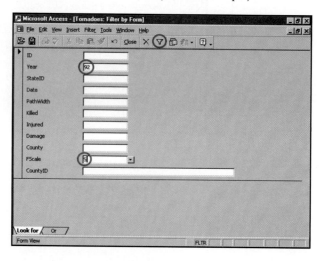

7 Click the **Apply Filter** button. This is an example of a compound filter that uses the logical And operator. Two criteria have been used together: tornadoes that occurred in 1992 and were rated a 5. The results show that only 2 of the 1,404 tornadoes in 1992 were rated a 5. The one shown in the figure occurred in Minnesota (state code 27).

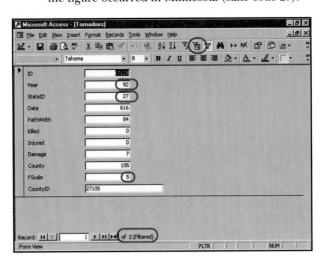

8 It is also possible to filter for Or conditions. Click the **Filter by Form** button again. Notice that the Year and FScale boxes still contain the previous filter conditions. Also notice the tab at the bottom labeled Or.

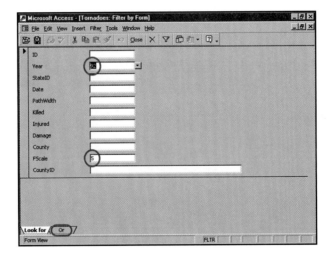

9 To also look for tornadoes rated 4 in 1992 click the **Or** tab. Type **92** in the Year field box and **4** in the **FScale** field box.

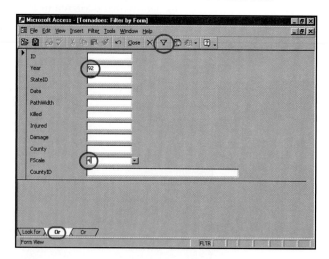

10 Click the **Apply Filter** button. Notice that there were 30 tornadoes in 1992 rated 4 or 5. The one shown in the figure occurred in Georgia (state code 13). This compound filter uses both the logical And operator and the logical Or operator. Use of the Or operator expands the results of the filter, whereas an And operator further restricts the results.

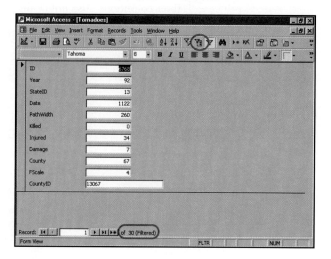

Caution: A form can have one filter at a time. The **Apply/Remove Filter** button does not erase the filter; rather, it turns the filter on and off. Once a filter is created, it will persist as an invisible part of a table or form. Any sorting you do will become the default method of displaying that table or form. Therefore, the last sort you do should be on the primary key field to restore it as the default choice for displaying the records.

11 Click the **Filter By Form** button. Click the **Clear Grid** button. This will remove the values entered for the filter.

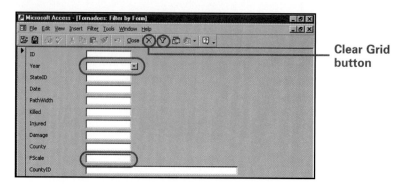

Clear Grid button

12 Click the **Apply Filter** button. This will replace the previous filter with a filter that has no conditions.

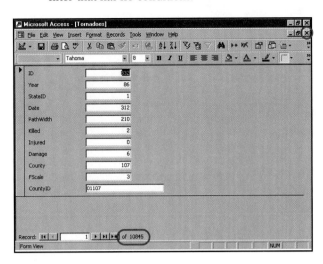

13 Click the **Close Window** button and click **No** when prompted to save the form. The Tornadoes table is displayed.

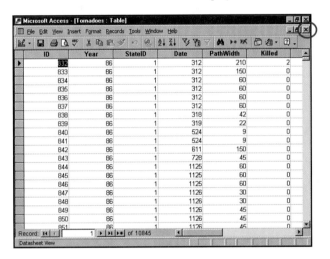

14 Click the **Close Window** button. The Database window is displayed.

TASK 5

Using Select Queries to Display Data

Why would I do this?

Filters are useful, but they are limited in what they can do. Queries are specifically designed to create useable subsets of the data found in large tables. After a query is designed, it is run against the current information in the tables. The results of a query are known as a *dynaset*. When you save a query, Access does not save the dynaset; rather, it saves the structure of the query so it can be used again. Often, reports are based on queries so the information in the reports is limited to the fields and records that are needed.

There are several types of queries, but the most commonly used are called *select queries*. Select queries may contain criteria, like a filter, but they can also limit the fields that are displayed, be sorted on particular fields, and calculate new values based on some of the fields.

In this task, you learn how to create a select query. You choose which fields in the Tornadoes table you want to display and enter criteria in the Year field.

1 Click the **Queries** object button. No queries have been created for this database.

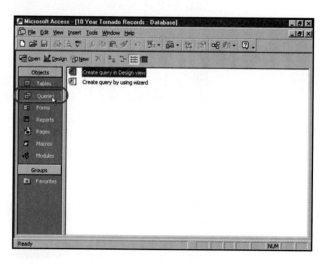

2 Click the **New** button. The New Query dialog box is displayed.

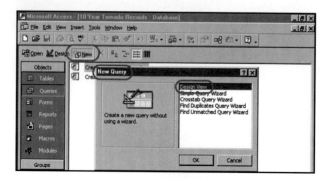

3 Click **Design View**, if it is not already selected, and click **OK**. The Show Table dialog box is displayed.

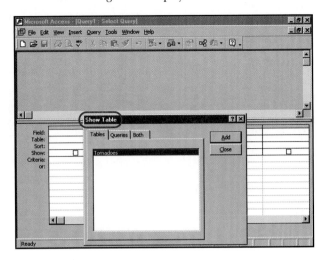

4 Click **Tornadoes**, if it is not already selected, and then click **Add**. A list of fields in the Tornadoes table is displayed in the upper portion of the window.

Table field list —

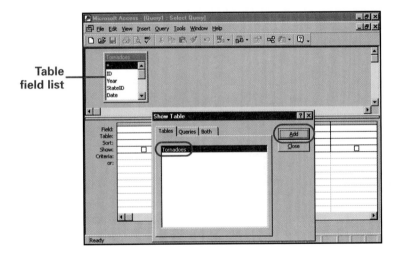

5 Click the **Close** button in the Show Table dialog box. The Query Design view shows a list of the fields in the Tornadoes table and an empty design grid.

Design grid—

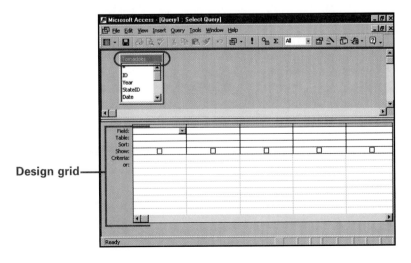

6 Double-click the **Year** field. It is placed in the first column of the design grid along with the name of the table from which it comes.

Source table of the field —

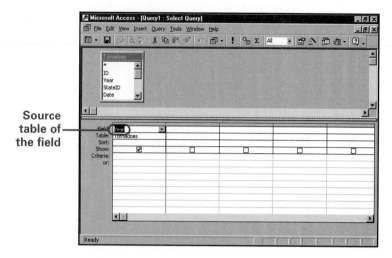

7 Scroll down the list of fields and double-click the **Killed**, **Injured**, and **PathWidth** fields, in that order. They are added to the design grid.

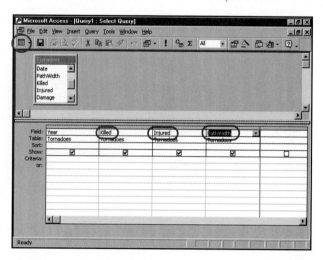

8 Click the **View** button to switch to **Datasheet** view. All of the records are represented, but only these four fields are displayed.

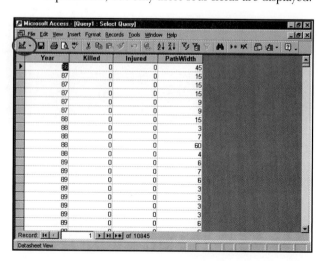

LEARN OFFICE 2000

9 Click the **View** button to return to the **Design** view. Click the **Criteria** box in the first column under **Year** and type **93**.

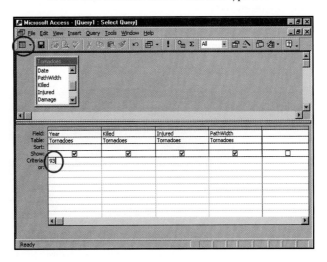

10 Click the **View** button to switch to **Datasheet** view. Only the 1993 tornado records are displayed. There were 1,258 tornadoes recorded that year. Leave the query open for the next task.

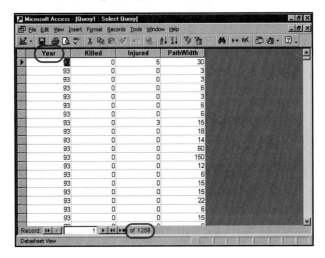

Calculating Values in a Query

Why would I do this?

Sometimes the information you want can be derived from data in the table. For example, in a personnel database, you may need to know an employee's age for various benefits. It is better to store their birth date, from which their age can be derived when needed, rather than an age field which would have to be updated every year.

In the Tornado database, the tornado's path width was stored in tens of feet in the original table provided by the weather service. This could easily be misunderstood when viewed, so it would be better to display it in feet.

To perform a calculation in a query you use the same operator symbols that are used in Excel: ⊞ for addition, ⊟ for subtraction, ⁎ for multiplication, and ⁄ for division. You can also sort on fields to have the records displayed in ascending or descending order based on one or more fields.

In this task, you learn how to create a new column in the table that is calculated from the PathWidth field. You also learn how to create a heading for the new column, hide unwanted columns, and sort on fields.

1 Click the **View** button to switch to **Design** view of the query you created in the previous task.

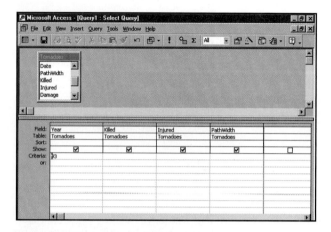

2 Right-click the **Field** box in the empty column to the right of the **PathWidth** column. A shortcut menu is displayed.

Empty Field box

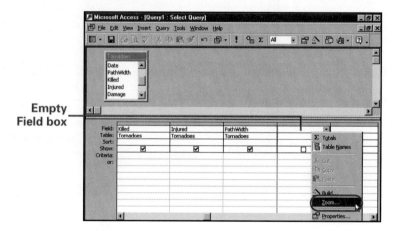

3 Click the **Zoom** option. The Zoom window opens. This window is useful when making long entries in small boxes.

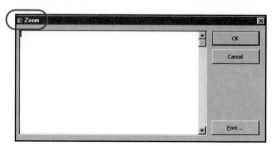

Caution: A calculated field uses square brackets, [], to enclose the field name, not parentheses, (), or braces, {}. It is easy to get these confused. It is also important that the field name is spelled exactly as it appears in the table field list. If it is misspelled, a parameter box (see D-1 at the end of this lesson) will open asking for more information when you run the query. If this happens, return to the query design and fix the spelling of the field name.

4 Type **Path Width (ft):[PathWidth]*10**. Make sure that the first two words are separated by a space, but the field name is all one word. (The parentheses around **ft** have no special function, they are just used as normal parentheses in this example.)

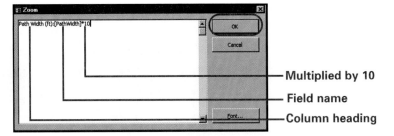

— Multiplied by 10
— Field name
— Column heading

5 Click **OK**. The statement is placed in the Field box in the new column.

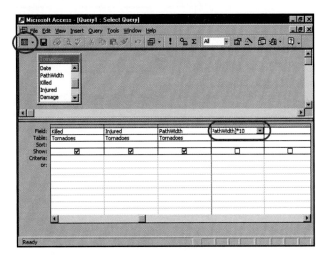

6 Click the **View** button to switch to the **Datasheet** view. Notice that the words that were entered to the left of the colon are used as the column heading. (Widen the last column if necessary to see the entire heading.) Compare the figures in the right two columns to verify the result of the calculation.

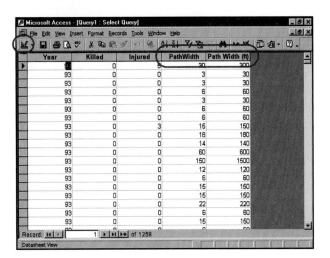

7 Click the **View** button to switch to **Design** view. Click the **Sort** row under the **Killed** field and click on the arrow. A drop-down menu is displayed. You can sort on fields in ascending (alphabetical, A to Z) or descending (Z to A) order.

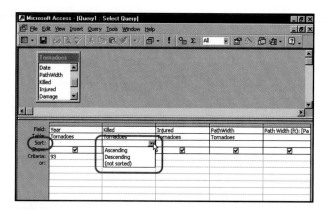

8 Click **Descending** to select it. Do the same for the **Injured** field. The data will be displayed with the tornadoes that caused the greatest number of fatalities and injuries at the top of the list.

In Depth: If you choose to sort on multiple fields, the leftmost one always takes priority. In this case, the program will sort on the Killed field first. When the numbers in this field are the same, it will then do a second sort on the Injured field

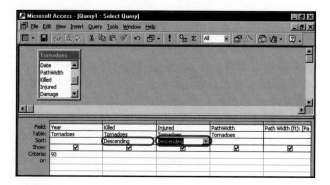

9 Click the **Show** check box in the **PathWidth** column to deselect it. Now this field will not show when you view the dynaset.

The Show check box

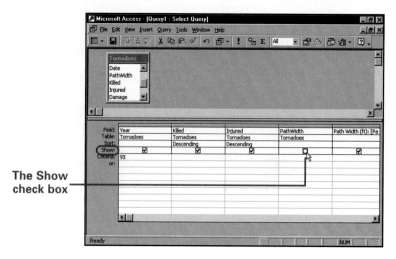

10 Click the **View** button to switch to **Datasheet** view. Notice that the original **PathWidth** column is not displayed, and the records are sorted to display the tornadoes that caused the greatest number of fatalities and injuries at the top of the list.

Sort in descending order

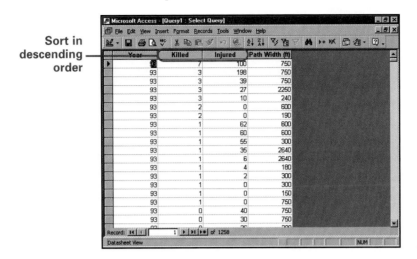

11 Click the **Save** button. The Save As dialog box is displayed. Type **Path Width** in the **Query Name** box.

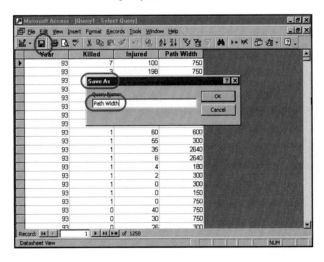

12 Click **OK**. The query is saved for later use. Close the query; it is listed in the Database window. This database will be used in the exercises that follow.

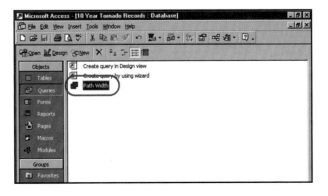

Comprehension Exercises

Comprehension exercises are designed to check your memory and understanding of the basic concepts in this lesson. You distinguish between true and false statements, identify new screen elements, and match terms with related statements. If you are uncertain of the correct answer, refer to the task number following each item (for example, T4 refers to Task 4) and review that task until you are confident that you can provide a correct response.

True-False

Circle either T or F.

T   F   **1.** In Access, you can save a database file with another name using the Save As command. **(T1)**

T   F   **2.** When you freeze a column, Access automatically moves that column to the far left position in the Datasheet view. **(T1)**

T   F   **3.** A calculated field is a field that is derived from other information in the database. **(T6)**

T   F   **4.** One way to find something in a particular field is to select the field and click the **Find** button, then type what you're looking for in the **Find What** box. **(T2)**

T   F   **5.** It is best to create indexes for very large databases before most of the records have been entered. **(T3)**

T   F   **6.** A form filter can be used to limit the data to specific records. **(T4)**

T   F   **7.** The form filter is limited because you cannot filter on more than one field at a time. **(T4)**

T   F   **8.** To erase a form filter, click the **Remove Filter** button. **(T4)**

T   F   **9.** In a query, you can view selected fields, sort on one or more fields, and set criteria in one or more fields. **(T5)**

T   F   **10.** A valid calculation in a query based on a table that contained a field named Amount would be **(Amount)/2**. **(T6)**

Identifying Parts of the Access Screen

Refer to the figure and identify the numbered parts of the screen. Write the letter of the correct label in the space next to the number.

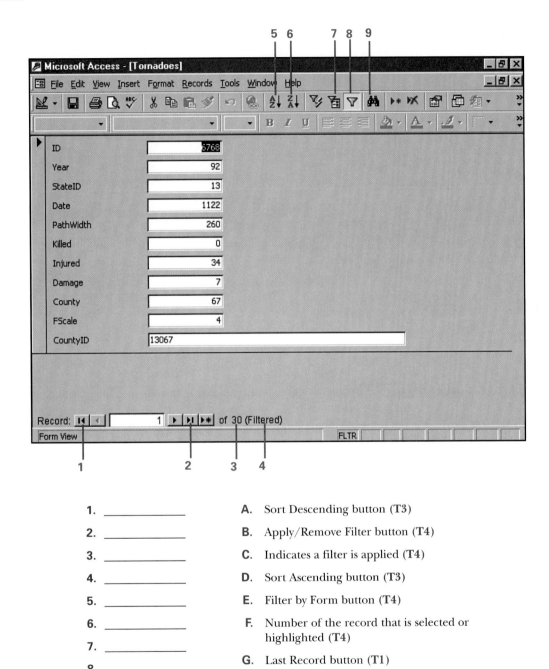

1. _____ **A.** Sort Descending button (**T3**)

2. _____ **B.** Apply/Remove Filter button (**T4**)

3. _____ **C.** Indicates a filter is applied (**T4**)

4. _____ **D.** Sort Ascending button (**T3**)

5. _____ **E.** Filter by Form button (**T4**)

6. _____ **F.** Number of the record that is selected or highlighted (**T4**)

7. _____
                    G. Last Record button (**T1**)
8. _____

                    H. Indicates a filter is in use (**T4**)
9. _____
                    I. Find button (**T4**)

                    J. Number of records filtered (**T4**)

Matching

Match the statements below to the word or phrase that is the best match from the list. Write the letter of the matching word or phrase in the space provided next to the number.

1. ___ Name of the button with a picture of binoculars on it

2. ___ Sort order that sorts in alphabetical order

3. ___ Used to restrict or limit the records displayed

4. ___ Action that places a field name in the query grid

5. ___ These are used in a query to surround a field name that is being used in a calculated field

6. ___ This action brings up a shortcut menu

7. ___ Used to select fields when adding fields to a query

8. ___ The most common type of query used in Access

9. ___ A command in Datasheet view that moves a column to the far left and keeps it in place as you scroll

10. ___ A large box used to write expressions so you can see more than what would fit in a small query grid box

A. Field list box (**T5**)

B. [] (**T6**)

C. Zoom (**T6**)

D. Freeze columns (**T1**)

E. Double-click a field name (**T5**)

F. Select (**T5**)

G. Ascending (**T3**)

H. Find button (**T2**)

I. Right-click (**T1**)

J. ⏎Enter (**T3**)

K. Criteria (**T5**)

Reinforcement Exercises

Reinforcement exercises are designed to reinforce the skills you have learned by applying them to a new situation. Detailed instructions are provided along with a figure, where appropriate, to illustrate the final result. The Reinforcement exercises that follow should be completed sequentially. Leave the database open at the end of each exercise for use in the next exercise until you are specifically directed to close it.

R1—Find Records

1. Launch **Access** and open the **10 Year Tornado Records** database. Open the **Tornadoes** table.

2. Freeze the **Year** column. Scroll to the right until the **FScale** column is next to the **Year** column.

3. These records were grouped together from individual state tables. Even though the Year column looks like it is sorted, if you scroll down you will see that the years start at 86 again for the next state. Sort the table in ascending order on the **Year** column.

4. Click anywhere in the **FScale** column and click the **Find** button.

5. Answer the following questions:

    a. What was the first year in which a tornado occurred that was rated 5 on the FScale? _____

    b. When the scale was created, it defined ratings from zero to 6. How many tornadoes have been rated a 6? ____

6. Close the table. Do not save the changes.

R2—Use a Form to Define a Filter

1. Open the **Tornadoes** table and create an **AutoForm**.

2. Click the **Filter by Form** button. Enter **90** for the **Year** and **5** for the **FScale**.

3. Apply the filter and look at the number of records that match the criteria. This is the number of F5 tornadoes in 1990.

4. Use this method to answer the following questions:

   a. How many tornadoes were rated 5 on the FScale in 1990? _____

   b. How many tornadoes were rated 5 on the FScale in 1991? _____

   c. How many tornadoes were rated 5 on the FScale in 1992? _____

5. Clear the grid and use the **Or** feature to determine the number of tornadoes that occurred in 1995 that were rated 3 or 4. _____

6. Clear the grid. Determine the number of tornadoes that have killed more than 20 people. (Hint: In the **Killed** box, enter **>20.**) _____

7. Close the form. Do not save the form.

R3—Create a Simple Select Query

1. Click the **Queries** object button and click **New** to create a new query. Select **Design** view and click **OK**.

2. Add the **Tornadoes** table and close the **Show Table** dialog box.

3. Add the **Year**, **Date**, **Damage**, and **FScale** fields to the query grid

4. Sort the query in descending order by **Year**.

5. In the **Criteria** box, under the **Date** field, type **401** for April 1.

6. Click the **View** button to see the results of your query and answer the following questions:

   a. How many tornadoes occurred on April 1? _____

   b. For tornadoes recorded on this date, what is the most recent year in which a tornado resulted in a damage rating of 4 or higher? _____

7. Save the query with the name **April Fool's Day Tornadoes**. Close the query.

R4—Create a Select Query with a Calculated Field

1. Create a new query that contains the **Year**, **StateID**, **Killed**, and **Injured** fields.

2. You are going to determine how many tornadoes killed more people than they injured. Create a calculated field that has the heading **Killed to Injured Ratio** and divides the number **Killed** by the number **Injured**. (Note: Remember that each field needs to have brackets around it.)

3. Use a criteria of **>0** in the **Killed** and **Injured** fields to eliminate tornadoes where no one was killed or injured. Use a criteria of **>1** in the newly created column to show only those tornadoes where the ratio will be greater than 1, indicating that the number killed was greater than the number injured.

4. Sort in descending order on the new **Killed to Injured Ratio** field.

5. View the datasheet. How many recorded tornadoes killed more people than they injured? _____

6. In the **Design** view, change the criteria to **>=1** in the new ratio field you created. This will give you all of the tornadoes with the number of fatalities equal to or greater than the number of injuries.

7. In the **Datasheet** view, resort the query on the **StateID** field. From visual examination, how many states are represented more than once? _____

8. In the **Datasheet** view of the query, click the **Print** button to print the results of your query. It should print on one page.

9. Close the query and save it as **Fatality and Injury Ratio**.

10. Close the database.

Challenge

Challenge exercises are designed to test your ability to apply your skills to new situations with less detailed instruction. These exercises also challenge you to expand your repertoire of skills by using Access commands that are similar to those you have already learned. The desired outcome is clearly defined, but you have more freedom to choose the steps needed to achieve the required result.

The following Challenge exercises use the file **45 Year Tornado Records** that is on the CD-ROM disc in the **Student\Lesson17** folder. This file is approximately five megabytes in size and has more than 38,000 records. It contains the tornado history in the United States from 1950 to 1995. In the following exercises, you will use this file in the same way that you might use a company's database. You will not be able to change any of the data, but you can answer questions and do some basic research. You will also find out what difference, if any, it makes to search a database that is read-only.

C1—Find Records in the 45 Year Tornado Records Database

Goal: Answer a set of questions regarding the data in the **45 Year Tornado Records** database.

1. Launch **Access**. Locate and open the **45 Year Tornado Records** file which can be found in the **Student\Lesson17** folder on your CD-ROM disc. You will work with this database from your CD-ROM disc. (Your instructor may have also placed this database in a network folder for your use.)

2. Sort the **Tornado** table by the **Year** column in ascending order. Find the first instance of a tornado with an **FScale** ranking of **5**. In what year did this occur?

3. Does this table contain any tornadoes with an **FScale** rating of **6**?

4. Close the table. Leave the database open for use in the next exercise.

C2—Use a Form to Define a Filter

This database has been provided with a form that may be used by anyone who has permission to read the database. It can be used to define a form filter.

Goal: Use the **Tornadoes** form to create filters to answer the same questions asked of the **45 Year** database.

1. Open the **Tornadoes** form. Use the **Form Filter** method to answer the question, "How many tornadoes have killed more than 20 people?" (Hint: The > character can be used with a number in a form filter to mean "greater than.") _____

2. Close the form. Leave the database open for use in the next exercise.

C3—Hide Columns

You can suppress the display of columns by using the **Format, Hide columns** option. This will greatly simplify the display of data.

Goal: Hide all the columns in the **Tornadoes** table except Year, Date, Time, Killed, and Injured.

1. Open the **Tornadoes** table in **Datasheet** view.

2. Select the **ID** column and hide it.

3. Rather than hide each column individually, choose **Format, Unhide columns** to display a check list. Remove the checks to hide all the columns except Year, Date, Time, Killed, and Injured.

4. The **Form Filter** feature may be used in the Datasheet view of the table. Use a form filter to limit the records displayed to those that killed more than 25 people.

5. Sort the table in ascending order by **Year**.

6. Print the table.

7. Close the table and do not attempt to save your changes. Leave the database open for use in the Discovery exercises.

Year	Date	Time	Killed	Injured
52	321	1730	29	180
52	321	1650	50	325
53	608	1930	116	785
53	609	1425	90	1228
53	1205	1745	38	270
53	511	1610	114	597
55	525	2245	75	270
57	520	1937	37	176
65	411	1815	31	252
65	411	1715	31	252
66	303	1830	57	504
67	421	1724	33	500
68	515	2150	34	350
70	511	2035	26	500
71	221	1635	30	411
74	403	1330	36	1150
74	403	1435	31	257
79	410	1755	42	1700
87	522	1916	30	121
90	828	1437	29	350

Discovery

Discovery exercises are designed to help you learn how to teach yourself a new skill. In each exercise, you discover something new that is related to the topic taught in this lesson. You may be directed to use built-in wizards or some of the extensive Help features provided in Access to discover new features and learn new skills with minimum assistance from books or instructors. The required outcome demonstrates your ability to apply the new skill. You determine the choice of topic, worksheet design, and steps of execution.

The following Discovery exercises use the file **45 Year Tornado Records** that is found in the **Student\Lesson17** folder on your CD-ROM disc. You create a query using parameter criteria, then use the skills you have learned in this lesson to answer questions about this database.

D1—Using Parameter Queries

If you wanted to examine data on a year-by-year basis, it would be time consuming to change the criteria in the query design each time and then run the query. Fortunately, there is a way to write the criteria so that a dialog box appears each time you go to Datasheet view. This enables you to enter the value for that field at the time the query is run.

Goal: To create a parameter query that enables you to enter a different year each time the query is run.

1. Use Help to learn how to create a parameter query.

2. Create a new query based on the **Tornadoes** table that contains the **Year**, **Killed**, **Injured,** and **FScale** fields. Sort the query in descending order in the **Killed** field.

3. In the criteria box for the **Year** field, enter this prompting message: **[Enter the Year]**.

4. In the criteria box for the **FScale** field, enter this prompting message: **[Enter an FScale Code from 0 to 5]**.

5. Limit the records to display only those tornadoes that resulted in fatalities. (Hint: Use > with a number to mean "greater than.")

6. Use this parameter query to answer the following questions:

a. How many F5 tornadoes caused fatalities in 1955? ___

b. How many F4 tornadoes caused fatalities in 1967? ___
   (Hint: Use ◆Shift + F9 to bring up the parameter value boxes again.)

c. How many F5 tornadoes caused fatalities in 1988?____ What does the record number show at the bottom? ____

d. How many F4 tornadoes caused fatalities in 1979?____

7. Close the query without saving it. Leave the database open for the next exercise.

D2—Time of Day

Time of day is given based on local time using a 24-hour clock (4 p.m. is represented as 1600). If you want to filter the number of records to display those tornadoes that occurred between 3 and 4 in the afternoon (including those at exactly 3 and 4), you can use the filter condition **between 1500 and 1600**. The Between operator includes the numbers used to define the range.

Goal: Determine the hour of the day in which the most tornadoes occur.

1. Predict what two-hour period of the day you think tornadoes are most likely to occur.

2. Examine the number of recorded tornadoes that have occurred each two-hour period of the day.

3. Write down the number of records that qualify for each time period. Add up the numbers you get. The total should agree with the number of records in the database.

4. What conclusions can you draw from this research? Is there a time of day when tornadoes are most likely? When are they least likely?

5. Close the table and leave the database open for use in the next exercise.

D3—Using a Database for Comparative Analysis

Goal: Compare the number of deaths and injuries in 1995 to deaths and injuries from other causes.

Filter the table to show only those tornadoes that killed or injured at least one person in 1995. How many people were killed? How many were injured? Compare the number of deaths and injuries from tornadoes to other causes. Use an almanac or search the Internet to find statistics about automobile accidents, boating accidents, lightning strikes, floods, earthquakes, or hurricanes. What was the leading cause of accidental death and injury in 1995 among the group of statistics you researched? How did this compare to deaths and injuries caused by tornadoes that year?

Introduction to PowerPoint

One of the most powerful ways to present an idea, plan, or report to a group is to use a series of slides that illustrate the important points. PowerPoint provides the tools you need to create dynamic and colorful presentations, complete with customized animations, sounds, video clips, and transitions. Using PowerPoint, you can display a presentation electronically on a computer screen or projection panel, create overhead transparencies, or print handouts.

How PowerPoint Works

PowerPoint is a graphical presentation program that uses an outline structure to create slides that can be used to present an idea, or report information to a group. Each main idea in your topic is usually presented on its own slide with sub-points used to expand the idea, like the sub-points and supporting information used in an outline structure.

There are several ways of working with the information in a presentation. The Normal and Outline views are best used to focus on the overall content and flow of ideas, while the Slide view is used to concentrate on the layout, graphics, and design elements. In Slide view, you can add clip art, charts, drawing objects, and other graphics elements that help to illustrate the point that is being explained.

The Slide Sorter View is used to rearrange the order of the slides and to apply animations and transitions to the whole presentation. There is also a Note Pages View that is used to create notes for the speaker to use during the presentation.

Finally, the Slide Show view is used to preview the presentation or display it in an electronic format.

In addition to creating an electronic slide show, you can create overhead transparencies, audience handouts, and speaker notes. These options offer a variety of tools that provide the flexibility to create a presentation in a format that is suited for any presentation environment.

PowerPoint provides several graphics tools than can be used to enhance the impact of your presentation. You will learn how to add clip art, WordArt, drawing tools, charts, and a number of other graphic tools. The animation features that come with PowerPoint allow you to control the pace of a presentation and the manner in which text and other objects appear on your screen during an electronic slide show. These tools add a dynamic dimension to an electronic presentation.

Overall, PowerPoint is fun and easy to use. Once you learn a few basic techniques, you will be able to create dynamic and exciting PowerPoint presentations.

Lesson: 18

The Basics of Using PowerPoint

Introduction

PowerPoint is a presentation graphics program. It provides features and tools for creating a presentation consisting of a collection of slides, overheads, or handouts. If you need help creating a presentation, you can use the *AutoContent Wizard* to help you organize the content. In other cases, you may already know what needs to be included in the presentation, in which case you start with a blank presentation and create the content from scratch. This lesson is designed to provide you with the basic skills to create, edit, view, and save a simple presentation.

In this lesson, you learn how to create a PowerPoint presentation, edit the presentation, create speaker notes, preview the presentation, print the outline, and save the presentation.

Visual Summary

When you have completed Task 6, you will have created a presentation and printed the outline.

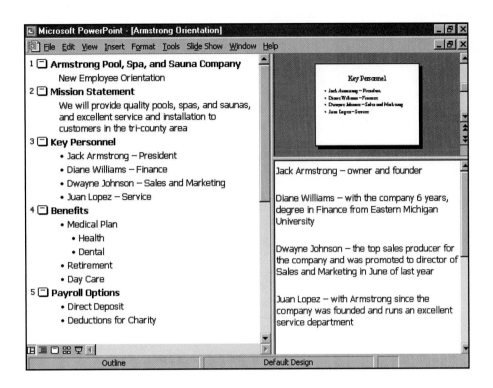

TASK 1

Opening a Blank Presentation

Why would I do this?

There are several ways to create a presentation. In this example, you create a short presentation to welcome new employees to the Armstrong Pool, Spa, and Sauna Company. You know what you want to say, and you have prepared an outline of your main points. In this case, it is recommended that you start with a blank presentation and enter your points in the Normal view.

In this task, you learn how to open a blank presentation.

1 Launch **PowerPoint**. The PowerPoint dialog box is displayed. If the Office Assistant appears, decline its offer for help.

2 Confirm that **Blank presentation** is selected, and then click **OK**. The New Slide dialog box opens. PowerPoint assumes that you want the first slide in the presentation to be a title slide. The title slide is highlighted with a dark blue border.

Title slide ──────

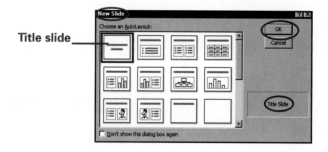

3 Click **OK**. PowerPoint opens in Normal view.

In Depth: You can also use the **Promote** or **Demote** buttons that appear on the Formatting toolbar if you do not remember the keyboard method. If you are using PowerPoint with the Standard and Formatting toolbars sharing the same line, these buttons may not appear if they have not been used recently. They are on the drop-down menu of buttons.

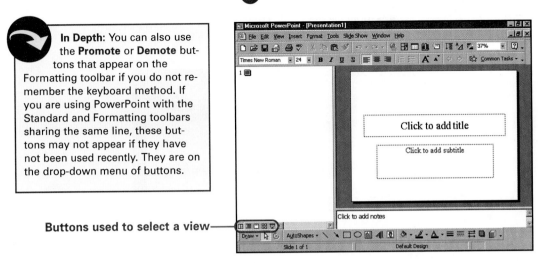

Buttons used to select a view

4 Locate the view buttons at the left end of the horizontal scrollbar. These buttons enable you to quickly change views. Click each of the first four view buttons to see what the views look like (do not click the Slide Show button). Click the **Normal View** button to return to Normal view.

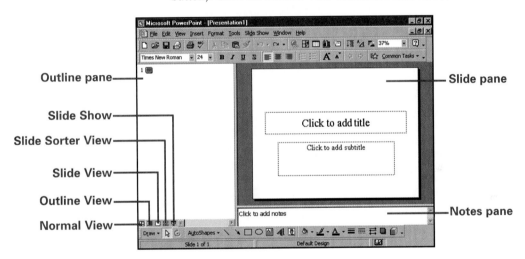

Outline pane — Slide pane

Slide Show

Slide Sorter View

Slide View

Outline View

Normal View — Notes pane

Entering Text in Normal View

Why would I do this?

There are several advantages to entering text in Normal view. First, you can enter text in the outline or the slide part of the window. As you enter text, you can see how it will be displayed on the slide. As you move from one topic to the next, you continue to see the full content of your presentation in the outline while the slide displays the content for the topic you are currently writing. This enables you to see how your ideas flow from one slide to the next while, at the same time, allowing you to see how the words fit on a slide. In addition, you can make notes for the speaker to use during the presentation if you wish.

In this task, you learn how to enter text in the Normal view, first using the slide pane for the title, then the outline pane for the body of the presentation.

1 Click on the *placeholder* where it says **Click to add title**. Type **Armstrong Pool, Spa, and Sauna Company**. Then click in the placeholder for the subtitle and type **Employee Orientation**. While you type, the words are added to the slide and to the outline on the left.

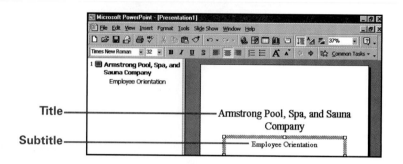

Title——

Subtitle——

In Depth: Your presentation may be viewed one of five ways: *Normal view* is the most commonly used option because it is the most flexible. It can be used to enter text in an outline or on a slide, or to add speaker notes. You can also use this view to add graphics to your slides. *Outline view* is used to type in the text of a presentation. *Slide view* is used to view and edit each slide individually. *Slide Sorter view* is used to see many slides at once, to rearrange their order, and to add transitions and animations. *Slide Show* utilizes the full screen and may be used to project the slides for viewing by an audience. If you select the slide show, press Esc to stop the show (there is nothing to see yet). Click **Normal View** button to return to Normal view.

2 Click on the outline pane on the left side of the window and move the *insertion point* to the end of the subtitle, if necessary. You will enter the body of the presentation in the outline pane where you can focus on the flow of ideas.

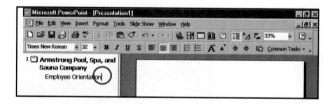

3 Press ⏎Enter. The insertion point moves to the next line on the same slide, but you want to create a new slide. Hold down the ⬆Shift key and press Tab↹. This *promotes* the insertion point to a title for the new slide. The layout of the slide is a bulleted list, which is the most commonly used slide in a presentation.

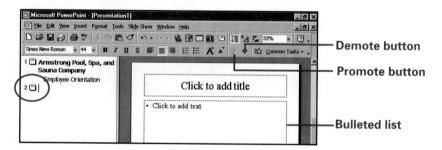

——Demote button

——Promote button

——Bulleted list

4 Type **Mission Statement** and press ⏎Enter. The title for the second slide is entered in the outline and on the slide. When you press ⏎Enter the program starts another line of the outline at the same level of importance, which in this case is another new slide.

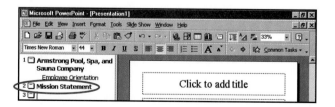

5 Press `Tab`. This *demotes* the line to a lower level of importance, and moves the insertion point to the first bullet point. Type **To provide quality pools, spas, and saunas to customers in the tri-county area**. If a light bulb appears, click it. Then click **OK** to close it.

In Depth: You may see a *Tip Bulb* appear next to the first bullet point. The Office Assistant recognizes keywords that correspond to clip art categories and offers help in selecting appropriate clip art. Adding clip art will be covered in a later lesson, so ignore the Office Assistant at this time.

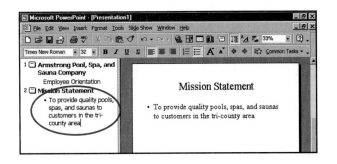

6 Press `Enter`, then `Shift`+`Tab`. This action promotes the next point and moves the insertion point to the title for slide 3. A new slide is displayed on the right.

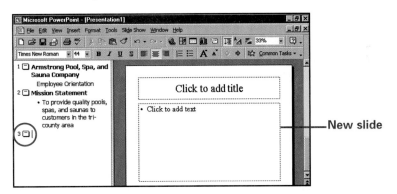

New slide

7 Refer to the figure and enter the text for slides **3** through **5** as shown.

Caution: If the frame on the left, where the outline is displayed, is not wide enough to display the full length of the line, it will wrap the text to fit in the frame. This does not affect the text in the slide. Do not use `Enter` to force **President**, **Finance**, or **Sales** onto a second line.

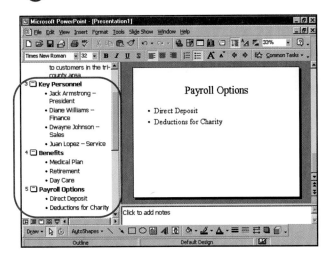

TASK **3**

Editing Text

Why would I do this?

Once you have completed the first draft of your presentation, you may want to show it to someone else to see if there is anything else that should be covered. It is likely that you will modify the text of any presentation several times before it is finished. You can edit the text in Normal view, or you may prefer working in Outline view where you can focus more fully on the content and the flow of ideas. You can also edit in Slide view, which is a preview of the final slide. This view shows what the *font* will look like, and whether the *font sizes* and text location are appropriate. Slide view is also useful when evaluating the overall layout of the slide when graphic elements are added.

In this task, you learn how to add additional text to some slides using Outline view, then change to the Slide view to change the slide layout for the Mission Statement slide.

1 Click the **Outline View** button at the bottom of the window. Move the pointer (in the shape of an I-beam) to the right of the word **Sales** in slide **3** and click. The blinking insertion point is moved. Press the (Spacebar), then type **and Marketing**.

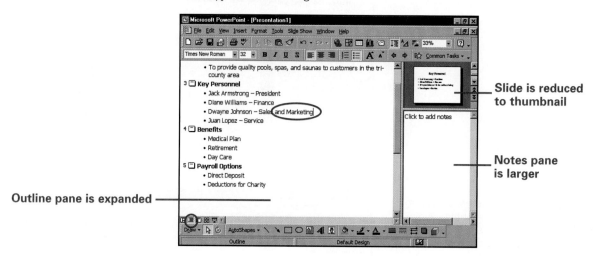

Outline pane is expanded

Slide is reduced to thumbnail

Notes pane is larger

2 Click to the right of **Medical Plan** on slide **4**. Press (Enter), then press (Tab). You are ready to enter a subpoint under Medical Plan. Type **Health**, press (Enter), then type **Dental**. Two subtopics have been added to this topic.

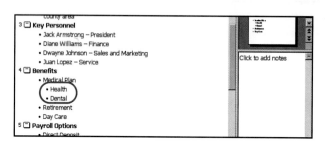

3 The mission statement has recently been modified. Change the mission statement on slide **2** to read as follows:

We will provide quality pools, spas, and saunas, and excellent service and installation to customers in the tri-county area

In Depth: The same techniques that are used with a word processor can be used to edit text in PowerPoint. Use [◆Backspace] to delete characters to the left of the insertion point and [Del] to delete characters to the right. You can also use the mouse to drag across text and then type over the highlighted text to change it, or press [Del] to remove it.

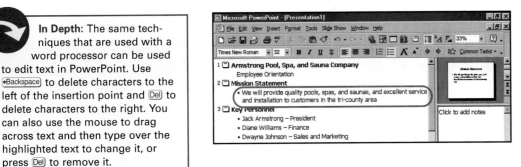

4 Click the **Slide View** button to change to Slide view. This slide only has one bullet point. It would look better if the the style was changed from a bulleted list to a title slide. It is easiest to see the effect of this type of change in Slide view.

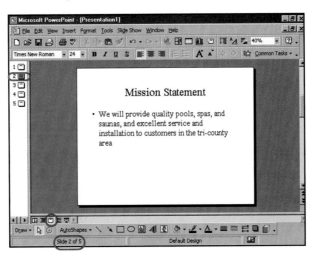

Quick Tip: In Slide view, you can move quickly from one slide to the next by clicking on one of the numbered slide icons displayed on the left side of the screen.

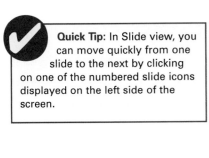

5 Click the **Common Tasks** button at the right end of the Formatting toolbar at the top of the window. Three options are displayed.

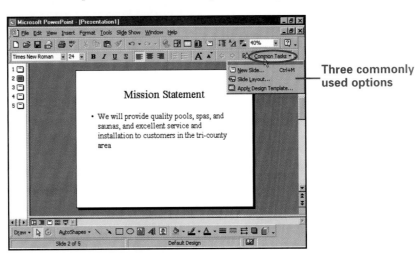

Three commonly used options

6 Click **Slide Layout**. The Slide Layout dialog box opens.

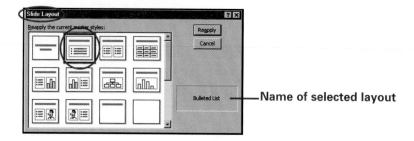

Name of selected layout

7 Click the **Title Slide** layout, the first option in the first row.

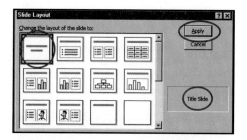

8 Click **Apply**. The slide layout changes to a title slide. Now you will reposition the title and subtitle boxes by moving them up on the slide.

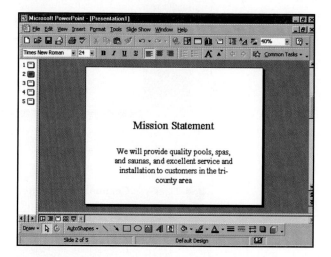

9 Click anywhere on the title of the slide. The outline of the title placeholder is displayed. The square *sizing handles* around the edge of the box can be used to change the size and shape of the placeholder. Move your mouse pointer to the upper border of the placeholder. The pointer changes to a four-headed arrow.

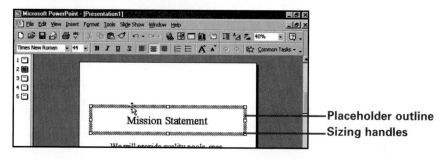

Placeholder outline
Sizing handles

10 Click and drag the box up to the top third of the slide as shown in the figure. As you drag you see the new location for the placeholder outlined with a dashed box.

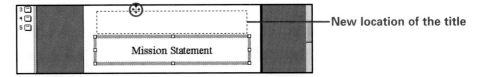

New location of the title

11 Release the mouse. Click anywhere on the subtitle of the slide. Move your mouse pointer to the upper edge of the placeholder. Click and drag it up to the middle of the slide as shown in the figure.

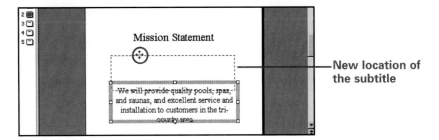

New location of the subtitle

12 Release the mouse. The subtitle placeholder needs to be widened so the statement fits on three lines. Move the mouse pointer to the square sizing handle on the right edge of the placeholder. The pointer changes to a two-headed arrow.

13 Click and drag to the right, almost to the edge of the slide. As you drag, you see the new shape for the placeholder outlined with a dashed box. Release the mouse. Confirm that the text now fits on three lines. Widen the box further, if necessary. Click on the placeholder border and drag the entire box to the left to center it under the title.

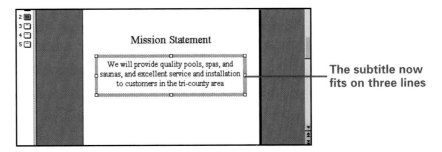

The subtitle now fits on three lines

TASK 4

Saving a Presentation and Adding Speaker Notes

Why would I do this?

PowerPoint creates temporary files on your computer's hard disk. These files are used to protect your work in case of unexpected power failure and loss of memory, but as with all computer files, after you have spent some time creating, it is important to save your work. Similarly, notes used by a speaker during a presentation help to ensure that nothing is left out. Notes can provide useful reminders about details that need to be added, and can help a speaker keep on track. They also add a bit of insurance against a temporary memory loss when talking in front of a group. PowerPoint contains a feature that makes it easy to create effective speaker notes.

In this task, you learn how to save your presentation and create speaker notes.

1 Click the **Save** button on the Standard toolbar. The Save As dialog box is displayed.

2 Confirm that the default filename is selected in the **File name** box and replace it by typing **Armstrong Orientation**.

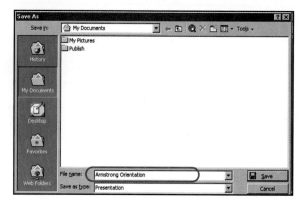

3 Place a formatted disk in the **A** drive. Click the down arrow at the right end of the **Save in** box. Select the **3 1/2 Floppy (A:)** drive.

4 Click **Save**. The presentation is saved to your floppy disk. The filename is displayed on the title bar.

5 Click the **Next Slide** button at the bottom of the vertical scrollbar. Slide 3 is displayed.

> ✔ **Quick Tip:** In Slide view, there are three ways to move from slide to slide. You can use the **Next Slide** and **Previous Slide** buttons on the vertical scrollbar, you can click on a particular slide icon on the left of the screen, or you can use the vertical scrollbar. If you click on the scroll box and drag it up or down the vertical scrollbar, it reveals the slide number and the title as you scroll from one slide to the next. This is useful if you want to go to a particular slide when you know the title but not the slide number.

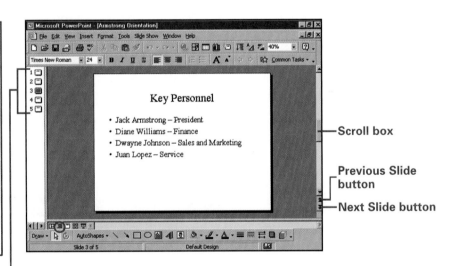

Slide icons

6 Click the **Outline View** button. Move the mouse pointer to the right border of the outline pane. When the mouse pointer changes to a two-headed arrow, click and drag to the left until the notes pane is expanded to a little more than half of the window.

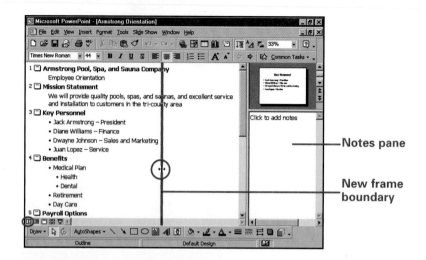

Notes pane

New frame boundary

7 Release the mouse. The view button selection changes to Normal. Click in the **Click to add notes** area. The insertion point is placed in the upper-left corner of the notes pane.

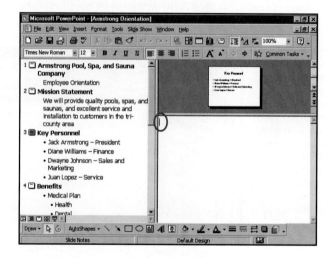

8 Type the following notes as shown in the figure:

Jack Armstrong – owner and founder

Diane Williams – with the company 6 years, degree in finance from Eastern Michigan University

Dwayne Johnson – the top sales producer for the company and was promoted to director of Sales and Marketing in June of last year

Juan Lopez – with Armstrong since the company was founded and runs an excellent service department

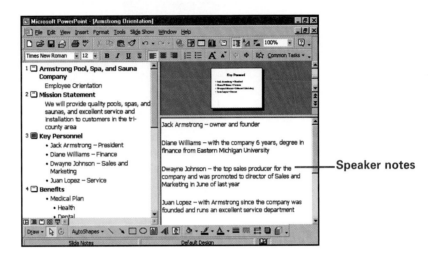

Speaker notes

9 Click **View**, **Notes Page**. Now you can see what the notes page will look like when it is printed. The top part of the page displays the slide, and the notes show below it. When you are giving a presentation, it is helpful if the notes are in a font size and style that is easy to read at a glance.

Caution: When you click the View menu, not all of the options are immediately displayed. Wait a moment for the menu to expand. You can also click the arrow at the bottom of the menu list to reveal the other menu commands.

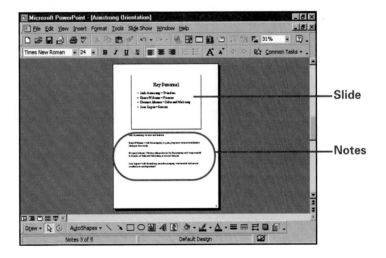

Slide

Notes

10 Click and drag across the notes in the lower part of the screen to select the text. Click the down arrow to the right of the **Font Size** box and select **18** to change the font to a larger size.

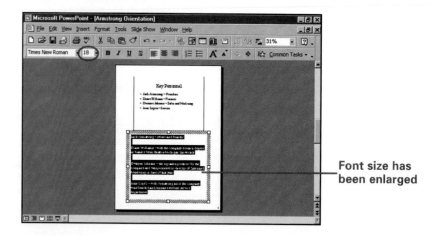

Font size has been enlarged

11 Click the down arrow at the right end of the **Zoom** box and select **75%**. The **Notes** view is enlarged and you can now easily read the notes that have been added for this slide. Click outside of the slide to deselect the text.

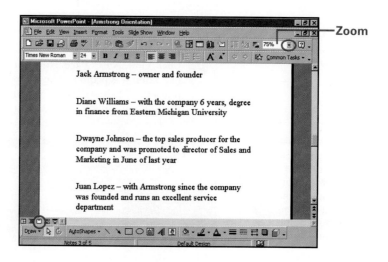

Zoom

12 Click the **Slide View** button, and then click the **Save** button to save your work. The changes made to the Armstrong Orientation presentation are saved.

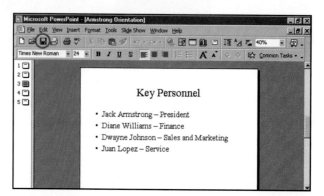

TASK 5

Previewing a Slide Show

Why would I do this?

At any time during the creation process, you may want to see how the slides will actually look when they are projected for an audience. The slide show is a view that uses the entire screen for each slide. Running the slide show allows you to preview what your audience will see when you give your presentation, whether the presentation is given using a computer screen, a projection device, or overhead transparencies.

In this task, you preview your entire series of slides.

1 Click on the scroll box and drag it to the top of the scrollbar to scroll to the first slide of the presentation.

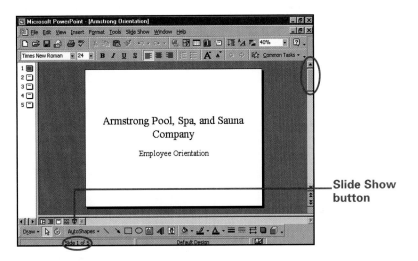

Slide Show button

2 Click the **Slide Show** button at the bottom of the window. The slide fills the entire screen. You can view the slide show beginning from any view in PowerPoint. When you are done, PowerPoint will return to the view from which you started.

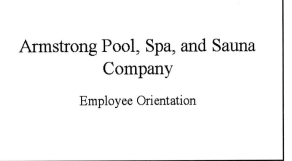

3 Click the mouse to proceed from one slide to the next. After you have viewed all of the slides, a blank screen is displayed with the message **End of slide show, click to exit**.

4 Click again to exit the slide show. The program returns to the first slide.

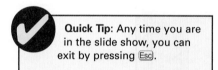

Quick Tip: Any time you are in the slide show, you can exit by pressing Esc.

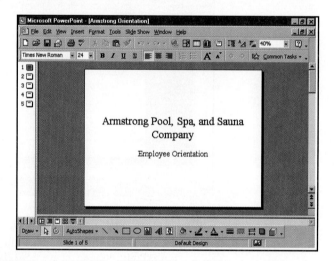

TASK 6

Printing an Outline

Why would I do this?

It is often useful to print an outline so that you can review the presentation and consider changes when you are away from a computer. There will be times when others want to see your outline so they, too, can make changes or respond to your suggested changes.

In this task, you learn how to print the outline for your Armstrong Orientation presentation.

① Choose **File**, **Print** from the menu. The Print dialog box opens.

Caution: In PowerPoint, it is best to use the **File**, **Print** menu option rather than the Print button on the Standard tool-bar. The default setting used by the Print button will print all of the slides on individual pages. Several other print options will probably serve your needs, use less ink and paper, and print faster. It is always best to go to the **Print** dialog box and select what you want to print.

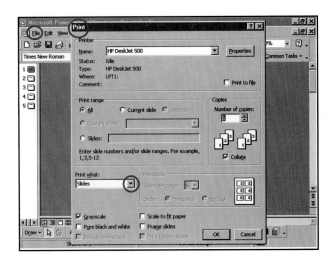

② Click the down arrow on the **Print what** box to display a list of options.

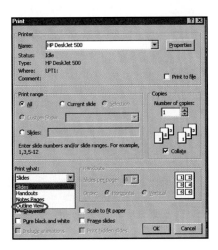

③ Click **Outline View**. Outline View is displayed in the Print what box. Make sure the **Grayscale** check box is selected.

In Depth: The **Grayscale** option is the default option for printing. The **Pure black and white** option changes everything to black and white. In both cases, dark backgrounds are replaced by white backgrounds to reduce ink or toner consumption when printing most of the designs. You can check this by printing a single slide or by printing handouts.

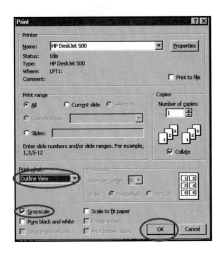

④ Click **OK**. If the Office Assistant appears, click **OK** to close it. The outline prints and you return to Slide view.

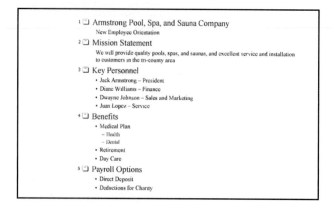

⑤ Click the **Save** button on the Standard toolbar. The presentation is saved with any changes you have made.

Close Window button

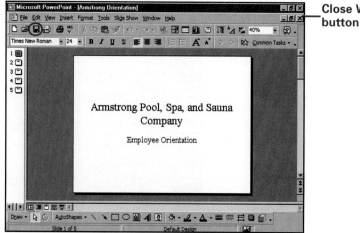

⑥ Click the **Close Window** button at the upper-right corner of the presentation window. Leave PowerPoint open for use in the end of lesson exercises.

Caution: The Close Window button for the presentation is directly below the Close button for the PowerPoint program. If you accidentally close the program instead of the presentation, no harm is done. If you have not yet saved the presentation, you will be asked if you want to do so. Choose **Cancel** to stop the process.

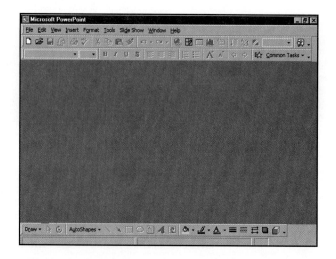

Comprehension Exercises

Comprehension exercises are designed to check your memory and understanding of the basic concepts in this lesson. You distinguish between true and false statements, identify new screen elements, and match terms with related statements. If you are uncertain of the correct answer, refer to the task number following each item (for example, T4 refers to Task 4) and review that task until you are confident that you can provide a correct response.

True-False

Circle either T or F.

T   F   **1.** To print an outline, select **Outline View** in the **Print what** box. **(T6)**

T   F   **2.** Each time you press ⏎**Enter** in Outline view, a new line of the outline is started that is the same level as the previous line. **(T2)**

T   F   **3.** To demote a heading, press ⇥**Tab**. **(T2)**

T   F   **4.** Placeholders designate different areas on the slide in Slide view. **(T2)**

T   F   **5.** You can add notes for the speaker in Slide view. **(T1)**

T   F   **6.** In Slide view, when you move the pointer to the edge of a text box placeholder, the pointer changes shape. **(T1)**

T   F   **7.** To change a slide's layout from a bulleted list slide to a title slide, click the **Change Outline** button on the Standard toolbar. **(T3)**

T   F   **8.** To move a placeholder on a slide, click on the border of the placeholder. **(T3)**

T   F   **9.** To preview or display a slide so that it fills up the entire screen, click the **Slide Show** button. **(T5)**

T   F   **10.** If you are viewing the third slide in Slide view and click the **Slide Show** button, the slide show automatically starts at the first slide. **(T5)**

Identifying Parts of PowerPoint's Normal View

Refer to the figure and identify the numbered parts of the screen. Write the letter of the correct label in the space next to the number.

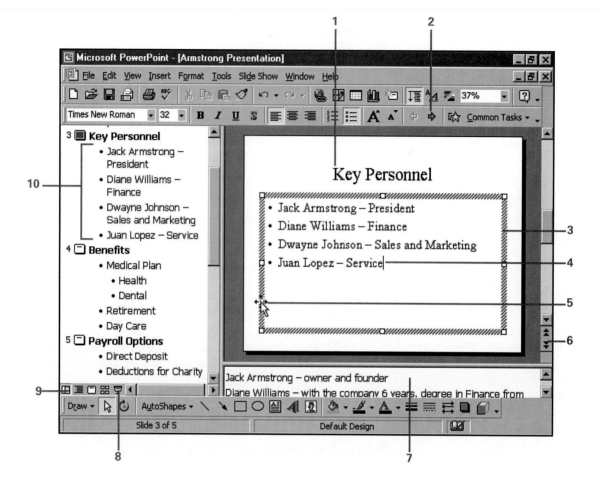

1. _____   **A.** Slide title (**T1**)

2. _____   **B.** Next Slide button (**T2**)

3. _____   **C.** Shape of pointer when a placeholder can e moved (**T3**)

4. _____

5. _____   **D.** Normal View button (**T1**)

6. _____   **E.** Bulleted list (**T3**)

7. _____   **F.** Demote button (**T2**)

8. _____   **G.** Slide Show button (**T1**)

9. _____   **H.** Notes pane (**T1**)

10. _____   **I.** Placeholder border (**T3**)

   J. Insertion point (**T2**)

Matching

Match the statements below to the word or phrase that is the best match from the list. Write the letter of the matching word or phrase in the space provided next to the number.

1. ___ The vertical line that shows where text will be inserted

2. ___ Used to enter text in an outline, on slides, or in speaker notes

3. ___ Utilizes the full screen to display one slide at a time

4. ___ Button with an X in it used to exit PowerPoint

5. ___ Most common slide layout

6. ___ Type of slide layout that shows a centered main heading followed by centered subheadings

7. ___ Method used to advance slides during a slide show

8. ___ Term used to describe the organization of the text and graphics on a slide

9. ___ The button that displays the current slide on the full screen

10. ___ Area in Normal view and Outline view that can be used to add details for a speaker to use

A. Slide show (**T5**)

B. Bulleted list (**T2**)

C. Layout (**T2**)

D. Click left mouse button (**T5**)

E. Close (**T6**)

F. Slide View button (**T1**)

G. Insertion point (**T2**)

H. Normal view (**T2**)

I. Notes pane (**T4**)

J. Title (**T1**)

K. Slide Show button (**T1**)

Reinforcement Exercises

Reinforcement exercises are designed to reinforce the skills you have learned by applying them to a new situation. Detailed instructions are provided along with a figure, where appropriate, to illustrate the result.

Each exercise depends upon the previous exercise. Leave the presentation open at the end of each exercise for use in the next. You may want to do these and succeeding exercises in groups.

R1—Launch PowerPoint and Start a Blank Presentation

1. Launch **PowerPoint**.

2. Choose <u>**B**</u>**lank presentation** from the PowerPoint dialog box.

3. Click **OK** to select the title slide layout.

R2—Enter the Text for a Short Presentation

1. Click in the title placeholder and type the following title: **Sales Meeting**

2. Click the subtitle placeholder and type **Your Name**.

3. Click after your name in the Outline pane. Press (←Enter) to move the insertion point to the next line. Press (⬆Shift)+(Tab⇄) to create the second slide. Use the outline pane to enter the following information for the next three slides:

New Sales People

Bill Martin - Adrian

Mary Jones - Taylor

Sue Miller - Troy

New Product Promotions

20% off on the Blue Deluxe Spa Group

15% rebate on Esther Williams pools

10% reduction on all pool chemicals

Monthly Sales Awards

Mary Shepherd - 110% of goal

Charity Hawken - 95% of goal

Robert Reid - 93% of goal

4. Print the outline.

R3—Edit the Text

1. Click the **Slide View** button and click the slide **2** icon.

2. Change the name of the third person from Sue to **Susan**.

3. Click the **Next Slide** button and change the first item to **25% off on the Blue Deluxe Sauna**.

4. Go to the fourth slide and change the percentage for Charity to **105%** and for Robert to **103%**.

5. Print the outline again.

R4—Add Notes for the Speaker and Save the Presentation

1. Click the **Outline View** button.

2. Choose slide **2**.

3. Expand the notes pane and enter the following information:

Bill Martin comes to us from Caesar Pools and Spas.

Mary Jones is just out of college and has a degree in Marketing. She has worked in retailing for 5 years.

Sue Miller is new to the area and has worked at several pool and spa related enterprises.

4. Click **View**, **Notes Pages**.

5. Select the text in the notes area. Click the down arrow in the **Font Size** box and change the size to **18**.

6. Save the presentation on your 3 1/2 inch floppy disk and name it **Sales Meeting**.

R5—Preview, Save, and Close the Presentation

1. Scroll to the first slide.

2. Click the **Slide Show** button.

3. Click the mouse to advance through the slides and then again to return to Slide view.

4. Click the **Save** button.

5. Close the presentation and exit PowerPoint.

Challenge

Challenge exercises are designed to test your ability to apply your skills to new situations with less detailed instruction. These exercises also challenge you to expand your repertoire of skills by using PowerPoint commands that are similar to those you have already learned. The desired outcome is clearly defined, but you have more freedom to choose the steps needed to achieve the required result.

C1—Creating a Presentation Based on a Report

Launch Word and open the **Less1801** file located in the **Student\Lesson18** folder on the CD-ROM disc that came with your book. Click the **Print** button to print the document, then close the file and close Word.

This paper is about new technologies in distance education. Assume your instructor has to give a presentation on this topic to his or her colleagues and has asked you to create PowerPoint slides that will cover the presentation's main topics.

Goal: Create a PowerPoint presentation based on the Distance Education paper that includes a title slide and four to six bulleted list slides that cover the following main topics:

- Overview
- Video Conferencing
- Computer-Based Communications
- Conclusion

1. Each bulleted slide should have at least four to six sub-points.

2. Use the view of your choice to create the basic outline for this presentation.

3. On the title slide, add your name in the subtitle as **Prepared by: <your name>**.

4. Print the outline.

5. Save the presentation on your floppy disk with the name **New Technologies**.

C2—Creating a Presentation with Speaker Notes

Goal: Create a short (three to four slide) presentation on a procedure with which you are familiar, and add notes for another speaker to use.

Use the Normal view to create this presentation and add speaker notes so someone else could deliver the presentation in your absence. The topic might be registering for classes, applying for a parking permit, changing a flat tire, or any procedure that requires specific steps that need to be followed in a particular order. Make sure you add notes to at least two of the slides. Save the presentation on your floppy disk with an appropriate title.

C3—Using Help to Learn About Importing an Outline from Word

Goal: To locate and print a Help topic on importing an outline from Word.

1. Click **Help** on the menu and select **Microsoft PowerPoint Help**.

2. Type **Importing an outline from Word** and press **⏎Enter**.

3. Select **Create a presentation from an existing outline**. Then select **Create a presentation by importing an outline** from the Help window.

4. Read the explanation about importing an outline from Word.

5. Click the **Print** button to print the Help topic.

6. Close Help and close the Office Assistant.

Discovery

Discovery exercises are designed to help you learn how to teach yourself a new skill. In each exercise, you discover something new that is related to the topic taught in this lesson. You may be directed to use built-in wizards or some of the extensive Help features provided in PowerPoint to discover new features and learn new skills with minimum assistance from books or instructors. The required outcome demonstrates your ability to apply the new skill. Choice of topic, design of presentation, and steps of execution are determined by the learner.

D1—Using the AutoContent Wizard to Create a Presentation

Launch **PowerPoint** and choose the **AutoContent Wizard** option from the PowerPoint dialog box. Follow the steps in the AutoContent Wizard dialog box to select your choice of presentation type, style, and options. Following the basic content that is suggested for the type of presentation you chose, replace the words with your own words and content. Feel free to make up a product, company, or any other information needed to complete the outline. Print the outline, and save your presentation on your floppy disk with the name **Wizard**.

D2—Creating an Outline from a Word Document

Launch **Word**. Locate and open the file named **Less1802** in the **Student\ Lesson18** folder on the CD-ROM disc that came with your book. Review the file, then close it and close Word.

Launch **PowerPoint**. Refer to the information printed in Challenge 3 to complete this Discovery exercise. Follow the steps listed to import the **Less1802** Word file into PowerPoint. The Word document will convert to a PowerPoint outline. Change the first slide to a title slide layout. In the subtitle area of the title slide, add **Presented by <your name>**. Print the PowerPoint outline and save it on your floppy disk with the name **Computer Update**. Close the file and close PowerPoint.

Lesson: 19

Improving the Design of the Presentation

Introduction

You can emphasize points in your message by the careful use of images and sound. PowerPoint offers a wide selection of clip art and other graphic sources that can be used to enhance your presentation and increase the interest of your audience. The judicious use of graphics adds to the visual appeal of your presentation, and helps to keep the attention of your audience. WordArt is a special graphic program that turns text into a graphic drawing object. Many different WordArt styles and effects can be used to give pizzazz to a title on a slide. WordArt can be printed horizontally, vertically, or at an angle.

You have seen how text can be added to a PowerPoint presentation through the use of bulleted points, titles, and subtitles. There are times, however, when freeform text is advantageous. You will often want to add text boxes to describe charts, graphs, or illustrations. PowerPoint also enables you to add lines to connect two or more screen objects together, which can help demonstrate a process or flow of ideas.

In this lesson, you learn how to add a design template and clip art to an existing presentation and add a new slide using WordArt, text boxes, and connectors. You also learn how to print several slides per page to create handouts to accompany your presentation.

Visual Summary

When you have completed Task 5, you will have applied a design, added clip art, inserted text objects with connector lines, and printed all five slides on a handout.

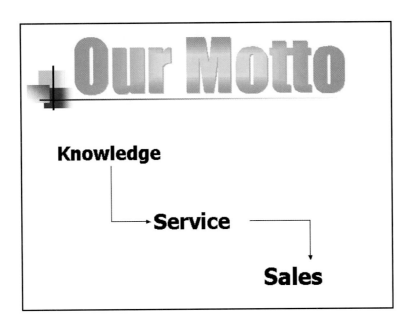

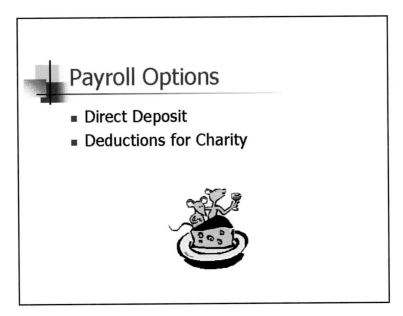

TASK 1

Opening an Existing Presentation and Applying a Design
Why would I do this?

PowerPoint offers a variety of design templates that can be used to enhance the overall appearance of your slides. A presentation looks more professional when a background design is added. It is possible to design your own background patterns for a presentation, but it is much faster to pick one of the designs that come with the program. When you select a design, try to match it to the audience and the environment. Some designs are playful, while others are serious. Some designs are rich in color, but require very bright projection systems if they are used in partially lit rooms. Fortunately, it is easy to change designs to find the best one for the task.

In this task, you learn how to apply one of PowerPoint's design templates to the Armstrong Orientation presentation.

1 Launch **PowerPoint**. The PowerPoint dialog box is displayed. If the Office Assistant appears, decline its offer for help. If the file you need has been opened recently, it will appear in the list at the bottom of the PowerPoint dialog box and you can select it from that list.

2 Click **Open an existing presentation**, and then click **OK**. The Open dialog box opens so you can select the file you want.

Caution: The files you see on your screen will be different from the files listed in the figure. Also, depending on the option selected in your Open dialog box, it may show a list of files on the left side and a preview of the selected presentation on the right side. To see a preview, click the down arrow on the **Views** button and select **Pre̲view**.

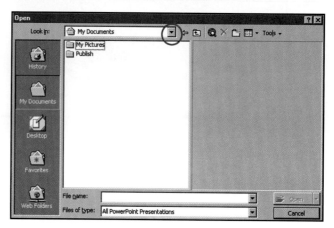

3 Locate and open the file named **Less1901** in the **Student\Lesson19** folder on the CD-ROM disc that came with your book. PowerPoint opens the file in Normal view, the view it was in when it was saved. The name of the file is shown in the title bar, and the first slide is displayed.

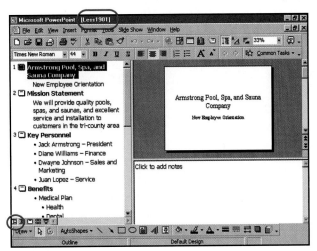

4 Choose **File**, **Save As** from the menu bar. The Save As dialog box opens.

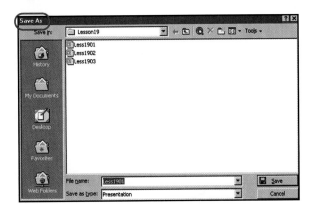

5 Type **Armstrong Employee Orientation** in the **File name** box. Make sure a formatted floppy disk is inserted in the **A:** drive and change the **Save in** box to the **3 1/2 Floppy (A:)** drive.

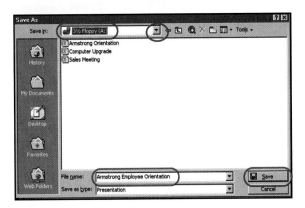

6 Click the **Save** button. The presentation is saved on the floppy disk and the new name is displayed in the title bar.

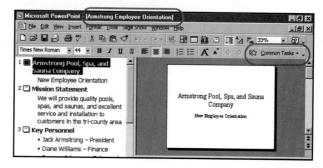

7 Click the **Common Tasks** button and select **Apply Design Template** from the three options. The Apply Design Template dialog box opens. The left side of the dialog box shows a list of design templates, and the right side shows a preview of the selected design. Take a moment to click on some of the different design options to see what is available.

Selected design

List of design templates

Preview of selected design

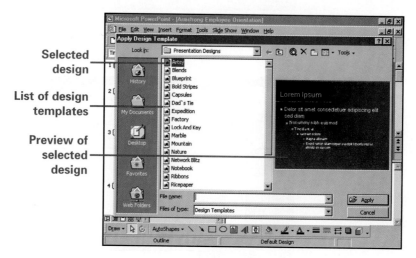

8 Select the **Blends** design option. The design is displayed in the Preview area.

Preview of the Blends design

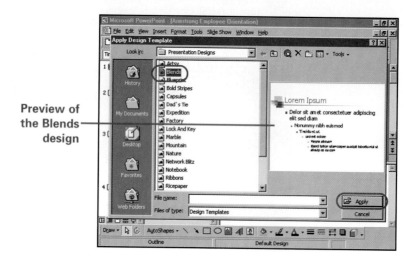

9 Click **Apply**. The design is applied to all of the slides. Click the **Slide Show** button to view the slides. Click the mouse button to proceed through the slide show. When you are done, click to end the slide show and return to **Normal** view. Leave the file open for use in the next task.

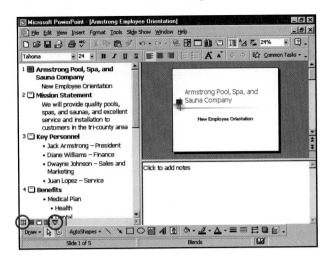

TASK 2

Inserting and Resizing Clip Art

Why would I do this?

PowerPoint comes with a wide variety of predefined images. This collection of images includes photographs, drawings, and other types of graphics that can be "clipped" and inserted into your presentation. You can insert a clip art image to add visual interest, emphasize an important point, add humor, or add a graphical expression of an idea. Clip art is fun and easy to use.

In this task, you learn how to add a piece of clip art to the Payroll Options slide, then move and resize the clip art image.

1 Click the **Slide View** button, if necessary, then click the icon for slide **5** on the left side of your window. The Payroll Options slide is displayed in Slide view.

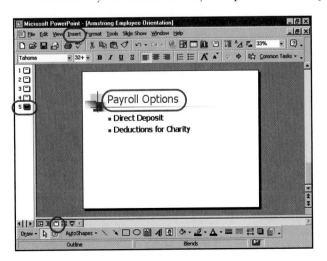

2 Click **Insert**, **Picture**, **Clip Art** from the menu bar. The Insert Clip Art dialog box opens. The categories of clip art are displayed. There are several images available in each category.

> **Caution:** When the clip art images are installed on a computer, there is an option to leave most of them on the CD-ROM disc to save room on the hard disk drive. If you are using this software in a computer lab, the images may be stored on a network server or they may not have been installed at all. Check with your instructor if the clip art image you want to use is not available. If you have the installation CDs, insert the disc with the clip art in the CD-ROM drive to use the full library of available images.

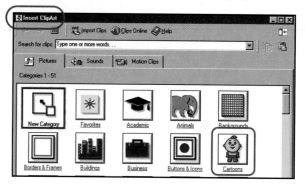

3 Locate the **Cartoons** category. Click **Cartoons** and click a cartoon of your choice. The image is selected, and a shortcut menu with four buttons is displayed.

> **Caution:** If you see images listed in the catalog that do not actually paste into the figure, there are several possible reasons. Most of the clip art is on one of the Office CD-ROM discs. The correct disc must be in the CD-ROM drive to use them or they have to be installed to a network drive. Some of the clip art images are installed on the hard disk, but the catalog does not tell you which ones. If you installed Office 2000 over an existing version of Office 97, you may see some clip art images listed that are no longer available.

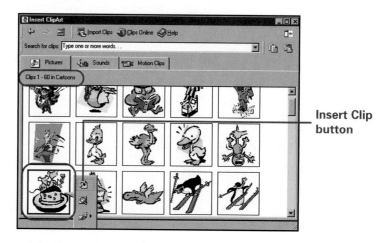

Insert Clip button

4 Click the **Insert Clip** button on the shortcut menu. Click the **Close** button on the dialog box. The image is placed on the slide, and the Picture toolbar opens.

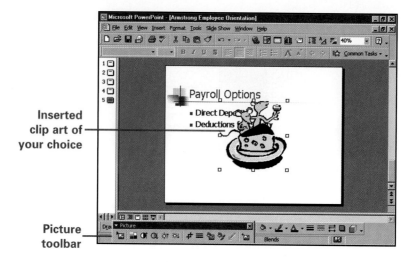

Inserted clip art of your choice

Picture toolbar

5 Move the pointer to the sizing handle in the upper-right corner. The pointer changes into a two-headed arrow.

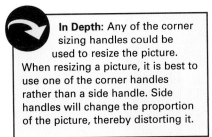

In Depth: Any of the corner sizing handles could be used to resize the picture. When resizing a picture, it is best to use one of the corner handles rather than a side handle. Side handles will change the proportion of the picture, thereby distorting it.

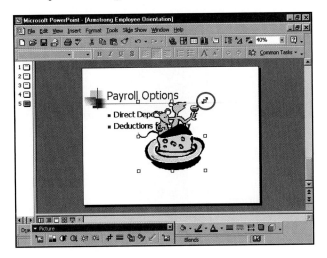

6 Click and drag the corner handle toward the middle of the image until the image is about half its original width and height. Release the mouse button.

Click and drag sizing handle to make image smaller

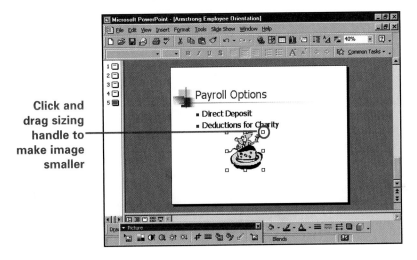

7 Move the pointer onto the picture. It turns into a four-headed arrow. You can move the entire picture when the pointer is in this shape.

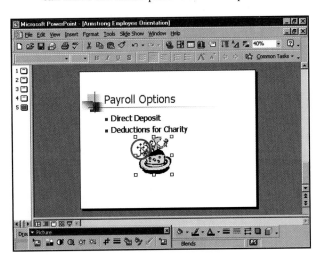

8 Click and drag the picture to the middle of the lower part of the slide. A dotted outline shows the proposed placement of the image.

Future position of the image ────

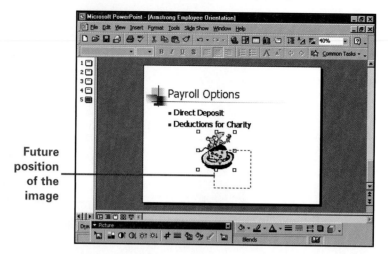

9 Release the mouse button and click outside the image to deselect the clip art.

Sizing handles do not appear when the image is not selected ────

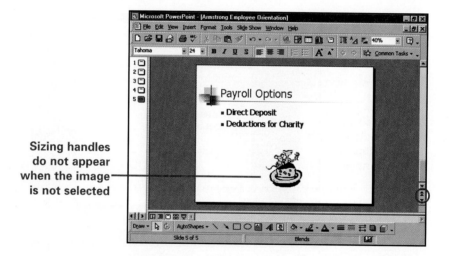

10 Click the **Previous Slide** button to move to slide **4**. Insert a clip art image of your choice that would be relevant to medical benefits.

Clip art image of your choice ────

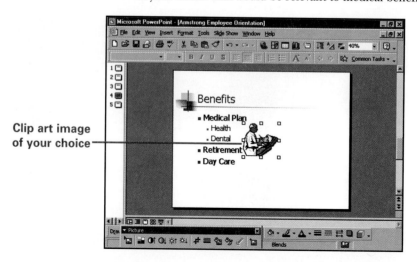

11 Resize the image as needed and reposition it in the lower-right quarter of the slide. Click the **Save** button to save your work. Leave the file open for use in the next task.

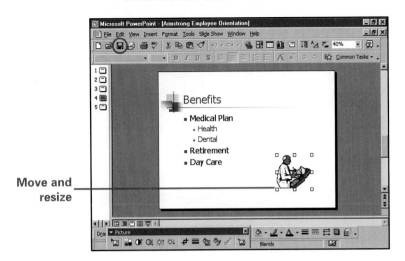

Move and resize

TASK 3

Inserting and Resizing WordArt

Why would I do this?

If you want to create customized titles, PowerPoint has a very powerful tool called WordArt that allows you to be very creative with text. WordArt is a feature that creates text as a drawing object, allowing you to add special colors, shadows, and 3-D effects. WordArt is not restricted to slide titles, but that is where WordArt objects are most often used.

In this task, you learn how to create a WordArt object for a conclusion slide for the employee orientation. Then you will move and resize the image using the same techniques that you learned working with clip art.

1 Click the **Next Slide** button on the vertical scrollbar to move to slide **5**. Slide 5 is displayed. Now you will add a new slide.

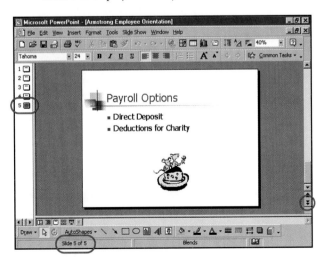

2 Click the **Common Tasks** button, then click the **New Slide** button. The New Slide dialog box is displayed.

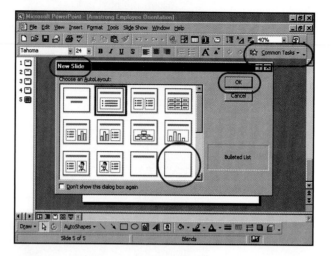

3 Click the **Blank Slide** option, then click **OK**. A new blank slide is displayed.

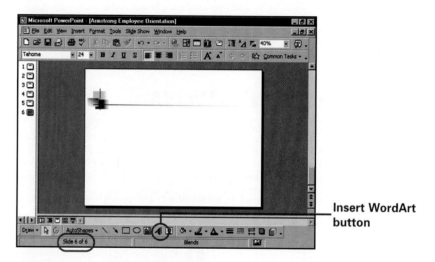

Insert WordArt button

4 Click the **Insert WordArt** button on the Drawing toolbar. The WordArt Gallery dialog box is displayed.

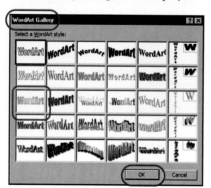

5 Select the third option in the first column. Click **OK**. The Edit WordArt Text dialog box opens with the phrase **Your Text Here** highlighted.

Your words go here. Do not press Enter when done →

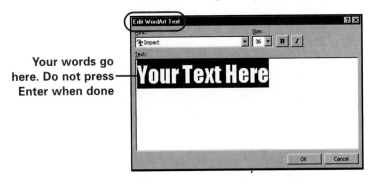

6 Type **Our Motto**, then change the font size to **72** point and click the **Bold** button.

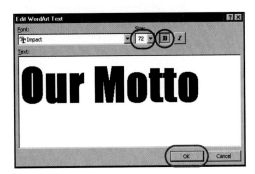

7 Click **OK**. The WordArt drawing object is placed in the center of the blank slide, and the WordArt toolbar opens. Make sure the WordArt object is selected. The sizing handles surrounding the image indicate that it is selected.

Sizing handles indicate selection ⎯

WordArt toolbar ⎯

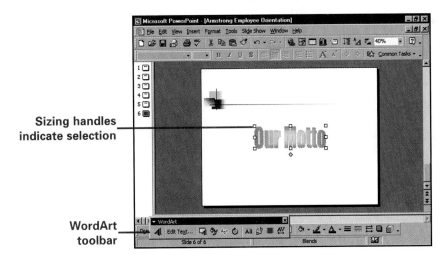

8 Move the mouse pointer onto the image until it is a four-headed arrow. Click and drag the image so it is centered in the top part of the slide. As you move the image, dotted lines known as guides are displayed to indicate the boundary and placement of the WordArt object.

Placement guides

Pointer

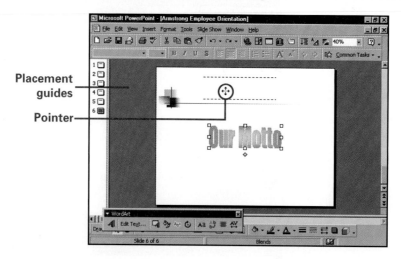

9 Release the mouse button. The WordArt is moved. Use the sizing handles to adjust the size to match the figure. Click the **Save** button and leave the presentation open for use in the next task.

Resized and repositioned WordArt

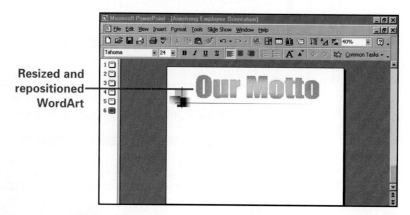

TASK 4

Adding Text Objects and Connector Lines
Why would I do this?

In the previous task, you used WordArt to create a fancy title for a slide. You may also want to add text to a slide in addition to the title. A *text box* is a drawing object that is used to add general-purpose freeform text. This drawing object can be used to add text that can be placed anywhere on a slide and resized just like clip art or WordArt. Connector arrows can also be used to connect these boxes to indicate relationships.

In this task, you learn how to add three text boxes to the slide with the WordArt object and then connect them.

1 Click the **Text Box** button on the Drawing toolbar. The pointer changes shape. Position the pointer on the left side of the slide under the WordArt, and click and drag down and to the right until you have a text box as shown in the figure. Release the mouse button.

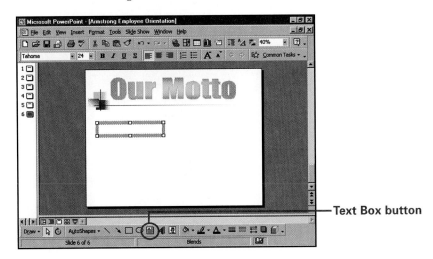

Text Box button

2 Change the font size to **36** point using the Font Size drop-down menu, and then click the **Bold** button. Type **Knowledge** in the text box.

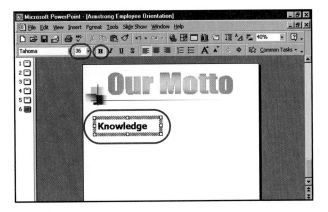

3 Create a second text box as shown. Change the font to **40** point Bold and type **Service** as shown. Adjust the size of the text box as necessary.

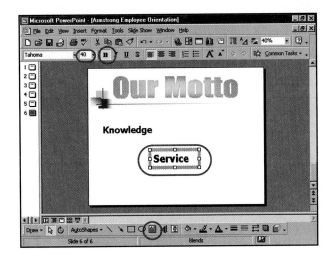

4 Create a third text box as shown. Change the font to **44** point Bold and type **Sales**. Adjust the size of the text box as necessary.

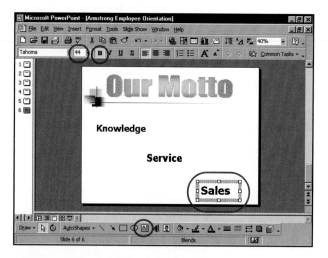

5 Click the **AutoShapes** button on the **Drawing** toolbar. Select **Connectors**. The connector options toolbar is displayed.

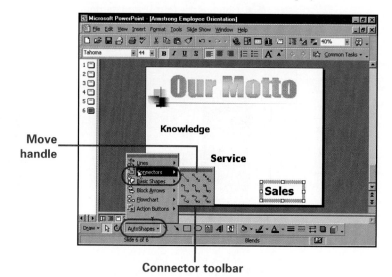

Move handle

Connector toolbar

6 Move the pointer to the move handle at the top of the connector options toolbar. A ScreenTip is displayed that says, "Drag to make this menu float". Click the move handle and drag the toolbar onto the screen. This toolbar is now displayed as Connectors, and the AutoShapes menu closes. This enables you to work with the connectors without having to reopen the AutoShapes menu each time.

In Depth: Some submenus may be separated from the rest of the menus and exist by themselves on top of the presentation. These are called *floating menus*. Such submenus have a gray bar across the top called a *move handle*. The submenu may be made into a floating menu by clicking and dragging the menu onto the screen using the move handle.

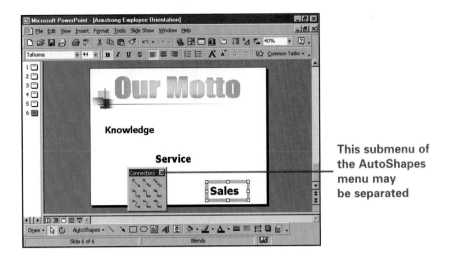

This submenu of the AutoShapes menu may be separated

7 Click the middle button in the second row, called the **Elbow Arrow Connector**, and release the mouse button. Move the pointer just below the word **Knowledge**. Blue connector handles show on the left, right, top, and bottom, and the pointer changes shape. These small blue boxes are used to connect one drawing object to another.

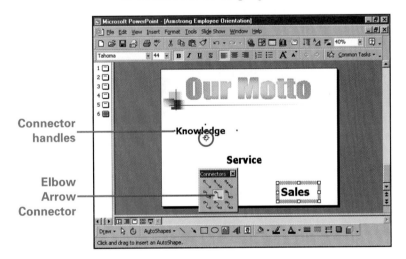

Connector handles

Elbow Arrow Connector

8 Place the pointer on top of the bottom handle of the word **Knowledge**, then click and drag a connector to the handle that is left of the word **Service** (connector handles will appear when the pointer nears the text box). Release the mouse button. A connector with handles is displayed.

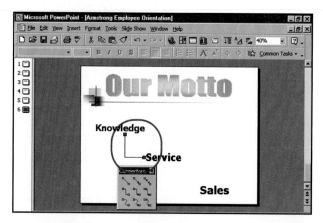

9 Click the **Elbow Arrow Connector** button again. Place the pointer on top of the right handle next to the word **Service**; then drag a connector to the top handle next to the word **Sales** and release the mouse button.

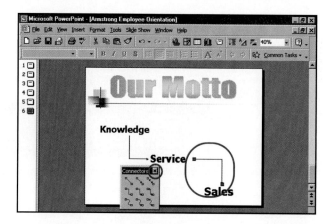

10 Click the **Save** button to save your changes. Click the **Close** button on the Connectors toolbar. Click on an empty area of the slide to deselect the connector box. Leave the file open for use in the next task.

TASK 5

Printing Audience Handouts
Why would I do this?

Audience handouts are printouts that display images of your slides or the outline. When you give your handouts to your audience, it frees them to concentrate on the presentation and participate in a discussion rather than writing down the bullet points on your slides. Participants can add clarifying information to the handouts or jot down questions they might have. Handouts are useful in a teaching or training environment where specific facts are provided.

In this task, you print an audience handout that displays all six slides on one page.

1 Choose **File**, **Print** from the menu. The Print dialog box opens.

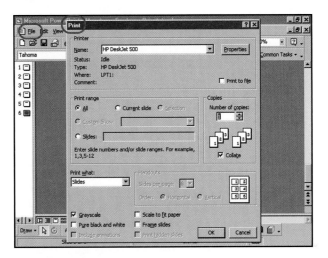

2 Click the down arrow on the **Print what** box and select **Handouts**.

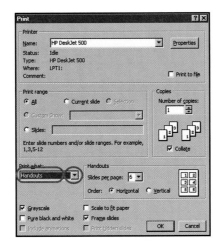

3 Click the **Slides per page** box in the **Handouts** area and select **6**. This option will print six slides per page in two columns of three each in portrait layout.

> **In Depth:** If you want your audience to take notes during your presentation, choose three per page. Three slides will be printed on the left side of the page, and space will be available on the right side for note taking.

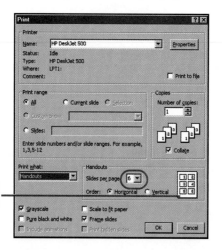

Arrangement of slides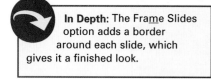

4 Check to make sure the **Grayscale** and **Frame Slides** check boxes are selected.

> **In Depth:** The Frame Slides option adds a border around each slide, which gives it a finished look.

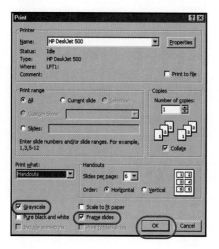

5 Click **OK** to print the handouts. If the Office Assistant appears, click **OK** to turn it off. Click the **Save** button to save your changes. Click the **Close Window** button to close the presentation. Leave PowerPoint open for use in the following exercises.

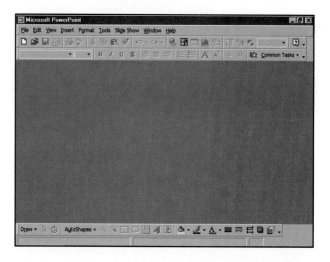

Comprehension Exercises

Comprehension exercises are designed to confirm your knowledge of basic facts that are necessary to advance to higher levels of understanding and performance. The task upon which the question is based is indicated following each question (for example, T4 refers to Task 4). If you are unsure of the correct answer to any of these questions, review the task that is indicated.

True-False

Circle either T or F.

T   F   **1.** If you save a presentation with a new name, the new name will display in the title bar. **(T1)**

T   F   **2.** When you open an existing presentation, it always displays first in Slide view. **(T1)**

T   F   **3.** When you insert clip art, the program automatically adjusts the size to the available empty space on the slide, and places the image in that space. **(T2)**

T   F   **4.** The best way to change the size of a clip art image without distorting it is to click and drag one of the side sizing handles rather than a corner handle. **(T2)**

T   F   **5.** Clip art is grouped into categories to make it easier to locate the appropriate image. **(T2)**

T   F   **6.** Text typed in as WordArt is really a drawing object. **(T3)**

T   F   **7.** Square handles around the outside of a WordArt object indicate that the object has been selected. **(T3)**

T   F   **8.** Guides display to show you the new size or placement of a WordArt object. **(T3)**

T   F   **9.** You can increase the length of a text box by dragging one of its sizing handles. **(T4)**

T   F   **10.** Audience handouts are valuable because your audience does not have to write down what is on the slide and can concentrate on what you are saying. **(T5)**

Identifying Parts of PowerPoint's Slide View

Refer to the figure and identify the numbered parts of the screen. Write the letter of the correct label in the space next to the number.

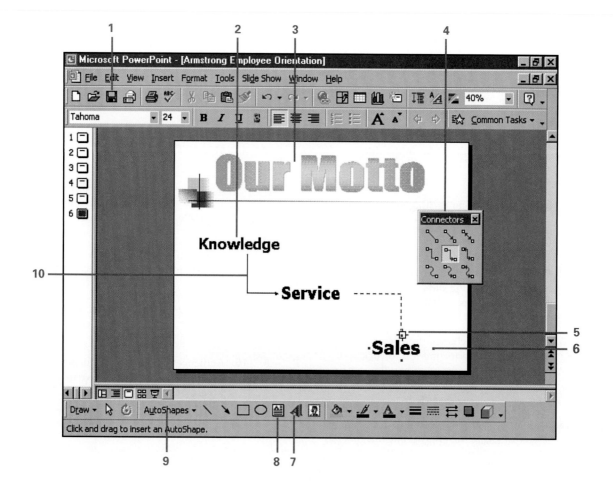

1. _____   **A.** AutoShapes button (T3)

2. _____   **B.** Save button (T2)

3. _____   **C.** WordArt button (T3)

4. _____   **D.** Connectors toolbar (T4)

5. _____   **E.** WordArt object (T3)

6. _____   **F.** Text box (T4)

7. _____   **G.** Connector (T4)

8. _____   **H.** Text Box button (T4)

9. _____   **I.** Pointer (T4)

10. _____   **J.** Connector handle (T4)

Matching

Match the following statements to the word or phrase that is the best match from the list. Write the letter of the matching word or phrase in the space provided next to the number.

1. ___ Button that provides a list of operations that are frequently used

2. ___ A selection of colors and symbols that may be applied to all the slides to create a uniform style

3. ___ A group of clip art images that share a common theme

4. ___ A small square on the perimeter of an object that is currently selected

5. ___ Used to advance to the next slide

6. ___ Slide that has nothing in it

7. ___ Method used to advance slides during a slide show

8. ___ Used to separate a submenu from a menu

9. ___ A menu that is not attached to the side of the window

10. ___ Several slides printed per page

A. Category (**T2**)

B. Click the mouse (**T2**)

C. Floating menu (**T4**)

D. Design template (**T1**)

E. Next Slide button (**T2**)

F. Common Tasks (**T1**)

G. Move handle (**T4**)

H. Handout (**T5**)

I. Blank slide (**T3**)

J. Sizing handle (**T3**)

Reinforcement Exercises

Reinforcement exercises are designed to reinforce the skills you have learned by applying them to a new situation. Detailed instructions are provided along with a figure, where appropriate, to illustrate the result.

Each exercise depends upon the previous exercise. Leave the presentation open at the end of each exercise for use in the next. You may want to do these and succeeding exercises in groups.

These exercises use the file **Less1902**.

R1—Open an Existing File, Rename It, and Apply a Design

1. Locate the file **Less1902** in the **Student\Lesson19** folder on your CD-ROM disc and open it. Save the file as **Getting Ahead** on your floppy disk.

2. Click **Common Tasks**, **Apply Design Template**. Review the different options.

3. Select **Lock And Key** and click **Apply**.

R2—Insert Clip Art

In this exercise, you add a clip art image to the first slide.

1. Go to Slide view of slide **1**.

2. Click **Insert**, **Picture**, **Clip Art**. Select the **Transportation** category and then select the airplane in the first row. If this image is not available, pick another image.

3. Move the image to the right so that it does not overlap the text.

R3—Insert, Resize, and Move Clip Art

In this exercise, you add another clip art image, and then you resize and move it on the slide.

1. Use the Next Slide button to advance to slide 2.

2. Insert the clip art image of an owl reading a book. It is in the **Animals** category. Choose another image if this one is not available.

3. Enlarge the image without distorting its proportions.

4. Move the image to center it in the available empty space.

R4—Insert a WordArt Image

In this exercise, you create a WordArt image.

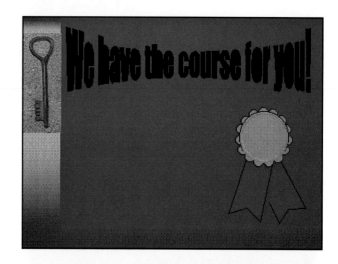

1. Click the slide **5** icon to move to slide 5.

2. Click the **Insert WordArt** button and select the fourth option in the first row and click **OK.**

3. Type **We have the course for you!** and click **OK.**

4. Move the WordArt to the top of the slide and increase its size as shown in the figure.

R5—Add Text Boxes and Connectors

In this exercise, you add text boxes and connectors to slide 5. Use the figure as a guide.

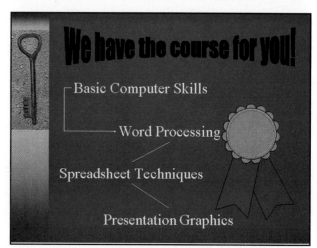

1. Add four text boxes and type the text as shown in the figure.

2. Add an elbow connector between the first and second box.

3. Add straight-line connectors between the second and third, and third and fourth boxes.

4. Save the presentation.

5. Print the presentation as an audience handout with six slides to a page.

Challenge

Challenge exercises are designed to test your ability to apply your skills to new situations with less detailed instruction. These exercises also challenge you to expand your repertoire of skills by using PowerPoint commands that are similar to those you have already learned. The desired outcome is clearly defined, but you have more freedom to choose the steps needed to achieve the required result.

C1—Change a Clip Art Image into a Watermark

Pictures and clip art images can be displayed in four different states: Automatic (the colors as displayed by the image), Black and White, Grayscale, or Watermark. A watermark image is often used as a background for text.

Goal: Create a bulleted slide for a notice about a nature walk, similar to the one shown in the figure, that includes a watermark image.

Create a bulleted slide as shown in the figure to announce a field trip to a local bird sanctuary. Add the text, and then insert the clip art image. The figure is found under the Animals category. Follow these steps to change the image to a watermark:

1. Open a blank presentation and a new bullet list slide. Enter the text shown in the figure.

2. Insert a clip art image of a bird.

3. Change the figure to a watermark by choosing **Format, Picture.**

4. Click the **Picture** tab and use the drop-down arrow next to **Color** under the **Image Control** area to select **Watermark.**

5. Close the Format Picture dialog box, and enlarge and reposition the bird as needed.

6. To have the text print on top of the bird, right-click on the image and choose **Order, Send to Back** from the shortcut menu.

7. Click the **Print** button to print the slide.

8. Save the file on your floppy disk under the name **Watermark**, and then close it.

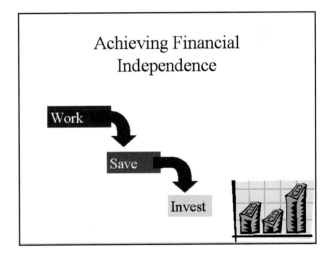

C2—Adding Colors to Text Boxes, Text Font, and Drawing Objects

There are many tools you can use with drawing objects, such as changing the background color, font color, size, or style, or changing the border.

Goal: Create a slide similar to the one shown in the figure that adds colors to text boxes and changes text font color.

1. Open a new presentation and select the title slide.

2. Add the title for the slide as shown.

3. Add three text boxes with the words **Work, Save,** and **Invest,** and position them on the slide as shown. Increase the font size to at least **36** point.

4. Use the **AutoShapes** button and select **Bent Arrow,** which is located under the **Block Arrows** group.

5. Use the **Free Rotate** button to rotate the arrow 180°, and position it between the words **Work** and **Save** as shown.

6. With the arrow still selected, click the **Copy** button and then the **Paste** button to make a copy of the arrow.

7. Click on the new arrow and drag it to a position between the words **Save** and **Invest** as shown.

8. Add a clip art image of your choice having to do with accumulation of wealth and position as shown.

9. Select each text box and add a color by clicking on the drop-down arrow next to the **Fill Color** button on the drawing toolbar. Use the **More Fill Colors** option to increase your color choices.

10. Select each text box and change the font color to a contrasting color by clicking the drop-down arrow

next to the **Font Color** button on the drawing toolbar. Choose the colors so the text will show clearly.

11. Use the **Fill Color** button to add a color to the two arrows.

12. Save the slide on your floppy disk with the name **Investing.**

13. Print the slide and close the presentation.

C3—Adding Connectors and Applying Formats to Text Boxes by Using the Format Painter

Processes can be diagrammed using the Flow Chart symbols, which are a group of AutoShapes. In this Challenge exercise, a diagram on how to register for class has been created. You will add the connecting arrows and change the format of the flow chart boxes. You then use the Format Painter to apply the format from one box to another.

Goal: Add connectors to a registration diagram slide as shown in the figure, and change the format of the text and text boxes by using the Format Painter tool.

1. Locate the file **Less1903** in the **Student\Lesson19** folder on your CD-ROM disc. Save the file on your floppy disk as **Registration**.

2. Using the figure as a guide, add the missing text to the chart objects as needed. (Hint: Click the text box and type to insert the text. Press (⬆Shift) + (⏎Enter) to force text to the next line as needed.)

3. Add the connecting arrows. Use the curved arrows where appropriate as shown.

4. Use the **Fill Color** button to change the color of the first box to a color of your choice.

5. Use the **Line Color** button to change the color of the line on this object to match the fill color.

6. Use the **Font Color** button to change the font color on this object to a contrasting color. (Choose something other than black.)

7. With the first box still selected, double-click the **Format Painter** button on the Standard toolbar. The mouse pointer will have a paintbrush attached.

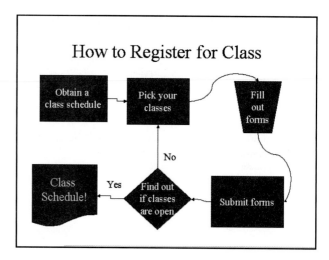

8. Click on the next four boxes to copy the format from the first box to the next four boxes as shown.

9. Save the slide and print it. Close the file.

C4—Creating a Vertical WordArt Design for an Orientation Slide

WordArt offers many different styles and formats. One of the unusual styles is vertical WordArt. This can be useful for something that is short, such as a one-word greeting. Anything that is much longer will be harder to read in a vertical arrangement. In this Challenge exercise, you create an orientation slide that is an overview to topics to be covered in a presentation.

Goal: Create an orientation slide that includes a vertical WordArt object to the left of a bulleted list.

1. Open a blank presentation and choose the bulleted list slide.

2. Click the title placeholder, and then click on the drop-down arrow next to the **Font** box on the Standard toolbar and change the font to one of your choice. (The figure shows Comic Sans MS as the font style.)

3. Add the title as shown in the figure.

4. Click the bulleted list placeholder, change the font to the same one you selected for the title, and then add a list of topics for a student orientation. You can use the ones shown in the figure, or create your own list of six or seven topics.

5. Click the sizing handle on the left side of the bulleted list placeholder and reduce the size of the bulleted list box as shown, leaving room on the left to add the WordArt object.

6. Add a vertical WordArt object for the word **Welcome**. Choose one of the four vertical options that are available in the WordArt Gallery and make the text bold.

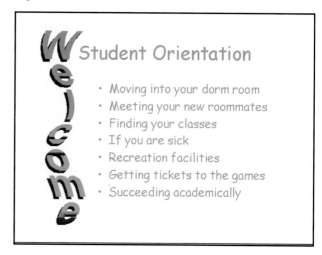

7. Reposition the WordArt as shown and expand it to fill the space.

8. Print the slide and save the presentation as **Student Orientation**.

Discovery

Discovery exercises are designed to help you learn how to teach yourself a new skill. In each exercise, you discover something new that is related to the topic taught in this lesson. You may be directed to use built-in wizards or some of the extensive help features provided in PowerPoint to discover new features and learn new skills with minimum assistance from books or instructors. The required outcome demonstrates your ability to apply the new skill. Choice of topic, design of presentation, and steps of execution are determined by the learner.

D1—Using Other Drawing Tools

In this lesson, you learned how to use a text box and connectors, which are tools on the Drawing toolbar. There are many other tools that can be used from the Drawing toolbar. The figure shows you several shapes that are available and color options that can be used.

In this Discovery exercise, explore the different Drawing toolbar options. Create a blank slide that utilizes four to six different AutoShapes, then add fill colors, add text boxes, and change the color of the text. Use at least one other new option and add a text box that identifies the option you have chosen to use. Save the file on your floppy disk with the name **Drawing Objects**.

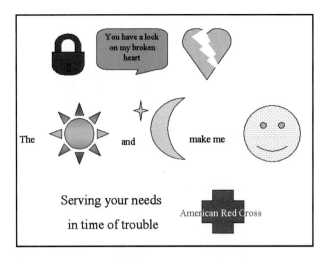

D2—Creating a Circular WordArt Design

One of the more impressive WordArt designs that can be created is a circular design as shown in the figure. The trick to creating this type of a design is to press ⏎Enter between the words so the first line is at the top of the circle, the middle line is in the middle and the last line is the bottom part of the circle. It also works best if the text for the top and bottom of the circle is longer and approximately the same length, while the text in the middle is shorter. Use the figure as a model for creating this type of WordArt design.

In this Discovery exercise, you create a slide that looks like the one shown in the figure. The figure uses the WordArt style that is in the last row, fourth from the left of the WordArt Gallery window. Enter the text with the returns in the appropriate places to create the three lines of text. The following is a list of other options and changes that need to be made to create this image:

- **Impact** is the font style used for both the WordArt object and the text box at the bottom.

- The yellow diamond handle needs to be used to straighten the text horizontally.

- The **Tilt Right** button on the 3-D Settings toolbar needs to be used to straighten the text so it has a flat perspective.

- The **WordArt Shape** button on the WordArt toolbar offers a variety of shapes that can be applied to WordArt. The one used for this design is called **Button (Pour)** and is the last one in the second row.

- **3-D Style 15** was used in this image.

- You will need to enlarge the WordArt object and center it before you add the text box at the bottom of the image.

- Save the file as **WordArt Design**, and then print the slide.

D3—Creating a Flow Chart Showing Your Family Tree

Use the various shapes found in AutoShapes to create a diagram of your family tree. Start with your grandparents (or great-grandparents if you know the information), then include any siblings, spouses, or children. At a minimum, you should have seven boxes. Add connecting lines to show relationships and use a symbol of your choice to show marriages, divorces, etc. Add the name of each family member by typing the name on the appropriate box. (Hint: You do not have to use a text box for this—rather, you select the box and just type to add the text.) Add a banner at the top of the slide and add your family name, i.e., Preston Family Tree. Save the file with the name **Family Tree**, then print the slide.

Lesson: 20

Charting Numerical Data

Introduction

Many presentations include charts. That is because charts are much better at communicating trends and relationships than columns of numbers. This lesson is designed to show you how to create these charts for the Armstrong Pool and Spa company. There is a wide variety of chart types available to display numerical information. You can modify any of the chart components, change colors of chart elements, change font or font size of labels, or even customize a chart.

In this lesson, you learn how to add a basic number chart to a presentation.

Visual Summary

When you have completed Task 5, you will have created a PowerPoint slide that look like this:

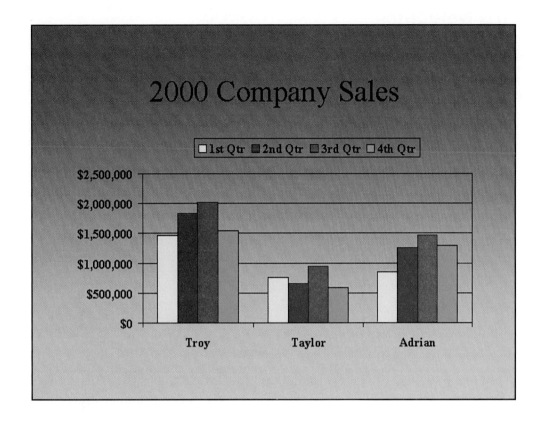

TASK 1

Inserting a New Slide
Why would I do this?

If you plan a presentation perfectly, you will not need to add any new slides. It is rare, however, for this to happen. Normally, you will need to insert new slides in nearly all presentations. As the presentation day approaches, you or your co-presenters will likely decide to cover topics not originally planned, and new slides will be required.

In this task, you will add the first of two new slides to a company year-end report.

1 Launch **PowerPoint**. Open **Less2001** from the **Student** folder on your CD-ROM disc and save it on your floppy disk as **Year End Report**. Click the **Slide View** button.

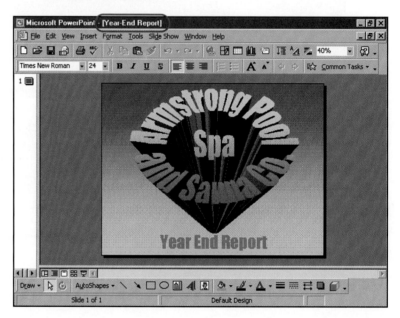

2 Click the **Common Tasks** button on the Formatting toolbar and select **New Slide**. The New Slide dialog box opens. Select the **Chart** option.

Common
Tasks button

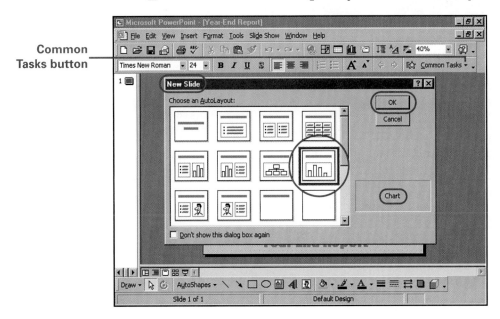

3 Click **OK**. A new slide is shown, with placeholders reserving areas for the slide title and for a chart.

Slide title
placeholder

Chart
placeholder

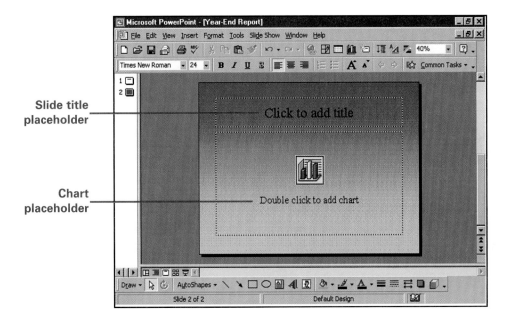

TASK 2

Replacing Sample Data

Why would I do this?

There are two parts to a PowerPoint chart—the chart itself and the datasheet upon which the chart is based. A *datasheet* is similar to a spreadsheet because it contains the data used to build the chart. When you insert a chart into a PowerPoint presentation, the datasheet includes sample data. To create the chart, you change the data, edit the row and column headings, and add or delete rows or columns as needed. The underlying chart changes to reflect the new data as you enter it.

In this task, you learn how to change the data from which the chart is generated.

1 Using the chart slide created in Task 1, double-click anywhere in the **Double click to add chart** box. *Microsoft Graph*, a graph creation and editing program, is activated. The chart and datasheet are displayed with the default values.

Data sheet —

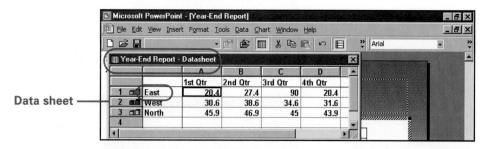

2 Click the word **East** in the first data row, then type in **Troy**. Change **West** and **North** to **Taylor** and **Adrian** as shown on the datasheet in the figure. Use the ⬇ on your keyboard to move from one cell to the next. You now have three stores for which to enter data. Each entry is displayed on the chart when you move your insertion point to another cell.

New data is
shown on the chart —

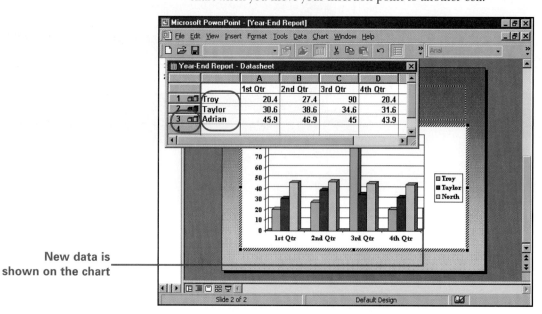

3 Change the quarterly sales data for each of the stores as shown in the figure. Watch the chart change in the background as you make changes.

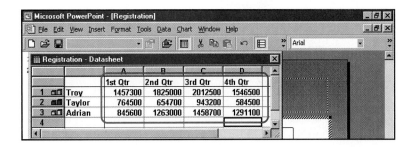

4 Click the **Close** button in the Datasheet window. The datasheet is closed, but the chart remains selected and the Microsoft Graph program remains active.

Chart button on the toolbar

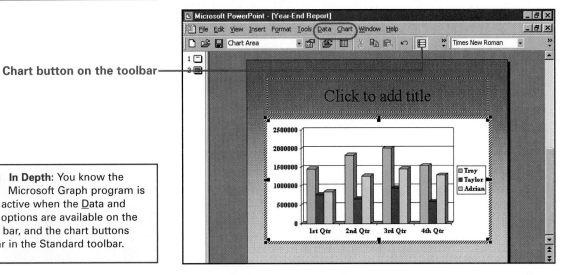

5 Click the **Save** button to save your work.

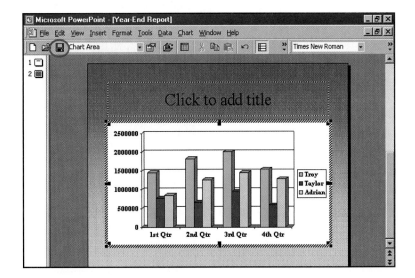

TASK *3*

Choosing a Chart Type
Why would I do this?

Different chart types give the viewer a different perception of the same data. Some chart types are more effective with certain types of data. For example, to show parts of a whole, a pie chart works best. To show a sequence over time, a line chart is usually best. PowerPoint gives you an easy way to change the chart type. You may need to try several chart types before you find one that is just right.

In this task, you learn how to change the chart type to see which type works best with your data.

1 Make sure the chart you created in Task 2 is active. If the **Data** and **Chart** options are not shown on the menu bar, double-click on the chart to activate Microsoft Graph.

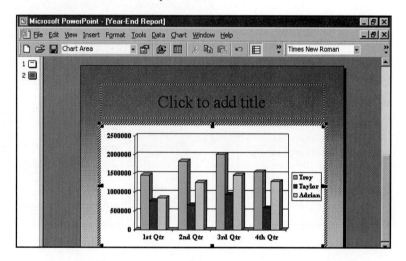

2 Click the **More Buttons** button and point to the **Chart Type** button. The Chart Type submenu is displayed.

More Buttons button

Chart Type toolbar

Caution: The Chart Type button may be displayed on the toolbar in the Microsoft Graph program, particularly if this button has been used previously. If this button is showing on the toolbar, click on the down arrow next to it to display the list of chart options.

3 Point to the bar at the top of the Chart Type toolbar. This is called the move handle. Click and drag it onto your screen. The Chart Type toolbar is displayed as a floating toolbar.

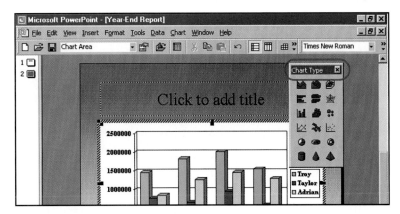

4 Click the **Area Chart** button on the Chart Type toolbar. The area chart provides the same information as the column chart you created in Task 2, but it is much more difficult to interpret.

Area chart ———

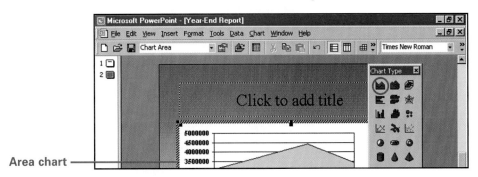

5 Click the **Line Chart** button, the first button in the fourth row of the Chart Type toolbar. The line chart is somewhat easier to interpret than the area chart, but is still not very clear.

Line Chart ———

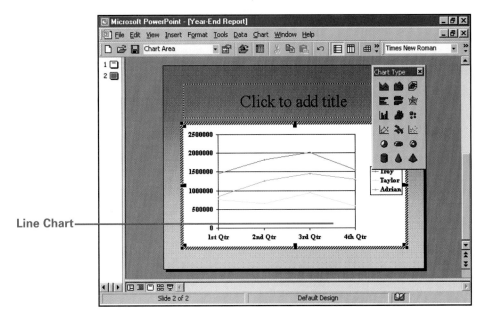

6 Click the **Column Chart** button, the first button in the third row of the Chart Type toolbar. The column chart, which is the default chart type, is actually best for this type of data.

In Depth: You can view a wider assortment of chart types by choosing **Chart**, **Chart Type** from the menu. (The Office Assistant might open if you use this method. Right-click on the Assistant and click **Hide** to close it.) The Chart Type dialog box gives you several different options under each basic category of chart. You can also use this dialog box to create a custom chart.

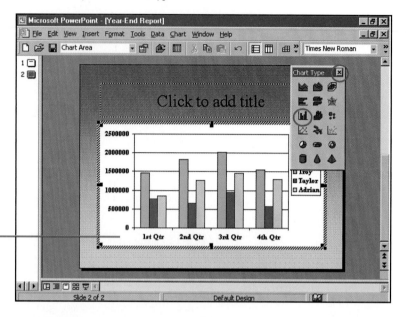

Column chart—

7 Click the **Close** button on the **Chart Type** toolbar. Click the **Save** button to save your work.

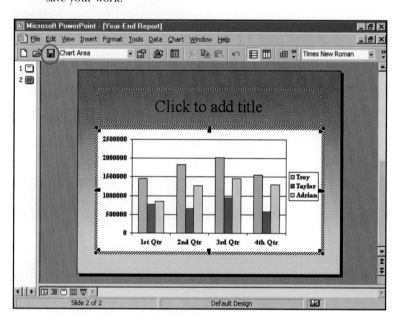

Switching Columns and Rows

Why would I do this?

The chart you created in Tasks 2 and 3 displays the four quarters of the year along the category axis for all three stores. If you wanted to display the sales for each store for the whole year, you would need to view the data by column rather than by row.

In this task, you learn how to change the chart from row format to column format.

1 Make sure the chart is active. If the **Data** and **Chart** options are not shown on the menu bar, double-click the chart to activate **Microsoft Graph**. Notice that the category axis at the bottom of the graph is divided into quarters.

In Depth: As you move the mouse pointer around on the graph, ScreenTips are displayed that identify different parts of the graph. These ScreenTips are used when you want to edit a particular part of the graph.

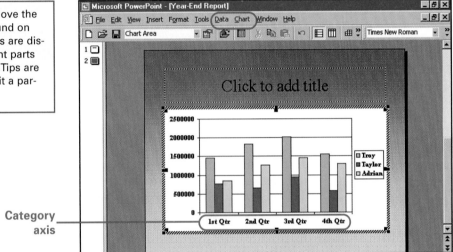

Category axis

2 Click the **By Column** button on the toolbar. The category axis now shows the data by store, rather than by quarter.

By Column button

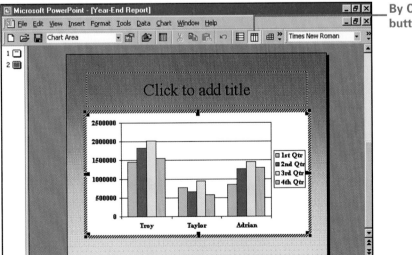

3 Click outside the selected graph area to leave Microsoft Graph. Click in the **Click to add title** area and type in **2000 Company Sales**.

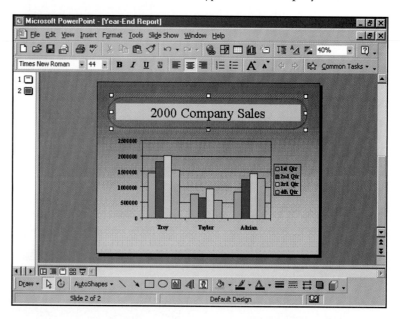

4 Click the **Save** button to save your work.

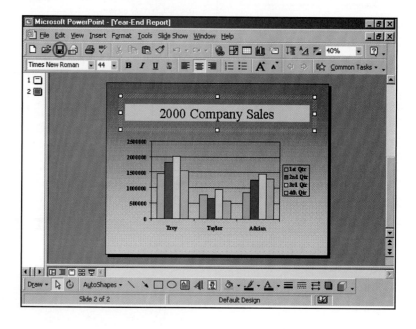

Modifying a Chart

Why would I do this?

Once you have created a chart, you can modify it in a number of ways to better suit your needs. For instance, you can change the colors of the bars or lines in the chart to colors you prefer, or to colors that match ones your company might use to designate the quarters of the year, various departments, or product lines. You can change the scale on a chart to create more or less emphasis, or change the format of your numbers. You can move the legend to another location on the chart. There are two or three approaches that can be used to access the dialog boxes that are used to modify a chart. One of the easiest is to point to the part of the screen that you want to change, right-click to open the related shortcut menu, then select the appropriate menu option from the list. This is the method that will be demonstrated.

In this task, you will learn how to make some basic modifications to the chart you have created.

1 Double-click the graph to reactivate the **Microsoft Graph** program. To modify a chart, you must first be in the graphing program. If necessary, click the **Close** button to close the **Year End Report Datasheet**.

Border with resizing handles indicates chart may be edited

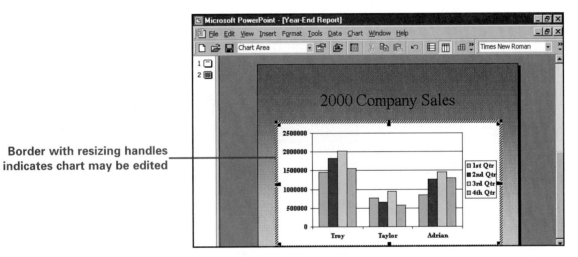

2 Right-click on one of the light-blue bars on the graph. A shortcut menu is displayed and a dark square appears in each of the light-blue bars to indicate that this series has been selected.

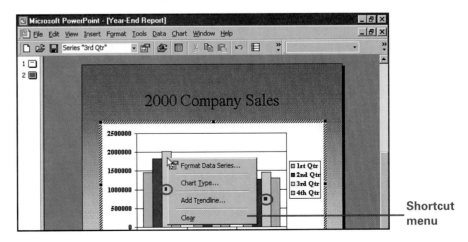

Shortcut menu

3 Click **Format Data Series**. The Format Data series dialog box opens. Click the bright red color at the bottom of the color chart. The sample color changes to red.

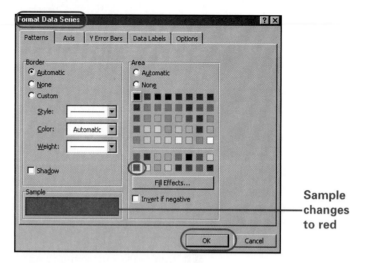

Sample changes to red

4 Click **OK**. The selected series changes to red. Repeat Steps 2 and 3 to change the green bar to yellow and the gray bar to a dark green.

Colors are changed for the first and fourth quarters

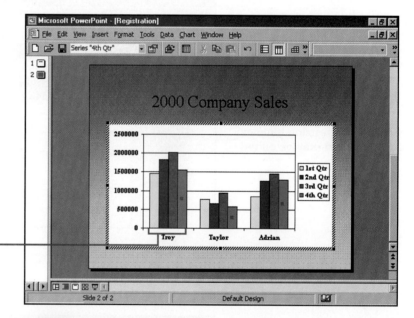

Quick Tip: When you change the color of a series, the legend color changes automatically to match it. Also notice that when you point to a particular bar, a ScreenTip is displayed showing the value of that particular bar.

5 Right-click the **Value Axis**. This is the vertical line on the left side of the graph where the numbers are displayed. A shortcut menu opens.

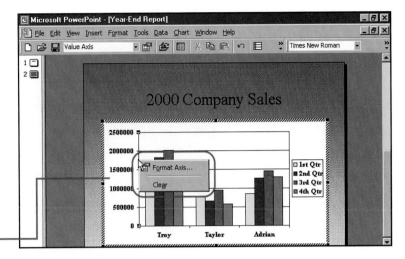

Value axis

6 Select **Format Axis** to open the Format Axis dialog box. Click the **Number** tab. Select **Currency** in the **Category** box and change the **Decimal places** to **0**.

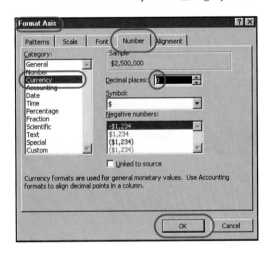

7 Click **OK**. The figures are formatted as currency. Next, you will move the legend to the top of the chart.

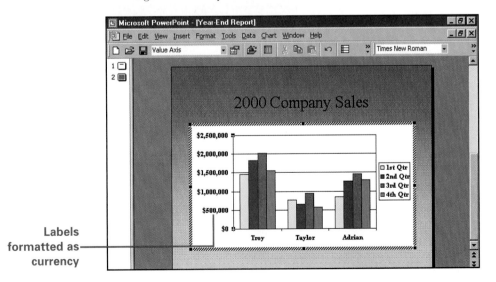

Labels formatted as currency

8 Right-click on the **Legend** and select **Format Legend**. Select the **Placement** tab, then click the **Top** option button.

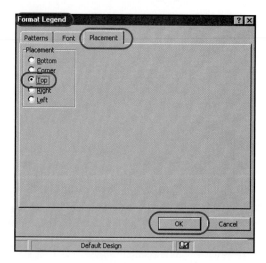

9 Click **OK**. The legend moves to the top of the chart. Click off the chart to view your changes and exit the Microsoft Graph program. Save your work and close the presentation.

The legend is placed above the chart

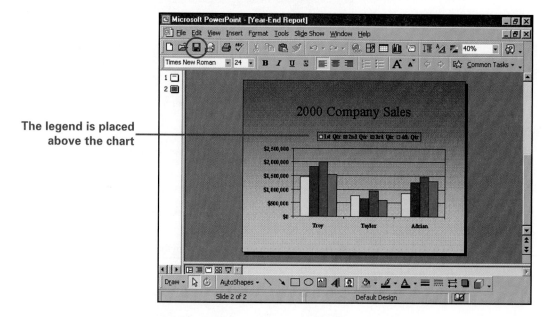

Comprehension Exercises

Comprehension exercises are designed to confirm your knowledge of basic facts that are necessary to advance to higher levels of understanding and performance. The task upon which the question is based is indicated following each question (for example, T4 refers to task 4). If you are unsure of the correct answer to any of these questions, review the task that is indicated.

True-False

Circle either T or F.

T   F   **1.** The New Slide button is one of the tasks listed on the Common Tasks button. **(T1)**

T   F   **2.** You can add or delete both rows and columns in a chart datasheet. **(T2)**

T   F   **3.** If you want to chart a series of numbers in PowerPoint, you would use a subprogram called Microsoft Graph. **(T2)**

T   F   **4.** To delete a row in a datasheet, put the insertion point in any cell of that row, then press ⌦. **(T2)**

T   F   **5.** You know you are in Microsoft Graph when the Data and Chart options are available on the menu. **(T2)**

T   F   **6.** The type of chart you choose should be determined by the type of data you are going to display. **(T3)**

T   F   **7.** You can modify a chart using the tools in the regular PowerPoint program. **(T5)**

T   F   **8.** The type of chart that shows how parts relate to the whole is a line chart. **(T1)**

T   F   **9.** To show a trend in the data over a period of time, a line chart is useful. **(T1)**

T   F   **10.** A shortcut menu is available for many parts of the screen and may be opened by double-clicking on the area of interest. **(T1)**

Identifying Parts of the PowerPoint Screen

Refer to the figure and identify the numbered parts of the screen. Write the letter of the correct label in the space next to the number.

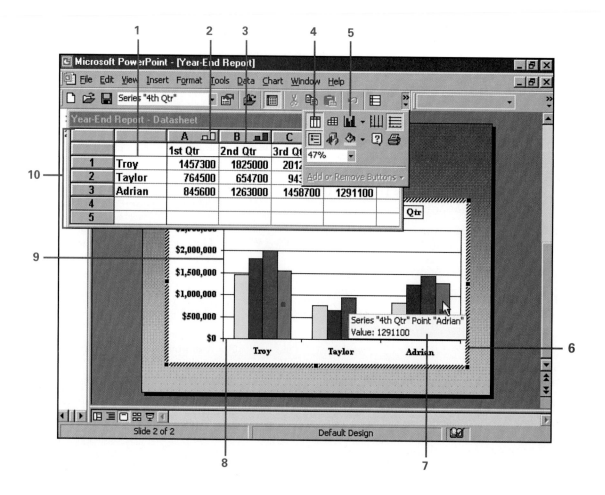

1. _____	A. Category label (T5)
2. _____	B. Chart Type button (T5)
3. _____	C. Category axis (T4)
4. _____	D. Value axis (T5)
5. _____	E. Series label (T4)
6. _____	F. Datasheet (T2)
7. _____	G. Color of series (T5)
8. _____	H. Border with resizing handles (T5)
9. _____	I. ScreenTip (T4)
10. _____	J. By Column button (T4)

Matching

Match the following statements to the word or phrase that is the best match from the list. Write the letter of the matching word or phrase in the space provided next to the number.

1. ___ Used to change from a pie chart to a line chart

2. ___ The area where chart data is stored

3. ___ Used to change the magnification of the view of a chart

4. ___ Button that contains the New Slide option among frequently used options

5. ___ Microsoft subprogram that builds charts from numbers

6. ___ A device that is used to enter numeric data quickly

7. ___ Identifies different parts of a chart

8. ___ These two options are available on the menu bar when the Microsoft Graph program is active

9. ___ Changes the order of the data on the data axis

10. ___ A section of a chart that identifies the colors used to identify a data series

A. Common Tasks button (T1)

B. Office Assistant (T3)

C. Numeric keypad (T2)

D. ScreenTips (T4)

E. Data, Chart (T2)

F. Legend (T5)

G. By Column button (T4)

H. Datasheet (T1)

I. Chart Type button (T3)

J. Zoom button (T1)

K. Microsoft Graph (T1)

Reinforcement Exercises

Reinforcement exercises are designed to reinforce the skills you have learned by applying them to a new situation. Detailed instructions are provided along with a figure, where appropriate, to illustrate the result. The Reinforcement exercises that follow should be completed sequentially. Leave the computer on at the end of each exercise for use in the next exercise until you are specifically directed to close it.

R1—Create a New Chart Slide

1. Launch **PowerPoint**. Open **Less2002** from your CD-ROM disc and rename it on your floppy disk as **Final Year-End Report**.

2. Move to slide **3**.

3. Click **Common Tasks**, **New Slide**.

4. Select the **Chart** slide type and open it.

5. Double-click to open the Microsoft Graph program and enter the text and numbers in the datasheet as shown in the figure.

Final Year-End Report - Datasheet

		A	B	C	D
		1st Qtr	2nd Qtr	3rd Qtr	4th Qtr
1	Pools	3	34	47	5
2	Spas	56	52	44	61
3	Saunas	23	12	8	43
4					

R2—Modify a Chart

1. Change the chart type to **Column Chart**.

2. Change the colors of the bars in the chart to colors of your choice.

3. Right-click on the **Category Axis**, and then select **Format Axis**. Click the **Font** tab and change the font to **Arial**.

4. Select the **Value Axis** and change the font to **Arial**.

5. Click the title on the slide and add the title **Taylor Store - Units Sold**.

6. Print a black and white copy of this column chart slide.

7. Save your work and close the presentation.

Challenge

Challenge exercises are designed to test your ability to apply your skills to new situations with less detailed instruction. These exercises also challenge you to expand your repertoire of skills by using PowerPoint commands that are similar to those you have already learned. The desired outcome is clearly defined, but you have more freedom to choose the steps needed to achieve the required result.

C1—Changing Chart Types Using the Menu Options

In this lesson, you learned how to change chart types by using the Chart Type button. Many more options are available to you when you use the Chart menu option. In this Challenge exercise, you change the chart type by using the Chart menu option and then make other changes to the resulting line chart.

Goal: To change a chart to a line chart by using the Chart menu option, and change other chart features. When you have completed this Challenge exercise you will have created a slide that looks similar to the one in the figure.

1. Locate the file **Less2003** in the **Student\Lesson20** folder on the CD-ROM disc and open it. Save the file on your floppy disk with the name **Line Chart**.

2. Activate the chart and choose **Chart, Chart Type**. Click on the various **Chart type** options to see the choices that are available. On the **Standard Types** tab, select the default line chart (**Line with markers ...**) for this graph.

3. Click the **Press and Hold to View Sample** button. A sample of the chart is displayed. As you can see, you will need to make some changes to have this chart work properly. Click **OK** to select the line chart type.

4. Change the chart to display the data **By Column**.

5. Select **Chart, Chart Options** and add **Age** as the label for the **Category Axis** and **% Attending** as the label for the **Value Axis**.

6. Select the line for the boys and open the **Format Data Series** dialog box. Change the line color for boys to blue and select the largest **Weight** option available for the line. Change the **Foreground** and **Background** for the marked object to blue, and increase the **Size** to 10 point.

7. Select the line for the girls and make the same changes you did for the other line, but use pink as the color choice.

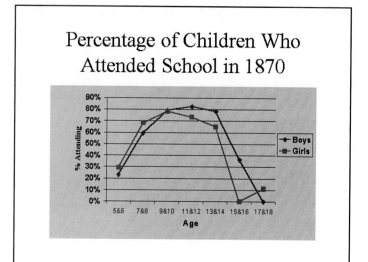

8. Select the **Category Axis** and change the font to **Arial** and the font size to **14** (not bold).

9. Change the font on each of the following to **Arial**:

   Category Axis Title, **Value Axis Title**, **Value Axis**, and **Legend**

10. Right-click in an open area on the chart to open the **Format Chart Area** dialog box. Select the **Patterns** tab and choose a pale, contrasting color for the background of the chart.

11. Save your changes and print the slide.

C2—Creating a Pie Chart and Changing Pie Chart Options

A pie chart is very useful for showing parts of a whole. It gives the viewer a perspective on how much each part is contributing to the whole. In this Challenge exercise, you will create a pie chart that shows the total number of casualties (injuries and deaths) caused by tornadoes in the state of Michigan for the past four decades.

Goal: Create a chart of the tornado casualties in Michigan by decade using a pie chart that displays the colors, legend placement, and data labels as shown in the figure.

1. Open a blank presentation and choose the **Chart** layout option. Add **Michigan Tornado Casualties by Decade** as the title as shown in the figure.

2. Activate the chart and enter the following data:

1950s	1695
1960s	1236
1970s	384
1980s	79

   Delete the columns that will not be used on the datasheet. (Hint: Select the column headings, not just the data in the columns.)

3. Change the chart to display the data **By Column**, then change the **Chart Type** to the 3-D Pie Chart. Close the Datasheet.

4. Right-click on the **Legend** and choose **Format Legend**. Change the **Placement** to the **left** of the chart.

5. Select an individual segment of the pie chart. Right-click on the selected piece and use the options found in the **Format Data Point** dialog box to change the color to match the figure and show the corresponding value. Change the colors of the other segments to match the figure. Use the legend to determine which segment represents each decade. (Hint: You can also click once, then click a second time to select one wedge of the pie.)

6. Select the **Plot Area**. Right-click on the chart and use the options in the **Format Data Series** dialog box to show the value next to each segment.

7. Select one of the values displayed next to a pie segment. Right-click on the value and use the options in the **Format Data Labels** dialog box to change the format of the numbers to **Number** with **0** decimal places and select the **Use 1000 Separator (,)**

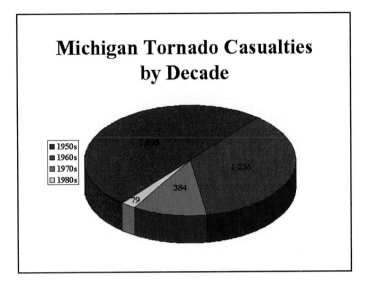

checkbox. Change the position of the values to center them in the segments and change the **Font** to **Arial**.

8. Click once to select the value label for 1980s. Click a second time to select just that label and not the other three. You will see handles around just the value label for 1980. Right-click and open the Format Data Labels dialog box. Change the Label Position on the Alignment tab for this one label to Inside End.

9. Choose **Chart**, **3-D View**. Click the upward pointing arrow until the **Elevation** box shows **30**. Click the left or right rotation arrow until the **Rotation** box shows **220**. Click **Apply** and **Close**.

10. Click outside the pie to select the **Plot Area**. Use the sizing handles in the corner or the placeholder to increase the size of the chart.

11. Right-click in Plot Area and select **Format Plot Area**. Select **None** for the **Border** options.

12. View your slide in the **Slide Show** view, and save it with the name **Tornado**. Print the slide.

C3—Create an Organization Chart Slide

PowerPoint contains a subprogram to generate organization charts. It helps you diagram relationships between people and their responsibilities. Like the Microsoft Graphing program, the organization chart program has its own set of tools and toolbars.

Goal: Create a new slide that diagrams the reporting relationships within the organization and then modify it.

1. Open the **Final Year-End Report** presentation you created in the Reinforcement exercises. If you did not create that file, open **Less2002** from the **Student\Lesson20** folder on your CD-ROM disc and rename it **Final Year-End Report**. Select the last slide.

2. Click **Common Tasks**, **New Slide**.

3. Select the **Organization Chart** slide type.

4. Open the new chart slide. Add the information as shown in the first figure.

5. Use the buttons on the toolbar to add the subordinates and assistant shown in the second figure.

6. Close Microsoft Organization Chart and update the chart as prompted.

7. Resize the organization chart as shown.

8. Add the title **Taylor Staff**.

9. Print the new organization chart slide only.

10. Save your work and close the presentation.

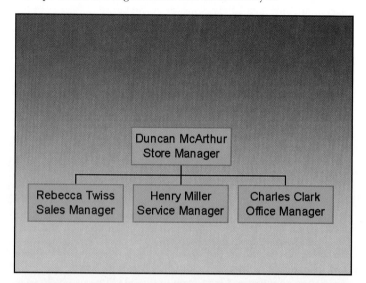

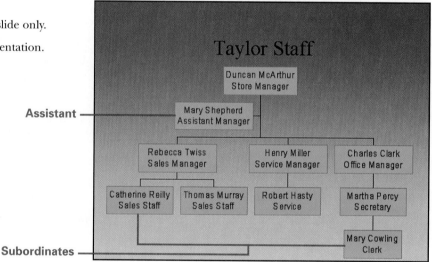

Discovery

Discovery exercises are designed to help you learn how to teach yourself a new skill. In each exercise, you discover something new that is related to the topic taught in this lesson. You may be directed to use built-in wizards or some of the extensive Help features provided in PowerPoint to discover new features and learn new skills with minimum assistance from books or instructors. The required outcome demonstrates your ability to apply the new skill. The learner determines choice of topic, design of presentation, and steps of execution.

D1—Creating a Table

Open a new presentation. Select the **Table** slide as the type of slide you want. Create a table with the appropriate number of rows and columns to accommodate the data shown below. Enter the data and the title shown in the figure. Apply a style of your choice.

Ages	Boys	Girls
5&6	23%	29%
7&8	59%	68%
9&10	79%	78%
11&12	82%	73%
13&14	78%	65%
15&16	36%	0%
17&18	0%	11%

Save the presentation as **Attended School**.

D2—Inserting a Microsoft Excel Chart as an Object

Sometimes it is preferable to insert a chart that has been created previously in another program, such as Microsoft Excel. One advantage of this approach is that the data does not have to be reentered, thereby reducing the risk of error. A second advantage is that the chart can be linked to the original file so that any changes to the data in the source file are also reflected in the inserted chart in the PowerPoint presentation.

Activate **Help** and type **Inserting an Excel chart**. Click on **Insert a Microsoft Excel chart in a presentation** and read the instructions.

Start a new presentation with a title-only slide and follow the instructions given in Help to insert the chart. Use the **Create from file** option on the **Insert Object** dialog box, and use the **Browse** button to locate the **1999 Sales** file in the **Student\Lesson20** folder on the CD-ROM disc that came with your book. Mark the **Link** checkbox on the **Insert Object** dialog box to make sure the chart is linked to the data source file. Reduce the size of the chart slightly so it does not overlap the title area of the slide. Title the slide **Real Estate Brokers**.

Double-click on the pie chart that is inserted. This will launch Excel, which enables you to make changes to the chart or to the data. The same charting tools that are used in PowerPoint are used in Excel. Click on the **1999 Sales** tab at the bottom of the window. (Maximize your window if you do not see the tabs at the bottom.) Double-click in the cell for the **2nd Qtr** for the **South** (cell **C5**), and change the data from **42.1** to **82.1**. Press ⏎Enter and notice the change in the totals. Click on the **Chart1** tab at the bottom of the window to see the changes in the Excel chart. Use the taskbar to go back to PowerPoint and see the change in the chart in PowerPoint. Save the file as **1999 Sales Chart**. If the slide did not update properly, choose **Edit**, **Links**, **Update** now. Save the file as **1999 Sales Chart**. Print the slide.

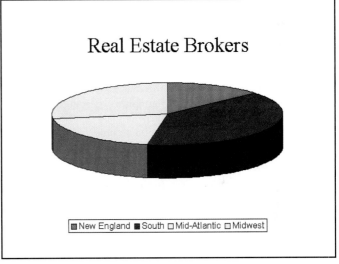

Percentage of Children Who Attended School in 1870

Ages	Boys	Girls
5 & 6	23%	29%
7 & 8	59%	58%
9 & 10	79%	78%
11 & 12	82%	73%
13 & 14	78%	65%
15 & 16	36%	0%
17 & 18	0%	11%

Real Estate Brokers

New England ■ South □ Mid-Atlantic □ Midwest

Lesson: 21

Sorting and Animating the Slides

Task 1   Using Slide Sorter View to Change Sequence

Task 2   Animating the Transition from One Slide to the Next

Task 3   Animating Text

Task 4   Dimming Previously Displayed Text

Introduction

Once you have created a slide show, you should review it to see if you can make it better. You may want to rearrange the slides so they are presented in a different order. When photographers rearrange a set of traditional 35mm slides, they place them side by side on a piece of glass that has a light behind it. This method enables them to see all of the slides at the same time and make judgments about how they look as a group or how the sequence from one slide to another will flow. PowerPoint uses the same type of layout in Slide Sorter view to let you make similar decisions about a set of slides.

In this lesson, you learn to control the transition between slides, the order in which the text and graphics appear on the slide, and the color of current and previously discussed bullet points.

Visual Summary

When you have completed Task 4, you will have animated a bulleted list so that the points appear one at a time, and the previous points are shown in a new color. Your slides will look like this:

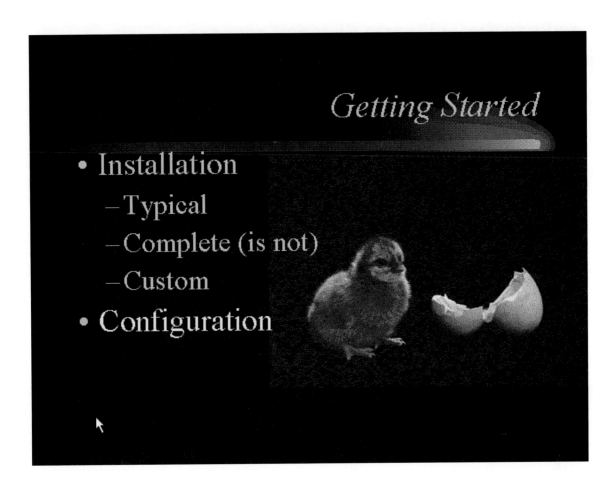

TASK 1

Using Slide Sorter View to Change Sequence

Why would I do this?

Most slide shows benefit from examination and revision. The Slide Sorter view enables you to see several slides at once so you can examine the sequence of the slides and see how they look next to each other. Slide Sorter view is also the best place to rearrange the order of the slides.

In this task, you learn how to use the Slide Sorter view to change the order of the slides in a presentation.

1 Launch **PowerPoint**. Choose **Open an existing presentation**, and click OK. Locate the file **Less2101** in the **Student\Lesson21** folder on the CD-ROM disc. Open it, then save it on your floppy disk as **Install Office**.

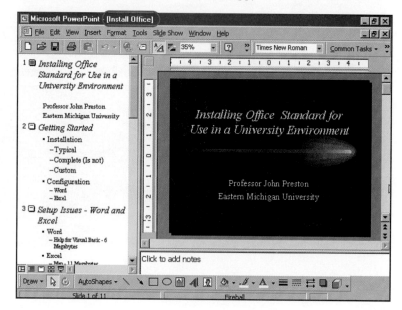

2 Click the **Slide Sorter View** button. The slides are displayed side by side. Use the scrollbar to view slides **7-11**.

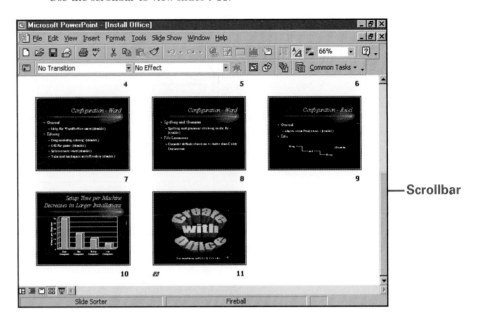

Scrollbar

3 Click the down arrow next to the **Zoom** box and click **33%**. All of the slides in this show are displayed on one screen, but they are difficult to read.

Slide sorter view button

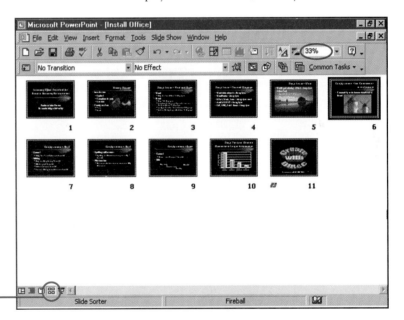

4 Click the **Show Formatting** button to turn off the details of the slides' formatting. Each slide's title will still be displayed, but in a larger font.

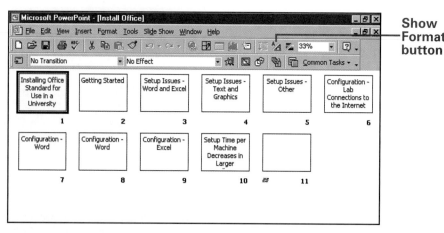

Show Formatting button

5 The sixth slide, which deals with Internet connections, should be moved to the next-to-last position. Click the sixth slide to select it.

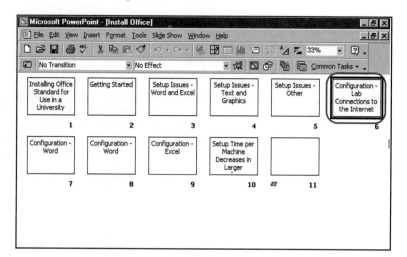

6 Click and drag the pointer to a position between slides **10** and **11**.

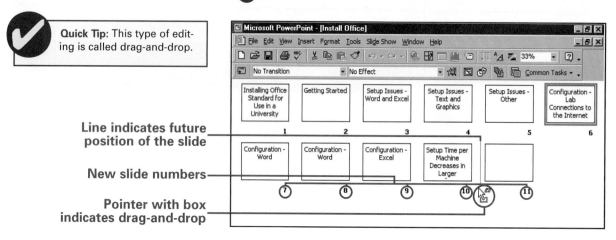

Line indicates future position of the slide

New slide numbers

Pointer with box indicates drag-and-drop

7 Release the mouse button. The Internet slide is now slide **10**, and all of the affected slides are renumbered.

TASK **2**

Animating the Transition from One Slide to the Next

Why would I do this?

When you run the slide show, it will present the slides one after the other when you click the mouse button. The slides will simply appear on the screen in their entirety. You can make the way a slide comes into view, known as the *transition*, more interesting by animating this transition.

In this task, you learn how to control the transitions from one slide to the next.

1 Choose **Edit**, **Select All** from the menu. All of the slides are selected.

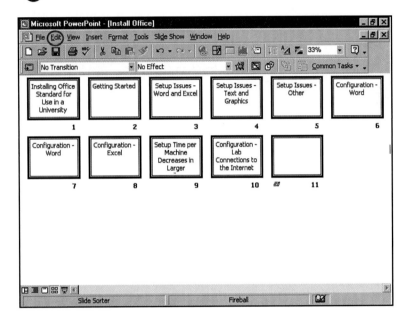

② Click the down arrow next to the **Slide Transition Effects** box to reveal a list of transition options.

Slide Transition Effects box—

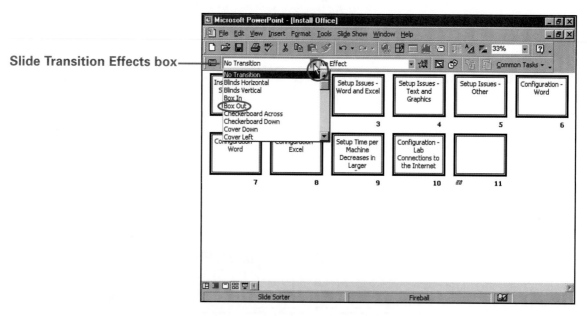

③ Click **Box Out**. A small icon is placed beneath each slide to indicate that a transition has been applied.

Slide Transition icon—

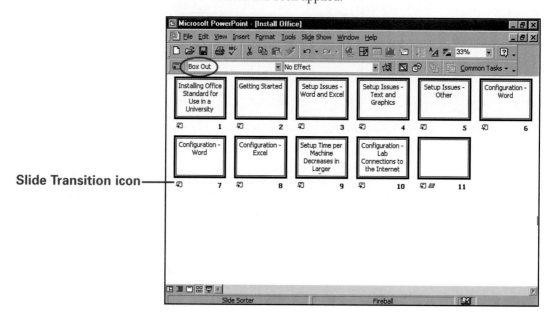

4 Click the **Show Formatting** button. The detail of each slide is shown.

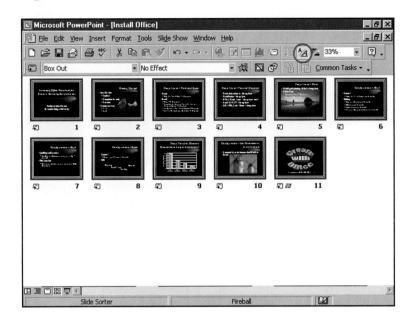

5 Click the down arrow next to the **Zoom** box. Click **66%**. The slides are enlarged.

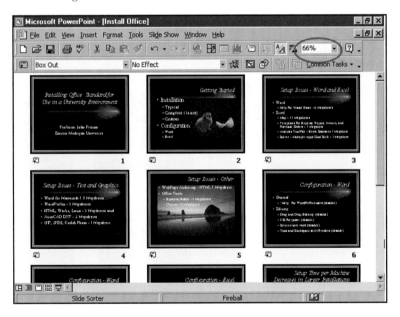

6 If necessary, scroll to display the first slide. Click in a white space between the slides to deselect the slides, then click on the first slide to select it.

Dark border indicates the
slide is selected

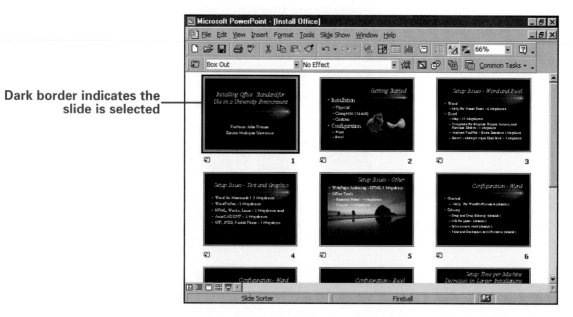

7 Click the **Slide Transition** icon below slide 1. The Box Out transition is demonstrated on slide 1. This gives you the opportunity to review the transition style that has been selected.

In Depth: Slide transitions can be different for each slide. You can select the random option, which will vary the transition randomly, or you can individually select a slide and set the transition.

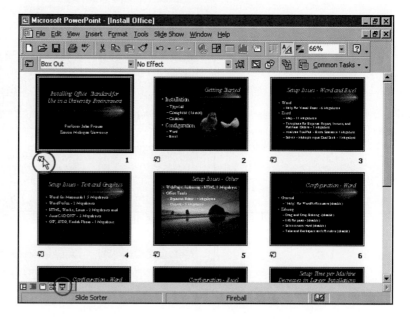

8 Click the **Slide Show** button to start the slide show. Click the mouse button to advance from one slide to the next to observe the Box Out transition. Stop at slide **10**, titled **Configuration – Lab Connections to the Internet**.

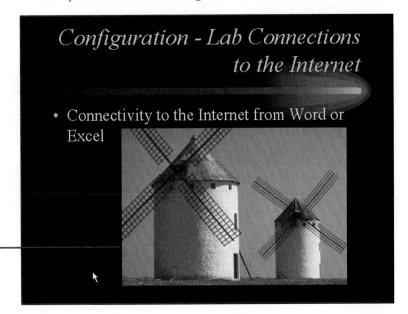

Stop the slide show at slide 10 ——

9 Right-click to reveal the shortcut menu.

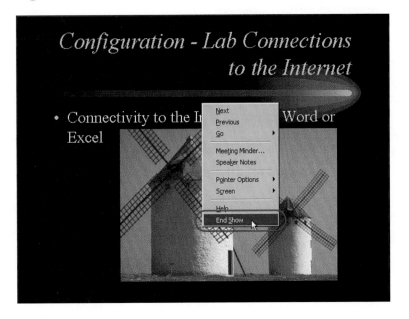

10 Click **End Show** to return to Slide Sorter view.

> **Quick Tip:** You can also exit a slide show at any point by pressing the [Esc] key on your keyboard.

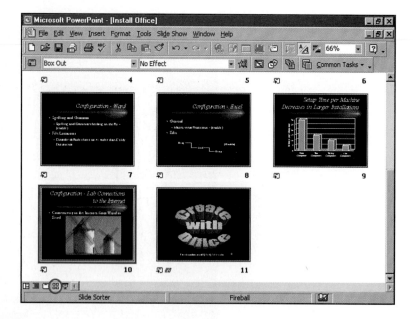

TASK **3**

Animating Text

Why would I do this?

Just as you select an animation style for the transitions between your sides, you can also control the manner in which text is displayed on the slide. For example, people read text from left to right, so you may want to reveal the text from left to right. It is also desirable to display your bulleted points one at a time to prevent your audience from reading ahead.

In this task, you learn how to select all of the slides and animate the appearance of the text. You also learn how to remove the transition effect from individual slides.

1 Select **Edit**, **Select All** from the menu.

Preset Animation box

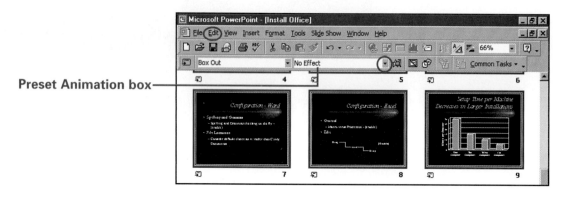

2 Click the down arrow next to the **Preset Animation** box and scroll near the bottom of the list of options.

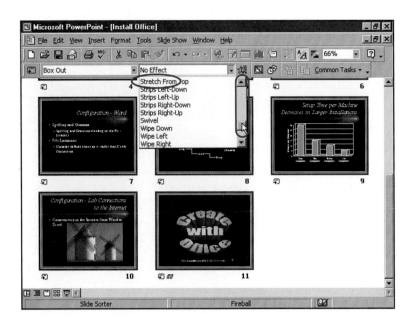

3 Click **Wipe Right**. This effect reveals the text from left to right in Slide Show view. Notice the text animation icon below each slide with the exception of slide 8.

In Depth: Slide 8 does not show the animation icon because the original file contains a custom animation for no animation effects on this slide. The Select All option does not override custom animations.

Preset Animation icon⎯⎯⎯⎯

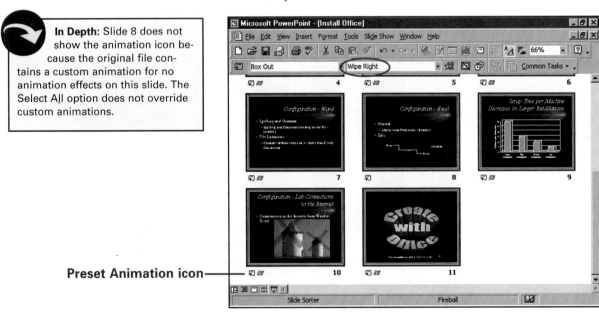

4 Click the **Slide Show** button to start the slide show. Click the mouse repeatedly to observe the text transition. Notice that the text transition is probably not necessary on the title slide.

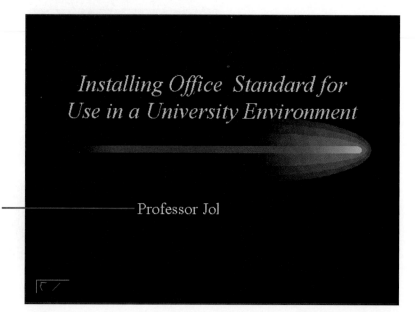

Text partially revealed during
the Wipe Right text animation

5 Click the right mouse button and click **End Show** to return to the Slide Sorter view.

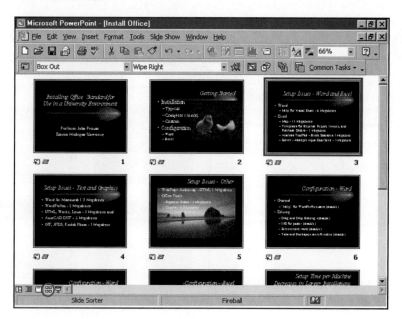

6 Click slide **1** to select it. Click the down arrow next to the **Preset Animation** box and scroll to the top of the list.

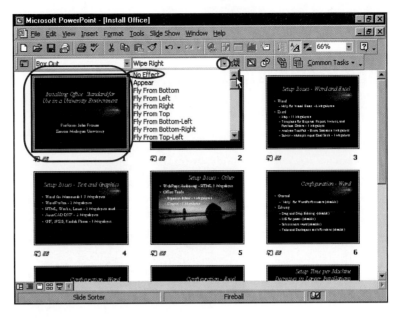

7 Click **No Effect**. The text animation is removed from slide 1.

Text animation removed from slide 1

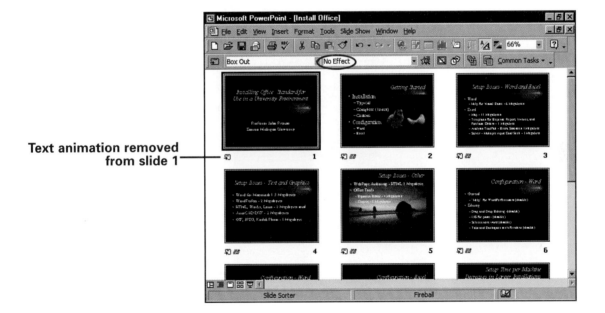

TASK 4

Dimming Previously Displayed Text

Why would I do this?

You can emphasize the text you are currently talking about by dimming those bulleted points that have already been discussed. This helps the audience keep track of where you are in your presentation. You may also want to reveal the subpoints of a section one at a time. You can individually control the timing of items that appear on your slide using the *Custom Animation* feature.

In this task, you learn how to use the Custom Animation feature to *dim* previous points and to reveal subpoints one at a time.

1 Click slide **2** to select it, then click the **Slide View** button.

In Depth: If the ruler shows in the Slide view window, you can turn it off by clicking **View**, **Ruler** from the menu. If there is a check mark showing next to **Ruler**, the ruler is turned on; no check mark means the ruler is turned off.

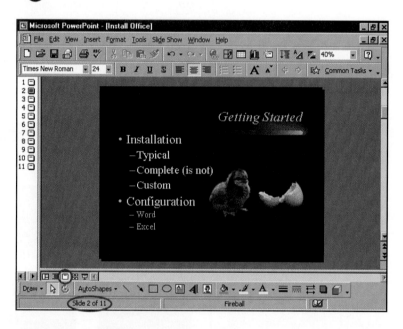

2 Point at the text and click the right mouse button. The text area is selected, and a shortcut menu opens.

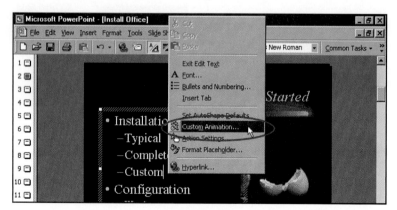

3 Click **Custom Animation**. The Custom Animation dialog box opens. Make sure the **Effects** tab is selected.

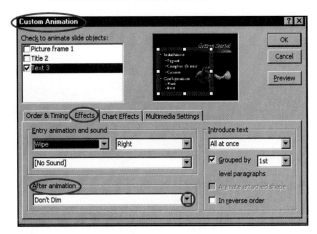

4 Click the list arrow next to the **After Animation** box. Several options are displayed.

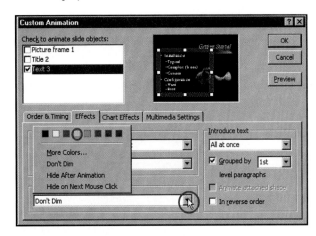

5 Click the fourth color box from the left to select a darker color than the yellow that is used for text.

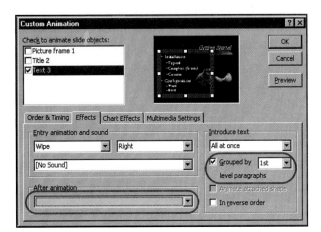

6 Click the list arrow next to the **Grouped by level paragraphs** box and select **2nd** from the list. This type of animation will list the second level subpoints of the bulleted text one at a time.

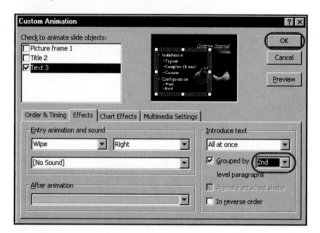

7 Click **OK** to return to Slide view.

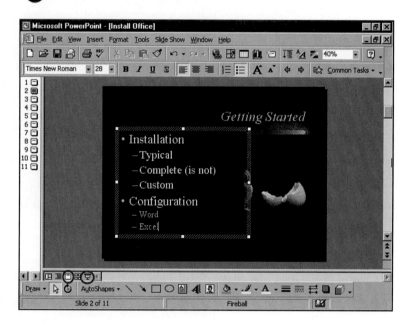

8 Click the **Slide Show** button. Click the left mouse button repeatedly to reveal each bullet point and its subpoint individually. Notice that each point changes color after the next point is presented.

Color changes after the next point is selected

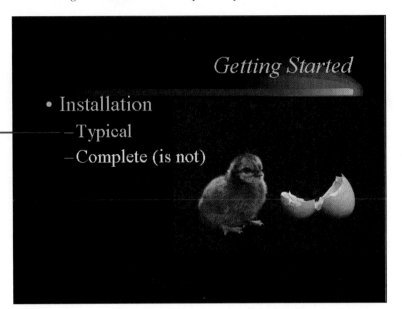

9 Right-click to display the shortcut menu and click **End Show**. The slide is displayed in Slide view. Save your work.

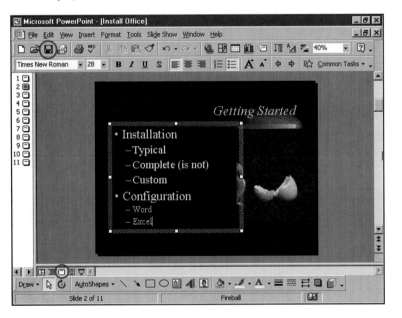

Comprehension Exercises

Comprehension exercises are designed to check your memory and understanding of the basic concepts in this lesson. You distinguish between true and false statements, identify new screen elements, and match terms with related statements. If you are uncertain of the correct answer, refer to the task number following each item (for example, T4 refers to Task 4) and review that task until you are confident that you can provide a correct response.

True-False

Circle either T or F.

T   F   **1.** You can change the sequence of slides by clicking and dragging a slide to a new position in Slide Show view. **(T1)**

T   F   **2.** In Slide Sorter view, you turn off the details of a slide and just show the slide's title by clicking the **Show Formatting** button. **(T1)**

T   F   **3.** The Slide Transition Effects box displays how each line of bulleted text will be revealed. **(T3)**

T   F   **4.** If you are in Slide Sorter view and want to see how a particular slide transition will look, you can click on the small icon below the slide to preview the transition (Show Formatting must be turned on). **(T3)**

T   F   **5.** The **After Animation** option will dim the previous slide during a slide show. **(T4)**

T   F   **6.** If you use a Wipe Right transition to display a new slide, the entire slide will appear to move as an intact image from the left of the screen. **(T2)**

T   F   **7.** Dimming previous points affects the text in the slides that have already been shown, but does not affect any of the text in the current slide. **(T4)**

T   F   **8.** You can use some of the same types of transition on lines of text in a slide as were used to transition from one slide to the next. **(T3)**

T   F   **9.** When you dim a previous point, you choose a color that is still visible against the background, but not as bright as the most recently displayed bullet point. **(T4)**

T   F   **10.** When you drag a slide to its new position in the sequence of slides in the Slide Sorter view, the slides are renumbered automatically. **(T1)**

Identifying Parts of the PowerPoint Screen

Refer to the figure and identify the numbered parts of the screen. Write the letter of the correct label in the space next to the number.

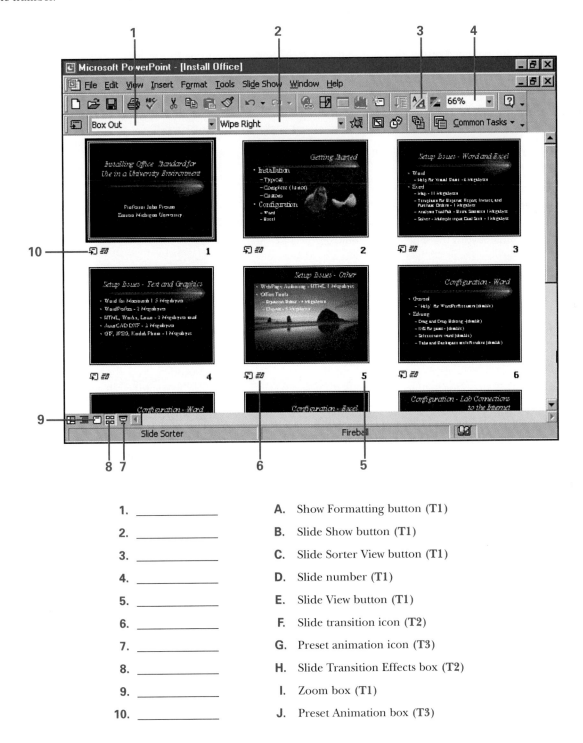

1. _____	**A.** Show Formatting button (**T1**)
2. _____	**B.** Slide Show button (**T1**)
3. _____	**C.** Slide Sorter View button (**T1**)
4. _____	**D.** Slide number (**T1**)
5. _____	**E.** Slide View button (**T1**)
6. _____	**F.** Slide transition icon (**T2**)
7. _____	**G.** Preset animation icon (**T3**)
8. _____	**H.** Slide Transition Effects box (**T2**)
9. _____	**I.** Zoom box (**T1**)
10. _____	**J.** Preset Animation box (**T3**)

Matching

Match the statements below to the word or phrase that is the best match from the list. Write the letter of the matching word or phrase in the space provided next to the number.

1. ___ View that displays the slides in a presentation simultaneously

2. ___ Button that turns on and off the details of the slides when viewed in Slide Sorter view

3. ___ A transition option that will use different transitions each time the slide show runs

4. ___ Pressing this key will end the slide show quickly

5. ___ A type of slide transition that reveals the next slide from the center outward

6. ___ A text animation option that displays the bulleted points that have already been displayed in a different color

7. ___ A transition that reveals the slide or text from left to right

8. ___ Option that is used to remove animation from a selected slide

9. ___ Menu choice used to select all the slides at once in the Slide Sorter view

10. ___ When you select an object and then move it with the mouse

A. Box Out **(T2)**

B. Dim **(T4)**

C. Esc **(T2)**

D. Slide Sorter **(T1)**

E. Wipe Right **(T2)**

F. Show Formatting **(T1)**

G. Drag-and-drop **(T1)**

H. Edit, Select All **(T1)**

I. No Effect **(T3)**

J. Random **(T2)**

Reinforcement Exercises

Reinforcement exercises are designed to reinforce the skills you have learned by applying them to a new situation. Detailed instructions are provided along with a figure, where appropriate, to illustrate the final result. The Reinforcement exercises that follow should be completed sequentially. Leave the presentation open at the end of each exercise for use in the next exercise until you are specifically directed to close it.

These exercises all use the same presentation. Leave the presentation open at the end of each exercise for use in the next. Launch **PowerPoint**. Open the file **Less2102** from the **Student\Lesson21** folder on the CD-ROM disc and save it on your floppy disk as **Nucleus in the News**. (This is a presentation created by the author to help people understand current events that are related to nuclear physics.)

R1—Rearrange a Slide Show Using the Slide Sorter

1. Click the **Slide Sorter** button.

2. Change the **Zoom** to **33%**.

3. Click the **Show Formatting** button to turn it off and display the slide titles.

4. Slides **21**, **22**, and **23** deal with the radon issue. Move these three slides to the end of the presentation. The last three titles should be: **Radioactive Isotopes Turn into Stable Isotopes**, **Radon**, and **Radon**.

5. Choose **File**, **Print** from the menu.

6. Choose **Slides**, and type **22-27**.

7. Select **Handouts** in the **Print what** box, then select **6** in the **Slides per page** box.

8. Select **Pure black & white**, and **Frame Slides**, then click **OK** to print.

R2—Apply a Slide Transition to All of the Slides

1. Click the **Show Formatting** button to display the details of the slides.

2. Choose **Edit, Select All** from the menu.

3. Click the list arrow next to the **Slide Transition Effects** box and pick **Cover Right**.

4. Click the small transition icon below one of the slides to preview the transition.

5. Choose **File, Print** from the menu.

6. Choose **Current slide** (it doesn't matter which slide is printed). Select **Slides** in the **Print what** box. Select **Pure black & white** and **Frame slides**. Click **OK** to print the slide.

7. Below the printed slide, write a description of what the Cover Right transition looks like. Draw an arrow to indicate the direction of motion. Write your name on the slide.

R3—Animate Text Transitions

1. If necessary, click the **Slide Sorter View** button to show the slides.

2. Choose **Edit, Select All** from the menu.

3. Click the list arrow next to the **Preset Animation** box.

4. Select **Dissolve** from the list.

5. Click between the slides to deselect them.

6. Click slide **4** to select it.

7. Click the **Slide Show** button to start the slide show.

8. Click the mouse button repeatedly to display each line of text using the Dissolve transition.

9. Press Esc to end the slide show. Click slide **4** to select it again.

10. Choose **File, Print** from the menu.

11. Choose **Current slide**. Select **Slides** in the **Print what** box. Select **Pure black & white** and **Frame slides**. Click **OK** to print.

12. Below the printed slide, write a description of what the Dissolve transition looks like. Write your name on the printout.

R4—Dimming Previous Points

1. Click the **Slide View** button to display slide **4** in Slide view.

2. Right-click on the text portion of the slide and choose **Custom Animation** from the shortcut menu. Click the **Effects** tab if necessary.

3. Click the list arrow next to the **After Animation** box.

4. Select the gray color at the right end of the line of colors.

5. Click **OK**.

6. Click the **Slide Show** button to display this slide. Click the mouse button repeatedly to see how the previous points are dimmed. Press Esc to return to Slide view.

7. Save your presentation and close it.

Challenge

Challenge exercises are designed to test your ability to apply your skills to new situations with less detailed instruction. These exercises also challenge you to expand your repertoire of skills by using PowerPoint commands that are similar to those you have already learned. The desired outcome is clearly defined, but you have more freedom to choose the steps needed to achieve the required result.

C1—Animating Drawing Objects

The transitions that you learned to use on slides can also be applied to lines of text within the slide.

Goal: Apply animation to the text as each line of a bulleted slide is revealed.

1. Open the **Install Office** file that you created in this lesson. Select the **Slide Sorter** view. Click the slide **8** icon and select the text portion of the slide.

2. Right-click on the text and choose **Custom Animation** from the shortcut menu. Click the **Order & Timing** tab.

3. Click the check box next to **Text 3** to add it to the **Animation order** box. Select the other objects in the following order:

   Elbow connector 6
   Text 4
   Elbow connector 7

   Text 5
   Text 8

4. Click the **Effects** tab. Click **Text 3**, then hold ⬆Shift and click **Elbow connector 7** to select the first five objects.

5. In the **Entry animation and sound** area, click the down arrow and select **Wipe**. In the same area, click the down arrow next to the box on the right and select **Right**.

6. Click **OK**, then use the slide show to view this slide and its animations. Save the changes you have made and close the presentation.

C2—Animate Drawing Objects

Objects such as arrows may be animated to illustrate a point. This exercise uses the **Nucleus in the News** file that was created in the Reinforcement exercises. If you have not done those exercises, locate **Less2102** in the **Student\Lesson21** folder on your CD-ROM disc and save it as **Nucleus in the News** on your floppy disk.

Slide 13 is used to describe how moderators are used to slow down neutrons so they can cause additional fission to occur. The animations are chosen to indicate sequence and relative speeds of the neutrons.

Goal: Animate the drawing objects to demonstrate a process.

1. Select and display slide **13** in Slide view.

2. Right-click one of the drawing objects and select **Custom Animation** from the shortcut menu.

3. Move between the **Order & Timing** tab and the **Effects** tab to animate each of the objects in the order and with the effect shown in the list below:

Object	Effect
Group9	Crawl from Left
Line4	Stretch Across
Group3	Wipe Right
Group8	Appear
Group6	Wipe Right
Line7	Wipe Right
Group2	Appear

4. Click **OK** when finished.

5. Click the **Slide Show** button. Click the mouse button repeatedly to observe how the animations show the process. Press Esc to return to Slide view.

6. Make sure that slide **13** is selected, and then choose **File**, **Print** from the menu.

7. Choose **Current slide**. Select **Slides** in the **Print what** box. Select **Pure black & white** and **Frame slides**. Click **OK** to print the slide.

8. Below the printed slide, write a description of how the Crawl from Left, Stretch Access, and Wipe Right transitions were used to simulate the process. Draw a line from each of your descriptions to an object in the slide that was animated with that transition. Write your name on the printout.

9. Save your changes and close the presentation. Exit PowerPoint.

 In Depth: There are several other animated drawings in this presentation. If you are interested, you can look at them to see how they were designed.

C3—Animating Charts

Charts can be made more effective with the use of animation. Charts that indicate a trend in time such as a line or column chart are particularly effective if the chart elements are revealed sequentially.

Goal: Animate the columns in a chart so that they appear one group at a time.

1. Open the **Install Office** file that you worked with in this lesson. In Slide view, select slide **9** and right-click on the chart.

2. Select **Custom Animation** from the shortcut menu and click the **Chart Effects** tab in the dialog box.

3. Click the down arrow next to the **Introduce chart elements** box and select **by Element in Series**.

4. Click the **Animate grid and legend box** to animate them as well. Click **OK**. Use the slide show to view the results.

5. Save your changes. Close the presentation.

Discovery

Discovery exercises are designed to help you learn how to teach yourself a new skill. In each exercise, you discover something new that is related to the topic taught in this lesson. You may be directed to use built-in wizards or some of the extensive Help features provided in PowerPoint to discover new features and learn new skills with minimum assistance from books or instructors. The required outcome demonstrates your ability to apply the new skill. The learner determines choice of topic, design of presentation, and steps of execution.

D1—Changing the Order of Topics in an Outline

In this lesson, you learned how to change the order of slides using the drag-and-drop method in the Slider Sorter view. Sometimes you need to change the order of topics within a slide. The drag-and-drop technique can be used to move topics within a slide, but it requires a little more finesse. Generally, it is easier to use the Outlining toolbar to move topics.

Locate **Less2103** in the **Student\Lesson21** folder located on the CD-ROM disc that came with your book. Save the file on your floppy disk with the name **Ex2101**. Add your name to the first slide after the words **Presented by**. Open **Help** and type **Rearrange topics**. Select **Change the order of paragraphs in an outline** and read the resulting Help screen. Change to the Outline view and open the Outline toolbar. On slide **3**, select the second topic and make it the first topic. You can drag the selected text to the new location or use the up arrow on the Outline toolbar. On slide **4**, select the first topic and use the down arrow to move it down to the second topic. Make sure the entire topic moves. On slide **5**, move the first topic to the third position. Save your changes and print slides 3 through 5.

D2—Setting a Presentation to Run Continuously

One of the features of PowerPoint is the ability to have a slide show run continuously. This technique can be used to create a slide show to highlight the features and benefits of your product and have it play continuously at a trade show or convention booth. This gives potential customers something to look at when they stop by your booth. It can be created to run with or without assistance.

To learn more about a self-running presentation, open **Help** and type **Self-running presentations**. Select the appropriate topic to read, then print it. Locate **Less2104** in the **Student\Lesson21** folder located on the CD-ROM disc that came with your book and open it. Save the file on your floppy disk with the name **Ex2102**. Add your name to the first slide after the words **Presented by**. Follow the procedure described in Help to set this presentation to run automatically. Choose either the manual or rehearsal option to set the timing for each slide. Be sure to set the timing in seconds, not minutes. The timing will apply to each item on the slide. View the slide show to see how the automatic timing works. Make any adjustments necessary. Save your changes and close the presentation.

D3—Adding Animation Sounds

PowerPoint has several animation sounds that can be added to a presentation for special effects. It is advisable to limit the use of these animation sounds so they do not detract from the message. An animated sound in the beginning or end of a presentation can add some humor and grab the audience's attention.

Locate and open the **Less2105** file located in the **Student\Lesson21** folder on the CD-ROM disc that came with your book. Save the file on your floppy disk with the name **Ex2103**. Using the **Animation Effects** button on the toolbar, or the **Slide Show**, **Preset Animation** menu, add sound animation to at least two text boxes and three lines. Preview the changes using Slide Show view and make any adjustments that are necessary. Save your changes.

Glossary

Absolute reference   A cell reference that will not change when copied or filled into other cells.

Animate   To control the pace or timing of items on a slide.

Animation features   Controls that can be used to make items on a slide appear one at a time or in groups, and at a variety of speeds and directions.

Application   One of the components of the Microsoft Office 2000 suite, such as Word, Excel, or PhotoDraw. An application is also referred to as a program in this book.

APR   Annualized Percentage Rate.

Arguments   Numbers or words used by a function to perform its operation.

Arial   A Microsoft True Type font that does not have horizontal lines at the end of each vertical letter stroke. This is known as a sans serif font, often used for labels and titles.

AutoContent Wizard   A PowerPoint wizard that provides a general outline and content suggestions for various types of presentations.

AutoFit   A wizard that automatically adjusts the widths and heights of columns and rows in a table to fit the contents of the table.

Autoform   A form that will list all of the fields in a table.

AutoFormat   A tool in the **Table** menu that enables you to choose from many different table styles.

AutoNumber   A data type used for unique sequential numbers incremented by 1.

Bar chart   A chart that compares values across categories. The data bars are horizontal.

Boldface   A darker version of characters, used to add emphasis.

Borders   The sides of the cells in a table.

Browser   A program such as Netscape or Internet Explorer that helps you connect to the Internet and view Web pages.

Calculations   Mathematical operations involving data in the worksheet cells.

Category axis   The vertical axis on a chart in PowerPoint. Also known as the X-axis in Excel.

CD-ROM   Compact Disc-Read Only Memory. An optical storage device from which you can read and open files, used to store data permanently. You cannot save files to these discs.

Cell   The intersection of an individual row and column in a table.

Cell address   The column letter and row number that designates the location of a cell.

Center   Each line of text is placed in the middle between the margins.

Chart   A graphic representation of a series of numbers; sometimes referred to as a graph.

Chart subtype   A variation on a basic chart type that allows for different emphasis and views of a chart.

Chart Wizard   A mini-program that walks you through the steps involved in creating a chart.

Click-and-drag   A method of selecting with the mouse. To select a group of cells in Excel, click the left mouse button and hold it down. While holding the button down, move the mouse to cover the area that you want to select, and then release the mouse button.

Click-and-type   A feature that enables you to double-click to place the insertion point outside the current text area. It does not work in Normal view.

Clip art   A graphic image that you can place in a document to convey an idea.

Clipboard   See *Office Clipboard*.

Column chart A chart that compares values across categories. The data columns are vertical.

Column heading The letter at the top of each column of an Excel worksheet that identifies the column.

Column Selector In Access, the thin gray line above the field name in the table Datasheet view, or on the query grid. When you click the column selector, the whole column is selected.

Combo box On a form, a text box that presents a drop-down list of options for data that can be selected for a field. With a combo box, you also have the option to enter data manually if the options presented do not contain the correct information.

Connector handles Small blue boxes that are used to connect one drawing object to another.

Connectors Lines that link shape and design options together. The ends automatically go from a handle on one object to a handle on another.

Control Any graphic object on a form or a report that is used to display data, perform an action, or make a form or report easier to read.

Copy [in Excel] A command used with the Paste command to duplicate values or formulas to other cells.

Copy [in Word] A command used with the Paste command to duplicate text from one part of a document and place it in a second location.

COUNTIF function A function that will survey a specified range of cells and count the number of occurrences of a specified word or number.

Criteria Used in a query to restrict data to those records that meet certain conditions.

Custom Animation Used to selectively control the appearance of items on a slide.

Cut-and-paste A method used to move text from one location to another using the **Cut** and **Paste** commands.

Data type Used in a table to specify the kind of information that will be entered in a field. The most common data type is text.

Database A group of related records.

Database window A window that displays a list of the table, query, form, report, macro, and module objects that comprise a database.

Database Wizard A program that creates a database by guiding you through a series of options.

Datasheet The spreadsheet-like matrix that contains the data for a PowerPoint chart.

Datasheet view Displays the data in rows and columns.

Date/Time A data type used to store and display dates and times.

Default A setting in the program that will be used unless it is changed by a specific action. Depending on the type of default, you can change it by going to the appropriate dialog box, selecting a new setting, and then specifying it as the default.

Default values Values that are preset. Default values will automatically be filled in when a new record in Access is added unless overwritten.

Demote To decrease the level of importance of a bulleted point in a slide.

Design template A background design with preset graphics, fonts, alignments, bullet symbols, and other elements. Using a design template adds a professional appearance to a PowerPoint presentation.

Design view A view of a database object that is used to examine or modify the object.

Desktop The basic screen from which Windows and programs are run. The desktop consists of program icons, a taskbar, a Start button, and a mouse pointer.

Desktop publisher   A program that enables you to create sophisticated page layouts for such things as newsletters, cards, posters, and even Web pages. Microsoft Publisher is the Office 2000 desktop publisher.

Destination disk   The disk to which you want to copy the original (source) disk in the Copy Disk procedure. All other information on the destination disk is deleted in this procedure.

Detail section   The area of a form or report where records from the form or report source are displayed.

Dialog box   A box that asks you to make a decision about an individual object or topic. Dialog boxes do not have Minimize buttons.

Dim   When lines of text on a slide change to a lighter color for less emphasis as new lines of text come into view.

Display settings   The default choices that affect such things as how many rows and columns will be shown on the screen. They can be found by clicking on the **Start** button and choosing **Settings, Control Panel, Display**. It is not proper etiquette to change them if you do not have permission from the computer's owner.

Double density   An older disk formatting method that only stores 720 kilobytes of data per floppy disk.

Drag-and-drop   The method used to move text from one location to another by first selecting the text, and then dragging it with the mouse to a new location and releasing the mouse button to drop the text in the new location.

Dynaset   The results of running a query.

Elbow connector   One of the AutoShape connector types.

Field   A single category of data or information that makes up a record.

Field selector   The column label at the top of each column in the Table view.

File   Work that you save and store on a disk drive.

File extension   The three characters to the right of the period in a filename. Extensions tell the computer what program to open the file in. Extensions can be displayed or hidden. Use when opening the file.

Fill   The method used to complete a group of adjacent cells with values, formulas, or a series such as dates, numbers, days of the week, or months of the year.

Fill handle   A small black square in the lower-right corner of selected cells. When you point to this area, the square turns into a cross. You can click on the cross to drag the contents of one cell to other adjacent cells or to create a series, such as a series of dates.

Filter   A method used on a form to limit the data to records that meet certain conditions.

Floating menu   A menu that is not attached to the edge of the window.

Floppy disk   A small, round, magnetic storage device encased in hard plastic and used to store data that can be written to and read. Floppy disks enable you to carry your computer files with you.

Floppy-disk drive   Provides storage on a floppy disk.

Folder   A directory used to organize files and programs on a computer, represented by icons that look like file folders. Folders are created and named by the user.

Font   A typeface style that determines the appearance of text.

Font size   The height and width of letters, numbers, and characters, measured in points. Seventy-two points equals one inch.

Footer   A specific space between the margin and the bottom of the page that is reserved for text, dates, or page numbers that will appear on every page.

Footer   [in PowerPoint] One of the placeholders at the bottom of a master page.

Form   A database object used to display and edit records.

Format a disk   To set up a floppy disk to receive data. Formatting a disk sets up a special location for a disk directory and marks the disk magnetically so information can be written and found.

Formatted   Data storage areas are already marked electronically on the disk. The disk is ready to receive data.

Format Painter   A tool that enables you to copy the formatting of one paragraph and paint it onto another paragraph. This tool can help you apply formatting characteristics quickly and easily.

Formula bar   A bar below the Formatting toolbar that displays the address of the currently selected cell and any data in the cell.

Frame   The container for an object on a Publisher page. All objects, including pictures, clip art, and text, are contained in a frame.

Graphical User Interface (GUI)   A computer operating system that shows documents as they will look in their final form, and uses icons to represent programs and commands.

Graphics software   A program that enables you to create drawings, modify clipart images, and work with photographs. Microsoft PhotoDraw is the Office 2000 graphics software.

Gridlines   Lines that show on a worksheet that separate one cell from another. Gridlines can be turned off both on the worksheet itself and on the printout.

Handout Master   A slide that controls the information placed in the header and footer areas of printed handouts.

Hanging indent   The first line of text in the paragraph is not indented, but the rest of the lines of text are indented.

Hard disk drive   Generally referred to as the hard drive, the main storage device on your computer. It stores the programs that run on your computer, as well as the files you save.

Header   A specific space between the top of the page and the margin that is reserved for text, dates, or page numbers that will appear on every page.

Header   [in PowerPoint] One of the placeholders at the top of a master page.

Headings   Letters or numbers used to identify a row or column.

High density   A common formatting method that stores 1.44 million bytes (megabytes) of data per floppy disk.

Horizontal scrollbar   The bar at the bottom of a window that enables you to move left and right to view information too wide for the screen.

HTML   A computer language used for documents that are put on the Web. You can save Office applications as HTML documents for easy translation to a Web site. HTML stands for Hypertext Markup Language.

Hyperlink   A connection between the different elements of Web pages or other files that use colored or underlined text or a small picture, called an icon, on which the user places the pointer and clicks on a mouse.

Icon   A graphic representation; often a small image on a button that enables you to run a program or program function.

Information Manager   A program that enables you to keep track of contacts, oversee email, and maintain a calendar and task list. Microsoft Outlook is the Office 2000 information manager.

Input mask   A field property applied in a table that creates a format so data containing dashes or parentheses is entered in a consistent way. Common examples include Social Security numbers, zip codes, and phone numbers.

Insertion point   A flashing vertical line that indicates where text will be entered.

Internet   A worldwide communications network of computer connections that allows people to have access to thousands of online resources.

Intranet   A closed network that uses the same technology as the Internet, but restricts access to authorized users.

Justified   The lines of text in a paragraph begin at the same distance from the left side of the page and end at the same distance from the right side of the page. To accomplish this alignment, additional space is added between words in the line.

Kilobyte   One thousand bytes. It usually takes one byte of memory to store a single character.

Label   Text in a form or report that is not data, usually the field name.

Label box   A control on a form or report that contains descriptive text such as a title or caption.

Landscape orientation   The horizontal orientation of a printed page.

Launch   A synonym for start, begin, or open. Windows 95 has a special button named the Start button, so we say that we "launch" a program to avoid using the same word.

Leaders   A series of characters such as dashes or periods that provide a visual connection between widely separated text on the same line. They are commonly used in tables of contents where the page number is at the far right of the page.

Left-aligned   The lines of text in a paragraph begin at the same distance from the left side of the page.

Legend   A list that identifies a pattern or color used in an Excel worksheet chart.

Line chart   A chart that includes a line running through each data point. It is usually used to show trends.

List box   On a form, a text box that presents a list of options from which to choose data. With a list box, the list always shows on the screen and you can only select from the options that are presented.

Local area network (LAN)   A system that uses telephone lines or cables to join two or more personal computers, enabling them to communicate with each other.

Macros   One of the seven objects in a database. Macros are used to automate existing Access commands. Sometimes macros consist of a series of commands that may be attached to buttons on forms, tables, or queries.

Margins   The empty spaces between the left, right, top, and bottom edges of the paper and text in your document.

Marquee   A box of moving, blinking lines that resembles the flashing lights around the marquee of a theater.

Maximize   To increase the size of a window to fill the screen, using the Maximize button.

Memo   A data type used for lengthy text and numbers such as comments or descriptions

Menu bar   The bar, just under the title bar, that contains command options. These commands are words, not icons.

Microsoft Graph   A Microsoft subprogram that is activated when you create or edit a PowerPoint chart.

Microsoft Organization Chart   A Microsoft subprogram that is activated when you create or edit a PowerPoint organization chart.

Minimize   To remove the window from the screen without closing it, using the Minimize button. Minimized windows can be reopened by clicking the appropriate button on the taskbar.

Modules   One of the seven objects in a database. Modules are programs in the Visual Basic programming language used to customize the database for special needs.

Mouse pointer   The moving arrow (or other object) on the screen that is controlled by moving the mouse. It is used to select or activate objects and programs.

Move handle   A bar at the top of a submenu that may be used to drag the submenu away from the rest of the menu and turn it into a floating menu.

My Computer   A program used to manage files.

Navigation bar   A frame containing the navigation buttons.

Navigation buttons   Labeled buttons that enable the user to move easily from page to page in a Web site.

Navigation buttons   [in Access] Enable you to move through the records by moving to the next record, previous record, to the end, or to the beginning of the records.

Network file server   A computer that connects many computers. It usually has a large hard drive and may be used to store files used by computers on the network.

Normal   A view that enables you to write your presentation in an outline format or directly on slides, and also has a space to add notes for the speaker.

Notes Page view   A view that allows you to create a separate page of speaker notes for each slide that includes the slide plus the comments you want to make.

Notes pane   An area in the PowerPoint window that displays any notes that have been added which would be printed in a format known as speaker notes.

Objects   A general term for the seven parts of an Access database: tables, queries, forms, reports, pages, macros, and modules.

Office Assistant   A Microsoft Office Help program that enables you to ask questions by typing in sentences or phrases. When you ask a question of the Office Assistant, a series of possible related topics are displayed, from which you can pick one of the topics to expand on it.

Office Clipboard   A temporary storage area for text or objects that have been copied or cut. Commonly referred to as just the clipboard, the Office Clipboard differs from the Windows Clipboard in that it can be used to temporarily store multiple items instead of a single item.

OLE Object   A data type that uses object linking and embedding protocol to display objects such as spreadsheets, pictures, or sounds.

One-to-many relationship   A relationship where data in a field occurs one time on the first table and many times in the related table.

Outline pane   The area that displays the outline for your PowerPoint presentation.

Outline view   A view that displays the text of the presentation in outline form.

Page break   An artificial break that is placed in a document to move the text following the break to a new page.

Parameter queries   Queries that use values to define output as part of the query structure.

Parameters   Values that define output.

Paste   A command used to insert a value or formula from another cell or range of cells.

Paste Function   A button on the toolbar that allows the user to select from a library of preprogrammed calculations.

Payment function   A formula used to calculate the periodic payment amount for money that is borrowed based on the length of time money is borrowed and a specified interest rate.

Pie chart   Displays the contribution of each value to the total.

Pixel   A unit of screen display.

Placeholder   An area on the screen reserved for an object, or a rectangle that shows the position of an object that is being moved.

Point size   The height of a character. One inch is 72 points.

Pointer   See *Mouse Pointer.*

Presentation manager   A program that enables you to create computer slide presentations, overhead transparencies, and Web slide shows. Microsoft PowerPoint is the Office 2000 presentation manager.

Primary key   A field in Access that has unique values for each record, and that are used to speed up sorting and finding data in a large table and to link tables together.

Print Preview   Displays the layout of the document as it will appear when it is printed.

Program   One of the components of the Microsoft Office 2000 suite, such as Word, Excel, or PhotoDraw. A program is also referred to as an application in this book.

Promote   To increase the level of importance of a bulleted point in a slide.

Queries   One of the seven objects in a database. Queries are used to sort, search, and limit the data to just those records that you need to see.

Read-only   A file property that indicates that the file has been opened but cannot be changed. This occurs when you open a database file on a CD-ROM.

Record   A group of data pertaining to one event, transaction, or person. The categories of information in a record are called *fields.*

Record Selector   The small box to the left of each record on the table's Datasheet view that enables you to select all of the fields in a record.

Registered programs   When you install a program, Windows records this fact. Most Windows programs use unique extensions to identify the files they create.

Relational databases   Databases that use related tables.

Relationship   Connection between a field in one table to a field in a second table, allowing you to draw information from more than one table at a time for forms or reports.

Relative reference   A cell reference that will change when the formula is copied, moved, or filled into other cells.

Reports   One of the seven objects in a database. Reports are used to summarize information for printing and presentation of the data.

Restore   Returns a window to the size it was before it was maximized.

Screen resolution   The number of picture elements displayed across and down the screen. The examples in this book represent a resolution of 640×480. If your screen is set to a higher resolution such as 800×600, you will see more columns and rows on your screen.

ScreenTip   A short, descriptive message that pops up when the pointer is placed and held on an object such as a button, icon, hyperlink, or some other part of the window.

Scroll box   A small box in a horizontal or vertical scrollbar that indicates the relative location in a window. It can also be dragged to view information off the screen.

Scrollbar   The bars located on the right side and bottom of the screen that allow you to move a document up and down or side to side on the screen.

Select a cell   When you click on a cell, it is outlined with a dark border, indicating it is ready to be edited by entering or changing the data in the cell.

Select query   A query that can be used to filter records, sort, and limit the fields included.

Sheet A synonym for worksheet, identified by tabs at the bottom of the window.

Sheet tab A tab near the bottom of the workbook window that displays the name of the worksheet.

Shortcut menu A menu activated by placing the pointer over an object and clicking the right mouse button.

Sizing handles Small square boxes that are displayed at the corners and along the sides of an object when you click on it. When an object is selected, it can be resized, moved, or edited.

Slide pane The area that displays the layout of a PowerPoint slide.

Slide show Shows the slides one at a time on the full screen, used for previewing or final presentation.

Slide Sorter view A view used to see many slides at once and rearrange their order.

Slide view Shows the slides one at a time; may be used for editing.

Source disk The original disk that you want to copy in the Copy Disk procedure.

Spreadsheet A program that enables you to compute, analyze, and chart numerical data. Spreadsheets can also perform some database functions. Microsoft Excel is the Office 2000 spreadsheet.

Standard toolbar The toolbar at the top of the screen that has the Save and Print buttons on it.

Start button The button on the left side of the taskbar that is used to launch programs, change system settings, or shut down the computer.

Status bar The bar at the bottom of a window that gives additional information about the window.

Subfolder A folder that is stored inside another folder; a subdirectory.

Submenu A second menu, activated by selecting a menu option.

Tab order The order the cursor follows in moving from field to field in a form.

Tables One of the objects in an Access database. Tables store data in row-and-column format, and are the foundation of the database. A table in Word or Excel also features lists of information set up in a row-and-column format, somewhat like the layout of a spreadsheet.

Taskbar A bar, usually at the bottom of the screen, that contains the Start button, buttons representing open programs, and other buttons that will activate programs.

Text A data type in a table that is readable content. May be used to store short phrases or words, or numbers that will not be used in calculations, such as phone numbers or Social Security numbers.

Text box [in PowerPoint] A rectangular area used for displaying text on a slide.

Text boxes [in Access] Controls on a form or report that contain data.

Times New Roman Microsoft True Type font similar to Times Roman. This is known as a serif font because it has horizontal lines at the end of each letter, which helps the reader track words across a page.

Tip Bulb An icon indicating that the Office Assistant has a suggestion for this item.

Title bar The line at the top of a window that contains the name of the application and document, along with the Minimize, Maximize/Restore, and Close buttons.

Toolbar The bar, usually just under the menu bar, that contains command options. These commands are buttons with icons, not words.

Toolbox Used in Access to add controls to forms and reports.

Transition The way a slide comes into view in a slide show.

Value axis The vertical line on the left side of a chart where values for the chart are displayed. In Excel, this is also known as the Y-axis.

Vertical scrollbar The bar at the right side of a window that enables you to move up and down to view information too long for the screen.

Web Formally known as the World Wide Web or simply WWW, a system of computers and files by which users may view and interact with a variety of information.

Web creation and management tool A program that enables you to create and maintain a Web site. Microsoft FrontPage is the Office 2000 Web creation and management tool.

Wildcard A symbol used to search for unspecified characters. An asterisk can be used as the first or last character in a string of characters to match any number of characters.

Window A box that displays information or a program, such as a letter, a list of programs, or a calculator. Windows usually consist of title bars, toolbars, menu bars, and status bars. A window will always have a Minimize button.

Windows A Graphical User Interface (GUI) operating system required to run Office 2000. It works in the background while you are using an office application.

Windows Explorer Displays the files and folders on the various drives and computer desktop. You can copy, delete, move, and rename files in Windows Explorer.

Word processor A program that enables you to create documents such as letters, memos, and research papers. Microsoft Word is the Office 2000 word processor.

WordArt A program within Office applications that creates text as a drawing object, allowing you to add special colors, shadows, and 3-D effects. WordArt can be displayed horizontally, vertically, or at an 0angle.

Word wrap The word processing function whereby the first word to reach the right margin automatically moves to the next line.

Workbook A collection of worksheets saved under one filename.

Worksheet A set of cells that are identified by row and column headings. Also referred to as a *sheet*.

XML (Extensible Markup Language) A Web language that allows the program to attach additional information to data.

Yes/No A data type used for an either/or condition, Yes/No, True/False, On/Off.

Zoom The percent of screen magnification. It may be set by using a control found on the right side of the Standard toolbar.

Index

A

absolute formulas (Excel), 332-334. *See also* formulas
Access
  commands
    Change To Combo Box, 432
    Change To List Box (Format menu), 428
    Tab Order (View menu), 397
    Unfreeze All Columns (Format menu), 448
  databases. *See* databases (Access)
  default values, 424
    configuring, 422
  dialog boxes
    Input Mask Wizard, 421
    List Box Shift Properties, 428
    New Query, 460
    Report Wizard, 399
    Show Table, 461
  fields
    adding, 387
    deleting, 388
    modifying, 416-419
  forms, 390-392
    combo boxes, 431-434
    defining filters, 454-459
    list boxes, 427-430
    tab orders, 397-399
  input masks, 419-422
  labels, 393-396
  primary key fields, assigning, 425-426. *See also* fields
  queries, 460-463
    calculating values, 463-467
  records
    entering, 383-384
    finding, 448-450
    indexing, 451-453
    sorting, 451-453
  reports, 399-402
    printing, 402-406
  tables, 444-448
  text, 393-396
  toolbars, Form Design, 428
  Toolbox, 393
  Views, Design, 464
  wizards
    Database, 378
    Form, 390-392
    Report, 399-402
adding. *See also* inserting
  clip art to tables (Word), 195-199
  combo boxes (Access), 431-434
  connector lines (PowerPoint), 512-516
  fields (Access), 388
  input masks (Access), 419-422
  labels (Access), 393-396
  list boxes (Access), 427-430
  rows to tables (Word), 189-190
  slides (PowerPoint), 528-529
  Speaker Notes (PowerPoint), 486-490
  text (Word), 101-102
  text boxes (PowerPoint), 512-516
  toolbars, 64
  words to dictionaries (Word), 86
aligning text, 134. *See also* formatting; indenting
  Excel, 253-256
  Word, 124-125
animating
  text (PowerPoint), 558-561
    customizing, 562-565
  transitions (PowerPoint), 553-558
Annual Percentage Rate, 335
applications, starting, 52-55
Apply Design Template dialog box (PowerPoint), 504
applying designs (PowerPoint), 502-505. *See also* templates
APR (Annual Percentage Rate), 335
arguments, 338. *See also* values (Access)
assigning primary key fields (Access), 425-426
AutoContent Wizard (PowerPoint), 476
AutoFit (Word), 191-195
AutoForm (Access), 390-392
AutoFormat (Word), 191-195
AutoNumbers, 416
AutoRecover (Word), 89
AutoShapes (PowerPoint), 515

B

backspace keys (Word), correcting errors, 82-86
bar charts (Excel), 358-359. *See also* charts
Blank Database Option (Access), 378
boldface text (Word), 122. *See also* formatting, (Word) text
borders (Excel), 258-262
Break command (Insert menu), Word, 170
Break dialog box (Word), 170
breaks (Word), 169-170. *See also* page breaks (Word)
built-in formulas, 337-341. *See also* formulas (Excel)
bulleted lists (Word), 129-133

C

calculating
  Excel, 322-324
    columns, 227-228
    formulas, 324-329, 340-341
  values (Access), 463-467
Calculator, 9
cartoons, 506. *See also* clip art; graphics (Word)
cells (Excel)
  copying, 300-302
  data, 221-223